The
Sugar-Free
KITCHEN

The Sugar-Free KITCHEN

LOVE FOOD™

This edition published by Parragon Books Ltd in 2014
LOVE FOOD is an imprint of Parragon Books Ltd

Parragon Books Ltd
Chartist House
15—17 Trim Street
Bath BA1 1HA, UK
www.parragon.com/lovefood

ISBN: 978-1-4723-5804-2

Printed in China

New recipes and food styling by Georgina Besterman
Created and produced by Pene Parker and Becca Spry
New photography by Haarala Hamilton

Notes for the Reader

This book uses both metric and imperial measurements. Follow the same units of measurement
throughout; do not mix metric and imperial. All spoon measurements are level: teaspoons are
assumed to be 5 ml, and tablespoons are assumed to be 15 ml. Unless otherwise stated, milk is
assumed to be full fat, eggs and individual vegetables are medium, and pepper is freshly ground
black pepper. Unless otherwise stated, all root vegetables should be peeled prior to use.

Garnishes, decorations and serving suggestions are all optional and not necessarily included in the
recipe ingredients or method. Any optional ingredients and seasoning to taste are not included in
the nutritional analysis. The times given are an approximate guide only. Preparation times differ
according to the techniques used by different people and the cooking times may also vary from
those given. Optional ingredients, variations or serving suggestions have not been included in the
time calculations.

CONTENTS

INTRODUCTION

Sugar seems to be in almost everything we eat, from ready-meals to natural ingredients such as fruit and vegetables. It is thought that many of us consume ten or more teaspoons of sugar every day. The negative impact of this high-sugar diet on our health is increasingly evident in the rising levels of obesity, and it may be a factor in type two diabetes. But the problems don't stop there. It is thought that sleep disturbances and mood disorders can also be linked to over-indulgence in sugar. Health issues aside, a sugar binge can quickly be followed by a 'crash', where your energy levels plummet, leaving you feeling exhausted.

This book is about becoming aware of where sugar is found, both openly and concealed, within day-to-day cooking, and then taking action to avoid it. The problems aren't only associated with refined sugars; sugar is sugar after all, and natural sugars need to be restricted too, in particular those containing fructose (see page 9).

In this book you'll find sugar-free or very low-sugar versions of the things you love to eat, such as Coffee and Pecan Mini Breakfast Muffins on page 30, a reduced-tomato Bolognese Sauce on page 81 and Black Rice Risotto with Parma Ham and Charred Chicory on page 82. No one wants to have their favourite foods adapted so much that they bear no resemblance to the original, though. If you bake a cake, then you want to end up with something that looks and tastes like a cake. The Courgette Loaf Cake with Cream Cheese Frosting on page 110 and the Sweet Potato Brownies on page 112 are sure to delight cake lovers.

Of course, you are unlikely to eradicate all sugar from your diet; it would be unrealistic and inadvisable to permanently stop eating all fruit, for example. However, the recipes in this book include no more than 6 g of sugar per 100 g of ingredients. If you keep your intake to this low-to-negligible level you can be confident that you are managing your sugars well.

WHAT IS FRUCTOSE?

Sugar, or sucrose as it is scientifically known, comes in the chemical forms of glucose and fructose. Glucose is the basic stuff of life: every single cell in every single thing growing or moving produces and uses it. We do not need to go out of our way to consume glucose, as the body's digestive system releases it from a lot of foods.

Fructose in particular can be damaging if we eat too much of it. Through human evolution it was only periodically available in very ripe fruit, and the human body is not designed to deal with it in large amounts. While every cell in the body is slurping up glucose, only the liver can process fructose in significant amounts. If the liver is overloaded with fructose it converts it straight into fat, which has the result of weight gain and has been linked to type two diabetes and heart disease.

A further problem with fructose is that while some natural sugars stimulate the release of insulin in the body, fructose sneaks under our natural radar system. Insulin produces leptin, which is responsible for regulating fat storage and, when it is not released, the fructose is unregulated and stored as fat, leading to weight gain and associated diseases.

Fructose is hiding in many day-to-day foods, from some ready-meals and diet products to sugary drinks. It is also found naturally in fruit and vegetables. Many of us feel we are making a healthy choice if we reach for an apple or raw carrot, but it is important to limit how much high-sugar fruit and vegetables we eat too. While they are nutritious, the sugar they contain quickly adds up.

HIDDEN SUGARS

Sugar might not be as easy to detect as you think it is. It is essential to check the packaging when buying any ready-made food product. On the front of the packet it may advertise the food's fat and calorie content, but you usually need to check the back for sugars. Often, when the fat is removed from a product, sugar is added to enhance the flavour. Look for the section labelled 'carbohydrates'; beneath that it will usually say 'of which sugars'.

It is best to cook home-made food as often as possible in order to effectively control your sugar intake. Yet even this has potential pitfalls. Many natural foods, including most fruit, are full of sugar. Fruit juice and dried fruit should be avoided.

Vegetables can also have a high sugar content; sugarsnap peas, artichokes and beetroot are just some of the vegetables that are high in sugar and should therefore be eaten sparingly.

If you are eating a product that does not conveniently come with a helpful breakdown of its nutritional components, simply avoid a sweet taste, and remember that 'low-calorie' does not necessarily mean 'low-sugar'.

It is also important to look out for refined carbohydrates. The body reacts to most carbohydrates by breaking them down into sugar. Therefore white flour should be avoided, which means most pastries, breads and cakes should not be eaten. White rice, noodles, pasta and potatoes are also off the menu.

GOOD FATS AND PROTEIN

The low-sugar eater has two great allies: protein and fat. Since the 1980s, it has been fashionable to label fat as 'the enemy' and carbs as 'the good guys'. A big bowl of pasta has long been considered a healthy choice. Now, the rise of the low-carb lifestyle has turned these beliefs on their head, and a small portion of wholewheat pasta is considered a healthy portion. If you're keeping your sugar intake down and avoiding refined carbohydrates, you will need protein and fat to replace this energy.

The body naturally produces leptin to regulate and distribute fat. The body's regulatory gland, the hypothalamus, is sensitive to leptin and will tell the brain the stomach is full when there is leptin in the blood, thus suppressing appetite.

The avocado, a food that is naturally low in sugar but loaded with mono-unsaturated fats, which play a big role in reducing cholesterol, is a good choice for anyone watching their sugar intake. Heroic mono-unsaturated fats are found all over the food aisles, in products from olive oil and oily fish to animal fats, nuts and dairy. These foods often contain virtually no sugar, and so are used as the basis for many low-sugar recipes, adding a sense of indulgence to a dish. Of course, as with everything, it is important to manage your intake of foods containing mono-unsaturated fats; they should be eaten in moderation.

Fat's fondly regarded cousin is protein. Lean meats and eggs have always been in the healthy eater's arsenal and they can certainly be enjoyed in the sugar-free kitchen. Protein has a marvellous ability to make you feel full; if you eat enough of it, a hormone called PYY is triggered, which is effective in creating a sense of fullness and removing the desire to eat.

Protein-rich products are incredibly diverse. They include meat and fish, dairy products such as cheese and yogurt, seeds and nuts and some surprising grains such as quinoa.

Natural, high-protein ingredients tend to be low in sugar too. However, watch out again for processed products advertising themselves as high protein, as they can also contain hidden sugars used to add extra flavour or texture.

CRASHES AND CRAVINGS

Living a low-sugar lifestyle should protect you against energy crashes, which are particularly common mid-morning and mid-afternoon. Sugar crashes occur when sugar quickly enters the blood-stream, making blood sugar levels spike. Then, as the body releases large amounts of insulin to encourage the cells to absorb the glucose, blood glucose levels drop rapidly, leaving you feeling fatigued and lethargic. Healthy fats, protein and fibre contain little if any sugar, and provide slow-release energy without having the same effect on the body.

According to research, cravings are quite simply all in your head. It is thought that the sections of the brain most active during cravings are the parts responsible for memory and sensing pleasure and fulfilment, which suggests that memory rather than bodily needs often triggers cravings.

In order to trigger the strong mental sequence that is a craving, the body tends to want (although not need) something, and often that something is sugar after a blood glucose dip. These are the moments when self-control is necessary. It can help to have something on hand to snack on, such as a bag of nuts or piece of cheese. There are some recipes for low-sugar snacks in this book, such as the Crunchy Parmesan and Kale Crisps on page 64. You'll also find portable snacking recipes, such as the Chocolate and Brazil Nut Bars on page 66 or the Ginger and Oat No-Bake Biscuits on page 70. Responding to cravings by snacking on low-sugar foods such as these will help you through them.

HOW TO STOCK YOUR CUPBOARD

Sugar is often synonymous with celebration and pleasure. Dessert is the crescendo of a dinner, cake is considered a treat, holidays are associated with sugary foods, and we often cheer up children with chocolate. Therefore, facing a kitchen devoid of sugar can seem rather joyless, but you will discover that it is anything but.

There are both natural and chemical sugar alternatives that are easy to use and effective in baking. Stevia is a natural plant extract, and is grainy and exceptionally sweet, making it an excellent alternative to sugar. Rice malt syrup is made from fermented cooked brown rice and contains no fructose. With these two allies to hand there are few baking challenges that cannot be overcome.

The best way to start with your sugar-free eating plan is by making your diet almost completely sugar-free, to keep temptation at bay. Meats and cheeses can be enjoyed in moderation conscience-free, but choose carefully when buying processed products such as bacon, ham and smoked cheese, which can be made using sugar. The same goes for dairy products: flavoured yogurts and creams are often loaded with sugar, so always read the label and, if necessary, go for a sugar-free alternative.

Another common source of processed sugar is refined carbohydrates, such as white flour and potatoes, and these should be avoided. Replace wheat flours with nut flours, ground almonds, coconut flour and polenta. A number of the replacement flours contain some sugar, so use them in small quantities.

Nuts and seeds are a splendid addition to your kitchen. They are great for texture and taste, and come in various forms such as butters and flours. Snacking on unsalted nuts is a good way to diminish cravings and resist temptation.

Many vegetables are rich in carbohydrates and sugars. Leafy greens, from lettuce and spinach to kale and chard, are fine. Root vegetables, however, can be more problematic: beetroot, parsnips and carrots all contain high levels of sugar so should only be eaten in moderation. The sweet potato is acceptable in moderation too, as it releases its sugar slowly into the bloodstream. The main family of veggies on your side are cruciferous veg, including cauliflower, cabbage, broccoli and sprouts. Most of these are bulky and full of vitamins and fibre.

Lastly, berries are acceptable in moderation as they are relatively low in sugar. Blueberries, raspberries, strawberries, cranberries and redcurrants are all packed with flavour and fibre.

BREAKFASTS

Avocado, bacon and chilli frittata	20
Courgette rosti with smoked salmon and scrambled eggs	22
Mushrooms on rye toast	24
Eggs Florentine	27
Coconut flour pancakes with lemon	28
Coffee and pecan mini breakfast muffins	30
Blueberry and oat breakfast bars	32
Creamy porridge with blackberries	34
Nutty muesli medley	36
Greek-style yogurt with orange zest and toasted seeds	38
Red pepper pep-up juice	41

AVOCADO, BACON AND CHILLI FRITTATA

Inspired by the flavours of Mexico, this protein-packed frittata is lovely lingered over on a lazy morning. You can make it ahead and store it in the refrigerator for two days.

SERVES: 4   PREP: 15 MINS   COOK: 14 MINS

1 tbsp vegetable oil
8 streaky bacon rashers, roughly chopped
6 eggs, beaten
3 tbsp double cream
2 large avocados, peeled and sliced
1 red chilli, deseeded and thinly sliced
½ lime
sea salt and pepper

1 Preheat the grill to medium. Heat the oil in a 20–cm/8–inch ovenproof frying pan over a medium heat. Add the bacon and fry, stirring, for 4–5 minutes, or until crisp and golden. Using a slotted spoon, transfer to a plate lined with kitchen paper. Remove the pan from the heat.

2 Pour the eggs into a bowl, add the cream and season with salt and pepper, then beat. Return the pan to the heat. When it is hot, pour in the egg mixture and cook for 1–2 minutes, without stirring. Sprinkle the bacon and avocado on top and cook for a further 2–3 minutes, or until the frittata is almost set and the underside is golden brown.

3 Place the frittata under the grill and cook for 3–4 minutes, or until the top is golden brown and the egg is set. Scatter with the chilli and squeeze over the lime juice. Cut into wedges and serve.

COOKING BACON

The soft texture of the frittata works best with really crispy bacon. To achieve this, cook the bacon over a medium heat until it has a dark golden colour, then remove it from the pan and drain on kitchen paper.

PER SERVING: 525 CALS | 41.6G FAT | 15G SAT FAT | 8.8G CARBS | 1.5G SUGARS | 2.5G SALT | 4.8G FIBRE | 23.5G PROTEIN

COURGETTE ROSTI WITH SMOKED SALMON AND SCRAMBLED EGGS

*Courgettes make a brilliant substitute for potatoes in this tasty rosti;
their subtle creamy flavour complements the luxurious egg and salmon perfectly.*

SERVES: 2   PREP: 30 MINS   COOK: 18 MINS

3 large eggs
1 tbsp double cream
2 tsp finely snipped fresh chives
15 g/½ oz butter
2 large slices of smoked salmon, to serve
sea salt and pepper

ROSTI
300 g/10½ oz courgette, grated
2 tsp quinoa flour
20 g/¾ oz Parmesan cheese, grated
1 large egg yolk
1 tbsp double cream
1 tbsp vegetable oil

1 Preheat the oven to 110°C/225°F/Gas Mark ¼. To make the rosti, lay a clean tea towel on a work surface and pile the courgette in the centre. Holding the tea towel over the sink, gather the sides together and twist them tightly until all the liquid from the courgette has run out.

2 Put the courgette, flour, Parmesan, egg yolk and cream in a bowl and mix well. Roll the mixture into two balls and flatten them with the palms of your hands to make thick patties.

3 Heat the oil in a small frying pan over a medium–low heat. Cook the rostis for 5–8 minutes on each side, or until golden brown. Remove from the heat, transfer to a baking sheet and put them in the oven to keep warm.

4 To make the scrambled eggs, crack the eggs into a bowl, add the cream and chives and season with salt and pepper. Beat with a fork until evenly mixed.

5 Wipe the frying pan clean with kitchen paper, then melt the butter in the pan over a low heat. Pour in the egg mixture and cook, stirring, for 5–6 minutes, or until the eggs are just set.

6 Put the warm rostis on two plates. Spoon the scrambled eggs over them, then top with the salmon. Grind over some black pepper and serve immediately.

PERFECT SCRAMBLED EGGS

When cooking scrambled eggs, the trick any chef will tell you is 'low and slow' – keep the heat down and stir patiently until the eggs start to bind. They will keep cooking all the time they're in the pan, so serve them quickly.

PER SERVING: 428 CALS | 33.2G FAT | 13.4G SAT FAT | 7.3G CARBS | 4G SUGARS | 2.2G SALT | 1.6G FIBRE | 25G PROTEIN

MUSHROOMS ON RYE TOAST

This quick and easy breakfast is a real treat. If you can't find wild mushrooms, just increase the amount of chestnut mushrooms instead. The rye bread is packed with fibre.

SERVES: 4   PREP: 8 MINS   COOK: 8 MINS

3 tbsp olive oil
2 large garlic cloves, crushed
225 g/8 oz chestnut mushrooms, sliced
225 g/8 oz wild mushrooms, sliced
2 tsp lemon juice
2 tbsp finely chopped fresh flat-leaf parsley
4 slices of rye bread
sea salt and pepper

1 Heat the oil in a large frying pan over a medium-low heat. Add the garlic and cook for a few seconds.

2 Increase the heat to high. Add the chestnut mushrooms and cook, stirring continuously, for 3 minutes. Add the wild mushrooms and cook for a further 2 minutes.

3 Stir in the lemon juice and parsley, and season with salt and pepper.

4 Lightly toast the rye bread then transfer to a serving plate. Spoon the mushroom mixture over the toast and serve immediately.

MMM, MUSHROOMS

Darker mushrooms provide the antioxidant mineral selenium, and are immune-boosting.

PER SERVING: 197 CALS | 11.3G FAT | 1.6G SAT FAT | 20.3G CARBS | 3.2G SUGARS | 1.3G SALT | 2.5G FIBRE | 5.5G PROTEIN

EGGS FLORENTINE

This rich, classic dish is simple to prepare and is perfect for a special occasion or a lazy weekend brunch.

SERVES: 4   PREP: 20 MINS   COOK: 40 MINS

450 g/1 lb spinach leaves, destalked and washed
55 g/2 oz butter, plus extra to grease
55 g/2 oz button mushrooms, sliced
55 g/2 oz pine nuts, toasted
6 spring onions, thinly sliced
4 eggs
25 g/1 oz wholemeal plain flour
300 ml/10 fl oz milk, warmed
1 tsp prepared English mustard
85 g/3 oz mature Cheddar cheese, grated
sea salt and pepper

SERVE IT WITH

Chunky slices of spelt bread, plain or toasted, make a good accompaniment to this dish and soak up the tasty juices.

1 Preheat the oven to 190°C/375°F/Gas Mark 5. Lightly grease a shallow ovenproof dish with butter.

2 Drain the spinach well, then put it in a large saucepan. Place the pan over a medium heat and sprinkle with a little salt. Cover and cook for 2–3 minutes, or until the spinach has wilted. Drain, pressing out any excess liquid, then chop and transfer to the prepared dish.

3 Melt 15 g/½ oz butter in a small saucepan over a medium heat. Add the mushrooms and cook for 2 minutes, stirring often. Add the pine nuts and spring onions and cook for a further 2 minutes. Remove from the heat, season with salt and pepper and scatter the mixture over the spinach, then keep warm.

4 Meanwhile, heat a wide, shallow pan of water until it is simmering but not quite at a rolling boil. Crack one egg into a cup, then stir the water to make a whirlpool. As the whirlpool slows almost to a stop, gently slip the egg into its centre. Cook for 2–3 minutes, or until set, then remove with a slotted spoon and place on top of the mushrooms. Repeat with the remaining three eggs.

5 Melt the remaining 40 g/1½ oz butter in a saucepan over a medium heat. Stir in the flour, then cook for 2 minutes. Remove from the heat and gradually stir in the milk. Return to the heat and cook, stirring constantly, until the mixture comes to the boil and has thickened. Add the mustard, then 55 g/2 oz cheese and stir until it has melted. Season with salt and pepper, then pour on top of the eggs, completely covering them. Sprinkle with the remaining 30 g/1 oz cheese.

6 Bake for 20–25 minutes, or until piping hot and the top is golden brown and bubbling. Serve immediately.

PER SERVING: 455 CALS | 35G FAT | 15G SAT FAT | 17.5G CARBS | 6G SUGARS | 1.6G SALT | 4.5G FIBRE | 22G PROTEIN

COCONUT FLOUR PANCAKES
WITH LEMON

Pancakes are the ultimate breakfast treat and this version, made with coconut flour, really hits the spot. Pile them up and spoon over the home-made lemon drizzle.

SERVES: 4   PREP: 15 MINS   COOK: 10 MINS

2 large eggs
100 ml/3^{1}/$_{2}$ fl oz coconut milk
125 ml/4 fl oz cold water
1 tsp vanilla extract
1 tbsp stevia
50 g/1^{3}/$_{4}$ oz coconut flour
1 tsp bicarbonate of soda
1 tbsp coconut oil
salt
4 tbsp crème fraîche, to serve (optional)

LEMON DRIZZLE
finely grated zest and juice of 1 unwaxed lemon
2 tsp rice malt syrup

1 Crack the eggs into a bowl, then add the coconut milk, water, vanilla, stevia, flour and bicarbonate of soda and season with a pinch of salt. Whisk to a smooth batter, then leave to rest for a moment.

2 Meanwhile, to make the lemon drizzle, put the lemon zest and juice and rice malt syrup in a small bowl and mix well.

3 Heat the coconut oil in a large frying pan over a medium heat. Pour in a tablespoon of the batter, leave to settle for a moment, then add more tablespoons, allowing a little space between each one. Fry for 2 minutes, or until the bottom of each pancake is light brown and the sides are set. Carefully flip over the pancakes using a fish slice and cook for a further 2 minutes.

4 Transfer the pancakes to warm serving plates. Cook the remaining pancakes in the same way. Top each plate of pancakes with a tablespoon of crème fraîche, if using, and spoon over the lemon drizzle.

GRATING LEMON ZEST

It is best to grate a lemon with a fine Microplane grater, so you can ensure you take off just the zest and not the bitter white pith.

PER SERVING: 157 CALS | 14G FAT | 10.3G SAT FAT | 4.7G CARBS | 1.6G SUGARS | 1.3G SALT | 1.2G FIBRE | 4.5G PROTEIN

COFFEE AND PECAN MINI BREAKFAST MUFFINS

Sometimes you feel you need a sweet hit in the morning to get you through the first few hours. These little muffins provide that with none of the sugar highs and crashes.

MAKES: 9 MUFFINS   PREP: 25 MINS   COOK: 20 MINS

50 g/1³/4 oz coconut flour
¹/4 tsp baking powder
¹/2 tsp bicarbonate of soda
1 tbsp stevia
30 g/1 oz pecan nuts, roughly chopped
150 ml/5 fl oz soured cream
5 tbsp vegetable oil
2 large eggs, beaten
5 tbsp prepared espresso or strong instant coffee
1 tsp rice malt syrup
sea salt

1 Preheat the oven to 170°C/325°F/Gas Mark 3. Put nine mini muffin cases into a mini muffin tray.

2 Put the flour, baking powder, bicarbonate of soda, stevia, 20 g/³/4 oz pecan nuts and a small pinch of salt in a large bowl and mix well. Add the soured cream, oil, eggs and 4 tablespoons of espresso, and stir until evenly mixed. Leave to stand for a moment, then spoon the mixture into the mini muffin cases.

3 Bake for 20 minutes, or until well risen and the tops spring back when pressed with a fingertip. Leave to cool for 5 minutes, then transfer to a wire rack.

4 To make the topping, put the rice malt syrup and remaining 1 tablespoon of espresso in a bowl and mix. Spoon a small drizzle over each muffin. Sprinkle on the remaining 10 g/¹/4 oz pecan nuts and serve warm, or store in an airtight container for up to two days.

RICE MALT SYRUP

Baking with rice malt syrup is similar to baking with sugar in terms of quantity and texture. However, be aware that it can burn quickly. If you are concerned, loosely place a sheet of baking paper over the top of your bake to protect the exposed areas while allowing the rest to continue to bake.

PER MUFFIN: 170 CALS | 16.6G FAT | 3.2G SAT FAT | 1.6G CARBS | 1.1G SUGARS | 0.5G SALT | 0.5G FIBRE | 3.6G PROTEIN

BLUEBERRY AND OAT BREAKFAST BARS

These are like a cross between a biscuit and flapjack with their moist explosion of blueberries, and they will give you an energetic start to the day.

MAKES: 12 BARS   PREP: 15 MINS   COOK: 25 MINS

115 g/4 oz unsalted butter
100 g/3$\frac{1}{2}$ oz quinoa flour
100 g/3$\frac{1}{2}$ oz rolled oats
pinch of sea salt
$\frac{1}{2}$ tsp freshly grated nutmeg
1 tsp ground cinnamon
$\frac{1}{2}$ tsp ground allspice
$\frac{1}{2}$ tsp baking powder
$\frac{1}{2}$ tsp bicarbonate of soda
2 tbsp rice malt syrup
1 large egg, beaten
60 g/2$\frac{1}{4}$ oz blueberries
30 g/1 oz cranberries, roughly chopped (optional)

1 Preheat the oven to 160°C/325°F/Gas Mark 3. Line a 26 x 16-cm/10$\frac{1}{2}$ x 6$\frac{1}{4}$-inch cake tin with baking paper. Melt the butter in a small saucepan, then pour it into a large bowl.

2 Put all the remaining ingredients apart from the blueberries and cranberries in the bowl and mix to a chunky batter. Carefully stir in the blueberries and cranberries, if using.

3 Pour the mixture into the prepared tin and spread it into an even layer using the back of a spoon. Bake for 20–25 minutes, or until golden brown and set.

4 Transfer to a wire rack to cool. After 10 minutes, cut into 12 bars, then leave to cool completely. Serve or store in an airtight container for up to three days.

COOL CRANBERRIES

Cranberries are packed with vitamin C and fibre, but have a terrific array of phytonutrients. They are also high in sugar, so eat in moderation.

PER BAR: 141 CALS | 8.9G FAT | 5G SAT FAT | 12G CARBS | 0.6G SUGARS | 0.3G SALT | 1.7G FIBRE | 3.3G PROTEIN

CREAMY PORRIDGE WITH BLACKBERRIES

Oats are a complex carbohydrate that provide slow-release energy to keep you sustained throughout the morning.

SERVES: 2   PREP: 5 MINS   COOK: 8 MINS

100 g/3½ oz large rolled oats
small pinch of sea salt
600 ml/1 pint cold water
3½ tbsp double cream, plus extra to serve
1 tbsp stevia
1 tbsp pumpkin seeds
6 large blackberries, quartered

1 Put the oats and salt in a medium-sized saucepan and pour over the water. Bring to the boil, then reduce the heat to medium-low and simmer, stirring regularly, for 5–6 minutes, or until the oats are thick but have a dense pouring consistency.

2 Stir in the cream and stevia. Spoon the porridge into two bowls, top with the pumpkin seeds and blackberries, and serve immediately with a little extra cream for pouring over.

ALSO TRY THIS

The Scottish have made porridge with just water for generations, so you can omit the cream if you prefer. However, it does provide calcium.

PER SERVING: 268 CALS | 9G FAT | 2.9G SAT FAT | 38G CARBS | 1.5G SUGARS | 0.7G SALT | 7.2G FIBRE | 11G PROTEIN

NUTTY MUESLI MEDLEY

Muesli makes an excellent start to the day, but a handful of this crunchy nut and seed mixture is equally delicious as a snack when you're on the go.

SERVES: 6   PREP: 10 MINS   COOK: 15 MINS

100 g/3¹/2 oz large rolled oats
10 g/¹/4 oz shredded coconut
20 g/³/4 oz pumpkin seeds
20 g/³/4 oz flaked almonds
20 g/³/4 oz pecan nuts
55 g/2 oz flaxseeds
20 g/³/4 oz almond flour
1 tbsp stevia
1 tsp ground cinnamon
¹/2 tsp ground ginger
pinch of sea salt
55 g/2 oz almond butter
70 g/2¹/2 oz unsalted butter
2 tbsp natural yogurt, to serve

1 Preheat the oven to 160°C/325°F/Gas Mark 3. Put the oats, coconut, pumpkin seeds, flaked almonds and pecan nuts in a food processor and pulse briefly to break everything into small chunks. Transfer the mixture to a large bowl, then add the flaxseeds, almond flour, stevia, spices and salt, then mix well.

2 Melt the butters together in a small saucepan, stirring. Pour them over the dry ingredients and stir.

3 Spread the mixture evenly in a large roasting tin. Bake for 15 minutes; it should release a toasty aroma and be a light golden brown when ready. Leave to cool completely.

4 Shake the pan to break up the ingredients into a chunky crumb, with some larger shards. Serve with a tablespoon of natural yogurt or store in an airtight jar for up to one week.

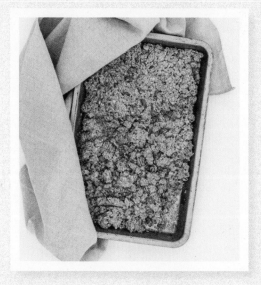

PROTEIN FOR ENERGY

The nuts and seeds in this muesli are packed with protein and fibre – the ideal weekday breakfast to keep you going until lunch.

PER SERVING: 302 CALS | 24.5G FAT | 8.8G SAT FAT | 15.2G CARBS | 0.8G SUGARS | 0.7G SALT | 4.3G FIBRE | 7.3G PROTEIN

GREEK-STYLE YOGURT WITH ORANGE ZEST AND TOASTED SEEDS

Toasting the seeds in this recipe enhances their flavour, so they contrast wonderfully with the smooth, creamy yogurt.

SERVES: 2 PREP: 5 MINS COOK: 3 MINS

2 tsp flaxseeds
2 tsp pumpkin seeds
2 tsp chia seeds
200 g/7 oz Greek-style natural yogurt
grated zest of 1 small orange, plus 1 tsp juice

1 Place a small frying pan over a medium heat. When it is hot, tip in the seeds. Toast, stirring constantly with a wooden spoon, until they start to turn brown and release a nutty aroma. Tip them onto a plate and leave to cool.

2 Spoon the yogurt into two glass pots or serving bowls, then scatter the seeds on top, followed by the orange zest. Sprinkle over the orange juice and serve immediately.

FLAXSEEDS FOR HEALTH

Flaxseeds are high in omega-3s, which are essential fatty acids that some studies show can help reduce the risk of heart disease and stroke.

PER SERVING: 172 CALS | 10.6G FAT | 4.3G SAT FAT | 8.1G CARBS | 4.3G SUGARS | TRACE SALT | 3.3G FIBRE | 12G PROTEIN

RED PEPPER PEP-UP JUICE

Full of disease-fighting, anti-ageing antioxidants,
this juice provides lots of energy to help you get through the day.

SERVES: 2   PREP: 5 MINS

2 fennel bulbs with leaves, halved
1 apple, halved
1 small red pepper, halved
1 carrot, halved
200 ml/7 fl oz cold water

1 Remove a few leaves from the fennel and reserve.

2 Feed the apple, then fennel and pepper, then carrot through a juicer.

3 Pour into a jug, top up with the water and mix well.

4 Pour into two glasses, garnish with the fennel leaves and serve immediately.

AMAZING APPLES

Apples are a good source of vitamin C, soluble pectin (which is thought to help lower cholesterol) and the minerals calcium, magnesium and phosphorus.

PER SERVING: 93 CALS | 0.5G FAT | TRACE SAT FAT | 21.9G CARBS | 10.9G SUGARS | 0.2G SALT | 1.5G FIBRE | 2.6G PROTEIN

LUNCHES AND SNACKS

BEEF AND HERB SOUP

*Forget ready-made soups, which often contain hidden sugars —
this substantial home-made soup will keep you full for hours!*

SERVES: 6 PREP: 20 MINS COOK: 1 HOUR

2 onions
2 tbsp sunflower oil
1 tbsp ground turmeric
1 tsp ground cumin
100 g/3½ oz green or yellow split peas
1.2 litres/2 pints beef stock
225 g/8 oz beef mince
200 g/7 oz long-grain wholegrain rice
1 tbsp roughly chopped fresh coriander, plus
extra to garnish
1 tbsp finely snipped fresh chives
55 g/2 oz baby spinach, finely chopped
25 g/1 oz butter
2 garlic cloves, finely chopped
3 tbsp roughly chopped fresh mint
sea salt and pepper
6 tbsp Greek-style natural yogurt, to serve

1 Grate one of the onions into a large bowl and finely chop the other. Heat the oil in a large saucepan over a medium–low heat. Add the chopped onion and cook, stirring occasionally, for 8–10 minutes, or until golden. Stir in the turmeric and cumin, add the split peas and pour in the stock. Bring to the boil, then reduce the heat to low, cover and simmer for 15 minutes.

2 Meanwhile, add the mince to the grated onion, season with salt and pepper and mix. Shape the mixture into small balls.

3 Add the meatballs to the soup, re-cover the pan and simmer for 10 minutes. Add the rice and stir in the coriander, chives and spinach. Simmer, stirring frequently, for 25–30 minutes, or until the rice is tender and the meatballs are cooked.

4 Melt the butter in a frying pan over a low heat. Add the garlic and cook, stirring frequently, for 2–3 minutes. Stir in the mint and cook for a further minute.

5 Transfer the soup to bowls and sprinkle over the garlic mixture. Add a spoonful of yogurt to each bowl and sprinkle with the remaining coriander.

SPLIT PEAS

Brimming with soluble fibre, split peas also contain lots of protein and two B vitamins. They are an inexpensive nutrient powerhouse!

PER SERVING: 344 CALS | 12.7G FAT | 5G SAT FAT | 40.8G CARBS | 3.9G SUGARS | 2.4G SALT | 6.3G FIBRE | 17G PROTEIN

SWEET POTATO SOUP

*This thick, colourful and filling soup has a lovely sweet flavour,
yet the sugar levels are low – brilliant!*

SERVES: 6   PREP: 25 MINS   COOK: 30 MINS

1 tbsp vegetable oil
1 onion, finely chopped
2.5-cm/1-inch piece fresh ginger,
peeled and finely chopped
1 tsp medium curry powder
1 tsp sea salt
500 g/1 lb 2 oz sweet potatoes, roughly chopped
400 ml/14 fl oz canned coconut milk
1 litre/1³⁄4 pints vegetable stock
juice of 1 lime
2 tbsp roughly chopped fresh coriander, to garnish

1 Heat the oil in a large, heavy-based saucepan over
a medium-high heat. Add the onion and ginger and cook,
stirring, for 5 minutes, or until soft. Add the curry powder and
salt and cook, stirring, for a further minute. Add the sweet
potatoes, coconut milk and stock, and bring to the boil. Reduce
the heat to medium and simmer, uncovered, for 20 minutes, or
until the sweet potatoes are soft.

2 Purée the soup, either in batches in a blender or food
processor, or using a hand-held blender. Return the soup to
the heat, bring back up to a simmer, then stir in the lime juice.
Transfer the soup to bowls and sprinkle with the coriander.

SWEET POTATOES

High in vitamin C, potassium and beta-carotene
(which the body converts to vitamin A), sweet
potatoes make a healthy addition to any meal.
They are also a source of manganese.

PER SERVING: 242 CALS | 13.3G FAT | 9.8G SAT FAT | 27G CARBS | 7.2G SUGARS | 1.6G SALT | 3.8G FIBRE | 3G PROTEIN

CLAMS IN BACON, LEEK AND CREAM BROTH

Leeks pack lots of flavour and are very low in sugar. The bacon really complements the clams in this recipe.

SERVES: 4   PREP: 45 MINS   COOK: 1³/4 HOURS

1.5 kg/3 lb 5 oz live clams, scrubbed
1 tsp butter
12 streaky bacon rashers, roughly chopped
200 g/7 oz leeks, sliced
1 garlic clove, finely chopped
100 ml/3¹/2 fl oz brandy
300 ml/10 fl oz cold water
100 ml/3¹/2 fl oz single cream
25 g/1 oz fresh flat-leaf parsley, finely chopped

1 Discard any clams with broken shells or any that refuse to close when tapped.

2 Melt the butter in a deep, heavy-based saucepan over a medium heat. Add the bacon and fry, stirring, for 4–5 minutes, or until crisp and golden. Using a slotted spoon, transfer to a plate lined with kitchen paper.

3 Put the leeks and garlic in the pan and cook, stirring regularly, for 5 minutes, or until softened but not browned.

4 Pour in the brandy and leave it to bubble for a minute to burn off the alcohol (brandy in a hot pan can easily flame, so take care). Add the water and stir well. Turn up the heat to medium-high and, when the water starts to boil, toss in the clams. Put on the lid and steam for 5 minutes, or until the clams have opened.

5 Take the pan off the heat. Discard any clams that remain closed. Stir in the bacon and cream. Sprinkle with the parsley and serve in bowls, with a large empty bowl to collect the shells.

BUYING BACON

Try to find a brand of bacon that has no sugar content in the cure.

PER SERVING: 380 CALS | 20.5G FAT | 9.6G SAT FAT | 9.8G CARBS | 3G SUGARS | 2.2G SALT | 0.9G FIBRE | 25G PROTEIN

WARM QUINOA, ROAST PUMPKIN AND PINE NUT SALAD

Quinoa is considered a sacred food by the Incas, and has long been prized for its flavour and ability to keep you feeling full. Loaded with protein and vitamins, it is perfect for a salad.

SERVES: 2 PREP: 20 MINS COOK: 30 MINS

100 g/3½ oz white quinoa, rinsed
350 ml/12 fl oz cold water
200 g/7 oz pumpkin flesh, cut into bite-sized chunks
4 tbsp olive oil
pinch of cayenne pepper
20 g/¾ oz pine nuts
25 g/1 oz fresh flat-leaf parsley, roughly chopped
20 g/¾ oz baby spinach
juice of ¼ lemon, plus lemon wedges to serve
sea salt and pepper

1 Preheat the oven to 180°C/350°F/Gas Mark 4. Put the quinoa in a saucepan. Add the water, bring to the boil, then cover and simmer over a very low heat for 10 minutes. Remove from the heat, but leave the pan covered for a further 7 minutes to allow the grains to swell. Fluff up with a fork.

2 Meanwhile, put the pumpkin and 2 tablespoons of oil in a large roasting tin, sprinkle with the cayenne and a pinch of salt and toss well. Roast for 25 minutes, or until crisp on the edges and tender. Tip into a large bowl.

3 Toast the pine nuts in a dry frying pan over a high heat until they are light brown, then tip them into the bowl. Gently mix in the quinoa, parsley and spinach, taking care that nothing breaks up, then season with salt and pepper.

4 Divide the salad between two plates, drizzle with the remaining oil and the lemon juice, and serve with lemon wedges for squeezing over.

COOKING QUINOA

Cooked quinoa should have a texture similar to slightly chewy couscous, but be careful not to overcook it. If the pan boils dry during cooking, add a splash more water and turn off the heat, then leave for 10 minutes with the lid on; the trapped steam should be enough to finish cooking the quinoa without saturating it.

PER SERVING: 521 CALS | 37G FAT | 4.5G SAT FAT | 40.5G CARBS | 2G SUGARS | 1.5G SALT | 4.6G FIBRE | 9.9G PROTEIN

GREEK SALAD CROSTINI

Crisp, toasted high-fibre country bread topped with a classic salad packed with vibrant Mediterranean flavours.

SERVES: 4   PREP: 20 MINS   COOK: 5 MINS

1 garlic clove, crushed
4 tbsp olive oil
2 slices of seeded wholemeal bread
200 g/7 oz feta cheese, diced
¼ cucumber, finely diced
25 g/1 oz black olives, stoned and sliced
4 plum tomatoes, roughly chopped
½ small onion, roughly chopped
2 tbsp fresh mint leaves, shredded
2 sprigs fresh oregano, chopped
1 lettuce heart, finely shredded
½ tsp toasted sesame seeds
2 tsp pine nuts (optional)
pepper

1 Preheat the grill to medium–high. Put the garlic and oil in a large bowl and mix well.

2 Put the bread on the grill rack, brush lightly with some of the garlic oil and toast well away from the heat for 2–3 minutes, or until crisp and golden. Turn the bread and brush lightly with more oil, then toast again.

3 Add the feta cheese to the remaining garlic oil in the bowl and season with pepper. Mix in the cucumber, olives, tomatoes, onion, mint and oregano, then gently mix in the lettuce.

4 Transfer the toasts to a serving plate and spoon the salad and its juices over the top. Sprinkle with the sesame seeds and pine nuts, if using, then cut them in half and serve half a crostini per person.

SESAME SEEDS

Sesame seeds are packed with minerals, vitamins and antioxidants. They are especially rich in monounsaturated fatty acids, which are considered to help prevent heart disease and stroke.

PER SERVING: 379 CALS | 28.8G FAT | 9.7G SAT FAT | 20.2G CARBS | 6.7G SUGARS | 2.8G SALT | 3.6G FIBRE | 11.5G PROTEIN

FLATBREAD PIZZA WITH GARLIC COURGETTE RIBBONS

This fresh, Mediterranean-style lunch with a satisfying crunchy base and fresh vegetable topping is sure to keep hunger pangs at bay.

SERVES: 2 PREP: 20 MINS COOK: 10 MINS

50 g/1³/4 oz crème fraîche
150 g/5¹/2 oz courgettes, shredded into ribbons
using a vegetable peeler
55 g/2 oz cherry tomatoes, quartered
50 g/1³/4 oz ricotta cheese
1 garlic clove, crushed
2 tbsp olive oil
green salad leaves, to serve (optional)

PIZZA BASES

100 g/3¹/2 oz wholemeal plain flour, plus extra to dust
50 g/1³/4 oz quinoa flour
³/4 tsp bicarbonate of soda
1 tbsp olive oil
2 tbsp warm water
sea salt

1 Preheat the oven to 200°C/400°F/Gas Mark 6. To make the pizza bases, put the flours and bicarbonate of soda in a mixing bowl, season with salt and stir. Add the oil, then gradually mix in enough of the warm water to make a soft but not sticky dough.

2 Lightly dust a work surface with flour. Knead the dough on the surface for 2 minutes, or until smooth and slightly elastic.

3 Put two large, flat baking sheets in the oven to get hot.

4 Divide the dough into two pieces. Roll out each piece to a circle about 5-mm/¹/4-inch thick. Remove the hot baking sheets from the oven and, working quickly, lay the dough on top. Spread the crème fraîche over the dough, then sprinkle with the courgettes and tomatoes. Blob the ricotta cheese in small dollops on top.

5 Bake the pizzas for 7–10 minutes, or until the crust is crispy and slightly puffed up, and the ricotta is tinged golden.

6 Mix the garlic and oil together in a jug, and drizzle over the pizzas. Serve with salad leaves, if using.

KNEADING DOUGH

Push the dough down, stretching it out in front of you, using the heels of your hands. You are trying to stretch the gluten strands in it. Fold the top half of the dough back towards you and press down and stretch again. Continue like this until the dough is smooth and elastic.

PER SERVING: 568 CALS | 31.4G FAT | 8G SAT FAT | 57.6G CARBS | 3.7G SUGARS | 2.1G SALT | 8.2G FIBRE | 14G PROTEIN

ASPARAGUS WITH HOT-SMOKED SALMON AND POACHED EGG

Asparagus, salmon and poached eggs with lemony butter makes a luxurious lunch or summer starter.

SERVES: 2 PREP: 25 MINS COOK: 21 MINS

50 g/1³/4 oz unsalted butter, softened
finely grated zest of ½ unwaxed lemon, plus ½ tsp juice
sprig of fresh dill, roughly chopped
400 g/14 oz hot-smoked salmon
10 asparagus spears, woody stems removed
2 large eggs
sea salt and pepper

1 Preheat the oven to 180°C/350°F/Gas Mark 4. Put the butter, lemon zest and juice and dill in a small bowl, season with salt and pepper and mix. Pat the butter into a rough square with the back of a spoon, wrap it in clingfilm and chill in the refrigerator while you make the rest of the dish.

2 Wrap the hot-smoked salmon in kitchen foil and bake for 15 minutes. Flake the fish into bite-sized pieces and keep warm.

3 Cook the asparagus in a pan of lightly salted boiling water for 2 minutes. Drain and run under a cold tap briefly to stop the cooking process, then set aside.

4 Heat a second wide saucepan of water until it is almost at simmering point. Crack one egg into a cup, then stir the water to make a whirlpool. As the whirlpool slows almost to a stop, gently slip the egg into its centre. Cook for 2–3 minutes, then remove with a slotted spoon. Repeat with the second egg.

5 Put five asparagus spears on each of two plates, top with half the flaked salmon, then balance a poached egg on top and crown with a dab of lemon butter. The remaining heat from the egg should melt the butter into a scrumptious lemon herb sauce. Serve immediately.

ALSO TRY THIS

If you don't like lemon, replace it with parsley and a little crushed garlic.

PER SERVING: 618 CALS | 40G FAT | 18.6G SAT FAT | 3.5G CARBS | 1.7G SUGARS | 2.5G SALT | 1.7G FIBRE | 58G PROTEIN

NO-CRUST SQUASH, CHORIZO AND GOAT'S CHEESE QUICHE

This simple quiche is brimming with energy-boosting chorizo and vitamin-packed butternut squash – and is ideal for packing into a lunchbox.

SERVES: 4   PREP: 30 MINS
CHILL: 30 MINS   COOK: 1 HOUR 20 MINS

400 g/14 oz butternut squash flesh, diced
1 tbsp olive oil
200 g/7 oz chorizo, cut into small, irregular chunks
3 eggs
100 ml/3½ fl oz crème fraîche
2 tbsp fresh thyme leaves
100 g/3½ oz semi-hard goat's cheese
sea salt and pepper
green salad leaves, to serve (optional)

PASTRY
50 g/1¾ oz cold butter, diced
100 g/3½ oz wholemeal plain flour, plus extra to dust
2 tbsp cold water

CHILLING PASTRY

Just before you put the wrapped pastry in the refrigerator, shape it into a roughly flat-topped disc – a bit like a big burger. This will make it easier to roll.

1 Preheat the oven to 190°C/375°F/Gas Mark 5. To make the pastry, put the butter in a mixing bowl, add the flour and season with salt and pepper. Rub the butter into the flour until it resembles fine breadcrumbs. Alternatively, process it in a food processor. Gradually mix in enough of the water to make a soft but not sticky dough.

2 Lightly dust a work surface with flour. Pat the dough into a disc (see tip below), then wrap it in clingfilm. Chill in the refrigerator for at least 30 minutes.

3 Meanwhile, to make the filling, put the butternut squash and oil in a large roasting tin, season with salt and pepper and toss well. Roast for 15 minutes, then stir and add the chorizo. Roast for 15 minutes more, or until the squash is crisp on the edges and tender, and the chorizo is crisp. Set aside to cool.

4 Dust the work surface with more flour. Knead the pastry gently, then roll it out to a circle just under 23 cm/9 inches in diameter. Place on a baking sheet and prick all over with a fork. Bake for 20 minutes. Remove from the oven and, using the base of a 20-cm/8-inch loose-bottomed tart tin as a template, cut a circle in the pastry. Set aside to cool.

5 Meanwhile, crack the eggs into a large bowl and lightly beat with a fork. Stir in the crème fraîche and thyme and season with plenty of pepper.

6 Line the 20-cm/8-inch tart tin with baking paper. Carefully place your cooled pastry circle in the tin, then scatter with the chorizo and butternut squash. Pour over the egg mixture, then crumble the goat's cheese on top. Reduce the oven temperature to 160°C/325°F/Gas Mark 3. Bake the quiche for 30 minutes, or until the egg in the centre is set. Serve warm or cold, with salad leaves, if using.

PER SERVING: 677 CALS | 49.7G FAT | 23.5G SAT FAT | 32G CARBS | 3.9G SUGARS | 3G SALT | 4.7G FIBRE | 27.5G PROTEIN

BLUE CHEESE AND HERB PATE

*An easy-to-make light lunch, this filling pâté is also ideal for a starter
or for packing in a summer picnic.*

SERVES: 4   PREP: 20 MINS
CHILL: 30 MINS   COOK: 1 MIN

150 g/5¹/2 oz full-fat soft cheese
350 g/12 oz fromage frais
115 g/4 oz blue cheese, crumbled
15 g/¹/2 oz dried cranberries, finely chopped
25 g/1 oz fresh herbs, such as flat-leaf parsley,
chives, dill and tarragon, finely chopped
85 g/3 oz butter
25 g/1 oz walnuts, roughly chopped
4 slices of wholegrain bread, to serve

1 Put the soft cheese in a bowl and beat well with a metal
spoon to soften. Gradually beat in the fromage frais until
smooth. Add the blue cheese, cranberries and herbs, and stir
well. Spoon the mixture into four 150-ml/5-fl oz ramekins or
small dishes and smooth the tops.

2 Melt the butter in a small saucepan over a low heat. Skim
any foam off the surface and discard it. Carefully pour the
clear yellow top layer into a small jug, leaving the milky liquid
in the pan. The yellow layer is the clarified butter; discard
the remaining liquid in the pan.

3 Pour a little of the clarified butter over each ramekin of
pâté and sprinkle with the walnuts. Cover with clingfilm and
chill in the refrigerator for at least 30 minutes, or until firm.

4 Toast the bread and serve the pâté alongside it, spreading
some onto the toast.

SLOW-RELEASE ENERGY

Protein from the cheese provides the
slow-release energy you need to keep going
without feeling the need to top up with sugar.

PER SERVING: 455 CALS | 40G FAT | 24G SAT FAT | 9.8G CARBS | 7.8G SUGARS | 1.8G SALT | 0.5G FIBRE | 15.5G PROTEIN

SMOKY PAPRIKA SWEET POTATO CHIPS WITH SOURED CREAM DIP

Starchy and sweet, with crunchy edges and fluffy insides, these chips make a really satisfying snack. Always use the best paprika you can find.

SERVES: 2   PREP: 10 MINS   COOK: 40 MINS

300 g/10½ oz sweet potatoes, unpeeled, scrubbed and cut into chips
2 tbsp olive oil
1 heaped tbsp smoked paprika
sea salt and pepper

SOURED CREAM DIP
4 stalks of chives, finely snipped
150 g/5½ oz soured cream

1 Preheat the oven to 180°C/350°F/Gas Mark 4. Put the sweet potatoes, oil and smoked paprika in a large bowl, season with salt and pepper and toss well.

2 Arrange the chips in a single layer on a large baking sheet. Bake for 30–40 minutes, or until crisp.

3 To make the dip, put the chives and soured cream in a bowl and mix. Season with salt and pepper and divide between two small dipping bowls.

4 Line two larger bowls with kitchen paper. Transfer the chips to the bowls and serve immediately with the dip.

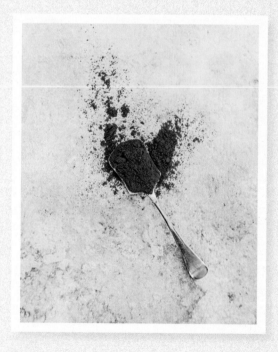

ALSO TRY THIS

This dip works well with 2 tablespoons of finely chopped fresh flat-leaf parsley instead of chives, or try mixing in ½ teaspoon of smoked paprika.

PER SERVING: 399 CALS | 28.4G FAT | 10.4G SAT FAT | 32.8G CARBS | 8.8G SUGARS | 1.1G SALT | 5G FIBRE | 4G PROTEIN

CRUNCHY PARMESAN AND KALE CRISPS

This recipe for kale crisps is one of the simplest you'll ever make. They're deliciously crisp, with a salty kick from the Parmesan.

SERVES: 4   PREP: 10 MINS   COOK: 15 MINS

200 g/7 oz kale, woody stalks removed
1 tbsp olive oil
pinch of cayenne pepper
100 g/3½ oz Parmesan cheese, finely grated
sea salt

1   Preheat the oven to 180°C/350°F/Gas Mark 4. Put the kale and oil in a bowl, season with the cayenne pepper and salt, then toss.

2   Arrange the kale in a single layer on a large baking sheet. Sprinkle the cheese over the kale. Bake for 10–15 minutes, or until the leaves are dry and crisp but just a little brown at the edges.

3   Leave to cool and crisp up for 5 minutes, then serve.

BAKING KALE

Watch your kale very closely; if it overcooks and the leaves turn brown they will be bitter.

PER SERVING: 153 CALS | 10.2G FAT | 4.6G SAT FAT | 5.8G CARBS | 0.2G SUGARS | 1.4G SALT | 1G FIBRE | 10.6G PROTEIN

CHOCOLATE AND BRAZIL NUT BARS

These bars are ideal for anyone with a sweet tooth. They have a crunchy, chewy texture and are perfect for when you're out and about.

MAKES: 9 BARS   PREP: 20 MINS
COOK: 4 MINS   CHILL: 30 MINS

100 g/3½ oz flaked almonds
125 g/4½ oz Brazil nuts, roughly chopped
70 g/2½ oz unsalted butter
70 g/2½ oz almond butter
1 tsp vanilla extract
50 g/1¾ oz ground almonds
30 g/1 oz desiccated coconut
1½ tbsp rice malt syrup
2 tsp cocoa powder
20 g/¾ oz plain chocolate with 85% cocoa, cut into small chunks
sea salt

1 Line a 19-cm/7½-inch square cake tin with baking paper. Toast the flaked almonds and Brazil nuts in a dry frying pan over a high heat until they are light brown, then tip them into a large mixing bowl.

2 Melt the butters together in a small saucepan over a low heat. Stir in the vanilla and a pinch of salt.

3 Add all the remaining ingredients to the toasted nuts, then stir. Add the melted butter mixture and stir again. Tip the mixture into the prepared tin and, using the back of a spoon, spread it out to reach all the corners. Cover and chill in the refrigerator for 30 minutes, or until set.

4 Cut into nine bars and wrap each in baking paper. Store in an airtight container in the refrigerator for up to two days.

SAVE TIME

Pulse the Brazil nuts momentarily in a food processor to chop them. If you buy whole rather than flaked almonds, they can be chopped in this way too.

PER BAR: 334 CALS | 31.5G FAT | 9.6G SAT FAT | 9.9G CARBS | 3G SUGARS | 0.2G SALT | 4.1G FIBRE | 7.8G PROTEIN

PLAIN CHOCOLATE AND PEANUT BUTTER ENERGY BALLS

Chocolate containing more than 80 per cent cocoa is one of the star ingredients of the low-sugar kitchen if used in small amounts.

MAKES: 8 BALLS   PREP: 15 MINS   CHILL: 30 MINS

50 g/1³/4 oz almond flour
60 g/2¹/4 oz unsweetened peanut butter
20 g/³/4 oz unsalted peanuts, roughly chopped
3 tbsp flaxseeds
30 g/1 oz plain chocolate with 85% cocoa, finely chopped
1 tsp cocoa powder
sea salt

1 Put the almond flour in a food processor and process for a minute, until you have the texture of rough flour.

2 Put the peanut butter, peanuts, flaxseeds, chocolate and a small pinch of salt in a bowl and mix. Add the almond flour, reserving 1¹/2 tablespoons. Mix until you have a texture resembling chunky clay.

3 Sprinkle the remaining almond flour and the cocoa powder onto a plate and mix with a teaspoon. Form a tablespoon-sized blob of the peanut mixture into a ball using your palms. Roll it in the cocoa powder mixture, then transfer to a plate. Make a further seven balls in the same way.

4 Cover and chill in the refrigerator for at least 30 minutes, or up to two days.

ALSO TRY THIS

If the coating of cocoa powder is too bitter and strong for your taste, substitute it with a teaspoon of ground cinnamon.

PER BALL: 144 CALS | 11.9G FAT | 2.1G SAT FAT | 5.9G CARBS | 1.7G SUGARS | 0.3G SALT | 3G FIBRE | 4.9G PROTEIN

GINGER AND OAT NO-BAKE BISCUITS

This is a low-sugar version of the beloved flapjack. Sweet, gingery and oaty, it has an irresistible flavour and lots of texture.

MAKES: 8 BISCUITS   PREP: 10 MINS
COOK: 8 MINS   CHILL: 25 MINS

50 g/1³/4 oz unsalted butter
200 ml/7 fl oz double cream
1 heaped tbsp unsweetened smooth peanut butter
3 tbsp rice malt syrup
1 tbsp ground ginger
200 g/7 oz large rolled oats

1 Put the butter, cream and peanut butter in a saucepan and bring to the boil over a medium heat, stirring from time to time. Turn the heat down to medium–low and cook for 5 minutes.

2 Tip all the remaining ingredients into the pan and stir.

3 Line a baking sheet with baking paper. Drop tablespoons of the mixture onto the tray – it should make eight biscuits – then, cover and chill in the refrigerator for 25 minutes before serving.

ALSO TRY THIS

If you're not a fan of ginger, try using the same amount of ground cinnamon or allspice instead.

PER BISCUIT: 175 CALS | 11.8G FAT | 6.3G SAT FAT | 14G CARBS | 1.6G SUGARS | 0.2G SALT | 2G FIBRE | 3.8G PROTEIN

MAINS

Rib-eye steak, chimichurri sauce and sweet potato mash	74
Steak, broccoli and sesame seed stir-fry	76
Hearty beef stew with herby cheese dumplings and kale	78
Bolognese sauce	81
Black rice risotto with Parma ham and charred chicory	82
Spicy fried chicken with red cabbage and chilli coleslaw	84
Chicken satay with sweet potato and spinach stir-fry	86
Monkfish in pesto and Parma ham with ricotta spinach	88
Crispy Parmesan-coated sea bass	91
Squid with saffron aioli	92
Pumpkin and Gruyère bake	94
Butternut squash and lentil stew	97
New potato, feta and herb frittata	98

RIB-EYE STEAK, CHIMICHURRI SAUCE AND SWEET POTATO MASH

Chimichurri is an Argentinian herb sauce with a texture similar to rough pesto. Most regions have a variation on it, such as adding anchovies or removing the chilli.

SERVES: 2   PREP: 30 MINS   COOK: 22 MINS

1 tbsp olive oil
· 2 x 125 g/4¹/2 oz rib-eye steaks
¹/2 tsp ground cumin
sea salt and pepper

CHIMICHURRI SAUCE
15 g/¹/2 oz fresh flat-leaf parsley, roughly chopped
15 g/¹/2 oz fresh oregano
3 small garlic cloves, roughly chopped
¹/2 shallot, roughly chopped
¹/4 red chilli, deseeded and roughly chopped
3 tbsp extra virgin olive oil
1 tsp red wine vinegar
juice of ¹/4 lemon

MASH
250 g/9 oz sweet potatoes, cut into
2-cm/³/4-inch chunks
20 g/³/4 butter

1 To make the mash, cook the sweet potatoes in a large saucepan of lightly salted boiling water for 12–15 minutes, or until very soft. Drain, then leave off the heat to steam dry in the pan for at least 5 minutes. Using a potato masher, mash the potatoes to a smooth consistency.

2 Meanwhile, to make the chimichurri sauce, put all the ingredients in a food processor, season with salt and pepper, and process until you have a paste of a similar consistency to pesto. Add a little extra olive oil if the mixture appears too . thick. Spoon into a serving bowl, cover and set aside.

3 Return the mash to the heat and warm through before stirring in the butter. Season with salt and pepper, and keep warm.

4 Massage the oil into both sides of each steak, then sprinkle with salt and the cumin. Heat a griddle pan over a high heat until smoking hot. Cook each steak for 2–3 minutes on each side, or for longer if you prefer it well done. Allow the steaks to rest for 2 minutes.

5 Serve a steak on each of two plates with the chimichurri sauce spooned over and the mash on the side.

STEAK POWER

Steak is crammed with selenium and zinc and contains moderate amounts of iron and phosphorus. It is also a good source of protein and B vitamins.

PER SERVING: 691 CALS | 52.8G FAT | 15.7G SAT FAT | 26.4G CARBS | 5.2G SUGARS | 2G SALT | 3.8G FIBRE | 27G PROTEIN

STEAK, BROCCOLI AND SESAME SEED STIR-FRY

Vibrant green broccoli and juicy beef are the stars of this stir-fry,
and the sesame oil introduces a nutty depth and richness.

SERVES: 2

PREP: 15 MINS PLUS MARINATING   COOK: 10 MINS

1 tbsp soy sauce, plus extra to serve
1 tbsp sesame oil, plus extra to serve
200 g/7 oz sirloin beef steak, cut into strips
2 tsp sesame seeds
1 tbsp groundnut oil
1 large garlic clove, thinly sliced
½ red chilli, deseeded and thinly sliced lengthways (optional)
250 g/9 oz broccolini
3 tbsp water

1 Mix the soy sauce and sesame oil in a large bowl, add the steak and toss. Cover and leave to marinate for 10 minutes.

2 Toast the sesame seeds in a large dry wok over a high heat until they are just beginning to brown, then tip them into the bowl with the steak and set aside.

3 Remove the wok from the heat and wipe it clean with kitchen paper. Return to the heat and pour in the oil. Remove the steak from the marinade and quickly cook it, turning from time to time, until browned on all sides and cooked to your liking. Transfer it to a plate and set aside.

4 If the pan is dry, add a splash more oil, then fry the garlic and chilli, if using. Add the broccolini, steak marinade and water, stir and cook for 1 minute, until the broccolini is bright green and just beginning to soften.

5 Return the steak to the wok and stir well. Divide the stir-fry between two plates and drizzle with extra soy sauce and sesame oil. Serve immediately.

ALSO TRY THIS

Add a 2.5-cm/1-inch piece of fresh ginger, finely grated, with the garlic and chilli in step four and stir in a handful of finely chopped fresh coriander with the steak in step five.

PER SERVING: 366 CALS | 24.5G FAT | 4.8G SAT FAT | 10.5G CARBS | 2.2G SUGARS | 1.4G SALT | 4.1G FIBRE | 28.6G PROTEIN

HEARTY BEEF STEW WITH HERBY CHEESE DUMPLINGS AND KALE

Rich, deep and comforting, this delicious winter stew will draw everyone to the table and fill up the hungriest of diners.

SERVES: 4   PREP: 30 MINS   COOK: 3¹/4 HOURS

4 tbsp olive oil
1/2 onion, finely chopped
1 leek, thinly sliced
1 celery stick, roughly chopped
4 garlic cloves, finely chopped
1 level tsp tomato purée
900 g/2 lb beef shin, cut into bite-sized chunks
45 g/1¹/2 oz quinoa flour
125 ml/4 fl oz brandy
800 ml/1 pint 7 fl oz beef stock
1 tbsp fresh thyme leaves
2 tbsp finely chopped fresh flat-leaf parsley
2 tsp smoked paprika
6 cloves
2 fresh bay leaves
sea salt and pepper
200 g/7 oz kale, roughly chopped, to serve
juice of 1/4 lemon, to serve

DUMPLINGS
125 g/4¹/2 oz quinoa flour
20 g/³/4 oz beef suet
60 g/2¹/4 oz mature Cheddar cheese, grated
1 tsp baking powder
1 tbsp fresh thyme leaves
2 tbsp finely chopped fresh flat-leaf parsley
4 tbsp water

1   Heat 2 tablespoons of the oil in a large lidded casserole over a medium heat. Add the onion, leek and celery, and fry for 5 minutes, or until softened. Add the garlic and tomato purée, stir well, then turn the heat down to medium–low and leave to simmer while you cook the meat.

2   Heat the remaining 2 tablespoons of the oil in a large heavy-based frying pan over a high heat until smoking hot. Season the beef with salt and pepper, then add it to the pan in batches and cook for a few minutes, turning, until browned on all sides. Using a slotted spoon, transfer the first batch to a plate while you brown the rest of the meat. Toss the browned meat into the casserole, then stir in the quinoa flour.

3   Turn the heat down to medium–high. Deglaze the beef frying pan with the brandy, being careful as it can flame. Scrape all the meaty goodness off the bottom of the pan into the bubbling brandy with a wooden spoon, then tip into the casserole. Pour in the stock, then add the thyme, parsley, paprika, cloves and bay leaves, and season with salt and pepper.

4   Bring to a light boil, then turn the heat down to low and put on the lid. Simmer for 2–2¹/2 hours, or until the sauce is thick and the meat is soft enough to pull apart with a spoon.

5   To make the dumplings, put the quinoa flour, suet, cheese, baking powder, thyme and parsley in a large bowl and mix well. Add the water a little at a time, mixing, until you have a firm dough. Shape the mixture into 12 small balls.

6   After 2–2¹/2 hours cooking, remove the lid from the stew and arrange the dumplings on top. Put the lid back on and cook for 20 minutes, or until cooked through.

7   Cook the kale in a large pan of lightly salted boiling water for 2 minutes. Drain, then squeeze over the lemon juice and toss lightly. Serve immediately with the stew.

PER SERVING: 830 CALS | 39.7G FAT | 14.5G SAT FAT | 41G CARBS | 3G SUGARS | 3.9G SALT | 5G FIBRE | 60G PROTEIN

BOLOGNESE SAUCE

A rich, filling, classic Italian sauce that tastes delicious served stirred into wholewheat tagliatelle.

SERVES: 4   PREP: 10 MINS   COOK: 1¹/4 HOURS

25 g/1 oz dried ceps
125 ml/4 fl oz lukewarm water
1 tbsp butter
55 g/2 oz pancetta, diced
1 small onion, finely chopped
1 garlic clove, finely chopped
2 small carrots, finely chopped
2 celery sticks, finely chopped
300 g/10¹/2 oz beef mince
pinch of freshly grated nutmeg
1 level tbsp tomato purée
125 ml/4 fl oz red wine
250 ml/9 fl oz passata
sea salt and pepper
400 g/14 oz fresh wholewheat tagliatelle (optional)

1 Soak the ceps in the water for 20 minutes, then drain well, reserving the soaking water.

2 Meanwhile, melt the butter in a heavy-based saucepan over a medium heat. Add the pancetta and fry, stirring, for 4 minutes, or until cooked.

3 Add the onion and garlic and fry for 4 minutes, or until translucent. Add the carrots and celery, and fry for a further few minutes, stirring often.

4 Add the mince and fry, stirring constantly, for 5 minutes, or until browned. Season with salt and pepper and add the nutmeg. Stir in the tomato purée and cook for 1–2 minutes, then pour in the wine and passata.

5 Thinly slice the ceps, then add them to the sauce. Pour in the soaking water through a fine sieve. Cook for 1 hour, or until you have a thickened sauce and the mince is cooked.

6 Meanwhile, cook the tagliatelle, if using, according to the packet instructions, then drain well. Serve the Bolognese with the tagliatelle.

CHOICE OF PASTA

Italians would traditionally serve Bolognese with tagliatelle rather than spaghetti.

PER SERVING: 272 CALS | 11G FAT | 5.1G SAT FAT | 14.6G CARBS | 5G SUGARS | 1.6G SALT | 3G FIBRE | 21G PROTEIN

BLACK RICE RISOTTO WITH PARMA HAM AND CHARRED CHICORY

Black rice (or 'forbidden' rice) contains large amounts of antitoxins and fibre, as well as being low in sugar, and makes a change from traditional risotto rice.

SERVES: 4   PREP: 10 MINS   COOK: 1 HOUR

200 g/7 oz black rice
6 Parma ham slices
1 tbsp olive oil
2 small heads chicory, quartered lengthways
15 g/1/2 oz butter
2 garlic cloves, thinly sliced
1 small shallot, roughly chopped
500 ml/17 fl oz chicken stock
2 level tbsp mascarpone cheese
2 tbsp roughly chopped fresh flat-leaf parsley
sea salt

1 Cook the rice in a large pan of lightly salted boiling water for 45 minutes, or until tender but slightly chewy.

2 Heat a deep frying pan over a medium–high heat. Add the Parma ham and dry-fry for 30 seconds on each side, or until crisp. Transfer to a plate.

3 Add the oil to the pan, then fry the chicory for 2 minutes on each side, or until darkly golden. Remove from the pan, wrap in kitchen foil to keep warm and set aside.

4 Reduce the heat to medium, then melt the butter in the pan. Add the garlic and shallot and fry for 4 minutes, or until softened. Add the cooked and drained rice and stock, bring to a simmer, then cook gently for 5 minutes, or until two-thirds of the liquid has been absorbed. Stir in the mascarpone and parsley, then return the chicory to the pan and warm through.

5 Crumble the Parma ham into large shards. Serve the risotto heaped into four bowls with the crisp ham on top.

WHY EAT BLACK RICE?

Black rice is arguably even better for you than wholegrain rice, because the bran hull contains significantly higher amounts of vitamin E, which boosts the immune system.

PER SERVING: 346 CALS | 17.6G FAT | 8.3G SAT FAT | 38G CARBS | 2.8G SUGARS | 2.8G SALT | 2.9G FIBRE | 12G PROTEIN

SPICY FRIED CHICKEN WITH RED CABBAGE AND CHILLI COLESLAW

Instead of the usual breadcrumbs, this chicken has a crunchy coating of polenta, quinoa flour and wholemeal flour, which works brilliantly with the zingy flavours of the coleslaw.

SERVES: 4
PREP: 20 MINS PLUS MARINATING   COOK: 35 MINS

200 ml/7 fl oz soured cream
1/2 tsp cayenne pepper
1 garlic clove, crushed
4 chicken thighs and 4 chicken drumsticks (about 850 g/1 lb 14 oz)
2 tsp coarse polenta
2 tbsp quinoa flour
2 tbsp wholemeal plain flour
vegetable oil, for deep-frying
sea salt and pepper

COLESLAW
200 g/7 oz red cabbage, shredded
400 g/14 oz fennel, shredded
1 red chilli, deseeded and thinly sliced lengthways
100 g/3½ oz Greek-style natural yogurt
juice of ¼ lemon

1 Put the soured cream, cayenne and garlic in a large bowl and season well with salt and pepper. Add the chicken and toss well. Cover the bowl with clingfilm and chill in the refrigerator for 2–3 hours, or overnight if you have time.

2 To make the coleslaw, put all the ingredients in a large bowl and toss well, then season with salt and pepper to taste. Cover and chill in the refrigerator.

3 Mix together the polenta and flours on a plate and season with salt and pepper. Half-fill a heavy-based frying pan with oil and place it over a medium-high heat. Heat the oil to 180°C/350°F, or until a cube of bread browns in 30 seconds. While it heats, sprinkle the flour mixture over the chicken.

4 Cook the chicken in two batches, as too much chicken in the pan will make the oil temperature drop. Using tongs, carefully place half the chicken in the oil. Cook for 6–8 minutes, then turn and cook for a further 6–8 minutes, until the coating is a deep golden brown, the chicken is cooked through to the bone, and the juices run clear with no sign of pink when a skewer is inserted into the thickest part of the meat.

5 Using a slotted spoon, transfer the cooked chicken to kitchen paper to drain, then keep warm in a low oven while you cook the second batch.

6 Serve the chicken on a sharing board with the coleslaw.

PER SERVING: 695 CALS | 47.4G FAT | 14.5G SAT FAT | 30G CARBS | 6G SUGARS | 1.3G SALT | 6G FIBRE | 38G PROTEIN

CHICKEN SATAY WITH SWEET POTATO AND SPINACH STIR-FRY

*This seriously flavoursome dish is packed with Asian punch,
and the satay sauce has a mildly sweet and satisfying flavour.*

SERVES: 4
PREP: 20 MINS PLUS MARINATING   COOK: 20 MINS

8 small skinless and boneless chicken thighs
(550 g/1 lb 4 oz), cut into 1.5-cm/ ½-inch chunks

MARINADE
1 small stick of lemon grass, finely chopped
1 small shallot, finely chopped
1 large garlic clove, finely chopped
1 red chilli, deseeded and finely chopped
2.5-cm/1-inch piece fresh ginger,
peeled and finely chopped
2 tbsp finely chopped fresh coriander
2 tbsp soy sauce
1 tbsp groundnut oil

PEANUT SATAY SAUCE
2 level tbsp unsweetened peanut butter
100 ml/3½ fl oz coconut milk

STIR-FRY
1 tbsp groundnut oil
½ red chilli, deseeded and thinly sliced
2-cm/¾-inch piece fresh ginger,
peeled and thinly sliced
200 g/7 oz sweet potatoes, cut into strips
using a vegetable peeler
200 g/7 oz baby spinach
dash of soy sauce

1 Soak eight bamboo skewers in water for at least 10 minutes.

2 Put all the marinade ingredients in a blender and process
to a fine paste.

3 Put the chicken in a deep bowl. Scrape the marinade into
the bowl and stir well so that all the chicken is thoroughly
coated. Cover the bowl with clingfilm and chill in the
refrigerator for 2–4 hours.

4 To make the satay sauce, put the peanut butter and
coconut milk in a bowl and stir well. Transfer to a dipping bowl.

5 Thread the marinated chicken evenly onto the skewers.
Heat a griddle pan over a high heat until smoking hot. Cook
the skewers for 2 minutes on each side, or until the
chicken is cooked through and a little charred at the edges
and the juices run clear with no sign of pink when a piece is
cut in half.

6 Meanwhile, to make the stir-fry, heat the oil in a large wok
over a high heat. Add the chilli and ginger and stir-fry for
30 seconds. Add the sweet potatoes and stir-fry for
1 minute, then add the spinach and soy sauce and stir-fry
for 30 seconds.

7 Serve the skewers on a platter with the dipping sauce and
individual portions of the stir-fry in bowls.

PER SERVING: 451 CALS | 26.6G FAT | 8.3G SAT FAT | 16.7G CARBS | 4.1G SUGARS | 2.2G SALT | 4.2G FIBRE | 35.7G PROTEIN

MONKFISH IN PESTO AND PARMA HAM WITH RICOTTA SPINACH

Monkfish can dry out during cooking, but by wrapping it in Parma ham you can keep it moist and add lots of extra flavour and texture.

SERVES: 4   PREP: 25 MINS   COOK: 25 MINS

8 Parma ham slices
3 tbsp fresh green pesto
8 large fresh basil leaves
600 g/1 lb 5 oz monkfish tail, separated into 2 fillets
1 tbsp olive oil

RICOTTA SPINACH
2 tbsp olive oil
1 garlic clove, thinly sliced
150 g/5¹/₂ oz baby spinach
2 tbsp ricotta cheese
sea salt and pepper

1 Preheat the oven to 180°C/350°F/Gas Mark 4. Lay two large sheets of clingfilm side–by–side on a work surface. Arrange the Parma ham slices vertically on the clingfilm so they overlap by 1 cm/¹/₂ inch. Spread the pesto all over the ham, leaving a 2–cm/³/₄–inch border around the edge. Scatter the basil over the top.

2 Put one monkfish fillet on top of the pesto and basil, then lay the other fillet next to it the other way round, so its thick end is against its neighbour's thin end.

3 Fold the ham over the ends of the fish and then, using the clingfilm, roll and encase the whole fillet tightly in the ham. Remove the clingfilm. Transfer to a roasting tin so the join in the ham is on the bottom, and lightly drizzle with the oil. Roast for 20–25 minutes, or until cooked through but still moist. Cover the tin with kitchen foil to keep the fish warm.

4 To make the ricotta spinach, heat the oil in a large frying pan over a medium–high heat. Add the garlic and cook for 30 seconds, or until it is soft but not burnt. Stir in the spinach and cook, stirring all the time so the oil coats the leaves, for 1 minute, or until it is wilted but not completely collapsed. Transfer to a serving bowl, dot with blobs of the ricotta and season well with salt and pepper.

5 Place the fish on a serving platter, carve into slices and pour over any cooking juices from the roasting tin. Serve with the spinach.

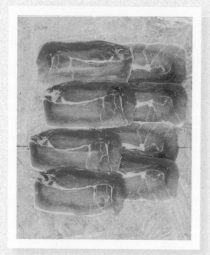

MMM, MONKFISH

Monkfish is loaded with protein and includes vitamins B6 and B12, which are essential for brain function. It also includes the minerals phosphorus and selenium.

PER SERVING: 341 CALS | 22G FAT | 5G SAT FAT | 2.5G CARBS | 0.6G SUGARS | 2.3G SALT | 0.8G FIBRE | 35.2G PROTEIN

CRISPY PARMESAN-COATED SEA BASS

Parmesan cheese, parsley and lemon make a top-notch trio to spooon over sea bass, adding a delicious flavour without overpowering the delicate fish.

SERVES: 4   PREP: 15 MINS   COOK: 4 MINS

3 tbsp olive oil
4 x 125 g/4^1/$_2$ oz sea bass fillets, skin on and pin-boned
finely grated zest and juice of 1 unwaxed lemon, plus 1 lemon, cut into wedges to serve
100 g/3^1/$_2$ oz Parmesan cheese, finely grated
25 g/1 oz fresh flat-leaf parsley, finely chopped
sea salt and pepper
70 g/2^1/$_2$ oz watercress, rocket or mixed leaves, to serve

1 Preheat the grill to its highest setting. Brush the grill rack with a little of the oil and lay the sea bass fillets on top, skin side-down. Drizzle over a little of the remaining oil, give each fillet a good squeeze of lemon juice and season with salt and pepper.

2 Put the lemon zest, cheese and parsley in a bowl and mix well, then scatter the mixture evenly over the fish. Drizzle over the remaining oil.

3 Grill for 4 minutes, or until the fish is just cooked and golden – the exact cooking time will depend on the thickness of the fillets. Serve immediately with the salad and lemon wedges for squeezing over.

PARMESAN PLEASE

Parmesan cheese is an excellent source of bone-building calcium and phosphorus. It also includes good levels of protein, vitamin B12, zinc, selenium and riboflavin.

PER SERVING: 339 CALS | 19.6G FAT | 6.3G SAT FAT | 2G CARBS | 0.5G SUGARS | 2G SALT | 0.2G FIBRE | 37G PROTEIN

SQUID WITH SAFFRON AIOLI

In this take on a classic squid dish, the celebrated crispy coating of the squid is made from cornflour, which has a low sugar content.

SERVES: 2 PREP: 30 MINS COOK: 9 MINS

500 g/1 lb 2 oz whole small squid,
skinned, cleaned and gutted
3 level tbsp cornflour
vegetable oil, for deep-frying
sea salt and pepper
2 lemon wedges, to serve (optional)

AIOLI
small pinch of saffron strands
1 tsp lukewarm water
3 heaped tbsp whole egg mayonnaise
1/2 small garlic clove, finely chopped

SALAD
head of red chicory, leaves separated
25 g/1 oz watercress
10 g/1/4 oz Parmesan cheese, shaved
juice of 1/4 lemon
1 tbsp extra virgin olive oil

1 To make the aioli, put the saffron and water in a small bowl and leave for 5 minutes. Stir during the soaking to release the flavour. Meanwhile, put the mayonnaise and garlic in a bowl and mix well. When the saffron has turned the water vibrant yellow, discard the saffron strands and stir the liquid into the mayonnaise. Transfer to two dipping bowls, cover with clingfilm and chill in the refrigerator.

2 To make the salad, put the chicory and watercress in a large bowl, then scatter over the cheese. Put the lemon juice and oil in a small jug and mix well with a fork.

3 Slice the squid body into 1-cm/1/2-inch rounds and cut the tentacles in half. Wash under the cold tap, then dry on kitchen paper. Put the cornflour on a plate and season with plenty of salt and pepper, then toss the squid lightly in it to coat.

4 Heat the oil in a deep heavy-based saucepan, being careful not to fill the pan too high. To test whether it is hot enough, drop in a small cube of bread. If it takes about 30 seconds to turn golden, the oil is ready.

5 Cook the squid in two batches, as too much squid in the pan will make the oil temperature drop. Scatter half the squid in the oil and cook for 2–3 minutes, until the coating is just tinged a golden colour.

6 Using a slotted spoon, transfer the cooked squid to kitchen paper to drain, then keep warm in the oven while you cook the second batch.

7 Season the squid with salt and pepper. Pour the dressing over the salad. Serve the squid immediately with the salad and aioli, and lemon wedges for squeezing over, if using.

COOKING SQUID

Smaller squid are often less tough than their large counterparts and require less cooking.

PER SERVING: 783 CALS | 51.8G FAT | 8.4G SAT FAT | 35G CARBS | 2G SUGARS | 2.6G SALT | 1.3G FIBRE | 43.1G PROTEIN

PUMPKIN AND GRUYERE BAKE

This creamy, wholesome dip served in a pumpkin shell is great fun and will be loved by the whole family.

SERVES: 4   PREP: 15 MINS   COOK: 1 HOUR 10 MINS

1 large pumpkin
300 ml/10 fl oz double cream
3 garlic cloves, thinly sliced
1 tbsp fresh thyme leaves, plus sprigs to garnish
125 g/4½ oz Gruyère cheese
sea salt and pepper
4 slices of wholegrain crusty bread, to serve
70 g/2½ oz watercress salad, to serve (optional)

1 Preheat the oven to 180°C/350°F/Gas Mark 4. Cut horizontally straight through the top quarter of the pumpkin to form a lid. Scoop out the seeds. Put the pumpkin in a large, deep ovenproof dish.

2 Put the cream and garlic in a saucepan, then place over a medium heat and bring to just below boiling point. Remove from the heat, season with salt and pepper and stir in the thyme. Pour the mixture into the pumpkin and replace the pumpkin lid.

3 Bake for 1 hour, or until the flesh is tender. Take care not to overcook the pumpkin, or it may collapse. Remove from the oven, lift off the lid and scatter over the cheese. Bake for a further 10 minutes with the lid off.

4 Scatter over the thyme sprigs. Serve the soft pumpkin flesh with a generous portion of the cheesy cream, a slice of the bread, and the salad, if using.

PUMPKIN POWER

Pumpkin is rich in beta–carotene, which the body converts into vitamin A, a powerful antioxidant that helps us maintain good skin and sight. It is also a good source of B vitamins, including B6 and folates.

PER SERVING: 453 CALS | 38G FAT | 23.3G SAT FAT | 18.4G CARBS | 3.5G SUGARS | 1.8G SALT | 1.2G FIBRE | 13.3G PROTEIN

BUTTERNUT SQUASH AND LENTIL STEW

Brown lentils have a powerful savoury flavour and are a great choice for vegetarians and meat-eaters alike. They are also super-rich in iron and protein.

SERVES: 4   PREP: 10 MINS   COOK: 30 MINS

1 tbsp olive oil
1 onion, finely chopped
3 garlic cloves, finely chopped
2 level tbsp tomato purée
2 tsp ground cumin
1 tsp ground cinnamon
1/4 tsp cayenne pepper
450 g/1 lb butternut squash flesh, cut into cubes
100 g/3½ oz brown lentils
450 ml/15 fl oz vegetable stock
juice of 1/4 lemon
sea salt and pepper

TO SERVE
2 tbsp finely chopped fresh coriander
2 tbsp flaked almonds
4 tbsp natural yogurt

1   Heat the oil in a large saucepan over a medium–high heat. Add the onion and garlic and cook, stirring occasionally, for 5 minutes, or until soft.

2   Add the tomato purée, cumin, cinnamon and cayenne and season well with salt and pepper, then stir. Add the squash, lentils and stock, and bring to the boil. Reduce the heat to low and simmer uncovered, stirring occasionally, for 25 minutes, or until the squash and lentils are tender.

3   Just before serving, stir in the lemon juice. Serve hot, sprinkled with the coriander and almonds, with a dollop of the yogurt on top.

LOVELY LENTILS

Lentils contain high levels of soluble fibre, which studies show can help to reduce the risk of heart disease. They are also rich in protein, folate and magnesium.

PER SERVING: 234 CALS | 7G FAT | 1.1G SAT FAT | 35G CARBS | 6G SUGARS | 2.6G SALT | 11G FIBRE | 9.7G PROTEIN

NEW POTATO, FETA AND HERB FRITTATA

This easy-to-make treat is perfect for a main course, or leave it to go cold, then wrap it in foil and enjoy for lunch or take on a picnic.

SERVES: 4   PREP: 20 MINS   COOK: 35 MINS

250 g/9 oz new potatoes, scrubbed
85 g/3 oz baby spinach
5 eggs
1 tbsp finely chopped fresh dill, plus extra to garnish
1 tbsp snipped fresh chives, plus extra to garnish
115 g/4 oz feta cheese, crumbled
10 g/¼ oz butter
1 tbsp olive oil
sea salt and pepper

1 Cook the potatoes in a large saucepan of lightly salted boiling water for 25 minutes, or until tender.

2 Put the spinach in a colander and drain the potatoes over the top to wilt it. Set aside until cool enough to handle.

3 Cut the potatoes lengthways into 5-mm/¼-inch thick slices. Squeeze the excess water from the spinach.

4 Crack the eggs into a bowl and lightly beat with a fork. Add the dill and chives and beat again. Season with pepper and add 85 g/3 oz feta. Preheat the grill to high.

5 Heat the butter and oil together in a 20-cm/8-inch frying pan over a medium heat until melted and foaming. Add the potatoes and spinach and cook, stirring, for 1 minute. Pour in the egg mixture. Cook, stirring, for 2 minutes, or until half set, then cook for a further 2–3 minutes without stirring, until set and golden brown underneath.

6 Sprinkle with the remaining feta, then grill for 3–4 minutes, until golden brown on top. Serve hot or cold, sprinkled with the remaining dill and chives.

EXCELLENT EGGS

Eggs are a wonderful source of protein, vitamins A and D, and B vitamins.

PER SERVING: 272 CALS | 18.3G FAT | 8.2G SAT FAT | 12.3G CARBS | 2.2G SUGARS | 1.9G SALT | 2G FIBRE | 14.5G PROTEIN

DESSERTS AND BAKING

LEMON CHEESECAKE WITH ALMOND BASE

A crunchy-based, zesty and creamy cheesecake that's perfect for when friends come over for dinner.

SERVES: 8   PREP: 20 MINS   COOK: 1^1/4 HOURS

20 g/^{3}/4 oz butter, plus extra for greasing
100 g/3^1/2 oz ground almonds
50 g/1^3/4 oz almonds, finely chopped
2 tbsp smooth sugar-free almond butter
2 tbsp quinoa flour
2 tbsp stevia

TOPPING
250 g/9 oz mascarpone cheese
300 g/10^1/2 oz full-fat cream cheese
2 large eggs
finely grated zest and juice of 1 large unwaxed lemon
1 tbsp quinoa flour
4 tbsp stevia

1   Preheat the oven to 180°C/350°F/Gas Mark 4. Lightly butter a 20-cm/8-inch round non-stick springform cake tin and line the base with baking paper.

2   To make the base, melt the butter in a small saucepan over a medium-low heat. Pour it into a large bowl and add the ground almonds, chopped almonds, almond butter, quinoa flour and stevia, then mix well. Spoon the mixture into the prepared tin and, using the back of a fork, press down into an even layer. Bake for 25 minutes, then remove from the oven and reduce the temperature to 120°C/250°F/Gas Mark ^{1}/2.

3   To make the topping, put the mascarpone cheese and cream cheese in a large bowl and whisk until loose. Beat for a further 30 seconds, then add the eggs, one at a time, beating between each addition. Add the lemon zest and juice, quinoa flour and stevia, then whisk again until well mixed.

4   Pour the topping over the base. Bake for 50 minutes, or until the sides are set and the middle still has a slight wobble. Leave to cool, then cover and chill in the refrigerator for 1–2 hours.

LOVE YOUR LEMONS

If your lemons are old and hard, put them in the microwave on high for 30 seconds – this makes them easier to zest and juice.

PER SERVING: 402 CALS | 35.6G FAT | 16.2G SAT FAT | 11G CARBS | 3.7G SUGARS | 0.5G SALT | 2.4G FIBRE | 10.6G PROTEIN

PUMPKIN PIE WITH PECAN NUTS

Pumpkin pie is ideal for a dinner party or cosy family lunch. The almond pastry adds a sweet nuttiness.

SERVES: 8   PREP: 35 MINS   COOK: 1^{1}/4 HOURS

PASTRY
80 g/2^{3}/4 oz ground almonds
20 g/^{3}/4 oz butter, diced
1 tbsp coconut flour
1 tbsp stevia
1 egg
pinch of sea salt

FILLING
700 g/1 lb 9 oz pumpkin, peeled and diced
2 tbsp coconut flour
2 tbsp stevia
1^{1}/2 tsp ground cinnamon
1 tsp freshly grated nutmeg
20 g/^{3}/4 oz butter, diced
2 eggs
3 tbsp double cream
20 g/^{3}/4 oz pecan nuts, roughly chopped

1 Preheat the oven to 160°C/325°F/Gas Mark 3. Line a 23–cm/9–inch fluted non–stick tart tin with baking paper.

2 To make the pastry, put all the ingredients in a food processor and process until it forms a soft dough. Press the pastry into the prepared tin, pushing it up the sides so it evenly covers the base. Prick all over with a fork. Bake for 15 minutes, or until the sides are golden. Set aside to cool.

3 Meanwhile, to make the filling, cook the pumpkin in a large saucepan of lightly salted boiling water for 10 minutes, or until soft. Drain, then leave to cool. Put the coconut flour, stevia, cinnamon, nutmeg and pumpkin in a food processor and process until smooth. Add the butter, eggs and cream and process again. Tip the mixture into the tart case.

4 Sprinkle over the pecan nuts. Bake for 55–60 minutes, or until the sides are set and the centre still has a slight wobble. Serve warm or cold.

LINING A TIN MADE EASY

To make baking paper really pliable, screw it up into a ball before you use it; all the creases will then fit easily into the fluted edge of the tin.

PER SERVING: 224 CALS | 19.1G FAT | 8.4G SAT FAT | 9.5G CARBS | 2.2G SUGARS | 0.3G SALT | 2.6G FIBRE | 6.4G PROTEIN

MOCHA SOUFFLES WITH MASCARPONE

A soufflé is the most glamorous of desserts, puffing up when it comes out of the oven and collapsing before the eyes of the diner.

SERVES: 4   PREP: 15 MINS   COOK: 15 MINS

2 tsp butter, to grease
2 tbsp ground almonds
1 tbsp cocoa powder, plus a little extra to dust
1 tbsp prepared strong espresso
small pinch of sea salt
5 tbsp cold water
3 egg whites
1 tbsp rice malt syrup
4 level tbsp mascarpone cheese, to serve

1 Preheat the oven to 190°C/375°F/Gas Mark 5. Lightly butter four ramekins, then sprinkle with the ground almonds. Roll and rotate the ramekins so the almonds stick to the butter, coating all sides.

2 Put the cocoa powder, espresso, salt and water in a small saucepan and cook, stirring over a low heat, until smooth. Increase the heat to medium-high and bring to the boil, then cook for a further 1 minute. Pour the mixture into a large bowl and leave to cool.

3 Put the egg whites in a separate large, clean glass bowl and whisk until they form soft peaks. Add the rice malt syrup and whisk again until you have stiff peaks. Using a metal spoon, gently fold a spoonful of the egg white into the cocoa mixture, preserving as much air as possible, then fold in the rest.

4 Spoon the mixture into the prepared ramekins. Bake for 10–12 minutes, or until the soufflés are towering out of the ramekins.

5 Add a tablespoon of mascarpone to each ramekin and sprinkle with cocoa powder. Serve immediately, before the soufflés start to collapse.

SOUFFLE TIPS

For successful soufflés, it's a good idea to have everything measured out before you start. Ensure all equipment is clean and grease-free and all ingredients are at room temperature. Don't open the oven door while the soufflés cook.

PER SERVING: 172 CALS | 15.1G FAT | 9.1G SAT FAT | 5G CARBS | 2.7G SUGARS | 0.5G SALT | 0.9G FIBRE | 4.9G PROTEIN

KEY LIME POTS

*Small and rich, these decadent chocolate and zesty lime pots
make a rich yet surprisingly refreshing end to a meal.*

SERVES: 4   PREP: 10 MINS
COOK: 8 MINUTES   CHILL: 4 HOURS

250 ml/9 fl oz double cream
1½ tbsp rice malt syrup
30 g/1 oz plain chocolate with 85% cocoa,
broken into pieces
finely grated zest of 1 lime, plus 1½ tbsp juice
1 tsp cocoa powder

1   Put the cream in a saucepan and slowly bring to the boil over a medium heat. Add the rice malt syrup and stir well, then boil for 3 minutes. Stir in the chocolate, most of the lime zest and all the lime juice, until the chocolate has melted.

2   Pour the mixture into four espresso cups. Cover with clingfilm and chill in the refrigerator for at least 4 hours.

3   Decorate the pots with the cocoa powder and remaining lime zest and serve.

ALSO TRY THIS

If you would prefer these pots a little less rich, then leave out the chocolate.

PER SERVING: 276 CALS | 26G FAT | 16.3G SAT FAT | 9.4G CARBS | 3.8G SUGARS | TRACE SALT | 1G FIBRE | 2G PROTEIN

COURGETTE LOAF CAKE WITH CREAM CHEESE FROSTING

Courgette cake is just as delicious as carrot cake. It's super-moist, with a creamy and fresh flavour.

SERVES: 10   PREP: 25 MINS   COOK: 1 HOUR

175 g/6 oz ground almonds
1/2 tsp baking powder
1/2 tsp bicarbonate of soda
3 tbsp stevia
40 g/1 1/2 oz chopped mixed nuts
50 g/1 3/4 oz butter
2 large eggs, beaten
1 tsp vanilla extract
200 g/7 oz courgettes, coarsely grated

FROSTING
200 g/7 oz full-fat cream cheese
1 tbsp stevia
finely grated zest and juice of 1/4 unwaxed lemon

1 Preheat the oven to 160°C/325°F/Gas Mark 3. Line a non-stick loaf tin with baking paper.

2 Put the ground almonds, baking powder, bicarbonate of soda, stevia and half the nuts in a large bowl and stir well.

3 Melt the butter in a small saucepan over a medium-low heat. Pour it onto the dry ingredients. Add the eggs, vanilla and courgettes, and mix well.

4 Spoon the mixture into the prepared tin and spread it into an even layer. Bake for 55–60 minutes, or until well risen and a skewer comes out clean when inserted into the centre of the cake. Leave to cool for 15 minutes, then remove from the tin, peel off the baking paper and transfer to a wire rack.

5 To make the frosting, put the cream cheese and stevia in a large bowl and whisk until light and airy. Add the lemon zest and juice, and whisk again briefly. Using a spatula, spread the frosting over the top of the cake. Decorate with the remaining nuts and serve.

UNWAXED LEMONS

If you are intending to use the zest, it is important to buy unwaxed lemons. If you can't find them, scrub the lemons well before use. Choose firm, heavy lemons with a thick, knobbly skin that has no tinges of green.

PER SERVING: 237 CALS | 21.9G FAT | 6.5G SAT FAT | 5.3G CARBS | 2.2G SUGARS | 0.6G SALT | 2.4G FIBRE | 7.2G PROTEIN

SWEET POTATO BROWNIES

Sweet potatoes make gooey, sweet brownies. Once you have tried these, you are sure to bake them again and again!

MAKES: 12 BROWNIES   PREP: 30 MINS   COOK: 20 MINS

150 ml/5 fl oz olive oil, plus extra to grease
175 g/6 oz sweet potatoes, coarsely grated
100 g/3¹/2 oz stevia
50 g/1³/4 oz cocoa powder
¹/2 tsp baking powder
¹/2 tsp bicarbonate of soda
50 g/1³/4 oz ground almonds
2 eggs, beaten
20 g/³/4 oz walnuts, roughly chopped

1 Preheat the oven to 180°C/350°F/Gas Mark 4. Lightly oil a shallow 19-cm/7¹/2-inch square cake tin, then line it with a large square of baking paper, snipping into the corners diagonally then pressing the paper into the tin so that the base and sides are lined.

2 Put all the ingredients in a large bowl and stir well. Pour the mixture into the prepared tin. Bake for 20 minutes, or until well risen and the centre is only just set.

3 Leave to cool in the tin for 15 minutes. Lift out of the tin using the baking paper, then carefully remove the paper. Cut into 12 brownies to serve.

ALSO TRY THIS

If this recipe is too chocolatey for your taste, reduce the amount of cocoa to 35 g/1¹/4 oz.

PER BROWNIE: 182 CALS | 17.2G FAT | 2.6G SAT FAT | 6.6G CARBS | 1G SUGARS | 0.2G SALT | 2.4G FIBRE | 3.4G PROTEIN

REALLY RICH AVOCADO
CHOCOLATE MOUSSE

Avocados add creaminess and richness to this delicious mousse, while chocolate is decadent and flavoursome – wonderful!

SERVES: 4   PREP: 10 MINS

2 ripe avocados, peeled, stoned and roughly chopped
35 g/1¼ oz cocoa powder
2 tbsp rice malt syrup
1 tsp vanilla extract
small pinch of sea salt
2 tbsp unsweetened almond milk

1 Put all the ingredients in a blender or food processor and process until combined. Scrape down the sides and process for a further minute, or until the mousse is airy. If it is still too thick, add a splash more almond milk and process again briefly.

2 Spoon the mousse into small teacups or serving bowls and serve immediately, or cover and chill in the refrigerator for up to 4 hours.

RIPENING AVOCADOS

If your avocados are too hard, put them in a sealed paper bag with a ripe tomato for 24 hours and they should ripen to perfection.

PER SERVING: 151 CALS | 11.8G FAT | 2.1G SAT FAT | 15G CARBS | 2.7G SUGARS | 0.4G SALT | 7.5G FIBRE | 3G PROTEIN

VANILLA PANNA COTTA WITH PISTACHIOS AND ROSEWATER

Panna cotta is an elegant dessert. Here, the dairy milk is replaced by unsweetened almond milk, which complements the fragrant rosewater and emerald pistachios.

SERVES: 4   PREP: 15 MINS
COOK: 4 MINS   CHILL: 2^1/4 HOURS

3 sheets of leaf gelatine
300 ml/10 fl oz double cream
200 ml/7 fl oz unsweetened almond milk
1 vanilla pod, split lengthways
2 tbsp stevia
2 tbsp rosewater
2 tbsp unsalted pistachio nuts, roughly chopped

1   Soak the gelatine in a shallow bowl of cold water for 5–10 minutes, or until floppy.

2   Meanwhile, pour the cream and almond milk into a large heavy-based saucepan. Scrape in the vanilla seeds using a blunt knife, then drop in the pod. Bring to the boil over a medium-high heat, stirring from time to time. Leave to cool for 5 minutes, then stir in the stevia and, using a fork, remove the vanilla pod.

3   Squeeze the water out of the gelatine and stir the gelatine into the custard until dissolved. Pour the custard into four ramekins, then leave to cool for 15 minutes. Cover with clingfilm and chill in the refrigerator for at least 2 hours, or overnight if you have the time.

4   Half-fill a bowl with boiling water. Dip each ramekin into the water briefly, making sure it doesn't splash over the top, then turn out onto serving plates. Drizzle the panna cottas with the rosewater and sprinkle over the pistachio nuts.

USING GELATINE

It is important the mixture cools to lukewarm before you add the gelatine; if the heat is too high the gelatine won't set the dessert. Test it with your finger.

PER SERVING: 313 CALS | 31.1G FAT | 17.6G SAT FAT | 4.2G CARBS | 0.5G SUGARS | 0.1G SALT | 0.8G FIBRE | 6.2G PROTEIN

BAKED PASSION FRUIT CUSTARDS

Light and fluffy with a refreshing tropical flavour, this simple dessert tastes every bit as good as it looks.

SERVES: 4   PREP: 15 MINS   COOK: 45 MINS

2 passion fruit
4 large eggs
175 ml/6 fl oz coconut milk
3 tbsp stevia
1 tsp orange flower water

1   Preheat the oven to 180°C/350°F/Gas Mark 4. Halve the passion fruit, scoop out the flesh from three of the halves and push it through a sieve using the back of a spoon to remove the seeds.

2   Crack the eggs into a large bowl. Add the passion fruit juice, coconut milk, stevia and orange flower water, and whisk until smooth and airy.

3   Pour the passion fruit custard into four ramekins, place them in a roasting tin and pour in hot water to reach halfway up the dishes. Bake for 40–45 minutes, or until just set.

4   Scoop the pulp from the remaining passion fruit half and spoon a little onto each dish. Serve immediately, or cover with clingfilm and chill in the refrigerator for up to 8 hours.

PASSION FRUIT

Passion fruit is an excellent source of fibre and vitamins A and C, which help boost the immune system.

PER SERVING: 185 CALS | 15.4G FAT | 10.2G SAT FAT | 3.8G CARBS | 2.5G SUGARS | 0.2G SALT | 0.9G FIBRE | 9G PROTEIN

RASPBERRY AND MASCARPONE ICE CREAM

Fresh raspberries and extra creaminess from the mascarpone mean you will be fighting people off the last scoops of this classic ice cream.

SERVES: 8   PREP: 20 MINS
COOK: 10 MINS   FREEZE: 4 HOURS

1 large egg, plus 4 large egg yolks
2 1/2 tbsp stevia
100 g/3 1/2 oz mascarpone cheese
1 tsp vanilla extract
400 ml/14 fl oz double cream
80 g/2 3/4 oz raspberries, halved

1 Crack the egg into a large heatproof bowl, add the yolks and stevia, and whisk with an electric hand-held mixer for 30 seconds. Place over a saucepan of gently simmering water, making sure the bowl doesn't touch the water, and whisk until the mixture is pale and airy. This cooks the eggs and makes a sweet custard, but be careful not to overcook them.

2 Pour cold water into a basin and put the custard bowl into it, so the base of the bowl is in the water, to cool. Continue to whisk for 2 minutes, then lift the bowl out of the water and set aside.

3 Put the mascarpone and vanilla in another large bowl and whisk briefly until loose. Pour in the cream and whisk again until it forms soft peaks.

4 Using a metal spoon, gently fold the custard into the cream mixture, preserving as much air as possible. Stir in the raspberries.

5 Pour the mixture into a freezerproof container, cover with a lid and freeze for 4 hours, or until set. Take the ice cream out of the freezer 10 minutes before you serve it to allow it to soften. Scoop it into glasses or small bowls and serve.

ALSO TRY THIS...

If you prefer vanilla ice cream, simply leave out the raspberries.

PER SERVING: 285 CALS | 28.6G FAT | 16.5G SAT FAT | 3.9G CARBS | 1.2G SUGARS | 0.1G SALT | 0.8G FIBRE | 4.2G PROTEIN

CHOCOLATE AND CHERRY SORBET

The chocolate makes this sorbet rich and thick, while the frozen cherries add instant glamour.

SERVES: 4   PREP: 10 MINS
COOK: 10 MINS   FREEZE: 4 HOURS

300 ml/10 fl oz cold water
3 tbsp stevia
25 g/1 oz cocoa powder
1/4 tsp ground allspice
4 cherries, stoned and chopped, plus 4 whole cherries to decorate
70 g/2 1/2 oz plain chocolate with 85% cocoa, broken into small pieces

1 Pour the water into a saucepan, then add the stevia, cocoa powder, allspice and chopped cherries. Whisk lightly, then slowly bring to the boil over a medium–high heat.

2 Remove the pan from the heat and leave to cool for 2–3 minutes. Stir in the chocolate. Pour the mixture into a freezerproof container, cover with a lid and freeze for 4 hours, or until set. Stir with a fork every 30 minutes to break up the ice crystals. Put the four whole cherries in the freezer too.

3 Take the sorbet out of the freezer 10 minutes before you serve to allow it to soften. Scoop it into glasses or small bowls, decorate with a frozen cherry and serve.

PLAIN CHOCOLATE

Tests have found that plain chocolate is packed with antioxidants and polyphenols, which are thought to protect the body from some cancers and heart conditions.

PER SERVING: 129 CALS | 8.3G FAT | 4.7G SAT FAT | 14.3G CARBS | 6.3G SUGARS | TRACE SALT | 4.4G FIBRE | 2.6G PROTEIN

FROZEN YOGURT CUPS

Containing calcium-rich yogurt and heart-protecting berries, these little ices are good for you and a really tasty summer treat.

MAKES: 12   PREP: 10 MINS
FREEZE: 2 HOURS

450 g/1 lb natural yogurt
finely grated zest of 1/2 orange
225 g/8 oz mixed strawberries, blueberries
and raspberries
12 fresh mint sprigs, to decorate

1   Line a 12-hole muffin tin with paper cases.

2   Put the yogurt and orange zest in a large bowl and mix well. Cut two-thirds of the strawberries into pieces and add them to the yogurt. Add two-thirds of the blueberries and raspberries, and mix well.

3   Spoon the mixture into the paper cases. Freeze for 2 hours, or until just frozen. Decorate with the remaining berries and the mint sprigs, and serve.

SAY YES TO YOGURT

Flavoured yogurts tend to be full of sugar, so mixing fruit into natural yogurt is a great solution.

PER SERVING: 33.7 CALS | 1.2G FAT | 0.8G SAT FAT | 4G CARBS | 2.7G SUGARS | TRACE SALT | 0.7G FIBRE | 1.4G PROTEIN

INDEX

Fourth edition

International Business

Stuart Wall

Sonal Minocha

Bronwen Rees

PEARSON

Harlow, England • London • New York • Boston • San Francisco • Toronto • Sydney
Auckland • Singapore • Hong Kong • Tokyo • Seoul • Taipei • New Delhi
Cape Town • São Paulo • Mexico City • Madrid • Amsterdam • Munich • Paris • Milan

Pearson Education Limited
Edinburgh Gate
Harlow CM20 2JE
United Kingdom
Tel: +44 (0)1279 623623

Web: www.pearson.com/uk

First published in 2001 (print)
Second edition published 2004 (print)
Third edition published 2010 (print)
Fourth edition published 2015 (print and electronic)

The Financial Times. With a worldwide network of highly respected journalists, *The Financial Times* provides global business news, insightful opinion and expert analysis of business, finance and politics. With over 500 journalists reporting from 50 countries worldwide, our in-depth coverage of international news is objectively reported and analysed from an independent, global perspective. To find out more, visit **www.ft.com/pearsonoffer**.

ISBN: 978–1-292–01668–9 (print)
　　　978–1-292–01671–9 (PDF)
　　　978–1-292–01673–3 (eText)

British Library Cataloguing-in-Publication Data
A catalogue record for the print edition is available from the British Library

Library of Congress Cataloging-in-Publication Data
Wall, Stuart, 1946-
　International business / Stuart Wall, Sonal Minocha, Bronwen Rees. — Fourth edition.
　　pages cm
　ISBN 978-1-292-01668-9
　1. International business enterprises. 2. International economic relations. 3. Globalization. I. Minocha, Sonal. II. Rees, Bronwen. III. Title.
　HD62.4.W343 2015
　658'.049—dc23
　　　　　　　　　　　　　　2014048756

10 9 8 7 6 5 4 3 2 1
19 18 17 16 15

Print edition typeset in 9.5/12.5 pts Charter ITC Std by 71
Printed by Ashford Colour Press Ltd, Gosport
NOTE THAT ANY PAGE CROSS REFERENCES REFER TO THE PRINT EDITION

Brief contents

Contents

7   International strategic issues

List of figures

Preface: using this book

In the past decade the interconnectedness of our global economy has been brought into sharp focus by the worldwide impact of the so-called 'credit crunch', which many saw as having its origin in the ('subprime') housing market of the USA. Problems which began with excessive lending by financial intermediaries to non-creditworthy house purchasers in the USA quickly escalated into a worldwide recession, brought about by 'financial engineering' which created a wide range of derivative assets based on these high-risk mortgages. The impacts of holding such 'toxic' assets in the portfolios of financial institutions of many countries have been felt by companies and individuals worldwide, with liquidity shortages reducing global demand, output and employment. Similarly, current 'turbulence' in various Middle Eastern, North African and Eastern European countries is having extensive global impacts on production and trade, quite apart from devastating individual lives.

This book is primarily written for students taking modules in *international business* on a range of undergraduate and postgraduate programmes. Any text on international business must, of necessity, span a wide variety of topic areas and embrace a number of different subject disciplines. In that sense it is clearly difficult to locate its boundaries precisely. What we can be sure about is that we are studying a vibrant, ever-changing set of issues and relationships, which will almost certainly have major impacts on all our lives. It could hardly be otherwise when almost one-quarter of the world's recorded output is exported and when changes in business practices or technology in Beijing (China), will have major implications for a workforce as far away as Detroit (USA) or Birmingham (UK)! It has become increasingly clear that a proper understanding of worldwide patterns and trends in international business must draw upon far more than the conventional economic discipline of 'international trade and finance', or the in-depth analysis of 'multinational firm activity', or even the study of key functional areas such as marketing, management, finance and accounting. Important though all these contributions undoubtedly are, attention is increasingly being paid to the often subtle, but highly significant, organisational and cultural characteristics that underpin production and trade in a globalised economy. In fact, today's study of international business draws heavily on disciplines as diverse as law, sociology, anthropology, psychology, politics, history and geography, as well as those previously mentioned.

The first chapter of this text identifies some current patterns and trends, which are of key concern to those engaged in international business, whether from a corporate or national perspective. Chapters 2 to 6 then concentrate on issues that affect most types of international business, whatever their sector of activity, nature of operations or stage reached in the internationalisation process. The principles, practices and institutions underpinning international trading relationships are reviewed, as are a wide variety of external 'environmental factors', which play a key role in determining both the direction and outcome of international business activity. These include political, legal, sociocultural, ethical, ecological, economic and technological factors, all of which shape the environment in which the international business must operate. After considering these 'universal' aspects of international business, the more 'firm-specific' aspects are investigated in Chapters 7 to 10 with an in-depth analysis of the alternative courses of action facing the international business, whether in terms of corporate strategy, human resource management, marketing, accounting and finance, operations management or logistics.

Throughout the text you will find up-to-date case materials to illustrate many of the international issues involved. A number of questions will help direct your thoughts to some of the principles underpinning the facts and events presented in each case study. In a similar vein, you will also find a number of 'pause for thought' sections within the text of each chapter. A number of 'Boxes' are presented to take further some of the analysis presented in the text. You can find full details of any sources referenced within each chapter in the References section at the end of the text.

There is a full range of interactive questions (with solutions) and other teaching support materials in the lecturer encrypted website to accompany this text.

For this fourth edition all data, empirical and case study materials and analysis have been thoroughly updated and revised with a large number of entirely new cases integrated within the text. On occasion the text has been further developed to reflect contemporary debate, as with the more detailed scrutiny of the international financial system and associated accounting conventions and standards in Chapter 10.

Acknowledgements

We would like to thank Alan Griffiths, Sandhya Sastry, Professor Rolf Meyer and Geoff Black for contributing important case materials at various parts of the text.

We would also like to express our gratitude for all the help received from Eleanor Wall in helping develop case studies and other applied materials for the book. Our thanks also to all those who have given permission for the use of material in the book.

Stuart Wall
Sonal Minocha
Bronwen Rees

Publisher's acknowledgements

We are grateful to the following for permission to reproduce copyright material:

Figures
Figure 1.4 from *World Investment Report 2014* (UNCTAD), Figure 7 (p. xxiv), Copyright © 2014 United Nations. Used by permission of the United Nations; Figure 1.5 from Boston Consulting Group (BCG), *Analysis of the World's Largest Manufacturing Economies,* April 2014; Figure 1.6 adapted from OECD (2014), *Factbook 2014: Economic, Environmental and Social Statistics,* OECD Publishing. **http://dx.doi.org/10.1787/factbook-2014-en**; Figures 2.2, 3.5 adapted from *Applied Economics,* 12th ed., Financial Times Prentice Hall (Griffiths, A. and Wall, S. (eds), 2012), © Pearson Education Limited 2012; Figure 5.1 adapted from *International Business: Managerial Perspective,* 1st Ed., Addison-Wesley (Griffin, R.W. and Pustay, M.W. 1996), © 1996. Reprinted and Electronically reproduced by permission of Pearson Education, Inc.; Figure 5.2 adapted from *Cultures and Organizations: Software of the Mind,* 3rd ed., McGraw Hill (Hofstede, G., Hofstede, G.J. and Minkov, M. 2010), © Geert Hofstede B.V. quoted with permission; Figures 5.3, 6.1, 6.2, 6.4, 8.3 from *Applied Economics,* 12th ed., Financial Times Prentice Hall (Griffiths, A. and Wall, S. (eds), 2012), © Pearson Education Limited 2012; Figure 7.2 from *The BCG Product Portfolio Matrix,* © 1970, The Boston Consulting Group; Figure 7.3a from *Strategies of Diversification* by H.I. Ansoff, Sep/Oct 1957. © 1957 by the Harvard Business School Publishing Corporation, all rights reserved; Figure 7.4 adapted from Changes in the Competitive Battlefield, *Mastering Strategy* (Prahalad, C.K. (1999)), Financial Times Prentice Hall, © Pearson Education Limited 1999; Figure 8.2 from Human resource management: An agenda of the 1990s, *International Journal of Human Resource Management,* 1(1) (Hendry, C. and Pettigrew, A. 1990), reprinted by permission of the publisher (Taylor & Francis Ltd, **http://www .tandfonline.com**); Figure 9.1 from *International Business: Theories, Policies and Practices,* Financial Times Prentice Hall (Tayeb, M. 2000), © Pearson Education Limited 2000; Figure 10.2 from SIV manager dig out their manuals, *Financial Times,* 30/08/2007 (Davies, P.), © The Financial Times Limited 2007. All Rights Reserved.

Tables
Tables 1.1, 1.2, 1.9–1.11 adapted from *World Investment Report 2014* (UNCTAD), Copyright © 2014 United Nations. Used by permission of the United Nations; Table 1.3 from Boston Consulting Group (BCG), *Analysis of the World's Largest Manufacturing Economies,* April 2014; Table 1.5 adapted from *The Global Competitiveness Report 2013–2014* (Schwab, K. (ed)), Table 3, World Economic Forum,

Switzerland, 2014; Table 2.1 adapted from Building competitive advantage: managing strategic alliances to promote organisational learning, *Journal of World Business,* 32(3) (Lei, D., Slocum, J. and Pitts, R.A. 1997), Copyright 1997, with permission from Elsevier; Table 2.2 from OECD (2014), *Taxing Wages 2014.* OECD Publishing. **http://dx.doi.org/10.1787/tax_wages-2014-en**; Table 2.3 from OECD (2008), *Removing Barriers to SME Access to International Markets,* OECD Publishing. **http://dx.doi.org/10.1787/9789264045866-en**; Table 5.3 adapted from *Cultures and Organizations: Software of the Mind,* 3rd ed., McGraw Hill (Hofstede, G., Hofstede, G.J. and Minkov, M. 2010), © Geert Hofstede B.V. quoted with permission; Table 5.4 adapted from Use of transnational teams to globalize your company, *Organizational Dynamics,* 24(4), pp. 90–107 (Snow, C.C., Davison, S.C., Snell, S.A. and Hambrik, D.C. 1969), Copyright (1969), with permission from Elsevier; Table 5.6 from *International Human Resource Management,* 3rd ed., Chartered Institute of Personnel and Development (Brewster, C., Sparrow, P. and Vernon, G. 2011) p. 35; Table 7.6 from *Operations Management,* 7th ed., Financial Times Prentice Hall (Slack, N., Chambers, S., Harland, C., Harrison, A. and Johnson, R. 2013), © Pearson Education Limited 2013; Table 8.3 adapted from *Managing Cultural Differences,* Gulf Publishing, Houston (Harris, P.R. and Moran, R.T. 1991); Table 9.6 adapted from The Big Mac index, *The Economist,* 25/01/2014, p. 67, © The Economist Newspaper Limited, London 2014; Table 10.1 from International Accounting Standards Board (IASB) (2001) *Framework for the Preparation and Presentation of Financial Statements,* © Copyright IFRS Foundation.

Text

Case Study 1.2 from A local hero's fight for American jobs, *Financial Times,* 11/08/2014 (Donnan, S.), © The Financial Times Limited 2014. All Rights Reserved; Case Study 1.3 from Industry: Future factories, *Financial Times,* 10/06/2012, p. 9 (Marsh, P.), © The Financial Times Limited 2012. All Rights Reserved; Case Study 1.4 adapted from JCB digs in for growth after Indian demand stalls, *Financial Times,* 06/05/2014 (Crabtree, J. and Mallet, V.), © The Financial Times Limited 2014. All Rights Reserved; Case Study 1.5 from China's Vancl Trials Production Overseas, *Financial Times,* 08/08/2012, 21 (Waldmeir, P.), © The Financial Times Limited 2012. All Rights Reserved; Case Study 1.6 adapted from Reshoring offers 200,000 jobs, *Financial Times,* 12/03/2014 (Powley, T.), © The Financial Times Limited 2014. All Rights Reserved; Case Study 1.7 adapted from Korean shipbuilders struggle to keep Chinese in their wake, *Financial Times,* 27/03/2007 (Fifield, A.), © The Financial Times Limited 2007. All Rights Reserved; Case Study 2.1 adapted from Producers pin hope of Agoa trade pact to drive exports, *Financial Times,* 06/08/2014, p. 5 (England, A.), © The Financial Times Limited 2014. All Rights Reserved; Case Study 2.3 from Asda sees gap in Malta market for George shop, *Financial Times,* 22/04/2013 (Felstead, A.), © The Financial Times Limited 2013. All Rights Reserved; Case Study 2.5 adapted from An odd corporate vehicle for doing business in China: Is your joint venture really necessary?, *Financial Times* 14/05/2013, p. 14 (Hill, A.), © The Financial Times Limited 2013. All Rights Reserved; Case Study 2.6 from Renault and Nissan seek €4.3bn in synergies, *Financial Times,* 31/01/2014, p. 17 (Foy, H.), © The Financial Times Limited 2014. All Rights Reserved; Case Studies 2.7, 5.2, 5.5 from Cultural determinants of competitiveness: The Japanese experience (Griffiths, A. 2000), *Dimensions of International Competitiveness: Issues and Policies,* Lloyd-Reason, L. and Wall, S. (eds), Edward Elgar Publishing; Case Study 2.8 from High European energy prices drive BMW to US, *Financial Times,* 27/05/2013, p. 19 (Bryant, C.), © The Financial Times Limited 2013. All Rights Reserved; Case Study 2.9 adapted from Asia's bankers milk china's thirst for dairy, *Financial Times,* 13/11/2013 (Noble, J.), © The Financial Times Limited 2013. All Rights Reserved; Case Study 2.10 with permission from Toyota (GB) PLC; Case Study 2.11 adapted from Nokia: A bet with a safety net, *Financial Times,* 22/08/2013 (Milne, R. and Thomas, D.), © The Financial Times Limited 2013. All Rights Reserved; Case Study 3.1 adapted from Do not blame free trade for the sins of conservatives, *Financial Times,* 22/07/2014 (Posen, A.), © The Financial Times Limited 2014. All Rights Reserved; Case Study 3.3 adapted from India digs in heels over incentives for cereal farmers, *Financial Times,* 26/07/2014

(Kazmin, A.), © The Financial Times Limited 2014. All Rights Reserved; Case Study 3.4 adapted from Luxembourg tax regime: under siege, *Financial Times,* 23/07/2014 (Houlder, V.), © The Financial Times Limited 2014. All Rights Reserved; Case Study 4.2 from Sugar and onions pose commodity conundrum for Modi, *Financial Times,* 12/08/2014, p. 6 (Kazmin, A.), © The Financial Times Limited 2014. All Rights Reserved; Case Study 4.4 from Stricter US rules drive a pickup in fuel efficiency, *Financial Times,* 15/01/2014, p. 19 (Wright, R.), © The Financial Times Limited 2014. All Rights Reserved; Case Study 4.5 adapted from Consumers see the light over lower energy costs, *Financial Times,* 17/02/2014, p. 4 (Chazan, G.), © The Financial Times Limited 2014. All Rights Reserved; Case Study 4.6 adapted from Engineering the future – smartphone patents, *Financial Times,* 18/06/2014 (Bradshaw, T.), © The Financial Times Limited 2014. All Rights Reserved; Case Study 4.7 adapted from Redskins lose trademark protection, *Financial Times,* 10/06/2014 (Bond, S.), © The Financial Times Limited 2014. All Rights Reserved; Case Study 4.10 adapted from Retail banks go digital with gusto, *Financial Times,* 05/08/2014, p. 10 (Goff, S. and Arnold, M.), © The Financial Times Limited 2014. All Rights Reserved; Box 5.1 adapted from Overcoming multicultural clashes in global joint ventures, *European Business Review,* 98(4), pp. 211–6 (Elashmawi, F. 1998), © Emerald Group Publishing Limited, all rights reserved; Case Study 5.3 adapted from The modelling of issues and perspectives in MNEs (Kidd, J. and Xue, Li 2000), *Dimensions of International Competitiveness,* Lloyd-Reason, L. and Wall, S. (eds), Edward Elgar Publishing; Case Study 5.4 adapted from Apple agrees to China pollution audit, *Financial Times,* 15/04/2012, p. 22 (Nuttall, C.), © The Financial Times Limited 2012. All Rights Reserved; Box 6.1 from Ethics and cultures in international business, *Journal of Management Inquiry,* 8(3) (Beyer, J. and Nino, D. 1999), Copyright 1999 by Sage Publications, Inc. Reprinted by permission of Sage Publications; Case Study 6.2 from Apple in supply-chain purge at Africa mines, *Financial Times,* 14/02/2014 (Bradshaw, T.), © The Financial Times Limited 2014. All Rights Reserved; Case Study 6.5 adapted from Emissions trading: cheap and dirty, *Financial Times,* 13/02/2012, p. 9 (Chaffin, J.), © The Financial Times Limited 2012. All Rights Reserved; Case Study 7.3 from Publishers must become giants to take on Amazon, *Financial Times,* 29/05/2014, p. 15 (Gapper, G.), © The Financial Times Limited 2014. All Rights Reserved; Case Study 7.4 adapted from Apple hopes to open door to smarter homes, *Financial Times,* 28/05/2014, p. 17 (Bradshaw, T.), © The Financial Times Limited 2014. All Rights Reserved; Case Study 7.6 adapted from Retail banks go digital with gusto, *Financial Times,* 05/08/2014, p. 10 (Arnold, M.), © The Financial Times Limited 2014. All Rights Reserved; Case Studies 7.7, 9.4 from E-tailers in India prepare for showdown, *Financial Times,* 12/08/2014, p. 15 (Kazmin, A.), © The Financial Times Limited 2014. All Rights Reserved; Case Study 7.9 from Treating patients faster, *Financial Times,* 24/07/2012 (Schmenner, R.), © Roger W. Schmenner; Case Study 7.10 from Walmart's English experiment, *Financial Times,* 22/04/2014, p. 12 (Felsted, A.), © The Financial Times Limited 2014. All Rights Reserved; Case Study 8.1 from Hire the young and old to avoid 'workforce cliff', *Financial Times,* 31/03/2014, p. 19 (Groom, B.), © The Financial Times Limited 2014. All Rights Reserved; Case Study 8.2 from Sastry, S. (2015) 'Optimising intercultural synergies in post-merger integration contexts: an alternative framework for organisational leadership', PhD thesis, Anglia Ruskin University, Cambridge; Box 8.2 adapted from National culture, choice of management and business performance: The case of foreign firms in Greece (Kessapidou, S. and Varsakelis, N. (2000)), *Dimensions of International Competitiveness: Issues and Policies,* Lloyd Reason, L. and Wall, S. (eds), Edward Elgar Publishing; Case Study 8.3 from China factory chiefs struggle to maintain worker loyalty, *Financial Times,* 04/02/2014 (Sevastopulo, D.), © The Financial Times Limited 2014. All Rights Reserved; Case Study 8.5 from Skills training urged for low paid, *Financial Times,* 28/04/2014, p. 3 (Groom, B.), © The Financial Times Limited 2014. All Rights Reserved; Case Study 8.6 from Mindset of a Toyota manager revealed, *Financial Times,* 27/11/2008 (Mitchell A.), © The Financial Times Limited 2008. All Rights Reserved; Case Study 9.1 from How Lego and others turned to anthropology, *Financial Times,* 26/02/2014, p. 14 (Jack, A.), © The Financial Times Limited 2014. All Rights Reserved; Case Study 9.2 from Britons use smart devices for longer than they sleep, *Financial Times,* 07/08/2014, p. 3 (Thomas, D.), © The Financial Times Limited 2014. All Rights Reserved; Case Study 9.5 from Morrison's discounts all pain and no gain, *Financial Times,* 09/05/2014, p. 21 (Felsted, A.), © The Financial Times Limited 2014. All Rights Reserved; Case Study 9.7 from Indian stores in search of drama, *Financial Times,* 30/12/2008 (Yee, A.), © The Financial Times Limited 2008. All Rights Reserved; Case Study 10.1 from Accounts shake-up promises boost for growth,

Financial Times, 30/05/2014, p. 3 (O'Connor, S.), © The Financial Times Limited 2014. All Rights Reserved; Extracts 10.1, 10.2 from *Accountancy Age,* 18 February 1999; Case Study 10.2 adapted from New accounting rule a boost for investors, *Financial Times,* 28/05/2014 (Agnew, H. and Burgess, K.), © The Financial Times Limited 2014. All Rights Reserved; Case Study 10.3 adapted from Moody's cuts Puerto Rico deeper into junk, *Financial Times,* 01/07/2014 (Rodrigues, V.), © The Financial Times Limited 2014. All Rights Reserved; Case Study 10.4 adapted from Capital markets: Moody's faces new conflict of interest claim, *Financial Times,* 31/07/2014 (Alloway, T.), © The Financial Times Limited 2014. All Rights Reserved; Case Study 10.5 adapted from IMF says 'overvalued' pound preventing rebalancing, *Financial Times,* 28/07/2014 (Giles, C.), © The Financial Times Limited 2014. All Rights Reserved; Case Study 10.6 adapted from Sliced and diced debt deals make roaring comeback, *Financial Times,* 04/06/2014 (Alloway, T. and Thompson, C.), © The Financial Times Limited 2014. All Rights Reserved; Case Study 10.8 from Insight: Risk needs a human touch but models hold the whip hand, *Financial Times,* 23/01/2009 (Davies, P.), © The Financial Times Limited 2009. All Rights Reserved.

In some instances we have been unable to trace the owners of copyright material, and we would appreciate any information that would enable us to do so.

Abbreviations

APEC	Asia-Pacific Economic Corporation
ART	Alternative risk transfer
ASB	Accounting Standards Board (London)
ASEAN	Association of South East Asian Nations
B2B	Business-to-business
BIT	Bilateral investment treaties
CAP	Common Agricultural Policy
CCFF	Compensatory and Contingency Financing Facility
CDO	Collateralised debt obligations
CED	Cross elasticity of demand
CFF	Compensatory Financing Facility
CIM	Chartered Institute of Marketing
CIMA	Chartered Institute of Management Accountants (London)
CIS	Commonwealth of Independent States
CJV	Cooperative joint venture
DTT	Double taxation treaties
EAGGF	European Agricultural Guarantee and Guidance Fund
ECU	European Currency Unit
EER	Effective exchange rate
EFF	Extended Fund Facility
EJV	Equity joint venture
EPZ	Export processing zone
ERM	Exchange Rate Mechanism
ERP	Enterprise resource planning
EU	European Union
fdi	Foreign direct investment
FSC	Foreign sales corporation
GAAP	Generally accepted accounting practices
GATT	General Agreement on Tariffs and Trade
GDP	Gross domestic product
GM	Genetically modified
GNP	Gross national product
HICPs	Harmonised Indices of Consumer Prices
HRM	Human resource management
IASB	International Accounting Standards Board
IASs	International Accounting Standards
IBRD	International Bank for Reconstruction and Development
IDA	International Development Association
IED	Income elasticity of demand
IFC	International Finance Corporation
IHRM	International human resource management
II	Internationalisation index
IJV	International joint venture
ILO	International Labour Office

IMF	International Monetary Fund
IMM	International Monetary Market
IPLC	International product life cycle
IPR	Intellectual property rights
ISCT	Integrated Social Contract Theory
LDC	Less-developed country
LIBOR	London Interbank Offer Rate
LIFFE	London International Finance and Futures Exchange
LRAC	Long-run average cost
LSE	London Stock Exchange
M & A	Mergers and acquisitions
MAI	Multilateral agreement on investment
MES	Minimum efficient size
MGQ	Maximum Guaranteed Quantity
MID	Modularity-in-design
MIP	Modularity-in-production
MIU	Modularity-in-use
MNE	Multinational enterprise
NAFTA	North American Free Trade Association
NGO	Non-governmental organisation
OECD	Organisation for Economic Co-operation and Development
OTC	Over the counter
PED	Price elasticity of demand
PEST	Political, economic, social and technological environmental analysis
PESTEL	Political, economic, social, technological, legal and ecological analysis
Plc	Public limited company
PPP	Purchasing power parity
R & D	Research and development
RCEP	Regional Comprehensive Economic Partnership
RER	Real exchange rate
RPI	Retail Price Index
RTA	Regional trading arrangement
RULC	Relative unit labour costs
SAF	Structural Adjustment Facility
SAL	Structural Adjustment Lending
SDR	Special Drawing Right
SEC	Securities and Exchange Commission (USA)
SFF	Supplementary Financing Facility
SIV	Structured investment vehicle
SKU	Stock-keeping unit
SME	Small to medium-sized enterprise
SWF	Sovereign wealth funds
TNI	Transnationality index
TPP	Trans-Pacific Partnership
TRIPS	Trade-Related Aspects of Intellectual Property Rights
TTIP	Transatlantic Trade and Investment Partnership
UNCTAD	United Nations Conference on Trade, Aid and Development
UNIDO	United Nations Industrial Development Organisation
VER	Voluntary export restraint
WIPO	World Intellectual Property Organisation
WOFE	Wholly owned foreign enterprise
WTO	World Trade Organisation

Chapter 1

Introduction to international business

By the end of this chapter you should be able to:

- outline some of the key patterns and trends in international business activity;
- explain the various dimensions of the term 'globalisation';
- examine the role and importance of the multinational enterprise (MNE) in the global economy;
- discuss the contribution of different disciplines to an understanding of international business activity.

Introduction

A useful starting point for a text on international business is to identify some of the more recent patterns and trends in business activity worldwide. Of course, these patterns and trends are in part the *result* of some of the strategic choices taken by firms with an international orientation and in part the *stimulus* for future changes of direction by such firms. We shall examine each of these perspectives in later chapters.

Patterns and trends in international business

Let us first identify some of the more important and measurable trends in international business activity.

Rapid growth in world trade and investment

Figure 1.1 indicates some aspects of the growth in international trade and capital flows using *index numbers* based on 1980 = 1 for exports and foreign direct investment (fdi) respectively. (The term fdi refers to international investment in productive facilities such as plant, machinery and equipment.) Between 1980 and 2014 *world exports* of goods and services have more than doubled in real terms, reaching over $23,000 billion in 2014 and accounting for over 31% of world gross domestic product.

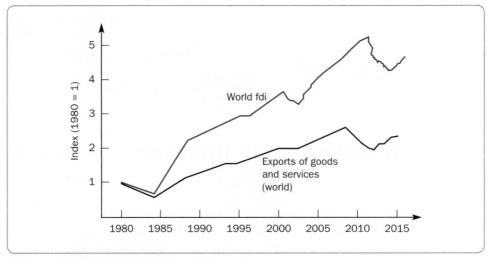

Figure 1.1 Changes in trade and capital flows
Source: World Bank, UNCTAD (various years).

Put another way, global exports of goods and services have increased at the astonishing rate of almost 5% per year in real terms between 1980 and 2014. It is worth noting that, while the developed 'high-income economies' (GNP of $12,616 per capita or more) have accounted for most of this growth in absolute value of global exports, the developing 'low-income economies' (GNP of $1,035 or less) have substantially increased their share of global exports, with the developing economies' exports rising at an above average 6% per annum in real terms between 1980 and 2014. This trend has resulted in the *exports-to-GDP ratio* of the 'developing economies' rising much faster than that of the 'developed economies'. As a result the export:GDP ratio of developing economies now exceeds that of the developed economies, with exports accounting for some 25% of GDP in developing economies in 2014, but only some 24% of GDP in developed economies at that date. The contribution of developing economies to international business is an issue we return to at various points in this text.

During the same time period flows of *world foreign direct investment* have increased over fivefold in real terms since 1980, reaching around $1,500 billion in 2014, some $200 billion below the previous peak year in 2007. Figure 1.2 provides more detail on this growth in world fdi inflows over the period 1995–2014. The developed, developing and transition economies, the latter including South East Europe and the Commonwealth of Independent States (Russia and states of the former Soviet Union), have all seen continued growth in inward fdi, despite occasional global dips, as in the 2000–03, 2007–09 and 2011–12 periods.

Rapid growth in cross-border mergers and acquisitions

There has been a rapid growth in cross-border mergers and acquisitions (M&A) since 1990. Between 1990 and 2013 the value of global cross-border M&A has risen sharply, rising more than eightfold to reach over $1,000 billion per annum in 2007, before falling back in the subsequent recessionary period. Much of this activity has been concentrated in financial services, insurance, life sciences, telecommunications and the media, with M&A being a key factor in accounting for the rise in fdi noted in Figures 1.1 and 1.2.

Largely as a result of cross-border mergers and associated 'greenfield investment' we can see from Table 1.1 that in 2013 the 100 largest MNEs were highly integrated within the global

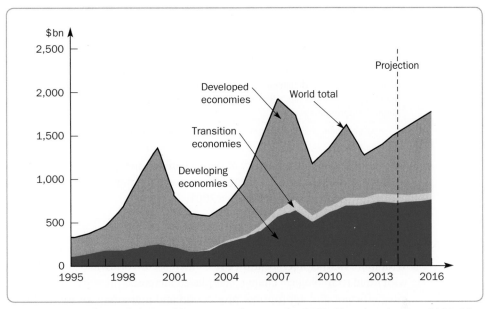

Figure 1.2 FDI inflows: global and by groups of economies 1995–13 and projections 2014–16
Source: World Development Report (2014), p. xiii.

economy with foreign assets making up 59% of their total assets, foreign sales 65% of their total sales and foreign employment 57% of their total employment. We review the contribution of MNEs to international business activity in much greater detail later in this chapter (pp. 30–36) and in Chapter 7.

More liberalised markets on a global scale

We noted in Figures 1.1 and 1.2 the rapid growth of foreign direct investment (fdi) and its relevance for cross-border mergers and acquisitions by multinational enterprises. Table 1.2 uses data from the United Nations Conference on Trade, Aid and Development (UNCTAD) to indicate the growth in regulatory changes affecting fdi by national governments. We can see

Table 1.1 Snapshot of the world's 100 largest MNEs, 2013

Variable	2013	Percentage change
Assets ($bn)		
Foreign	8,035	+2.0
Total	13,656	+2.0
Foreign to total (%)	59	2.0
Sales ($bn)		
Foreign	6,057	+3.0
Total	9,321	+4.0
Foreign to total (%)	65	−1.0
Employment (000)		
Foreign	9,810	+0.0
Total	17,292	+2.0
Foreign to total (%)	57	+2.7

Source: Adapted from *World Investment Report* 2014 (UNCTAD), Copyright © 2014 United Nations. Used by permission of the United Nations.

3

Table 1.2 **National regulatory changes, 1993–2013**

Item	1993	1997	2001	2005	2009	2013
Number of countries that introduced change	56	76	52	78	47	59
Number of regulatory changes	100	150	97	144	88	87
More favourable to fdi (liberalisation/promotion)	99	134	85	118	61	61
Less favourable to fdi (restriction/regulation)	1	16	2	25	23	23
Neutral/indeterminate	–	–	10	1	4	3

Source: Adapted from *World Investment Report* (UNCTAD 2014), p. 106.

that the overwhelming majority of these changes are regarded as being 'more favourable' to fdi flows, although there has been an increase in the number (and percentage) of regulatory changes 'less favourable' to fdi since 2001.

More globally dispersed value chains

With more market liberalisation comes increased worldwide competition which, together with rapid technological change, has placed increased pressures on large firms to adopt the most efficient and appropriate production and marketing locations if they are to survive and prosper. With improved international communications helping MNEs to co-ordinate and control geographically dispersed activities, including service functions, the result has been an increased propensity for MNEs to shift certain production and service activities to low-cost centres overseas. Put another way, MNEs are engaged in an unending search for increased competitive advantage in terms of costs, resources, logistics and markets and are increasingly willing to reconfigure the geographical locations of their activities accordingly.

> **Pause for thought 1.1**
>
> Can you give one or more recent examples of MNEs adjusting the geographical location of their production or support activities?

We can, for example, use the so-called *Transnationality Index* (TNI) to illustrate the increased international dispersion of production and service activities by multinational enterprises. The TNI is a simple average of three ratios for a multinational enterprise, namely foreign assets:total assets, foreign sales:total sales and foreign employment:total employment. As we note below (Table 1.9, p. 34), whereas for the world's largest 100 MNEs this average across the three ratios was only 51.1% in 1990, by 2012 the average had risen sharply to 60.8%, indicating a rapid growth in international orientation by the top 100 global MNEs. We return to this issue in more detail below (pp. 30–36) and in Chapter 7.

Bi-polar to tri-polar (triad)

The old *bi-polar* world economy, which was dominated by North America and Europe, has moved on to a *tri-polar* world economy dominated by the 'triad' of North America, the European Union and South-East Asia. These three regions now account for around 80% of the total value of world exports and 84% of world manufacturing value added.

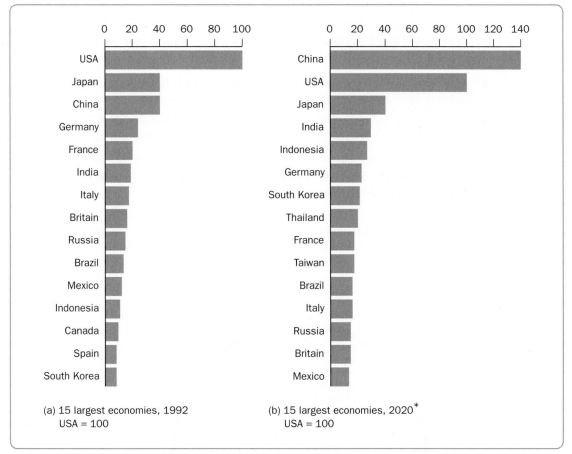

(a) 15 largest economies, 1992
USA = 100

(b) 15 largest economies, 2020*
USA = 100

Figure 1.3 Growth of the global economy, 1992–2020 (index number, USA = 100)

*Forecasts assume countries grow at regional rates projected in the World Bank's *Global Economic Prospects* Report.
Source: World Bank and author's own work.

The inclusion of the third leg of the triad, namely East and South-East Asia, is further reinforced by projections into the future. Figure 1.3 provides some World Bank projections for changes in national contributions to the world economy over the period 1992–2020. Although in terms of market size the global economy is currently dominated by the rich industrial economies of the USA, Japan, Germany, France, Italy and the UK, it is projected that by 2020 economies such as China, India, Indonesia, South Korea, Thailand and Taiwan will all have moved into the 'top ten'. This is an important pattern, suggesting that the attention of market-oriented companies will be increasingly drawn to these regions.

Growth of regional trading arrangements

As we note in Chapter 3, there has been a rapid growth in regional trading blocs and in associated regional trading arrangements (RTAs), which give preferential treatment to trade in goods and services between members of these blocs. Only countries *within* the particular regional trading bloc (e.g. the EU, NAFTA) benefit from these RTAs, which have increased substantially in number over the past decade or so. This has led to the growth of 'insiderisation', i.e. attempts by MNEs to locate productive facilities inside these various regional trading blocs in order to avoid the protective and discriminatory barriers which would otherwise face their exports to countries within these blocs.

In fact there is now a movement towards 'mega-regional' integration initiatives, with three major developments underway in 2014, as can be seen from Figure 1.4.

- *Transatlantic Trade and Investment Partnership* (TTIP) which is being negotiated between the US and EU, accounting for some 30% of global fdi flows.

- *Trans-Pacific Partnership* (TPP) which is being negotiated between the US and a range of other mainly Pacific located countries, accounting for some 32% of global fdi flows.

- *Regional Comprehensive Economic Partnership* (RCEP) which is being negotiated between the ten ASEAN member states (see p. 100) and their six free trade agreement partners. This group accounts for some 24% of global fdi flows.

Certainly there is evidence to support the belief of MNEs that being inside such blocs confers considerable advantages. For example Roberts and Deichmann (2008) found that spillovers of growth between members of RTAs averaged around 14% in the period

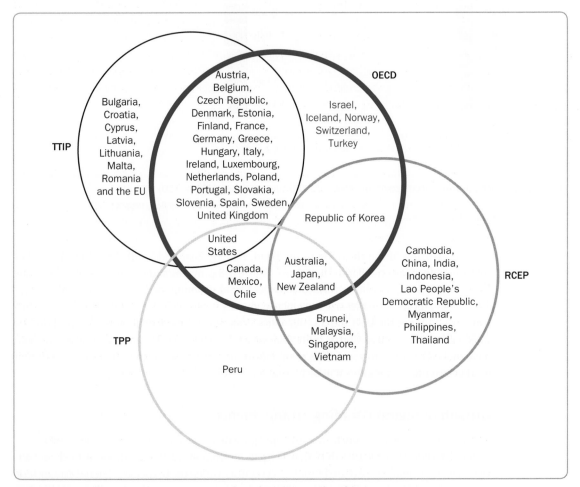

Figure 1.4 Participation in key megaregionals and OECD membership

Source: World Investment Report (2014), Figure 7, p. xxiv.

1970–2000. In other words, every 1% increase in the average growth rate of RTA partners brought a 'growth bonus' of 0.14% to other members of the RTA. In Europe and East Asia, where historically regional integration has been strongest, the average growth spillover was even larger at around 0.17% over the period 1970–2000. In a similar vein, as regards the benefits of membership of a regional trading bloc, Frankel (1997) noted that during the early 1990s, intra-regional trade within one such regional trading bloc – the Andean community of Bolivia, Colombia, Ecuador, Peru and Venezuela – was 2.7 times higher than the levels of national income and geographic separation of those economies would have led us to expect.

Growth of bilateral investment and trade treaties

Nor is it only within the broad-based regional trading blocs that preferential treatment is available to participating countries and companies. For example, there has been a rapid growth in *bilateral (two-country) investment and trade treaties,* which can take various forms, the major ones being *bilateral investment treaties* (BITs) and *double taxation treaties* (DTTs). Over 2,600 BITs had been notified to the World Trade Organisation (WTO) by 2014 which, while they may encourage foreign direct investment (fdi) flows between the two countries concluding the investment treaty, arguably discriminate against fdi flows involving countries that are *not* signatories to the BIT. Similarly, around 2,700 DTTs had been notified to the WTO by 2014, again arguably reducing tax rates and stimulating investments and trade between the two countries involved, but creating a complex patchwork of investment and taxation regimes which are difficult to manage on a global scale. We consider the impact of such bilateral treaties in more detail in Chapter 3.

Growth of sovereign wealth funds (SWFs)

Sovereign wealth funds (SWFs) are government-owned investment vehicles managed separately from the official reserves of the country. They have usually been accumulated by those governments as the result of high global commodity prices for their exports. High energy (e.g. oil), food and other primary product prices over recent years have meant that an estimated $5,000 billion is now available for potential investment by countries such as the United Arab Emirates, Saudi Arabia, Dubai, Kuwait, China, Norway, the Russian Federation and Singapore, amongst others. The SWFs will often be invested in projects with higher risks but higher expected future returns. Professional portfolio management techniques are often adopted with a view to generating a sustainable future income stream via investments in bonds, equities and other assets. In 2009 Barclays Bank raised $7 billion of funds from this source rather than accept UK government funding to help it cope with the liquidity crisis of the 'credit crunch' (see Chapter 10, p. 355). In 2014 there were 70 SWFs in 44 countries with assets ranging in value from $20 million (São Tomé and Príncipe) to more than $500 billion in the United Arab Emirates.

Growth of 'defensive techniques' to combat global insecurity

The global growth of foreign direct investment and the increasingly 'footloose' activities of MNEs have already been documented as widely used indicators of globalisation. Many commentators have also drawn attention to parallels between the rapid growth in formal, legal cross-border relationships and the rapid growth in a wide range of illegal cross-border relationships. Some of the characteristics of globalisation reviewed in Box 1.2 (p. 16) are seen as conducive to such growth, especially the weakening of power and control by nation states and the proliferation of new, less detectable methods of communication.

While a proper investigation of so complex an issue is beyond the scope of this section, we can perhaps draw attention to what many believe is a new global business environment since 11 September 2001 (9/11), which is perhaps the date most closely associated with the advent of global insecurity. The additional insurance premiums required since 9/11 is one important indicator of the costs to international business of such 'defensive techniques', as are the monetarised values for the increased time costs to individuals and businesses of additional security-related delays as well as the extra costs associated with more security-related personnel and equipment. For example, it has been estimated that the *actual* growth of global GDP has fallen since 9/11 by around 1% per annum relative to the previously *projected* growth.

Pause for thought 1.2

Can you suggest which sectors/industries have been the main 'losers' with the heightened concerns over global terrorism and which the main 'beneficiaries'?

Changing area patterns of international costs

Of particular interest to international business location is the area pattern of *international labour costs,* both wage and non-wage (employers' social security contributions, holiday pay, etc.). Comparable data is notoriously difficult to derive, both within broad geographical regions and between such regions. In any case it is not just overall labour costs that are important but these costs in relation to labour productivity. For example, if labour costs double but labour productivity doubles, then labour costs per unit of output remain the same. We return to this idea of Relative Unit Labour Costs below (p. 9).

The Boston Consulting Group (BCG) has constructed the *Global Manufacturing Cost-Competitiveness Index* to show how the production costs in the world's ten largest goods-exporting countries have changed, relative to the US, in the ten years from 2004 to 2014. The four key components of the Index are labour costs per hour, labour productivity (output per hour), energy costs per unit output and national currency exchange rates vis-à-vis the US dollar.

Figure 1.5 uses index numbers (US = 100) to compare manufacturing costs per unit of output across the top ten export economies over the period 2004 to 2014.

Figure 1.5 indicates some important shifts in cost competitiveness over the past decade. For example China's cost advantage over the US has fallen from 14% (100% against 86%) to only 4% (100% against 96%), hardly surprising when Chinese average labour costs have almost trebled over the ten-year period, far exceeding growth in Chinese labour productivity and thereby raising labour costs per unit output. The ten-point rise in the Chinese cost-competitiveness index over the past decade vis-à-vis the US is higher for China (in absolute and percentage terms) than the rise for eight out of the other nine countries. Clearly China's manufacturing cost competitiveness has therefore declined against these other eight countries also.

The US can be seen to be the second most competitive manufacturing location out of the ten largest global exporters, with the UK broadly maintaining its cost competitiveness with the US over the past decade, and the Netherlands becoming marginally more cost competitive. Figure 1.5 suggests that the other major manufacturing nations of Western Europe have become even less cost competitive with the US over the past decade, as well as becoming less cost competitive with the UK and the Netherlands.

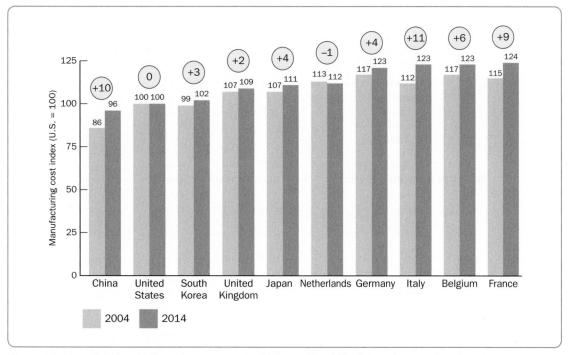

Figure 1.5 How global manufacturing cost competitiveness has shifted over the past decade
Source: Boston Consulting Group (BCG), *Analysis of the World's Largest Manufacturing Economies,* April 2014.

Table 1.3 uses the same BCG Index as that for Figure 1.5 but provides a broader coverage of the world's top 25 export economies in terms of cost competitiveness in 2014.

The data in Table 1.3 reveals some striking changes in manufacturing cost competitiveness. Mexico is now less expensive than China as a manufacturing location; Brazil is now a high-cost location for manufacturing; the UK is the lowest-cost location for manufacturing throughout Western Europe. Indeed, this BCG data challenges a number of simple, long-held assumptions that North America and Western Europe are high-cost locations and Asia and Latin America are low-cost locations. What is becoming increasingly clear is that there are low- and high-cost locations in *all* geographical regions of the world and that multinationals and others making global investment and locational decisions must do so on the basis of cost-related contemporary evidence, rather than basing such decisions on 'inherited wisdom' as to low-cost geographical locations!

Pause for thought 1.3

What other conclusions might be drawn from the data in Figure 1.3?

Labour costs and labour productivity

A more complete assessment of true labour costs would use the idea of Relative Unit Labour Costs (RULC), which are explored further in Box 1.1. Three of the four elements included in the BCG Index are also included in this, the most widely used indicator of international competitiveness.

Table 1.3 **Cost competitiveness in manufacturing across the world's top 25 export economies in 2014 (US = 100)**

Country	Global Manufacturing Cost Competitiveness Index (US = 100)
Australia	130
Austria	111
Belgium	123
Brazil	123
Canada	115
China	96
Czech Republic	107
France	124
Germany	121
India	87
Indonesia	83
Italy	123
Japan	111
Mexico	91
Netherlands	111
Poland	101
Russia	99
South Korea	102
Spain	109
Sweden	116
Switzerland	125
Taiwan	97
Thailand	91
UK	109
US	100

Source: Boston Consulting Group (BCG), *Analysis of the World's Largest Manufacturing Economies*, April 2014.

BOX 1.1 Relative Unit Labour Costs (RULC)

Labour costs per unit of output (unit labour costs) are determined by both the wages of the workers and the output per worker (labour productivity). International competitiveness, in terms of unit labour costs, is also influenced by exchange rates. For example, depreciation of the currency makes exports cheaper in terms of the foreign currency (see Chapter 3) and therefore can even compensate for low labour productivity and high money wages. When we bring all these three elements together and express each of them relative to a country's main competitors, we can derive the most widely used measure of labour cost competitiveness, namely *Relative Unit Labour Costs* (RULC).

The calculation of RULC is as follows:

$$\frac{\text{Relative labour costs}}{\text{Relative labour productivity}} \times \text{exchange rate} = \text{RULC}$$

This formula emphasises that lower RULC for, say, the UK could be achieved either by reducing the UK's relative labour costs, or by raising the UK's relative labour productivity, or by lowering the UK's relative exchange rate, or by some combination of all three.

The BCG Index used in Figure 1.5 and Table 1.3 contained four key elements: labour costs, labour productivity, energy costs and currency exchange rates. Here we focus on the contribution of the first two elements, namely labour costs and labour productivity to international competitiveness.

Table 1.4 uses data from the US Bureau of Labour Statistics (August 2013) to compare *hourly compensation costs* across 19 of the 25 countries presented in Table 1.3 above.

Table 1.4 indicates some sharp shifts in hourly compensation costs in both absolute terms and as a percentage of US labour costs, over the period 1997 to 2012. The labour cost *disadvantage* of Australia and many Western European countries has increased vis-à-vis the USA and other economies. However, it is clear from this table that while labour costs are indeed an important element in locational decisions for manufacturing firms, they are far from being decisive in terms of *overall* cost competitiveness. For example, hourly compensation costs in Brazil are only 31% (in 2012) of those in the USA, yet we have already seen in Figure 1.5 and Table 1.3 that Brazil's overall BCG competitiveness index was 23% *above* that of the USA!

Part of the answer as to why hourly compensation costs are only *part* of the competitiveness equation involves the issue of labour productivity. This is made clear for a number of countries in Figure 1.6.

As we can see from Figure 1.6, all countries except for Norway, Luxembourg and Ireland, and all groups of countries (e.g. OECD, G7 countries) have labour productivity data per hour worked which falls well below that of the USA. For example, Mexico has 70% less output (GDP) per hour worked than the USA, Russia has 63% less output per hour worked than the USA and the OECD group of advanced industrialised economies has average output per hour worked some 30% less than that of the USA.

Table 1.4 Hourly compensation costs in manufacturing, US dollars and as a percentage of costs in the USA

Country	Hourly Compensation Costs			
	In US dollars		In Index numbers US = 100	
	1997	2012	1997	2012
Australia	18.93	47.68	82	134
Austria	24.91	41.53	108	116
Belgium	28.92	52.19	125	146
Brazil	7.07	11.20	31	31
Czech Republic	3.25	11.95	14	34
France	24.86	39.81	108	112
Germany	29.16	45.79	127	128
Italy	19.76	34.18	86	96
Japan	21.99	35.34	95	99
Korea, Republic of	9.22	20.72	40	58
Mexico	3.47	6.36	15	18
Netherlands	22.45	39.62	97	111
Poland	3.15	8.25	14	23
Spain	13.95	26.83	61	75
Sweden	25.02	49.80	109	140
Switzerland	30.42	57.79	132	162
Taiwan	7.04	9.46	31	27
United Kingdom	19.31	31.23	84	88
United States	23.04	35.67	100	100

Source: Adapted from US Bureau of Labour Statistics, *International Labour Comparisons,* August 2013.

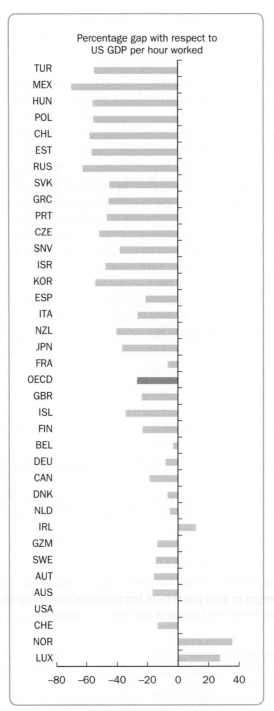

Figure 1.6 Labour productivity per hour worked: % differences with respect to the US, 2012

Source: Adapted from *OECD Factbook 2014: Economic, Environmental and Social Statistics,* 5 May 2014.

Table 1.5 Ranking of countries in terms of business competitiveness*

Country	Rank	Country	Rank
Switzerland	1	Australia	21
Singapore	2	Luxembourg	22
Finland	3	France	23
Germany	4	Malaysia	24
US	5	South Korea	25
Sweden	6	Brunei	26
Hong Kong	7	Israel	27
Netherlands	8	Ireland	28
Japan	9	China	29
UK	10	Puerto Rico	30
Norway	11	Iceland	31
Taiwan	12	Estonia	32
Qatar	13	Oman	33
Canada	14	Chile	34
Denmark	15	Spain	35
Austria	16	Kuwait	36
Belgium	17	Thailand	37
New Zealand	18	Indonesia	38
United Arab Emirates	19	Azerbaijan	39
Saudi Arabia	20	Panama	40

Note: *Including competitiveness of company operations.

Source: Adapted from Schwab, K. (ed.) *The Global Competitiveness Report 2013–2014,* Table 3. World Economic Forum.

Overall business competitiveness

Table 1.5 provides some interesting international comparisons when 'business competitiveness' is defined in terms of a wide range of microeconomic determinants in addition to labour costs and labour productivity. The top ten most competitive countries listed in the table are certainly not in the category of the 'low-wage economies' or even 'low-productivity economies'! We can therefore see how important other aspects of the business environment (e.g. access to R&D, access to business clusters, legal protection of property rights, corruption-free dealings, etc.) really are as regards overall business competitiveness. Switzerland (1st), Finland (3rd), Germany (4th), US (5th), Sweden (6th), the Netherlands (8th), Japan (9th) and UK (10th) are hardly low-wage or low-productivity economies, yet their advantages as regards the business environment in which they operate give them a ranking in the 'top ten' economies in terms of overall business competitiveness (Schwab 2014).

Such changes in area patterns of international costs have had a significant impact on the international location of business activity, as is indicated in Case 1.1.

CASE 1.1 Dyson revisits its international location

In January 2014 Dyson announced that it was to create 3,000 new science and engineering jobs in the UK by 2020 as part of the largest expansion in its 20-year history. This news came at a time when JCB, the world's third largest maker of construction equipment, announced in 2014 that it would create a further 2,500 jobs in the UK by 2018.

The news from Dyson reverses the earlier trend in which Dyson had moved production of its washing machines from the UK to Malaysia in 2008, which

Case 1.1 (*continued*)

followed an even earlier decision in 2002 to shift production of its revolutionary dual cyclone bagless vacuum cleaner to Malaysia with the loss of over 800 jobs at the Dyson factory in Malmesbury, Wiltshire, which had previously produced some 8,000 vacuum cleaners per day. Dyson had been keen to point out back in 2002 that the company was operating in a price-cutting market in which its competitors were able to pass on to their customers the lower costs from manufacturing vacuum cleaners outside the UK. In contrast, Dyson had faced a situation in which direct labour costs in Britain had doubled over the previous ten years, partly because of the need to pay high wages in an area around Swindon with almost zero unemployment.

Dyson had claimed that the sums no longer added up and it faced going out of business if it had continued manufacturing its product in the UK, and as of September 2002 all vacuum cleaner production had shifted to Malaysia. The company argued that its production costs would benefit from the much lower wages in Malaysia, equivalent to £1.50 per hour as compared to the then £4.10 per hour in the UK. Indeed, the company estimated that lower wages would reduce its unit production costs by around 30%. Further cost savings would also come from its now having most of its component suppliers nearby (South-East Asian component suppliers having progressively replaced those from the UK) and being much closer to emerging new markets in Japan, Australia and the Far East. In addition, the Malaysian government had offered various 'subsidies' in the form of grants for setting up the Dyson factories there, as well as lower taxes and other benefits.

While lamenting the loss of UK jobs, Dyson announced that in moving vacuum cleaner manufacturing to Malaysia it would now generate enough cash to maintain the company's commitment to reinvesting up to 20% of turnover in research and development (R&D). Dyson believed that it was the technological advantages secured by R&D that would keep the company alive and ensure that 1,150 other jobs in Malmesbury were safe, more than 300 of which involved engineers, scientists, designers and testers – the brains that ensure Dyson products remain a step ahead of the rest. Dyson claimed to have exported the brawn, keeping the higher-level value-added parts at home since Dyson's comparative advantage lies in researching and designing new products to ensure the company stays two steps ahead of its rivals, most of whom manufacture in the Far East. Indeed, he claimed that to have followed the rest of British industry, which invests an average of only 2% of turnover, would have been to neglect Dyson's engineering and technological heritage and to follow in the faltering footsteps of Britain's car, television and other domestic appliance industries. The innovative nature of the company has continued with the introduction in October 2006 of the Dyson 'Airblade', the first hygienic hand dryer which was shown to be 83% more energy efficient than its competitors.

Dyson argued that the lower costs from outsourcing had secured its future, helping it to beat the previous US market leader, Hoover, to such an extent that Dyson now has around 21% of the US vacuum cleaner market, ahead of Hoover's 16%. Although Hoover sells more vacuum cleaners by volume, the higher-technology Dyson cleaners command a premium price, giving greater sales value from lower-volume sales. James Dyson points to the key outsourcing decisions it had made as the foundation for this success.

Questions

1 How can Dyson argue that it was in the interests of his British workforce that he had relocated production to Malaysia?

2 Can you suggest any linkages of this study with the patterns and trends indicated in Tables 1.3 and 1.4, and Figure 1.5 above?

3 Can you apply the idea of Relative Unit Labour Costs (RULCs) in Box 1.1 to this situation?

◼ Other international patterns/trends

As well as the factors already discussed, a number of other patterns and trends are evident which are likely to be relevant to different types of international business activity.

- *International communications.* There have been dramatic increases and changes in various modes of international communications. Recent data suggests that there are almost as many mobile phones as there are people on earth, i.e. around 7 billion. Internet usage is also rising exponentially, with the percentage of individuals using the internet rising from less than 10% in 2001 to over 34% in 2014, with the figure as high as 70% in the developed economies.

- *International travel.* The number of international tourists has more than trebled from 260 million travellers a year in 1980 to over 900 million travellers a year in 2014. The growth of tourism is closely correlated with the growth of world GDP and is an important source of income and employment for many developed and developing countries alike.

- *International growth in leisure pursuits.* In 1880 some 80% of the time left over after necessities such as sleeping and eating were attended to was used for earning a living. Today that percentage has fallen to below 40% over the average lifetime of an individual in the advanced industrialised economies and is projected to continue falling to around 25% over the next decade. This dramatic increase in leisure-time availability in the higher-income advanced industrialised economies clearly has major implications for consumption patterns and therefore for the deployment of productive resources.

- *International growth in ageing populations.* Between 1950 and 2014 the median age (with 50% of the population below and 50% above) of the world's population rose by only three years, from 23.6 years in 1950 to 26.5 years in 2014. However over the next 35 years or so the UN projects that the median age will rise dramatically to 37 years by 2050, with 17 advanced industrialised economies having a median age of 50 years or above. Indeed in 2014 some 17% of the UK population was aged over 65 years, compared to only 11% in 1950, and some 5% of the UK population was aged over 80 years, compared to only 1.4% in 1981. Such sharp changes in the age profile of the global population have major implications for international business in terms of productive location (e.g. adequate supply of labour of working age) as well as in terms of the range of products likely to be in global demand.

- *International growth in currency transactions.* The daily turnover in foreign exchange markets has dramatically increased from $15 billion in the mid-1970s to over $5,300 billion in 2014. This growth in international currency transactions has contributed to greater exchange rate volatility, on occasion putting severe pressure on national economies and currencies.

- *International growth in countertrade.* When conventional means of payment for international transactions are difficult, costly or not available, then a range of barter/swap-type transactions may be used instead. Whereas such 'countertrade' only accounted for 2% of world trade in 1975, by 2014 over 25% of world trade was estimated as involving some element of barter, with the former Soviet Union and the Eastern European economies particularly active in using countertrade.

Pause for thought 1.4

Can you think of any other patterns and trends that might be of interest to a multinational enterprise? Explain your reasoning in each case.

Globalisation

Globalisation is much talked about in the media and is often used to refer to more closely integrated economies worldwide, with products, people and money moving more easily and in greater volume and value throughout the world. Hill (2012) usefully illustrates the realities of globalisation with an example of an American driving a car, designed and produced in Germany, which was assembled in Mexico from components made in Japan, using fabricated steel for the chassis from Korea and rubber for the wheels from Malaysia. The car is filled with petrol refined in the US, from oil extracted by a French oil company from oil reserves off the coast of Africa, and transported to the US refinery by a ship owned by a Greek shipping line.

Globalisation as a multi-dimensional process

Of course the term 'globalisation' is by no means the preserve of economists alone. Indeed it has been approached from the perspective of at least four academic disciplines, within each of which it tends to take on different characteristics:

- *economists* focus on the growth of international trade, the increase in international capital flows and the progressive dominance of the multinational enterprise (MNE) form of business organisation within domestic and global business activity;
- *political scientists* view globalisation as a process that leads to the undermining of the nation state and the emergence of new forms of governance;
- *sociologists* view globalisation in terms of the rise of a global culture and the domination of the media by global companies;
- *international relations experts* tend to focus on the emergence of global conflicts and global institutions.

Different perspectives on globalisation

Certainly the world is seen as becoming increasingly interconnected as the result of economic, political, sociological and cultural forces. A one-dimensional view of globalisation, which thinks purely in terms of market forces, is likely to result in only a partial picture at best. Box 1.2 presents a range of perspectives and definitions of globalisation.

BOX 1.2 Definitions of globalisation

- '. . . the process of transformation of local phenomena into global ones. It can be described as a process by which the people of the world are unified into a single society and function together. This process is a combination of economic, technological, socio-cultural and political forces' (Croucher 2003: 10).
- '. . . a widening, deepening and speeding up of interconnectedness in all aspects of contemporary social life from the cultural to the criminal, the financial to the spiritual' (Held *et al.* 1999: 2).

Box 1.2 (*continued*)

- '. . . increasing global interconnectedness, so that events in one part of the world are affected by, have to take account of, and also influence, other parts of the world. It also refers to an increasing sense of a single global whole' (Tiplady 2003: 2).
- '. . . the worldwide movement towards economic, financial, trade and communications integration. Globalisation implies opening out beyond local and nationalistic perspectives to a broader outlook of an interconnected and inter-dependent world with the free transfer of capital, goods and services across national frontiers' (*Business Dictionary*).
- '. . . refers to the shift toward a more integrated and interdependent world economy . . . [through] the merging of historically distinct and separate national markets into one huge global market place' (Hill 2005: 6).
- '. . . process by which the whole world becomes a single market. This means that goods and services, capital and labour are traded on a worldwide basis, and information and the results of research flow readily between countries' (Black 2002).
- '. . . reflects a business orientation based on the belief that the world is becoming more homogenous and that distinctions between national markets are not only fading but, for some products, will eventually disappear' (Czinkota and Ronkainen 1999: 454).

Some argue that globalisation is a long-standing phenomenon and not really anything new, pointing out that world trade and investment, as a proportion of world GDP, is little different today from what it was a century ago and that international borders were as open at that time as they are today with just as many people migrating abroad. Indeed Adam Smith, as long ago as 1787, defined the businessmen of his time as 'men without country'.

However, those who believe that globalisation really is a new phenomenon tend to agree that at least three key elements are commonly involved.

1 *Shrinking space.* The lives of all individuals are increasingly interconnected by events worldwide. This is not only a matter of fact but one which people increasingly perceive to be the case, recognising that their jobs, income levels, health and living environment depend on factors outside national and local boundaries.

2 *Shrinking time.* With the rapid developments in communication and information technologies, events occurring in one place have almost instantaneous (real-time) impacts worldwide. A fall in share prices in Wall Street can have almost immediate consequences for share prices in London, Frankfurt or Tokyo.

3 *Disappearing borders.* The nation state and its associated borders seem increasingly irrelevant as 'barriers' to international events and influences. Decisions taken by regional trading blocs (e.g. EU, NAFTA) and supranational bodies (e.g. IMF, World Trade Organisation) increasingly override national policy making in economic and business affairs as well as in other areas such as law enforcement and human rights.

Pause for thought 1.5

How might events in the aftermath of 9/11 relate to these three elements? Would this be evidence for or against the view that globalisation really is a new phenomenon?

Others identify four key features as indicative of globalisation being different from what has gone before.

- **New markets:** rapidly developing global and more deregulated markets in goods and services.

- **New tools of communication:** rapid growth in the use of internet, electronic and cloud-based communications on a global scale.

- **New actors:** increased presence and influence of a wide range of global 'players', including multinational corporations, non-governmental organisations (e.g. WTO), trading blocs involving regional groupings of countries (e.g. EU, NAFTA, ASEAN) and global policy co-ordination groups (e.g. G7, G8).

- **New rules and norms:** growth in privatisation, deregulation, impacts of conventions on issues such as human rights, environmental sustainability, etc.

In Chapter 3 we review in some detail the contribution of 'new actors', such as the various international institutions, to the growth of world trade and increased international activity. In particular we review the attempts by institutions such as the World Trade Organisation (p. 109) to create a 'level playing field' in an increasingly globalised economy. Case 1.2 examines the strategies and responses available to international businesses to compete effectively when facing the four key features outlined above which impose new pressures on international business activity.

CASE 1.2 A local hero's fight for American jobs

Most people in business have a story about how China has changed their industry; how over the past 30 years it has upended supply chains and grabbed daunting market share. But very few have the sort of China story that John Bassett III has. One day in November 2002, Mr Bassett, a third-generation furniture maker from Virginia, found himself in China meeting the Communist party official and businessman intent on putting him out of business. This man's ambitions and instructions were clear and direct: his company would soon be the biggest furniture manufacturer in the world and resistance was futile. Mr Bassett should shut his US factories and contract his production to China. It was the only way his business would survive. 'He was not belligerent, but it was just like you were speaking to a judge,' Mr Bassett tells Beth Macy in *Factory Man*, the new book that recounts his struggle to save his business and take on China. 'He was absolutely serious and confident in what he was saying.'

Mr Bassett's reaction was to do the very opposite. Within a year he had mobilised much of the US furniture industry and hired a top lawyer to mount a trade case against Chinese manufacturers for dumping bedroom furniture suites below cost on the US market. And if his furniture business is alive today it is largely because Mr Bassett won his fight. We have for some time been awash in books detailing the costs in shut factories and lost jobs that has come with the rise in China and the advent of truly international supply chains. But *Factory Man* deserves to be read by anyone wanting to wrap their heads around the present-day dynamics and politics of globalisation. Macy's book is an important read, whether or not you agree with its premise and economics.

There is an element of Don Quixote about it, as some of Mr Bassett's critics point out. *Factory Man* tells the story of one mans' fight to save a dying industry and the small southern towns that depend on it. But it is also about the much bigger theme of US competitiveness and the angst over lost manufacturing jobs that has been at the heart of the debate over trade ever since Bill Clinton signed the North American Free Trade Agreement in 1993.

The figures are stunning. In the two years after China joined the World Trade Organisation in 2001 and cheap Chinese-made furniture began

Case 1.2 (*continued*)

flooding the US market, almost a million jobs were lost as American furniture factories were shuttered, many of them in the rural Virginia and North Carolina company towns that over the previous century had become the focus of the industry in North America. In truth, as Macy acknowledges, China did to those southern towns what they had done in Grand Rapids, Michigan, just a few decades before, by paying lower wages and shamelessly turning out cheaper copies of popular furniture to grab market share.

The book does a good job of showing how some successful US businesses have learnt to adapt and compete with China and started to 'reshore'

their production. Mr Bassett relentlessly invests in new machinery for his factories and decides that he will beat his Chinese competitors on quality and service rather than just price. The answer to China is not just to hire lawyers, the message goes, but to innovate.

It is also clear that there is an element of futility in fighting globalisation. After punitive anti-dumping duties are levied by the US the production of bedroom furniture does not come home to Virginia as Mr Bassett hopes, it moves to Vietnam. And the fight is costly: one economist estimates that the legal battle ends ups costing $800,000 per job saved.

Questions

1 What lessons about globalisation can be learned from this account?
2 What policies are suggested as needed if a business or country is to effectively compete in a globalised world?

Outcomes of globalisation

Of course there are different schools of thought as to the possible outcomes of globalisation even among those who do accept its reality.

- *Hyperglobalists* envisage the global economy as being inhabited by powerless nation states at the mercy of 'footloose' multinational enterprises bestowing jobs and wealth creation opportunities on favoured national clients. National cultural differences are largely seen by these progressively powerful multinationals as merely variations in consumer preferences to be reflected in their international marketing mix.

- *Transformationalists* recognise that globalisation is a powerful force impacting on economic, social and political environments, but take a much less prescriptive stance as to what the outcomes of those impacts might be. Predictions as to any end-state of a globalised economy can only be tentative and premature. Globalisation involves a complex set of intermittent, uneven processes with unpredictable outcomes rather than a linear progression to a predictable end-state.

It is this more pragmatic transformationalist approach that is most commonly encountered in debates on globalisation. While there may be many theories as to the causes of globalisation, most writers would agree that globalisation is a discontinuous historical process. Its dynamic proceeds in fits and starts and its effects are experienced differentially across the globe. Some regions are more deeply affected by globalisation than others. Even within nation states, some sectors may experience the effects of globalisation more sharply than others. Many have argued that globalisation is tending to reinforce inequalities of power both within and across nation states, resulting in global hierarchies of privilege and control for some, but economic and social exclusion for others.

Giddens (1990) subscribes to the 'transformationalist' approach:

> Globalisation is a complex process which is not necessarily teleological in character – that is to say, it is not necessarily an inexorable historical process with an end in sight. Rather, it is characterised by a set of mutually opposing tendencies.

McGrew (1992) has tried to identify a number of these opposing tendencies.

- *Universalisation versus particularisation.* While globalisation may tend to make many aspects of modern social life universal (e.g. assembly line production, fast-food restaurants, consumer fashions), it can also help to point out the differences between what happens in particular places and what happens elsewhere. This focus on differences can foster the resurgence of regional and national identities.

- *Homogenisation versus differentiation.* While globalisation may result in an essential homogeneity ('sameness') in product, process and institutions (e.g. city life, organisational offices and bureaucracies), it may also mean that the general must be assimilated within the local. For example, human rights are interpreted in different ways across the globe, the practice of specific religions such as Christianity or Buddhism may take on different forms in different places, and so on.

- *Integration versus fragmentation.* Globalisation creates new forms of global, regional and transnational communities that unite (integrate) people across territorial boundaries (e.g. the MNE, international trade unions, etc.). However, it also has the potential to divide and fragment communities (e.g. labour becoming divided along sectoral, local, national and ethnic lines).

It may be useful to review globalisation in rather more detail under four separate headings:

1 Globalisation and markets.
2 Globalisation and production.
3 Globalisation and the role of the nation state.
4 Globalisation and new rules and norms.

The rest of the chapter then goes on to discuss globalisation and the multinational enterprise.

1 Globalisation and markets

Case 1.3 uses recent global developments in manufacturing to review the suggestion that the forces of globalisation would establish global markets for standardised products purchased in huge volumes by consumers worldwide. The marketing guru Theodore Levitt, a professor at Harvard Business School, made a statement on 1 May 1983 which has subsequently been seen by supporters of his views as prophetic and by opponents as delusional!

'The globalisation of markets is at hand', he declared in a *Harvard Business Review* article, written at a time when the word 'globalisation' was virtually unknown. Professor Levitt's message was simple. As new technology extended the reach of global media and brought down the cost of communications, the world was shrinking. As a result, consumer tastes everywhere were converging, creating global markets for standardised products on a previously unimagined scale.

CASE 1.3 Manufacturing futures and markets

A cavernous factory in Charlotte, North Carolina, is among the newest and shiniest in the empire of Siemens, the German engineering group. There is a palpable buzz as workers put the finishing touches to a new breed of 300-tonne gas turbines – workhorses of the global electricity industry. The turbines cut production times by a third and costs by 15 per cent but their improved efficiency is not the most striking feature of what is happening in Charlotte. More fundamentally, the Siemens operations offer a microcosm of the factors behind a far-reaching new industrial revolution that is altering the global balance of power in goods production.

This new period has the potential to turn winners into losers and also-rans into champions. It provides high-cost nations with a way back into areas of manufacturing some of them thought they had lost to emerging economies such as China and India. In many countries, policy makers are re-examining the potential of production industries to generate jobs and growth at a time of great economic uncertainty. 'Everywhere I go, re-industrialisation is at the forefront of political thought,' says Peter Loscher, Siemens chief executive.

There are seven key features that define this new era in which manufacturers, once dismissed as grimy and uncompetitive, can once again be seen as powerful engines of growth.

- First, 'networked manufacturing'. This makes it easier for businesses to operate in dispersed locations, drawing on skills spread across their empires. In the North Carolina unit, workers are connected with 350 global parts suppliers and about 3,000 engineers scattered around the world in other Siemens centres. Through such ties, the Charlotte plant has gained access to new ideas in production and design, some of which are derived from industries as diverse as medical equipment and car production, helping the unit to be competitive despite the handicap of relatively high wage costs.
- Second 'combining technologies'. The US factory uses an array of new ideas from new types of surface coatings to advances in computer-aided design. In the new era, says Omar Ishrak, Chief Executive of US medical equipment maker Medtronic, combining technologies – in anything from electronics to biotechnology – will prove crucial. 'It's not enough to know about different technologies, you have to be able to combine them,' he says.
- Third, 'industrial democracy'. More countries now have a role in manufacturing, with China leading the way. This can be seen at Charlotte, which can take advantage of its 40 per cent stake in Shanghai electric, giving Siemens access to the latest Asian trends and production facilities.
- Fourth, 'personalised production'. This is illustrated in techniques to ensure that most of the gas turbines being made in the plant incorporate bespoke features for consumers.
- Fifth, 'niche industries'. The turbine plant also depends on ideas that have been produced in a number of 'niche' industries. Large manufacturing operations are creating more work for boutique operations. The North Carolina plant is a big user of machines for boring tiny holes in turbine blades produced by UK-based niche manufacturer Winbro.
- Sixth, 'cluster dynamics'. While networked manufacturing widens the geographical options, companies also see a virtue in 'cluster dynamics' – having groups of suppliers concentrated in small areas to help ideas flow more freely. The Charlotte unit has 15 local suppliers and managers are keen for a three-fold increase in this number in five years.
- Seventh, 'environmental imperatives'. This is the final component of the new revolution. The turbines produced in the factory have higher standards of efficiency than previous generations, assisting in reducing emissions of carbon dioxide from power stations.

'There's a sense that we are seeing a global manufacturing renaissance,' says Jeff Immelt, chief executive of General Electric, and innovation is at its core.'

Questions

1 Match each of the following examples with the feature outlined in the Case to which the example most closely relates.

Mindray (China): a maker of medical equipment and a leading high-tech business from China. It has added a US marketing and development base to its Chinese operations. Mindray bases nearly all production in China because of low labour costs, while locating product development and marketing teams in the US, Sweden, Germany, the UK and India.

Starkey Hearing Technologies (US): the world's biggest maker of customised hearing aids. It has 16 factories in countries including France, Germany, the US, Britain, Mexico and China. The plants produced 600,000 'tailored' hearing aids in the past year, each configured to meet the dimensions of a single person's ear.

EBM-Papst (Germany): maker of low-energy fans. The company says its location in southern Germany – close to key suppliers and also many customers – helps it compete. It identifies the closeness of its relationship with 15 important suppliers within a 50-km radius of its headquarters as contributing to developing new technologies.

Element Six (Luxembourg): This is the world's largest producer of synthetic diamonds – made by subjecting carbon to high pressure. In the past year it accounted for about a quarter of global sales of $2 billion. This area of technology, used in cutting tools and semiconductors, requires a deep knowledge of high-pressure processes and materials science.

Interface (US): a large carpet maker that for the past decade has been a leader in using environmental standards as a way to sell more products. Of the company's sales in the past year of about $1 billion, roughly 90% came from carpets sold with an 'environmental product declaration'. These provide an assessment of some of the environmental factors linked to the product's manufacture, such as energy use production of waste and greenhouse gases.

Danfoss (Denmark): one of the world's biggest producers of central-heating valves. It operates 58 factories in about 20 countries. Danfoss has a group of 1,200 technical specialists of whom half are in Denmark, with the rest spread globally. The company can direct the production of new valves to plants with the most suitable know-how.

Komatsu (Japan): the world's second-biggest maker of construction machines. It develops new technical ideas, such as using improved and lighter steels in the tippers of dump trucks, thereby cutting the weight of the vehicle and reducing the fuel consumption.

2 To what extent does the Case support or challenge the view of globalisation held by Theodore Levitt?

While global markets do indeed exist for some standardised products such as microchips, energy sources (e.g. oil and gas) and other goods and services where little product differentiation is feasible or wanted by users, for many other goods and services varying international tastes and preferences mean that product differentiation is vital to appeal to local markets. What Levitt failed to appreciate was that technology would not only provide the mechanisms for large-scale, low-cost standardised production but would also permit customised, bespoke production at reduced cost, using the new methods of batch and modular production now available (see Chapter 7).

Similarly, new techniques for researching and analysing segmented markets (see Chapter 9) would also allow global companies to identify the product differentiation actually needed to meet differing global tastes.

Case 1.4 suggests that businesses may need to consider the 'local' as well as the 'global' when developing market-based strategies.

CASE 1.4 JCB adapts to the Indian market

Economic growth has many indicators, but in India one is more visible than most – the sight of ever more bright yellow diggers bearing the logo of Britain's JCB, moving earth around the nation's building sites. India is now easily the manufacturer's largest market by sales; such is its dominance, with more than half the construction equipment market, that all earth movers and excavators tend to be termed 'JCBs', whether they are or not. This makes the Staffordshire-based business a relatively rare example of British manufacturing success in Asia's third largest economy. JCB in January 2014 began operations at a £63m factory in the northern city of Jaipur, its third manufacturing site in the country and the culmination of a £250m investment that now sees roughly half the components fabricated in its Pune plant exported back for use in the UK.

JCB entered India in 1979; its first venture outside the UK. It was a personal project of Chairman Lord Anthony Bamford, a self-confessed Indiaphile and son of company founder Joseph Cyril Bamford. Originally part of a joint venture, it went solo in 2003, enjoying speedy growth on a boom in infrastructure spending. This early start provided an edge over larger competitors such as US-based Caterpillar and Hitachi of Japan, while its relatively inexpensive entry-level digger, otherwise known as a backhoe loader, proved popular with price-sensitive customers.

Moves to cut vehicle running costs also won buyers, according to Ravie Venkatesan, the former head of Microsoft India, who wrote glowingly about JCB's performance in a recent book on successful foreign companies in the country. 'They optimised for local tastes, they got rid of the bells and whistles, and in particular they changed the fuel system, to make it cheaper,' he says. A stable Indian management team operating with little interference from the UK helped too, as did investment in after-sales service, earning a reputation for reliability.

More quirky factors also played a part says JCB's Mr Sondhi, at least once the company noticed how many people tended to cram into its vehicles on busy Indian construction sites leading to a design rethink. 'We now have the largest cabin, able to accommodate about three or four', he says. 'And if the guy works off-site, he can now sleep for a while in the cab, it's more comfortable.'

Question
Consider the relevance of JCB's business strategy to the debate on globalisation.

2 Globalisation and production

We have already noted that differences in relative unit labour costs (RULCs) will provide incentives to firms to select particular countries for the production of part or all of a product. Case 1.1 (p. 13) examined the reasons for Dyson outsourcing parts of its production process to Malaysia, although we also noted a more recent trend by Dyson and others to return investment and jobs to the higher-wage, more developed economies. Here we review some further aspects on the issue of globalisation and its impacts on the location of production.

Outsourcing and the supply chain

Costs of production depend not only on the size of the production unit (plant) or enterprise (firm) but also on the geographical location of different elements of the supply chain. In an increasingly global economy new opportunities are available for many multinational enterprises (MNEs) to outsource activities which can reduce the costs of producing any given level of output.

For example, while car assembly includes robotic and highly automated systems, it still requires labour and Renault estimates that wage costs account for around 15% of the value of a car. When, in February 2012, Renault announced it would open a new €1.1 billion plant in Tangiers, Morocco, to produce a new 'people carrier', it contrasted the €4.50 per hour it would pay workers in Morocco with the €30 per hour it would need to pay in France. The factory in Tangiers will employ 6,000 workers by 2015, making 400,000 lower-priced 'people carriers'. Responding to sharp criticism of outsourcing jobs at a time when 2.87 million were unemployed in France, Renault argues that every car made in Morocco will still generate €800 for the French economy – €400 in parts and €400 in engineers' salaries.

Pause for thought 1.6

What are the advantages and disadvantages to Renault of outsourcing the 'people carrier'? What are the advantages and disadvantages to France of Renault outsourcing the 'people carrier'?

Of course, as we have already noted (pp. 8–14) there are sometimes some surprises in outsourcing, with countries which once received substantial inward investment as low-cost production locations themselves becoming relatively expensive over time. As a result businesses in those countries have begun to look for still lower-cost sources of manufacture and supply, as can be seen in the case of China.

CASE 1.5 Outsourcing in action: China outsources clothes

China's largest independent online clothing retailer by sales has started shifting production overseas in an effort to cut labour rates and beat the country's rapidly rising production costs. Vancl is sourcing part of its products from Bangladesh and plans to increase the proportion of clothes made outside China. Vancl said the main incentive for the move was cheaper labour costs. 'One Bangladesh worker's monthly salary would be Rmb500 to Rmb600 ($80 to $95), while one Chinese worker now costs at least Rmb 2,000 per month,' it said, noting that even after paying higher transport and other costs it could save 5–10% of total costs by outsourcing. In fact monthly pay for Chinese workers has risen by over 30% in the past 3 years.

Difficulty recruiting workers was another reason for the move, Vancl said, noting that the 'new generation' of Chinese workers did not like factory jobs. A Vancl official said the company was contacting manufacturers in Indonesia, Cambodia and other South-East Asian countries as part of the outsourcing effort, although it has not yet decided how significant a proportion of its production it will source overseas.

Case 1.5 (*continued*)

'The production cycle can be as long as four to six months (in Bangladesh),' said a company official, while domestic suppliers are required to deliver in 30 to 45 days. The online retailer said it also felt proud of its traditional 'made in China' label.

'Vancl only sells to the China market,' said Shaun Rein of China Market Research in Shanghai. One of the reasons they win is they can introduce new products, tailored specifically for China, very quickly.' Mr Rein added that sourcing from Bangladesh could jeopardise that.

 Source: China's Vancl Trials Production Overseas, *Financial Times*, 08/08/2012, 21 (Waldmeir, P.), © The Financial Times Limited 2012. All Rights Reserved.

Questions

1 What are the advantages to Vancl of outsourcing clothing production to Bangladesh and other South-East Asian countries?
2 What are the disadvantages of such outsourcing?

We have already noted (pp. 18–22) a tendency for jobs to return to the higher-wage developed economies from the lower-wage developing economies. Case 1.6 reviews such 'reshoring' in rather more detail for the UK and US.

CASE 1.6 Reshoring creates new jobs

Companies bringing production back to the UK from overseas could create up to 200,000 jobs in Britain over the next decade, as a small but growing trend gains strength. Manufacturing starts to benefit most from 'reshoring', particularly sectors such as textiles, electrical equipment and machinery.

The textiles industry, which has been hit hard by low-cost manufacturing in Asia, could see between 30,000 and 60,000 jobs return, according to research by PwC, the consultancy. The government hopes to boost output by encouraging companies to bring back production. In January 2014 it launched a service, Reshore UK, to help companies do so.

In recent years, more companies have brought production back to the UK. According to a recent study of almost 300 businesses by EEF, the manufacturers' trade association, one in six British companies has done so in the past three years. The EEF found that a desire to improve quality, rather than rising wage costs overseas, lay behind the trend. However, experts have warned that high energy costs and skills shortages remain barriers and the number of companies reshoring is relatively small.

According to PwC's research, the creation of 200,000 jobs could boost UK gross domestic product by 0.4 to 0.8 per cent over the next ten years – equating to £6bn to £12bn in today's values. Reshoring could also have a knock-on effect on other industries. PwC estimates 20,000 jobs could be created in areas such as business support services and telecommunications. In the US, reshoring has grown more quickly, with about 80,000 manufacturing jobs having been brought back to the US in the past three and a half years, driven by the shale gas boom.

John Hawksworth, Chief Economist at PwC, noted that 'reshoring . . . is still at a very early stage, but our analysis suggests that the impact on jobs and output could build up gradually to material levels over the next decade or so'.

Case 1.6 (*continued*)

However, he admits that jobs will continue to move overseas, but says there should be more of a 'two-way street' in the future!

While job creation would be welcomed by the government and industry, the numbers pale compared with the drop in UK manufacturing employment over the past 30 years from 6.4m in 1980 to 2.5m in 2014. The number of jobs in textiles has fallen from 800,000 in 1980 to as few as 100,000 in 2014. Even if more production is reshored, much of the work is likely to be done by machines rather than people.

 Source: Adapted from Reshoring offers 200,000 jobs, *Financial Times*, 12/03/2014 (Powley, T.), © The Financial Times Limited 2014. All Rights Reserved.

Questions

1 Examine the reasons behind the trend towards 'reshoring' jobs to the higher-wage, more advanced economies.
2 What does this suggest about the various perspectives towards globalisation?

3 Globalisation and the role of the nation state

It has been argued that one of the major effects of globalisation is to threaten the notion of the territorial nation state in at least three key respects: its competence, its autonomy and, ultimately, its legitimacy.

- *Loss of competence.* In a global economic system, productive capital, finance and products flow across national boundaries in ever-increasing volumes and values, yet the nation state seems increasingly irrelevant as a 'barrier' to international events and influences. Governments often appear powerless to prevent stock market crashes or recessions in one part of the world having adverse effects on domestic output, employment, interest rates and so on. Attempts to lessen these adverse effects seem, to many citizens, increasingly to reside in *supranational bodies* such as the IMF, World Bank, EU, etc. This inability of nation states to meet the demands of their citizens without international cooperation is seen by many as evidence of the declining *competence* of states, arguably leading to a 'widening and weakening' of the individual nation state.

- *Loss of autonomy.* In such a situation, the *autonomy* and even *legitimacy* of the nation state are also subtly altered. The increased emphasis on international cooperation has brought with it an enormous increase in the number and influence of inter-governmental and non-governmental organisations (NGOs) to such an extent that many writers now argue that national and international policy formulation have become inseparable. For example, whereas in 1909 only 176 international NGOs could be identified, by the year 2014 this number exceeded 30,000 and was still growing! The formerly monolithic national state, with its own independent and broadly coherent policy, is now conceived by many to be a fragmented coalition of bureaucratic agencies each pursuing its own agenda with minimal central direction or control. State autonomy is thereby threatened in economic, financial and ecological areas.

- *Loss of legitimacy.* Of course, any loss of competence or autonomy for the nation state is, to many, an implied loss of legitimacy. However, proponents of an alleged 'loss of legitimacy' in the UK often point more directly to the new EU constitutional arrangement adopted in 2003 and earlier adjustments of UK law and practice into conformity with the European Court of Justice and other supranational bodies.

However, as we saw earlier, globalisation consists of a series of conflicting tendencies. While there is some evidence that the relevance of the nation state is declining, other writers claim the alternative view. Some argue that the state retains its positive role in the world through its monopoly of military power, which, though rarely used, offers its citizens relative security in a highly dangerous world. Further, it provides a focus for personal and communal identity and, finally, in pursuing national interest through cooperation and collaboration, nation states actually empower themselves. The suggestion here is that international cooperation (as opposed to unilateral action) allows states simultaneously to pursue their national interests and at the same time, by collective action, to achieve still more effective control over their national destiny. For example, the international control of exchange rates (e.g. the EU Single Currency) is seen by some as enhancing state *autonomy* rather than diminishing it, since the collective action implicit in a common currency affords more economic security and benefits for nationals than unilateral action.

Globalisation is therefore redefining our understanding of the nation state by introducing a much more complex architecture of political power in which authority is seen as being pluralistic rather than residing solely in the nation state.

Case 1.7 would suggest that the nation state, as well as the business itself, may have strategic reasons to support or oppose transnational production activities in globalised economies.

CASE 1.7 Competing in a globalised economy

Emblazoned across the huge blue barns of the Daewoo shipyards on Koje island, off the southern coast of South Korea, are signs of declaring 'No change, no future'. Certainly it is a frequent mantra in Korea, as Hyundai Heavy Industries, Samsung Heavy Industries and Daewoo Shipbuilding and Marine Engineering strive to maintain their positions at the top of the global industry. Right now, the top three are in a sweet spot – orders are rolling in fast, deep hedging means they are insulated against the strong Korean won and their share prices have been sky-rocketing. All are frantically extending their docks and building new quays to allow them to increase capacity.

'Korean shipbuilders are enjoying this very bullish market', says Koh Youngyoul, chief strategy officer at Daewoo, which has a three-year backlog of orders worth $29 billion. But how long will it last? Korean shipbuilders are being threatened by China, which is set to have 23 docks for construction of large ships by 2015, many more than Korea's 15. Meanwhile, Chinese manufacturers, already churning out standard container ships, are trying

to make high-tech liquefied natural gas carriers and large containers – the Korean industry's bread and butter.

Korean estimates of the time China will take to close the technological gap range from four years to ten years. Industry operators know they must not be complacent. 'At the moment, China is simply building low-value-added ships while Korea is making much more high-technological oriented ships,' says Mr Koh of Daewoo, which expected to win orders worth $11 billion this year but had to revise this up to $17 billion after achieving its target in the first half. 'There is no serious competition from China right now but it is only a matter of time until China catches up with Korea like Korea caught up with Japan ten years ago,' says Mr Koh.

Korea came from nowhere to become the world's biggest shipbuilding country and, thanks largely to Hyundai, Samsung and Daewoo, has a global market share of around 40%. The rise of Chinese industry has caused Korean manufacturers to look at Japan's mistakes and make sure that they do not

Case study 1.7 (*continued*)

fall into the same trap. 'Japan failed to diversify,' says Park Chung-Heum, executive vice-president of project planning at Samsung Heavy, which likewise received $10 billion in orders in the first half and raised its projected orders to $15 billion.

About 90% of all Korean orders are for run-of-the-mill container carriers and tankers but the other 10% is made up of vessels such as floating production storage and offloading oil facilities that Korean shipbuilders hope will be their future. Already Daewoo has built the Agbami FPSO vessel for Chevron, the US oil giant, for a record $1.6 billion offshore oil production facility for Abu Dhabi Marine. Samsung is increasingly concentrating on offshore vessels such as barge-mounted power plants and drilling rigs. It has also built an Arctic tanker for Lukoil and ConocoPhillips that can break 1.5m-thick ice. 'Six years ago the average price of a Samsung ship was $50 million or $80 million at today's prices – but now it is $170 million,' Mr Park says from his office overlooking the Koje shipyards, illustrating both the sophistication of the ships being built and the recent escalation of prices shipyards can command.

But all this new added value carries a risk, namely technology leakage. Korea's National Intelligence Service has been investigating leaks from Korean companies to Chinese competitors and a former Daewoo employee has been arrested for selling drawings to a Chinese company. 'We are very concerned about this sort of leakage,' says Mr Park of Samsung. 'Now we are putting watermarks on our drawings and we always print them on paper, not on CD. This is a very critical time and China would like to be able to catch up with Korea.'

Sanjeev Rana, a shipbuilding analyst at Merrill Lynch in Seoul, nevertheless says Korean shipbuilders will be able to remain market leaders in high-value ships for some time, although he adds that this is not necessarily a recipe for success.

Korea will maintain their lead in the value-added segment but they need to maintain conventional shipbuilding in their portfolio – you can't have everything value added,' Mr Rana says. 'So even if they increase the high-tech component of their portfolio to 65%, they will still be 40 or 35% exposed to China.

Strategy of cheap labour

China might present a threat to Korean shipbuilders, but it also offers significant opportunities. Samsung Heavy Industries and Daewoo Shipbuilding and Marine Engineering, Korea's second and third largest shipbuilders, respectively, have both opened yards across the Yellow Sea. There, Chinese workers construct the blocks that form the basis for Korean ships, which are then transported back to Korea for value-added production. This enables Korean producers to utilise China's cheap labour without – in theory – giving away core technology.

'China is supplying the one-third of the blocks used in our ships, which are put together in the Koje yards,' says Park Chung-Heum, executive vice-president of project planning at Samsung Heavy. 'The price of block fabrication in Korea has become very expensive so we are very happy to do this in China.'

Samsung's factory in Ningbo, Zhejiang province, now produces 200,000 tonnes of ship blocks a year, while Daewoo's subsidiary in the north-eastern port city of Yantai, Shandong province, will churn out 220,000 tonnes of ship blocks when it reaches full capacity. However, Hyundai Heavy, Korea's largest shipbuilder, does not have a joint venture in China and has no plans to open one, says Kevin Chang, a company spokesman. 'Shipbuilding is a very labour-intensive industry and Hyundai Heavy wants to supply jobs for Koreans,' he said.

 Source: Adapted from Korean shipbuilders struggle to keep Chinese in their wake, *Financial Times*, 27/03/2007 (Fifield, A.), © The Financial Times Limited 2007. All Rights Reserved.

Questions

1 Why does Korea look to Japan when reviewing its strategies?
2 Consider the opportunities and threats to Korean shipbuilding from globalisation.

Pro- and anti-globalisation issues

Public announcements of jobs being relocated overseas often help to fuel the impression that globalisation equates with job losses for many countries. It is hardly surprising therefore that many trade union representatives and their members swell the numbers in the broad-based coalition sometimes referred to as the 'anti-globalisation movement'. Since this often finds expression in protests against *global institutions* (such as the WTO, World Bank, IMF, Group of 7/8, etc.), the basis of these anti-globalisation protests is considered in more detail in Chapter 3, where these institutions are reviewed – see, for example, discussions of the WTO (pp. 109–114) along with arguments in favour of globalisation.

4 Globalisation and new rules and norms

Not only are new international institutions and trading blocs characteristic of a more globalised economy in which nation states have progressively less influence, but so too are the 'rules and norms' by which they seek to operate (see p. 00). Market-oriented policies, democratic political frameworks, consensus goals involving social and environmental responsibility and growing multilateral applications of agreed rules were all identified as characteristics of globalisation. Here we note the importance of good governance and transparency, an absence of corruption and appropriate property rights to the establishment of a sustainable globalised economic environment.

Benefits of good governance

The World Bank has pointed out that *good governance* – including independent agencies, mechanisms for citizens to monitor public behaviour and rules that constrain corruption – is a key ingredient for growth and prosperity. Indeed the *Worldwide Governance Indicator* has been developed by the World Bank, as an average of six indicators reflecting broad dimensions of governance – namely accountability, political stability and absence of violence, government effectiveness, regulatory quality, rule of law and control of corruption. In the 2014 *World Development Report* the top five ranked countries (based on 2011 data) were Denmark (1), Finland (2), New Zealand (3), Sweden (4) and the Netherlands (5), with the bottom five ranked countries (based on 2011 data) including Somalia, Afghanistan, Congo (Democratic Republic), Zimbabwe and South Sudan.

That these types of indicators are important to good governance is clear from earlier academic studies. For example Barro (1991) found a positive correlation between economic growth and measures of political stability for 98 countries surveyed between 1960 and 1985. Other empirical research points in a similar direction, for example confirming that fdi inflows are *inversely* related to measures of corruption, as with Lipsey (1999) observing a strong negative correlation between corruption and the locational choice of US subsidiaries across Asian countries. Similarly Claugue *et al.* (1999) and Zak (2001) found that productivity and economic growth will improve when governments impartially protect and define property rights. Underpinning these findings is the perception by firms that a non-transparent business environment increases the prevalence of information asymmetries, raises the cost of securing additional information, increases transaction costs (e.g. risk premiums) and creates an uncertain business environment which deters trade and investment. For example, Wallsten (2001) found a strong inverse relationship between investment intentions and the threat of asset expropriation, as well as a propensity for firms to charge higher prices to help pay back their initial capital outlays more rapidly when they felt less secure about the intentions of host governments, the higher prices often inhibiting the penetration and growth phase of product life cycles.

Knowledge and information in globalised economies

Management specialist Stephen Kobrin describes globalisation as driven not by foreign trade and investment but by information flows. It is this latter perspective, which sees globalisation as a process inextricably linked with the creation, distribution and use of knowledge and information, which is the focus here. Many contributors to the globalisation debate regard the technological convergence of information, computer and telecommunications technologies in the late twentieth century as having acted as a key catalyst in the rapid growth of these information-based activities, seen here as the hallmark of the globalised economy.

International communications have grown dramatically, as we noted earlier (p. 14). Contemporary discourse often seeks to express globalisation in terms of the exponential growth in the creation, processing and dissemination of knowledge and information. For example, an 'index of globalisation' compiled jointly by the Carnegie Foundation and ATKearney (a global consultant) gives considerable weight to the economic, social and political indicators, including data on information flows such as the proportion of national populations online as well as to the number of internet hosts and secure servers per capita. These indicators of access to information technology and associated information flows are seen here as proxy variables for 'global openness', to be used in association with the more conventional indicators of investment, capital flows, foreign income as a proportion of national income and convergence between domestic and international prices when compiling the overall globalisation index. Singapore often appears as one of the 'most globalised' countries in this index, helped by the fact that it currently has 1,010 mobile phones per 1,000 people and 571 internet users per 1,000 people, as well as a recorded outgoing telephone traffic per head per year some four times that in the US.

The multinational enterprise (MNE)

Put simply, a multinational enterprise (sometimes called a transnational) is a company that has headquarters in one country but has operations in other countries. It is not always obvious that a firm is a multinational. The growth in alliances, joint ventures and mergers and acquisitions means that consumers tend to recognise the brand, rather than know who the parent company is. Who, for example, now owns Jaguar or Land Rover? The answer in this case is the India-based Tata Motor Corporation.

Pause for thought 1.7

Can you think of brands for three different types of product and identify the multinational company that owns those brands in each case?

Table 1.6 World's top ten multinationals ranked by foreign assets (and transnationality index), 2012

Ranking					
Foreign assets	Transnationality index	Company	Country	Industry	Transnationality index (%)
1	81	General Electric	USA	Electrical and electronic equipment	48.8
2	34	Royal Dutch/Shell	UK	Petroleum	72.8
3	67	Toyota Motor	Japan	Motor vehicles	58.6
4	56	Exxon/Mobil Corporation	USA	Petroleum	62.6
5	21	Total SA	France	Petroleum	79.5
6	38	British Petroleum (BP)	UK	Petroleum	69.7
7	9	Vodafone Group plc	UK	Telecommunications	88.9
8	68	Volkswagen	Germany	Motor vehicles	58.6
9	66	Chevron	USA	Petroleum	59.3
10	36	Eni SpA	Italy	Petroleum	71.2

Source: Adapted from *World Development Report* (UNCTAD 2014), Annex Table 28.

Dunning (1993) defines the multinational as a firm 'that engages in foreign direct investment and owns or controls value-adding activities in more than one country'. Typically the multinational would not just own value-adding activities, but might buy resources and create goods and/or services in a variety of countries. While the central strategic planning takes place at the headquarters, considerable latitude will usually be given to affiliates (subsidiaries) to enable them to operate in harmony with their local environments.

Ranking multinationals

From a statistical point of view, there are two main methods of ranking the world's top multinationals. First, ranking them according to the amount of foreign assets they control and, second, ranking them in terms of a 'transnationality index'.

- *Foreign assets.* Table 1.6 ranks the top ten multinationals according to the *value of foreign assets* they control and we can see that three of the top ten are from the USA, three from the UK and one from Japan, France, Germany and Italy. They are primarily based in the petroleum/energy, telecommunications and motor vehicle sectors.

- *Transnationality index.* However, Table 1.6 also provides each company's transnationality index and its transnationality ranking. The *transnationality index* takes a more comprehensive view of a company's global activity and is calculated as the average of the following three ratios:

  1 foreign assets:total assets;
  2 foreign sales:total sales;
  3 foreign employment:total employment.

For example, we can see that the largest multinational company is General Electric in terms of the foreign assets it owns. However, its transnationality index of 48.8% means that it is only ranked 81st in terms of this criterion. The reason for this is that even though it has large investments overseas in absolute value, in *percentage* terms most of its assets, sales and employment are still located in the USA. This is in contrast with British Petroleum where

Table 1.7 World's top ten multinationals ranked by the transnationality index (and foreign assets), 2012

Ranking					
Transnationality index	Foreign assets	Company	Country	Industry	Transnationality index
1	15	Nestlé SA	Switzerland	Food, beverages and tobacco	97.1
2	43	Anglo American plc	UK	Mining and quarrying	95.9
3	13	Anheuser-Busch InBev NV	Belgium	Food, beverages and tobacco	93.3
4	76	British American Tobacco plc	UK	Food, beverages and tobacco	91.0
5	74	Linde AG	Germany	Chemicals	91.0
6	89	Barrick Gold Corporation	Canada	Gold/Mining	89.2
7	55	SABMiller plc	UK	Food, beverages and tobacco	89.1
8	23	ArcelorMITTAL	Luxembourg	Metal and metal products	89.0
9	7	Vodafone Group plc	UK	Telecommunications	88.9
10	93	WPP plc	UK	Business Services	87.8

Source: Adapted from *World Investment Report* (UNCTAD 2014), Annex Tables 28 and 29.

69.7% of its overall activity in terms of the three ratios is based abroad, and Vodafone Group where this figure rises to as high as 88.9%.

If we wanted to find the companies that operate mostly outside their home country, we would have to look at the ten top multinationals ranked in terms of the transnationality index only. These are shown in Table 1.7 and here we see the dominance of EU companies (especially the UK) in sectors such as mining, food/beverages and tobacco, telecommunications, chemicals and business services. The companies with the highest transnationality index are often from the relatively smaller countries as a more restricted domestic market creates incentives to operate abroad if they are to maximise their growth in terms of revenue or profits.

Technical definitions of multinationals, however, fail to convey the true scope and diversity of global business, which covers everything from the thousands of medium-sized firms that have overseas operations to the truly gigantic multinationals like IBM, General Motors and Ford. Some multinationals are *vertically integrated,* with different stages of the same productive process taking place in different countries (e.g. British Petroleum). Others are *horizontally integrated,* performing the same basic production operations in each of the countries in which they operate (e.g. Marks & Spencer). Many multinationals are household names, marketing global brands (e.g. Rothmans International, IBM, British Airways). Others are holding companies for a portfolio of international companies (e.g. Diageo) or specialise in capital goods that have little name-recognition in the high street (e.g. BTR, Hawker Siddley, GKN).

How important are the multinationals?

In 2013 an estimated 83,000 multinational enterprises collectively controlled a total of around 900,000 foreign affiliates (subsidiaries), employed almost 71 million people worldwide and accounted for sales revenues of over $34,000 billion, yielding a value added of $7,492 billion and accounting for over 10% of world GDP. Table 1.8 provides an overview of such multinational activity. Indeed, in 2013 the sales of multinationals' foreign affiliates (subsidiaries) far exceeded the total global export of goods and services.

Table 1.8 **Multinational activity in a global context**

	2013 ($bn)
Sales of foreign affiliates of MNEs	34,508
Total exports of goods and services	23,160
Employment of foreign affiliates (thousands)	70,726
Total assets of foreign affiliates	96,625

Source: Adapted from *World Development Report* (World Bank 2014), p. 30.

We have already seen in Table 1.1 (p. 3) that the world's 100 largest MNEs alone accounted for over 9.8 million jobs and for annual sales in excess of $6,000 billion in value. Only 14 nation states have a GDP that exceeds the turnover of Exxon, Ford or General Motors.

Historically, the bulk of multinational activity has been concentrated in the developed world. Indeed, as recently as the mid-1980s, half of all multinational production took place in only five countries – the United States, Canada, the UK, Germany and the Netherlands. This pattern is now changing rapidly. The rapid industrialisation and economic growth in the so-called 'Bric' economies of Brazil, Russia, India and China and in other newly industrialising nations of the world has led to a sharp increase in multinational investment in Asia and (to a lesser extent) in South America. Some of these countries, such as Taiwan, South Korea, Hong Kong and Singapore, now have per capita GDP levels that exceed those of most European nations, and indigenous companies from India, China and elsewhere are now beginning to establish production facilities in the 'old world'.

We noted earlier (p. 4) that the old bi-polar world economy has now been replaced by the 'triad' of North America, the European Union and East and South-East Asia, with these three regions accounting for approximately 80% of the world's exports and 84% of world manufacturing output.

Multinationals and globalised production

Table 1.9 throws further light on the increasing globalisation of productive activity by showing the progressive growth in the transnationality index (TNI) for the world's largest 100 MNEs in their home economies between 1990 and 2012 (UNCTAD 2014). The TNI has been defined above as the average of the three ratios: foreign assets:total assets; foreign sales:total sales; and foreign employment:total employment. A rise in the overall TNI index of almost 10% between 1990 and 2012 suggests still more international involvement of the top 100 MNEs outside their home countries.

The European Union is home to half of the world's largest MNEs and we can see from Table 1.9 that the average transnationality index (TNI) for such MNEs based in the EU has risen from 56.7% in 1990 to 64.2% in 2012. A similar rapid growth in the TNI is also indicated for MNEs with North America (41.2% to 53.1%) or Japan (35.5% to 59.5%) as their 'home' base over the period 1990 to 2012. For 'all economies' the greater internationalisation of production is indicated via the TNI rising from 51.1% to 60.8% in the 1990–2012 time period. Closer scrutiny of this data reveals that the driving forces behind these observed increases in the TNI have been the growth in the foreign sales/total sales and in the foreign employment/total employment components of the TNI.

Table 1.9 Transnationality Index for the world's largest 100 MNEs in their home economies, 1990 and 2012

Economy	Average TNI (%)		Number of MNEs	
	1990	2012	1990	2012
European Union	56.7	64.2	48	50
France	50.9	63.6	14	11
Germany	44.4	66.0	9	10
UK	68.5	78.5	12	16
North America	41.2	53.1	30	23
US	38.5	51.5	28	22
Canada	79.2	89.2	2	1
Japan	35.5	59.5	12	10
China	n.a.	50.4	n.a.	5
Rest of the world	n.a.	n.a.	10	12
All economies	51.1	60.8	100	100

Source: Adapted from World Investment Report (UNCTAD 2014).

Multinationals and the developing economies

An increasing number of MNEs have 'home' economies outside Europe, North America and Japan. Here we review the growing importance of the *developing economies* as the source of MNE activities.

The foreign assets, foreign sales and foreign employment of the 100 largest MNEs from developing and transition economies are shown in Table 1.10. We can see that they accounted for $1,506 billion of foreign assets, $1,690 billion of foreign sales and over 4.1 million foreign employees. Of these largest 100 MNEs from developing countries, the top ten in size accounted for about half of these respective totals, with Hutchinson Whampoa (Hong Kong, China) at the head, followed by CITIC Group (China), Samsung Electronics

Table 1.10 Snapshot of the world's 100 largest MNEs from developing economies 2012 (billions of dollars, thousands of employees and %)

Variable	2012
Assets ($bn)	
Foreign	1,506
Total	5,531
Foreign to total (%)	27
Sales ($bn)	
Foreign	1,690
Total	3,863
Foreign to total (%)	44
Employment (000)	
Foreign	4,103
Total	10,596
Foreign to total (%)	39

*In percentage points.

Source: Adapted from World Investment Report (UNCTAD 2014), Table 1.10.

Table 1.11 Ranking of top 15 MNEs from developing economies (by foreign assets) and their transnationality index (TNI)

Foreign assets	Corporation	Home economy	Industry	TNI (%)
1	Hutchinson Whampoa Limited	Hong Kong, China	Diversified	80.9
2	CITIC Group	China	Diversified	17.1
3	Hon Hai Precision Industries	Taiwan Province of China	Electrical and electronic equipment	84.3
4	Petronas – Petroliam Nasional Bhd	Malaysia	Petroleum exploration, refining and distribution	39.2
5	Vale SA	Brazil	Mining and quarrying	44.5
6	China Ocean Shipping (Group) Company	China	Transport and storage	48.9
7	China National Offshore Oil Corp	China	Petroleum exploration, refining and distribution	18.6
8	America Movil SAB de CV	Mexico	Telecommunications	49.4
9	Lukoil OAO	Russian Federation	Petroleum and natural gas	42.8
10	Cemex S.A.B. de C.V.	Mexico	Non-metallic mineral products	80.1
11	Petroleos de Venezuela SA	Venezuela, Bolivarian Republic of	Petroleum exploration, refining and distribution	18.2
12	Samsung Electronics Co. Ltd.	Korea, Republic of	Electrical and electronic equipment	26.9
13	Singapore Telecommunications Ltd.	Singapore	Telecommunications	63.5
14	Hyundai Motor Company	Korea, Republic of	Motor vehicles	25.6
15	Jardine Matthews Holdings Ltd.	Hong Kong China	Diversified	57.9

Source: Adapted from World Investment Report (UNCTAD 2014), Web Table 29.

(South Korea), Cernex (Mexico), Hyundai Motor (South Korea) and Singtel (Singapore), respectively.

A further breakdown of the largest (by foreign assets) MNEs from developing economies is provided in Table 1.11, with associated transnationality indices (TNIs).

East and South-East Asia are clearly the major home location of the 15 largest MNEs from developing and transitional economies, with an average transationality index across these 15 MNEs of around 47%. These 15 largest MNEs from developing and transitional economies have a smaller overall TNI Index (47%) than the 15 largest MNEs from the developed economies (70%), suggesting a less globally integrated chain of operations. This is also reflected in the fact that the 100 largest MNEs in the developing and transitional economies have, on average, only nine affiliates in foreign countries, compared to the average of 41 affiliates in foreign countries for the 100 largest MNEs from the developed economies.

Types of MNE

The wide variety of strategies embraced by MNEs has led some writers to distinguish between different types.

- *Global corporations* that view the whole world as their marketplace, with goods and services standardised to meet the needs of consumers worldwide.
- *Multidomestic corporations* that comprise a relatively independent set of subsidiaries, each producing goods and services focused on a particular local market.

- *Transnational corporations* that integrate a geographically dispersed set of specialised activities into a single production process.

For the purposes of this text we will use the term 'multinational enterprise' (MNE) to apply to all three categories discussed above. However, from time to time we will apply terms such as 'market oriented' or 'cost oriented' to different multinationals, but only to indicate the broad strategic thrust behind their activities rather than the 'type' of multinational. The nature of many of today's MNEs will reflect, in part, the methods the company has used in its attempts to internationalise in the past. We discuss these different approaches to internationalisation in more detail in Chapters 2 and 7, respectively.

Of course, the nature of many of today's MNEs and of their activity in the UK and elsewhere also reflects broader changes in a globalised economy, including changing patterns of consumer behaviour and technological changes.

Chapter 2

Internationalisation process

By the end of this chapter you should be able to:

- explain the pressures for internationalisation and why firms move production facilities abroad;
- outline the various methods available to firms seeking to enter foreign markets;
- assess the advantages and disadvantages of each method;
- discuss some of the principles that may contribute to successful international alliances;
- evaluate the different theoretical approaches to internationalisation;
- review the barriers that must be overcome for successful internationalisation.

Introduction

As we note in Chapter 3, there has been a rapid growth in international trade in both goods and services. Such global competition has forced corporations to seek new markets, both at home and abroad, and to speed up the cycle of product development. The costs of entry into these new markets can be formidable. The days of large corporations working solely by themselves would seem to be numbered. Few firms can afford to be sophisticated in all areas of technology or to develop distribution channels and new markets in numerous countries. In addition, rapid technical change and newly emerging patterns and locations of international specialisation place continual pressure on the cost base of the modern corporation. As a means of meeting these challenges, many firms realise that they must find partners to share the risks of expansion. Partnership and collaboration are the order of the day. This in turn creates new and difficult challenges for international managers. The choice of direction is almost infinite. Which markets to expand into? Which products to develop? How much can we afford to invest? Which partners to choose? Which areas of business to keep as core competencies and which to develop with others?

But why and how do firms internationalise? The reasons for going international and the conditions under which firms choose to do so are complex and have been the subject of much debate. In this chapter we examine the history of internationalisation, the reasons firms choose to internationalise, the ways in which this has been done and the theoretical frameworks that seek to explain this process. Chapter 7 looks further into international strategic choice and Chapter 8 considers the types of international organisational structure often adopted by MNEs during the internationalisation process.

Once a firm has decided to go international, this may take place in a wide variety of ways, most of which fall into three broad categories:

1 export-based methods;

2 non-equity methods;

3 equity methods.

Export-based methods for internationalisation

This is the most common way in which a firm begins to go international. It continues to produce its product in the domestic market, but exports a proportion of this output to foreign markets. This may involve physical movements of products by air, sea, road or rail, but it increasingly involves the cross-border transfer of less tangible items such as computer software, graphics, images and the written word.

Exporting is the oldest and most straightforward way of conducting international business. In 1990 the global export of goods and services accounted for 18.4% of global GDP; by 2013 global exports had risen to as much as 31.2% of global GDP. Much of this growth can be put down to the liberalisation of trade that has taken place globally and within regional trading blocs over recent decades, with the World Trade Organisation significantly reducing tariff rates and quotas imposed on most imports (see Chapter 3, p. 109). Other protectionist measures are gradually being phased out or lowered at the regional level in free trade areas such as NAFTA (North American Free Trade Association), ASEAN (Association of South-East Asian Nations) and the APEC (Asia-Pacific Economic Cooperation), in customs unions such as the Andean Pact and Mercosur and in economic unions such as the European Union. In addition to these regional arrangements a host of bilateral free trade treaties have been concluded, providing further direct exporting opportunities. At the same time, international transportation costs are still falling and cultural barriers to trade are now more readily recognised and overcome than has previously been the case. Governments may further stimulate trade by providing various export-promoting initiatives in order to improve the country's balance of payments.

These export-based methods of internationalising are sometimes broken down into 'indirect exporting' and 'direct exporting'.

Indirect exporting

Indirect exporting happens when a firm does not itself undertake any special international activity but rather operates through intermediaries. Under this approach the exporting function is outsourced to other parties, which may prepare the export documentation, take responsibility for the physical distribution of goods and even set up the sales and distribution channels in the foreign market. The role of the intermediary may be played by export houses, confirming houses and buying houses:

- *Export house*: this buys products from a domestic firm and sells them abroad on its own account.
- *Confirming house*: this acts for foreign buyers and is paid on a commission basis, bringing sellers and buyers into direct contact (unlike an export house) and guaranteeing payment will be made to the exporter by the end-user.
- *Buying house*: this performs similar functions to those of the confirming house but is more active in seeking out sellers to match the buyer's particular needs.

The advantages of such an approach clearly involve the fact that no additional costs need be incurred or expertise acquired in order to access the overseas market. However, there are disadvantages of resorting to indirect exports, which include having little or no control over local marketing issues and little contact with the end-user, so that there is no feedback for product development or marketing.

Such indirect exporting may take different forms. For example, independent *export management companies* will sometimes handle the export arrangements for a number of clients, providing them with purchasing, shipping, financing and negotiation services (e.g. setting up contracts, providing localised overseas knowledge, etc.) as regards dealing with foreign orders. This is more likely to be the approach adopted by small and medium-sized businesses to indirect exporting. However, larger companies, such as MNEs, will sometimes set up their own subsidiary export management companies to deal with the overseas sales of their entire range of products and brands – as in the case of Unilever, which has established Unilever Export to deal with all its exports from the UK. This enables any scale economies within the exporting function to be gained on behalf of all the products and brands of the MNE.

Indirect exporting sometimes involves unexpected alliances rather than competition between firms. 'Piggybacking', for example, is where different companies share resources in order to access foreign markets more effectively. Here a firm with a compatible product (known as the 'rider') pays to get on board the distribution system already being operated by a firm active in the overseas market (known as the 'carrier'). The 'rider' thereby gains immediate access to the network of outlets operated by the existing 'carrier' while the 'carrier' can reduce various costs by operating closer to full capacity as well as add more value to its activities by offering its clients a greater product range.

Direct exporting

Direct exporting would typically involve a firm in distributing and selling its own products to the foreign market. This would generally mean a longer-term commitment to a particular foreign market, with the firm choosing local agents and distributors specific to that market. In-house expertise would need to be developed to keep up these contacts, to conduct market research, prepare the necessary documentation and establish local pricing policies. However the advantages of such an approach are that it:

- allows the exporter to closely monitor developments and competition in the host market;
- promotes interaction between producer and end-user;
- involves long-term commitments, such as providing after-sales services to encourage repeat purchases.

You are the managing director of a manufacturing firm, which currently sells all its product on the domestic market. What factors might encourage you to consider exporting abroad (whether directly or indirectly)?

Export processing zones (EPZs)

Direct exporting has been encouraged in recent years by the establishment of *export processing zones* (EPZs) by countries, which are a specific type of *free trade zone* established by governments to promote industrial and commercial exports. EPZs are currently used by over 120 countries, creating employment for over 66 million people worldwide in 2014. These EPZs are designated geographical areas within a country that provide appropriate infrastructure and incentives to encourage inward fdi that is focused on direct exporting from the EPZs. Various analysts have noted that most of the countries identified as 'winners' in terms of their export competitiveness within designated product groups used EPZs or their equivalents to promote the export-oriented inward fdi which has underpinned their subsequent export performance. Successful EPZs can be found, for example, in Brazil, China, Colombia, Costa Rica, the Dominican Republic, India, Mexico, the Philippines and Singapore, all of which provide incentives such as lower (or zero) taxes, less regulation and free or subsidised training. India, for example, removed many of its restrictive labour laws in the 17 Special Economic Zones it created in 2003, to meet the concerns of foreign investors as regards its low labour productivity and highly regulated labour market.

However, the effective performance of such export processing zones depends not only on the incentives provided but on other policies directed towards enhancing human resources and other aspects of the infrastructure needed to attract and develop export-oriented fdi. The operations of EPZs have, however, been criticised as providing 'unfair' competition and the financial incentives offered are now limited by the WTO's *Agreement on Subsidies and Countervailing Measures*.

Other supports for exporting, especially from developing countries, is provided by the importing countries offering developing countries special access to their markets. One such arrangement by the US to improve the access of African exports to its market is reviewed in Case 2.1.

CASE 2.1 Producers pin hope on Agoa trade pact to drive exports

The factory in Maseru, capital of Lesotho, is buzzing with activity. On one side, men load box after box of ladies' hooded sweatshirts destined for the US. Elsewhere, hundreds of workers cut and sew cloth, iron the finished products and put them on hangers. Even the price tag and Walmart logo are included. 'When they get to America, they just have to hang them up and start to sell them,' says David Cheng, managing director of TZICC Clothing Manufactures, which runs the factory.

The scene is common at clothing plants across Lesotho, a small landlocked country that has taken advantage of a US trade agreement to build one of Africa's leading textile industries. The growth of Lesotho's US exports, worth

Case 2.1 (continued)

about $321m last year, was made possible by the *African Growth and Opportunity Act* (Agoa), a piece of legislation crafted under the presidency of Bill Clinton in 2000 and extended under his successor, George W. Bush.

Aimed at boosting African trade by offering duty-free access to lucrative US markets, Lesotho is one of the best examples of Agoa's success: from a handful of factories in the 1990s, Lesotho now boasts 40 textile producers employing some 40,000 people – the largest private sector employer in the country. John Kerry, the US Secretary of State, recently hailed Agoa as a key driver of trade and investment with Africa.

'Whether it is cocoa and cashews from Ghana, textiles from Mauritius or petrochemical products from Angola, Agoa has served as a catalyst for greater trade and prosperity,' he said. But the Agoa initiative is due to expire in 2015, threatening a US–Africa economic relationship worth nearly $460bn for businesses on both sides of the Atlantic.

Although a renewal of Agoa is expected, the White House is pushing for broader measures to boost African trade. Mr Obama said this week that while tariff preferences provided by Agoa 'were important, they alone are not sufficient to promote transformational growth in trade and investment'. He added: 'For beneficiary countries to be able to utilise Agoa to its fullest, this programme must be linked to a comprehensive, co-ordinated trade and investment capacity-building approach with clearly stated goals and benchmarks.'

Although African apparel exports to the US have surged from $264m in 2001 to more than $900m in 2013, few other industries have taken advantages of the trade agreement to grow on such a scale. Agoa-related trade is dominated by oil: last year $22bn of the $27bn of exports to the US under the deal came from oil and gas, along with petroleum products and coal. With

the exception of South Africa, the continent's most industrialised country, which exports high-end goods to the US, including cars, the main beneficiaries of Agoa are oil-producing nations, notably Nigeria, Angola, Chad and Gabon.

Indeed, total Agoa imports have slipped from a high of $467bn in 2008, partly because of slowdown in the US economy but also because of a fall in US imports of African oil and gas. US officials note that non-oil exports under Agoa have increased from less than $1bn in 2001 to about $5bn last year. But they cite constraints ranging from a dearth of infrastructure in many nations to productivity issues and a lack of skills that act as a brake on African trade.

Lesotho also offers a glimpse of where more could be achieved. The creation of 40,000 jobs – about the same as the kingdom's entire public sector employment – has been critical to the impoverished nation. But its garments industry has remained under the control of foreigners, mostly Taiwanese, who could pack up easily and move to another country if Washington did not renew the legislation.

Officials also believe Agoa has made Lesotho too dependent on the US. The country has largely failed to tap Europe, where it also enjoys duty free access. Mr Cheng, who also chairs the Lesotho Textile Exporters Association, said: 'We have tried Canada and Europe, but their orders are much smaller than the US.'

Ricky Chang at Formosa Textile, a denim mill set up by Taiwan's Nien Haign Group as part of a $150m investment in Lesotho, says his company is committed to the country, but 'if the environment changes we would have to adjust to it'. He added: 'the exit strategy we have if Agoa terminates is that we might scale down or . . . we might just relocate our production capacity to some other area.'

Questions

1 Identify and explain who are the potential winners and losers from the Agoa trade pact.

2 Does the case have any relevance to the free trade versus protection debate?

Exporting by either indirect or direct methods is considered less risky than other methods of internationalisation and can be a 'way in' for firms testing out the waters before making the more resource-intensive fdi decision. Of course, some risks are still present when exporting – for example, exchange rates may change unexpectedly, affecting the anticipated profitability of the export transactions. However, the majority of today's international trade (and therefore exporting activity) takes place between firms that are themselves part of a single MNE. In fact, over a half of all world trade takes place within the company (intra-trade), as we note in Chapter 3. As regards this 'intra-trade', approximately 50% consists of exports by the MNE or its affiliates of finished products to its own distribution affiliates for sale in the host country or neighbouring markets. Around a further 50% involves the export of intermediate products for final assembly by the MNE's own production affiliates in other countries.

Besides exporting, the firm can internationalise by investing in foreign markets. A distinction is often made between non-equity and equity-based methods of fdi.

Non-equity-based methods for internationalisation

In this form of internationalisation, firms sell technology or know-how under some form of contract, often involving patents, trademarks and copyrights. These are often referred to as *intellectual property rights* and they now form a major part of international transactions, having grown enormously since the 1980s. These non-equity methods of internationalisation often take the form of licensing, franchising or other types of contractual agreement based on these intellectual property rights (see Chapter 4, pp. 139–145).

Licensing

At its most simple, *licensing* can mean permission granted by the proprietary owner (licensor) to a foreign concern (the licensee) in the form of a contract to engage in an activity that would otherwise be legally forbidden. The licensee buys the right to exploit a fairly limited set of technologies and know-how from the licensor, who will usually have protected the intellectual property rights involved by a patent, trademark or copyright. This tends to be a low-cost strategy for internationalisation since the foreign entrant makes little or no resource commitment. The licensor benefits from the licensee's local knowledge and distribution channels, which would otherwise be difficult and time-consuming to develop and maintain. Such agreements are often found in industries where R&D and other fixed costs are high, but where aggressive competition is needed at the local level to capture market share. The pharmaceutical and chemical industries provide licensing agreements, as do the industrial equipment and defence industries. For example, McDonnell-Douglas and General Dynamics have licensing arrangements with different Japanese and European governments to produce jet fighters.

In manufacturing industries the patent is the most common form of protecting intellectual property rights and licensing is often used as a means of controlling industry evolution: for example, Japanese manufacturers have in the past successfully cross-licensed VHS-formatted video recorders to one another as well as to foreign firms that produce them under licence. This helped the VHS standard become dominant worldwide and displaced the competing Sony and Philips versions. In high-tech industries, where breakthroughs tend to occur discontinuously, licensing helps firms avoid excessive costs from expensive plant and product obsolescence. IBM, for example, has previously linked up with Motorola Communications and Electronics Inc. to advance the state of X-ray lithography for making superdense chips. Licensing can be costly, however, if a firm transfers its core competencies into those of a competitor. RCS licensed its colour television technologies to Japanese firms during the 1960s only to be leapfrogged by new but related technologies emanating from those competitors. Licensors (the granters of licences) may therefore find themselves under pressure to continuously innovate in order to sustain the licensee's dependence on them in the relationship. Microsoft's various updated Windows systems have been widely criticised as having been introduced primarily as a means of maintaining the dependence of licensees on Microsoft itself, rather than as a source of new capabilities for existing users.

In general, the use of licensing, with its technological associations, has tended to be less readily adopted by the service industries, where franchising and other methods of internationalisation are more common. Nevertheless, the various intellectual property rights do permit service sector licensing, as in the case of copyright protection (see also Chapter 4, p. 144) of Walt Disney characters. For example, a medium-sized UK stationery company may decide it wishes to produce a range of stationery based on Walt Disney characters. In order to do this, the company would need to approach Disney and discuss the possibility of gaining a licence to sell Disney branded goods in the UK. The licensee (in this case the UK stationery company) pays a fee to Disney in exchange for the rights to use their brand name/logo.

An advantage of licensing to licensors is that they do not have to make a substantial investment in order to gain a presence in overseas markets and they need not acquire the local knowledge which may be so important for success in such markets. Licensing is also an effective way of increasing levels of brand awareness. However, a licensor can be damaged if a licensee produces products of an inferior standard. Licensing is very common in the film and music industry. Products include calendars, videos, books, posters and clothing.

Pause for thought 2.2

In 2013 the US alone issued 302,948 patents, more than six times the number it issued 20 years ago. Despite the rapid growth of patents worldwide, many observers believe that because of 'global shift' we should pay less attention to this particular indicator of intellectual property rights than we used to. Can you explain their reasoning?

Case 2.2 looks at the various arguments for and against using patents as a means of internationalising sales into the EU pharmaceuticals market.

CASE 2.2 Patents and the EU pharmaceuticals market

The arguments for using patent protection for internationalising pharmaceutical products are well known. They include the opportunity for pharmaceutical firms to access global markets to recoup the large expenditures on innovative R&D when only relatively few products eventually pass the rigorous and time-consuming tests to demonstrate both efficacy of

---

Case 2.2 (*continued*)

treatment as well as meeting health and safety standards. However, an EU report in 2008 has criticised aspects of the current operation of patents by international pharmaceutical companies operating in EU markets. On 28 November 2008 the European Commission unveiled the results of its year-long investigation into the pharmaceutical sector. The report criticised the use of the 'patent cluster', whereby a firm keen to defend a 'blockbuster' drug about to go off-patent, files large numbers of new patents for slight modifications to the existing product, allegedly to confuse and intimidate other pharmaceutical firms considering producing generic versions of the previously patented product. The report cited an example of a major pharmaceutical company taking out 1,300 new patents across the EU on a single drug about to go off-patent! Such delaying tactics have meant that generic competition in EU pharmaceuticals only begins, on average, some seven months after patent protection has lapsed. As a result the report says EU taxpayers paid about €3 billion more than they would have done had the generics been available immediately the patent expired.

Nor is it merely a matter of time delay. The EU report found that when generics do eventually enter the EU market they do so at a much higher price than in, say, the US market. Generics were found to enter the EU pharmaceutical market at an average price some 25% below that of the branded drug, and drop a further 40% in price after two more years. However, in the US pharmaceutical market generic prices were, on average, over 80% below the branded drug price within a year.

Questions

1 Can you suggest reasons for the observed differences in generic drug prices between the EU and US markets?

2 How might the EU seek to tackle the problem? Consider the costs and benefits of any proposed 'solution'?

Franchising

In *franchising* the franchisee purchases the right to undertake business activity using the franchisor's name or trademark rather than any patented technology. The scale of this activity varies from so-called 'first-generation franchising' where the franchisor usually operates with a light touch, to 'second-generation franchising' in which the franchisor transfers a much more comprehensive business package to the franchisee to help establish a 'start-up position'. This may include detailed guidance on how to operate the franchise, even extending to specialist staff training.

In second-generation franchising, the franchisor exerts far more control on the day-to-day running of the local operations. This type of franchising is common in the hotel, fast-food restaurant and vehicle rental industries, such as Holiday Inn, McDonald's and Avis respectively. It is estimated that currently there are over 1 million established franchised businesses worldwide, accounting for around $1,000 billion of output and some 9% of all private sector employment, i.e. over 11 million jobs. The US is the lead country in terms of franchised businesses, as it has been since the Great Depression of the 1930s when it used this approach to support the growth of fast-food restaurants, food inns and motels. In fact around 4% of all businesses in the US are franchise-worked. The US is headquarters for major franchising firms, such as McDonalds, which currently has around 38,000 franchised partners worldwide, and Subway with over 23,000 franchised partners.

Mature domestic service-based industries have chosen franchising as a means of internationalising because:

- it establishes an immediate presence with relatively little direct investment;
- it employs a standard marketing approach helping to create a global image;
- it allows the franchisor a high degree of control.

For instance, Coca-Cola's franchising arrangements with its numerous partners would seem to have given it an advantage over its arch-rival PepsiCo. Franchising also helps build up a global brand that can be cultivated and standardised over time. Before opening its first restaurant in Russia, McDonald's flew all key employees to its 'Hamburger University' for a two-week training session. During these sessions, Russian employees learned the McDonald's philosophy and the McDonald's way of addressing customers and maintaining quality standards.

McDonald's and Burger King are perhaps the two best-known examples of international franchises. However, franchising is a very popular method of market entry and is not limited to the fast-food industry. Examples include cleaning (Chem-Dry), clothing (Benetton) and childcare (Tiny Tots).

In international franchising, a supplier (franchisor) permits a dealer (franchisee) the right to market its products and services in that country in exchange for a financial commitment. This commitment usually involves a fee upfront and royalties based on product sales.

- Advantages for the *franchisee* are that they are buying into an existing brand and should receive full support from the franchiser in terms of marketing, training and starting up. When customers walk into a McDonald's restaurant they know exactly what to expect. This is one advantage of global branding.
- Disadvantages for the *franchisee* include restrictions on what they can and cannot do. For example, McDonald's have very strict regulations concerning marketing, pricing, training, etc. A franchisee cannot simply change the staff uniform, alter prices or vary opening hours as the company operates a standardised approach to doing business.
- Advantages for the *franchisor* are that overseas expansion can be much less expensive and that any local adaptations can (with agreement) be made by those well acquainted with cultural issues in that country (see Case 2.3 below).
- Disadvantages for the *franchisor* include possible conflict with the franchisee for not following regulations and agreements as well as a threat that the franchisee may opt to 'go it alone' in the future and thus become a direct competitor.

Interestingly, McDonald's has reacted to more difficult trading conditions by giving franchisees more freedom than had previously been the case. It sold some 1,500 restaurants in the deepest world recessionary period in 2007/8 to local entrepreneurs across 20 countries, who could invest in running the outlet and in introducing elements of 'customisation' of the product and its delivery to meet local requirements, while still retaining McDonald's support in marketing and supply chain provision. These 'developmental licensees' represented a shift by McDonald's in the direction of first-generation franchising.

Case 2.3 emphasises the benefits to the franchisor George (range of clothing) in terms of overseas expansion as a result of a carefully chosen franchisee (Asda/Walmart).

CASE 2.3 Asda sees gap in Malta market for George shop

Asda will this week open a dedicated clothing store in Malta, taking its George business's international franchise footprint into Europe for the first time. Its George franchised store in Malta will start to trade on Friday, joining stores in the Channel Islands, Sharjah, Abu Dhabi and Jordan. 'Malta is a good location for us,' said Andrew Moore, chief merchandising officer at Asda, and head of its George clothing business.

'It has a great connection to the UK. There's a lot of well-known retailers out there. We do think there's a gap in the Malta market for a great-value fashion retailer.' The franchise is part of a step up in George's international expansion – both by means of physical stores and online.

George's online business has also begun to ship to markets outside the UK.

It is already delivering to the Republic of Ireland, France, Belgium, Luxembourg, Spain and Holland. By July, it will deliver to 34 countries across the European Union. 'We've got a bit of a pincer movement taking place because we've got Malta, but also we're testing the market in a very cost-effective way through our dot-com business,' Mr Moore said.

But he says of the possibility of physical stores in continental Europe: 'That is a big step. We haven't got to that stage yet'. Asda, the UK arm of Walmart, the world's biggest retailer, is not only accelerating the international expansion of George, which is estimated to have annual sales of more than £2bn, but is also putting its firepower behind development of other non-food lines, such as homewares, now they're under Mr Moore's remit.

Fiona Lambert, brand director for George, is also looking after product development for 'soft lines', which includes cushions, curtains and towels. Asda has identified certain product areas in which it wants to be the first or second main presence in the market. But Mr Moore said the 'real game-changer' was to harness parent Walmart's 'buying strength'. Mr Moore is to make a presentation to US investors and analysts this week as Walmart's British operations are showcased.

George and Walmart are already collaborating to an increasing extent in areas such as fabric, while George clothing designed in the UK is already on sale in Walmart stores in Chile and Japan and it will soon be available in the Canadian outlets. Mr Moore said George was the UK's fastest growing online clothing retailer, with cash sales up about 50 per cent year on year. It is the third-biggest UK clothing retailer by volume, behind Marks and Spencer, and Primark, breaking through the 11 per cent market share threshold for the first time. In cash sales, George accounts for more than 5 per cent of the UK market, while it is Britain's biggest children's clothing retailer by volume.

With the acquisition last year of the sourcing division of its Turkish long-term supply partner GAAT, George has been concentrating on cutting its lead times, in order to get garments from the drawing table to the supermarket aisle in only six weeks. The shorter lead times have also helped George to 'weather proof' its spring ranges, adding cream or white lightweight knitwear and short-sleeved cardigans, as well as longer sleeved and longer legged garments and in some cases heavier weight fabrics.

'Womens-wear is having a good time at the moment,' said Mr Moore. George saw like-for-like sales increase last year.

Questions

1 Consider the benefits to Asda/Walmart as the franchisee from this link-up with George.
2 Consider the benefits to George as the franchisor from this link-up with Asda/Walmart.

Other contractual modes of internationalisation

Besides licensing and franchising, non-equity forms of internationalisation may involve activities such as *management contracting,* where a supplier in one country undertakes to provide to a client in another country certain ongoing management functions, which would otherwise be the responsibility of the client. Other examples include *technical service agreements* that provide for the supply of technical services across borders, as when a company outsources the operation of its computer and telecommunications networks to a foreign firm. India, with its highly educated and inexpensive labour force, has won many such contracts in many types of teleworking and increasingly in a wide range of 'back-office' functions, such as those involving legal and accountancy work (see Case 2.4 below). *Contract-based partnerships* may also be formed between firms of different nationalities in order to share the cost of an investment. For example, agreements between pharmaceutical companies, motor vehicle companies and publishing houses may include cooperation, co-research and co-development activities.

CASE 2.4 Legal process outsourcing in India

The global legal process outsourcing (LPO) market in 2014 has been estimated as being worth more than £1.5 billion and is expected to continue growing. India is the major provider of LPO, with over a million lawyers engaged in such activities for around 130 outsourcing law firms worldwide. The Philippines is another favoured source for LPO, with over 40,000 of its lawyers engaged on such work.

LPO has been aided by a variety of factors, including the unbundling of legal services into distinct and separate activities, many of which are seen as more routine and which can be provided at larger scale and lower cost. For example, while legal counsel, negotiation support, identifying and evaluating legal options and contract drafting require higher legal skills and are usually retained in-house, billing services, database management, secretarial services and e-functions require lower levels of legal skills and are increasingly outsourced.

Certainly there are considerable cost advantages from outsourcing these more scalable, lower legal skill activities. For example, a fully qualified lawyer in India will earn an average salary of around £12,000 per annum compared to a UK equivalent expecting an initial salary of £40,000 per annum rising to over £100,000 as a salaried partner. Less qualified 'para-legal' workers would earn around £35,000 to £45,000 per annum in London compared to £5000 to £10,000 per annum in India or the Philippines.

Interestingly, there is now a tendency for LPO to also involve ownership of the overseas supplier, as a means of quality control. Baker and McKenzie in the Philippines and Clifford Chance in India have already established their wholly owned off-shore legal centres, and others are treading the same path.

Question

Consider the implications of this contractual mode of internationalisation for (a) UK legal graduates, (b) Indian legal graduates, (c) the UK economy and (d) the Indian economy.

Equity-based methods for internationalisation

These essentially refer to the use of fdi by the firm as a means of competing internationally in the modern global economy. The major advantage of this method is that the firm secures the greatest level of control over its proprietary information and therefore over any technological advantages it might have. In addition, profits need not be shared with any other parties such as agents, distributors or licensees.

In practice, firms can use different approaches to fdi by acquiring an existing firm, by creating an equity joint venture overseas, by establishing a foreign operation from scratch ('greenfield' investment) or by creating various consortia.

Joint ventures

Unlike licensing agreements, *joint ventures* involve creating a new identity in which both the initiating partners take active roles in formulating strategy and making decisions (see also Chapter 7). Joint ventures can help:

- share and lower the costs of high-risk, technology-intensive development projects;
- gain economies of scale and scope in value-adding activities that can only be justified on a global basis;
- secure access to a partner's technology, its accumulated learning, proprietary processes or protected market position;
- create a basis for more effective future competition in the industry involved.

Joint ventures are particularly common in high-technology industries. For instance, Corning Incorporated of the USA has numerous global joint ventures, such as those to produce medical diagnostic equipment with CIBA-Geigy, fibre optics with Cie Financière Optiques and Siemens, colour television tubes with Samsung and Asahi and ceramics for catalytic converters with NGK Insulators of Japan.

Joint ventures usually take one of two forms, namely specialised or shared value-added.

1 *Specialised joint ventures.* Here each partner brings a *specific competency*; for example, one might produce and the other market. Such ventures are likely to be organised around *different functions.* One specialised joint venture has involved JVC (Japan) and Thomson (France). JVC contributed the specialised skills involved in the manufacturing technologies needed to produce optical and compact discs, computers and semiconductors, while Thomson contributed the specific marketing skills needed to compete in fragmented markets such as Europe.

2 *Shared value-added joint ventures.* Here both partners contribute to the *same function* or value-added activity. For example, Fuji-Xerox is a case of a shared value-added joint venture with the design, production and marketing functions all shared.

The major benefits of *specialised joint ventures* include an opportunity to share risks, to learn about a partner's skills and proprietary processes and to gain access to new distribution channels. However, they carry risks as well, perhaps the greatest being that one partner's exposure of its particular competencies may result in the other partner gaining a competitive advantage, which it might subsequently use to become a direct competitor. This happened to GE when it entered into a specialised joint venture with Samsung to produce microwave ovens. Samsung now competes with GE across the whole range of household appliances. Another risk relates to the high co-ordination costs often involved in assimilating the different types of value-added activity of each partner. Sometimes a partner can be relegated to a position of permanent weakness. For example, the GM–Fanuc venture was originally intended to co-design and co-produce robots and flexible automation systems, but GM was unable to learn the critical skills needed from its partner and has ended up as little more than a distributor.

Shared value-added joint ventures pose a slightly different set of risks: partners can more easily lose their competitive advantage since the close working relationships involve the same function. If the venture is not working, it may be more difficult to exit since co-ordination costs tend to be much higher than they are in specialised joint ventures, with more extensive administrative networks having usually been established.

'Success factors' for joint ventures

Critical success factors for joint ventures might include the following:

- *Take time to assess the partners.* Extended courtship is often required if a joint venture of either type is to be successful; Corning Incorporated of the USA formed its joint venture with CIBA-Geigy only after two years of courtship. Being too hurried can destroy a venture, as AT&T and Olivetti of Italy discovered when they formed a joint venture to produce personal computers that failed because of an incompatibility in management styles and corporate cultures as well as in objectives.

- *Understand that collaboration is a distinct form of competition.* Competitors as partners must remember that joint ventures are sometimes designed as ways of 'de-skilling' the opposition. Partners must learn from each other's strengths while preserving their own sources of competitive advantage. Many firms enter into joint ventures in the mistaken belief that the other partner is the student rather than the teacher.

- *Learn from partners while limiting unintended information flows.* Companies must carefully design joint ventures so that they do not become 'windows' through which one partner can learn about the other's competencies.

- *Establish specific rules and requirements for joint venture performance at the outset.* For instance, Motorola's transfer of microprocessor technology to Toshiba is explicitly dependent on how much of a market share Motorola gets in Japan.

- *Give managers sufficient autonomy.* Decentralisation of decision making should give managers sufficient autonomy to run the joint venture successfully. Two of the most successful global value-adding joint ventures are those between Fuji-Xerox and Nippon-Otis, which are also among those giving management the greatest autonomy.

It has been found that extensive training and team building is crucial if these joint ventures are to succeed. There are three ways in which effective human resource management (HRM) is critical (see also Chapter 8):

1 developing and training managers in negotiation and conflict resolution;

2 acculturation (i.e. cultural awareness) in working with a foreign partner;

3 harmonisation of management styles.

Problems with international joint ventures in China

When the first Sino-foreign joint venture, the Beijing Aviation Food Co., was established in 1980, it led to the beginning of intensive foreign direct investment (fdi) into China, which in turn has contributed to China's continuous growth of 8% every year for the last 20 years. World Trade Organisation (WTO) entry has also boosted inward fdi into China. Combine this with Beijing successfully hosting the Olympics in 2008 and a population of nearly 1.3 billion and it soon becomes evident why so many foreign firms have hurriedly tried to gain a presence in China. With Chinese people having a well-earned reputation for thrift, holding savings of more than US$1000 billion, nowhere is this desire more apparent than in the finance sector. For example, in the early years of the new millennium, Newbridge Capital, the US-based multinational finance corporation, sought to tap into this huge savings stockpile and paid US$1.8 billion for nearly 20% of Shenzhen Development Bank, while HSBC paid US$600 million for 10% of Pingan Insurance.

Many foreign companies turn to the *international joint venture* (IJV) as their chosen mode of entry into China. To foreign investors there exist three modes of foreign entry, the first two of which are types of IJV – *equity joint venture* (EJV), *cooperative joint venture* (CJV) and *wholly owned foreign enterprises* (WOFE). However, IJVs continue to experience high rates of dissolution.

The problems associated with IJVs in China have been well documented. One reason for foreign investors to shy away from IJVs is their fear of leaking proprietary technology and know-how to Chinese partners and thus losing long-term competitive advantages. To the Chinese partner gaining invaluable knowledge is a main strategic objective for entering into an IJV. For the Western partner, the problem is knowing how much of their technical expertise should be shared with their partner. A key factor that allows for sharing information is the establishment of trust between parties. In Chinese culture, trust is very much built on personal relationships and involves socialising and working together in order to build trust. In Western society, trust between business partners is underlined by the contract, therefore there is likely to be less importance placed on building relationships. It is often very difficult to build trust between two companies that originate from very different cultural backgrounds. Lack of cultural understanding and different strategic objectives are two of the main reasons why IJVs continue to experience high failure rates.

Most Western companies have sought to enter China via the joint venture route, sharing day-to-day control of the business with a local partner. Having a local partner in a joint venture does provide certain advantages, as in securing contracts that often depend on political linkages and being better able to use guanxi-type relationships (see Chapter 5). However, sharing operational control with the local partner can paralyse decision making. Lucent, for example, has seen its share of the market for optical-fibre equipment in China fall from 70% to 30% largely because, in the view of analysts, it has had to negotiate each technological change in its product base with the local partner. Such time delays in rapidly evolving high-technology markets can be extremely adverse.

Worse still, Chinese regulations are often geographically and product specific, forcing Western companies to have separate local partners in different Chinese regions and for different product groups. This restricts the benefits available to joint ventures in terms of economies of scale and scope. For example, Unilever has separate joint ventures in Shanghai for making soap, skin cream and laundry detergent. Adopting a uniform strategy across all these product groups and across different geographic regions has proved difficult to implement as individual partners fear that such co-ordination may be at the expense of their particular joint venture.

In recognition of these problems, some Western companies have established wholly owned foreign enterprises (WOFEs). Unfortunately, while this has helped avoid the lengthy decision-making process of joint ventures, it has proved a difficult vehicle for securing contracts and for establishing the local alliances and networks so important in a guanxi business culture.

Case 2.5 compares and contrasts the use of IJVs, WOFEs and other market entry methods for China.

CASE 2.5 Market entry into China

Shanghai GKN Driveshaft, a car parts venture between GKN of the UK and Saic, dates from 1988, making it one of the oldest in the sector. Xue Jinda, its managing director, says it combines the 'successful characteristics of both Chinese and western parties' – so extended it for another 50 years, and has just expanded its scope. But in other industries, where joint ventures are not mandatory, they are usually shorter-lived and, in many cases, may not even be necessary.

Richard Grans, who runs the Shanghai office of Benesch, the US law firm, says very few partnerships work after year three. Often, in that time, 'the company has spent as much or more time managing the relationship with the JV partners than they have pursuing the business.'

Unlike the carmakers, which operate via larger, more rigid equity joint ventures, a growing number of international companies in China are now using flexible 'contractual' or 'co-operative' agreements, under which more than two partners can have different shareholdings, pay off schedules and objectives. Non-Chinese companies may also prefer to link up selectively with specific local companies for one product or activity – for instance, distribution – rather than for the entire business.

Where there are likely to be large upfront costs or difficult negotiations with government officials, it makes sense to use a Chinese partner. But John Huang of Chinese law firm MWE China says that since 2000 more foreign groups have set up 'WOFEs', wholly owned foreign enterprises, than joint ventures. As Andy Reynolds Smith, GKNs chief executive of automotive points out, businesses with many customers lower down the supply chain may find it easier to serve China through a wholly owned subsidiary, as GKN does in the power metallurgy division he also oversees.

 Source: Adapted from An odd corporate vehicle for doing business in China: Is your joint venture really necessary?, *Financial Times* 14/05/2013, p.14 (Hill, A.), © The Financial Times Limited 2013. All Rights Reserved.

Question

Discuss the contribution of this case to the international joint venture (IJV) or wholly owned foreign enterprise (WOFE) debate for market entry into China.

Alliances

An 'alliance' can take many forms and is much less structured than a joint venture or an acquisition. Jeffrey Reuer has suggested that the 'Four Is' of collaboration (Figure 2.1) will crucially determine whether to enter into an alliance rather than a joint venture

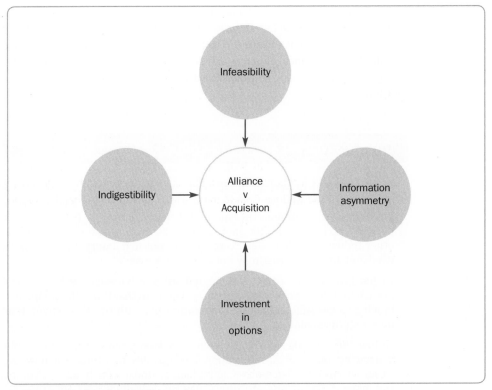

Figure 2.1 The four 'Is' of collaboration
Source: Based on Reuer (1999).

or acquisition, namely infeasibility, information asymmetry, investment in options and indigestibility.

1 *Infeasibility.* Alliances are more likely when acquisitions contain elements of infeasibility. For example, competition legislation may effectively prevent large corporate acquisitions or may impose conditions deemed unacceptable if they are to go ahead. Restrictions on inward fdi to some industrial/service sectors or countries may have the same effect.

2 *Information asymmetry.* Alliances are more likely the greater the degree of (actual or perceived) information asymmetry. In other words, companies may be more likely to resort to alliances rather than acquisitions when one company knows more than some other company. Even after due diligence, the acquiring company may have reservations as to the true value of the assets to be acquired. In a large-scale analysis of US companies by Reuer and Koza (2000), the announcements of joint ventures and alliances led to higher rises in the stock market prices of the affected companies the greater the degree of information asymmetry perceived as existing between the proposed allies.

3 *Investment in options.* Alliances are more likely the greater the degree of uncertainty as to the future prospects of the combined activity. For example, alliances form a higher proportion of total linkages between companies in uncertain industrial sectors such as biotechnology. An alliance can develop into greater or lesser linkage between two or more companies depending on the degree of success actually achieved by the initial joint activity. This 'staged engagement' can be expressed in terms of *call options*: these confer the

right, but not the obligation, for an allied party to expand its equity stake at a pre-specified price at some future date. Put another way, alliances are more likely the greater the perceived need to invest in call options rather than in an immediate equity stake.

4 *Indigestibility*. Alliances are more likely the greater the perceived indigestibility of the potential target for acquisition. (This term arises from the need of an acquiring company to 'digest' the assets of the acquired company.) Such 'indigestibility' raises the anticipated transactions costs of acquisition (i.e. the post-acquisition integration costs). In such circumstances alliances will prove relatively attractive, giving the respective allies greater freedom to link *selected* assets only. As Reuer (1999) pointed out, Nestlé established a joint venture for breakfast cereals with General Mills in Europe, but the parties made no attempt to link any of their other businesses. The same happened with Nestlé allying its coffee and tea operations with Coca-Cola to make use of the latter's global distribution system.

Case 2.6 reviews the reasons behind the continuing Franco-Japanese alliance between Renault and Nissan.

CASE 2.6 Renault and Nissan seek €4.3bn in synergies

Renault and Nissan will fully combine their manufacturing and research and development for the first time since the alliance was founded. The 15-year old Franco-Japanese alliance, which has kept the carmakers from financial ruin, involves sharing purchasing and investment resources and has allowed them to compete with the likes of Toyota and General Motors. 'Over €4.3bn is a commitment, not a target . . . We have got to continue to move on and move up,' said Carlos Ghosn, chief executive of both carmakers and the driving force behind the alliance. 'In our industry, a big part of competition is scale. If you do not have scale, then you cannot be competitive.'

In an industry where acrimonious divorces and failed joint ventures are the norm, Renault–Nissan's global partnership has saved them €10bn and become a blueprint for co-operation, as rival carmakers grapple with huge investment costs, increasing competition and the need to increase global scale. The alliance has essentially created the world's fourth largest car group with sales in 2013 of 8.3m cars, and the two companies already share some procurement of parts, a handful of factories and products. It saved a combined €2.8bn last year through such synergies. Under the deepening of the alliance, it will appoint four 'tsars' to oversee manufacturing, R&D, human resources and purchasing in a root and branch integration from design studio to factory gate that will see Renault and Nissan cars, parts and factories become ever more homogenous and drive down costs.

'This is an evolution,' Mr Ghosn told the *Financial Times*. 'All the areas where you had two different teams, two different opinions, are now disappearing. There's now one person.' Factories owned and run by Renault and Nissan separately will adopt shared production procedures and engineering techniques as a move to streamline costs and unite product research teams under one roof.

Renault–Nissan could have single product platforms making as many as 3m vehicles yearly, Mr Ghosn said. Renault owns 43.4 per cent of Nissan which in turn holds 15 per cent of the French carmaker. While Mr Ghosn has stressed he has no intention of fully merging the two, the deeper integration is seen as underlining their interdependence in the longer term.

Consortia, keiretsus and chaebols

In the USA and Europe there has been little success in building cross-industry consortia, largely as a result of the difficulties involved in getting firms to pool their resources into an integrative organisational design. The one exception in Europe is perhaps the Airbus Industrie. In the Far East, on the other hand, consortia such as the Japanese *keiretsus* and the South Korean *chaebols* are much more commonplace.

The Japanese *keiretsu* is a combination of 20–25 different industrial companies centred around a large traditional company. Integration is achieved through interlocking directorates, bank holdings and close personal ties between senior managers. Group members typically agree not to sell their holdings. Examples include Sumitomo, Mitsubishi, Mitsui and Sanwa. Case 2.7 looks at the impact of the *keiretsu* in supporting the post-war Japanese export drive, which has largely been based on the competitive advantages of Japanese firms.

CASE 2.7 The Japanese *keiretsu*

Whereas macro-environmental factors have provided the direction and stability needed to sustain Japan's rapid post-war growth in competitiveness, the actual mechanisms underpinning many of its efficiency gains have involved the dynamic behaviour of companies at the corporate level. To understand this process we need to look at the structure of Japanese industry, which consists of two key dimensions. First, there is the large-firm sector dominated by six major groupings of firms (*Kigyo Shudan*). Second, there is the important sector of small and medium-sized firms (*Chusho Kigyo*) whose members often act as sub-contractors to the larger firms.

The six major groupings are Mitsubishi, Mitsui, Sumitomo, Fuyo, Dai-ichi Kangyo (DKB) and Sanwa. The 'core' of each group consists of a number of large enterprises from different sectors of the economy, e.g. metals, oil, electrical, automobiles, etc., together with at least one major bank. Each group maintains its internal cohesiveness through regular meetings of the presidents of the larger companies and by the exchange of shares and directorships between member companies of the group (interlocking directorships). In addition, the various companies within the group would hold each other's shares as a means of affirming their relationship. Such shares would not be actively traded, making it difficult for companies to be taken over under this system as buying sufficient shares to gain control would be extremely difficult. In other words, the corporate governance of Japan was of a type that encouraged stable, long-term relationships between the members of large industrial groupings. However, inter-group rivalry was often intense – for example, Mitsubishi motors (Mitsubishi Group) competed actively with Toyota (Mitsui Group) and Isuzu motors (DKB Group) so that the market was often oligopolistic in nature. Surveys in the 1990s that asked Japanese companies for the reasons that motivated them to introduce new technology found that 36% of companies cited domestic competition with other Japanese companies as a major motivating factor.

However, the success of these large exporting firms depends ultimately on the numerous small and medium-sized firms that act as primary,

Case 2.7 (continued)

secondary and tertiary sub-contractors to the large firms. Many of the large Japanese companies, such as Toyota, are basically assemblers of parts produced by sub-contractors. For example, Toyota has 158 primary sub-contractors, 4,700 secondary sub-contractors and almost 31,600 tertiary sub-contractors – most situated in relatively close proximity to the main parent company. This vertically organised production group or *keiretsu* provides a vital source of competitiveness for Japanese industry. Cost savings derive from the fact that the major firms can save on overheads while, at the same time, also asking the various layers of small companies to trim their costs. As a result, the potential total cost reduction throughout the *keiretsu* can be substantial. The nature of the contractual relationship between companies in Japan is based more on unwritten, long-term contracts founded on trust, rather than the more legally framed, one-off 'spot' contracts more prevalent in Europe and the USA.

In terms of production and innovation, Japanese managers began concentrating on the 'focused factory', i.e. on fewer product lines with a view to maximising benefits from economies of scale and scope. Together with these cost benefits came those based on the learning curve that measured the savings made year after year as a result of increases in cumulative output. For example, between 1984 and 1990 the CD-player market grew very rapidly and Sony, Sharp and Rohm produced their low-powered laser diodes for the CD player. Over this time the costs per unit for the diodes fell from 2000 yen to 200 yen each, showing clearly how cumulative production helps companies to learn how to produce laser diodes more efficiently.

In their continuous quest for lower costs and increased competitiveness, Japanese production managers also concentrated on some basic but important factors:

- First, the Japanese concept of *kaizen* (i.e. the constant search for small incremental improvements in all aspects of company behaviour) was a powerful tool for improving competitive behaviour, especially when economic conditions were relatively difficult and when introducing new technology was expensive. For

example, Toyota workers have been recorded as providing 1.5 million suggestions a year for small improvements in production.

- Second, Japanese production managers, led by those at Toyota Motors, concentrated on the development of the just-in-time or *kanban* system whose aim was to create a continuous process flow both within large firms and also between large assemblers and their various sub-contractors. This meant that each workstation supplied a component to the next station ahead of it on the production line only when needed, saving the costly build-up (both purchase and storage) of inventories. The perfection of this process took Toyota over 25 years to achieve.

- Third, the management of quality was also critical for Japanese competitiveness and here the approach was based very much on the ideas of William Edwards Deming, who visited Japan in the 1950s and who helped Japan to reverse the usual American approach to quality management by stressing that 85% of the responsibility for quality should be in the hands of plant workers and only 15% should be dependent on line managers. In other words, the Japanese identified in their approach to *total quality management* that the individual worker was the main quality controller and not the manager, as is often thought to be the case in a high proportion of US and European firms.

It would seem that these approaches by Japanese production managers are continuing to yield productivity gains, with annual data regularly showing that Japanese car component makers are still more efficient than their US or European counterparts.

However, the strength of such inter-group relationship is subject to change as economic forces pressurise the groups to modify their behaviour. For example, during the period 1990–2014 the tendency for *keiretsu* members to hold each other's shares in order to cement their relationship and prevent takeovers (i.e. cross-holdings) has decreased from 32% to 12% in terms of the total value of shares held. In addition, there has been a tendency for large parent companies in manufacturing to try to extend their *ownership* of their affiliate companies

Case 2.7 (*continued*)

rather than continue the more traditional relationships with *independent* subcontractors. In addition, Japanese firm takeovers of foreign firms increased over the past decade, indicating the greater willingness of such companies to be more aggressive or market driven than before.

On the other hand it is also important to understand that *keiretsu* members continue to be prone to over-investment in their financially weak group members so that major changes in their 'group habits' will not disappear as rapidly as forecast by various observers.

 Source: Griffiths (2000); Griffiths and Wall (2012).

Questions

1 As well as helping Japanese export performance, what other impacts might you expect the *keiretsu* system to have in the internationalisation process?
2 Can you identify any factors in today's global economy that might put this system under strain?

The South Korean *chaebols* are similar agglomerations, which are also centred around a holding company. These are usually dominated by the founding families. While a *keiretsu* is financed from group banks and run by professional managers, *chaebols* usually get their funding from government and are managed by family members who have been groomed for the job. Prominent examples include Samsung, Daewoo and Sunkyong. Such alliances are usually initiated by merchant and industrialist families and the company keeps the shares in family hands.

Consortia of these types are essentially sophisticated forms of strategic alliances designed to maximise the potential benefits of joint ventures – namely risk sharing, cost reductions, economies of scale, etc. In both Japan and South Korea governments have played an important role in encouraging such developments. Such consortia tend to have a long-term focus and are uniquely positioned to share the risks of investing in high-fixed-cost projects in order to stay at the forefront of technology-based industries. At the same time, risk is diversified because the different companies are involved in many different industries. This encourages investment in the more volatile industries such as satellites, biotechnology, microelectronics and aerospace. The members of the consortia also benefit from strong buyer–supplier relationships, with costs reduced by bulk purchase discounts, etc. It often means extensive resource sharing of components and end products that can produce fast responses to changed consumer requirements, so essential when employing mass customisation techniques.

Pause for thought 2.3

Conglomerate mergers have been widely used in Western economies; (a) give some examples; (b) suggest the benefits they confer; (c) consider why they have become less popular in recent times.

It is worth noting that the *keiretsus* and *chaebols* benefit from government in the form of preferential interest rates and capital allocations that, arguably, only a managed economy can deliver. They are also characterised by close ties and shared values leading to mutual understanding and sacrifices that cannot easily be duplicated in the West. These organisations are linked together by networks and personal relationships, so the corporate culture needs to be able to embrace both hierarchical and horizontal integration. Fraternal relationships, mutual long-term commitment and pride in membership are characteristics that are less commonly found in the individualised cultures of the USA or UK (see Chapter 5).

Table 2.1 provides a useful summary of some of the benefits and costs of the various types of global alliances or related collaborations previously discussed.

Acquisitions and 'greenfield' investment

Some of the problems faced by joint ventures (especially those involving decision making and culture clashes) and by the various kinds of consortia can be avoided by wholly owning the foreign affiliates. This can be achieved through acquisition of, or merger with, an existing firm or through establishing an entirely new foreign operation ('greenfield' investment).

Acquisition of an existing foreign company has a number of advantages compared to 'greenfield' investment; for example, it allows a more rapid market entry, so that there is a quicker return on capital and a ready access to knowledge of the local market. Because of its rapidity, such acquisition can pre-empt a rival's entry into the same market. Further, many of the problems associated with setting up a 'greenfield' site in a foreign country (such as cultural, legal and management issues) can be avoided. By involving a change in ownership, acquisition also avoids costly competitive reactions from the acquired firm. Strategic aspects of acquisitions and mergers policies are considered in more detail in Chapter 7 (pp. 242–249).

Why invest abroad?

Of course, the 'bottom line' may simply be an estimated higher present value of future profits from establishing a production facility in a foreign country as opposed to the alternatives (e.g. continuing to export to the foreign country). Nevertheless, an fdi decision is a complex process that may be influenced by social relationships within and outside the firm and for which there may be a whole array of other motivating factors. Some approaches seek to classify these *motivating factors* into supply factors, demand factors and political factors.

Supply factors

A number of *supply factors* may encourage the firm to resort to foreign direct investment. These may be particularly important for those firms sometimes described as *cost-oriented multinationals,* i.e. those for which the major objective is to reduce costs by internationalising their operations.

Production costs

Foreign locations may be more attractive because of the lower costs of skilled or unskilled labour, lower land prices, tax rates or commercial real-estate rents. We noted earlier (pp. 40–42) the growth of incentives to attract inward fdi, as in the establishment of special economic zones. There has also been a trend to reduce corporate income taxes in both developed and developing countries.

Particular locations can change in terms of their relative popularity as low-cost centres of production, as we noted in Chapter 1 (pp. 8–14). For example, South Korea was once a production centre for low-priced training shoes, but as the country began to prosper, wages

Table 2.1 Characteristics of different types of global alliance

Type of global alliance	Benefits	Costs	Critical success factors	Strategic human resources management
Licensing – manufacturing industries	• Early standardisation of design • Ability to capitalise on innovations • Access to new technologies • Ability to control pace of industry evolution	• New competitors created • Possible eventual exit from industry • Possible dependence on licensee	• Selection of licensee likely to become a competitor • Enforcement of patents and licensing agreements	• Technical knowledge • Training of local managers on-site
Licensing – servicing and franchises	• Fast market entry • Low capital cost	• Quality control • Trademark protection	• Partners compatible in philosophies/values • Tight performance standards	• Socialisation of franchisees and licensees with core values
Joint ventures – specialisation across partners	• Learning a partner's skills • Economies of scale • Quasi-vertical integration • Faster learning	• Excessive dependence on partner for skills • Deterrent to internal investment	• Tight and specific performance criteria • Entering a venture as 'student' rather than 'teacher' to learn skills from partner • Recognising that collaboration is another form of competition to learn new skills	• Management development and training • Negotiation skills • Managerial rotation
Joint ventures – shared value-adding	• Strengths of both partners pooled • Faster learning along value chain • Fast upgrading of technological skills	• High switching costs • Inability to limit partner's access to information	• Decentralisation and autonomy from corporate parents • Long 'courtship' period • Harmonisation of management styles	• Team-building • Acculturation • Flexible skills for implicit communication
Consortia, kairetsus, and chaebols	• Shared risks and costs • Building a critical mass in process technologies • Fast resource flows and skill transfers	• Skills and technologies that have no real market worth • Bureaucracy • Hierarchy	• Government encouragement • Shared values among managers • Personal relationships to ensure co-ordination and priorities • Close monitoring of member-company performance	• 'Clan' cultures • Fraternal relationships • Extensive mentoring to provide a common vision and mission across member companies

Source: Reprinted and adapted from *Journal of World Business*, 32(3), Lei, D., Slocum, J. and Pitts, R.A. 'Building competitive advantage: managing strategic alliances to promote organizational learning'. Copyright 1997, with permission from Elsevier.

rose and this market is now dominated by China. Despite recessionary problems in recent years, Ireland is still attractive as a location for many MNEs with its low labour costs, English-speaking population, tax abatement opportunities and an infrastructure containing modern fibre-optic telephone networks. McGraw-Hill publishers moved the maintenance of the circulation files of its 16 magazines to Loughrea, Ireland, while retaining a direct link to its mainframe computers at its New Jersey headquarters.

This type of globalised production decision may often involve *vertical integration*. For example, many US and European companies have integrated forwards by establishing assembly facilities in South-East Asia in order to take account of the relative abundance of cheap, high-quality labour. Companies like America's ITT ship semi-manufactured components to the region, where they are assembled by local labour into finished products, which are then re-exported back to the home market. Such host countries for foreign direct investment are sometimes termed 'production platforms', which underscores their role as providers of a low-cost input into a global, vertically integrated production process.

Of course, even when looking solely at the factor of labour, we have already noted in Chapter 1 that it is not only labour costs that are important, but also labour productivity. Figure 1.6 (p. 12) usefully pointed out that sometimes countries with low labour costs may be less attractive because of low labour productivity, and vice versa for high-labour-cost countries. In fact, the most revealing overall statistic is relative unit labour costs (RULC), as outlined in Box 1.1 (p. 10).

Case 2.8 provides further insights into cost-based influences on internationalisation strategies.

CASE 2.8 High energy costs drive EU industry abroad

When BMW, the German carmaker, was considering where to build an energy intensive plant to manufacture carbon fibre for its forthcoming 13 urban electric vehicle, it did not pause long before selecting Moses Lake, Washington. The $100m plant, operated with joint venture partner SGL Group, relies on hydro-electric power produced by dams on the nearby Columbia River. They generate electricity that costs just 3 dollars per kWh. The equivalent electricity in Germany, to where the lightweight carbon fibre is shipped for processing and construction, would cost six times as much.

Joerg Pohlman, managing director of the joint venture, said: 'the main reason for wanting to be based there was to secure an adequate supply of energy from renewable sources. But another decisive factor was the low energy price.' Europe's comparatively high energy costs are increasingly a source of concern for its industry, which fears a loss of competitiveness. Last year gas prices in the US were about three times lower than in Europe and electricity prices were about 50 per cent lower.

Critics say two factors are driving the divergence: the US shale gas revolution, which has lowered US natural gas prices and, more controversially, European climate and energy policies, including emissions trading and renewable energy subsides.

About 58 per cent of business leaders surveyed in an Accenture study are pessimistic that European industry will in three years' time remain cost competitive on energy compared with rivals such as US, China or Russia.

In Europe, population density, environmental concerns and technical difficulties are holding back shale gas exploration and the continent remains reliant on expensive Russian and Norwegian gas.

Case 2.8 (continued)

Peter Loscher, chief executive of Siemens, said 'The shale gas agenda should be an enormous game changer (for the US), and Europe has no big game changer at this point in time. We have higher energy costs and we have higher labour costs.'

Wolfgang Eder, chief executive of Voestalpine, the Austrian steel company, sees the threat to Europe's' competitiveness in much starker terms. 'The exodus has started in the chemical, automatic and steel industries. If Europe doesn't change course, that process will accelerate and at some point will not be reversible.'

 Source: High European energy prices drive BMW to US, *Financial Times*, 27/05/2013, p.19 (Bryant, C.), © The Financial Times Limited 2013. All Rights Reserved.

Question

How might Europe become more cost competitive in the energy context?

Taxation

Table 2.2 indicates a wide variation in effective tax rates in 2013 between various OECD countries. It used the concept of the 'tax wedge' to measure differences between countries in the taxation of their employees. The 'tax wedge' is the *gap* between what an employer in a given country pays to its employees and what the employee actually takes home after paying the various types of tax levied on his/her income.

The average 'tax wedge' from all OECD (developed) economies was 35.9% in 2013, but Table 2.2 shows a wide divergence between effective taxation across the countries listed. For example, Belgium's tax wedge is the highest at 55.8%, some 24% higher than the figure for the US and Britain and almost 20% higher than the OECD average.

The figures for the tax wedge in South Korea, Mexico, New Zealand and especially Chile point to considerable tax advantages for such countries.

Distribution costs

Where transportation costs are a significant proportion of total costs, firms may choose to produce from a foreign location rather than pay the costs of transportation. Heineken, whose products are mainly water-based, finds it cheaper to brew in locations geographically closer to the foreign consumer. International businesses may find it cheaper to establish distribution centres in the foreign location, rather than to send individual consignments directly to sellers. For example, Citrovita, a Brazilian producer of orange concentrate, operates a storage and distribution centre in Antwerp, Belgium, so that it can benefit from low shipping rates when transporting in bulk. Mechanisms for minimising distribution costs are considered in more detail in Chapter 7.

Availability of natural resources

This is very important in certain industries such as oil and minerals. Indeed, this reason has often led to *backwards vertical integration* in search of cheaper or more secure inputs into the productive process. Oil companies, such as Exxon, Shell and BP, have provided well-known examples of this approach. In order to secure control of strategic raw materials in oil fields

Table 2.2 **Difference between labour costs and take-home pay (as % of total labour costs) in 2013**

Country	'Tax wedge' (%)*
Belgium	55.8
Britain	31.3
Chile	7.8
France	49.8
Germany	49.8
Italy	48.6
Japan	31.4
Mexico	19.8
New Zealand	17.5
Poland	35.9
Portugal	41.0
South Korea	21.1
Spain	40.8
US	31.2
OECD average	35.9

*Single person without children and with average earnings.

Source: OECD (various).

around the world, they established overseas extraction operations in the early years of the twentieth century with the aim of shipping crude oil back to their home markets for refining and sale.

Access to key technology

Many firms find it cheaper to invest in an existing firm rather than put together a new team of research specialists. Many Japanese pharmaceutical manufacturers have invested in small biogenetics companies as an inexpensive means of finding cutting-edge technology. Mitsubishi Electronics took over Apricot in the UK, while Fujitsu is now the second-largest computer corporation in the world, after acquiring ICL, at that point the largest UK computer company.

Demand factors

A number of *demand factors* may also encourage the firm to resort to foreign direct investment. These may be particularly important for those firms sometimes described as *market-oriented multinationals,* i.e. those for which the major objective is to internationalise with a view to accessing new markets and greater sales. In this case the internationalisation process is more likely to take the form of *horizontal* (rather than vertical) *integration* into new geographic markets.

Case 2.9 illustrates the 'pull' factors of demand for milk in China resulting in overseas dairy businesses entering into joint ventures with and acquisitions of dairy businesses in China.

Figure 2.2 presents a stylised version of this process with companies gradually switching from exporting (or licensing) to establishing first a sales outlet and finally full production facilities overseas. Underpinning this process may be a number of identifiable motivating factors of a demand type.

CASE 2.9 China's thirst for dairy

The average Holstein Friesian cow can grow to 600 kilos, stand 150 cm tall and produce as much as 10,000 litres of milk a year. They can calve after 24 months and produce milk for as long as 15 years. Bovine biology may not appear obvious required reading for Asia's investment bankers, but thanks to China's rapidly growing thirst for milk products, the regions' dairy sector is in the middle of a wave of deal-making, driving up asset prices from New Zealand to Inner Mongolia.

Milk is already big business in China, and it is getting bigger. A drive by the Chinese government to provide all Chinese children with half a litre of milk a day has caused demand for milk in China to increase by around 25% a year over recent years. Around one-third of all the world production of milk is now exported to China. Macquarie expects Chinese dairy consumption to rise at a compound rate of 13% a year between now and 2017, while high-end milk products are likely to see 20% annual growth rates.

Because of the capital intensity of the sector, the overhang from years of safety concerns, domestic dairies are struggling to catch up with demand.

International groups are picking up some of the slack, prompting them to increase their own supply base and strike deals with Chinese dairy companies. In May, France's Danone announced a joint venture with China Mengniu to produce yoghurt.

The flood of interest in the sector has raised some questions as to whether buyers and investors are overpaying for a seat at the table. This week, Mengniu – China's largest dairy by sales – announced it had sold a stake in Yashili, the baby formula producer, worth more than $200m to investors including Temasek and China's Hopu investment.

The deal marked the return to the private equity scene of Fang Fenglei, one of China's best known financiers. Shares in Yashili, which had been suspended since August, rose more than 20% after the announcement.

The same day YuanShengTai, a 'premium' raw milk producer based in northern China, filed its prospectus at the Hong Kong exchange, where it hoped to list a stake worth about $500m. YuanShengTai will seek to build on the success of Huishan Dairy, which raised $1.3bn from its initial public offering in September and attracted cornerstone investors including Norges Bank, the investment arm of Norway's central bank. While some fund managers questioned the pricing of the deal at the time, the stock has since risen more than 20%. Saputo's A$8 a share offer for WCB implies a price/earnings ratio of about 20 times, and compares with a share price of less than $4 in July.

Listed Chinese dairies in Hong Kong now trade at a price/earnings ratio of between 22, in the case of Yashili, and 46 for China Modern Dairy, compared with an average of just 8 for the Hong Kong market.

Questions

1 What are the key factors behind the increased Chinese demand for milk and milk products?
2 How is the market responding to such a sustained increase in demand?

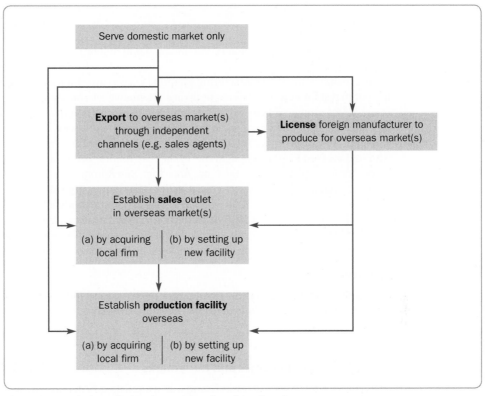

Figure 2.2 Evolution of a market-oriented multinational

Source: Adapted from *Applied Economics*, 12th ed., Financial Times Prentice Hall (Griffiths, A. and Wall, S. (eds)), 2012), © Pearson Education Limited 2012.

Marketing advantages

There are several types of marketing advantage that may be reaped from investing in overseas enterprises or setting up foreign affiliates. The physical presence of a factory may give a company visibility and the company may also gain from a 'buy-local' attitude, as indicated in Case 2.10.

CASE 2.10 Toyota wins support for its US operations

In San Antonio, Texas, the heart of America's pick-up truck country, Toyota makes one of the biggest passenger vehicles on the road. At its sixth and newest functioning US vehicle plant, the car company that propelled itself to the top of the global car industry largely by selling American reliable fuel-efficient compact cars, makes nothing but the Tundra large pick-up truck, which gets only about 17 miles to the gallon.

In launching the new Tundra, Toyota is breaching one of the last bastions of America's three struggling Detroit-area carmakers. Toyota's new extra-large version of the truck competes squarely with the Ford F-Series, General Motors' Chevrolet Silverado and Chrysler's Dodge Ram, which are among the respective companies' top-selling and most profitable vehicles.

Roughly one in seven pick-up trucks in the US is sold in Texas, and Toyota has described the new Tundra as one of its most important product launches in 50 years in the US. Its

> ## Case 2.10 (*continued*)
>
> 2.2 million sq foot, $1.28 billion (£780 million, €930 million) plant turns out one vehicle every 73 seconds.
>
> By expanding its US manufacturing footprint to keep up with its growing sales, Toyota has put to rest for now old jibes about taking automotive jobs overseas, which at one point in the 1990s prompted Ford workers to smash Japanese cars with sledgehammers. Local officials and employees describe the company as a positive presence in the city and a model employer. 'Toyota gave 4,000 of our people jobs,' says Phil Hardberger, San Antonio's mayor, who sold his Ford F150 and bought one of the first Tundras off the assembly line last year. 'These are not Japanese jobs – these are American, San Antonio jobs.'
>
> Toyota appears to be winning the crucial battle over its status as a good corporate citizen in the US. For example, a December 2006 report by Thomson Datastream identified Toyota as creating 34,675 direct jobs in the US in 2006 via production and supply-related activities. However, it also identified 386,314 indirect jobs via the spending of the Toyota company in the US on components and supply and via the spending of those employed by Toyota on other goods and services.
>
> ### Question
>
> As a public relations specialist for Toyota, how might you use the above information to support a 'buy local' attitude towards this Japanese-owned company?

Preservation of brand names and trademarks

In order to maintain control over its brands, an established firm may choose to manufacture in the host country rather than merely license its name and run the risk of licensees using inferior materials.

Customer mobility

A firm may be motivated to move its operations close to a business customer if that customer sets up operations elsewhere, in order to reduce the possibility that a host-based competitor might step in and replace it as the supplier. For example, Japanese firms supplying parts to the major Japanese automobile companies have responded to the construction of Japanese automobile assembly plants in the USA and UK by building their own factories, warehouses and research facilities there. This need to move abroad was heightened by the fact that Japanese automobile companies use just-in-time techniques, and it is difficult to be just-in-time when the parts suppliers are thousands of miles away. Of course, subsequently the Japanese car firms have helped to develop the abilities of local firms to supply the quality of parts and components with a frequency compatible with their manufacturing practices.

Political factors

At least three reasons with a 'political edge' may influence a fdi decision: one is to avoid political/judicial uncertainties, a second is to avoid trade barriers erected by governments (or regional trading blocs) and the third is to take advantage of economic development incentives offered by the government in the host country.

Avoidance of political/judicial uncertainties

As Case 2.11 suggests, when businesses are 'surprised' by unexpected quasi political/judicial decisions which have economic impacts, this may influence fdi decisions.

CASE 2.11 Nokia offers a taxing tale

Can India ever match China's manufacturing prowess? The fate of Nokia's flagship facility in the southern city of Chennai suggests the task will be far from easy. At first glance the state of the art factory seemed to prove that India could emulate the gleaming facilities of Guangzhou and Shenzhen. The Chennai plant was at one point the Finland-based company's largest, employing more than 8,000 workers and sending high-tech mobile phone handsets to dozens of countries – providing the type of export-led growth that brought prosperity to countries such as Vietnam and Thailand.

But while Nokia coped with unreliable electricity and uneven local roads, it was caught out by a more unexpected foe, India's revenue office! Nokia received a $321m bill for unpaid tax last year and a second claim followed this year in 2014. The original wrangle meant Nokia was unable to transfer its factory to Microsoft last month as part of the sale of its €5.4bn phone business to the US company. Nokia describes the claims as 'unreasonable and meritless', but the company still faces a lengthy legal battle over a factory it no longer wishes to operate. Workers have been offered voluntary redundancy and analysts say the plant will now have to be sold cheaply or closed.

Nokia's troubles matter because of India's notably weak record in manufacturing consumer electronics. The country's growing middle classes demand ever more flatscreen televisions and laptops, leading consultants Deloitte to predict a £296bn gap between domestic electronics demand and local production capacity by 2020. That will mean a flood of imports and damaging consequences for India's balance of payments.

The government has plans to boost domestic supplies, in part by persuading global companies such as Samsung and LG Electronics to expand their local facility.

But Sanjeev Prasad, director at Kotak Institutional Equities in Mumbai, says global groups are now likely to be more cautious: 'any major electronics manufacturer looking to open a big plant in India would only have to look at Nokia and think why would I take that risk, when there are other places to go?'

 Source: Adapted from Nokia: A bet with a safety net, *Financial Times*, 22/08/2013 (Milne, R. and Thomas, D.), © The Financial Times Limited 2013. All Rights Reserved.

Question

What issues are raised by this case for both the host government and potential investors?

Avoidance of trade barriers

Firms often set up facilities in foreign countries in order to avoid trade barriers (see also Chapter 3). For example, over recent decades US automobile companies have placed consistent pressure on their government to restrict Japanese and other low-cost imports of cars into the USA. To get around these restrictions, many Japanese companies set up factories in the USA, with the objective of reducing US consumer opposition to Japanese cars since US jobs would now be directly involved (see Case 2.10, p. 63).

Economic development incentives

Most governments see fdi as creating new employment opportunities, raising the techno-logical base and generally increasing the economic welfare of its citizens. Governments have therefore been ready to offer various incentives to firms to induce them to locate new facili-ties in their countries, including tax reductions or tax holidays, free or subsidised access to land or buildings (e.g. zero business rates), specially constructed infrastructure (road, rail, air links) and so on. We noted earlier that an increasing number of countries have developed 'export processing zones' (EPZs) providing various incentives to encourage inward fdi that can help these countries to improve their export competitiveness.

Other factors

The decision to internationalise is complex and the reasons cannot always be neatly contained in the supply, demand and political categories already considered. Other concerns include:

- *The role of management.* The ambitions of management are often crucial in the first stages of the decision to go international. Often a change of chief executive can prompt activity in this area.

- *Motives of the organisation.* Some commentators identify three broad motivations for inter-nationalisation: namely *market seeking* (the lure of additional revenue and profit from new overseas markets), *efficiency seeking* (the lure of lower production costs) and *resource seeking* (the lure of access to specific types of natural resource).

- *Saturation of the home market.* Restrictions in the size of the home market may mean that further growth requires the firm to gain access to overseas markets.

- *The bandwagon effect.* Intense rivalry can mean that a decision by one firm to enter an overseas market tends to be followed by other firms. The bandwagon effect has doubtless played some part in inducing some firms to enter the Chinese, Eastern European and ex-Soviet markets.

- *International product life cycle.* The internationalisation process may be more than simply an attempt to start new product life cycles elsewhere or to extend the maturity stage of an existing product life cycle. The suggestion here is that there may exist an *international product life cycle* for many products which will govern the geographical location of produc-tion in each stage (see Chapter 3).

Theoretical explanations

Attempts have been made to bring together various arguments to form theories or models of the internationalisation process. Some of these theories are taken further in Chapter 3.

Ownership-specific advantages

Here the focus is on the assets owned by the firm which might give it a competitive edge vis-à-vis other firms operating in overseas markets. Such ownership-specific advantages might include superior technology, a well-known brand name, economies of scale or scope (see Box 7.1, pp. 243–245, managerial or organisational skills, etc.

Internalisation

The focus here is on the costs of entering into a transaction, e.g. the costs of negotiating, monitoring and enforcing a contract. The firm decides whether it is cheaper to own and operate a plant or establishment overseas or to contract with a foreign firm to operate on its behalf through a franchise, licensing or supply agreement. Foreign direct investment is more likely to occur (i.e. the process to be *internalised*) when the costs of negotiating, monitoring and enforcing a contract with a second firm are high. On the other hand, when such transaction costs are low, firms are more likely to contract with outsiders and internationalise by licensing their brand names or franchising their business operations.

Location-specific advantages

These theories have mainly sought to answer the 'where' question involving MNE activity outside the home country as well as the 'why'. The availability and price of natural and human resources in overseas territories, of transport and communications infrastructure, market-size characteristics and other locational attributes are the focus of attempts by these theories to explain the internationalisation process.

Eclectic theory

John Dunning (1993) has sought to bring together all three of these theories, namely ownership, internalisation and locational factors, in one combined approach. His so-called 'eclectic paradigm' suggests that firms transfer their *ownership-specific* assets to *locational settings* which offer the most favourable opportunities for their sector of activity while seeking wherever possible to *internalise* these processes in order to retain control of the subsequent revenue generation.

Dunning concluded that companies will only become involved in overseas investment and production (fdi) when the following conditions are all satisfied:

- companies possess an 'ownership-specific' advantage over firms in the host country (e.g. via assets which are internal to the firm, including organisation structure, human capital, financial resources, size and market power);
- it must be more profitable for the multinational to exploit its ownership-specific advantages in an overseas market than in its domestic market. In other words, there must additionally exist 'location-specific' factors which favour overseas production (e.g. special economic or political factors, attractive markets in terms of size, growth or structure, low 'psychic' or 'cultural' distance, etc.); and
- these advantages are best exploited by the firm itself, rather than by selling them to foreign firms. In other words, due to market imperfections (e.g. uncertainty), multinationals choose to bypass the market and 'internalise' the use of ownership-specific advantages via vertical and horizontal integration (such internalisation reduces transaction costs in the presence of market imperfections).

The decisions of multinationals to produce abroad are, therefore, determined by a mixture of motives – ownership-specific, locational and internalisation factors – as noted above.

Sequential theory of internationalisation

Adherents of this approach (sometimes called the 'Uppsala model') include Johanson and Widersheim-Paul (1975), who examined the internationalisation of Swedish firms. They found a regular process of gradual change involving the firm moving *sequentially* through four discrete stages: (1) intermittent exports; (2) exports via agents; (3) overseas sales via knowledge agreements with local firms, for example by licensing or franchising; and (4) foreign direct investment in the overseas market.

This particular sequence is sometimes called the *establishment chain,* the argument being that each of these stages marks a progressive increase in the resource commitment by the firm to the overseas markets involved. There is also a suggestion that as firms move through these sequential stages, the knowledge and information base expands and the 'psychic distance' between themselves and the overseas markets involved contracts, making progression to the next stage that much easier. In this sense the model is dynamic, with the stage already reached by the firm in the internationalisation process helping determine the future course of action likely to be taken. Put another way, the greater the resource commitment to the overseas market and the information and knowledge thereby acquired, the smaller the uncertainty and the perceived risks associated with further internationalisation, leading eventually to foreign direct investment and the establishment of a production affiliate overseas. Firms will move initially to countries that are culturally similar to their own (a close psychic distance) and only later move into culturally diverse geographical areas.

Such a sequential pattern and trajectory has been discernible in Portugal's internationalisation efforts. Typically the first moves were made into the neighbouring economy, Spain. An example of this 'toe in the water' stage was the acquisition by Cimpor, the leading Portuguese cement maker, of Corporación Noroeste, a Spanish cement maker based in Galicia. The next move was for Portuguese firms as diverse as Cenoura, Petrogal, Transportes Luis Simões and Caixa Geral de Depósitos to penetrate the wider Spanish market. As a result of these rapidly expanding two-way flows, an EU regional bloc based in the Iberian peninsula then came into existence during the 1990s as a buoyant new trading area. Using Spain as a springboard, the next natural step for Portugal was into North Africa and the countries that were formerly Portugal's African colonies. The latter were attractive because of language and cultural affinities but also because they were undertaking privatisation programmes, while Brazil became a focal point for economic relations with Mercosur (see Chapter 3). The most recent stage has involved investments in the more advanced EU economies. In some cases, a presence has also been established in Eastern Europe, notably Poland, Hungary and Russia.

Simultaneous theory of internationalisation

Other writers have put forward a *simultaneous view* of internationalisation, based on global convergence. For example, they suggest that customers' tastes around the world are becoming progressively homogeneous, citing the success of such global products as Coca-Cola or Sony Walkman. This approach contends that the economies of scale and scope available for standardised products in such global markets are so substantial that a gradual, sequential approach to internationalisation is no longer practicable. Proponents of this approach point to studies which suggest that the global awareness of brands has fallen dramatically over time, with less than two years now needed for making consumers worldwide aware of high-profile brand images. Critics, however, suggest that there is little evidence for the notion of 'homogenisation' of consumer tastes, indeed quite the opposite, with sophisticated customers demanding greater customisation (see p. 22). Further, although simultaneous entry into a variety of overseas markets may be possible for highly resourced and established firms, it may be out of the question for smaller or less experienced firms.

Network theory

In a network perspective the process of internationalisation is seen as building on existing relationships or creating new relationships in international markets, with the focus shifting from the organisational or economic to that of the social. It is *people* who make the decisions and take the actions.

The series of networks can be considered at three levels.

1 *Macro* – rather than the environment being seen as a set of political, social and economic factors, network theory would see it as a set of diverse interests, powers and characteristics, which may well impinge on national and international business decisions. To enter new markets a firm may have to break old relationships or add new ones. A new entrant may find it difficult to break into a market that already has many stable relationships. Those firms better able to reconfigure their existing networks or which are seeking to enter overseas markets with few existing networked relationships, may be more successful in the internationalisation process.

2 *Inter-organisational* – firms may well stand in different relationships to one another in different markets. They may be competitors in one market, collaborators in another and suppliers and customers to each other in a third. If one firm internationalises, this may draw other firms into the international arena.

3 *Intra-organisational* – relationships within the organisation may well influence the decision-making process. If a multinational has subsidiaries in other countries, decisions may well be taken at the subsidiary level that increase the degree of international involvement of the parent MNE, depending on the degree of decentralisation of decision making permitted by the firm.

The network approach would suggest that internationalisation can be explained, at least in part, by the fact that the other firms and people who are involved in a particular national network themselves internationalise.

International product life cycle (IPLC)

The suggestion here is that the pattern and extent of internationalisation achieved by the firm, and future prospects for continuation of that process, will depend in part on the stage in the IPLC reached by the firm. This approach also sees internationalisation as a process and is considered in more detail in Chapter 3 (p. 86).

Barriers to internationalisation

Whatever the method of internationalisation proposed or undertaken, there are well-documented *barriers* to the internationalisation process. Particular attention has been paid to the barriers faced by small to medium-sized enterprises (SMEs), i.e. companies with fewer than

Table 2.3 Top 10 barriers to SME access to international markets as reported by member economies

Rank	Classification of barrier	Description of barrier
1	Capabilities	Inadequate quantity of and/or untrained personnel for internationalisation
2	Finance	Shortage of working capital to finance exports
3	Access	Limited information to locate/analyse markets
4	Access	Identifying foreign business opportunities
5	Capabilities	Lack of managerial time to deal with internationalisation
6	Capabilities	Inability to contact potential overseas customers
7	Capabilities	Developing new products for foreign markets
8	Business Environment	Unfamiliar foreign business practices
9	Capabilities	Meeting export product quality/standards/specification
10	Access	Unfamiliar exporting procedures/paperwork

Source: Table 1.4, Top ten barriers to SME access to international markets as reported by member economies, *Removing Barriers to SME Access to International Markets* (OECD 2008).

500 employees, when attempting to internationalise. Table 2.3 identifies the top ten barriers identified by the OECD in a large-scale survey within its member economies.

Table 2.3 demonstrates that member economies consider problems which are internal to SMEs to be the main barriers to access to international markets rather than barriers with the external environment, with five out of the top ten citing barriers falling within the *capability* category, and with just one falling within the *business environment* category. A lack of knowledge and scarce internal resources, both financial resources and human resources, feature within the top ten barriers as perceived by SMEs in member economies. External barriers, especially those imposed by governments, score relatively low. 'Unfavourable foreign rules and regulations' is ranked number 22 and 'unfavourable home rules and regulations' is ranked number 44. These findings suggest that knowledge barriers and problems with the development of key capabilities as well as further internal barriers, such as a lack of financial resources and management time and commitment, seem to constitute more serious problems to SMEs trying to internationalise than government-imposed or more general regulatory barriers.

Government support programmes to overcome barriers

Member economies report a wide range of support programmes, some of which are targeted specially at SMEs, while others are open to all firms, subject to specific conditions, such as those operating within special sectors or those offering high growth potential. Individual regions within individual member economies offer additional support programmes, which only firms from this specific region can apply for.

Four categories of support programme have been identified (OECD 2008).

1 *Capabilities support programmes* focus on helping firms to develop internal capabilities which form a critical element of the internationalisation process. This type of programme generally aims at providing firms with the critical resources required for success within their international markets and can be understood theoretically as part of the resource-based view of the firm. Typically, the programmes reported seek to develop the capabilities of the firm and its employees in the following areas: business planning, marketing, training in the area of cultural differences in international markets, language capabilities and knowledge of export procedures. These programmes also support research into

specific technologies, such as production processes, logistics and machinery, aimed at providing a competitive edge to the SME receiving the support.

2 *Access to markets support programmes* focus on gaining initial market access to individual markets, for exporting, sourcing (importing) or local operations. This classification includes the provision of general market information, specific market analysis, the organisation of trade fairs and off-shore assistance through the foreign consulates of the member economies.

3 *Business environment support programmes* tend to concentrate on seeking to remove international trade barriers and on improving the business environment in the home market to give firms a competitive edge, for example through improvements in the domestic taxation.

4 *Financial support programmes* provide support to firms in one of three categories: export insurance and loan guarantees, development finance and venture finance, and direct financial support to cover costs of international activities otherwise not possible, such as export promotion, visits to trade fairs and so on.

Arguments against internationalisation

So far we have reviewed the arguments in favour of an internationalisation strategy and the various methods available. It may, however, be useful to caution against the sometimes excessive enthusiasm for such a strategy. Alexander and Korine (2008) outline various reasons why companies should think carefully before embarking on a global strategy. They propose a 'going-global self-assessment'.

1 *Are there potential benefits for our company?*
   - Where and when would the benefits of globalisation show up in our financial statements?
   - What is the expected economic value of each benefit?
   - How detailed and solid is our understanding of each one?
   - What is the hard evidence that other companies in similar circumstances have been able to realise these benefits in practice?

2 *Do we have the necessary management skills?*
   - What skills are required to realise these benefits?
   - Do we have a clear track record of exhibiting them in the past?
   - Do we know how to further develop them?

3 *Will the costs outweigh the benefits?*
   - What will it cost, in terms of management time and business process investment, to realise the benefits of our globalisation strategy?
   - What would sceptics inside our various business units say about the cost of globalisation and its potential impact on their local performance?
   - What would be the most productive alternative use of all the resources that we plan to devote to our globalisation strategy?

Certainly 'failed' internationalisation strategies have been well documented in recent years (Case 2.12) and a stringent self-assessment *prior* to embarking on internationalisation strategies might have helped avoid some of these.

CASE 2.12 Internationalisation may not always deliver!

The experience of many multinationals in recent years would suggest a cautionary approach be taken to internationalisation. Royal Ahold is a Dutch supermarket operator which began its international expansion in the 1970s, acquiring related businesses throughout Europe, Asia, Latin America and the US, and eventually becoming the fourth largest retailer in the world in the early years of the millennium. Yet in 2007 the pressure of dissatisfied shareholders had forced the company to abandon its globalisation strategy and sell most of its US and other global operations to private equity firms. Critics point to unrealistic expectations of global-scale economies (see Chapter 7) in food retailing, with purchasing economies available mainly on items provided by global suppliers to all markets – typically no more than 20% of all supermarket items. The need to match cultural differences in food tastes and methods of serving food products is important here. Critics also point to a failure by Royal Ahold to integrate effective management and IT systems across its far-flung international operations, for example key suppliers were still able to charge Ahold different prices in different countries as recently as 2007.

Daimler Benz (Germany) merged with Chrysler (US) in 1998 to create a global car company. Karl Benz had constructed the first automobile in 1886, at which time Gottlieb Daimler was active in the same field of business. After years of partnership their businesses were formally integrated in 1926 as the Daimler-Benz Company. In the 1980s Daimler-Benz pursued a strategy of diversification, acquiring MTU, AEG, the aeroplane companies Dornier, MBB and Fokker, the latter completing the aviation arm of Daimler-Benz. The vision of the chairman (Mr Reuter) was to transform the firm from a car maker into an integrated technology group along the lines of General Electric or the Japanese Mitsubishi conglomerate. His vision included generating cross-border synergies between the automobile, aeroplane and electronics industries, exchanging skills and knowledge, and spreading the company's risks over the many businesses in its portfolio. On 6 May 1998 a new chapter in Daimler's M&A history began: Daimler-Benz AG and Chrysler Corporation announced their merger and the creation of the new DaimlerChrysler AG.

Expected synergies included a more complete product portfolio, with DaimlerChrysler stronger in the high price end of the market and Chrysler in the medium to low price end. Indeed, except in the 'off-road' segment there were no product overlaps – rather the respective product portfolios complemented one another. This was also the case in terms of their geographical markets, with Chrysler a strong player in the NAFTA region, while Daimler-Benz was a leading company in Europe. Daimler-Chrysler AG subsequently moved to acquire a third leg in the Asian market to consolidate its position in all regions of the triad. Further synergies were expected in fields such as procurement, common use of parts and sales.

In the event, after years of poor financial returns, Chrysler was sold for $1 to the private equity firm Cerberus in 2007, with cultural dissonance between the German and US arms of the company cited by many as a key underlying factor in this corporate failure.

A similar story can be recounted as regards the Dutch financial services firm ABN Amro, which acquired banks worldwide but failed to generate the expected return on its global investments. Critics point to unrealistic expectations of the Dutch bank being able to dominate overseas retail banking markets such as Italy and Brazil, when consolidation of local banks with other international banks had already taken place in these countries. ABN Amro was sold off, in 2007, with various parts going to Royal Bank of Scotland, Fortis (Belgium) and Banco Santander (Spain).

Questions

1 Identify some of the factors lying behind these and other 'failures' of internationalisation strategies in recent years.

2 Suggest approaches that might reduce the risks of such 'failures'.

Chapter 3

International business: theory and practice

By the end of this chapter you should be able to:

- outline the arguments used to support free trade between nations;
- identify the sources of comparative and competitive advantage between nations;
- discuss the nature and importance of both inter-industry and intra-industry trade in a global economy;
- assess the arguments and practices used to support protectionism;
- examine the impacts of a range of government policies and practices on inter-national business;
- review the role of organisations such as the World Trade Organisation (WTO), World Bank, International Monetary Fund (IMF) and others in the conduct of inter-national business.

Introduction

Most international business is conducted in a context in which the major players believe such business to be of benefit to themselves, to the nation states they represent and even to the broader international community. It would therefore seem appropriate to review the theoretical basis for trade at the outset of this chapter before moving on to discuss some of the issues and practices involving protectionism. The institutions and organisations that underpin the present system of global trade and payments, such as the World Trade Organisation (WTO), World Bank and International Monetary Fund (IMF) are reviewed, together with some recent proposals for reform. Since the European Union plays such a key role in the UK's international business environment, it is considered in some detail in this chapter.

Gains from trade

Absolute advantage

As long ago as 1776, Adam Smith in his *Wealth of Nations* suggested that countries could benefit from specialising in products in which they had an *absolute advantage* over other countries, trading any surpluses with those countries. By 'absolute advantage' Smith meant the ability to produce those products at lower resource cost (e.g. fewer labour and capital inputs) than the other countries.

This was an essentially limited view as to the benefits of international business. For example, in a simple two-country, two-product model, each country would have to demonstrate that it was absolutely more efficient than the other in one of these products if specialisation and trade were to be mutually beneficial.

This can be outlined by reference to Table 3.1, which presents hypothetical data for countries A and B.

With one unit of resource, country A can produce 20 units of textiles or 40 units of steel. With the same amount of resource country B can produce 80 units of textiles or 20 units of steel.

In terms of steel production, one unit of resource in country A can produce twice as much output as one unit of resource in country B. However, in terms of textile production, one unit of resource in country B can produce an output which is four times greater than that in country A. In this situation country A is said to have an *absolute advantage* in the production of steel and country B an *absolute advantage* in the production of textiles.

It can be shown that both countries can then gain by specialising in the production of the product in which they have an absolute advantage. This can be seen in Table 3.2, where, by real locating one unit of resource from textiles to steel in country A and one unit of resource from steel to textiles in country B, world output of *both* products can be increased. This additional world output of both textiles and steel is then traded to the benefit of both countries. There are gains to be made, therefore, from specialisation and trade according to absolute advantage.

Comparative advantage

David Ricardo sought, in 1817, to broaden the basis on which trade was seen to be beneficial by developing his theory of *comparative advantage*. Again, we can illustrate this by using a simple two-country, two-product model. In this approach even where a country has an absolute

Table 3.1 **Absolute advantage**

	Output from one unit of resource:	
	Textiles	Steel
Country A	20	40
Country B	80	20

Table 3.2 **The gains made from the movement of one unit of resource**

	Textiles	Steel	Movement of one unit of resource from:
Country A	−20	+40	textiles to steel
Country B	+80	−20	steel to textiles
World output	+60	+20	

Table 3.3 **Comparative advantage**

	Output from one unit of resource:	
	Textiles	**Steel**
Country A	320	40
Country B	80	20

advantage (less resource cost) over the other country in *both* products, it can still gain by specialisation and trade in that product in which its *absolute advantage is greatest,* i.e. in which it has a *comparative advantage.* Similarly, the other country that has an absolute disadvantage (higher resource cost) in both products can still gain by specialisation and trade in that product in which its *absolute disadvantage is least,* i.e. in which it also has a *comparative advantage.*

This example is illustrated in Table 3.3, where country A is more efficient in the production of both textiles and steel. The difference between Tables 3.3 and 3.1 is that country A has improved its output of textiles per unit of resource, possibly through technological change in the textile industry. Although country A is better at producing (has an absolute advantage in) both products, there are still gains to be made through specialisation and trade since country A is *relatively* more efficient in the production of textiles.

This can be seen by referring to Table 3.3, which shows country A is four times better at producing textiles than country B but only two times better at producing steel. In this situation country A is said to have a *comparative advantage* in the production of textiles. Country B is one-quarter as good as A at producing textile but half as good as A at producing steel. While B has, therefore, an absolute disadvantage in both products, it is *relatively* least inefficient in the production of steel. In this situation Country B is said to have a *comparative advantage* in the production of steel.

The result of specialisation in the two countries according to comparative advantages means there are gains to be made through trade which can benefit both countries, as illustrated in Table 3.4.

By reallocating resources within the two countries so that each produces more of the product in which it has a comparative advantage (A in textiles, B in steel) it is possible to increase world output, and so there are gains to be made from specialisation and trade. For example, by reallocating one unit of resource from steel to textiles in country A and three units of resource from textiles to steel in country B, it is possible to increase world output by 80 units of textiles and 20 units of steel.

Comparative advantage and opportunity cost

In developing the theory of comparative advantage it is possible to use the concept of *opportunity cost,* defined here as the output forgone by producing one more unit of a particular

Table 3.4 **Gains made from the reallocation of resources in a comparative advantage situation**

	Textiles	**Steel**	**Movement of resources:**
Country A	+320	−40	1 unit of resource from steel to textiles
Country B	−240	+60	3 units of resource from textiles to steel
World output	+80	+20	

Table 3.5 **Opportunity cost ratios**

	Opportunity cost of producing one extra unit of textiles	**Opportunity cost of producing one extra unit of steel**
Country A	$^1/_8$ unit of steel	8 units of textiles
Country B	$^1/_4$ unit of steel	4 units of textiles

product. Referring back to Table 3.3, if it is assumed that all resources are fully employed then it is only possible to produce one more unit of one commodity if resources are reallocated from the production of the other commodity. In country A, the production of one extra unit of textiles requires one-eighth of a unit of steel to be sacrificed. In country B, the production of one extra unit of textiles requires one-quarter of a unit of steel to be sacrificed. In country A, the production of one extra unit of steel requires eight units of textiles to be sacrificed, whereas in country B the production of one extra unit of steel only requires four units of textiles to be sacrificed. The opportunity cost ratios are summarised in Table 3.5.

Ricardo's theory of comparative advantage for a two-country, two-product model can be re-expressed in terms of *opportunity costs*:

A *country* has a comparative advantage in that product for which it has a lower opportunity cost than the other country.

In terms of Table 3.5, country A has a comparative advantage in *textiles* (one-eighth steel sacrificed is less than one-quarter steel sacrificed), whereas country B has a comparative advantage in steel (four units of textiles is lower than eight units of textiles sacrificed).

Let us now check whether specialisation and trade according to the comparative advantage we have identified really does provide potential benefits for both countries. Suppose country A produces one extra unit of textiles and country B one less unit of textiles (it specialises in steel). We then have the outcome shown in Table 3.6.

In producing one *extra* unit of textiles, A *sacrifices* one-eighth unit of steel. However in producing one *less* unit of textiles, B *gains* four units of steel. By this marginal re-allocation of resources according to our revised definition of comparative advantages (lower opportunity costs), total output of textiles is unchanged but total output of steel has risen. There is clearly potential for this extra output of steel to be traded to the benefit of *both* countries, provided the terms of trade are appropriate.

Limitations of the theory of comparative advantage

Limitations of the theory can be seen as:

- *Returns to scale.* The theory assumes constant opportunity costs, i.e. constant returns to scale, thus ignoring the possibility that economies or diseconomies of scale can be obtained as output increases.

Table 3.6 **Specialisation according to comparative advantages (lower opportunity costs)**

	Textiles	Steel
Country A	+1	$-^1/_8$
Country B	1	+ 4
	0	$3^7/_8$

- *Full employment.* The assumption is made that there is full employment of the factors of production. Thus, as specialisation takes place, those resources freed by one sector are automatically transferred to the sector in which the country is specialising. This assumption means that it is possible to calculate the opportunity costs.

- *Reciprocal demand.* The theory assumes what is known as *double coincidence of wants*. This means that in the example we have used, following specialisation, country A should demand steel from country B, and country B textiles from country A.

- *Transport costs.* Transport costs are not included in the theory of comparative advantage. Transport costs, however, increase production costs and therefore offset some of the potential gains made through specialisation.

- *Factor mobility.* The theory assumes that resources can be reallocated from the production of one product to another. In the real world, however, resources are likely to be immobile. In the example used above, it is unlikely that resources can be freely moved from steel to textile production or from textile to steel production.

- *Free trade.* Free trade is an obvious assumption of the theory of comparative advantage. There are no trade barriers such as tariffs and quotas, for these would limit the scope for specialisation in the two countries. This is unlikely to be the case in the real world.

Ricardo's theory is further developed in Box 3.1, with opportunity costs, terms of trade and diagrammatic representations all used to emphasise the potential benefits from specialisation and trade according to comparative advantages.

BOX 3.1 Comparative advantage and opportunity cost

Ricardo's theory can be illustrated using Table 3.7, where, for simplicity, we assume each country to have the same amounts of resources (e.g. labour and capital) available for producing two products: CDs and videos. Initially the analysis will also assume constant returns in producing each product. Table 3.7 shows the production possibilities if each country devotes all its (identical) resources to the production of either CDs or videos.

From Table 3.7 we can see that country A has an absolute advantage in both products (greater output for the same resource input) but a *comparative advantage in videos*. This is because although A is twice as efficient as B in CDs, it is four times as efficient as B in videos. Therefore, according to the principle of comparative advantage, country A should specialise in videos and trade these for the CDs that B produces.

By similar reasoning, from Table 3.7 we can see that country B has an absolute disadvantage in both products (less output for the same resource input) but *a comparative advantage in CDs*. This is because, although B is only one-quarter as efficient as A in videos, it is one-half as efficient as A in CDs. Therefore, according to the principle of comparative advantage, country B should specialise in CDs and trade these for the videos that A produces.

Table 3.7 Production possibilities in a two-product, two-country model

Country	Output of CDs	Output of videos
A	2,000	800
B	1,000	200

Box 3.1 (*continued*)

A country has a *comparative advantage* (in a two-product model) in that product in which its *absolute advantage is greatest* or in which its *absolute disadvantage is least*.

This idea of comparative advantage can be expressed in terms of *opportunity cost* (see Table 3.8), defined here as the output forgone by producing one more unit of a particular product. In country A, for example, the production of an extra video has an opportunity cost of only 2.5 CDs, whereas for country B the production of an extra video has an opportunity cost of 5 CDs. In other words, country A has a lower opportunity cost in video production than country B, and therefore has a *comparative advantage* in video production, even though it has an *absolute advantage* in both products.

Similarly, country B can produce an extra CD at an opportunity cost of one-fifth (0.2) of a video, whereas country A can only produce an extra CD at an opportunity cost of two-fifths (0.4) of a video. In other words, country B has a lower opportunity cost and therefore *comparative advantage* in CD production, even though it has an *absolute disadvantage* in both products.

A country has a *comparative advantage* (in a two-product model) in that product in which it has a *lower opportunity* cost than the other country. We would conclude that country A has a comparative advantage in videos and country B a comparative advantage in CDs.

Table 3.8 **Opportunity costs in a two-product, two-country model**

Country	Opportunity cost of 1 extra CD	Opportunity cost of 1 extra video
A	0.4 videos	2.5 CDs
B	0.2 videos	5.0 CDs

Gains from specialisation and trade

We can show the potential benefits from specialisation and trade according to comparative advantages in a number of different ways. Clearly a country will benefit if, by specialisation and trade, it can reach a consumption situation better than that which would result from being self-sufficient. Suppose that initially each country tries to be self-sufficient, using half its resources to produce videos and half to produce CDs. This gives us the *self-sufficiency* consumption bundles of *CA* (1,000 CDs, 400 videos) and *CB* (500 CDs, 100 videos) respectively. Provided that the *terms of trade* (i.e. the rate at which videos exchange for CDs) are appropriate, each country can be shown to benefit from specialisation and trade according to comparative advantages.

In Figure 3.1(a), with terms of trade of 1 video:3 CDs, country A specialises in videos and trades 250 of its 800 videos for 750 CDs (from B), ending at the consumption bundle of C'_A (750 CDs, 550 videos). Since C'_A is *outside* its production possibility frontier, country A could not have achieved this consumption bundle by being self-sufficient.

If the *terms of trade* are appropriate, both countries can gain from *specialisation and trade according to comparative advantages*.

In Figure 3.1(b), with the same terms of trade of 1 video:3 CDs, country B specialises in CDs and trades 750 of its 1,000 CDs for 250 videos (from A), ending at the consumption

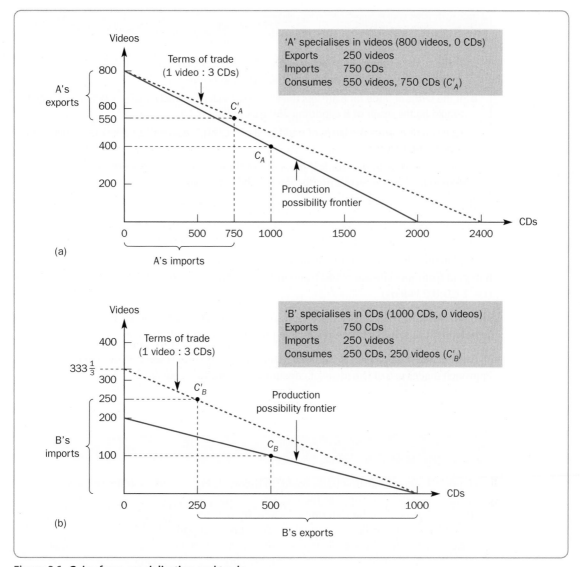

Figure 3.1 Gains from specialisation and trade

bundle of C'_B (250 CDs, 250 videos). Since C'_B is *outside* its production possibility frontier, country B could not have achieved this consumption bundle by being self-sufficient.

You should be able to see from Figure 3.1(a) that at terms of trade of *less than* 1 video:2.5 CDs, country A will be better off by being self-sufficient than by specialising in videos and trading them for CDs. In other words, the slope of A's production possibility frontier represents the 'worst' terms A is prepared to accept if it is to engage in specialisation and trade according to comparative advantages. Similarly, from Figure 3.1(b) we can see that at terms of trade of *less than* 1 CD:0.2 videos, country B will be better off by being self-sufficient than by specialising in CDs and trading them for videos. In other words, the slope of B's production possibility frontier represents the 'worst' terms B is prepared to accept if it is to engage in specialisation and trade according to comparative advantages.

We can therefore say that the terms of trade which will enable *both* country A and country B to gain from specialisation and trade must lie between 1 video:2.5 CDs and 1 video:5 CDs (i.e. 1 CD:0.2 videos).

The *terms of trade* which will enable both countries to gain from specialisation and trade must lie between the slopes of their respective production possibility frontiers.

An alternative approach to demonstrating the gains from trade is shown in Box 3.2. This approach makes use of the ideas of consumer and producer surplus.

BOX 3.2 Gains from trade

Figure 3.2 shows that free trade could, in theory, bring welfare benefits to an economy previously protected. Suppose the industry is initially completely protected. The domestic price P_D will then be determined solely by the intersection of the domestic supply ($S_D - S_D$) and domestic demand ($D_D - D_D$) curves. Suppose that the government now decides to remove these trade barriers and to allow foreign competition. For simplicity, we assume a perfectly elastic 'world' supply curve $P_W - C$, giving a total supply curve (domestic and world) of $S_D AC$. Domestic price will then be forced down to the world level P_W, with domestic demand being $0Q_3$ at this price. To meet this domestic demand, $0Q_2$ will be supplied from domestic sources, with Q_2Q_3 supplied from the rest of the world (i.e. imported). The *consumer surplus,* which is the difference between what consumers are prepared to pay and what they have to pay, has risen from $D_D BP_D$ to $D_D CP_W$. The *producer surplus,* which is the difference between the price the producer receives and the minimum necessary to induce production, has fallen from $P_D BS_D$ to $P_W AS_D$. The gain in consumer surplus outweighs the loss in producer surplus by the area ABC, which could then be regarded as the net gain in economic welfare as a result of free trade replacing protectionism.

Box 3.2 (continued)

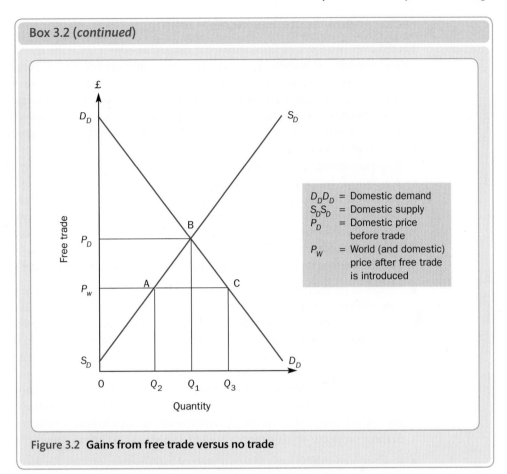

Figure 3.2 **Gains from free trade versus no trade**

Pause for thought 3.2

In the analysis above, what has happened to the area $P_W P_D BA$?

Sources of comparative and competitive advantage

We have seen that countries can gain from trade by specialising in those products in which they have a lower opportunity cost (i.e. a comparative advantage) vis-à-vis other countries and trading surpluses with those countries. An obvious question then presents itself: what is it that gives one country a comparative advantage in certain products over other countries? We briefly review a number of theories that have sought to answer this question.

Factor endowments: Heckscher–Ohlin

Named after two Swedish economists, the Heckscher–Ohlin (HO) theory suggests that *factor endowments* will broadly determine the pattern of trade between nations. The idea here is that those countries with an abundance of certain types of factor (labour, capital, natural resources, etc.) will be able to produce products that embody those abundant factors relatively more cheaply than other, less well endowed, countries. In its simplest form a labour-abundant country will be able to produce (and export) labour-intensive products relatively more cheaply than a labour-scarce country, and so on.

Empirical testing of the HO theory, however, has provided little support for it being a major explanation of observed patterns of trade, even when more complex forms of the theory have been devised. For example, international trade is larger in volume and value terms between the *similar* developed (advanced industrialised) economies rather than between the *dissimilar* (in terms of factor endowments) developed and less developed economies. This is, of course, the opposite to what we might have expected from the HO theory.

Possible reasons for these 'disappointing' empirical results might include the following:

- Factors of production – such as labour, capital, etc. – are hardly homogeneous so aggregate statements such as 'labour abundant' may be relatively meaningless. For example, labour can be broken down into many different skill levels, capital into different levels of technological intensity (e.g. high, medium and low technology), etc. In this case it may make little sense to regard a country as having a comparative advantage in, say, labour-intensive products merely because it is labour abundant vis-à-vis some other country. To compare 'like with like' we may need to disaggregate labour (and any other factor) into its component parts. Only then might we be able to say that a country is labour abundant in, say, high-skilled labour and might therefore be expected to have a comparative advantage in those products which intensively embody high-skilled labour inputs.

- Products may exhibit *factor intensity reversal* in different countries. For example, producing certain types of car in Japan (with higher real wages) is likely to be a more capital-intensive process than producing the same car in, say, Spain (with lower real wages). The suggestion here is that the higher *relative* price ratio of labour:capital in Japan than in Spain may provide greater incentives to substitute capital for labour in Japan than would be the case in Spain. Where substantial differences in such factor price ratios exist, there might even be factor intensity reversal, with a given product using relatively capital-intensive processes in one country but relatively labour-intensive processes in another.

- Factor and product markets must be competitive if differences in factor endowments and therefore factor productivities are to be reflected in differences in product costs. In reality, imperfections in factor markets (existence of unions, large employers, employer confederations, etc.) and in product markets (monopoly or oligopoly, public sector involvement, etc.) may well result in prices diverging markedly from actual marginal production costs.

- The *terms of trade* between the potential exported and imported products may lie outside the limits which would permit trade to be beneficial to both parties (see pp. 78–80). For example, the export:import price ratio may be influenced in arbitrary ways by unexpected fluctuations in relative exchange rates, etc.

- A host of other market imperfections may distort the linkage between factor endowment, actual production costs and the relative prices at which products are exchanged on international markets. Differences between countries in the degree of multinational or governmental involvement in a given sector, in the market structure of production in that sector or in terms of other types of 'market failure' can be expected to break any simple linkage between relative factor endowment and relative product prices.

For all these reasons it may be unsurprising that little empirical evidence exists to suggest that different national factor endowments have played a major part in explaining the observed patterns of international trade flows.

The discussion on increasing *intra-regional* and *inter-regional* trade (pp. 91–92) also has a bearing on why the factor endowment theory appears to be less useful in recent times as an explanation of actual trade patterns.

Disaggregated factor endowments

More refined versions of HO have tried to disaggregate the factors of production into units that are more homogeneous for purposes of comparison between countries.

- *Efficiency units.* Here labour and capital inputs are adjusted to take account of productivity differentials. So if American workers are twice as productive in manufacturing as, say, Thai workers, the number of American workers should be multiplied by two when comparing labour factor endowment between the two countries in terms of 'efficiency units'.

- *Human capital.* Workers can be disaggregated by *level* of human capital (e.g. years of education, experience, etc.) and by *type* of human capital (e.g. vocational/non-vocational, marketing/non-marketing, etc.). Again, we can then apply 'weights' to any raw data we might have when comparing labour factor endowment between countries.

Revealed comparative advantage

The suggestion here is that the sources of comparative advantage can be determined indirectly by *observing* actual trade flows between countries. For example, it is interesting to note that in the more dynamic sectors of UK industry, there are signs of a shift towards the higher end of the quality market for both UK manufacturing exports and for the production of substitutes for manufacturing imports. In other words, the data arguably suggests a *revealed comparative advantage* for the UK in terms of more technologically intensive manufacturing exports and imports (substitutes).

Competitive advantage: Porter

Michael Porter (1990) has attempted to explain the critical factors for success in both national and international production and exchange in terms of *competitive advantages.*

Competitive advantage: corporate

In the *corporate* context, the competitive advantages of a company are defined in terms of the 'marginal' company in that sector of economic activity. In other words, they are the collection of reasons that allow the more successful companies to create positive added value (profits) in that sector of economic activity as compared to the 'marginal' company, which is just managing to survive. Reasons for such competitive advantages could include some or all of the following:

- *architecture,* benefits to the company from some distinctive aspect of the set of contractual relationships the company has entered into with suppliers and/or customers;

- *innovation,* benefits to the company from being more innovative than rivals (perhaps re-inforced by legal structures, e.g. patent laws);
- *incumbency advantages,* benefits to the company from being an early 'player' in that field of activity (reputation, control over scarce resources, etc.).

Pause for thought 3.3

Can you give examples of these sources of competitive advantage using major international businesses?

The essential feature about many of these sources of competitive advantage is that they are usually *temporary.* Distinctive contractual relationships that prove to be successful (e.g. franchising arrangements) can be replicated by other firms, patents that protect innovation eventually expire and even incumbency advantages may not last. New sources of raw materials or other factor inputs may be found, technical change may alter production possibilities and even reputations can be transposed from other fields of economic activity (e.g. Virgin taking its reputation for quality/efficiency in entertainment/transport, etc. into financial services operations). Companies must continually seek new sources of competitive advantage if they are to avoid becoming themselves the 'marginal' firm in any sector of economic activity.

Competitive advantage: national

In the *national* context, Porter has again used this perspective of a dynamic, ever-changing set of competitive advantages as a basis for explaining trade patterns between countries. Porter sees both *product innovation* and *process innovation* as key elements in determining national competitive advantages. In his view these dynamic elements far outweigh the more static elements of 'factor endowments' in determining success in international trading relationships; still more so when technology is constantly changing the optimal combination of capital/labour/natural resource inputs for a product, when multinationals are so 'footloose' that they can readily relocate across national boundaries and when capital markets provide investment finance on an increasingly global basis.

Porter identifies six key variables as potentially giving a country a competitive advantage over other countries:

1 *demand conditions:* the extent and characteristics of domestic demand;

2 *factor conditions:* transport infrastructure, national resources, human capital endowments, etc.;

3 *firm strategies: structures and rivalries:* the organisation and management of companies and the degree of competition in the market structures in which they operate;

4 *related and supporting industries:* quality and extent of supply industries, supporting business services, etc.;

5 *government policies:* nature of the regulatory environment, extent of state intervention in industry and the regions, state support for education and vocational training, etc.;

6 *chance.*

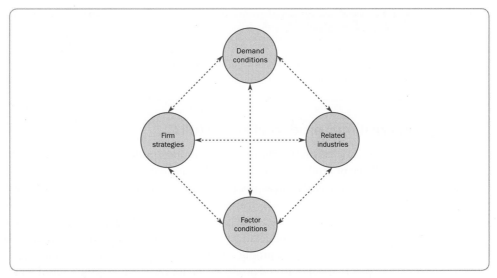

Figure 3.3 The determinants of national competitive advantage
Source: Based on Porter, M. (1998); Griffiths, A. and Wall, S. (2011); Sloman, J. and Jones, E. (2014).

Porter's diamond

The first four of these variables form a *diamond* shape, as shown in Figure 3.3, when mapped as the most important determinants of national competitive advantage.

In Porter's view, the four determinants are interdependent. For example, favourable 'demand conditions' will only contribute to national competitive advantage when combined with appropriate 'factor conditions', 'related and supporting industries' and 'firm strategies: structures and rivalries' so that companies are *able* and *willing* to take advantage of the favourable demand conditions. To sustain national competitive advantages in modern, high-technology industries and economies, Porter argues that all four determinants in the 'diamond' must be favourable. However, in less technology-intensive industries and economies, one or two of the four determinants being favourable may be sufficient for a national competitive advantage: e.g. natural resource dependent industries may only need favourable 'factor conditions' (presence of an important natural resource) and appropriate infrastructure to extract and transport that resource.

The last two determinants – 'government policies' and 'chance' – outlined above can interact with the four key determinants of the diamond to open up new opportunities (and threats) for national competitive advantage. For example, government policies in the field of education and training may help create R&D and other knowledge-intensive competitive advantage for a nation. Similarly, 'chance' events can play a part, as in the case of Russia supporting a greater US presence in Uzbekistan during the war in Afghanistan, thereby creating new opportunities for US oil companies to exploit the huge oil resources in that country. More recently, Russian annexation of Crimea in 2014, and the subsequent turmoil in Eastern Ukraine, has resulted in increased support for 'fracking' and other policies for promoting energy independence from Russian oil and gas supplies.

Pause for thought 3.4

Can you identify some possible impacts of increased international security concerns in terms of national competitive advantage?

International product life cycle (IPLC)

The suggestion here is that the pattern of products traded between countries will be influenced by the stage of production reached in the international life cycle of a variety of knowledge-intensive products. The *new product stage* (invention/development) will typically occur in the (advanced industrialised) innovating country but then the balance between production and consumption (and therefore between export and import) may shift *geographically* as different stages of the product life cycle are reached. In Figure 3.4 we can see a stylised IPLC for a knowledge-intensive product over three stages of the product life cycle (new product, mature product, standardised product) and for three broad geographical regions (innovating country, other advanced countries, less developed countries – LDCs).

- *New product stage.* Here production is concentrated in the *innovating country,* as is market demand. A typical scenario for this stage would be where the (initially) relatively low output is sold at premium prices to a price-inelastic domestic market segment (with few, if any, exports). There may be a small amount of production via subsidiaries in 'other advanced countries' but little or none in the LDCs.

- *Mature product stage.* Both production and consumption typically continue to rise in the *innovating country,* with scale economies beginning to reduce costs and price to a new, more price-sensitive mass market segment. Exports to other countries become a higher proportion of total sales. Output of the generic product also rises in the 'other advanced countries', via the output of subsidiaries or of competitors in these countries which have the knowledge-intensive capability of developing close substitutes. These countries typically import a high proportion of their sales from the innovating country, as do the LDCs.

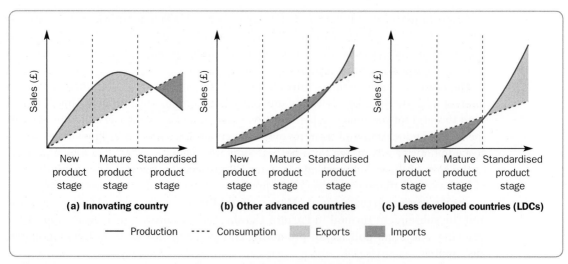

Figure 3.4 **The international product life cycle (IPLC) for knowledge-intensive products**

● *Standardised product stage.* At this stage the technology becomes more widely diffused and is often largely 'embodied' in both capital equipment and process control. Low-cost locations become a more feasible source of quality supply in this stage, often via MNE outsourcing and technology transfer. The LDCs may even become net exporters to the innovating country and to other advanced countries.

Some of the issues previously discussed are raised in Case 3.1, which looks at the North American Free Trade Agreement (NAFTA) in the 20 years since its signature by the US, Canada and Mexico.

CASE 3.1 Free trade and its impacts: NEFTA

In 2014, twenty years after Bill Clinton signed the North American Free Trade Agreement, its very name chills the spines of US voters and congressmen alike. Even advocates of new regional trade agreements insist that they are not proposing 'another NAFTA'. Yet NAFTA-phobia is irrational. None of the terrible things that were, according to its opponents, supposed to result from its implementation have in fact occurred. Members of the free-trade area – Canada, Mexico and the US – enjoy a large joint market and a common supply chain. Consumers in all three countries have gained.

It is true that America's less-skilled workers have received an increasingly raw deal since the 1970s. But NAFTA is not to blame. To claim otherwise is at best to mistake coincidence for causation. At worst it is a cynical tactic employed to protect special interests at the expense of the common good. Econometric studies have established that when US companies invest abroad the net result is increased employment, stronger demand and more investment at home. This makes sense, since it should on average be the more competitive businesses that have the resources and opportunities to expand abroad, and investing should increase their productivity. This conclusion applies specifically to US companies that have invested in Mexico. Recent research has found that, on average, for every 100 jobs US manufacturers created in Mexican manufacturing, they added nearly 250 jobs at their larger US home operations, and increased their US research and development spending by 3%.

At least until the 2008 financial crisis, US unemployment rates were much lower in the decades following NAFTA than before the agreement came into effect, even at a time when the US labour force was growing steadily. Doomsayers claimed that after NAFTA, US exports of corn and other agricultural products would lead to a surge of displaced Mexican farmers drifting northward, which did not in fact occur.

True, there have been job losses as a result of competition from Mexican (and Canadian) exports. Some critics of NAFTA estimate these at an average of 45,000 a year over the past two decades. But out of a US workforce of 135m workers – between 4m and 6m of whom leave or lose their jobs every month – that is less than 0.1% of turnover. What about the 4m or more other American workers who change jobs every month, many of whom are forced to do so through no fault of their own? It is unclear why someone who loses their job because digital photography replaces film, or because the taste for business-casual clothes decreases demand for suits, or because an industrial plant moves from California to Texas, is any less deserving of support than someone who loses their job because assembly of computers and flat screen televisions moves to Mexico. It is clear, though, that since such a tiny fraction

➡

Case 3.1 (*continued*)

of total labour force churn in the US is due to NAFTA that the NAFTA deal cannot be a significant cause of wage or employment conditions at home.

Many on the left in the US nevertheless use international trade, and especially NAFTA, as a scapegoat for the weakening of labour rights and growing inequality. Others have tried to use trade legislation as a bargaining chip with which to secure concessions on extending the American welfare state – something that conservatives oppose.

Questions

1 Examine the arguments in favour of free trade in general, and free trade between the three members of NAFTA in particular.

2 What arguments are used against NAFTA by its critics?

Trade and the world economy

The rapid growth of world trade over the past century reflects, at least in part, the fact that nations have become more interrelated as they have attempted to gain the benefits of freer trade. Table 3.9 compares the *relative growth* of world trade and world output from 1870 to the present day. It shows that the growth rate of world merchandise trade (exports) has exceeded the growth of world output (GDP) in five of the six periods. The only exception to this pattern occurred in the period 1913 to 1950 when two world wars and a major world depression resulted in the widespread adoption of protectionist trade policies. The post-Second World War period (1950–73) saw an unprecedented growth of world trade which far outstripped the growth of world production, as continued to a lesser extent in the 1973–2007 period. Even the recessionary period of 2008–13 has still recorded strong annual growth in exports. While such data cannot prove causation, we can at least say that growth in world trade is consistent with rising economic prosperity.

It may be useful at this point to consider the *type* of trade flow which underlies the recorded growth in world trade.

Table 3.9 Growth in world GDP and merchandise trade 1870–2013 (average annual % change)

	1870–1900	1900–13	1913–50	1950–73	1973–2007	2008–13
GDP	2.9	2.5	2.0	5.1	3.0	2.3
Trade (exports)	3.8	4.3	0.6	8.2	5.1	3.2

Source: Adapted from WTO, *International Trade Statistics* (various) and *Annual Reports* (various).

Type of trade flow

A distinction is frequently made between inter- and intra-industry trade.

- *Inter-industry* trade refers to situations where a country exports products that are fundamentally different in type from those that it imports. The UK exporting computer software to Switzerland but importing precision watches from Switzerland would be an example of inter-industry trade between two countries.

- *Intra-industry trade* refers to situations where a country exports certain items from a given product range while at the same time importing other items from the same product range. The UK exporting certain types of car to Germany but importing other types of car from Germany would be an example of intra-industry trade. Over half of world trade today is intra-industry trade, which consists of final goods, intermediate goods and primary goods (raw materials, etc.).

World *intra-industry* trade in intermediate goods, such as components, semi-finished manufactures, etc., has grown the fastest, more than doubling since 1962, with the growth in intra-industry trade in final goods only narrowly behind.

It is worth noting that intra-industry trade in *intermediate goods* will be more sensitive to changes in transport costs than such trade in *final goods*. For example, if intermediate inputs are two-thirds of the value-added for producing a final good, then a 10% increase in transport costs is the equivalent of a 20% increase in VAT on the final product. This heightened sensitivity to transport costs of intermediate goods, which we have seen to be the fastest growing segment of international trade (not least because of progressively geographically dispersed value chains), emphasises the importance of transport costs to the potential growth of global trade.

Clearly the likely explanations for the growth of world trade will be different for each type of trade flow. Factor endowment and other comparative advantage theories are often used in attempts to explain *inter-industry* trade patterns, whereas the activities of multinationals, the international product life cycle and various types of competitive advantage theories are more usually used to account for *intra-industry* trade patterns.

This point is usefully emphasised in the following quotation from the *World Development Report* (World Bank 2009: 170):

> During the first wave [of globalisation] from about 1840 to World War 1, transport costs fell enough to make large scale trade possible between places based on their comparative advantage. So Britain traded machinery for Indian tea, Argentine beef and Australian wool; trade increased between *dissimilar countries.* During the second wave [of globalisation] after 1950, transport costs fell low enough that small differences in products and tastes fuelled trade between *similar countries,* at least in Europe and North America. Neighbours traded different types of beer and different parts of cars, such as wheels and tyres. Trade in parts and components grew to take advantage of specialization and economies of scale. The first wave of globalization was characterized by 'conventional', *inter-industry* trade that exploited differences in natural endowments, the second by a 'new international trade' driven by economies of scale and product differentiation.

Most empirical studies suggest, therefore, that it is the growth in *intra-industry* trade flows that have made the greatest contribution to the recorded growth in world trade. The experience of Honda provides a useful case of the role the multinationals often play in promoting such patterns of trade.

CASE 3.2 Intra-industry trade: Honda

Figure 3.5 shows the Honda motorcycle network in Europe together with its outside supply links. Honda has been the world's largest motorcycle manufacturer since 1959, and is very much a multinational company with a transnationality index of over 80% in recent years. In other words, the average of the following ratios exceeds 80% for Honda: foreign assets/total assets, foreign sales/total sales and foreign employment/total employment. Honda began its operations by exporting motorcycles from Japan to Europe, but this was quickly followed by its first European overseas production affiliate in 1962. This affiliate, Honda Benelux NV (Belgium) was set up to provide a 'learning' opportunity before

Honda brought its motorcycle and automobile production to Europe. Figure 3.5 shows that Honda's operations have widened significantly, with its affiliates in Germany acting as its main European regional headquarters. Honda Deutschland GmbH co-ordinates the production and marketing side, while Honda R&D Europe is engaged in research, engineering and designing for all the affiliates in Europe.

Honda's key assembly affiliates are Honda Industriale SpA (Italy), which is wholly owned, and Montessa Honda SA (Spain) which is majority owned (88%). These companies were originally designed to concentrate on the assembly of specific types

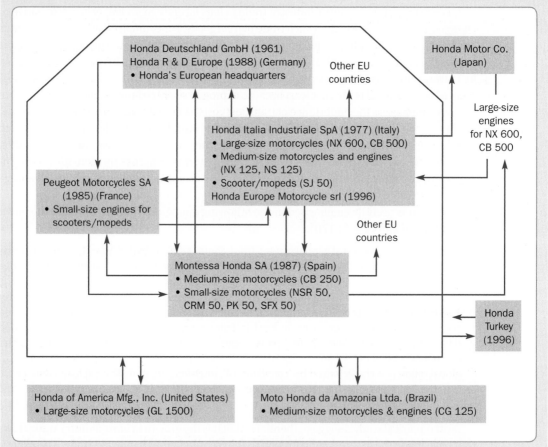

Figure 3.5 Honda: EU motorcycle networks and supply links

Source: Adapted from *Applied Economics*, 12th ed., Financial Times Prentice Hall (Griffiths, A. and Wall, S. (eds), 2012), © Pearson Education Limited 2012.

Case 3.2 (*continued*)

of motorcycle model appropriate to the different European locations in order to benefit from various economies of scale. At the same time, each assembler exported its own model to the other Honda locations in Europe in order to gain economies in joint production and marketing; in other words, any given model is produced in one location, but a full range of models is offered for sale in all locations. Finally, in the international context, Honda's European models are also exported to subsidiaries in the USA, Brazil and Japan, while its European network imports large and medium-sized motorcycles from its US and Brazilian affiliates.

As far as motorcycle parts are concerned, engines and key parts were initially supplied from Japan. However, in 1985 Honda acquired a 25% stake in Peugeot Motorcycles SA and began producing small engines in France for scooters and mopeds. These engines were then supplied to its Italian and Spanish assemblers of scooters and mopeds. Following this, medium-sized engines began to be produced in Honda Italia Industriale SpA, both for its own models and for Montessa Honda, while the latter began producing frames and other parts locally. Large-sized engines were still, however, supplied from Japan.

This study of Honda illustrates the types of motives underlying multinational activity in a globalised economy and the reasons for the consequent growth in intra-industry trade between countries. The traditional technical economies of scale were exploited to reduce average costs. The more market-based economies from producing and selling within the EU, with over 500 million consumers in 2014, have also benefited Honda. Some non-technical economies of scale have also been exploited, with R&D activities concentrated in the UK, Germany and Italy as well as Japan. In addition, the improved communications within the EU and the rise of more sophisticated corporate structures enabled Honda to integrate operations both horizontally, through affiliate specialisation in particular models, and vertically, through specialisation of affiliates in the production of parts. Honda was able to capitalise on its well-known ownership-specific advantages of excellent quality engineering and sound business skills, and to combine this with an intelligent strategy for locating production within the largest consumer market in the world.

The Honda experience helps to illustrate the nature of multinational inter-firm activity within a sophisticated market dominated by product differentiation, which in turn is the basis for much of the growth in the intra-industry trade already noted.

Questions

1 How might the Honda case relate to the various theoretical explanations of the basis for trade?

2 What benefits to Honda might result from integrating its operations both horizontally and vertically?

Intra-regional trade

It may be useful to enquire at this stage whether the expanding role of world trade seen in Table 3.9 was accompanied by an increase in the share of that trade conducted on a *regional* basis. It would seem natural that nations would tend to trade more with their immediate neighbours in the first instance, thereby raising the share of world trade occurring between nations within a specific geographical region. This tendency towards *intra-regional* trade can be seen in Table 3.10.

From Table 3.10 it can be seen that the share of intra-regional trade grew most rapidly in Western Europe between 1948 and 2006, while in Asia and North America the share of intra-regional trade also increased but to a lesser degree. Intra-regional trade occurring in other regions remained largely unchanged or even declined (i.e. de-regionalisation of trade), as seen in the early and mid-1990s in Central and Eastern Europe, though

Table 3.10 **Share of intra-regional trade in total trade 1928–2012 (% of each region's total trade in goods occurring between nations located in that region)**

Region	1928	1938	1948	1968	1979	1996	2006	2012
Western Europe	50.7	48.8	41.8	63.0	66.2	68.3	73.9	75.2
Central/Eastern Europe/USSR	19.0	13.2	46.4	63.5	54.0	18.7	22.8	25.3
North America	25.0	22.4	27.1	36.8	29.9	36.0	58.0	61.3
Latin America	11.1	17.7	17.7	18.7	20.2	21.2	24.5	28.2
Asia	45.5	66.4	38.9	36.6	41.0	51.9	52.6	54.1
Africa	10.3	8.9	8.4	9.1	5.6	9.2	9.9	10.8
Middle East	5.0	3.6	20.3	8.7	6.4	7.4	7.7	8.0

Source: WTO, Annual Reports (various).

some renewed growth in intra-regional trade has occurred since 1996. It is also clear from Table 3.10 that intra-regional trading is not a new phenomenon and that geographically adjacent nations in many areas of the world have been trading with each other for many years.

In Chapter 1 we have already noted the growth in preferential terms given to members of regional trading blocs (via regional trading arrangements – RTAs) which has, of course, been a key factor in the growth of intra-regional trade. Box 3.5 considers aspects of both 'trade creation' and 'trade diversion' resulting from regional trading arrangements which take the form of a customs union. We also review later in this chapter (p. 109) attempts by the World Trade Organisation (WTO) to remove some of the discriminatory effects (i.e. impacts on non-members) of such regional trading arrangements.

Forecasts suggest continued growth in intra-regional trade, especially should transport costs continue their downward trajectory. This perhaps somewhat surprising forecast is supported by data indicating notes that international freight costs per ton kilometre have halved since the mid-1970s. Air freight costs fell even more substantially, with air freight prices falling from $3.87 per ton kilometre in 1955 to less than $0.30 per ton kilometre in 2012 (using constant 2,000 US dollars). An earlier conclusion of the World Bank (*World Development Report* 2009: 21) was as follows:

> Falling transport costs increase trade more with neighbouring, not distant countries. With a decline in transport costs countries should trade more with countries that are farther away. But trade has become more localized than globalized. Countries trade more with countries that are similar because increasingly the basis of trade is the exploitation of economies of scale [via specialisation] . . . falling transport costs make specialization possible.

Barriers to trade

Those involved in international business face a number of methods by which individual countries or regional trading blocs (see p. 97) seek to restrict the level of imports into the home market. The World Trade Organisation (WTO) plays an important role in seeking to regulate and remove many of these impediments to trade, **as we note below (pp. 109–114).**

Tariff

A *tariff* is, in effect, a tax levied on imported goods, usually with the intention of raising the price of imports and thereby discouraging their purchase. Additionally, it is a source of revenue for the government. Tariffs can be of two types: *lump sum* (or *specific*) with the tariff a fixed amount per unit; *ad valorem* (or *percentage*) with the tariff a variable amount per unit. There is a general presumption that tariff barriers will discourage trade and reduce economic welfare. Box 3.3 considers the possible impacts of a tariff in rather more detail.

Non-tariff barriers

In recent years there has also been a considerable increase in trade that is subject to *non-tariff* barriers. The main types of non-tariff barrier in use include the following:

- *Quotas.* A quota is a limit applied to the number of units (or the monetary value) of an imported good that may be sold in a country in a given period.

- *Voluntary export restraints (VERs).* These are arrangements by which an individual exporter or group of exporters agrees with an importing country to limit the quantity of a specific product to be sold to a particular market over a given period of time. VERs are, in effect, quotas. VERs have been used in the past to restrict the import of cars from Japan into the EU and US, with Japanese producers agreeing to limit their sales into the EU or US to an agreed maximum number of cars (the figure excluded output from Japanese plants based in the EU or EU).

BOX 3.3 Impacts of a tariff

To examine the effect of a tariff, it helps to simplify Figure 3.6 if we assume a perfectly elastic world supply of the good S_W at the going world price P_W which implies that any amount of the good can be imported into the UK without there being a change in the world price. In the absence of a tariff, the domestic price would be set by the world price, P_W in Figure 3.6. At this price domestic demand D_D will be $0Q_2$, though domestic supply S_D will only be $0Q_1$. The excess demand, $Q_2 - Q_1$, will be satisfied by importing the good.

If the government now decides to restrict the level of import penetration, it could impose a tariff of, say, $P_W - P'_W$. A tariff always shifts a supply curve vertically upwards by the amount of the tariff, so that in this case the world supply curve shifts vertically upwards from S_W to S'_W. This would raise the domestic price to P'_W, which is above the world price P_W. This higher price will reduce the domestic demand for the good to $0Q_4$ while simultaneously encouraging domestic supply to expand from $0Q_1$ to $0Q_3$ and the government will gain tax revenue from the remaining imports which must now pay an import duty (area 3). All these are arguably 'positive' outcomes for governments. However, in terms of resource allocation, the impact of the tariff may be shown to be less favourable. Imports will be reduced from $Q_2 - Q_1$ before the tariff to $Q_4 - Q_3$ after the tariff. Domestic consumer surplus will decline as a result of the tariff by the area $1 + 2 + 3 + 4$, though domestic producer surplus will rise by area 1, and the government will gain tax revenue of $P'_W - P_W \times Q_4 - Q_3$ (i.e. area 3). These gains would be inadequate, however, to compensate consumers for their loss in welfare, yielding a net welfare loss of area $2 + 4$ as a result of imposing a tariff.

Box 3.3 (continued)

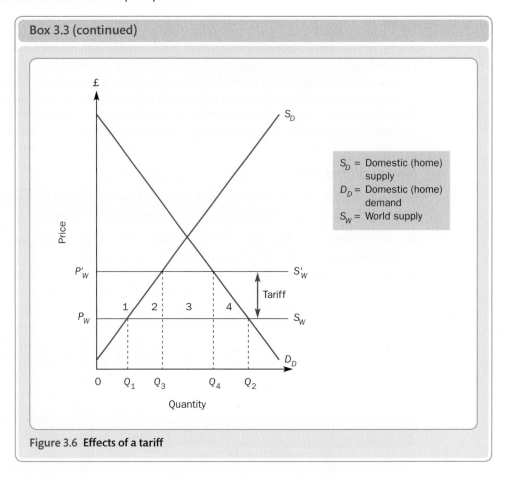

Figure 3.6 Effects of a tariff

- *Subsidies.* The forms of protection we have described so far have all been designed to restrict the volume of imports directly. An alternative policy is to provide a subsidy to domestic producers so as to improve their competitiveness in both the home and world markets. The effect of subsidies is considered in more detail in Box 3.4.

  Case 3.3 further investigates the impacts of subsidies, using the example of Indian subsidies for its cereal farmers, which have been criticised as violating WTO rules.

- *Exchange controls.* A system of *exchange controls* was in force in the UK from the outbreak of the Second World War until 1979 when, in order to allow the free flow of capital, they were abolished. They enabled the government to limit the availability of foreign currencies and so curtail excessive imports; for instance, holding a foreign-currency bank account required permission from the Bank of England. Exchange controls could also be employed to discourage speculation and investment abroad.

- *Safety and technological standards.* These are often imposed in the knowledge that certain imported goods will be unable to meet the specified requirements. The British government has in the past used such standards to prevent imports of French turkey and ultra-heat-treated (UHT) milk. Ostensibly the ban on French turkeys was to prevent

BOX 3.4 Impacts of a subsidy

Once again, with reference to Figure 3.7, we assume that the world supply curve is perfectly elastic at P_W. Under conditions of free trade, the domestic price is set by the world price at P_W. Domestic production is initially $0Q_1$ with imports satisfying the excess level of domestic demand, which amounts to $Q_2 - Q_1$. The effect of a general subsidy to an industry would be to shift the supply curve of domestic producers downwards (by the amount of the subsidy) and to the right. The domestic price will remain unchanged at the world price PW but domestic production will rise to $0Q_3$ with imports reduced to $Q_2 - Q_3$. If, however, the subsidy is provided solely for exporters, the impact on the domestic market could be quite different. The incentive to export may encourage more domestic production to be switched from the home market to the overseas markets, which in turn could result in an increased volume of imports to satisfy the unchanged level of domestic demand.

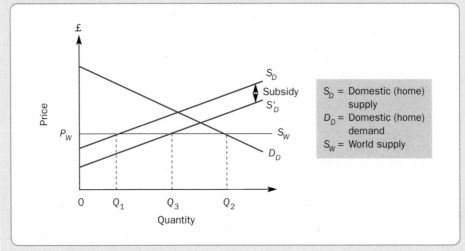

Figure 3.7 **Effects of a subsidy**

'Newcastle disease', a form of fowl pest found in Europe, from reaching the UK. The European Court ruled, however, that the ban was merely an excuse to prevent the free flow of imports.

- *Time-consuming formalities.* It has often been suggested that 'excessive invoicing require-ments' required by US and the EU importing authorities have hampered exports of com-petitors to the US and EU respectively. These problems abound in many parts of the world and often involve considerable administrative and capital costs for many companies. A similar problem in China can lead to a two- or three-week delay.

- *Public sector contracts.* Government often give preference to domestic firms in the issuing of public contracts, despite EU directives requiring member governments to advertise such contracts. Public contracts have been criticised in the EU as actually being placed outside the country of origin in only around 1% of cases.

● *Labour standards.* This bears some resemblance to the point made above concerning safety and technological standards but is rather more controversial. Does the enforcement of minimum labour standards represent a source of support for the poorest workers in the developing world or is it simply a covert form of protection? Low-cost producers, not surprisingly, believe the latter to be the case. The WTO has come under increasing pressure from governments in the industrialised world to take action on what is perceived as 'unfair' competition by countries which have few, if any, effective minimum labour standards.

CASE 3.3 Indian subsidies to cereal farmers

It is 1950, four years after independence from British colonial rule, and India is facing a food crisis after being hit by both floods and a drought, leaving its grain harvest some 4m tonnes short of requirements. Washington stepped in with urgent food aid, but its efforts to impose conditions on its help left a sour taste in New Delhi's mouth and an unflinching determination to meet its basic food needs without turning to international assistance. Today in 2014 India is sitting on a 33m-tonne stockpile of rice and wheat, nearly twice the level that experts say is needed for a strategic buffer stock. This mountain of grain is the result of extensive subsidies and incentives that have enabled India to become self-sufficient in basic food. 'We created a cereal economy,' says Subir Gokam, director of research at the Brookings Institution India Centre. 'That system remains in place, no matter how much consumer preferences have changed.'

While New Delhi sees its financial aid to cereal farmers as crucial for its national food security, the US and other countries argue that the extensive assistance violates WTO rules. Wheat-exporting countries are particularly aggrieved that New Delhi periodically dumps some of its wheat surplus on to international markets, which depresses global prices. It is not easy to calculate the precise amount India spends on subsidising agricultural production. New Delhi provides discounted farm inputs, such as fertiliser and diesel fuel for running irrigation pumps, while many

state governments in India provide free or deeply discounted electricity for irrigation pumps too. In the harvest season, New Delhi offers farmers 'minimum support prices' (MSP) for their wheat and rice, with the state-owned Food Corporation of India (FCI) obliged to procure grain from any willing seller at the set price. The MSP process serves as an effective floor price, whether farmers sell to private traders or to the FCI. Since 2007 the FCI has procured about 30 per cent of the country's annual wheat and rice harvest. Some of that grain is resold at cheap prices to the poor. According to US Department of Agriculture estimates, India has spent up to $14bn on fertiliser subsidies, and up to $12bn subsidising electricity to farmers in each of the past few years. Last year in 2013 the FCI paid farmers $15.2bn more for the wheat and rice it procured than the money it received through the public distribution. These subsidies and costs to the government could rise still further as New Delhi grapples with implementing a new 'right-to-food' law that is supposed to make subsidised grain available to more of the population.

Yet developed countries are not alone in questioning these policies. Within India, critics say that the strong incentives for cultivating cereals are distorting the entire domestic food market. Mr Gokam of Brookings says: 'What we want is reasonable availability of a variety of balanced foods at predictable prices over time. The strong incentive for producing cereals has to change.'

Questions

1 Outline the arguments in favour of subsidising cereal farmers in India.

2 Outline the arguments against subsiding cereal farmers in India.

Protectionist policies

In this section we briefly review the case for and against protectionist policies. Of course our earlier theoretical arguments supporting free trade (pp. 74–81) are themselves arguments against protectionist policies.

The case for protection

Protectionist measures may be applied on a selective or more widespread basis, with most of the measures currently in force falling into the first category. A number of arguments have been used to justify the application of both tariff and non-tariff barriers on a selective basis:

- to prevent dumping;
- to protect infant industries;
- to protect strategically important industries;
- to maintain employment by preventing the rapid contraction of labour-intensive industries.

Preventing dumping

Dumping occurs where a good is sold in an overseas market at a price below the real cost of production. We note below that under Article 6, the WTO allows retaliatory sanctions to be applied if it can be shown that the dumping materially affected the domestic industry. As well as using the WTO, countries within the EU can refer cases of alleged dumping for investigation by the European Commission. The Commission is then able to recommend the appropriate course of action, which may range from 'no action' where dumping is found not to have taken place, to either obtaining an 'undertaking' of no further dumping or imposing a tariff.

The prevalence of dumping is indicated by the number of anti-dumping cases initiated by the WTO, as Table 3.11 illustrates. Although 2001 saw a record number of anti-dumping cases of 348 in a single year, by 2013 these had fallen to only 102. The US has consistently been one of the main initiators of anti-dumping investigations and has had such success in securing WTO approval for retaliatory tariffs that the current official figures for average US tariffs on manufactured imports of 6% rises to around 23% when these additional retaliatory tariffs are included. Canada, India and the European Union have also initiated numerous actions. The main targets of anti-dumping probes have been the European Union, China, Chinese Taipai and India. The sectors where anti-dumping measures are most widely applied include chemical products and base metals, in particular steel, which is currently a battleground between the US and the EU. The US steel industry has previously alleged that financial support from European governments has given the EU steel industry an unfair advantage over US producers. In response the US

Table 3.11 Anti-dumping: cases initiated

1987	1993	2001	2005	2013
120	299	348	314	102

Source: WTO, Annual Reports (various).

government was allowed by the WTO to impose 'countervailing tariffs' of up to 30% on selected steel products in March 2002.

Protecting infant industries

The use of protection in order to *establish new industries* is widely accepted, particularly in the case of developing countries. Article 18 of the WTO explicitly allows such protection. An infant industry is likely to have a relatively high-cost structure in the short run, and in the absence of protective measures may find it difficult to compete with the established overseas industries already benefiting from scale economies. The EU has used this argument to justify protection of its developing high-technology industries.

Protecting strategically important industries

The protection of industries for *strategic reasons* is widely practised both in the UK and in the EU, and is not necessarily contrary to the WTO rules (Article 2). The protection of the UK steel industry has in the past been justified on this basis, and the EU has used a similar argument to protect agricultural production throughout the Community under the guise of the CAP. In the Uruguay round of the then GATT (now WTO) the developing countries used this argument in seeking to resist calls for the liberalisation of trade in their service sectors, which has been one of the few sectors recording strong growth in recent years and is still a highly 'regulated' sector in most countries.

Maintaining levels of employment

There is a small but growing body of opinion that advocates a degree of protection to maintain levels of employment and that questions the benefits to be derived from international trade and is hostile to the drive by the WTO to liberalise trade. This movement, which is quite diverse, comprises environmentalists, trade unions, charities, third-world activists, among many others, and has manifested itself in WTO/IMF demonstrations in Seattle, Prague and many other locations in recent years. Although not necessarily rejecting the theoretical benefits of free trade, opponents of the WTO contend that the gains are largely expropriated by big business, leaving both workers and developing nations no better off and in many cases actually worse off. Groups such as Global Trade Watch suggest that the WTO has little regard for democracy or for environmental standards and almost always acts against the public interest.

Case against protectionism

A number of arguments are often advanced as reasons for avoiding protectionist policies.

Retaliation

A major drawback to protectionist measures is the prospect of retaliation. The consequences of retaliation could be especially serious for countries increasingly dependent on international trade flows. For example, in 2014 German exports of goods and services totalled 38% of GDP, France 24%, Italy 22% and the UK 19%, with lower percentages for the export:GDP ratio in Japan (14%) and the USA (8%).

Misallocation of resources

Protectionism can erode some of the benefits of free trade. For instance, Box 3.3 showed that a tariff raises domestic supply at the expense of imports. If the domestic producers cannot make such products as cheaply as overseas producers, then one could argue that encouraging high-cost domestic production is a misallocation of international resources.

A related criticism also suggests that protectionism leads to resource misallocation on an international scale, but this time concerns the multinational. Multinationals are the fastest-growing type of business unit in the Western economies, and they are increasingly adopting strategies which locate particular stages of the production process in (to them) appropriate parts of the world. Protectionism may disrupt the flow of goods from one stage of the production process to another, and in this sense inhibit global specialisation.

Indeed, imposing tariffs on products derived by EU-based multinationals from their globally distributed value chains can have 'unexpected' consequences for both the multinationals and their 'home' countries. Peter Mandelson, then EU trade commissioner, argued that anti-dumping tariffs and quotas in the EU have harmed Europe's own manufacturers, which have used extensive outsourcing in the production of shoes, textiles, light bulbs and other goods, thereby aiming to maintain a competitive edge against cheaper Asian rivals. This was the reasoning behind Mr Mandelson supporting the 2007 EU decision to phase out anti-dumping duties on energy-efficient light bulbs made by European companies in China, noting that 'If producing cheaply in China helps generate profits and jobs in Europe, how should we treat these companies when disputes over unfair trading arise?'

A further case was leather footwear. The imposition of tariffs on shoes for two years in 2006 led to duties of 16% for China and 10% for Vietnam. A Swedish government report noted that these duties have caused heavy losses among shoe importers, despite the fact that these companies may be generating as much as 80% of each shoe's value in the EU through product design. Surveying five typical EU shoemakers, the Swedish government's National Board of Trade argued that companies have become 'globalised', creating jobs and investment in the EU. In their report it was noted that a €20 ($27, £13.50) pair of women's shoes adds value to the European economy. Intermedium, a Dutch company, pays €4.40 to bring the shoes to Europe, then sells them to retailers for €6.65. By that point, €2.45 of the total cost is classified as European value-added. Intermedium and its Chinese supplier make margins of less than 10% each. For a more expensive €150 pair of shoes, DC of Milan charges retailers €77.80, of which leather accounts for a third. But €40 of €50 value-added is classed as European, mostly going to research and development. 'The European value-added is 79%,' says the report. 'Is this a European or Vietnamese shoe?'

> ### Pause for thought 3.5
>
> What does this criticism of anti-dumping tariffs suggest in terms of the 'free trade versus protectionism' debate?

Regional trading arrangements

As we noted above, the resumption of rapid growth in world trade after the Second World War was tied up with the desire for the resumption of *multilateral trade* under the auspices of the GATT (now WTO). However, this movement towards free trade was accompanied by a parallel movement towards the formation of *regional trading blocs* centred on the EU, North and South America and East Asia. We noted in Table 3.10 that intra-regional trading is not a new phenomenon but one which has been active for at least a century or more. However, there is evidence to suggest that the nations of a given region have begun to create more formal and comprehensive trading and economic links with each other than was previously the case.

There are four broad types of regional trading arrangements (RTAs):

1 *free trade areas,* where member countries reduce or abolish restrictions on trade between each other while maintaining their individual protectionist measures against non-members;

2 *customs unions,* where, as well as liberalising trade among members, a common external tariff is established to protect the group from imports from any non-members;

3 *common markets,* where the customs union is extended to include the free movement of factors of production as well as products within the designated area;

4 *economic unions,* where national economic policies are also harmonised within the common market.

We can usefully review at this point examples of different types of regional trading arrangements across the globe.

● The European Union (EU) was founded in January 1958 as a *common market* with six member nations. By 2014 the EU included 27 nations with a population of over 500 million, and accounted for some 45% of world trade, with some 68% of EU exports going to other member countries. This group originated as a *common* market, the majority of members effectively progressing into a type of *economic union* with the Maastricht Treaty of 1992 and the advent of the euro and its related financial arrangements on 1 January 1999.

● In August 1993 the North American Free Trade Agreement (NAFTA) was signed between the US, Canada and Mexico, having grown out of an earlier Canadian–US Free Trade Agreement (CUFTA). NAFTA, as the name implies, is a *free trade area* with around 56% of NAFTA exports going to member countries, covering a population of 372 million and accounting for 31% of world output and 17% of world trade.

● MERCOSUR was established in South America in 1991, evolving out of the Latin American Free Trade Area, with the four initial members being Argentina, Brazil, Paraguay and Uruguay. It developed into a partial *customs union* in 1995 when it imposed a common external tariff covering 85% of total products imported.

● In Asia and the Pacific, the rather 'loose' Association of South-East Asian Nations (ASEAN) with a population of 300 million was formed in August 1967. In 1991 they agreed to form an ASEAN Free Trade Area (AFTA) by the year 2003. A Common External Preference Tariff (CEPT) came into force in 1994 as a formal tariff-cutting mechanism for achieving *free trade* in all goods except agricultural products, natural resources and services.

- On the western side of Latin America, a *free trade area* has been established by Venezuela, Columbia, Ecuador, Peru and Bolivia (Andean Pact).

- In Central and Eastern Europe, a *free trade area* has been established by Poland, the Czech Republic, Slovakia, Hungary, Slovenia, Romania and Bulgaria (CEFTA).

From the above examples it is possible to see that trading blocs have adopted various types of arrangements depending on their specific circumstances.

Three features have characterised post-war regional integration:

1 Post-war regional integration has been primarily centred in Western Europe. For example, of the 240 or so agreements notified to GATT/WTO between 1948 and 2013, more than half involved Western European countries, especially following the 1990 agreements between the EU and Central and Eastern European countries.

2 Only a small number of post-war regional agreements have been concluded by developing countries. This is mainly due to continuing competition between these countries involving trade in similar products (e.g. primary products) together with the difficulty in some developing countries of achieving the political stability which is so vital to trade.

3 The *type* of economic integration between the parties to agreements has varied quite significantly. Most of the notifications made to GATT/WTO have involved free trade areas, with the number of customs unions agreement being much smaller.

In recent years many of these free trade areas have taken the form of *bilateral trade treaties*, often involving the USA (see Chapter 1, p. 7).

Those who favour the regional approach argue that the setting up of trading blocs can enable individual countries to purchase products at lower prices because tariff walls between the member countries have been removed; this is the *trade creation effect*. They also argue that regional trading arrangements help to harmonise tax policies and product standards, while also helping to reduce political conflicts. Others argue that where the world is already organised into trading blocs, then negotiations in favour of free trade are more likely to be successful between these large and influential trading blocs than between a large number of individual countries with little power to bargain successfully for tariff reductions.

On the other hand, the critics of regionalism warn that regional trading blocs have, historically, tended to be inward looking, as in the 1930s when discriminatory trade blocs were formed to impose tariffs on non-members. Some also argue that member countries may suffer from being inside a regional bloc because they then have to buy products from within the bloc, when cheaper sources are often available from outside – i.e. the *trade diversion effect*. Further, it is argued that regionalism threatens to erode support for multilateralism in that business groups within a regional bloc will find it easier to obtain protectionist (trade diversionary) deals via preferential pacts than they would in the world of non-discriminatory trade practices favoured by the GATT/WTO. Finally, it is argued that regionalism will move the world away from free trade due to the increasing tendency for members of a regional group to resort to the use of *non-tariff barriers* (VERs, anti-dumping duties, etc.) when experiencing a surge of imports from other countries inside the group. Such devices can then easily be used by individual countries against non-members from other regional groups.

Box 3.5 looks in more detail at the trade creation and trade diversion elements related to the establishment of a customs union.

BOX 3.5 Customs union: trade creation and trade diversion

As already noted, a customs union is a protected free trade area. Those who favour this approach argue that the setting up of such regional trading blocs can enable individual countries within a broad geographical region to purchase products at lower prices because tariff walls between the member countries have been removed; this is the *trade creation effect*. They also argue that such regional trading arrangements may create opportunities for still deeper integration, such as harmonising tax policies and product standards, while also helping to reduce political conflicts. Supporters also argue that where the world is already organised into trading blocs, then negotiations in favour of free trade are more likely to be successful when individual countries combine to form large and influential trading blocs: a large number of individual countries will, on their own, have little power to bargain successfully with existing trade blocs to secure tariff or subsidy reductions.

On the other hand, the critics of integration warn that regional trading blocs have, historically, tended to be inward looking, as in the 1930s when discriminatory trade blocs were formed to impose tariffs on non-members. Some also argue that member countries may suffer from being inside a regional bloc because they then have to buy products from within the bloc, when cheaper sources are often available from outside – i.e. the *trade diversion effect*. Critics also argue that such regionalism threatens to erode support for multilateralism in that business groups within a regional bloc will find it easier to obtain protectionist (trade diversionary) deals via preferential pacts than they would in the world of non-discriminatory trade practices favoured by the GATT/WTO.

Figure 3.8 looks in more detail at the trade creation versus trade diversion impacts of establishing a regional trading bloc.

We assume that the domestic country initially has a tariff (t) imposed on imports from two separate countries, A and B, both of which are lower (and constant) cost producers, as indicated by their horizontal supply curves S_A and S_B respectively. We assume the tariff (t) imposed on imports from both A and B rules the less efficient country A out from competing in the domestic market altogether but still allows the relatively more efficient country B to compete.

The 'world' supply curve to the domestic market is therefore $S_d + (S_B + t)$, i.e. *LNK* giving a domestic price of P_d and domestic production of $0q_2$, with imports from country B of q_2q_3, but no trade at all with country A.

Suppose now a regional trading bloc, protected by the common external tariff t, is now formed between the domestic country and country A only. All tariffs between the domestic country and country A are abolished (it is a protected free trade area) so that the 'world' supply curve to the domestic market now becomes *LMZ*. Price in the domestic market falls to P'_d, with imports from country A of q_1q_4 but now no imports from country B.

We have in this example both trade creation and trade diversion.

- *Trade creation*: The result of removing the tariff t on trade with country A has created extra trade (with A) of the magnitude $q_1q_2 + q_3q_4$.

- *Trade diversion*: The result of removing the tariff t only on country A (i.e. forming a trading bloc with A) has enabled country A to undercut country B (the more efficient producer) in the domestic market. The volume of trade q_2q_3 previously undertaken with B prior to the trading bloc is now undertaken with the less efficient producer A. Trade has been 'diverted' by the formation of the trading bloc.

Using our earlier ideas of consumer and producer surplus, we can seek to measure gains and losses from trade creation and trade diversion. In Figure 3.8, the reduction in price from P_d to P'_d via creating the trading bloc has increased *consumer surplus* by area ($a + b + c + d$), but reduced *producer surplus* by area a, since domestic production has fallen from q_2 to q_1. The *tariff revenue* ($c + e$) previously earned on trade with country B is also lost as trade is diverted to tariff-free country A.

As long as the *net* benefits ($b + c + d$) brought about from trade creation exceed the losses ($c + e$) brought about from trade diversion, then the formation of the economic trading bloc can be regarded as beneficial overall.

Box 3.5 (*continued*)

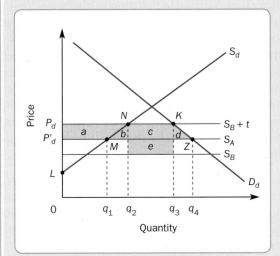

Figure 3.8 Customs union, trade creation and trade diversion

formation of an economic bloc, the greater the likelihood that the bloc will be a trade-creating one. If economies do not overlap, as in the case when a basically agricultural producing country joins a mainly manufacturing country, then there is little scope for trade creation but a great deal of scope for trade diversion.

- *The greater the differences in production costs between the potential members in their overlapping industries*, the greater the potential for trade creation. Conversely, if the differences in costs are small, so will be the potential gains.

- *The higher the tariff rates prior to the amalgamation of the economies*, the greater the gains from the associated tariff reductions.

It follows that the greatest gains from the formation of an economic group can be achieved if:

- The economic structure of the economies overlap.

- The industries that are common to both have a wide variation in their costs.

- The level of import tariffs placed by those countries on one another's products is high prior to the formation of the bloc.

Some general observations can be made from this analysis as to when the above condition is most likely to hold and to support the creation of a trading bloc.

- *The greater the degree of overlap in the economies of the countries contemplating the*

Government policies and international business

Government policies can influence international business in a variety of ways, some of which have already been considered in Chapter 2. For example, change in fiscal policies (involving government spending/taxation) or monetary policies (involving money supply/interest rates) will influence the macroeconomic environment in which domestic and international businesses operate. However, sometimes government policies can impact upon international business *indirectly*; for example, changes in interest rates may influence the price of currencies on the foreign exchange markets (see Chapter 4), which in turn may exert a strong influence on the prospects for exporting and importing products across national boundaries. It is to this issue of exchange rates that we first turn our attention.

Exchange rates

We note in Chapter 4 that few governments can now influence their exchange rates directly, via unilateral action. More usually they can only influence such rates indirectly whether intentionally or unintentionally. For example, high interest rates used as part of an anti-inflationary monetary policy may make a country's currency relatively attractive on foreign exchange markets, the extra demand then raises the price of that country's currency.

A *rise* in, say, the UK sterling exchange rate makes UK exports dearer abroad in terms of the foreign currency, and UK imports cheaper at home in terms of the domestic currency. Suppose, for example, sterling *appreciates* against the euro from £1:€1.10 to £1:€1.40. An item priced at £1,000 in the UK would have a euro-zone equivalent price of €1,100 prior to the sterling appreciation but €1,400 after that appreciation. Not only will exports be dearer abroad but imports will be cheaper at home. An item priced at €1,100 in the euro-zone would have a sterling equivalent price of £1,000 prior to the sterling appreciation but £785.7 after that appreciation.

The impact of higher export prices and lower import prices on business turnover (and the balance of payments) will depend to some extent on *price elasticities of demand* in the export and import markets respectively.

- If *price elasticity of demand for UK exports is relatively elastic* (greater than one), then any rise in euro-zone prices will reduce total expenditure in euros on those items. Since each euro is now worth less in sterling, this fall in the euro value of UK exports will mean a still more substantial fall in sterling turnover for UK exporters.

- If *price elasticity of demand for UK imports is relatively elastic* (greater than one), then any fall in sterling prices will raise total expenditure in sterling on those items. This is likely to imply a loss of turnover and market share from UK domestic producers to euro-zone producers.

Clearly the more elastic the respective price elasticities of demand for UK exports and UK imports, the greater the disadvantage for businesses located in the UK in trading with the euro-zone after sterling appreciates against the euro, and the greater the advantage for businesses located in the euro-zone in trading with the UK.

For illustrative purposes only we have used an example of sterling rising in value against the euro. This has indeed been the case in recent times (see Chapter 10, p. 354), but previously sterling has fallen substantially against both the euro and US dollar.

Pause for thought 3.6

Can you work through the previous analysis if sterling *depreciates* against the euro? (For example, suppose £1 is now worth €1.00 instead of €1.40.)

Import protection/export support

We have already seen how a variety of *protective trade barriers* (such as tariffs and quotas) can be used to discourage imports into a country, whether imposed unilaterally by a country or collectively as part of a regional trading bloc. An example of the latter would be the Common External Tariff imposed on industrial imports into the EU. Domestic producers can also be helped vis-à-vis overseas producers by a variety of support policies directed towards exporters.

The Common Agricultural Policy (CAP) of the EU provides a useful illustration of government-directed policies involving import protection/export support which exert a strong influence on the operations of farms and agri-businesses, both inside and outside the EU. Box 3.6 considers the operation of the CAP in rather more detail.

BOX 3.6 Impacts of EU policies on farms and agri-businesses

The formal title for the executive body of the CAP is the European Agricultural Guarantee and Guidance Fund (EAGGF), often known by its French translation of 'Fonds Européen d'Orientation et de Garantie-Agricole' (FEOGA). As its name implies, one of its key roles is in operating the 'guarantee system' for EU farm incomes.

Different agricultural products are dealt with in slightly different ways, but the basis of the system is the establishment of a 'target price' for each product (Figure 3.9(a)). The target price is not set with reference to world prices but is based upon the price which producers need to cover costs, including a profit mark-up, in the highest-cost area of production in the EU. The EU then sets an 'intervention' or 'guaranteed' price for the product in that area, about 7–10% below the target price. Should the price be in danger of falling below this level, the Commission intervenes to buy up production to keep the price at or above the 'guaranteed' level. The Commission then sets separate target and intervention prices for that product in each area of the Community, related broadly to production costs in that area. As long as the market price in a given area (there are 11 such

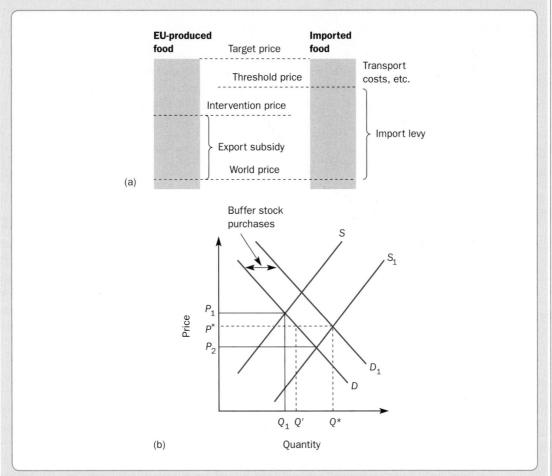

(a)

(b)

Figure 3.9 (a) CAP system: world price below target price; (b) Guarantee system: maintaining the intervention price (*P**)

Box 3.6 (*continued*)

areas in the UK) is above the intervention price, producers will sell their produce at prevailing market prices. In effect the intervention price sets a 'floor' below which market price will not be permitted to fall and is therefore the guaranteed minimum price to producers.

In Figure 3.9(b) an increase in supply of agricultural products to S_1 would, if no action were taken, lower the market price from P_1 to P_2 below the intervention or guaranteed price, P^*. At P^* demand is Q' but supply is Q^*. To keep the price at P^*, the EAGGF will buy up the excess $Q^* - Q'$. In terms of Figure 3.9(b), the demand curve is artificially increased to D_1 by the EAGGF purchase.

If this system of guaranteed minimum prices is to work, EU farmers must be protected from low-priced imports from overseas. To this end, levies or tariffs are imposed on imports of agricultural products. If in Figure 3.9(b) the price of imported food were higher than the EU target price then, of course, there would be no need for an import tariff. If, however, the import price is below this, say at the 'world price' in Figure 3.9(a), then an appropriate tariff must be calculated. This need not quite cover the difference between 'target'

and 'world' price, since the importer still has to pay transport costs within the EU to get the food to market. The tariff must therefore be large enough to raise the import price at the EU frontier to the target price minus transport costs, i.e. 'threshold price'. This calculation takes place in the highest-cost area of production in the EU, so that the import tariff set will more than protect EU producers in areas with lower target prices (i.e. lower-cost areas).

Should an EU producer wish to export an agricultural product, an export subsidy will be paid to bring his receipts up to the intervention price (see Figure 3.9(a)), i.e. the minimum price he would receive in the home market. Problems involving this form of subsidy of oil-seed exports have been a major threat to dealings between the EU and the USA, with the latter alleging a breach of WTO rules. The system outlined above does not apply to all agricultural products in the EU. About a quarter of these products are covered by different direct subsidy systems, e.g. olive oil and tobacco, and some products such as potatoes, agricultural alcohol and honey are not covered by EU regulation at all.

Reforms of the CAP over the past decade or so have modified this system which has proved an expensive method of supporting farm incomes. For example, Maximum Guaranteed Quantities (MGQs) have now been set for most agricultural products. If the MGQ is exceeded, the intervention price is cut by 30% in the following year. Further CAP reforms were also agreed in 2003, which came into effect from 2007 onwards. For example 'compulsory modulation' has been introduced whereby payments directly related to agricultural production have been progressively replaced by payments for a wide range of environmental protection activities by EU farmers.

Taxation policies

The ability of 'footloose' multinational enterprises to take advantage of tax discrepancies between countries or regions is well known, as in the examples of 'transfer pricing' (see Chapter 9, p. 331). Indeed the issue of 'tax havens' has risen to greater prominence in an era where governments are seeking greater tax revenues to fund their increased budget deficits from 'bailing out' endangered domestic firms and organisations during the so-called 'credit crunch'. There has been growing hostility to the tiny states and islands around the world that harbour an estimated $6,000 billion of offshore assets. The US adopted the *Stop Tax Haven Abuse Act* in 2007 and the *Incorporation Transparency and Law Enforcement Assistance*

Act in 2008, which seeks to make it easier for investigators to 'see through opaque corporate ownership structures' and stop the flow of offshore funds to the US from hedge funds and private equity that are 'of unknown origin' but do not have to pass money-laundering checks. It was noted that one building in the Cayman Islands supposedly housed 12,000 US-based corporations!

However, tax havens are not limited solely to developing economies. Delaware is a state in the US which is infamous for allowing corporate financial secrecy of the kind that regulators worldwide are seeking to overcome in offshore financial centres. Arguments over Delaware – whose more than 600,000 registered companies compare with an estimated 865,000 inhabitants – are part of a broader fight over what many havens see as rich-country double standards in international action to tackle money laundering and tax evasion. Delaware's corporations are under no obligation to file names of shareholders or beneficial owners, as the state offers a structure known as a limited liability company, which can be registered with not much more than a name and address.

Pause for thought 3.7

Examine the costs and benefits that might result from government policies to remove 'tax havens'.

Case 3.4 examines tax-related issues involving Luxembourg, seen by many as a source of tax distortion within the EU.

CASE 3.4 Luxembourg tax regime: under siege

Amid the rolling wooded farmland of the Ardennes, the highway from Brussels briefly hugs the Luxembourg frontier at Martelange, a small town famous for the border that runs down the middle of the busy main street. On one side – in low-tax Luxembourg – is a profusion of petrol stations offering some of the most lightly taxed fuel in Europe. It is a striking example of the 'gas pump tourism' that boosts Luxembourg's exchequer at the expense of its neighbours.

This is one face of Luxembourg: a tiny country at the crossroads of Europe that built a significant part of its wealth on its appeal to other countries' taxpayers. Its low fuel duties are just one facet of a distinctive tax system that has helped make its society one of the richest in the world. There is another face to Luxembourg. Its agility and financial expertise has built the world's second-largest fund administration industry. It has a reputation for stability and professionalism,

demonstrated by the resilience of its huge banking sector in the financial crisis. But the rumbling discontent over Luxembourg's tax practices is now threatening its prosperity. The world's last Grand Duchy has already bowed to pressure over accusations it helped other countries' citizens hide from the taxman. Xavier Betel, its prime minister, is 'fed up with being accused of being a defender of a tax haven and a hotbed of sin'.

Luxembourg is not overly a low-tax country for businesses: more than two-thirds of OECD countries have rates lower than its 29.2 per cent. But there are numerous deductions. Indeed, Luxembourg has been battling with its neighbours on tax matters for decades. As long ago as 1973, France and Germany demanded a crackdown on its 'letter box' subsidiaries – structures governed by a 1929 tax law that were often used to avoid tax. It was not until 2006 that the regime was outlawed under the European Commission's state aid rules.

Case 3.4 (*continued*)

For companies as well as individuals, Luxembourg's emphasis on discretion added to its appeal. Foreign tax inspectors trying to understand their multinationals' tax planning struggled to make sense of the sparse details in the companies' Luxembourg accounts and/or get hold of legal documents entrusted to lawyers. 'Luxembourg was phenomenally secret,' says one such official. 'Secrecy was more important to Luxembourg than anywhere else.' There was often a big gap between the letter of the law and how it was applied, with informal rulings playing an important role, he says. 'I would normally see nominal tax rates of around 9 to10 per cent in Luxembourg but they could be as low as 1 per cent in practice.'

Luxembourg is also under suspicion of offering 'sweetheart' deals to big companies, in breach of EU rules on state aid. Nerves are on edge in the Grand Duchy after the European Commission launched an investigation last month into tax 'rulings' embroiling Fiat, the car company, and potentially others. The commission is also suing Luxembourg for 'serious distortions of competition' over the 3 per cent rate of value added tax it charges Amazon and other eBook retailers. Its low VAT rates have made the Grand Duchy an ecommerce hub but it stands to lose €800m of revenues – 1.5 per cent of its gross domestic product – next year under a long-awaited shake-up of European tax rules.

Another threat is posed by a looming crackdown on corporate tax planning proposed by the Organisation for Economic Cooperation and Development in the wake of a public outcry over tax avoidance by companies such as Amazon and Apple. The OECD aims to stamp out 'treaty shopping' – routing income through 'brass-plate' companies in countries with attractive tax treaties – which will affect many of the Grand Duchy's finance and holding companies that own more than $2,000 billion of assets. It could spell the end of an era in which a country of 1,000 square miles receives more than a 10th of the world's foreign direct investment, as calculated by the International Monetary Fund. Consumption taxes are already set to rise as Luxembourg grapples with the loss of 'significant' revenues from these changes, the IMF said in May. Luxembourg's public finances are at a turning point.

In Luxembourg City, a glass and steel metropolis grafted on to a medieval fortress town, the impending changes are viewed with trepidation, tempered by a belief the Grand Duchy can both adapt and defend its interests. Much depends on whether the government is 'being seen to fight' the OECD proposals, according to PwC, the professional services firm in a May bulletin. The appointment of Jean-Claude Juncker, Luxembourg's former prime minister, as president of the European Commission, has sparked speculation that the Grand Duchy has won a powerful protector.

 Source: Adapted from Luxembourg tax regime: under siege, *Financial Times*, 23/07/2014 (Houlder, V.), © The Financial Times Limited 2014. All Rights Reserved.

Question

What are the likely impacts of the new approach towards taxation in Luxembourg (a) for Luxembourg itself and (b) for international business?

International institutions and world trade

Here we pay particular attention to the role of the World Trade Organisation, as successor to the earlier General Agreement on Tariffs and Trade. We also look in more detail at the role of other institutions that also play a key role in underpinning the world trading system, such as the International Monetary Fund (IMF) and the World Bank.

General Agreement on Tariffs and Trade (GATT)

The General Agreement on Tariffs and Trade was signed in 1947 by 23 industrialised nations that included the UK, USA, Canada, France and the Benelux countries. The objectives of GATT were to reduce tariffs and other barriers to trade in the belief that freer trade would raise living standards in all participating countries. Since 1947 there have been eight 'rounds' of trade negotiations with the average tariff in the industrialised nations falling from 40% in 1947 to below 5% in 1995 when the GATT was replaced by the WTO. Supporters of the role of GATT point to facts such as the volume of world trade rising by 1,500% and world output by 600% over the years of its existence.

The World Trade Organisation (WTO)

The World Trade Organisation replaced GATT in 1995 and had 160 members in 2014, with the People's Republic of China, Chinese Taipei, Cambodia and Yemen being among those joining since the beginning of the millennium. The WTO's members in total account for more than 90% of the value of world trade. The objectives of the WTO are essentially the same as GATT's, namely to reduce tariffs and other barriers to trade and to eliminate discrimination in trade, and by doing so contribute to rising living standards and a fuller use of world resources.

WTO authority

Trade disputes between member states now come under the auspices of the WTO, which has been given more powers than GATT to enforce compliance, using a streamlined disputes procedure with provision for appeals and binding arbitration. Whereas under GATT any single member (including the one violating GATT rules) could block a ruling of unfair trade, the findings of the WTO's disputes panels cannot be blocked by a veto of a member state. Countries found to be in violation of a WTO principle must remove the cause of that violation or pay compensation to the injured parties. If the offending party fails to comply with a WTO ruling, the WTO can sanction certain types of retaliation by the aggrieved party.

Since its creation in January 1995, more than 450 cases have been brought before the WTO against only 200 cases brought before GATT in the 47 years of its existence. Almost half of these have involved the USA and the EU while around one-quarter have involved developing countries. The WTO also seeks to provide a forum for further multilateral trade negotiations.

WTO principles

Both the GATT and its successor the WTO have sought to implement a number of principles:

- *non-discrimination:* the benefits of any trading advantage agreed between two nations (i.e. in bilateral negotiations) must be extended to all nations (i.e. become multilateral). This is sometimes referred to as the 'most-favoured-nation' clause;
- *progressive reduction in tariff and non-tariff barriers:* certain exceptions, however, are permitted in specific circumstances. For example, Article 18 allows for the protection of 'infant industries' by the newly industrialising countries, whereas Article 19 permits any country to abstain from a general tariff cut in situations where rising imports might seriously damage domestic production. Similarly, Articles 21–5 allow protection to continue where 'strategic interests' are involved, such as national security;

- *solving trade disputes through consultation rather than retaliation:* again, certain exceptions are permitted. For example, Article 6 permits retaliatory sanctions to be applied if 'dumping' can be proven, i.e. the sale of products at artificially low prices (e.g. below cost). Countries in dispute are expected to negotiate bilaterally, but if these negotiations break down then a WTO-appointed working-party or panel can investigate the issue and make recommendations. Should any one of the parties refuse to accept this outcome, the WTO can impose fines and/or sanction certain types of retaliation by the aggrieved party.

The WTO has inherited 28 separate accords agreed under the final round of GATT negotiations (the Uruguay round). These accords sought to extend fair trade rules from industrial products to agricultural products, services, textiles, intellectual property rights and investment.

Although almost half the cases heard by the WTO have been brought by the US and EU, there are signs that this is beginning to change. China and other rapidly developing countries are themselves using the WTO to challenge what they see as protectionist policies and actions by the developed economies. For example, in 2013 while the US and EU were 'complainants' in 5 of the 20 disputes in that year, mainly on alleged 'dumping' issues, they were cited in 6 of these 20 disputes.

Perspectives on WTO initiatives

Despite its greater authority, not everyone is convinced that the WTO is using that authority effectively or fairly, with many critics pointing to the fact that changes in the WTO rules require the agreement of all WTO members who must reach consensus through rounds of negotiations. It may be useful to briefly review the arguments of both critics and supporters of the WTO.

Critics of the WTO

- *Bias to the 'North'.* Developing countries ('South') exporting to the advanced industrialised countries ('North') face tariffs on their exports that are four to five times higher than those placed on exports from advanced industrialised countries. For example, the average tariffs on imports of textiles and garments from developing countries into industrialised countries are 15–20%, as compared to only 3% on the imports of industrial goods. As a result, Bangladesh, one of the world's poorest countries, pays the US over $300 million a year in import taxes – about the same as France, the world's fifth richest economy.

- *Inability to progress the Doha Round of negotiations.* The most recent round of multilateral negotiations by the WTO to reduce trade restrictions began in Doha, Qatar, as long ago as 2001 and have still not been completed, given the requirement for all WTO members to reach a consensus by the end of these negotiations. Promises were made to reduce restrictions on trade in textiles and agricultural products (among others) which together account for around 70% of the exports of developing countries. Little progress has been made in either. For example, industrialised countries promised to phase out an elaborate system of quotas applied to textile imports by 2005 but by 2014 many of these quotas still remained. Reducing tariffs on agricultural imports and the subsidies given to agricultural exports was also a key element of the Doha Round. Yet little progress has been made as the powerful agri-businesses in the EU and USA have lobbied effectively against such measures.

- *Undue pressure on the 'South'.* Critics argue that the WTO is only consistent and effective in pursuing its free trade credentials when it places intense pressures for import liberalisation on the developing ('South') countries. The impact of such pressures can be seen from the fact that indices of 'trade openness' currently place 17 African countries as more accessible to import penetration than either the EU or the US. Yet the most successful developing countries have been those of East Asia which have liberalised slowly and in a staged manner, only lowering trade barriers as domestic productivity rises and home industries become more competitive on world markets.

- *Undue emphasis on protecting trade-related aspects of intellectual property rights.* The countries of the 'North' account for some 90% of world patents and successfully secured increased protection for intellectual property rights in the WTO 'TRIPS Agreement' (see p. 145) in 1995. However, before agreeing to the current Doha Round of negotiations, the developing countries insisted that a declaration be made at Doha confirming their right to 'set aside patents in the interests of public health and to buy or make cheap generic versions of expensive drugs'. While the developing countries see this as applying to any condition which undermines public health, whether diabetes, cancer, asthma, HIV/Aids or whatever, the large pharmaceutical companies have sought to limit the list of diseases to which this 'right' applies to malaria, tuberculosis and HIV/Aids, and to give only the poorest countries the opportunity of exercising this 'right'. With no agreement yet reached, critics blame the WTO for being ineffectual in failing to secure a more broad-based application of this 'right' enshrined in the Doha Declaration.

- *Undue emphasis on liberalising trade in services.* Of course many other criticisms have been levelled at the WTO, as for example the suggestion that it is too compliant in seeking to open world markets in *services,* to the benefit of the 'North'. Major proposals for wholesale deregulation of services have been proposed by the EU and US, opening up everything from banking and insurance to energy, water, sanitation and a host of 'public services'.

- *'Localisation' as an alternative doctrine.* Critics of the WTO include adherents of a doctrine opposed to unbridled free trade, namely 'localisation', which proposes that everything that can be produced locally should be produced locally, and to that end nations should protect their economies using trade taxes and legal barriers, though some international trade is still envisaged. The author of the 'localisation' manifesto, Colin Hines, suggests that 'some long-distance trade will still occur for those sectors providing goods and services to other regions of the world that can't provide such items from within their own borders, e.g. certain minerals or cash crops'. However, this is clearly a minimalist world trading environment which, in this view, hardly needs a WTO to regulate and expand it!

Pause for thought 3.8

Outline the arguments that could be used both for and against 'localisation'.

Supporters of the WTO may even accept some of these criticisms, yet focus on its role in preventing still greater excesses in a global environment characterised by grossly unequal power relationships between 'North' and 'South'. We now review a number of counter-arguments presented by supporters of the WTO.

Supporters of the WTO

- *Unilateralism/bilateralism may be the alternative to multilateralism.* We noted (p. 109) that the WTO embodies a *multilateral* approach to trade negotiations, as in the 'most-favoured-nation' clause extending benefits to all. In Chapter 1 (p. 7) we also noted the growth of *bilateral* trade treaties and regional trade arrangements which threaten this multilateral approach. In seeking to avoid such discriminatory treaties and arrangements, the WTO has won considerable support. Indeed, some see powerful nations (e.g. US) or supranational bodies (e.g. EU) as seeking to impose their own *unilateral* rules on world trading practices and regard the WTO as an indispensable bulwark in the fight against such unilateralism.

- *Absence of rules may be the alternative to imperfect WTO rules.* Even critics of the WTO often hesitate to contemplate a world trading regime with no rules whatsoever.

- *WTO has not distorted trade patterns.* Various working papers for the National Bureau of Economic Research in the US have suggested that the World Trade Organisation scarcely merits the demonisation it receives. Traditional linkages among countries, such as belonging to the same regional trade pact, or sharing languages, borders or colonial histories, are suggested in these working papers as more powerful factors in explaining variations in trade. Membership of WTO and its predecessor organisation, the GATT, appears to have had no strong or consistent impact on policy either, judged by 64 measures of trade policy openness investigated in these working papers.

- *WTO is taking more robust action against trade restrictions from the 'North'.* The WTO has, in fact, taken firm action against trade distortions from advanced industrialised economies such as the US, as for example involving its impositions of steel tariffs on imports. The WTO ruled in July 2003 that the US had violated international trading rules when it imposed tariffs of up to 30% on steel imports in 2002. The decision, by a dispute settlement panel of the WTO, was in a case brought by the EU and seven other countries. The US had imposed tariffs of up to 30% in March 2002 on many imported steel products, saying that ailing US steel companies needed protection against a flood of cheap foreign steel. The tariffs particularly hit steelmakers in the EU, Japan and Korea, while excluding most developing countries as well as Mexico and Canada. Brussels had argued that the duties were illegal because they failed to meet the basic test for a safeguard action – a recent surge in imports. Under WTO rules, countries can extend temporary protection to industries hit by import competition, but only under strict conditions. The US had previously lost half a dozen WTO cases concerning safeguard measures, including curbs on steel, wheat, gluten and lamb. The WTO ruled that there was no evidence of such a surge in imports due, as alleged, to 'dumping' by non-US companies of steel in US markets, and the WTO gave permission for the disadvantaged countries to retaliate by imposing tariffs themselves on a range of specified US products to the estimated value of the losses they themselves had suffered from the unwarranted tariffs the US had imposed on their exports. (In the event the various countries chose not to exercise this option of retaliation.)

- *'Localisation'* is viewed by free-traders as diminishing the wealth of poorer nations rather than enhancing it. The World Bank has argued that increased openness to trade (the opposite of localisation) raises average incomes and the incomes of the poor – i.e. there is no relationship between increased openness to trade and rising inequality, if anything quite the opposite. Sebastian Edwards of the University of California also concludes in a study of 93 countries that there is a close link between openness to trade and rates of productivity growth. In this view 'localisation' is itself seen as a recipe for increased inequality. Colin Hines' model invents a whole new series of global bodies to impose localisation on nation states whether they like it or not. States would be forbidden to pass laws that diminish local control of industry and services. Hines, in other words, prohibits precisely the kind of political autonomy he claims to promote.

● *Reformed WTO may have much to commend it.* Even critics of the WTO see the potential for this body undergoing reform to the benefit of the global trading system. Many suggest that greater 'fairness' to the developing countries would result from the WTO placing greater emphasis on the short-term protection of infant industries and the short-term use of intellectual property rights in the developing countries. Developing countries could then follow the well-trodden path of the now developed countries which, historically, used trade barriers and the acquisition (legally or illegally) of intellectual property to grow themselves.

Case 3.5 reviews recent development and challenges to the role of the WTO in securing multilateral outcomes for trade negotiations.

CASE 3.5 WTO doubts grow over global role

Roberto Azevedo, the new head of the World Trade Organisation, struck a triumphal tone in Bali last December when he announced that the body's 159 members had reached the first global agreement in its 18 year history. 'The WTO is back!' the visibly sleep-deprived Brazilian told delegates, drawing cheers from all around. Mr Azevedo, it turns out, was speaking too soon. Seven months later, the WTO has been plunged into an existential crisis, after India's new government this week blocked the centrepiece of the Bali deal: a seemingly benign arrangement called the *Trade Facilitation Agreement* to reduce customs red tape around the world. As a result Mr Azevdeo is now facing doubts about both the future of his organisation and, more broadly, the liberal vision of a multilateral trading system that has guided the post-war era in the global economy.

The WTO, which took over in 1995 from the General Agreement on Tariffs and Trade, has grown out of the agreements struck at Bretton Woods in the US in 1944, which sought to keep world leaders from repeating the protectionist mistakes of the 1930s. There are bound to be efforts to revive negotiations. The government in New Delhi has already sought to play down the implications of its stand. Announcing the failure to reach a compromise to members on Thursday,

Mr Azevedo urged them to use the August break to ponder the future and return in September with ideas. However, the Bali agreement already amounted to a rescue operation and its failure bodes badly for the system.

'There is an element of significant dysfunction that you can't hide,' said one senior official yesterday.

India had originally given its blessing to the deal. But that was before a new government, led by Narendra Modi, came to power two months ago. New Delhi has in recent weeks insisted it wants to renegotiate deadlines set in Bali in order to bring forward negotiations to update the WTO rules that apply to subsidies it gives to farmers as part of a massive government programme to provide cheap food to poor people.

In an effort to get what it wanted, India carried out a threat this week to block a procedural measure to prevent the Trade Facilitation Agreement from making the July 31 deadline set in Bali for its implementation. The failure to meet the deadline means the WTO's members are even less likely to meet another in December to come up with a plan to deliver the rest of the Doha round of negotiations for a global trade deal. The Doha round was launched in 2001 and has since repeatedly broken down as a result of

Case 3.5 (*continued*)

the failure of rich countries such as the US, and emerging economies, such as China and India, to narrow their differences. Putting Doha back on track would mean tackling much more difficult issues such as agricultural subsidies in a new climate of distrust, say diplomats.

The irony is that India and other developing counties are likely to suffer most from any collapse of the Doha round, say trade analysts. The US, EU and other key players such as Japan all have big regional trade initiatives under way, and are likely to find moving on much easier than India or smaller and more vulnerable states.

Several members have threatened to enact the Trade Facilitation Agreement as a 'plurilateral' deal outside the WTO, a move that would further marginalise the Geneva-based organisation. The text to do so has already been drafted and translated into three languages. Up to 60 countries have indicated they are keen to see it implemented, which is contrary to the spirit of the WTO with multilateral agreements covering all 159 members.

Negations such as those now under way between the EU and US or between the US and 11 other countries to create a *Trans-Pacific Partnership* are increasingly focused on more complex, non-tariff barriers to trade. In Brussels and Washington, negotiators are also starting to tackle how to guarantee the free flow of data across borders or ease the way for the global supply chains so vital to modern business. These are discussions that are years beyond what is on the current agenda at the WTO.

The WTO will not come crashing down tomorrow, says Kimberly Elliott, a trade analyst at the Centre for Global Development think-tank in Washington. But its future looks bleak if the Doha negotiations go back into the coma that has been their dominant state in recent years.

While many celebrate the WTO's place as a venue for settling disputes, that function will be eroded if it is not updating its rules to reflect new issues. Without any progress in negotiations, 'there are going to be more and more disputes that cannot be resolved [at the WTO]' said Mrs Elliott.

FT *Source:* Donnan, S., 'WTO plunged into crisis as doubts grow over global role'. *Financial Times*, 2 August 2014.

Questions

1 Why did India block the Trade Facilitation Agreement?

2 What problems do many analysts see as a result of this and other 'failures' by the WTO?

The International Monetary Fund (IMF)

The IMF plays a key role in providing foreign currencies and other sources of world liquidity to support the growth of international trade and payments. It also provides specific packages of financial support for economies in times of need. This latter role involves a variety of 'stabilisation programmes' (see p. 118), which provide essential funding but only on condition that the countries receiving funds agree to implement specific programmes of change agreed with the IMF.

 ## Foreign currencies and world liquidity

In order to settle balance of payments deficits arising from international trade, theory tells us that deficit countries should be able to run down their foreign exchange reserves or to borrow from surplus countries. Both methods have, in reality, proved next to impossible.

The countries most likely to suffer balance of payments deficits are those with low per capita incomes and with few foreign exchange reserves – in other words, countries with low credit ratings on the international banking circuit, making borrowing from surplus countries difficult. It was in order to solve just these sorts of liquidity problems for deficit countries that the IMF was established.

The IMF began in 1946 with just 39 members, but is now a giant international organisation with 171 members. It has an unwieldy board of governors, with one governor from each member country. However, day-to-day decisions are taken by an executive board of 22 members, seven of whom are appointed by the USA, Germany, the UK, France, Japan, Saudi Arabia and China, with the remaining 15 elected from geographical constituencies.

Currency quotas

The IMF was originally set up to provide a pool of foreign currencies, which could be used by members to 'finance' temporary balance of payments deficits. This would give deficit countries time to 'adjust' their deficits, i.e. adopt policies which would eventually eliminate them without having to resort to immediate and massive deflations aimed at cutting spending on imports, or to sudden moves towards protectionist measures, or to reductions in the exchange rate to regain price competitiveness. By helping deficit countries to finance their deficits, the IMF was therefore seeking to promote the smooth growth of world income and trade.

Quotas

These have been assigned to each country to determine its access to foreign currency and also its voting rights within the IMF. Critics of the IMF point out that these quotas were allocated *pro rata* to each country's total value of trade, so that in practice the richer countries received much higher quotas than poorer, less trade-oriented countries. So, for example, in 2006 the US quota (against which it could access 125%, over five years, in foreign currencies) was equivalent to around $40 billion, while that for Tonga and Bhutan was a mere $7 million or so.

Borrowing facilities

There are, however, further facilities for borrowing, with varying degrees of strictness as to the conditions attached. As we shall see, these various facilities and practices, and especially the creation of SDRs (see p. 116), have together changed the nature of the IMF. It is no longer the rather conservative institution of its Articles, simply reallocating a *given* pool of world currencies, but one which can intervene actively to find varied sources of finance and even to *create* new world money.

- *Compensatory Financing Facility* (CFF). The CFF was introduced in 1963 to assist primary producing countries in difficulty due to a temporary fall in export earnings (e.g. crop failure or natural disaster).
- *Compensatory and Contingency Financing Facility* (CCFF). This superseded the CFF in August 1988. It has added the possibility of contingency financing to support agreed structural adjustment programmes.
- *Extended Fund Facilities* (EFF). The EFF began in 1974 and was introduced to provide countries with more time to adjust their financial affairs. Most IMF loans had to be repaid in three to five years, but the EFF initially gave up to eight years for repayment, and now even longer.

- *Oil Facilities*. These were temporary facilities established in 1974 to assist countries whose balance of payments had been severely hit by rising oil prices. In theory, the oil facility had an upper limit of 450% of quota (to enable less developed countries with very low quotas to receive significant assistance), but some countries received loans up to 800% of quota. The oil facilities were ended in 1976.

- *Bufferstock Facility*. This was established in June 1969 to finance the building up of bufferstocks by commodity producers at times of falling world prices. Up to 45% of the quota is permitted for this purpose.

In addition to its 'normal' resources, the IMF has a variety of other instruments and facilities at its disposal:

- *Supplementary Financing Facility* (SFF). This is actually a separate trust, established with the IMF as a trustee in February 1979. It originally borrowed SDR 7.5 billion from the oil producers to assist countries that had exceeded their Credit Tranche borrowing.

- *Enlarged Access Facilities*. Set up in May 1981 after SFF money became fully committed, it allows members to borrow up to 150% of quota in a single year, or up to 450% of quota over a three-year period. The intention is to assist countries with large deficits relative to quota.

- *Structural Adjustment Facility* (SAF). In 1986 a new 'structural adjustment facility' was implemented in order to recycle the loan repayments to some of the Fund's poorer members, the Low Income Developing Countries.

- *Enhanced Structural Adjustment Facility*. At the Venice Summit of 1987 it was agreed to expand the SAF on identical terms but with additional funds. Loans are now determined on need and there is no overall ceiling. However, the IMF operates a policy of 250% of quota as the maximum access unless there are 'exceptional circumstances'. Normal repayments are in ten half-yearly payments, beginning after five-and-a-half years and ending ten years after the date of the loan.

- *Trust Fund Facility*. Between 1976 and 1980 the IMF sold 25 million ounces of gold at market prices. It used most of the revenue to establish a trust fund to assist the lesser developed countries (LDCs). This facility ceased in 1981 when the fund had been exhausted.

- *Systemic Transformation Facility*. Established as a series of initiatives between 1990 and 1993, this facility was designed to channel restructuring funds and support to countries in the former 'Eastern Bloc'.

Intermediation

The role of the IMF does not end with these various facilities. It has been an intermediary in arranging *standby credits* at times when currencies have come under severe strain. These credits have not usually been used, but have helped restore market confidence in a country's ability to withstand speculative pressure, which itself has often eased that pressure. It has also from time to time arranged finance from the Group of Ten leading industrial countries.

Special Drawing Rights (SDRs)

These were introduced by the IMF in 1969, both to raise the total of world official reserves and to serve as a potential replacement for gold and foreign currency in the international monetary system. Special drawing rights were essentially a 'free gift' from the IMF to its members, which could be used to settle debt between countries. The SDR had no separate existence of its own, being simply a book entry with the IMF. It served as international money since it could be transferred to other countries in settlement of debt. The total of SDRs to be created was at the discretion of the IMF, but the allocation of that total was to be strictly in proportion to quotas. To make this new world currency acceptable it was initially valued in gold, with interest rates paid on credit balances. Special Drawing Rights were later valued in terms of a basket of 16 different currencies, the idea being to move away from depending on gold yet to retain confidence in the value of the SDR by avoiding dependence on any single currency. In 1981 this rather unwieldy basket was replaced by a smaller basket of five major currencies

The fact that SDRs have been given to members in amounts proportional to the size of their quotas has not been without criticism. It is the major trading countries that (as we have seen) have the largest quotas. The whole matter of SDRs has become much more controversial in recent years as their shortcomings have become more apparent. Although efforts were made to make them more attractive (e.g. providing market rates of interest to those holding them) they still only represent 2% of total world liquidity and are, essentially, being held by those who least need them (the richer trading countries).

General arrangements to borrow (GAB)

In 1962 the ten largest IMF members plus Switzerland (which is not an IMF member) constructed the GAB. Each of the signatories contributed an amount of its own currency towards a fund which now stands at over $19 billion and can be used to help alleviate the world banking crises.

'Swap' arrangements

In the 1960s the USA instituted a system of currency 'swaps' with other countries, whereby each central bank agrees to lend its own currency, or to acquire currency balances of the other, for a specified time period. Although these are relatively short-term arrangements, there is currently an additional $30 billion to $40 billion that could be added to total reserves under such schemes.

> ### Pause for thought 3.9
>
> Why has the IMF sometimes been termed 'the rich man's club'? Is this criticism fair?

Review of the role of the IMF

The IMF has undoubtedly helped to support the growth of international trade and payments through its various and substantial contributions to world liquidity. Nevertheless, where it has been involved in 'stabilisation programmes' in support of particular LDCs and transition economies at times of financial hardship, it has been the subject of some criticism (see Box 3.7).

Interestingly the BRIC economies, together with South Africa, announced in July 2014 that they were creating two new financial institutions, seen by many as an attempt by Brazil, Russia, India, China and South African to develop an alternative infrastructure to the IMF. The *New Development Bank* (NDB) will have $50 billion to finance infrastructure and sustainable development projects and the *Contingent Reserve Arrangement* (CRA) will have $100 billion to support members in financial difficulties.

BOX 3.7 IMF stabilisation programmes

IMF stabilisation programmes (see also p. 120) seek to address adverse balance of payments situations while retaining price stability and encouraging the resumption of economic growth. The main components of typical IMF stabilisation programmes include some or all of the following:

- *fiscal contraction* – a reduction in the public sector deficit through cuts in public expenditure and/or rises in taxation;
- *monetary contraction* – restrictions on credit to the public sector and increases in interest rates;
- *devaluation of the exchange rate* (this is often a pre-condition for the serious negotiation of a stabilisation programme, rather than part of the programme as such);
- *liberalisation of the economy* – via reduction or elimination of controls, and privatisation of public sector assets;
- *incomes policy* – wage restraint and removal of subsidies and reduction of transfer payments.

Criticisms of the IMF's stabilisation programmes in LDCs and the transition economies can be grouped as follows:

1 *IMF programmes are inappropriate.* The criticism here is that its approach to policy has been preoccupied with the control of demand, and too little concerned with other weaknesses stemming from problems with the productive system in LDCs and transition economies. By deflating demand, the IMF has imposed large adjustment costs on borrowing countries through losses of output and employment, further impoverishing the poor and even destabilising incumbent governments.

2 *IMF programmes are inflexible.* The criticism here is that the IMF has imposed its solutions on the country needing to borrow rather than negotiating a more flexible package. This has arguably infringed the sovereignty of states and alienated governments from the measures they are supposed to implement.

3 *IMF support has been too small, expensive and short term.* The programmes have been criticised for having been too small in magnitude and too short term in duration for economies whose underlying problems are rooted in structural weaknesses and that often face 'adverse' terms of trade (fall in export prices relative to import prices).

4 *The IMF is dominated by a few major industrial countries.* The criticism here is that the industrial countries have sometimes used their control of the IMF to promote their own interests, as for example in using the IMF to shift a disproportionate amount of the debt burden onto the debtor countries rather than forcing lenders (e.g. banks) to accept some of the debt burden, given their earlier readiness to lend huge funds at high rates of interest to 'risky' ventures.

Box 3.8 (p. 120) looks further at the principles involved in the IMF stabilisation programmes and contrasts those with some of the World Bank's attempts to support the global economic system.

World Bank

The World Bank is, in effect, a grouping of three international institutions, namely the International Bank for Reconstruction and Development, the International Development Association and the International Finance Corporation.

International Bank for Reconstruction and Development (IBRD)

The origins of the World Bank lie in the formation of the IBRD in 1946. The IBRD sought to help countries raise the finance needed to reconstruct their war-damaged economies. This often took the form of guaranteeing loans that could then be obtained at lower interest rates than might otherwise have been possible.

International Development Association (IDA)

In 1958 a second international institution was created to operate alongside the IBRD, namely the International Development Association. The main objective of the IDA was to provide development finance for low-income nations which had insufficient resources to pay interest on the IBRD loans.

International Finance Corporation (IFC)

The International Finance Corporation was established in 1959. Unlike the previous two bodies, the IFC concentrates on lending to *private* borrowers involved in development projects.

Initially much of this lending was for specific infrastructure projects such as dams, power facilities, transport links, etc. More recently, the focus of lending has shifted towards improving the efficiency and accountability of the administrative and institutional structures in the recipient countries.

The role of the World Bank has broadened in recent years to include the private sector as well as governments. In June 2003, the International Development Association – the bank's concessional arm, which deals with the world's poorest countries – gave grants of around $100 million (£60 million) to improve the financial services available to small and medium-sized companies. This marked a continued cultural shift away from the bank's traditional public sector focus.

World Bank 'Structural Adjustment Lending'

Since 1980 the World Bank has been involved in various types of Structural Adjustment Lending (SAL) which account for over 20% of its lending. These SAL programmes are non-project-related; rather they involve lending to support specific programmes or policy which may involve elements of institutional change. These SAL programmes are generally directed towards improving the 'supply side' of the borrowing countries, intending to initiate and fund changes which will ultimately raise productive efficiency in various sectors of their economies.

Box 3.8 provides a rather stereotyped but useful overview of the World Bank's SAL programmes and compares these with the IMF's 'stabilisation programmes' previously discussed (see Box 3.7).

BOX 3.8 World Bank structural adjustment and stabilisation

Structural adjustment. As noted earlier, most of the World Bank Structural Adjustment Lending (SAL) programmes have sought to improve the supply side of the economy. Where successful this will result in the downward, to the right, movement of the aggregate supply curve (AS) from AS_1 to AS_2, thus reducing the price level (from P_2 to P_3 with AD_2) and increasing output (from Q_2 to Q_3) – see Figure 3.10. Clearly the remedies involving structural adjustment are rather more palatable than the remedies which involve deflation (see below) in that both output and employment rise, but only after possibly difficult changes to labour and capital market practices and institutions to improve supply-side conditions.

It is also worth noting that the World Bank is seeking to offer progressively 'softer' loans to developing countries.

Stabilisation. As was noted earlier most of the policies in the IMF stabilisation programmes have been of a deflationary nature. This results in the downward movement, to the left, of the aggregate demand curve (AD) from AD_1 to AD_2 thus reducing the price level (from P_1 to P_2 with AS_1) but also reducing output (from Q_1 to Q_2). The debtor country may be made more competitive in its exports and import-substitute sectors, benefiting its balance of payments and reducing its debt, but at the cost of lost output and employment.

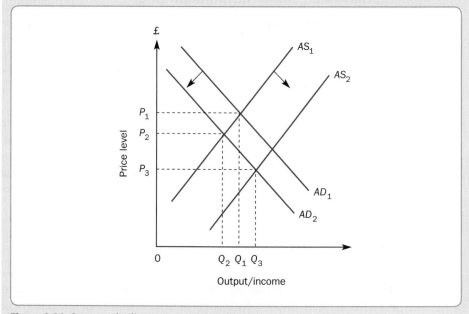

Figure 3.10 Structural adjustment and stabilisation

Chapter 4

The political, legal, economic and technological environment

By the end of this chapter you should be able to:

- assess the effects of globalisation on world political systems;
- explain the various ways in which political risk can be analysed and minimised;
- discuss the implications of different political and regulatory systems for international business;
- outline the issues that MNEs have to consider in relation to the legal environment, including the increasingly important areas of intellectual property rights and e-commerce legal risks;
- consider the main features of the different types of economic system in which international businesses operate;
- identify and explain some of the key economic variables which influence international businesses in the assessment of their economic environment;
- discuss the opportunities and threats to international business of technological change.

Introduction

In Chapters 1–3, we outlined how the internationalisation of business increasingly transcends national barriers. Nevertheless, the basic unit in which the MNE operates is still the nation state, each one of which has its own method of governance, institutional framework and legal environment. It would be folly indeed for any company thinking of going international to be unaware of these different factors, and to have failed to take them into account before making any significant strategic decisions. In this chapter, we look at the various political and legal elements that make up 'governance', highlight areas of political and legal risk, and suggest ways in which businesses may seek to address such risk.

In the widely used approach of PESTLE analysis (see p. 222) businesses seek to assess the political, economic, social, technological, legal and ecological environments in which they must operate. In this chapter, as well as the political and legal variables, we also pay particular attention to the economic and technological variables that may crucially determine the outcomes for international business of individual investment projects or broad strategic initiatives. Further discussions of the economic and technological issues facing the individual business also take place in Chapters 7–10. For example, Chapter 7 looks at the impacts of new technologies on the supply chain and on other logistical operations.

The following two chapters focus on the sociocultural, environmental and ethical aspects of international business decisions which may also play a part in more sophisticated PEST-type analyses.

Political environment

At the heart of governance is the notion of 'sovereignty', which implies the power to rule without constraint and which, for the last three centuries, has been associated with the nation state. We live in a world which is organised as a patchwork of nation states within which different peoples live, with their own systems of government exerting authority over the affairs within their territory. Of course, as has clearly been the case in recent years, groupings within those territories have arisen which seek a measure of independence from the central authorities, often claiming nation statehood themselves, with Iraq, Syria, Ukraine and Palestine among many such examples.

Many would also argue that the idea of the nation state has itself been challenged by the growth of globalisation. Before turning to this issue it may be useful to highlight some opposing and arguably contradictory tendencies in globalisation (see also Chapter 1).

- *Centralisation versus decentralisation.* Some aspects of globalisation tend to concentrate power, knowledge, information, wealth and decision making. Many believe this to be the case with the rise of the MNE, the growth of regional trading blocs (e.g. the EU), the development of world regulatory bodies such as the WTO, etc. However, such centralising tendencies may conflict with powerful decentralising tendencies as nations, communities and individuals attempt to take greater control over the forces that influence their lives (e.g. the growth of social movements centred on the global environment, peace and gender issues, etc.).

- *Juxtaposition versus syncretisation.* In the globalisation process, time and space become compressed, so that different civilisations, ways of life and social practices become juxtaposed (placed side by side). This can create 'shared' cultural and social spaces characterised by an evolving mixture of ideas, knowledge and institutions. Unfortunately this can also stimulate the opposite tendencies, such as a heightened awareness of challenges to the established norms of previously dominant groups, which can result in determined attempts to avoid integration and instead combine against a 'common opponent' (syncretisation).

While there may be many theories as to the causes of globalisation, most writers would agree that globalisation is a discontinuous historical process. Its dynamic proceeds in fits and starts and its effects are experienced differentially across the globe. Some regions are more deeply affected by globalisation than others. Even within nation states, some communities (e.g. financial) may experience the effects of globalisation more sharply than others (e.g. urban office workers). Many have argued that globalisation is tending to reinforce inequalities of power both within and across nation states, resulting in global hierarchies of privilege and control for some but economic and social exclusion for others.

We have already considered the ways in which globalisation has arguably influenced the notion of the nation state (Chapter 1), suggesting some loss of competence, autonomy, authority and ultimately legitimacy for such entities (pp. 26–27). We concluded that globalisation is redefining our understanding of the nation state by introducing a much more complex architecture of political power in which authority is seen as being pluralistic rather than residing solely in the nation state.

Political risk

While businesses are largely aware that the political climate in different countries varies enormously, for organisations wishing to go global a far more detailed analysis needs to take place. When considering penetrating or expanding into new markets, organisations need to be able to assess the political risk. Political risk is widely understood to include uncertainty that stems, in whole or in part, from the exercise of power by governmental and non-governmental actors.

Political risks can be classified into two broad categories, 'macropolitical' and 'micropolitical'.

1 *Macropolitical risks* potentially affect all firms in a country, as in the case of war or sudden changes of government. Such risks may even result in expropriation or confiscation, where governments seize the assets of the firm without compensation. Communist governments in Eastern Europe and China expropriated private firms after the Second World War, with the same happening at different times in the post-war period to private enterprises in Angola, Chile, Ethiopia, Peru and Zambia. Higher general levels of inflation or taxation might adversely affect all firms, as might security risks related to terrorism, etc.

2 *Micropolitical risks* within a country affect only specific firms, industries or types of venture. Such risks may take the form of new regulations or taxes imposed on specific types of businesses in the country. For example, the indebtedness of countries in South America has meant that many have introduced legislation to encourage certain types of exports and discourage certain types of imports. For firms focused on exporting products into these countries, such practices are extremely adverse. However, for MNEs looking for an international location ('platform') from which to produce and export products to other countries, these government policies may appear very attractive.

In globalised economies political decisions can bring benefits and/or costs to many sectors of an economy, arising from unexpected political sources, as Case 4.1 illustrates.

CASE 4.1 Chinese government and EU milk products

We have already noted the sharp increases in demand in 2014 for dairy cows and dairy output in Case 2.9 (p. 62). The sharp increase in Chinese demand for milk products in recent years can be seen to have its origins in the political arena. Indeed, in late 2007 EU producers and consumers of milk products become only too well aware of how political decisions in one part of the world can, with interconnected global markets, transmit market 'shocks' to all corners of the world. A drive by the Chinese government to provide all Chinese children

---

Case 4.1 (*continued*)

with half a litre of milk a day caused demand for milk to increase dramatically by around 25% a year, with around one-third of all the worldwide production of milk soon thereafter being exported to China. Prices of a litre of milk in the EU itself rose by over 25% in one week alone in August 2007, with a substantial price increase in dairy-based products such as cheese, butter and yogurt following closely behind. Kraft raised prices of its cheese-based products by 12% in 2007, linking the price rise explicitly to higher milk costs.

However, others blamed different political factors, namely over-regulation in the EU, for milk-based inflation. They argued that it had been the extremely tight milk quotas imposed by the EU and due to last until 2015 that has prevented the supply side of the EU market for milk from adjusting to this surge of Chinese demand. Even so some market adjustment has taken place, if only slowly, as for example with EU dairy farmers increasingly breeding high-performance milk cows and selling these to Chinese farmers, who have little or no tradition of dairy farming. Increased Chinese production of milk has also been helped by Chinese government subsidies for farmers to encourage them to switch to dairy farming.

Questions

1 In what ways does this case indicate one or more of the features (discussed in Chapter 1) often associated with globalisation?

2 What aspects of political risk are involved here and how might those political risks have been taken into account?

It may be useful to disaggregate the types of political risk further, as indicated in Table 4.1.

Pause for thought 4.1

You are the MD of a US-based multinational company considering establishing a major affiliate in the UK. Which types of political risk in Table 4.1 are likely to be of major concern?

Analysing political risk

Analysing political risk has, in the past, been a rather ad hoc affair, but in more recent times it has become increasingly sophisticated. A common criticism of political risk analysis is that it usually takes place too late, when projects are already underway. More management time and effort is now being directed towards appraising political risk at the initiation stage of projects as companies become more aware of its importance to their future operations. For example, organisations seeking to internationalise typically investigate the following factors in countries which might become the focus of fdi activity: the system of government, foreign capital controls, industrial regulations, history of civil unrest, diplomatic tensions, and so on.

Managers or their representatives may well visit the countries under investigation, as well as using information and data sources from libraries, the internet, industry associations, government agencies, banks and insurers. Country-risk reports are also available from risk assessment companies and specialists in particular business activities, often consisting of a

Table 4.1 **Types of political risk and their likely impacts**

Type	Impact on firms
Expropriation/confiscation of companies by foreign governments	Loss of sales Loss of assets Loss of future profits
Campaigns against imported goods by foreign governments	Loss of sales Increased cost of public relations campaigns to improve public image
Mandatory labour benefits legislation (e.g. new or higher minimum wage)	Increased operating costs
Kidnappings, terrorist threats, and other forms of violence	Disrupted production Increased security costs Increased managerial costs Lower productivity
Civil wars	Destruction of property Lost sales Disruption of production Increased security costs Lower productivity
Inflation	Higher operating costs
Currency devaluations or depreciation	Reduced value of repatriated earnings
Currency revaluations or appreciation	Less competitive in overseas markets and in competing against imports in home market
Increased taxation	Lower after-tax profits Relocation, where possible, to lower tax regimes

country profile and macro-level market/non-market risk assessment. However, such analyses may not include the fine detail that might be vital for particular ventures, and at best provide only an indication of the sociopolitical background.

Case 4.2 provides useful insights into the complex political interventions which international businesses may encounter in specific countries and product areas – in this case India and sugar and onion products.

CASE 4.2 Sugar and onions in India

After Indian inflation unexpectedly shot up in late 2014, driven by a sharp rise in the price of basic foodstuffs, the government of Narendra Modi responded with two apparently contradictory moves. First, it doubled the minimum export price of onions – a staple of Indian cookery – in effect making it tougher for farmers to sell the vegetable overseas. It seemed a strong signal of intent: New Delhi was ready to combat rising food prices by using trade as a lever. Second, a week later, it took a step that had the opposite impact on another important commodity. The government doubled tariffs on imported sugar to buoy the ailing local industry, which immediately led to a 1.5 per cent rise in the price of domestic sugar.

The back-to-back moves – discouraging onion exports to help cool local prices, then discouraging sugar imports to prop up local prices – highlight the conflicting pressures on Mr Modi's government as it seeks to chart a

Case 4.2 (continued)

coherent food policy in a country where changes in both food and farm prices are highly sensitive political issues.

On the one hand, about 25–30 per cent of India's population spends more than half of its monthly household income on food. These consumers, especially the urban poor and working classes, expect Mr Modi to fulfil his promise to tame persistently high inflation, which has eroded their purchasing power as earnings have failed to keep pace. But India is also a country where 60–70 per cent of households lie in rural areas, with at least some of their household income tied to agriculture. Mr Modi's Bharatiya Janata Party also has its eye fixed on a clutch of forthcoming state assembly elections, including in the sugar-growing state of Maharashtra, where the BJP hopes to seize power from the enfeebled Congress parties.

Alay Vir Jakhar, chairman of the Bharat Krishak Samaj – or Indian Farmers Forum – says the sugar tariff move was not fundamentally at odds with the clampdown on onion exports. Rather, he says, the effort to bolster local sugar prices was to prevent a sharp drop in production, as occurred in 2008–09, which would cause prices to spiral out of control. 'The policy of the government is very clean and clear,' he says. 'They want prices to remain low for urban consumers. Every policy stems from that.'

Ashok Gulaati, former chairman of the government's Commission for Agricultural Costs and Prices, which makes recommendations on minimum support prices for many commodities, agrees. 'In a country where the bottom 30 per cent of people are spending more than half their income on food, sensitivity to food prices will be very, very high,' he says. "If anything goes off-course, there will be a knee-jerk reaction, either to protect the farmers or to protect the poor consumers".

Onion prices are a political issue in India, where few dishes can be complete without the vegetable's pungent flavour. Voters have been known to give decision rebukes – via the ballot box – to governments that fail to keep onion prices stable. This year onion supply was affected by erratic weather and Mr Modi felt compelled to counteract the resulting upward pressure on prices. 'Over the last 20 to 30 years, governments have been booted out of office after onion price rises,' says Anwarul Hoda, professor of trade policy at the New Delhi-based Indian Council for Research on International Economic Relations.

The sugar industry's woes are deeper and more complex. In India – both the world's biggest sugar consumer and the second-largest producer – sugar is one of the most heavily regulated agricultural commodities. Every year New Delhi sets raw cane prices that private sugar millers must pay to all the farmers in a designated geographical area. But in the northern state of Uttar Pradesh, the local administration, seeking to bolster its popularity among farmers, mandated that millers pay a premium on top of the federally prescribed price, encouraging farmers to grow more cane, despite big sugar stockpiles. Squeezed between the government-mandated prices for buying cane, and the market price at which it sells processed sugar, millers have struggled to pay farmers for their crops, and have pleaded for New Delhi's help. As of July, mills owed about $1.8bn to farmers. Mr Jakhar says increasing import tariffs and a government subsidy for sugar exports are aimed at helping local millers liquidate stocks and raise cash to pay farmers, who were threatening not to grow sugar next year.

With so many players – and politics – in the game, ensuring adequate supplies of agricultural commodities at affordable prices looks set to remain a challenge for Mr Modi's government for the foreseeable future.

Questions

1 Why are the government policies for sugar and onions seen by many analysts as contradictory?

2 Explain the political factors involved in the policy proposals (a) for sugar and (b) for onions.

Quantifying political risk

There are various sophisticated ways of analysing political risk, one of which is to identify and then *quantify* the various elements involved. Table 4.2 outlines the criteria that might be used for such an analysis. We can see that some of the criteria in Table 4.2 have a wider minimum to maximum range than others, because that particular risk is perceived as varying more widely between different countries. For example, no country is viewed as having

Table 4.2 **Select criteria for evaluating political risk**

Major area	Criteria		Score	
			Minimum	Maximum
Political economic environment	1	Stability of the political system	3	14
	2	Imminent internal conflicts	0	14
	3	External threats to stability	0	12
	4	Degree of control of the economic system	5	9
	5	Reliability of the country as a trading partner	4	12
	6	Constitutional guarantees	2	12
	7	Effectiveness of public administration	3	12
	8	Labour relations and social peace	3	15
Domestic economic conditions	9	Size of the population	4	8
	10	Per capita income	2	10
	11	Economic growth over the last 5 years	2	7
	12	Potential growth over the next 3 years	3	10
	13	Inflation over the past 2 years	2	10
	14	Accessibility of the domestic capital market to outsiders	3	7
	15	Availability of high-quality local labour force	2	8
	16	Possibility of employing foreign nationals	2	8
	17	Availability of energy resources	2	14
	18	Legal requirements regarding environmental pollution	4	8
	19	Infrastructure, including transportation and communication systems	2	14
External economic conditions	20	Import restrictions	2	10
	21	Export restrictions	2	10
	22	Restrictions on foreign investments	3	9
	23	Freedom to set up or engage in partnerships	3	9
	24	Legal protection for brands and products	3	9
	25	Restrictions on monetary transfers	2	8
	26	Revaluation of the currency during the last 5 years	2	7
	27	Balance of payments situation	2	9
	28	Drain on foreign funds through oil and energy imports	3	14
	29	International financial standing	3	8
	30	Restriction on the exchange of local money into foreign currencies	2	8

Source: Adapted from Dichtl and Koeglmayr (1986), p. 6.

perfect 'stability of the political system', hence the minimum risk assessment is three rather than zero. At the other extreme some countries are viewed as extremely unstable in this respect, receiving the maximum risk assessment, for this criterion, of 14. The respective minimum and maximum scores are indicated for some 30 criteria across three major areas: political economic environment, domestic economic conditions and external economic conditions.

Suppose, for example, that a MNE wishes to evaluate the political risk of pursuing a joint venture in a particular country. If the country scores too highly over the selected criteria deemed appropriate to the joint venture or investment project under consideration, then the MNE will look elsewhere unless there is a way of reducing these risks. For some criteria this may be possible. For example, while the MNE may itself be unable to influence the first criterion in Table 4.2 of 'stability of the political system', it might believe that it can reduce the initial risk score ascribed, say, to the eighth criterion of 'labour relations and social peace'. For example, the MNE may well look at an initial risk score on this criterion for a particular country and then re-evaluate that assessment in the light of its own strategic intentions (e.g. adopting widespread worker consultation procedures, paying above the minimum wage, etc.) and any promises made to it by the authorities of a potential host country (e.g. assurances as to no-strike agreements, etc.). However, should the overall risk-assessment score for a particular project still be higher than that in other countries despite taking into account these planned risk-reduction strategies, this may cause the firm to reconsider its location decision.

Of course, these 'risk scores' for the various criteria will to some extent be subjective, based on management perceptions as to the likelihood (probability) of that risk factor actually occurring. These risk scores must continually be reviewed as events and circumstances (and associated probabilities) are ever-changing. For example, investment in Indonesia facilitated by a close confidant of the then President Suharto before 1997 will have very different political risk scores for the various factors after the fall of President Suharto in 1997, the instability induced by various independence movements (e.g. East Timor in 1999) and recent investigations into state corruption in the pre-1997 period.

Pause for thought 4.2

You are the MD of a US-based MNE specialising in heavy equipment (capital goods) manufacture. You are about to decide whether to establish a production platform in either Italy or Russia. Look at Table 4.2 and identify some of the political risk factors that might influence your decision. What other considerations might be taken into account?

Expected value and political risk

It is not only the probability of a particular political risk factor occurring but the magnitude of its potential impact on the objectives of the company that must also be taken into account. It is worth remembering that the expected value of an event is the sum of the probability of each possible outcome multiplied by the value (impact) of each outcome.

$$EV = \sum_{i=1}^{n} p_i x_i$$

where p_i = probability of outcome i (as a decimal)

x_i = value of outcome i

n = number of possible outcomes

So if the firm estimated a 60% probability of a 'strike' labour dispute (criterion 8 'labour relations and social peace' in Table 4.2) occurring so that profits are £10 million and a 40% probability of a 'work to rule' occurring so that profits are £20 million, the expected value (EV) should a labour dispute occur would be:

$$EV \ (£m) = (0.60 \times 10) + (0.40 \times 20)$$

$$= £14\,m$$

A change in the firm's assessment of the probabilities of these events occurring or the value of their impact should they occur would, of course, influence the expected value calculation.

Once identified and assessed, such political risks can be prioritised, as in Figure 4.1. The 'gross risks' (expected values) associated with the various political factors or events are sometimes placed by businesses in a two-by-two diagram, giving four 'boxes'. Box A shows risks (high impact/high likelihood) requiring immediate action, resulting in attempts by the firm to reduce either the probability of their occurrence or the impact should they occur. Perhaps it would also be sensible to have in place contingency plans to cover some of the risks in boxes B and C, but those in D would be of lesser concern.

Responses to political risk

Once the risk has been analysed and assessed, an organisation must decide if there are ways in which such risks can be managed. There are two common responses:

1 improve relative bargaining power;

2 adopt integrative, protective and defensive techniques.

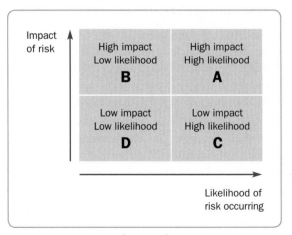

Figure 4.1 Prioritising (political) risk

Relative bargaining power

In an attempt to overcome political risk, some MNEs may seek to develop a stronger bargaining position than that of the host country itself. For example, the MNE might attempt to create a situation in which the host country loses more than it gains by taking action against the company. This could be the case when the MNE has proprietary technology that will be lost to the host country if the company is forced to meet certain governmental regulations or where the MNE can credibly threaten to move elsewhere (with significant job losses) to avoid such regulations.

Integrative, protective or defensive techniques

A second approach is to use a set of techniques to prevent the host government interfering with the operations of the MNE.

- *Integrative techniques* ensure that the subsidiary is as fully integrated as possible with the local economy, so that it becomes part of the host country's infrastructure. Techniques here may include: developing good relations with the host government and other local political groups; producing as much of the product locally as is possible; creating joint ventures and hiring local people to manage and run the operation; carrying out extensive local research and development; and developing good employee relations with the local labour force. These techniques raise the 'costs' to the host country economy of unwelcome interference in MNE activities.

- *Protective and defensive techniques* seek to limit, in advance, the 'costs' to the MNE should the host government interfere in its activities. Such techniques may include doing as little local manufacturing as possible, locating all research and development outside the country, hiring only those local personnel who are essential, manufacturing the same product in many other different countries, etc.

A risk management strategy involves adopting a comprehensive and systematic approach to dealing with the factors causing political risk. Clearly prioritising the areas of political risk in the manner of Figure 4.1 (above) is one step in such a process. Zonis and Wilkin (2000) suggest that a business might also try to break down the 'drivers' of political risk into three separate categories, namely external, interaction and internal drivers.

1 *External drivers* of political risk involve factors whose probability cannot be influenced by the firm. Examples include political instability (e.g. riots, civil war, coups) and weak public policy (e.g. hyperinflation, currency crisis). Although the company cannot influence these factors itself, it can try to assess accurately their probabilities of occurrence and potential impacts, as a preliminary to taking out appropriate levels of risk insurance.

2 *Interaction drivers* of political risk involve factors that are broadly related to company relationships. Examples include relationships with home-country and host-country governments, regional and local authorities, national and supranational institutions and regulatory bodies, pressure groups, local communities, and so on. Unlike the 'external drivers', the firm *can* influence these 'interaction drivers' by its own actions. It can influence both the probabilities and potential impacts of any breakdown in the various categories of relationship. It can seek to manage such risks by investing resources in fostering those relationships it has given the highest priority in terms of their potential for favourable or unfavourable corporate outcomes. For example, given the importance of *guanxi*-type relationships to business activities in Confucian societies, the politically 'risk-averse' firm

operating in China or Hong Kong might invest substantial resources in fostering such relationships (see Chapter 5).

3 *Internal drivers* of political risk involve factors which are specific to the organisation and *operation* of the company itself. Examples might include the extent to which internal incentive structures are aligned with corporate objectives. An executive remuneration scheme which links bonuses to turnover or market share may be less appropriate where the corporate objective is primarily profit related.

Case 4.3 provides an opportunity to consider political issues and political risk analysis in the context of major decisions involving the future of Rover, then owned by BMW.

CASE 4.3 BMW after Rover

Joachim Milberg took over as chief executive of BMW in 1999. His predecessor, Bernd Pischetsrieder, had been actively involved in the running of Rover, the British volume car maker that he had bought in 1994. Early March 2000, when the continuing strong pound was damaging Rover group exports, Milberg came to the conclusion that the German company couldn't turn round the ailing British subsidiary. Hence, the decision to sell Rover to Alchemy, a group of British venture capitalists who would have ended up making only a small number of sports cars under the MG label. This decision by BMW to sell Rover caused an uproar in the British press and among politicians in the West Midlands who feared large job losses in Rover and in the numerous component suppliers located around the region. The West Midlands has many parliamentary seats, often with only small majorities and which regularly change hands at general elections.

In the event Alchemy eventually withdrew from the bidding process and the bulk of Rover was sold to the Phoenix consortium for the princely sum of £10! Over the previous six years BMW had spent a total of DM9 billion (£3.4 billion) trying to turn Rover into a car maker with a future, but had posted large losses, as high as £2.5 billion in 1999, as well as writing down Rover assets by £3.2 billion in the same year. The disposal provoked a political storm in Britain, which was still rumbling in April 2000, when BMW bosses were summoned to appear before a parliamentary inquiry.

The British government was furious that it had learnt about the disposal from a leak in the German press. Mr Milberg retorted that the British government had been slow to hear the signals he sent in telephone calls before Christmas as Rover's situation worsened. Even this reply further infuriated the British government as it came under press criticism for failing to 'read' these alleged signals from BMW. BMW had bought Rover because its Board had doubted whether it could survive as a niche firm, then making around 600,000 cars a year. By buying Rover, it secured production of around 400,000 cars, plus the Land Rover business. Having abandoned this strategy, can BMW now survive on its own?

Major losses had resulted from trading Rover group products in the previous years (e.g. £3.2 billion lost in writing down the value of Rover assets in 1999 alone). The strong pound had provided added problems, making Rover group exports progressively less competitive in its major euro-zone markets. One of Rover group's key assets, Land Rover, was to be replaced by an own-brand product, which was much cheaper to produce (fewer basic platforms required). Land Rover could therefore be sold, raising

Case 4.3 (*continued*)

useful revenue. Underlying all this was the conviction that volume car production will be increasingly in the hands of only a few producers, given the huge scale economies involved. BMW will increasingly focus on niche markets, selling quality cars (e.g. acquisition of Rolls-Royce label from Volkswagen) at premium prices.

Today, giant firms dominate the industry to an even greater extent than they did in 1994. Only Honda, PSA Peugeot Citroen and BMW remain as smaller independents. Of those, BMW is the smallest, at around a third the volume of the others. BMW plans to remain in Britain, moving production of its new Mini from Birmingham to a modernised plant in Oxford. It also has a brand new factory in the Birmingham area producing engines for BMW models produced in the UK and overseas. Continuing good relations with the UK government, workers and consumers would still seem important for BMW.

Questions

1 What political problems were raised by the sale of Rover?
2 How might a more systematic approach to political risk analysis have influenced the outcome for BMW?

The international legal and regulatory environment

Legal systems and regulatory environments vary enormously throughout the world, and these have a significant impact on the ways in which international business is conducted. While many large organisations will employ their own lawyers to advise and settle any disputes, it is important that international managers themselves have some understanding of the likely impacts of legal systems in the countries in which the firm operates.

Types of legal system

The different types of legal system can generally be divided into the following categories: common law; statutory law; code law; religious law; and bureaucratic law. These categories need not be mutually exclusive: for example common law can coexist with various types of code law, e.g. civil law.

- *Common law.* This is the foundation of the legal system in the UK and its former colonies, including the USA, Canada, Australia, India, New Zealand and much of the Caribbean. Common law is essentially unwritten, has developed over long periods of time and is largely founded on the decisions reached by judges over the years on different cases. When a judge makes a particular decision, a *legal precedent* is then established. Such case law has evolved over the centuries, which means that there will obviously be legal variations between countries. For example, manufacturers of defective goods are more liable to litigation in the USA than they are in the UK.

- *Statutory law.* Common law countries depend not only on case law but also on statutory law – i.e. *legislation,* the laws passed by government. This can also be a source of legal variation between countries. For example, the US Freedom of Information Act is more far-reaching than similar UK legislation, so that transactions between the government and companies have to be more transparent in the USA than in the UK.

- *Code law.* This is the world's most common system. It is an explicit codification in written terms of what is and what is not permissible. Such laws can be written down in criminal, civil and/or commercial codes, which are then used to determine the outcome of all legal matters. When a legal issue is in dispute, it can be resolved by reference to the relevant code. Most continental European countries, together with their former colonies, follow this type of legal system.

- *Religious law.* Religious law is based on rules related to the faith and practice of a particular religion. A country that works in this way is called a *theocracy.* Iran is one such example. Here a group of mullahs (holy men) determine what is legal or illegal depending on their interpretation of the Koran, the holy book of Islam. This can pose interesting dilemmas for firms operating in these countries. For example, the Koran says that people should not charge others interest as this is an unfair exploitation of the poor. Thus banks, rather than charging interest, charge up-front fees, and owners of bank deposits are given shares of the bank's profits rather than interest. The emphasis within countries operating under religious laws tends to be on smaller family-owned businesses since the prohibitions we have mentioned often result in less capital being available through national banking systems, forcing a greater emphasis on borrowing from family members. Companies need to be cautious in countries relying on religious laws as there is often an absence of a due process and appeals procedure; for example, companies operating in Saudi Arabia often find that they need a local representative or sponsor to mediate between themselves and the Royal Family in many business disputes.

- *Bureaucratic law.* This occurs in dictatorships and communist countries when bureaucrats largely determine what the laws are, even if these are contrary to the historical laws of the land. MNEs operating in such countries have often found it difficult to manage their affairs as there tends to be a lack of consistency, predictability and appeals procedures.

Effects of national laws and regulations on international business

National laws affect international business in a variety of ways. There may be legal rules relating to specific aspects of business operations such as off-shore investment, the environment, ways in which financial accounts are prepared and disclosed, corporate taxation, employee rights and pension provisions. There may even be legal rules as to the amount of assets and shares companies may own and the proportion of profits they are allowed to remit back to their home country. Countries vary enormously in the amount of control they impose in these different areas.

National laws may also affect aspects of the companies' internal organisation such as its human resource management and health and safety policies. These might include factors such as the provision of maternity and paternity leave, payment of a statutory minimum wage, physical working conditions, protection of employees against hazards at work and pollution, pension and medical provisions and childcare facilities.

Case 4.4 reviews the relevance of national laws in the US regarding vehicle emissions on international corporate strategies in car making.

CASE 4.4 Stricter US roles drive fuel efficiency

It was presented as a decisive and savvy market move. In a semi-derelict factory building in Detroit, at the annual US auto show, General Motors unveiled the second of two vehicles with which it hopes to reconquer a neglected segment of the US market – the midsize pickup truck. But, as Ms Barra, who takes over as General Motors' chief executive tomorrow, trumpeted how the GMC Canyon would widen choice for a neglected group of consumers, she omitted any mention of another incentive for GM to introduce smaller pickups, improving the average fuel economy of its Canyon – and of the Chevrolet Colorado, unveiled in December 2013 – will give GM much-needed assistance in meeting tough new US emissions standards.

Manufacturers in the US need to meet government-set 'corporate average fuel efficiency' targets of 54.5 miles per gallon across their fleets by 2025, compared with only 27.5 mpg in 2012 when the new rules were announced. The fuel-economy standards sustained car makers' enthusiasm for fuel-efficient vehicles at this week's Detroit auto show.

The fuel-efficiency drive takes different forms for different manufacturers. It was on display most obviously at the launch of Ford's F150 pickup. The new vehicle boasts far better fuel efficiency thanks to lighter aluminium body parts and a more sophisticated engine. The vogue for fuel-efficiency stretched to the most unlikely corners of the market. Dan Ammann, GM's new president, boasted about the fuel efficiency of a new, racing version of the flagship Chevrolet Corvette sports car. The improvement meant the vehicle would be able to skip a pit stop on some endurance races, saving valuable seconds, he explained.

Jeff Luke, GM's executive chief engineer for full and midsize trucks, said the company estimated that the US market for midsize trucks was bigger than either Ford or Chrysler believed. Both of those domestic rivals of GM have withdrawn from midsize pickups. But Mr Luke added: 'For us, certainly there's a benefit [to focusing on that sector of the market]. It helps us to [meet] our government obligations and requirements.'

 Source: Stricter US rules drive a pickup in fuel efficiency, *Financial Times*, 15/01/2014, p.19 (Wright, R.), © The Financial Times Limited 2014. All Rights Reserved.

Question

How might the phrase 'across their fleets by 2025' in the US auto regulations influence the strategies for manufacturers of cars in the US?

Of course, the nature of these rules and regulations may, to some extent, reflect the national government's trade and industrial policies. Some governments positively encourage inward investment while others may create a whole web of red tape and bureaucracy, which may take months or even years to unravel. Certainly the MNE should be aware of national regulations in the following areas.

- *Trade restrictions*: as noted in Chapter 3, various types of regulations may be imposed to restrict trade, even to the extent of imposing sanctions or embargos on trade with particular countries. Sanctions can take many forms, such as restricting access to high-technology goods, withdrawing preferential tariff treatment, boycotting the country's goods or denying new loans.

- *Foreign ownership restrictions*: many governments may limit the foreign ownership of firms for economic or political reasons. This may sometimes be applied to particular industrial sectors, such as air transportation, financial services or telecommunications. For example, Mexico restricts foreign ownership in its energy sector, while the USA limits foreigners to a maximum 25% ownership of US television and radio stations.

- *Environmental restrictions*: sometimes domestic laws in a country can directly or indirectly affect the competitiveness of MNEs, as already reviewed in Case 4.4 above, as regards tighter vehicle emission regulations in the US. Similarly, the extensive legislation involving the environmental packaging of goods in Germany means higher costs if products are to meet these environmental restrictions.

- *Exit restrictions*: international businesses also need to take account of the costs of exiting a country, should they need to. Many countries impose legal restraints on the closing of plants in order to protect the rights of employees. For example, in Chinese law, if a partner in a joint venture wishes for any reason to shut down a factory, this would require not only the approval of the entire board, but also the approval of the Chinese government.

Effects of supranational regulations on international business

We have already noted the rapid rise in non-governmental organisations (NGOs) and supranational institutions (e.g. the EU) in Chapter 1. Multinational enterprises must pay careful attention to the regulations imposed by these bodies (and the interpretations placed on them) when devising corporate policy. Case 4.5 examines the impacts of new EU regulations involving the use of light bulbs in member countries.

CASE 4.5 Light bulbs reduce energy costs

Energy prices are rising in the UK but there is a small light on the horizon as people use nearly a third less electricity to light their homes than they did 16 years ago. The improvement is due to the recently introduced EU regulations phasing out inefficient incandescent light-bulbs and their replacement with energy efficient alternatives. Chief among them is the compact fluorescent bulb, which uses 80 per cent less electricity than the older kind but produces the same amount of light.

The regulatory inspired change is one of the reasons why peak electricity demand has been falling in the UK: average domestic electricity consumption dropped 5 per cent between 2008 and 2012, according to government statistics. Brenda Boardman, emeritus fellow at the University of Oxford's Environmental Change Institute, says that thanks to more efficient bulbs, the average amount of electricity needed annually to light a UK home fell from 720 kilowatt-hours in 1997 to less than 500 kWh in 2013, a drop of more than 30 per cent.

This has had a big impact on broader household energy consumption, since lighting makes up a quarter of total peak residential electricity demand. Lower consumption

Case 4.5 (*continued*)

also means lower bills. The Energy Saving Trust says the UK could save as much as £1.4bn on electricity bills every year if households phased out their remaining filament bulbs. And those savings could be even greater if people switch to light-emitting diode (LED) bulbs, which have long been used in car brake lights and the infrared beams of television remote controls but are now so powerful they can illuminate a whole room. While LED products still cost more to produce than conventional lighting, they last longer, produce more light and use very little energy.

The shift towards more efficient bulbs has been driven by policy. The European Commission has phased out the sale of standard incandescent bulbs, a technology that has remained unchanged since it was developed in the 1870s by rival inventors Joseph Swan of the UK and Thomas Edison of the US. The EU is also removing more inefficient halogen bulbs from sale by 2016.

Various UK government schemes have also helped to accelerate the rollout of energy-saving light bulbs, millions of which were given away for free by energy companies. National Grid estimates that electricity demand for lighting could halve by 2020, even as the number of bulbs increases. Much of that drop will be driven by the switchover to 'high-quality and low-cost LED bulbs', it says.

But while many households have opted for better bulbs, local councils have been slow to adapt. The UK's 7m street lights clock up an electricity bill of more than £300m a year and, although street lighting is one of the largest single items in local authorities' budgets, fewer than 1m lamps are low-energy models. However, there has been some progress. The UK Green Investment Bank is offering local authorities low, fixed rate loans to help finance the switch to low-energy street lights. The bank says such a transition could reduce their electricity bill by up to 80 per cent. Glasgow City Council, which plans to convert its 70,000 street lights to low energy, will be the first recipient of the loan.

 Source: Adapted from Consumers see the light over lower energy costs, *Financial Times*, 17/02/2014, p.4 (Chazan, G.), © The Financial Times Limited 2014. All Rights Reserved.

Questions

1 How might the case help explain the following: while the unit price of electricity in 2014 was 50% higher in Germany than the UK, the average German electricity bill was only around 10% higher?

2 What is the contribution of regulation in this case to reducing energy costs?

3 What other impacts might follow in the UK from this EU regulatory intervention?

When companies are offered governmental inducements to retain or initiate production facilities in particular countries within the EU, they must ensure that these inducements are compatible with EU directives on state aid. Otherwise, the aid inducements will be vetoed by the EU, and both the MNE's and host country's policies will be disrupted. An important issue in the initial BMW plan to build new production lines for its Rover Group affiliate in the UK was the 'legality' of a £200 million-plus aid package from the UK government. This part of the 'rescue package' was still being considered by the EU as to its legality when BMW decided instead to dispose of the Rover Group in early 2000 (see pp. 131–132). Box 4.1 looks in rather more detail at various EU regulations regarding state aid.

BOX 4.1 EU directives and state aid

The reasoning behind European competition policy is exactly that which created the original European Economic Community (EEC) over 45 years ago. Competition is viewed as bringing consumers greater choice, lower prices and higher-quality goods and services. The European Commission has a set of directives in this area which are designed to underpin 'fair and free' competition. They cover cartels (price fixing, market sharing, etc.), government subsidies (direct or indirect subsidies for inefficient enterprises – state and private), the abuse of dominant market position (differential pricing in different markets, exclusive contracts, predatory pricing, etc.), selective distribution (preventing consumers in one market from buying in another in order to maintain high margins in the first market), and mergers and takeovers. The latter powers were given to the Commission in 1990.

State aid

One of the most active areas of competition policy has involved state aid. The Commission has attempted to restrict the aid paid by member states to their own nationals through Articles 87 and 88 (formerly Articles 92 and 93 of the original Treaty of Rome). These Articles cover various aspects of the distorting effect that subsidies can have on competition between member states. However, it is likely that the progressive implementation of single-market arrangements will result in domestic firms increasing their attempts to obtain state aid from their own governments as a means of helping them meet greater Europe-wide competition. Overall the amount of aid given by member states to their domestic industry had been running at around 1.5% of their respective GDPs during the 1990s but by 2014 had been cut back to below 1%, though with considerable variation across member countries.

The main problem with state aid is that the big, industrially powerful countries – Germany, France, the UK and Italy – account for some 85% of the total state aid given by EU countries to their domestic industry. This arguably gives such economies considerable advantages over the other 23 countries.

To counter some of these trends, the European Commission has begun to scrutinise state aid much more closely – especially where the aid seems to be more than is needed to ensure the ultimate viability of the recipient organisations. For example, in April 1998 the Commission decided that aid paid to the German porcelain firm Triptis Porzellan GmbH should be recovered because it believed the aid to be more than was needed to restore the firm's viability, thereby distorting competition in the market.

Article 87 determines all state aid to be illegal, unless it conforms to one or more of a number of exceptions:

- aid to promote improvements of a social character;
- aid to promote economic development in areas with high unemployment or low living standards;
- aid to promote a project of common EU interest;
- aid to the former German Democratic Republic;
- aid to disaster areas;
- sectoral aid to assist in the restructuring of an individual sector in structural decline, e.g shipbuilding.

In recent years the European Commission has also recognised the importance of small and medium-sized enterprises (SMEs) within the EU, so that certain grants and low-interest loans for small businesses are now allowed, as is government support for SME start-ups involving innovation and research and development.

As regards the decision as to whether any governmental support constitutes state aid, the Commission uses the 'market investor principle' – i.e. would a rational investor get a reasonable return on the investment undertaken? If the answer is 'no', the state support is regarded as aid rather than as an economic investment. Even when a state aid programme is accepted, the Commission will continually review its implementation.

If a new aid scheme is to be introduced by a member state, the Commission must be informed in advance. The Commission will apply the concept of 'one time – last time', which means that aid for restructuring an industry or rescue aid should only be granted once.

In all these ways it is clear that both MNE and host government must tread carefully through a complex set of legal directives and rules as regards any support via state aid and many other aspects of EU competition policy.

Settling international disputes

The cross-border activities of MNEs can create problems in settling international disputes. At least four issues are often involved:

1 Which country's laws apply to the dispute?

2 In which country should the issue be resolved?

3 What techniques should be used to resolve the conflict – litigation, arbitration, mediation or negotiation?

4 How will the settlement be enforced?

The answers to the first two questions may be written into MNE contracts. If not, companies may seek to initiate the legal process in the country most favourable to their own interests (a process known as 'forum shopping'). For example, since monetary rewards for compensation are higher in the USA than elsewhere, many plaintiffs attempt to use USA courts to adjudicate lawsuits involving US companies.

- *Litigation.* The principle of *comity* provides for a country to honour and enforce within its own territory the decisions of foreign courts. 'Comity' requires three conditions to be met:

  1 reciprocity is extended between the countries;

  2 proper notice is given to the defendant;

  3 the foreign court's judgment does not violate domestic statutes or treaty obligations.

- *Arbitration or mediation.* Court cases can be costly and time-consuming, so many companies may prefer the process of arbitration whereby the two conflicting parties agree to abide by the decisions of a third party or mediation whereby a third party attempts to bring the positions of the conflicting parties closer together.

- *Governmental disputes.* Sometimes a company may be in dispute with a national government. There is little legal recourse here for companies. For example, the Foreign Sovereign Immunities Act of 1976 in the USA provides that the actions of foreign governments against US firms are beyond the jurisdiction of the US courts. If Germany, say, chose to nationalise IBM's German operation or impose taxes on IBM, there would be no redress for the company. If, however, a government reneges on a commercial agreement, such as repudiating a contract to purchase, then there is the possibility of legal proceedings.

- *Negotiation.* International negotiations bring with them a whole new set of problems over and above those faced when negotiating domestically. The bargaining power of the MNE with host governments or businesses will depend on factors such as the level of technology, nature of the goods or services, importance of its managerial expertise, value of its capital input, etc. The bargaining power of the host country will depend on factors such as the size of the consumer market, the degree of economic and political stability, etc.

Intellectual property rights

The international economy is becoming a 'knowledge-based' economy, so that questions of intellectual copyright are becoming ever more important. The value of intellectual property can quickly be destroyed unless countries enforce rights in this area. Intellectual property rights (IPRs) can take various forms, with patents, trademarks and copyrights being particularly important.

Patents

Patent law confers ownership rights on the *inventor*. To qualify as the subject matter of a patent the invention must be novel, involve an inventive step and be capable of industrial application. 'Novel' seeks to exclude granting monopoly ownership rights to something which already exists; 'inventive' seeks to establish that a step has been taken which would not be obvious to experts in the field; 'industrial application' seeks to avoid the restrictions which would result from ideas and principles being patentable, instead limiting such protection to specific applications of these ideas. Patents depend upon registration for their validity.

- *Paris Convention 1883.* This was the first major attempt to achieve international cooperation in the protection of patents (as well as trademarks and other intellectual property rights). This convention led to the setting up of the International Bureau for the Protection of Industrial Property Rights (BIRPI). One key provision is to grant reciprocity to foreigners whose countries are members of the convention. Another is to grant a 'period of grace' to patents registered in one country before they need to be registered in other countries. After registration a further 'transition period of protection' is granted before the patent holder has to make use of the patent in a particular market; once this transition period is exhausted with no use having been made of the patent, the patent is deemed to expire. The Uruguay Round of GATT agreed a transition period of one year in developed countries, five years in developing countries and 11 years in the least developed countries.
- Two other important treaties allow international recognition of patents granted in member countries:
  1 *European Patent Convention* (EPC);
  2 *Patent Cooperation Treaty* (PCT) of the World Intellectual Property Organisation (WIPO).

These respective treaties allow businesses to make a uniform patent search and application, which is then valid in all signatory countries.

These various methods provide some protection to owners of intellectual property rights, but not all countries have signed them, and enforcement by signatories can be lax. Certainly patents are receiving a much higher profile in terms of international business strategy. For example, the number of patents currently issued in the USA is more than double that of a decade ago. Patents are becoming global in scope, with reciprocity agreements and the work of international bodies (e.g. UN, WTO) ensuring that, say, a US patent will restrict attempts to exploit that process or product elsewhere in the world. However, there are international discrepancies, with court decisions in the US making biotechnology and genes (1980), computer software (1981) and business methods (1998) patentable. In 2014, in a big judgment, the US Supreme Court (*Alice* v *CLS' Bank*) affirmed that software inventions in the high-tech industry are indeed patentable. At present in the EU only biotechnology and genes of these particular categories are patentable.

The whole patenting issue is becoming a key part of MNE international business strategy, as can be seen from Box 4.2.

BOX 4.2 Strategic patenting

The USA has permitted more aspects of business activity to be patented than has been the case elsewhere and tends to be more supportive of the rights of patent holders when those patents are challenged. 'Strategic patenting' refers to attempts by MNEs to incorporate their approach to patenting into a more coherent strategic approach, which may be broadly defensive or offensive in its direction. Underlying all this is a general recognition that patents are a valuable 'barrier to entry' in an otherwise more open global economy and that intellectual property protected by patent can be a major factor in stock market evaluations.

- *Defensive patenting* involves the aggressive defence of established patents by holders. Texas Instruments and National Semiconductors aggressively and successfully defended themselves against perceived patent infringements by Japanese and other chip makers in the early 1990s. It has been argued that without such defence they would have been bankrupted by lower priced but similar quality chips available from other suppliers in their major markets.

- *Offensive patenting* involves exploiting patents to increase revenue. For example, IBM is reported as applying for ten new patents every working day, while Dell Computers now has around 80 patents for process operations involving manufacture and testing alone. Biotech and dot.com companies, many of which are currently unprofitable, have stock market valuations almost entirely dependent on the patents they possess or have applied for. Companies such as Walker Digital in the USA are now specialising entirely in the holding and development of patents, one of which, Priceline, involves 'reverse auctions' (customers set a price they are willing to pay, companies decide whether they are willing to supply) and is worth over $11 billion.

Case 4.6 provides further evidence of the importance of patents in the strategic approaches of corporations.

CASE 4.6 Engineering the future - Smartphone patents

When Apple and Samsung returned to the courtroom in April 2014 to fight it out over smartphone patents, the stakes seemed higher than ever. Apple was seeking more than $2bn in damages from the South Korean rival – twice what it was awarded by a jury in the same courtroom in 2012. But 18 months after that blockbuster verdict, Apple is still no closer to getting its hands on that compensation, as appeals drag on.

And at this time, the jury in San Jose, California, was not so sympathetic to Apple's cause. While Samsung was found to have infringed three patents, covering the iPhone's operating system, IOS, Apple was awarded just $120m. 'It's a fraction of what Apple sought and probably wasn't substantially more than Apple spent on lawyers,' says Mark McKenna, law professor at the University of Notre Dame. 'It's hard to imagine that Apple sees this as a real victory.' Richard Windsor, tech analyst with Radio Free Mobile, says the trial 'once again exposes the critical flaw of the patent system in its current form . . .'. The legal cycle is much longer than the device life-cycle, meaning that by the time an infringement finding can be won, the device is already obsolete and no longer shipping.

Apple has sought an injunction against US sales of Samsung phones that are 'not more than colourable different' from the ageing GalaxyS3 and Note 2 devices cited in court, but Samsung has proven capable of designing around infringing features to avoid a block on sales. In the meantime, smartphone sales have continued to soar. More than 1bn were sold last year, according to researchers at ICD, the market intelligence firm. Samsung's 31 per cent market share was more than double Apple's in the crucial fourth quarter. Mark Lemley, a professor at Stanford Law School, says 'We can continue fighting this out piece by piece forever, but it doesn't seem to be having any real effect on the marketplace.' He has represented tech clients, including Google, as a partner at the San-Francisco firm Duria Tangri. While the tech giants have been slugging it out between themselves, Prof Lemley says that a common enemy has grown stronger: the litigious 'non-practising entities' that hoard intellectual property without using it to create products better known as 'patent trolls'. Apple was sued 59 times in 2013 by trolls, according to Prof Lemley, bringing the total number of open lawsuits against it to more than 200.

In June, Interdigital, a mobile technology patent company, struck a licensing agreement with Samsung worth hundreds of millions of dollars and is pressing Apple for a similar deal. This approach may have, in part, motivated a settlement between Apple and Google in mid-May. While the two remain arch-rivals in the smartphone wars, responsible for the two dominant mobile operating systems, iOS and Android, they dismissed all outstanding litigation between them and agreed to 'work together in some areas of patent reform'. One person familiar with the agreement says this unlikely alliance is aimed at lobbying governments for greater protection from trolls. Nonetheless, progress in reforming the US patent system remains slow.

However, the lack of a cross-licensing agreement between the two companies, which would indemnify both from future litigation over smartphone patent infringement, was unusual, says Prof Lemley. 'It does not look like most of the ways you settle patent litigation.' One tactic may be that the agreement leaves Apple free to pursue Samsung, whose mobile devices use Android. After the last trial focused on Android software, any broader agreement between Apple and Google might have allowed Samsung to argue that any infringement found to its smartphones was covered by that deal too. Apple's litigation against Samsung was initiated by its late co-founder Steve Jobs, who described it as part of a 'holy war' against Android, which he saw as slavishly copying the iPhone. However, competition between the two mobile platforms has remained fierce, with each leapfrogging the other with the introduction of additional features every year.

Refinements to smartphones' hardware may have slowed, but software continues to improve at a rapid clip. Commentators see some of Apple's latest enhancements in iOS8 – such as an improved keyboard, cloud services integration and changes in the way apps can communicate

Case 4.6 (continued)

with each other – as playing catch up with Android, while Samsung and Google are still striving to match the iPhone's security, stability, and overall simplicity. Steve Mlunovich, an analyst at UBS, says: 'Although the Wall Street view is that smartphones are a mature market, there is plenty of innovation left as regards their uses.

 Source: Adapted from Engineering the future – smartphone patents, *Financial Times*, 18/06/2014 (Bradshaw, T.), © The Financial Times Limited 2014. All Rights Reserved.

Questions

1 Explain the strategic thinking behind the patent settlement between Apple and Google in May 2014.

2 Why might Apple and Google have resisted adopting a cross-licensing agreement which would have protected each of them against patent challenges from third-party users of their respective systems?

However, the use of patents as a means of protection of intellectual property rights is important to national as well as corporate strategies. It has become highly politicised and of major importance to the multinational enterprises involved. This was certainly the suggestion in August 2007, when an Indian court dismissed a challenge to the country's patent laws filed by Swiss pharmaceuticals maker Novartis, signalling a victory for health advocates who say they are protecting cheap generic drugs for the developing world. The decision by Chennai High Court was seen by critics as setting back the pharmaceutical industry's hopes of bringing drug patent protection in India up to international standards.

Novartis had sought to revise aspects of India's patent laws, which it said violated World Trade Organisation rules by giving the Indian government too much power in rejecting patent applications from international businesses. Novartis had disputed a crucial part of Indian law that restricts the patenting of small improvements to drugs, such as a change from tablet to capsule, which can give the maker 20 years more patent protection. It had challenged a decision by India's patent office to reject a patent application for its cancer drug Glivec. Novartis claimed the patent restrictions in the Indian Patents Act were not compliant with WTO rules. However, public health advocates insisted that India should be allowed to remain the 'pharmacy of the developing world'; 84% of the antiretroviral drugs that Médecins Sans Frontières (MSF) prescribes to HIV/Aids patients come from Indian generic companies.

Pause for thought 4.3

1 Why has Novartis reacted so strongly to the Indian court judgment?

2 What do you consider to be the potential benefits and costs to the Indian pharmaceutical industry of this judgment?

3 How might the WTO TRIPS Agreement be relevant to situations involving intellectual property rights in India?

Trademarks

Trademarks have been defined in the Trade Marks Act 1994 as 'any sign capable of being represented graphically which is capable of distinguishing goods or services of one undertaking from those of other undertakings'. This is sometimes referred to as the 'product differentiation' function. Such trademarks require less intellectual activity than patents or copyright to be deemed protectable, with the focus instead being on the commercial activity associated with such trademarks. As with patents, trademarks depend on registration for their validity, which gives the holder the exclusive right to use the mark in the UK for ten years, subject to further renewals for periods of ten years. Infringement occurs where others use the trademark without permission.

Trademarks can be a key element of worldwide 'branding' strategies by companies. Failure to register a brand name can be costly. For example, New Zealand growers of Chinese gooseberries began to market the product as 'kiwifruit' in the 1960s but unfortunately neglected to register a trademark, with the result that growers throughout the world can use this as a generic name for the fruit.

Trademarks are often the context for disputes between rival companies. For example, a trademark battle between confectionery giants Nestlé and Mars occurred in 2003 over the 'Have a Break' phrase and became a test case for the protection of advertising slogans. Swiss-based Nestlé, which makes Kit Kat, has for years had trademark protection over the 'Have a Break, Have a Kit Kat' slogan, as well as over 'Kit Kat' itself. But it wanted to gain similar intellectual property rights over the simpler 'Have a Break' tag-line, in respect of all chocolate products.

Nestlé's initial application to the Trade Mark Registry was turned down in 2002 after Mars, its US-owned rival, objected. However, to bolster its case, the company pointed to consumer research suggesting that use of the phrase 'Have a Break' did elicit the response 'Have a Kit Kat' from consumers. Even so, a High Court judge in the UK was unpersuaded that the public's association meant 'Have a Break' had actually acquired distinctiveness 'as a result of its use as a mark'. Accordingly, he upheld the registry hearing officer's decision.

- *Trademark Registration Treaty* (Vienna Convention). Once a trademark has been registered, each signatory country must accept it or provide grounds for refusal within 15 months of registration.

Trademark protection may be challenged not only in the more usual corporate arena, but also by groups that regard certain trademarks as offensive, as can be seen from Case 4.7.

CASE 4.7 Redskins lose trademark protection

The US patent agency has cancelled trademark protections for the name of the Washington Redskins professional football team, ruling that the term is 'disparaging of Native Americans'. The decision comes amid pressure from Native Americans and others who say the National Football league franchises' name is offensive. They have also been pressing Dan Snyder, the team's owner, for a change. The ruling does not prevent the team from continuing to use the name, and it would keep its trademark rights during an expected appeal.

But if upheld, the decision would allow anyone to sell merchandise using the name, which could eat into the team's income from sales of items from jerseys and hats to

Case 4.7 (continued)

Redskins-branded toasters and shower curtains. The six trademarks in question were registered between 1957 and 1990.

The Redskins were valued at $1.7bn in 2013 by Forbes magazine, ranking them third among the NFLs 32 teams, with 2012 revenue of $381m. The case was brought before the patent office's Independent Appeals Board in 2006 by five Native Americans who argued the name violated federal law, which blocks protection for trademarks that 'may disparage' individuals or groups or 'bring them into contempt or disrepute'. 'We presented a wide variety of evidence . . . to demonstrate that the word "'redskins" is an ethnic slur,' said Jesse Wiitten, the plaintiffs' lawyer. 'This victory was a long time coming'. It was the second time such a case has been filed. In 1999, the appeals board revoked trademark protection but that decision was overturned by a federal appeals court, which ruled the plaintiffs lacked standing to file the case.

Pressure has been escalating on Mr Snyder and the NFL. Last month, half the US Senate signed an open letter to the league's commissioner urging him to endorse a name change. Mr Snyder has been unmoved, telling USA Today that he will 'never' change the team's name, no matter what the outcome of the trademark case.

FT *Source:* Adapted from Redskins lose trademark protection, *Financial Times*, 10/06/2014 (Bond, S.), © The Financial Times Limited 2014. All Rights Reserved.

Question

Why is the Washington Redskins American football team so keen to retain its trademark protection?

Copyrights

Copyright law prevents the copying of forms of work (e.g. an article, book, play, poem, music score, etc.) rather than the ideas contained within these forms. However, sometimes the copyright can be extended to the 'structure' underpinning the form actually used (e.g. the plot of a book as well as the book itself).

Copyright (unlike patents and trademarks) applies automatically and does not require registration. For copyright to apply, there must be three key conditions:

1 *a recorded work which is 'original'*, in the sense that the work is different from that of its contemporaries;

2 *of an appropriate description*, i.e. literacy, dramatic, music, artistic, sound recordings, films and broadcasts all qualify. Even business letters can receive protection as 'literacy works';

3 *being sufficiently connected to the country in question*, since copyright is essentially national in character, at least in the first instance. So in the case of the UK, the author (or work) must be connected to the UK by nationality, domicile, source of publication or in some other acceptable way.

Berne Convention and the Universal Copyright Convention (UCC) are international agreements which extend the copyright laws of one country to the other signatory countries.

The period of copyright in the UK extends to the life of the author +50 years. Copyright protection is not absolute: for example, limited copying of copyright material is permitted for purposes of research or fair journalistic reporting. Breaching copyright beyond any existing provision can result in an injunction to desist and/or the award of damages.

However, there is a continued debate as to what, exactly, should be the appropriate period of time for copyright protection.

Trade-related Aspects of Intellectual Property Rights (TRIPS)

The WTO Agreement on *Trade-Related Aspects of Intellectual Property Rights,* the so-called TRIPS Agreement, is based on a recognition that increasingly the value of goods and services entering into international trade resides in the know-how and creativity incorporated into them. The TRIPS Agreement provides for minimum international standards of protection for such know-how and creativity in the areas of copyright and related rights, trademarks, geographical indications, industrial designs, patents, layout-designs of integrated circuits and undisclosed information. It also contains provisions aimed at the effective enforcement of such intellectual property rights, and provides for multilateral dispute settlement. It gave all WTO members transitional periods so that they could meet their obligations under it. Developed-country members have had to comply with all of the provisions of the Agreement since 1 January 1996, while for developing countries and certain transition economies, the general transitional period ended on 1 January 2000. For the least-developed countries (LDCs), the transitional period was originally set as 11 years (i.e. until 1 January 2006), but this has been repeatedly extended and in 2013 the transition period was extended further to 2021.

Economic systems

Free-market economies

Most international business takes place within the context of free-market economies in which the market is the key mechanism for resource allocation. It is here that buyers and sellers interact to determine the prices and quantities of the goods and services exchanged. Of course, the market need not be a particular physical location; for example, foreign exchange is bought and sold worldwide from numerous geographical locations.

Markets yield prices that act as 'signals' to both consumers and producers in resource allocation. For instance, in a situation of excess demand, price will typically rise, acting as a signal to discourage some consumer demand and encourage some additional producer supply, until the quantities bought and sold are once more in balance (equilibrium).

The 'profit motive' is seen as playing a key role here, with higher prices increasing the relative profitability of a product, thereby attracting more resources (labour, capital, land, etc.) into producing that product. In fact profit can be seen as performing at least four key functions:

1 acting as a 'signal' to firms in terms of allocating scarce resources;

2 rewarding risk taking;

3 encouraging productive efficiency (lower costs imply greater profit);

4 providing resources for expansion (e.g. 'ploughed back' profits).

Supporters of such a system see the 'invisible hand' of the free market as the most efficient means of co-ordinating the innumerable individual decisions which must be taken by consumers and producers every day in global markets. Critics of the free market point to the many examples of 'market failures' which often distort its operation. These can include imperfect information, non-competitive market structures and divergences between private and social costs (externalities), among many other types of market distortion. Occasional periods of economic recession, with declining output and rising unemployment, have helped to temper some of the more excessive claims made by free-market adherents.

Pause for thought 4.4

Choose one of these types of 'market failure' and suggest how it might prevent the market from allocating resources efficiently. Can you repeat your analysis for another type of market failure?

Case 4.8 shows how shifts in the demand for and supply of shares in Wellcome, a major pharmaceutical company, influenced the market price of these shares during the early 1990s.

CASE 4.8 Market influences on Wellcome share price

Figure 4.2 uses market analysis to explain some of the observed changes in the Wellcome share price during the early 1990s.

(a) American medical opinion expresses doubts over the effectiveness of Retrovir, a new anti-AIDS drug developed at great expense by Wellcome. There is an increased supply of Wellcome shares as people lose confidence and sell them. Price falls from P_1 to P_2.

(b) A major AIDS conference makes favourable comments on Retrovir. Demand for Wellcome's shares increases (shifts to the right). Price rises from P_1 to P_2.

(c) Enthusiasm for pharmaceutical stocks has been growing; Wellcome had benefited from this, being one of the major drugs companies. Demand had previously risen, but now US investors decide they are over-priced. Supply of Wellcome shares increases. Price falls from P_1 to P_2.

(d) The Wellcome shares provide investors with a high dividend. Demand further increases (shifts to the right). However, the supply of shares to the market decreases (shifts to the left) as shareholders speculate on a further rise in price and sell fewer shares than before. Price rises from P_1 to P_2 (but quantity of shares traded is little affected).

(e) The Wellcome Trust announces its decision to sell 38% of its shares. The market is taken by surprise. The supply curve shifts sharply to the right at a time when share prices are generally depressed. Wellcome's share price falls from P_1 to P_2.

Questions

Consider the likely impact on the Wellcome share price of each of the following:

1 Wellcome announces that it is to begin production of a best-selling ulcer treatment drug, which is currently produced by a rival whose patent is about to expire;

2 Wellcome introduces a rights issue of shares in order to raise new investment capital.

Case 4.8 (*continued*)

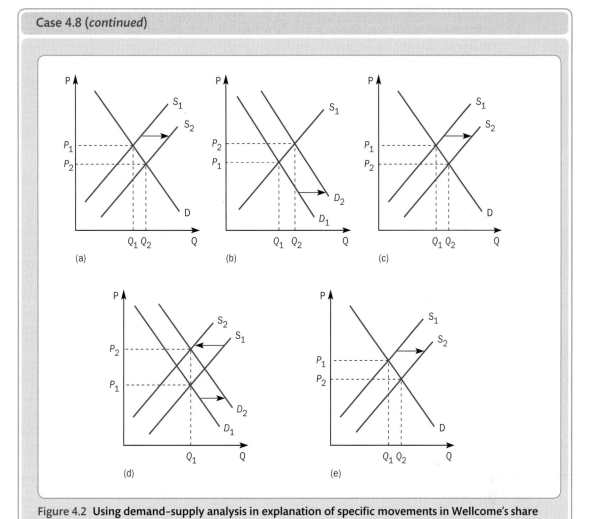

Figure 4.2 Using demand–supply analysis in explanation of specific movements in Wellcome's share price

Command economies

Although few examples of a command economy remain, this structure was previously used by many of the so-called 'transition economies' of Central and Eastern Europe. The command economy dominated every aspect of life, often involving the issue of explicit instructions to factories as to where to buy their inputs, how much to pay their workers, how much to produce and where to sell their output; individuals were trained in specialist schools and universities and directed to work at specific factories, which provided their wages, houses, healthcare – and even holidays in enterprise-owned hotels and sanatoria; the national bank was told how much to lend to which factories and how much cash to print to pay wages.

As a theoretical concept, central planning was very elegant. Using 'input–output' analysis (a planning framework which calculated the inputs required for each factory in order for it to deliver its planned outputs to the next stage in the production process), the planning ministry could calculate precisely how much labour, capital and raw materials each enterprise required to achieve its production targets. The various production targets for raw materials and intermediate and final products all fitted together to ensure a perfectly balanced expansion of the economy. Input and output prices were carefully set to ensure that all firms could pay their wage bills and repay loans from the national bank, while at the same time consumer goods were priced to encourage consumption of politically favoured goods (e.g. low prices for books, ballet, theatre, public transport, etc.) and to discourage consumption of politically unfavoured goods (e.g. higher prices for international telephone calls, cars, luxury goods).

The overall national plan was thus internally consistent. If each of the enterprises achieved its production targets, there could not be, by definition, shortages or bottlenecks in the economy. There would be full employment, with everyone working in an enterprise for which he/she had been specifically trained at school and/or university. The total wage bill for the economy, which was paid in cash, would be sufficient to buy all the consumer goods produced. There would be zero inflation and all the country's citizens would have access to housing, education and healthcare.

Of course, in reality this stylised account of a command economy was rarely, if ever, achieved. Plans were devised which were often internally inconsistent, leading to massive shortages or surpluses. Output frequently fell below target as workers saw little incentive to meet productivity targets. Poor-quality products often failed to satisfy either home or overseas consumer demands. The process of economic transformation from central planning to a market economy in Eastern Europe is now well underway, though it has been neither smooth nor uniform. States in the vanguard of reform like Poland, the Czech Republic and Hungary quickly succeeded in creating thriving, dynamic private sectors, generating new jobs and contributing to economy recovery, though encountering challenges with other EU countries in the recessionary period after 2008. States in the vanguard of reform like Poland, the Czech Republic and Hungary quickly succeeded in creating thriving, dynamic private sectors, generating new jobs and contributing to economic recovery though encountering challenges with other EU countries in the recessionary period after 2008. In contrast, in the 12 states of the former Soviet Union that now comprise the Commonwealth of Independent States (CIS) the slump in economic activity has been much more prolonged and economic recovery more fragile.

Nevertheless, the direction of movement is towards the market economy, as indeed has largely been the case within the People's Republic of China for more than two decades. This process of transition clearly has implications for both domestic firms within these economies and for multinational enterprises seeking to invest in, or trade with, them.

Economic variables and the business environment

Whatever stylised type of economic structure provides the context for international business, a number of key *economic variables* will shape the environment in which such business is conducted. Managers of international businesses must take into account a number of economic indicators in the countries with which they seek to do business if economic opportunities and threats are to be properly assessed.

Real income per head

The gross national product (GNP) is a widely used measure of economic well-being, reflecting the total value of output (or income) attributable to nationals of that country in a given year. To serve as a measure of the *standard of living* this is often expressed 'per head of population' and in 'real terms' (i.e. excluding inflation).

The World Bank and a number of other bodies use annual GNP per head to identify three broad groups of countries, one of which is further subdivided, making four groups in all:

1 *high-income economies*: countries with an annual GNP per head of $11,456 or more;

2 *middle-income economies*: countries with an annual GNP per head from $936 to $11,455.

Because this group is so broad it has been subdivided into:

(a) *upper-middle income economies*: annual GNP per head from $3,705 to $11,455;

(b) *lower-middle income economies*: annual GNP per head from $936 to $3,704.

3 *low-income economies*: countries with an annual GNP per head of $935 or less.

Of course, it is not just the *absolute* level of income per head of a country or group of countries that is important in assessing the prospects for business, but *changes* in that level.

Economic growth or recession

This is often expressed in terms of the percentage change in real national income per head and can be a key indicator for future business prospects. For example, where a business is trading in products which have a high *income elasticity of demand* (see Box 4.3), such as air travel, then prospective changes in economic growth rates can have a major influence on projected future profitability. As real incomes rise (or fall) by a given percentage, demand for these products increases (or decreases) by more than that percentage. For example, estimates for air travel have suggested income elasticities of demand as high as +4, suggesting that a 1% rise in real income will increase the demand for air travel by over 4%, but equally a 1% fall in real income will decrease the demand for air travel by over 4%.

BOX 4.3 Elasticity of demand

Businesses should be aware of at least three types of elasticity of demand if they are to accurately assess prospects for the future.

Income elasticity of demand (IED)

This measures the responsiveness of demand for a product to changes in the real income of consumers.

$$IED = \frac{\% \text{ change in quantity demanded of } X}{\% \text{ change in real income}}$$

For products with high (positive) values for IED, a rise in real income will *shift* the demand curve substantially to the right (*increase*), whereas a fall in real income will *shift* the demand curve substantially to the left (decrease). Figure 4.3(a) captures these effects of more or less of a product X being demanded at any given price of X due to a change in real income.

Products with a negative value of IED are often called 'inferior goods', with a rise in real income causing demand to shift to the left (decrease).

Box 4.3 (*continued*)

Price elasticity of demand (PED)

This measures the responsiveness of demand for a product to changes in its own price.

$$PED = \frac{\% \text{ change in quantity demanded of } X}{\% \text{ change in price of } X}$$

When this ratio is greater than 1 (ignoring the sign), we speak of a relatively elastic demand; when smaller than 1, a relatively inelastic demand.

Figure 4.3(b) captures these effects of a movement along the demand curve for X, due to a change in the price of X itself.

Box 9.5 (Chapter 9, p. 326) provides further explanation of the following link between PED and total revenue.

PED > 1 (relatively elastic demand): fall in price raises total revenue, rise in price reduces total revenue.

PED < 1 (relatively inelastic demand): fall in price reduces total revenue, rise in price increases total revenue.

Cross elasticity of demand (CED)

This measures the responsiveness of demand for a product to changes in the price of some other product.

$$CED = \frac{\% \text{ change in quantity demanded of } X}{\% \text{ change in price of } Y}$$

Where X and Y are substitutes in consumption, the sign of CED will be positive. A fall in the price of Y, the substitute, will decrease the quantity demanded of X ($-/- = +$)

Where X and Y are complements in consumption (fit together), the sign of CED will be negative. A fall in the price of Y, the complement, will increase the quantity demanded of X ($+/- = -$).

Figure 4.3(a) captures these effects of a shift in the demand curve for X, due to a change in the price of some other product, Y.

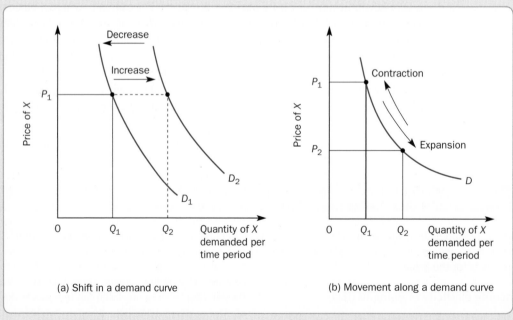

(a) Shift in a demand curve

(b) Movement along a demand curve

Figure 4.3 **Economic conditions and demand**

For the years 2008–13 the prevailing forecasts had been for a substantial reduction in real national income across developed countries in particular, and a slowing down of the rate of increase in real national income across developing and emerging economies. The reasons for the so-called 'credit crunch' are considered in more detail in Chapter 10 (pp. 355–360). Here we note that the economic recession created particular problems for products with high income elasticities of demand, as, for example, has been the case with many leisure and tourism related activities over this period.

Case 4.9 reviews the transport sector and provides a useful context for applying the various elasticities of demand outlined in Box 4.4.

CASE 4.9 Transport and elasticities of demand

Evidence from the developed economies suggests that for every 10% increase in real fuel prices, the demand for fuel will fall by around 6%. This consumer response to higher fuel prices may take several years to fully work through.

The demand for car ownership and for travel (and therefore the derived demand for fuel) is also closely related to the level of household income. Again, studies suggest that for every 10% increase in real income the demand for fuel eventually increases by around 12% within two years of the rise in real income.

Of course, the demand for fuel does not only depend on its own price and the level of real household income, but also on other factors. For example, whereas the real cost of motoring per kilometre travelled (fuel costs, car purchase, repairs, road tax, etc.) has barely changed over the past 20 years (e.g. more efficient engines result in more kilometres per litre of fuel), the real costs of rail and bus per kilometre travelled have risen by more than 30% and 35% respectively over the same 20-year period. Clearly this change in *relative* costs has given a boost to demand for car ownership and travel, and therefore to the demand for fuel.

Many people argue that fuel taxes should rise even higher than they are now, since the private motorist imposes costs on society that he or she does not actually pay for. Extra motorists bring about congestion on our roads and increased journey times, increase the need for more road building with the inevitable loss of countryside, result in more carbon dioxide (CO_2) and other toxic gas emissions which damage the ozone layer and lead to global warming. In other words, many believe that the *private costs* of the motorist do not fully reflect the *social costs* imposed by the motorist.

Higher taxes on fuel will, as we have seen, raise the price of motoring and discourage road travel. For example, it has been estimated that a 10% increase in the price of fuel will lead to an extra 1% of rail passengers on rail services and an extra 0.5% of bus passengers on bus services.

Of course, demand for some products may actually *decrease* as fuel prices rise. With less car usage there may be a decrease in demand for garage-related services and products.

The *net* effect of a rise in fuel prices will depend on the sign and size of all these elasticities, namely own-price, income and cross-elasticities of demand.

Case 4.9 (*continued*)

Questions

1 Can you calculate any own-price, income and cross-elasticities of demand from the information given in the case?

2 Why do some people believe that fuel taxes and fuel prices are too low?

3 Can you suggest why governments might be wary of making the motorist pay the full private and social costs of any journey?

Exchange rate

When comparing the standard of living (e.g. GNP per head) between different countries it is usual to use a common currency such as the US dollar in the World Bank classification above. Even this may be misleading, since converting the value of GNP expressed in the local currency into a $ equivalent using the *official* exchange rate may misrepresent the actual purchasing power in the local economy. This is because the official exchange rate is influenced by a range of complex forces in the foreign exchange markets and may not accurately reflect the purchasing power of one country's currency in another country. A more accurate picture is given if we use *purchasing power parities* (PPPs) rather than official exchange rates when making this conversion. Purchasing power parities measure how many units of one country's currency are needed to buy *exactly the same basket of goods* as can be bought with a given amount of another country's currency.

Quite apart from the role of the exchange rate in making more accurate international comparisons of GNP, we have seen (Chapter 3) that it is a crucial determinant of export/import competitiveness. Indeed, it is sometimes called an 'expenditure switching' economic variable. For example, a fall in the exchange rate will make exports cheaper overseas and imports dearer at home, encouraging consumers in overseas markets to switch from domestic to the now relatively cheaper foreign products and consumers in home markets to switch from the now relatively more expensive foreign products to domestic products. The opposite effects can be expected from a rise in the exchange rate, exports becoming relatively more expensive and imports relatively cheaper.

International business must clearly take into account actual and prospective changes in relative exchange rates when evaluating the economic environment in which they are doing business.

Pause for thought 4.5

China has pegged the exchange rate of its own currency the Renminbi to the US dollar. How will that influence the EU if the euro continues to weaken against the US dollar?

Inflation

Inflation is a persistent tendency for the general level of prices to rise. A modest rate of inflation is often regarded as 'favourable' by business as in such an economic environment any extra costs can more readily be passed on to consumers in the form of higher prices.

Of course, excessive rates of inflation can result in instability and rapid increases in costs, often followed by deflationary macroeconomic measures by governments resulting in sharp decreases in consumer demand.

In the UK the Retail Price Index (RPI) is the most widely reported measure of inflation, measuring the change from month to month in the cost of a representative 'basket' of goods and services of the type bought by a typical household. In the EU the Harmonised Index of Consumer Prices (HICP) has been calculated on a standardised basis to allow more accurate comparisons across countries. The HICP uses the geometric mean in its calculation and gives lower recorded rates of inflation for the UK than the RPI, which uses the arithmetic mean and a different 'basket' of goods and services. However, the UK itself adopted the HCIP as its official inflationary measure in 2003.

For a 'cost-oriented' multinational (see p. 36), locations with low and stable rates of inflation might prove more attractive in terms of foreign direct investment.

Taxes and subsidies

Variations in national tax rates and allowances (see Chapter 2, pp. 60–61) and in the provision of grants and subsidies can have a major influence on international business decisions. These can obviously include decisions as to where to locate particular elements of the globalised production process. They might also include decisions involving the 'transfer pricing' of internal transactions within the multinational enterprise (see p. 331).

This section has dealt with a number of economic variables that might influence the decisions taken by international business. Of course, in reality many of these (and other) variables are changing, or are about to change, in different directions at the same time.

Technological environment

Technological change can have important effects on the decisions taken by international business. Technological change can involve *new processes* of production, i.e. new ways of doing things which raise the productivity of factor inputs, as with the use of robotics in car assembly techniques which has dramatically raised output per assembly line worker. Around 80% of technological change has been process innovation. However, technological change can also be embodied in *new products* (goods or services) which were not previously available. Online banking and many new financial services are the direct result of advances in microprocessor-based technologies.

Technology and employment

One important issue to governments, firms, labour representatives (e.g. unions) and indeed society as a whole has been whether such process innovations have generally resulted in job losses. Each case must, of course, be judged on its separate merits. Box 4.4, however, indicates that there should be no presumption that the continuing technical change that often accompanies inward and outward foreign direct investment by multinational enterprises need necessarily result in job losses. In fact, provided that any cost reductions for productivity gains via the new technologies are passed on to consumers as lower prices and that the demands of consumers are sufficiently responsive (price elastic) to those lower prices, job gains can be anticipated. Of course, whatever the impact on the volume of labour required, there may also be changes in the patterns of skills required from those who remain, with the often repeated claim that many craft and intermediate levels of skill have been displaced by automated processes.

BOX 4.4 Creating or destroying jobs

New technologies have substantially raised output per unit of labour input (labour productivity) and per unit of factor input, both labour and capital (total factor productivity). There has been much concern that the impact of these productivity gains has been to reduce jobs, i.e. to create technological unemployment. We now consider the principles which will in fact determine whether or not jobs will be lost (or gained) as a result of technological change.

Higher output per unit of factor input reduces costs of production, provided only that wage rates and other factor price increases do not absorb the whole of any productivity gain. Computer-controlled machine tools are a case in point. Data from Renault show that the use of DNC machine tools resulted in machining costs one-third less than those of general-purpose machine tools at the same level of output. Lower costs will cause the profit-maximising firm to lower price and raise output under most market forms, as in Figure 4.4. A downward shift of the average cost curve, via the new technologies, lowers the marginal cost curve from MC_1 to MC_2. The profit-maximising price/output combination ($MC = MR$) now changes from P_1/Q_1 to P_2/Q_2. Price has fallen, output has risen.

The dual effect on employment of higher output per unit of labour (and capital) input can usefully be illustrated from Figure 4.4. The curve $Q = F(N)$ is the familiar production function of economic theory, showing how output (Q) varies with labour input (N), capital and other factors assumed constant. On the one hand the higher labour productivity from technical change shifts the production function outwards to the dashed line $Q' = F(N)$. The original output Q_1 can now be produced with less labour, i.e. with only N_2 labour input instead of N_1 as previously. On the other hand, the cost and price reduction has so raised demand that more output is required. We now move along the new production function Q' until we reach Q_2 output, which requires N_3 labour input. In our example the reduction in labour required per unit output has been more than compensated for by the expansion of output, via lower prices, so that employment has, in fact, risen from N_1 to N_3.

This analysis highlights a number of points on which the final employment outcome for a firm adopting the new techniques will depend:

1 the relationship between new technology and labour productivity, i.e. the extent to which the production function Q shifts outwards;

2 the relationship between labour productivity and cost, i.e. the extent to which the marginal cost curve shifts downwards;

3 the relationship between cost and price, i.e. the extent to which cost reductions are passed on to consumers as lower prices;

Box 4.4 (continued)

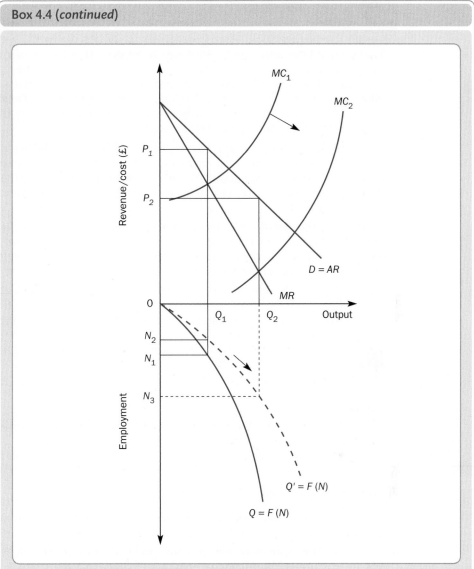

Figure 4.4 Technical change and the level of employment

4 the relationship between lower price and higher demand, i.e. the price elasticity of the demand curve (see Box 4.3, p. 150).

Suppose, for instance, that the new process halved labour input per unit output! If this increase in labour productivity (1 above), reduces cost (2 above), and price (3 above), and output doubled (4 above), then the same total labour input would be required. If output more than doubled, then more labour would be employed. The magnitude of the four relationships above will determine whether the firm offers the same, more, or less employment after technical change in the production process.

CASE 4.10 Eyeball scans are a fresh weapon against fraud

Banks around the world are trialling new technology that they expect to transform the way customers access their banking services and spend their money. Wells Fargo, the biggest US bank by market capitalisation in 2014, plans to pilot a system that allows customers to sign into their banking app by using voice and facial recognition systems on their mobile devices. It is also working on a technology that identifies people by scanning the veins in their eyeballs.

Meanwhile BBVA, Spain's second largest bank, is testing a system to reduce fraud by using the GPS signal from a customer's smartphone to check that they are in the same place as a retailer taking a payment from one of their cards. If not, the bank would send a request for the customer to approve a transaction, adding an extra security check to stop fraud.

Meanwhile a number of banks, including Wells Fargo Bank of America and Ukraine's PrivatBank, are developing so-called 'augmented reality' app's to use with Google Glass, the wearable headband computer. These apps are destined to provide the banks' customers with added information about their physical surroundings in real time.

US banks are also working on technology that would work with Google Glass in order to recognise that a customer was in a specific location, such as a car showroom, and provide that person with relevant details of loan options for different vehicles.

FT *Source*: Adapted from Retail banks go digital with gusto, *Financial Times*, 05/08/2014, p.10 (Goff, S. and Arnold, M.), © The Financial Times Limited 2014. All Rights Reserved.

Question

Identify the advantages and disadvantages to banks of this particular advance in technology.

 ## Technology and competitive advantage

Of course, technological change provides national and international businesses with both opportunities and threats, whether in the manufacturing or service sectors. Digital technologies often underpin many new products and many new processes, as can be seen in Case 4.10, in which new technology is being used to improve bank access, bank security and bank information.

Technology transfer

It is widely held that multinational activity by more efficient foreign multinationals promotes technology transfer to the benefit of domestic companies. For example, when Nissan established a car plant in north-eastern England, it demanded much higher standards of UK component suppliers than the incumbent national producers such as Ford and Rover. Nissan's engineers assisted these supplying companies to upgrade their production processes in order to meet their requirements. The result was the creation of a strong positive externality: the international competitiveness of the UK car supply industry was strengthened and, as a direct consequence, the quality of the inputs to the existing domestic car makers improved.

This so-called 'technology transfer' is clearly maximised by such 'direct linkages' with domestic suppliers, which occurs when incoming multinationals like Sony, Nissan, Honda and Toyota work closely with domestic suppliers to raise the standard of UK-produced inputs. Technology transfer may also bring with it some positive indirect 'demonstration effects' as less efficient local producers seek to imitate the superior processes and organisational advantages of the foreign multinationals.

Many analysts have pointed out there are, however, clear limitations to technology transfer. The inward fdi may, for example, reflect the multinational seeking to exploit an ownership-specific advantage over domestic companies. In such circumstances it is unlikely that the foreign multinational will willingly share the technological-based sources of its competitive advantage over local rivals. Moreover, in the case of Japanese multinationals, their historical advantage was built upon close relationships with Japanese suppliers. For example, the big four Japanese motorcycle companies (Honda, Yamaha, Suzuki and Kawasaki) rely heavily on a very limited number of domestic suppliers (e.g. Bridgestone for tyres, Nippon Denso for electronic components, etc.). Early dissatisfaction with UK suppliers with regard to quality and reliability of deliveries has led to a number of these Japanese suppliers following their major customers into the European market, thereby reducing the potential scope for technology transfer via linkages with local suppliers.

A further obstacle to technology transfer may involve the issue of cultural dissonance. The psychic distance between US and UK companies is relatively small. Both share a broadly common culture, a common language and they have a reasonably high level of mutual understanding. However, the success of multinationals from, say, Japan or other parts of East and South-East Asia is built on a very different set of social and cultural values, which are not easily transferable to the UK setting (see Chapter 5). Companies like Sony, Nissan and Honda have all reported difficulties in establishing Japanese-style work practices, which many economists regard as an integral part of that country's corporate success. The operation of 'just-in-time' production processes and 'quality circles' rely on employee loyalty to his or her company, which in Japan is reinforced by lifetime employment and a shared set of values which emphasises collectivism. Such techniques are much less easily transposed to Western cultures with their stress on individualism and self-determination.

An opposing view points to the potential damage to host countries of technology transfer when it enables foreign affiliates to dominate domestic markets and displace domestic producers. This argument holds still greater weight when such foreign affiliates largely import components and other intermediate inputs rather than using domestic suppliers located in the host country.

Types of technology transfer

Technology transfer usually occurs in one of two ways:

1 *internalised transfer* – this takes the form of direct investment by a parent company in its foreign affiliate. Such intra-firm technology transfer may be difficult to measure;

2 *externalised transfer* – this can take a variety of forms: licences, franchises, minority joint ventures, subcontracting, technical assistance, purchase of advanced equipment (embodied technical progress) and so on.

The following factors are widely regarded as increasing the probability of an MNE resorting to 'internalised transfer':

- the more complex and fast moving the technology;
- the larger and more transnational (see Chapter 1) the company;
- the more internationally experienced and more technologically specialised the parent company and its affiliates;
- the fewer obstacles placed in the way of fdi by host governments and the more inducements offered;
- the greater the focus of the parent company on utilising advanced technology as rapidly as possible without waiting for host country domestic firms to develop technological capabilities.

Benefits of internalised transfer to host country

The most important benefit to the host country of internalised technology transfer is that it gives host country firms access to new, up-to-date and more productive technologies, which are unlikely to be available by any other means. These technologies of the parent company are often based on expensive R&D related to branded products or to complex manufacturing processes, which are part of a globalised pattern of international specialisation. Such technologies would only be shared by the parent company with related parties such as wholly owned (or majority-stake) affiliates.

Other benefits often follow from access to such technologies, as in the case of the host economy being used by the parent company as a production platform for an export-oriented policy to that region (e.g. Japanese motor vehicle firms using the UK as a production platform to export to the EU). The host country affiliates may also gain access to expensive brand images which further aid overseas sales, as well as to substantial financial and other resources owned by the parent company. New operations management and other logistical techniques may be learned by the host country workers, with the general skill base of local labour being raised by exposure to more advanced operations and in-house training methods. In summary, internalised transfer gives the host country, at least in principle, access to the whole range of MNE technological, organisational and skill assets, including those related to tacit knowledge (see Chapter 7) as well as explicit knowledge.

Costs of internalised transfer to host country

Local firms may be disadvantaged by being dominated in their home and export markets by the production affiliates of the overseas parent company. This may reduce overall employment and income in the home economy, especially where the parent MNE uses few local resources in component supply or manufacture in its overseas affiliates. Parent companies may, in fact, share little of their tacit or explicit technological, organisational or operational knowledge with the local affiliates, thereby doing little to raise the skill and knowledge base of the local economy.

We consider many other aspects of technological change and their impacts on international business in Chapters 9 and 10, especially the impact of internet-related technologies on business-to-business and business-to-consumer activities.

Chapter 5

International sociocultural environment

By the end of this chapter you should be able to:

- explain the nature of culture and the differences between national, organisational and occupational culture;
- say why it is important to have an understanding of culture in international business;
- define the different dimensions of culture;
- outline the different ways of analysing national culture in business;
- suggest strategies for developing intercultural competence;
- show an understanding of how to develop multinational teams.

Introduction

Over the ages many philosophers, thinkers, novelists, anthropologists, social scientists and latterly management theorists have grappled with the concept of culture. Definitions have been used to try to capture the all-pervasive scope of cultural influence, as in the following examples.

- We can liken it to the air: it is everywhere, we cannot see it but we know it is there, we breathe it and we cannot exist without it. Culture is not a biological necessity and we will not die if we are deprived of it. But it is rather improbable if not impossible for a person to be devoid of the traces of his or her cultural upbringing and separated from his or her cultural context. (Tayeb 1994: 5)
- Culture should be regarded as the set of distinctive spiritual, material, intellectual and emotional features of society or a social group, and that it encompasses, in addition to art and literature, ways of living together, value systems, traditions and beliefs. (UNESCO 2002: 11)
- Culture . . . is that complex whole which includes knowledge, belief, art, morals, law, custom, and any other capabilities and habits acquired by man as a member of society. (*Encyclopædia Britannica* 2014)

While any definition of culture remains necessarily broad, we can at least see some of the processes by which culture is constructed. As human beings we are social animals and it is from a constant interaction with one another that we learn acceptable ways of being, of behaving, of thinking and of acting. In our day-to-day lives we learn how to act in different circumstances, modelling our behaviour on those around us to build up a coherent set of preferences, beliefs, values and meanings that create our cultural context. At least two features help to distinguish culture from other attributes, such as opinion. The first and most important is that it is enduring and changes very little over time. The second is that it has a social context in that it is expressed as part of a community.

National cultural characteristics

Elias, a famous social scientist and thinker, has made significant contributions to our understanding of culture. He suggested that the development of social institutions and accepted ways of behaving become so closely associated with the groups that historically have dominated particular societies that we can, with reason, speak of national cultural values. In his major work, *The Civilizing Process* (1994), Elias identifies gradual but discernible changes in the expectations of people's interpersonal conduct and in the ways in which they approach their emotions, and even bodily functions, as being distinctive between different European states such as Britain, France and Germany. He saw many of these national characteristics arising from variations in the routes by which the different bourgeois and courtly societies evolved. In France, for example, by the eighteenth century the most prominent bourgeois groups and the nobility read, spoke and behaved in roughly the same way, with courtesy, eloquence, respect for hierarchical differences and a sense of honour accepted by a broad strata of French society.

Elias has therefore focused on national cultures as being the outcome of historical power struggles between different groups for dominance in different nation states. The ideas and values associated with the 'successful' groups in such power struggles eventually evolve into 'national' cultures. Of course, other factors may also play a part in this process.

- *Religious background.* While the underlying values and assumptions of all world religions may share some common features, there are arguably some important differences. Weber (1930), for example, argued that individualism, expressed as a preference for personal choice, autonomy and the pursuit of personal goals, was the hallmark of Protestantism, with the result that these characteristics have been incorporated into the 'Protestant' work ethic of many northern European countries. He suggested that this work ethic was in part responsible for the creation of many of the attributes we ascribe to modern Western capitalism. In contrast, Confucianism of East and South-East Asia is characterised by family and group orientation, respect for age and hierarchy, a preference for harmony and the avoidance of conflict and competition, and a set of cultural values quite unlike the acquisitive behaviour of Western capitalism.

- *Ecological factors.* The environment may also play a part in the development of cultural characteristics. It has often been argued that harsh and 'unfriendly' climates and poor agricultural conditions can, over time and across generations, result in people who are hardworking, resilient, patient, tough and aggressive. Tayeb (2000) describes how this can happen using the example of the Arian tribes who, thousands of years ago, migrated from central Asia to India and Iran. Those who settled in India found a fertile land with plenty of water and rivers and a relatively mild climate. Those who settled in Iran faced harsh variable seasons, salt deserts and very few rivers. Tayeb suggests that it is hardly an accident that Hinduism and Buddhism took root in India, religions noted for their non-violence and passivity. By way of contrast, those from the same ethnic Arian tribes who settled under the harsher ecological conditions of Iran became aggressive, fought other nations and built up the Persian Empire, which ruled over a vast area for centuries.

High and low context cultures

Whatever their origins, attempts have been made to identify some of the differences in national cultural characteristics. For example, early work by Hall (1976) suggested that the various national cultures could be divided into 'high context' and 'low context' cultures in terms of the ways in which people in that culture communicate with one another. Table 5.1 briefly outlines some of the differences between each type. For Hall, the high context cultures include countries or regions such as Japan, China, the Middle East, South America and the southern European countries.

Geert Hofstede (1980) undertook a major research project to identify different national cultures within the same multinational organisation: IBM. Using the responses of some 116,000 IBM employees in 40 countries, Hofstede identified four important dimensions of national culture, namely individualism, power distance, uncertainty avoidance and masculinity/femininity, to which he later added a fifth dimension: long-term orientation (see Figure 5.1).

Individualism

- In *individualist* societies, people tend to put their own interests and those of their immediate family before others. People in such societies would have a high degree of self-respect and independence but a corresponding lack of tolerance for opposing viewpoints. Such people may put their own success through competition over the good of others. Hofstede found that people in the United States, the United Kingdom, Australia, Canada, New Zealand and the Netherlands tend to be relatively individualist in their values.

- In *collectivist* societies there is the belief that the group comes first. Such cultures would contain well-defined social networks in which people are expected to put the good of the group ahead of their own personal freedom, interests or success. Group members try to fit into their group harmoniously with a minimum of conflict or tension. Hofstede found that people from Mexico, Greece, Hong Kong, Taiwan, Peru, Singapore, Colombia and Pakistan tend to be relatively collectivist in their values.

Table 5.1 **High context and low context cultures**

High context cultures	Low context cultures
Define personality more in terms of the group than the individual	Are more individualistic than group-oriented
Tend to have a high sensory involvement (low boundaries in terms of personal space)	Tend to have a low sensory involvement (high boundaries in terms of personal space)
Initiate and receive more bodily contact when talking	Convey more information via explicit codes which do not rely so heavily on non-verbal language
Are polychronic, i.e. time does not have a totally linear aspect so that punctuality and scheduling have low priority	Are monochronic, i.e. time is viewed in more linear terms involving punctuality and tight scheduling

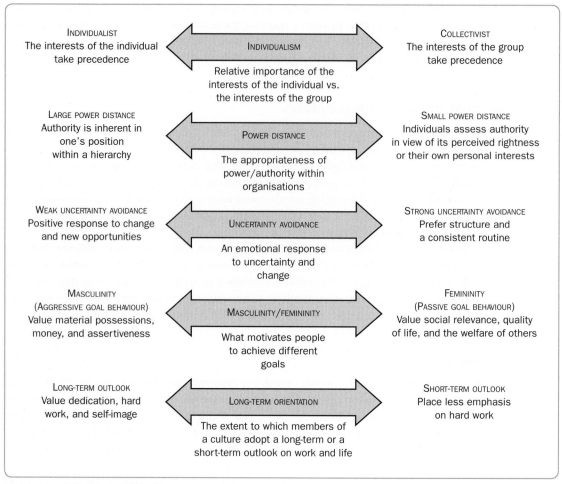

Figure 5.1 Hofstede's five dimensions of culture

Source: Adapted from *International Business: Managerial Perspective*, 1st ed., Addison-Wesley (Griffin, R.W. and Pustay, M.W. 1996), © 1996. Reprinted and Electronically reproduced by permission of Pearson Education, Inc..

Power distance

Hofstede refers to power distance as 'the extent to which the less powerful members of institutions and organisations within a country expect and accept that power is distributed unequally'.

- In *large power distance countries* there is considerable dependence of subordinates on bosses, and a preference for clearly demarcated hierarchy. The emotional distance between hierarchies will tend to be relatively large: subordinates will rarely approach and contradict their bosses. People in such a culture tend to accept the power and authority of their superiors simply on the basis of the superior's position in the hierarchy and to respect the superior's right to that power. Hofstede found that people in the Philippines, Mexico, Venezuela, India, Singapore, France, Spain, Japan and Brazil tend to be relatively power respecting.

- In *small power distance countries* there is limited dependence of subordinates on bosses, and a preference for consultation. The emotional distance between hierarchies will tend to be relatively small: subordinates will quite readily approach and contradict their bosses. People in such a culture are reluctant to accept the power and authority of their supervisors merely because of their position in the hierarchy. Hofstede found that people in Austria, Israel, Denmark, New Zealand, Ireland, Great Britain, Germany, Australia, Canada and the USA have relatively little power respect.

Uncertainty avoidance

Hofstede defines this as 'the extent to which the members of a culture feel threatened by uncertain or unknown situations. This feeling is, among other things, expressed through nervous stress and in a need for predictability: a need for written and unwritten rules'. An important aspect of the level of uncertainty avoidance in a society is the amount of trust between citizens and authorities.

- *Weak uncertainty avoidance* (uncertainty accepting) stands for citizen competence; i.e. a belief that ordinary citizens are able to influence their authorities, and that there is some degree of mutual trust among them. People in cultures characterised by weak uncertainty avoidance tend to be positive in their response to change, which is seen more in terms of providing new opportunities rather than as posing considerable threats. Nordic and Anglo-Saxon countries as well as most Asian and sub-Saharan countries score below average on this dimension (i.e. they exhibit weak uncertainty avoidance).

- *Strong uncertainty avoidance* implies that decisions should be left to experts; citizens and authorities tend to exhibit mutual distrust for each other. People in cultures characterised by strong uncertainty avoidance will avoid ambiguity whenever possible. These people prefer the structured routine and even bureaucratic way of doing things. Latin, Mediterranean and Central and Eastern European countries tend to score above average on 'uncertainty avoidance', along with Japan, South Korea and Pakistan (i.e. they exhibit strong uncertainty avoidance).

Masculinity/femininity

Hofstede used these labels for a dimension he believed to be the only one on which the scores of men and the women in his sample were consistently and significantly different.

- *Masculinity* refers to cultures in which the social gender roles are clearly distinct; men are supposed to be more assertive and acquisitive, valuing material possessions and money.

- *Femininity* refers to cultures in which social gender roles overlap; both men and women are supposed to be modest, tender and concerned with the quality of life.

In some respects the label for this dimension is somewhat confusing. Griffin and Pustay (1996) relabelled it as 'goal orientation', referring to the way in which people are motivated towards different types of goal. Those people towards the extreme 'masculine' side demonstrate *aggressive goal behaviour*: they place a high premium on material possessions, money and assertiveness. At the other extreme, people on the 'feminine' side who adopt *passive goal behaviour* place a higher value on social relationships, the quality of life and concern for others.

According to Hofstede, in cultures characterised by extremely aggressive goal behaviour, gender roles are rigidly defined: thus men are expected to work and to focus their careers in traditionally male occupations; women are generally expected not to work outside the home

Table 5.2 Impacts of different cultural dimensions at the workplace

Cultural dimension	Impacts at the workplace
Individualist	Same value standards apply to all: universalism
	Other people seen as potential resources
	Task prevails over relationship
	Calculative model of employer–employee relationship
Collectivist	Value standards differ for in-group and out-groups: particularism
	Other people seen as members of their group
	Relationship prevails over task
	Moral model of employer–employee relationship
Large power distance (power respect)	Hierarchy reflects on existential inequality of roles
	Subordinates expect to be told what to do
	Ideal boss is a benevolent autocrat (good father)
Small power distance (power tolerance)	Hierarchy means an inequality of roles, established for convenience
	Subordinates expect to be consulted
	Ideal boss is a resourceful democrat
Weak uncertainty avoidance (uncertainty acceptance)	Dislike of rules, written or unwritten
	Less formalisation and standardisation
	Readiness to accept change
Strong uncertainty avoidance	Emotional need for rules, written or unwritten
	More formalisation and standardisation
	Reluctance to accept change
Masculinity (aggressive goal behaviour)	Assertiveness appreciated
	Oversell yourself
	Stress on careers
	Decisiveness
Femininity (passive goal behaviour)	Assertiveness ridiculed
	Undersell yourself
	Stress on life quality
	Intuition

and to focus more on families. If they do work outside the home, they are usually expected to pursue work in areas traditionally dominated by women. Many people in Japan tend to exhibit relatively aggressive goal behaviour, whereas many people in Germany, Mexico, Italy and the United States tend to exhibit moderately aggressive goal behaviour. People from the Netherlands, Norway, Sweden, Denmark and Finland tend to exhibit relatively passive goal behaviour.

Table 5.2 gives a rather more detailed account of the impact of these different cultural dimensions.

Table 5.3 outlines the original scores obtained by Hofstede (1980) on the first four cultural dimensions across the 40 countries in his initial survey.

In later studies Hofstede (1991) added a fifth dimension to his national cultural classification, namely 'long-term orientation'.

Pause for thought 5.1

Look carefully at Table 5.3. Compare and contrast the results for Australia, Denmark, Japan and Singapore. What do these differences imply in terms of business practice?

Table 5.3 Scores of cultural dimensions (by country)

Country	Individualism	Power distance	Uncertainty	Masculinity
Argentina	46	49	86	56
Australia	90	36	51	61
Austria	55	11	70	79
Belgium	75	65	94	54
Brazil	38	69	76	49
Canada	80	39	48	52
Chile	23	63	86	28
Colombia	13	67	80	64
Denmark	74	18	23	16
Finland	63	33	59	26
France	71	68	86	43
Germany (FR)	67	35	65	66
Great Britain	89	35	35	66
Greece	35	60	112	57
Hong Kong	25	68	29	57
India	48	77	40	56
Iran	41	58	59	43
Ireland	70	28	35	68
Israel	54	13	81	47
Italy	76	50	75	70
Japan	46	54	92	95
Mexico	30	81	82	69
The Netherlands	80	38	53	14
New Zealand	79	22	49	58
Norway	69	31	50	8
Pakistan	14	55	70	50
Peru	16	64	87	42
Philippines	32	94	44	64
Portugal	27	63	104	31
Singapore	20	74	8	48
South Africa	65	49	49	63
Spain	51	57	86	42
Sweden	71	31	29	5
Switzerland	68	34	58	70
Taiwan	17	58	69	45
Thailand	20	64	64	34
Turkey	37	66	85	45
USA	91	40	46	62
Venezuela	12	81	76	73
Yugoslavia	27	76	88	21

Source: Adapted from *Cultures and Organizations: Software of the Mind*, 3rd ed., McGraw Hill (Hofstede, G., Hofstede, G.J. and Minkov, M. 2010), © Geert Hofstede B.V. quoted with permission.

Long-term orientation

Hofstede defines this as 'dealing with a society's search for virtue'. Long-term orientation means focusing on the future and implies a cultural trend towards delaying immediate gratification by practising persistence and thriftiness. The top long-term-oriented countries were found to be China, Hong Kong, Taiwan, Japan and South Korea in that order. Its opposite, short-term orientation, means a greater focus on the present and a more immediate gratification of need, such as spending to support current consumption even if this means borrowing money. The short-term-oriented countries in Asia included Pakistan, Philippines and Bangladesh. All Western countries showed a short-term orientation.

Hofstede later extended his survey from 40 to the current total of 74 countries. He also revised the original national scores (shown in Table 5.3) by conducting regular survey updates in each country and extending the sample beyond IBM employees to include students, civil service managers, airline pilots and consumers in subsets of countries for which occupational compatibility could reasonably be answered.

Figure 5.2(a) presents the worldwide average of the five Hofstede dimensions across the 74 countries using the most recent data set, and Figure 5.2(b), (c), (d) and (e) present these scores for India, China, the UK and the US respectively.

- *Power distance:* China has a much higher power distance score (80) as compared to the world average score of 60, as has India (77), unlike both the UK (35) and the US (40). This suggests much greater respect for position within hierarchies and for receiving direct instructions in China and India as compared to the UK and the US. In fact both China and India score well above the Far East Asian countries' average of 60 on this dimension.

- *Individualism:* China has a much lower individualism score (20) as compared to the world average score of 44, and the Asian average score of 24. The scores in the UK (89) and the US (91) are much higher for this dimension, indicating a much more collectivist outlook in China as compared to greater emphasis on self-reliance, and relatively loose bonds with others in the UK and the US. Interestingly, India (48) has an individualism score above the world average, quite different from the situation in China.

- *Masculinity/femininity:* the US has a high masculinity score (62) as has China (66) and the UK (66), compared to the world average of 50. This suggests a greater emphasis on assertiveness, decisiveness and career focus, amongst other 'male characteristics'. The score for India (56), while much lower than those of the UK, China and the US on this dimension, is above the world average for this dimension.

- *Uncertainty avoidance:* the US (46) and the UK (35) have scores for uncertainty avoidance well below the world average of 68. This suggests a high degree of 'acceptance' of uncertainty and ambiguity in these countries, i.e. members of these societies feel comfortable in unstructured situations. Interestingly, both India (40) and China (30) also score well below the world average of 68, which suggests a greater acceptance of unstructured situations than one might have expected!

- *Long-term orientation:* China (118) has an exceptionally high score for long-term orientation, with India (61) some distance behind but still well above the world average of 44. The US (29) has a very low score on this dimension, with the UK (25) in a similar position. The emphasis on materialism and immediate gratification in the UK, the US and many other Western countries is in sharp contrast to the greater emphasis on thrift, perseverance and tradition in China, and to a lesser extent India.

We have paid particular attention to Chinese cultural characteristics using the Hofstede dimensions of culture and associated national scores. Case 5.1 reviews the cultural dimensions of the other BRIC economies, using the same theoretical and empirical analysis of Hofstede.

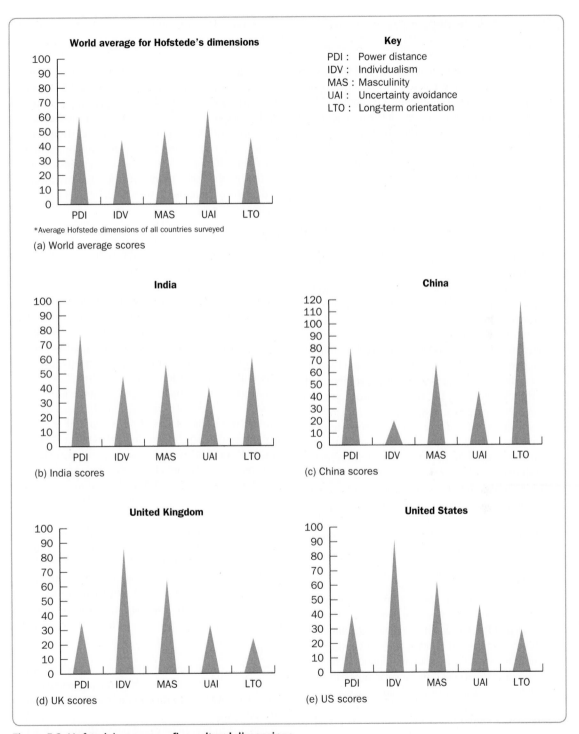

Figure 5.2 Hofstede's scores on five cultural dimensions

Source: Adapted from *Cultures and Organizations: Software of the Mind*, 3rd ed., McGraw Hill (Hofstede, G., Hofstede, G.J. and Minkov, M. 2010), © Geert Hofstede B.V. quoted with permission.

CASE 5.1 Brazilian, Russian, Indian and Chinese cultural characteristics

Figure 5.2 provided an outline of India's cultural characteristics using Hofstede's definitions, and compared these with another BRIC economy, China, and the world 'average' scores for the individual elements, as well as those for the UK and US.

Figure 5.3 extends this analysis further, by providing equivalent data for the other BRIC economies of Brazil and Russia.

Brazil

Figure 5.3(b) presents the Brazilian cultural characteristics identified by Geert Hofstede's analysis. We can see that Brazil has a higher *power distance* score of 69 than the world average (60), suggesting considerable respect for position within hierarchies and a willingness to receive direct instructions. However, its *individualism* score of 38 is below the world average of 44, suggesting a more collectivist and group-oriented outlook than in many other countries. In terms of *masculinity* characteristics, Brazil's score of 49 is broadly similar to the world average (50), i.e. similar to most countries in terms of assertiveness/materialism. However, its *uncertainty avoidance* score of 76 is above the world average (68), suggesting a preference for a more structured and predictable environment, as compared to a less certain one. Finally, in terms of *long-term orientation* Brazil has a score of 65, well above the world average (44) and suggesting a greater readiness to look further into the future and to postpone immediate gratification in favour of longer-term goals.

Russia

Figure 5.3(c) presents the Russian cultural characteristics identified by Geert Hofstede's analysis. We can see that Russia has a higher *power distance* score of 93 than the world average (60), suggesting considerable respect for position within hierarchies and a willingness to accept direct instructions. However, its *individualism* score of 39 is below the world average of 44, suggesting a more collectivist and group-oriented outlook than in many other countries. In terms of *masculinity* characteristics, Russia's score of 36 is below the world average (50), i.e. perhaps rather surprisingly suggesting less assertiveness/

materialism and other 'male' characteristics! However, its *uncertainty avoidance* score of 95 is well above the world average (68), suggesting a strong preference for a more structured and predictable environment, as compared to a less certain one. Finally, in terms of *long-term orientation* Russia has a score of 36, below the world average (44), suggesting a reluctance to look further into the future and to postpone immediate gratification in favour of longer-term goals

India

As we can see (Figure 5.3(d)), India is similar to China in terms of *power distance* (PDI), with its 'score' of 77 higher than the world average of 60, indicating significant respect for position within hierarchies and for accepting direct instructions. The India score for *individualism* (IDV) is 48, which is interestingly above the world average (44) and well above that for China (20). This suggests a less collectivist outlook in India than in China and a greater emphasis on self-reliance and less close bonds with others. As regards *masculinity* (MAS), the Indian score of 56 is again above the world average (50), suggesting a somewhat greater emphasis on decisiveness, career focus, assertiveness and other 'male' characteristics. As regards *uncertainty avoidance* (UAI), the Indian score of 40 is well below the world average (68), suggesting a higher degree of acceptance of uncertainty and change in India than perhaps might have been expected! Finally, in terms of *long-term orientation* (LTI), the Indian score of 61 is well above the world average (41), suggesting a lesser emphasis on materialism and instant gratification and a greater focus on long-term outcomes than in many other countries.

China

Figure 5.3(e) provides a useful summary of Chinese cultural characteristics from the perspective of Geert Hofstede's classification of national cultural characteristics.

Power distance: In terms of *power distance* (PDI) China has a much higher score (80) as compared to the world average score of 60, suggesting much greater respect for position within hierarchies and

Case 5.1 (*continued*)

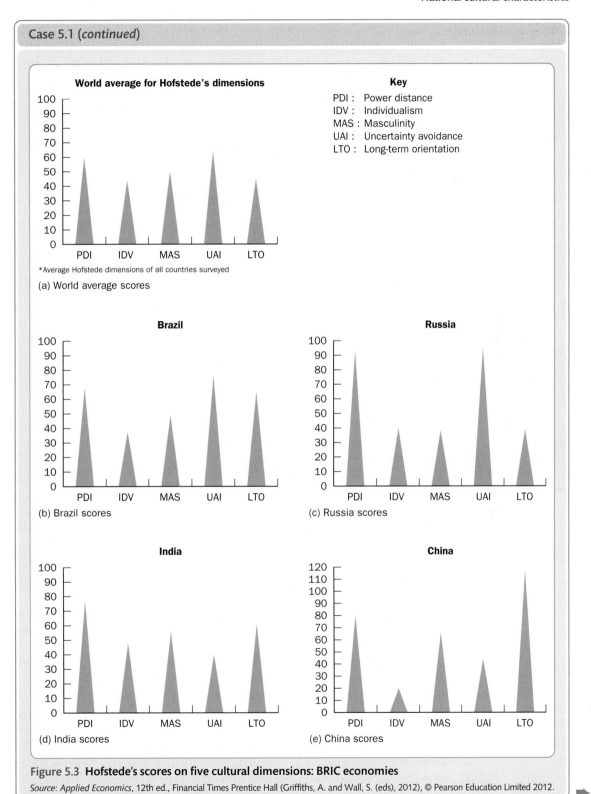

Figure 5.3 Hofstede's scores on five cultural dimensions: BRIC economies

Source: Applied Economics, 12th ed., Financial Times Prentice Hall (Griffiths, A. and Wall, S. (eds), 2012), © Pearson Education Limited 2012.

Case 5.1 (continued)

for receiving direct instructions in China as compared to, say, the UK (35), US (40), and most other countries which also have lower PDI scores than China.

Individualism: In terms of *individualism* (IDV) China has a much lower individualism score (20) as compared to the world average score of 44, and the UK (89) and US (91). This indicates the much more collectivist outlook in China as compared to the greater emphasis on self-reliance and relatively loose bonds with others in the UK, US and most other countries.

Masculinity: In terms of *masculinity* (MAS) China has a higher score (66) as compared to the world average score of 50, suggesting a greater emphasis on assertiveness, decisiveness and career focus amongst other predominantly 'male' characteristics.

Uncertainty avoidance: In terms of *uncertainty avoidance* (UAI) China has a much lower score (30) than the world average score of 68. This implies that China is much less concerned with uncertainty avoidance than many other countries, suggesting

that China has a much higher degree of acceptance of uncertainty and change than many might have expected.

Long-term orientation: In terms of *long-term orientation* (LTO) China has a much higher score (118) as compared with the world average score of 44. There is clearly a much greater readiness in China to postpone immediate gratification and materialism in favour of achieving longer-term objectives as a result of such abstinence.

Questions

1 Explain how the different cultural characteristics identified above might influence how a multinational business operating in all four countries might adjust its approach to managing a subsidiary company located in each country.

2 Apply your reasoning to a specific policy area for each country, e.g. recruitment policy for HR, advertising policy for marketing etc.

Cultural impacts on international business

In Chapters 1 and 2 we noted the rapid growth in joint ventures, strategic alliances and mergers and acquisitions in a globalised economy. At such times managers and executives often focus on the business needs of the new operations, such as raising finance, acquiring the capital infrastructure, drawing up operational plans and providing technical training. Unfortunately cultural issues at a national or organisational level have often been ignored during these periods of consolidation, as many firms have subsequently found to their cost. Box 5.1 brings this issue into focus.

The situation in Box 5.1 shows 'the clash between American values of individualism, directness and time consciousness and the Japanese interest in face-to-face discussion and consensus building. At the core of the clash are the differing values underlying task-oriented versus process-oriented cultures. Americans typically come to business meetings well informed, focused and expecting an open dialogue. They also expect to take action and assign responsibilities. However, their Asian and Japanese partners place more emphasis on group harmony, consensus and the need to discuss proposals and actions; they rarely make an immediate decision. Japanese people may come to a meeting, sit as a group, ask ten questions and leave with 20 more in mind. Decisions come later after reaching a consensus. The Indonesian team expects a senior person to open and close important meetings, frequent coffee breaks and snacks and perhaps sufficient time to conduct their daily prayers. Indonesians are used to inviting others to their meetings if they are subject specialists and do not mind side conversations if these are on important points. They also expect seating to be arranged according to seniority, as well as explicit invitations to participate during the course of the meeting. With three sets of competing values, cultural clashes can easily occur and teamwork can be seriously damaged.

> ## BOX 5.1 A clash of cultures
>
> Mike Burgess is an operations manager from the USA who is in charge of a multicultural team in Indonesia, which includes a number of Japanese experts on production control. At a team meeting beginning at 9.00 a.m. he is surprised to find that at 9.20 a.m. three of the remaining members of the Indonesian team are still arriving, each bringing with them an additional three uninvited participants. The room has to be reorganised and an extra nine chairs brought in. Four members of the Japanese team have reorganised themselves so that they are sitting together. Mr Budi, the senior Indonesian member, is due to deliver the opening formal comments and eventually arrives at 9.45 a.m. He begins his opening address immediately but exceeds his allotted five minutes, taking ten minutes in all. The meeting itself is finally underway at 9.55 a.m.
>
> Mike presents the agenda and outlines the objectives of the meeting and invites questions. To his surprise, no one volunteers with a first question. He then realises that Mr Budi, as senior, is expecting to be invited to make comments. After he does so the rest of the team joins in. The meeting is going well, but Mike becomes annoyed by side conversations among the Indonesian team members – as a rule he likes his meetings to maintain their focus on achieving the final results and objectives.
>
> Halfway through the meeting, Mike and his marketing director have a disagreement. The openness of the heated debate surprises the Indonesian and Japanese teams. By 10.30 a.m. everyone is irritated and Mike suggests a coffee break, at which point the Indonesians express surprise that Mike has not ordered any snacks. When the meeting reconvenes, Mike wants to reach a decision so he asks Mr Yamaguchi, the senior Japanese team member, to agree to a vote. Mr Yamaguchi replies by asking for a week to consult with his headquarters in Tokyo, which frustrates Mike whose project will now be delayed. Mr Yamaguchi decides this is an opportunity to vent his own frustrations and he questions Mike, who works on the upper floor, about his failure to reply directly to the e-mails he has been sent.
>
> Mr Yamaguchi does not understand why Mike cannot meet with him personally to discuss some of the issues contained in these e-mails.
>
> *Source:* Adapted from Elashmawi (1998).

It may be useful to briefly review some other possible impacts of Hofstede's analysis of national culture on international business practices.

● *Power distances:* If companies operate with others from nations with different degrees of power distance, misunderstandings can easily arise. For example, a firm from a country with a small power distance, when negotiating in a joint venture, may send a team of experts who are relatively junior. If this team is sent to a large power distance (power-respecting) culture, this may be viewed as an insult. The informality that characterises communication in countries with a small power distance may be misinterpreted by those from a power-respecting culture as an attempt to reduce their authority.

171

● *Uncertainty avoidance:* Those operating in strong uncertainty avoidance countries tend to adopt more rigid hierarchies and more elaborate rules and procedures for doing business. Risk taking may also be less preferred than in weak uncertainty avoidance (uncertainty accepting) countries such as the United States and Hong Kong. This can affect the way in which certain benefits are received. For example, Japanese firms operating in uncertainty accepting countries such as Canada and the United States have been forced to modify their pay and promotion policies because North American workers are more oriented towards an individualistic 'pay me what I'm worth attitude' and are less worried about job insecurity.

Pause for thought 5.2

What impacts might result in terms of international business practices if two companies involved with each other originate from countries with sharply different scores for 'individualism' and 'long-term orientation'?

Case 5.2 provides a useful illustration of national cultural influences on employer/ employee engagement practices.

The next section emphasises the types of understanding and awareness that may be needed of national cultural differences if international business negotiations are to be conducted effectively. It emphasises the differences between the collectivist/individualist dimension of national culture, with particular reference to conducting business with Confucian societies, such as China.

A more detailed analysis of management issues for multicultural teams is also presented below (pp. 184–187), including Case 5.5. Chapters 8 and 9 also draw heavily on these national cultural characteristics when reviewing international human resource management and international marketing, respectively.

CASE 5.2 National culture and Japanese competitiveness

Among the many factors contributing to Japan's post-war competitiveness has been the sociocultural underpinnings at the national level of its industrial and commercial activities. For example, during most of the post-war era Japan's workers had a strong preference for work over leisure so that as real incomes rose, a high percentage of the additional income was saved. This, coupled with relatively low inflation and low interest rates, helped stimulate investment.

The social framework of Japanese society also played a part, having been influenced by two powerful ideologies, namely Buddhism and Confucianism. Buddhism taught the importance of harmony and respect, reminding people that they should be prepared for change since this was an endemic part of life. Confucianism taught the importance of the individual's position in society and the vital significance of the interaction between a person and his or her immediate superior/inferior. With this background, Japan became a strongly 'vertical' society based on the household or 'ie'. Individuals were subservient to group interest, whether it was within a traditional family framework or in

Case 5.2 (continued)

a 'quasi' family-type situation based on the company. This aspect of Japan's nature has been characterised as a society in which work organisation is *gemeinschaft* rather than *gesellschaft* in nature – that is, one based on natural will and close face-to-face relationships rather than one which is based on rational will and is more utilitarian and goal directed in nature.

Competitiveness also depends to a great extent on how companies manage their most valuable asset – their workers. Japanese corporate strategy on labour management in the large-firm sector is very much about creating an efficient internal labour market. First, they hire individuals straight from school or college and employ them as far as possible until retiring at about 55 to 58 years. On average Japanese companies tend to hire people with 'neyaka', i.e. an optimistic, open-minded and wide-ranging set of interests as compared to the more specialist hiring policies of many European companies. Second, they mould workers into 'flexible assets' by rotating them between different departments within the company to ensure a broader perspective and a more flexible attitude. Third, they involve workers in in-company training schemes and stress the importance of on-the-job training. Finally, the pay system varies closely with age around the concept of providing workers in large and medium-sized firms with 'lifetime' employment. Japanese managers work hard at creating a stable internal labour market and treat workers as key resources deserving of attention. If workers feel that the company has a commitment to keep them employed, this gives them the confidence to release the 'tacit' knowledge or basic know-how, which often cannot be easily articulated. In other words, workers have the confidence to share any untapped knowledge they may have because they operate within a secure and dynamic environment.

Nevertheless, there have been pressures on Japanese companies and workers to adapt such long-standing cultural, social and workplace norms to a more globalised context. For example, in the past two decades the share of Japan in world outward fdi has halved to around 5% in 2014 and analysts have pointed to a more 'insular' and less flexible organisational culture within Japanese-owned MNEs as compared to their rivals. Even in 2014 the cultural attachment of Japanese employers to lifetime employment has resulted in around one-third of the permanent staff in the larger Japanese firms being identified in surveys as 'surplus to requirements' ('Business', *Economist*, 12 July 2014, p. 55). The Japanese labour laws are seen as extremely favourable to existing employees, so that voluntary severance packages are extremely costly for businesses, usually offering two to three years pay.

The MD of Rakuten, a Japanese e-commerce company valued at $16 billion, reflected on the need for changes in Japanese corporate cultures. 'We need to be global . . . to bring in ideas and people from all over the world. In our headquarters. Not just at the executive level but at the entry level. You are competing against global companies.' In November 2013 Honda announced it would start using English in all its global meetings, following a similar decision by Rakuten and other major Japanese MNEs.

Source: Griffiths (2000); Griffiths and Wall (2012).

Questions

1 How does the discussion above relate to Hofstede's five cultural dimensions?

2 Comment on the scoring for Japan in Hofstede's investigations in Table 5.3. Are there any surprises?

▇ Doing business in Confucian societies: the importance of guanxi (connections)

China became one of the world's four largest economies in 2010. The success has often been attributed to Confucianism, which stresses hard work, thrift and perseverance. Confucius lived from 551 to 478 BC and societies influenced by his thinking include China, Hong Kong,

Taiwan, Japan and Korea, all of which have prospects for sustained economic growth in the new millennium. In these societies 'who you know is more important than what you know'. These connections are known in Chinese as *guanxi*; in Japan they are known as *kankei*; and in Korea as *kwankye*. Here we pay particular attention to *guanxi*.

Under the influence of Confucianism these societies share the following characteristics: disdain for institutional law; strong bonds on the basis of blood, ancestral village and school and military ties; a clear demarcation between members of the in- versus out-groups; an ability to grasp the interdependent relationship situations that may not be obvious to Westerners; and a tendency to view matters from a long-term perspective. These characteristics mean that connections in virtually all social functions, including business, are of the utmost importance. In the West, institutional law and contracts establish what can and should be done and largely overshadow the role of connections.

The word *guanxi* contains two characters that make up the term 'gate/pass' or 'to connect'. Thus *guanxi* refers to the establishment of a connection between independent individuals to enable a bilateral flow of personal or social transactions. Both parties must derive benefits from the transaction to ensure the continuation of such a relationship.

How does this differ from 'networking' in the West? Yeung and Tung (1996) analyse these differences along six dimensions.

1 *Motives: role obligation versus self-interest.* Confucianism emphasises the importance of an individual's place in the hierarchy: individuals are part of a social system, not isolated entities. These include such relationships as ruler–subject, father–son, husband–wife, brother–brother and friend–friend. People have responsibility to the role and not merely to their own self-interest, as in the West.

2 *Reciprocation: self-loss versus self-gain.* In Confucianism everyone is encouraged to become a *yi-ren* (righteous person). To do so, a person must repay favours and increase the value of the favour given. There is a Chinese saying: 'If someone pays you an honour of a linear foot, you should reciprocate by honouring the giver with ten linear feet.'

3 *Time orientation: long-term versus short-term perspective.* In Confucian societies people understand all social interaction within the context of a long-term perspective. Their values are based on an understanding of the interdependence of events and of the relationship between events and time. Every *guanxi* relationship is regarded as 'stock' to be put away in times of abundance and plenty. The 'stock' will then be at their disposal in times of need and trouble. *Guanxi* is maintained through continuous, long-term interactions. Social interactions in the West are usually seen as one-offs with the main emphasis placed on immediate gratification from the situation.

4 *Power differentiation: xia versus power.* In Confucianism everyone striving to become a righteous person becomes a *xia* or knight, attempting to right the wrongs in the world. Those in positions of power and authority must assist the disadvantaged; it is their obligation to do so. In return, those in positions of power and authority gain face and reputation. While social conscience may be strong in the West, there is no obligation for the powerful to help the disadvantaged.

5 *Nature of power: personal power versus institutional authority.* Governance by ethics is preferred to governance by law. There is a general aversion to law and litigation in Confucian societies. The focus is on personal power and the importance of *guanxi,* since an individual (rather than authority) defines what is permissible in a given context in a given time.

6 *Sanction: shame versus guilt.* The primary sanction in Confucian societies is that of shame. There is great emphasis on face and face-saving. Face implies more than reputation. There is a Chinese saying that 'face is like the bark of a tree; without its bark, the tree dies'. People who lose face in these societies are more than social outcasts; a loss of face brings shame to the person and to his or her family members. Face can be given and taken away only in the broader context of social interactions. To maintain *guanxi,* extra care needs to be taken in acquiring and maintaining 'face' – often known as 'face works'. In the West, probably due to the influence of Judeo-Christianity, sanctions work on the basis of guilt. Thus, if the behaviour deviates from the norm, it is individuals who are required to internalise their understanding of sin.

To many in the West, *guanxi* can appear to resemble nepotism. For example, someone in authority may make decisions based on family ties instead of being based on an objective evaluation of ability. As with any system, it is open to abuse, though defenders of *guanxi* might also point to the arguably adverse impacts of excessive litigation in the USA!

Although *guanxi* may appear undemocratic, it is embedded in a rich cultural heritage which places a strong emphasis on the family and is drawn from the Confucian background in which most of the key relationships already discussed pertain to the family. In fact, the majority of Chinese businesses are family-run concerns. The importance of *guanxi* cannot be overestimated. In their research of 2,000 Chinese businesses surveyed in and around Shanghai, Gordon C. Chu and Yanan Ju (1993) found that 92.4% of those polled affirmed the importance of *guanxi* in their daily lives. Also 84.5% indicated that they did not trust strangers until they had had the opportunity to get to know them better, and 71.7% preferred to use *guanxi* connections rather than normal bureaucratic channels.

The following quotation from the chairman of the Lippo group, an Indonesian conglomerate, usefully summarises many of the above points; he stated that he devotes his time exclusively to cultivating relationships while delegating the daily functioning of the group's business to his two sons. In his words, 'I open the door and others walk through.'

Effective ways of cultivating guanxi

Yeung and Tung (1996) reported the results of their survey of executives who identified the following activities as being crucial for cultivating *guanxi*.

- *Group identification/altercasting.*Kinship and locality are the important bases for *guanxi*. Kinship is based on people's immediate and extended families, while locality refers to the ancestral village or province. Such 'ascribed' relationships are based on common or shared experiences, such as going to the same school, serving in the same military unit or working in the same organisation. As most non-Chinese investors cannot do this, 'altercasting' is an alternative possibility. This means rearranging the social network so that individuals can focus on some element of commonality. The most effective way of doing this is through an intermediary. According to Victor Fung, chairman of Prudential Asia, a Hong Kong investment bank: 'If you are being considered for a new partnership, a personal reference from a respected member of the Chinese business community is worth more than any amount of money you could throw on the table.' As another executive put it: 'The China market is like a pond full of hidden delicious food. A new fish in the pond can starve to death because he doesn't know how to locate the food. Your intermediary is an old fish who knows where every plant and plankton is. He can show you the precise location of this food so you can eat to your heart's satisfaction.'

- *Tendering favours.* Another way of establishing relationships is to offer immediate rewards. Gift giving, entertainment, overseas trips, sponsoring and support for the children of Chinese officials at universities abroad are common. When a gift has been received, there is a symbolic breaking down of the boundaries between the individuals, although these cannot be the basis for long-term *guanxi*.

- *Nurturing long-term mutual benefits.* The intent of this approach is to create an interdependence between two parties in the relationship so that there will be a great cost to either side in severing such ties.

- *Cultivating personal relationships.* *Guanxi* relations that are based exclusively on material benefits are fragile; many respondents felt that it was important to develop a personal relationship with the partner that cannot be readily imitated by others. 'Personal' means sharing inner feelings or secrets for which, in Chinese society, sincerity and frankness are absolutely essential. To do this you would need to acquire an in-depth knowledge of the Chinese business associate and know what appeals to his or her needs.

- *Cultivating trust.* Finally, cultivating trust is crucial. Around 85% of the companies interviewed indicated that this was an essential condition for cultivating *guanxi*. For many this was based on two factors: 'Deliver what you promise' and 'Don't cheat'. Another way is to learn all you can about the Chinese culture, including its language.

Case 5.3 casts further light on the relevance of *guanxi* relationships.

CASE 5.3 East meets West

When East meets West there are clashes with respect to their management practices. For example, in the context of strong global fdi and M&A activity, great demands are placed on joint-venture firms having all their subsidiaries working within a common form of governance, and conforming to the transparency of accounting practices that result from the adoption of GAAP (generally accepted accounting practices). This commonality allows the global management team to measure, contrast and control their operations in a straightforward way – but such operations are anathema to most Eastern managers. In fairness, we should note that opaqueness is not a unique East/West issue since the Channel Islands, Belgium, Spain and Switzerland all practise low levels of financial disclosure. However, research into the Oriental concept of probability and risk taking indicates that Asian cultures tend to be more 'fate-oriented' and less willing (than Occidentals) to take a probabilistic view of the world. The inclination towards a lack of disclosure in Asian accounting together with a reluctance to adopt management accounting poses serious problems for those seeking goal congruence in joint operations. It may be useful at this stage to consider in more detail some of the key differences between Western and Eastern practices as they may impinge upon international business activity.

- *Rules versus relationships.* In advanced economies, companies do business within a 'rules-based' system, with business generally conducted by using contracts under laws that are widely known and consistently enforced. Although it may not be apparent to those operating in a rules-based system that has grown up over decades or even centuries, such a system carries large fixed costs. These include the establishment of the legislation and the judiciary, the drafting and interpretation of laws, and the implementation of contracts, all of which involve high sunk costs. On the other hand, once such a system is in place, the incremental cost of enforcing an additional contract is minimal.

China's is not a rules-based economy, at least not yet; it is still an economy based on relationships.

Case 5.3 (*continued*)

Business transactions are made on the strength not of contracts but of personal agreements. Transactions are purely private, and are neither verifiable nor enforceable in the public sphere. However, the marginal costs of finding, screening and monitoring a potential partner are extremely high. For instance, the relationships have to be managed personally: you cannot afford to delegate the task. A telling difference with the West is that executives in China tend to answer their own phones. Given this marginal cost of cultivating new relationships, it makes sense to do business with close family, then with the extended family, then neighbours from your home town, then former classmates, and only then, reluctantly, with strangers.

- *Ethical norms.* In Western literature it has only been in relatively recent times that business ethics have impinged explicitly on decision-making techniques and structures. In China, however, there has always been a debate about *yi* and *li* – where *yi* is ethical value (justice) and *li* is economic value (profit). Indeed, both *yi* and *li* have been central concepts within Chinese Confucianism. It is said that one cannot 'have both fish and a bear's paw at the same time'. So man will favour *yi* and discard *li,* and thus it is to be understood that '*xiao-ren* (a mean person) is pushed by *li,* whereas *jun-zi* (a gentleman) is delighted by *yi*'. Of course, such attitudes are being increasingly challenged in an age of globalism as the world is effectively reduced to a single market economy.

- *Guanxi.* As already noted, Asians tend to deploy rather opaque accounting practices and to adopt 'gift giving' on a scale that seems to many Westerners little short of bribery, though in many cases this may be a misconception. In China there is the universal practice of *guanxi,* the maintenance of which will involve gift giving. In Chinese society the exchanges of favours involving *guanxi* are not strictly commercial, they are also social – involving *renqing* (social or humanised obligation) and the giving of *mianzi* (the notion of 'face'). More recently, as China opens up, *guanxi* has become known as 'social capital' and has been seen in the West as an important element in securing commercial contracts between corporations. Although 'gift giving' and 'banqueting' are both normal facets of Chinese *guanxi,* many Western firms' operations arguably go too far and operate too close to bribery. Western individuals can become known as 'eat and wine friends', defeating the object of true *guanxi* – which is the offering of favours during the development of a personal relationship. Confucianism is sometimes (many would argue unfairly!) accused of promoting corruption in East Asia given that its teachings call for individuals to improve and maintain relationships among relatives and friends through influence and contacts. The World Bank and the International Monetary Fund now seem more vigilant in acting as 'whistle blowers' whenever they detect funding diversions. Similarly, the United States seems more ready to implement its 1977 laws, which declare acts criminal if national personnel offer commercial payoffs to public servants abroad. Corporations themselves also seem more ready to tackle perceived corruption. For example, the Royal Dutch/Shell Group in its April 1998 annual report said it had fired 23 of its staff and had terminated contracts with 95 firms on ethical grounds. In China, there is a strong history of *guandao,* or official corruption, that is more pervasive than in Japan.

In terms of the management of projects and of joint ventures, there have clearly been examples of attempts by negotiators to ask for bribes in some form. From the Western ethical perspective, giving bribes should be resisted. In an attempt to tackle this issue, the OECD Council adopted in 1996 the 'Recommendation on Bribery of Foreign Public Officials in International Business Transactions' which calls on member countries to act to combat illicit payments in international trade and investment. As part of that recommendation, reference was made to the need 'to take concrete and meaningful steps including examining tax legislation, regulations, and practices insofar as they may indirectly favour bribery' (OECD 1996, C (94) 75). Following this, the OECD Committee on Fiscal Affairs undertook an in-depth review of tax measures that may influence the willingness

Case 5.3 (*continued*)

to make or accept bribes. The committee concluded that bribes paid to foreign public officials should no longer be deductible for tax purposes. They noted that many member countries would have to change their current practices.

Source: Adapted from Kidd and Xue (2000).

Questions

1 Consider some of the differences between a 'rules-based' system and a 'relationship-based' system.

2 How might *guanxi* relationships influence international business activity?

National, organisational and occupational cultures

As well as his major study on differences in national cultures within a given organisation (IBM), Hofstede undertook a study on variations in organisational culture within the same nation. He compared otherwise similar people in different organisations within the same countries (Denmark and the Netherlands). His results suggested that at the organisational level 'culture' differences consisted mostly of different practices rather than different values (this emphasis was reversed at the national level). Using the word 'culture' for both levels suggested that the two kinds of culture were identical phenomena, but to Hofstede this was clearly false. A nation is not an organisation and the two types of 'culture' are of a different kind.

This conclusion contradicts a popular notion about 'corporate culture' derived from Peters and Waterman's classic work, *In Search of Excellence,* which assumed that *shared values* represented the core of a corporate culture. Hofstede's work showed that while the values of founders and key leaders may undoubtedly shape organisational cultures, the ways in which these 'cultures' affect ordinary members is through *shared practices*. The fact that organisational cultures are shaped by management practices and not by values explains why such cultures can, to some extent, be managed. As Hofstede points out, values are shaped early in our lives, through family, school and peers, so that employers cannot readily change the values of their employees. The only way in which they can affect them is through selecting and promoting employees with the 'desired' values, where appropriate candidates are available. If, in order to change organisational cultures, employers had to change their employees' values, it would arguably be a hopeless task. However, because organisational cultures reside mainly in the more superficial arena of practices rather than values, they are somewhat more manageable.

Table 5.4 provides a brief outline of some aspects of national, corporate (organisational) and occupational cultures. Many of the terms presented are considered further in Box 5.2.

Pause for thought 5.3

Think of any particular company with which you are familiar. Can you identify any distinctive elements in its corporate culture? Can you trace the origin of any of these elements?

Table 5.4 Aspects of national, corporate and occupational cultures

National culture	Corporate culture	Occupational culture
An individual's orientation towards: ● universalism v particularism	A particular company's: ● values ● rituals ● heroes ● symbols	A given occupation's: ● analytical paradigm ● work norms and practices ● code of ethics ● jargon
● analysing v integrating	NB: Corporate culture can also refer to the values, systems and practices which influence the corporate behaviour of all firms in a country.	
● individualism v communitarianism ● Inner-directedness v outer-directedness ● time as sequence v time as synchronisation ● achieved status v ascribed status ● equality v hierarchy		

Source: Reprinted and adapted from *Organizational Dynamics,* vol. 24, no. 4, Snow, C.C., Davison, S.C., Snell, S.A. and Hambrik, D.C., Use of Transnational Teams to Globalize your Company, pp. 90–107. Copyright 1996, with permission from Elsevier.

BOX 5.2 National and organisational cultural dimensions

As well as Hofstede's seminal work, Trompenaars (1993) set out a cultural model consisting of seven dimensions, five of which are grouped under 'relationships with people' and the other two are concerned with time and the environment.

1 **Universalism v particularism.** In universal cultures 'rules' are favoured over 'relationships'. Contractual agreements are considered of the utmost importance, and logical, rational analytical thinking and professionalism are of great importance. In particularist cultures there are greater obligations to friendship and kinship and these are maintained through personalism, saving 'face' and paternalism.

2 **Individualism v communitarianism.** This is almost identical to Hofstede's dimension (see p. 161), with cultures towards the former end of the spectrum seen as reinforcing the role of the individual and those towards the communitarianism end of the spectrum seen as emphasising the role of groups and larger systems.

3 **Achieving or ascribing.** In achieving societies the emphasis is on esteem related to past achievements. In ascribing societies achievement is a more collective affair and organisations in these societies often justify a high power distance so that things get done. Power here does not need to be legitimised by title or qualification, with esteem often related more to position and age.

4 **Relating to nature.** This concerns beliefs about nature's ability to be controlled. 'Inner-directed' cultures want to overcome nature and depend a great deal on one's own control, while 'outer-directed' cultures see themselves more as a product of the outside world and external environment.

5 **Perceptions of time.** This reflects different attitudes to time: synchronic and circular attitudes allow parallel activities and are less concerned with punctuality. In a 'sequential culture' the focus is on rational efficiency and time is viewed in a more linear fashion.

Table 5.5 **Scores on four of Trompenaars' cultural dimensions**

Country	Universalism (%)	Individualism (%)	Achieved status (%)	Inner-directedness (%)
Australia	40	75	93	61
Belgium	37	61	n.a.	48
Canada	75	80	93	64
France	26	68	94	60
Germany	31	67	96	65
Italy	28	69	81	49
Japan	34	50	86	41
Netherlands	38	n.a.	96	55
Singapore	21	38	79	42
Sweden	n.a.	84	96	45
UK	42	74	94	51
US	77	79	90	68

Source: Adapted from THE SEVEN CULTURES OF CAPITALISM by Charles Hampden-Turner, Alfons Trompenaars, copyright © 1993 by Charles Hampden-Turner. Used by permission of Doubleday, a division of Random House, Inc.

The scores on four of these dimensions are shown in Table 5.5, following the work of Hampden-Turner and Trompenaars (1994).

Pause for thought 5.4

How do the Trompenaars' cultural dimensions in Table 5.5 compare with the cultural dimension scores of Hofstede in Table 5.3. What are the similarities in cultural awareness and are there any implied differences?

As noted in Table 5.4, corporate culture can refer to the individual company's values, rituals, heroes and symbols. Steve Jobs, the founder of Apple, has obviously had a major influence on the company he helped drive forward to global success. The organisational culture of confidence in the rigour and effectiveness of its own internal processes and procedures, especially as regards product innovation, quality and excellence, was seen by many as reflecting the founder's own personal characteristic and value. However, when key elements of the organisational culture are recognised as no longer in alignment with business imperatives, then there may be some modification to these elements, as is suggested by Case 5.4.

CASE 5.4 Apple

Apple agreed in 2012 to a jointly monitored audit of pollution controls at a supplier's factory in China. A maker of printed circuit boards for the Silicon Valley Company is due to be inspected by auditors, with Apple and the China-based Institute of Public and Environmental Affairs (IPE) jointly monitoring their efforts. Apple had held lengthy talks in 2012 with the IPE, a non-governmental organisation that has amassed a database of 97,000 environmental violations in China from official data. Apple was the only one of 29 companies that had failed to respond to an earlier 2010 report by the IPE on hazardous wastes from suppliers causing pollution and health problems in China.

Case study 5.4 (continued)

Ma Jun, IPE director, told the *Financial Times* that Apple's attitude changed in September 2011, two weeks after a second report said that pollution discharges were expanding and spreading in Apple's Chinese supply chain. Apple had been insisting earlier that details about its suppliers and its own audits of them were private and were sufficient to ensure environmental standards were being maintained. Ma Jun, commenting on Apple's change of policy, said 'it's now become about validation: we kept telling Apple that you can't just say that everything is fine – we need proof'. The IPE hopes that the first jointly monitored audit of pollution by Apple will act as a pilot for others to take place in 13 more Chinese factories where Apple had previously been carrying out only its own environmental checks.

With a $564bn market capitalisation, Apple is the world's most valuable company and environmentalists hope its responsiveness to their concerns will influence other companies to take action. Mr Ma cited Taiwan's HTC, Sweden's Ericsson and Japan's Canon as having also been slow in responding to pollution problems the IPE had highlighted in their supply chains.

 Source: Adapted from Apple agrees to China pollution audit, *Financial Times*, 15/04/2012, p. 22 (Nuttall, C.), © The Financial Times Limited 2012. All Rights Reserved.

Question

Use economic analysis to explain why Apple has changed its mind and is now cooperating with independent audits of its supply chain in China.

Corporate culture can also reflect the values, systems and practices which are generally accepted by *all home-country companies* within a given nation. Case 5.5 looks at these aspects of corporate culture, taking further the material on Japan presented in Case 5.2.

The linkages between national and corporate/organisational cultures prevalent across the majority of home-country companies is taken further in the next section, using investigatory material from a number of countries.

CASE 5.5 Corporate culture and Japanese competitiveness

Another important area of debate has been the nature and perceived weaknesses in the much-vaunted industrial groupings either of the *Kigyo-Shudan* or *keiretsu* types. The typical corporate governance system in Japan included such attributes as the long-term supply of funds to industry at low interest rates; the monitoring of industry by the main group bank; the extensive cross-holding of shares; the lack of non-corporate shareholders; and the absence of mergers and acquisitions as a means of extracting value from poorly performing firms. All these attributes arguably created a corporate culture which aided Japan's catch-up process.

However, weaknesses in such a corporate culture began to emerge during the rapidly changing environment of the 1980s, which began to erode the traditional corporate governance system. For example, banks found that large firms began to rely more on

Case 5.5 (continued)

the capital market for funds so that a greater proportion of their lending had to be directed to the small and medium-sized companies whose performance was more difficult to monitor. There was also an increasing realisation that the 'old' corporate culture of the *Kigyo-Shudan* form of industrial organisation based on six major industrial groupings (see Case 2.7) would have to change. Under this system company shares were mostly held by other companies in order to consolidate a relationship rather than as an active form of investment. This would have to change in a globalised environment in which cross-border mergers and acquisitions are increasingly the norm rather than the exception. Further, the changes brought about by financial deregulation will bring new investors into the equity market (pension funds, insurance companies) which are likely to be more active traders of shares.

The other main form of industrial organisation, the *keiretsu* system of parent company and vertically organised subcontracting suppliers, is also changing. For example, the Renault 'revival plan' for Nissan involved a reduction in its capacity by 25% together with the selling of its shareholdings in its affiliated companies where it owns less than 20% of those shares. This inevitably weakens the vertical *keiretsu* 'relationship' based on long-term 'family' type bonds between large firms and their subcontractors who lie below them in the production 'pyramid'. In fact 36% of subcontractors surveyed in 2001 stated an intention of reducing their dependence on specific parent companies. The unwinding of cross-holdings also continues, with a survey by Toyo Keizai estimating that cross-holdings have decreased by 10% between 1992 and 2000, with most of those acquiring the released shares being foreigners who are more interested in profits than the previous holders.

If shares become more easily traded as cross-holdings decrease, then the ownership of Japanese companies may change and restructuring through mergers and acquisitions may eventually become more prevalent. In the past, the importance of creating shareholder value has been relatively unimportant in Japan since managers were mostly recruited from the pool of workers within the company so that there was a lack of a pure profit motive. However, the changing industrial system and the banking reorganisation underway will inevitably shift Japanese corporations in the direction of a greater emphasis on raising short-term profits and increasing shareholder value. For example, in the past each *keiretsu* group would have its own 'main' bank, but now those banks have themselves been involved in large amalgamations in attempts to rationalise operations, such as the Mitsubishi-Tokyo Financial Group (MTFG), the Sumitomo-Mitsui Financial Group (SMFG) or the Mizuho Financial Group (MFG). These *keiretsu* groups therefore now include banks from different *keiretsu* and this could, of course, change the nature of individual groups' identity and funding.

Japanese firms are meeting the challenges of the new millennium by increasingly redeploying their assets, with the numbers of companies announcing restructuring plans increasing from an average of 42 per month in 1998 to 91 per month in 2001. Many firms are also placing relatively less emphasis on sales and total profits and more emphasis on returns on equity and the efficient use of capital. The much-vaunted Japanese car industry is a classic case of the restructuring process, with Toyota creating much closer links with Hino Motors and the Yamaha Motor company, while in March 2000 the German-American company Daimler-Chrysler secured control of 34% of Mitsubishi Motors' equity as a means of combining the companies more effectively in order to cut marketing and production costs. Indeed, by 2003 Renault owned 37% of Nissan, Daimler-Chrysler owned 34% of Mitsubishi Motors and Ford owned 33% of Mazda Motors. Corporate restructuring in Japan is being led by dynamic companies such as Toyota, which have begun diversifying into auto insurance and consumer finance, and Sony, which is in the process of transforming itself into a fully networked corporation by opening an online store.

On the human resource front, the basic pillars of the Japanese employment system have included employment for life, wages according to age/length of service and company-based unions. These have helped Japan to develop an 'internal' labour market where workers in large companies were 'grown' within the organisation in which they were trained.

Case 5.5 (continued)

However, the pressures of competition have begun to slowly modify this system. There has been a lowering of the age of retirement for permanent employees in order to decrease wage bills while at the same time there has been a decrease in yearly hirings. Also the number of mid-term employees (i.e. those who change job in mid-career) has increased as companies try to 'poach' good workers. In addition, wages are now being increasingly determined by merit rather than by age, although it should be remembered that only some 20% of Japanese workers are paid according to merit. Finally, more Japanese companies have been resorting to temporary workers as a way of cutting labour costs. In other words, a number of features more reminiscent of the 'external' labour markets familiar in the West are now gradually developing within large Japanese companies.

Some of these points have been reinforced by recent survey evidence. For example, a survey from the Japan Ministry of Health and Labour in 2003 showed that in 2002 only 48.6% of employers attached great importance to the lifetime employment system when hiring employees. The same survey also showed that some 55.9% of Japanese employers attached greater importance to the merit system of payment when deciding on employees pay.

The period from 2000 to 2013 has seen changes in Japan's corporate culture as companies have looked to restructure their operations. During this period, the importance of mergers and acquisitions has accelerated with the number of M&A deals involving at least one Japanese company surging to 2,775 in 2006 as compared to only 621 in 1996. In addition, the new Company law (*Kaisha Ho*) of 2006 has made it easier for foreign firms to buy Japanese firms so that overseas ownership of Japanese firms may rise in the future. However, this does not necessarily mean that there will be *rapid* changes in Japan since it is still a stakeholder environment as opposed to a shareholder one. For example, even though the number of attempts at hostile takeover had increased to 3% of the total of all takeover attempts by 2005, no hostile attempt at takeover in Japan had ever been successful up to that date. Similarly, the widespread practice of mutually holding shares in friendly companies (cross-shareholding) actually increased in 2006, after the custom had declined following the collapse of the bubble economy in the early 1990s. Therefore, although a number of changes in Japan's corporate environment are certainly affecting Japan's corporate culture, the pace of such change is difficult to predict.

Source: Griffiths (2000); Griffiths and Wall (2012).

Questions

1 Identify some of the corporate cultural changes underway in Japan and comment on their likely impacts.

2 What factors have been 'driving' these changes in corporate culture?

Interaction of national with organisational cultures

Hofstede has suggested that while management practices differ between organisations and societies they remain remarkably similar within each society. D'Iribane (1996) adopts a similar view and researched this area by carrying out in-depth interviews in the 1980s in three production plants of a French-owned aluminium company, one in France, one in the USA (Maryland) and one in the Netherlands. The plants were technically identical, but interpersonal interactions on the shop floor differed dramatically between them. D'Iribane identified three different 'logics' that controlled the interpersonal interactions at the sites: honour in France; fair contract in the USA; and consensus in the Netherlands. These philosophies represent patterns of thinking, feeling and acting which can be traced back to the national histories of these three societies over the centuries.

In France, for example, D'Iribane argues that the most important feature is that it is still largely a 'class-based' society. Within the plant the different 'classes' coexist on at least three levels: the cadres (managers and professionals), the maitrise (first-line supervisors) and the non-cadres (levels below maitrise). The relationships between these 'classes' are governed by antagonism, yet a sense of respect prevails, for the types of orders a supervisor can give are constrained by a need to respect the honour of the subordinates. In the USA, on the other hand, everybody is supposed to be equal and the relationship between management and workers is contractual. While this is less hierarchical than in France, American managers can get away with demanding things from their workers that in France would be impossible. In practice, some people in the USA would still seem to be more equal than others. D'Iribane attributes the US practices to the country's immigrant past: the heritage of the Pilgrim Fathers and other seventeenth- and eighteenth-century white settlers. Since there was no traditional aristocracy as in France, immigrants developed a middle-class society, with relationships governed by contractual agreements. D'Iribane calls them 'pious merchants'. In the Netherlands, while they have pious merchant ancestors, relationships have historically been based on compromise rather than contract. The Republic was born from a revolt against their Spanish overlords and, in order to survive, the former rebels learned to cooperate across religious and ideological lines. The Dutch tradition leaves room for contracts, but negotiations may be re-opened the day after conclusion if new facts emerge. D'Iribane is struck by everybody's respect for facts, which he finds stronger than in either France or in the USA. In France, status and power often prevail over facts; in the USA, moral principles are often seen as superseding facts. Dutch consensus is based on concern as to the individuals' quality of life, which should not be harmed by avoidable conflicts.

Strategies for developing intercultural competence

Having established the importance of cultural sensitivities to international business operations, how can managers develop their own intercultural competences as well as those of their subordinates? Research studies such as Brett *et al.* (2006) and Snow *et al.* (1996) has shown that the development of a healthy group process must take into account at least five major factors reflecting different elements of national and corporate cultures:

1 the degree of similarity among the cultural norms of the individuals on the team;
2 the extent to which such norms are manifested in the group;
3 the level of fluency in the common language used by the team;
4 the communication styles and expectations of what constitutes effective group behaviour;
5 the management style of the team leader.

Case 5.6 examines various challenges encountered by cross-cultural teams.

Fedor and Werther (1996) have outlined an eight-stage process that can help to create a culturally responsive joint-venture alliance, assuming, of course, that those involved have already accepted the strategic imperatives of such an alliance. By following this multi-step process, decision makers can systematically consider the organisational dynamics of both firms by adding the cultural dimension to the normal strategic, financial and legal considerations. Working through these issues should mean that deeply rooted values are brought to the surface before they damage the prospects of the alliance.

CASE 5.6 Challenges to cross-cultural team management

The dangers of imposing single-culture-based approaches when managing multicultural teams was highlighted in the results of a major study of global multicultural teams by Brett *et al.* (2006). They noted that the cultural differences which can create major problems for effective teamwork are often subtle and unrecognised until damage has actually been inflicted. Awareness of the challenges facing such teams from the outset can, however, help senior management resolve many of the problems before they become irreversible. Four types of challenge were identified as of particular importance in the study.

1 Direct versus indirect communication

In Western cultures communication is usually direct and explicit, whereas in many other cultures communication is indirect and implicit, often embedded in the means chosen to deliver the message and nuanced rather than communicated explicitly.

An example is cited of an American manager leading a project to build an interface for a US and Japanese customer data system.

When the American manager discovered that several flaws in the system would significantly disrupt company operations, she pointed that out in an e-mail to her American boss and the Japanese team members. Her boss appreciated the direct warnings; her Japanese colleagues were embarrassed, because she had violated their norms for uncovering and discussing problems. Their reaction was to provide her with less access to the people and information she needed to monitor progress. They would probably have responded better if she had pointed out the problems indirectly – for example by asking them what would happen if a certain part of the system was not functioning properly, even though she knew full well that it was malfunctioning and also what the implications were. (Brett *et al.* 2006: 86)

The result of 'inappropriate multicultural communication' was, in this case, for the American manager to be denied access to information by the Japanese members of the team, with those identified as violating accepted norms of behaviour typically isolated in Japanese culture.

2 Differing attitudes towards hierarchy and authority

Whereas teams may often have 'flat' structures, this may create problems for members from cultures which place considerable respect on the posts held rather than the qualities of the post-holder. They may then still exhibit characteristics within the team which would typically be used by them in more hierarchic organisational structures. For example, in the Mexican culture knowledge and information may be conveyed to other team members indirectly in the form of an open-ended question, rather than a statement, which may well be interpreted as a lack of knowledge and conviction by other team members from cultures with a large power distance (see p. 162).

Table 5.6 **Interpreting high-context communications**

What the British say	What they really mean
Not bad	Good, or very good
Quite good	A bit disappointing
Interesting	That is interesting, or it is interesting that you think it is interesting – it seems rather boring to me!
Oh, by the way,. . .	I am about to get to the primary purpose of our discussion
I hear what you say	I disagree and do not wish to discuss it any further
With the greatest respect. . .	I think that you are wrong (or a fool)
Perhaps we could consider some other opinions	I don't like your ideas

Source: Human Resource Management, 3rd ed., Chartered Institute of Personnel and Development (Brewster, C., Sparrow, P. and Vernon, G. 2011) p. 35.

Case 5.6 (*continued*)

3 Conflicting norms for decision making

The approach to time and to the openness of the process involved in decision making can vary significantly between cultures. In the study by Brett *et al.* (2006) it was noted that the US members of a US–Indian project team were much more optimistic (2–3 weeks compared to 2–3 months) as to the likely delivery date and much more willing to share setbacks encountered with other team members than was the case with the Indian team members. A major frustration was that US team members would only find out about problems when work was received, rather than being alerted earlier when the problems were encountered – thereby delaying resolution of such problems. Similarly, a frustrated Brazilian manager from a US company purchasing Korean products thought that agreement on three of the four points at issue had been made on day one, only to find that while the US team members wanted to proceed to point 4 on day two, the Korean team members wanted to review and re-discuss points 1 to 3.

4 Problems with accents and fluency

Native English speakers were found on occasions wrongly to attribute a lack of fluency in English with a lack of expertise by team members on the problems at issue, creating frustrations all round and inefficiencies in the failure to exploit team expertise to the full.

Questions

1 To what extent might the various cross-cultural issues encountered here have been predicted from the Hofstede 'scores' in Table 5.3?

2 What suggestions might you make for resolving each of the 'challenges' above for a multicultural team you are managing?

Eight-stage process for cultural compatibility

1 *Corporate cultural profiles.* You can't create cultural compatibility unless you first realise where you are coming from. For this reason, it is important to have an idea of the original corporate culture for each of the partners before working out cultural compatibility. There are, of course, many different ways of carrying out cultural audits. Fedor and Werther suggest that the corporate culture can be defined by the unique set of beliefs and methods of problem-solving which underpin each company's activities.

2 *Cultural incompatibility identification.* At this stage, teams can compare profiles and identify problem areas. Such exercises usually reveal ambiguities and inconsistencies that should not be ignored. It could also reveal areas of mutuality that may have gone unnoticed.

3 *Development of a joint business purpose.* Teams need to agree on the nature of their purpose by reaching consensus about business objectives – such as desired rates of return, market shares, salaries, growth and time targets. This should uncover areas where there is any divergence. Reconciling such divergences early might help avoid future misunderstandings.

4 *Operational independence.* Both parties need to agree the degree of operational independence they are hoping to achieve. The degree of independence will depend on how much each party is prepared to reveal about their working practices without making their partners more formidable competitors.

5 *Structural choice.* The legal structure chosen for the alliance must take into account the desired culture. The variety of structures are wide: from open-ended joint ventures with

varying ownership splits, through to time-specific technology-sharing contracts. The choice is likely to be driven by deep-seated cultural preferences. For example, American-based partners often gain operational control by choosing a structure that gives them the final say in significant decisions, typically secured through majority ownership. This may, however, create obstacles in the design of an international alliance.

6 *Management systems agreement.* It is vital that these factors be taken into consideration. Management systems reflect deeply embedded ways of working that are often manifested in working practices. For example, in the failure of the Colgate–Palmolive/Kao joint venture in shampoo production, it was the Colgate marketing force that set up the marketing and distribution programme. Even the Colgate people questioned whether the market perspectives and practices successful for toothpaste would work for shampoo. In this way, the culture of the joint venture emerged unconsciously from Colgate's desire to maintain control. These were the driving forces creating the international alliance, rather than the unique needs of the shampoo business.

7 *Staffing the international alliance.* Care needs to be taken in selecting the managing director and key senior officers, since corporate cultures tend to be embodied in the values and beliefs of the people who work in them. Careful discussion will also be needed as to the job specifications and responsibilities, which may reveal deep-seated values about how organisations should be run.

8 *Assessing the international alliance's demands on parent company culture.* It is equally important to have a clear picture of what changes may be required in the parent company's culture. How will those changes be made? By whom? These questions may yield further insights into the cultural expectations and capabilities of the respective companies.

Fedor and Werther suggest that assessing the cultural compatibility of international alliances is critical if failure is to be avoided. This is the fourth dimension, after the financial, legal and strategic deal has been struck. Knowing the cultural match between the partners helps define the type of deal most likely to succeed once the deal makers have gone.

Brett *et al.* (2006) compress this eight-stage process into four key 'strategies' team managers might use to enhance the effectiveness of multicultural teams.

1 *Adaptation*: team members adapt practices or attitudes themselves, without changing the team membership or the tasks allocated.

2 *Structural intervention*: removing sources of conflict or inter-personal frictions by formally reorganising the team or redistributing tasks.

3 *Managerial intervention*: leader(s) intervene to establish norms of behaviour and decision making that take account of the multicultural characteristics of the team and/or establish networks of communication that are tailored to suit the different subgroups in the team.

4 *Exit*: removing one or more members from the team.

Pause for thought 5.5

Under which situations might you advocate each of the four strategies identified above?

There is an increasing emphasis being placed on the corporate/organisational culture, even to the extent of adapting psychologically based personality tests for individuals to the corporate culture. Since, as we note in Chapters 2 and 7, many mergers and acquisitions, joint ventures and alliances fail as much because of *organisational* cultural incompatibility as *international* cultural incompatibility, this new emphasis is receiving much attention by the potential acquirers and acquired. Indeed, the Chartered Institute of Personnel and Development has argued that some 30% of the difference in performance between companies can be attributed to differences in culture. That compares with just 5% that can be attributed to differences in strategy. Other studies have repeatedly found that as many as 75% of mergers and acquisitions fail primarily because of cultural clashes. However, the key question is whether you can go one step further and improve performance by analysing corporate personality in the same way as you might analyse that of an individual.

That is the question raised by Cognosis, a management consultancy that has adapted the Myers–Briggs Type Indicator (MBTI), a personality test widely used in the recruitment and personal development of individuals; and it is now applying it to organisations. Using the averaged responses to a 15-minute test containing 30 questions, given to as few as a dozen executives, Cognosis claims to be able to use MBTI to identify four organisational character types. The organisation is then profiled on a number of characteristics, such as its approach to problem solving, how it deals with change, innovation and internal communications and how it will react to stress.

What sort of person is your company?

The Cognosis method of analysing company personality sorts companies into four types:

1 Rational – logical and ingenious, e.g. Diageo.

2 Sympathetic harmoniser, e.g. EasyJet.

3 Pragmatic – focused on the here and now, e.g. Nestlé.

4 Idealistic – enthusiastic and insightful, e.g. Interbrew.

While no type is better than any other, Cognosis argues that the results have important strategic implications since some organisational character types are better suited to the markets in which they compete and each character type has its own particular development needs. For example the Cognosis approach has met a mixed reception among organisational psychologists and academics, who argue that the idea of a simple way of identifying profound truths about a company sounds attractive, but is too simple.

Pause for thought 5.6

1. Why is such emphasis being placed on cultural aspects of organisational behaviour?
2. If companies could be categorised according to the MBTI test, what benefits might result and for whom?
3. Consider the arguments for and against this organisational approach.

Chapter 6

International ethical and ecological environment

By the end of this chapter you should be able to:

- explain why an awareness of ethical issues can be important for international business;
- outline the different ethical positions that can be adopted and examine the suggestion that ethics must be inversely related to profits;
- discuss the different ethical approaches that multinationals have taken when trading abroad;
- evaluate the reasons behind the increased emphasis by MNEs on Corporate Social Responsibility (CSR)
- examine some of the national/international agreements and regulations that have been adopted in an attempt to instil an ethical awareness into business practices, with particular reference to MNE activity;
- assess the importance of managing the ecological environment, for both individuals and companies;
- evaluate the impacts of sustainability-related issues on international business activities.

Introduction

What is an organisation for? Why does it exist? How are decisions taken within it? People often assume that organisations exist in order to make a profit or to provide a service in the most cost-effective way. In the West businesses have developed under the capitalist ethic, which focuses on the creation of surplus value (profit) and its distribution to shareholders in the form of dividends. Over time, national governments have increasingly sought to remedy aspects of 'market failure' in such economies, by providing minimum levels of public services in education or health or by seeking to prevent private businesses from abusing their market power. As societies become ever more complex, businesses are beginning to exert still more influence over the ways in which the economy is run, so that even social institutions are becoming more intimately linked with economic patterns. In the UK, for example, the powerful lobby of the supermarkets has exerted considerable influence on transport policies, on the types of goods we consume, on trading relationships with domestic and international suppliers and on the ways in which we define our leisure hours. Thus business organisations are carrying more and more responsibility for the ways in which wealth is both created and distributed and the ways in which we organise ourselves. In these various ways the ethical responsibilities of business are arguably growing. But what do we mean by business ethics?

Ethical standards are generally regarded as those ways of acting or being that are deemed acceptable by some reference group at a particular time and place. These standards can be implicit to the group or explicit, as in the case of a 'code of practice'. The objective of making such standards explicit usually involves an attempt to avoid an excess of self-interest that might work against the 'good of all'. Of course, the key question is, what is the good of all? One man's meat may be another man's poison! Further, even if a code of ethics were to be agreed by a reference group it must be flexible and capable of change, otherwise it can easily become institutionalised, dogmatic and ultimately self-defeating.

Business ethics

Too often, in the past, business ethics have been taken for an 'oxymoron' (a contradiction in terms). At the level of business the prevailing view has often seemed to be that as long as the business is profitable then 'anything goes'. Somewhere along the line business and ethics have become separated; no one in business talks about ethics and no one in the moral field of actions talks about business.

And yet, if we can define ethics or morality as the 'set of organising principles by which people live together', ethics must surely play a large part in organisational and business activities – based, as they are, on group dynamics and individual interactions. The reason that the process of applying ethical standards to business or management seems to be difficult may be because it might appear to contradict economic perspectives such as 'competition', which sets organisations (communities of beings) against one another.

This is, of course, a misperception: ethics are as much an integral part of business and commerce as they are of specialised functions, such as financing, accountancy, legal practices, etc. The fundamental issue here is that of choice – and in business choices are made each and every moment. Business decisions are choices in which the decision makers could have acted otherwise. Every decision or action affects people or relationships between people such that an alternative action or inaction would affect them differently. What criteria are these decisions based upon? Are they criteria of profit or of 'well-being'? It is far better for everyone concerned if managers are aware of the ethical significance of their actions and decisions and thus consciously, rather than inadvertently, lead and shape their corporate cultures.

A study by Collins and Porras (1994) cited a number of companies that survived major changes in management, new product development and the impacts of various business cycles. The companies that flourished over a long period were found to be companies that pursued a stable core mission, which provided the basis for all corporate activities and drove decision making through all the business changes encountered. According to Collins and Porras, the 'best' (longest lasting and most profitable) business organisations are those that do not focus on profitability as their primary mission. In their rankings, the highest performing corporations tended to be those that were governed by core beliefs, which transcended purely economic pursuits, seeking rather to produce the finest products in the marketplace, to win customer satisfaction, to serve employees, and so on. Such findings are contrary to much of the theory taught in our business schools.

The authors cited a number of international businesses that have thrived through the creation of ethical cultures. For example, Patagonia Inc. has created a strong corporate culture that values its employees and the social and natural environments in which it conducts business. Patagonia gives 1% of its annual sales revenue to environmental groups and grants employees up to two months off with full pay to work for non-profit environmental groups. Independent human rights organisations have been invited to audit any of their facilities on request. In response to the 1996 public dialogue on 'sweatshops', Patagonia implemented a corporate policy not to contract with any supplier engaging in such practices.

The Body Shop has also adopted overtly 'ethical' aims, which are explained further in Case 6.1.

CASE 6.1 The Body Shop

The Body Shop is a publicly quoted manufacturer and retailer of health and beauty products. It began in 1976 with the opening of the first shop in Brighton and is now an international company rapidly expanding throughout the world. Today The Body Shop has over 2,500 shops, operates in 60 countries and trades in 23 languages with over 3,000 staff directly employed and a similar number of staff working in franchised retail outlets. Its founder was the late Anita Roddick, a charismatic woman with very firm ideas, particularly about the values involved in business trading. Unlike other companies in this area, it does not use direct marketing or pay for advertising and believes that what differentiates the company is not so much the product but, as stated by a previous head of corporate services, 'what they represent as a company'.

The Body Shop is a known brand retailer which manufactures its own products, which means that, unlike other retailers, it does not work on short cycles. Traditional problems such as branding and design appear less important since the labels have tended to stay the same and the bottles in which the products are sold have also been largely unchanged. The company has often been the top seller in its market, with many new products simply being extensions of existing ones. For much of the time its competitors have had only a marginal impact on its market since its customer profile is that of 20–35-year-old females who have an interest in the environmental and social issues on behalf of which this organisation campaigns.

The Body Shop claims that its values are fundamentally very simple, and represent the initial values of the founders, namely that people, in relating to each other, should act with honesty, care, integrity and respect.

In previous mission statements The Body Shop has emphasised its dedication to the pursuit of social and environmental 'justice' and to furthering the interests of all its stakeholders, whether employees, customers, franchisees, suppliers or shareholders. It has also emphasised its commitment to ecological sustainability, especially as regards the protection of the environment and thereby safeguarding the interests of future generations who depend on that environment.

In more recent mission statements similar commitments have been made, including the pursuit of 'fair wages', the use of natural materials and ingredients, and support for campaigns to end the needless suffering of animals.

Case 6.1 (*continued*)

However, as the general manager for corporate culture at The Body Shop noted, though these basic values appear superficially quite straightforward, they are notoriously difficult to implement. Indeed, disappointing results from attempts to expand into the US and other acquisitions resulted in financial difficulties which have placed considerable pressure on the ethical focus of the company. Since 1985 The Body Shop has been a public company, quoted on the Stock Exchange and with a growing number of shareholders. Only 18% of shares were in the hands of the founder herself by the time of the takeover of The Body Shop by L'Oréal, the French cosmetics giant, in 2006. It was pointed out by critics that L'Oréal was in the bottom three companies as regards ethical rating from the *Ethical Consumer Magazine*, with particular concern being expressed as regards L'Oréal's animal testing policy and the use of chemicals in its cosmetics.

Questions

1 Can you suggest any hypothetical (or actual) ethical problems which The Body Shop might face (or has faced) in implementing its core values?

2 Consider the implications of the L'Oréal merger in terms of the ethical principles guiding The Body Shop.

Ethics and the corporate culture

In all organisations the same principles arguably apply. Organisations need certain 'ways of acting or being' (which can be either explicit or implicit) as a guide to 'acceptable' behaviour by members of the organisation. In the current business press two things stand out. One is the issue of global competitiveness and the other is a list of alleged wrongdoings by business leaders in virtually all countries. For Beyer and Nino (1999):

> It seems likely that the two are related, that the ethical and cultural fabrics of our business communities and whole societies are being weakened, virtually torn apart by the struggles inherent in unprecedented levels of economic competition. Clearly it is time for management scholars and academics everywhere to begin to address the ethical issues associated with the all-out economic war being waged throughout the world.

Beyer and Nino go on to tell a story which, in their view, has a number of parallels with modern international business practice (see Box 6.1).

BOX 6.1 An ethical dilemma

McCoy was in the mountains of Nepal on his way to a village considered a holy place with an American anthropologist named Stephen, a Sherpa guide and a group of porters. To get to the village they had to climb across a mountain pass at 18,000 feet (about 5,500 metres).

> **Box 6.1 (*continued*)**
>
> The night before the planned climb they camped at around 15,000 feet, near several other groups: four young men from New Zealand, two Swiss couples and a Japanese hiking club.
>
> At 3.30 the next morning the New Zealanders got the first start up the mountain. The American party left next, followed by the Swiss, while the Japanese lingered in their camp. When the Americans reached about 15,500 feet, Stephen began to feel ill and they stopped to rest. Soon thereafter one of the New Zealanders appeared with a body slung over his back. It was a sadhu (old man) he had found on the mountain – almost naked and unconscious, clearly suffering from hypothermia, but still alive. The New Zealander suggested that the porters travelling with the Americans take the old man down the mountain and then went back to join his group. Stephen and the Swiss couples attended to the sadhu, stripping off his wet clothes, wrapping him in clothing from their packs and giving him food and drink when he revived.
>
> Meanwhile the businessman McCoy was growing anxious about the delay because he feared that if he waited any longer to resume his climb, the sun would melt the steps carved in the snow that he needed to help him cross the mountain pass. Adding to his worry was the fact that previously he had suffered quite severe altitude sickness even at a lower altitude. Neither of these concerns led him to abandon his goal. He was still determined to cross the mountain pass and reach the sacred village. So he left to catch up with some of the porters who had gone ahead to prepare the way. His friend Stephen, who was still not feeling well, and the Swiss couples stayed behind with the sadhu.
>
> An hour or so later, after climbing most of the way, McCoy himself became dizzy and stopped to rest, allowing the Swiss to catch up with him. He asked them about the sadhu and was told he was fine and that his friend Stephen was on the way. When Stephen finally arrived he was suffering from altitude sickness and could only walk 15 steps at a time before resting. He was also very angry and accosted McCoy saying, 'How do you feel about contributing to the death of a fellow man?' McCoy was stunned and asked if the sadhu had died. 'No', Stephen replied, 'But he will.' He then explained that the Swiss had departed not long after McCoy and that the Japanese, when asked, refused to lend a horse they had with them to carry the man down the mountain to the nearest village. The Japanese then went on their way taking the horse with them. When Stephen asked the Sherpa and the remaining porters if they would take the sadhu they also refused, saying they would not have the strength or time to get across the pass if they first carried him down the mountain. Instead, the porters took the old man a short distance down the mountain, where they laid him on a large rock in the sun, and left him there, awake, but weak. No one in the four groups of climbers ever found out whether the sadhu lived or died but all got over the pass and on to the holy village that was their goal.
>
> *Source*: Beyer and Nino (1999). Copyright 1999 by Sage Publications, Inc. Reprinted by permission of Sage Publications.

We can usefully use this account to derive a number of ethical implications, which have some parallels in international business. Beyer and Nino pick out the following parallels.

- First, no one assumed ultimate responsibility for the sadhu. By focusing on reaching a holy place, they ignored their ethical responsibilities. Trying to reach the mountain top can be compared with the unremitting competition of global business with its elements of social Darwinism, namely the idea of the survival of the fittest. This modern business 'ethic' would see it as natural that others get left behind. 'Doing unto others as you would have them do unto you' would be suicidal in business. Such attitudes encourage people to set for themselves self-interested (organisational goals) and to pursue them relentlessly with little concern for their effects on others. Some forms of winning in business (getting a new product to market, achieving assigned targets, taking over another firm) can overwhelm broader-based ethical principles and impulses.

- Second, the groups involved had no prior experience or model for jointly arriving at a consensus about what to do. They came from four different cultures and lacked a commonality of mutually accepted values that would give them guidance as to what to do. Each group passed the problem on to the other group. There was no strong culture to glue their actions together. This 'buck-passing' between departments and multinational divisions is hardly uncommon.

- Third, there was a failure to act which then itself became the decision. This can often happen in business, especially when something has been going on for some time. The lack of guidance given to Nick Leeson, an inexperienced trader in Singapore in 1996, is arguably one such example.

- Fourth, the decision makers were physically and mentally stressed and under time pressures. It is precisely under these conditions in a hyper-competitive world that personal and corporate values are most severely tested.

- The final parallel is that even though one of the people saw through all of these considerations as regards his ethical responsibility, he did not get the support he needed from the others present to rescue the sadhu. It was beyond his individual capacity, a circumstance that often occurs in business. Many ethical decisions require the support of the corporate community. Ethically sensitive and courageous individuals cannot often perform ethically without the support of others.

The lesson here is that it is up to management to provide such support as part of the corporate culture. The ethical dilemma previously described was heightened by the fact that people of different cultures were attempting (or not attempting) to reach a decision. With increasing globalisation, such issues are becoming more common as multinational teams attempt to work together.

Pause for thought 6.1

Can you suggest how two MNEs from different national cultures, which are collaborating on a joint venture, may adopt different ethical positions on certain issues?

We have already noted that our actions as individuals are determined in part by the values we hold, which can be influenced by our surroundings and our experiences. But what happens in an organisation? An organisation is neither an individual nor a total social system. It is comprised of individuals in various roles which may be authorised by the larger 'society' to function for specific, often narrowly defined, purposes. The actions of an organisation are often the result of collective, rather than individual, decision making. We saw in Box 6.1 how the *sadhu* was left to die because no single group or person was prepared to take responsibility. This can be true within organisations, even more so when that organisation is trading internationally.

But who is acting in an organisation? Can we reduce the group action down to the level of each individual? Or do we treat an organisation as if the organisation itself was an individual directing the activity of its constituents? Ethically and academically many thinkers have sought to understand the nature of corporate responsibility. The Nobel Prize economist Milton Friedman declared: 'There is only one social responsibility of business – to use its resources and engage in activities designed to increase its profits so long as it stays within the rules of the game, which is to say, engages in open and free competition without deception or fraud' (Friedman 1970: 126).

This does not mean that 'anything goes': law and common morality should guide action. However, there is an assumption here that profit maximisation is the main responsibility of business. This is based on the so-called 'rational actor' theory. In this view when an individual acts rationally, he/she is seeking to maximise his/her own long-term self-interest. In Friedman's view, that self-interest will be allied to making an overt contribution to enhancing corporate profitability.

The idea of such a 'unity of purpose' impacting on the values of those who act on behalf of an organisation has been challenged in various ways.

The principal–agent problem

In the case of a sole trader, the principal (owner) and the agent (manager) are one and the same. However, to assume that it is the owners who control the firm neglects the fact that today the dominant form of industrial organisation is the public limited company (plc), which is usually run by managers rather than by owners. This may lead to conflict between the owners (shareholders) and the managers whenever the managers pursue goals which differ from those of the owners. This conflict is referred to as a type of *principal–agent* problem and emerges when the shareholders (principals) contract a second party, the managers (agents), to perform some tasks on their behalf. In return, the principals offer their agents some compensation (wage payments). However, because the principals are divorced from the day-to-day running of the business, the agents may be able to act as they themselves see fit. This independence of action may be due to their superior knowledge of the company as well as their ability to disguise their actions from the principals. Agents, therefore, may not always act in the manner desired by the principals. Indeed, it may be the agents' goals which predominate. This has led to a number of managerial theories on the behaviour of business organisations, such as sales revenue maximisation and growth maximisation, which see the salary and status of managers being more closely related to turnover and company size rather than to its pure profit performance.

Ethical responsibilities and codes of conduct

Over time a wide range of ethical theories have developed, with individuals and groups supporting or challenging them! Figure 6.1 gives a broad 'map' of the range of ethical theories available and it may be useful at this point to define the terms on the horizontal and vertical axes, before turning briefly to the ethical theories themselves.

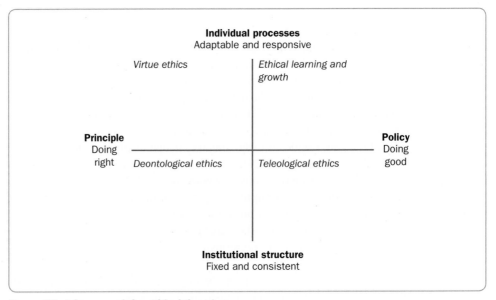

Figure 6.1 A framework for ethical theories

Source: Applied Economics, 12th ed., Financial Times Prentice Hall (Griffiths, A. and Wall, S. (eds), 2012), © Pearson Education Limited 2012.

Horizontal axis

- *Principles*: standards to be observed, seen as desirable in terms of fairness/justice or some other moral dimension in their own right, irrespective of the outcome of following those principles. This approach is sometimes referred to as a 'duties' view of ethical behaviour – things to be done (or avoided) because they are intrinsically right or wrong.

- *Policies*: approaches that achieve measurable outcomes which are regarded as improvements on the original situations. This approach is sometimes referred to as a 'consequential' view of ethical behaviour – things to be done (or avoided) because they will have consequences which result in an overall *net* benefit or loss.

Along this horizontal axis, some ethical theories are seen as focusing primarily on the 'rightness' of some action or approach or on the 'outcome' of that action or approach in terms of making a net overall improvement for the individual or group.

Vertical axis

- *Individual processes*: approaches that emphasise the responsibilities of individuals to develop/improve themselves or the group(s) to which they belong.

- *Institutional structure*: approaches that emphasise the importance of establishing institutions and structures that exist and operate independently of the individuals who devise them, but which determine the key principles which underpin ethical considerations.

Of course any such diagram is over-simplistic, but it does give us a useful starting point to consider various ethical theories in the context of our previous discussions.

- *Virtue ethics*: this broadly corresponds to theories which emphasise individuals having the responsibility to respond to the question 'What would a virtuous person do in this situation?' Plato is often associated with this approach, identifying the four virtues of wisdom, courage, self-control and justice. His follower, Aristotle, identified key personal qualities associated with achieving these virtues, particularly 'justice', namely liberality (especially as regards money), truthfulness, patience, and magnanimity. These virtues and personal qualities were seen as desirable ends in their own right, whatever the outcomes of practising them!

- *Deontological ethics*: while the emphasis is still on universal principles to be followed because of their intrinsic 'rightness', irrespective of outcomes, there is a recognition that individuals act within a social and institutional context which gives them a sense of shared identity and commitment to the values of their group. Kantian ethics come under this heading, with actions to be guided by universal principles and deemed morally acceptable only if carried out as a duty, rather than in expectation of any reward or reciprocity. Kant used the term 'categorical imperative' to refer to principles that must be obeyed, with no exceptions.

- *Ethical learning and growth*: located in the top-right quadrant of Figure 6.1, the emphasis here is on ethical behaviour being tested by outcomes, but ones that are based on individual morality, and cannot be imposed by institutional decree (e.g. codes of conduct). Ethical behaviour can only be encouraged indirectly from this perspective by providing learning experiences from which individuals derive their own ethical codes of behaviour.

- *Teleological ethics*: these are again outcome-oriented ethical theories, but which see institutions as necessary to achieve these desirable ethical outcomes. The term 'teleological' means that the rightness or goodness of an action is not intrinsic to that action, but must be judged on the merits of its outcomes. Utilitarianism is often placed under this heading, with the emphasis here on institutions or organisations seeking to achieve the greatest good of the greatest number: 'The greatest happiness of the greatest number is the foundation of morals and legislation' (Bentham 1823). In this sense utilitarianism is a calculated approach to ethics, with the costs and benefits of institutional actions assumed to be capable of valuation and ranking.

Perspectives

- *Friedman perspectives*: In terms of our earlier analysis, Friedman's view on businesses (not individuals) having the primary responsibility of achieving profit, and their having no right to engage in distracting philanthropy, would locate his perspective in the bottom-left quadrant of Figure 6.1, i.e. 'Deontological ethics'. His emphasis is on the 'rightness' of a shareholder focus by the business and on the business as an 'institutional' and social construct, dependent on legal definitions and legal protections for its existence (Friedman 1970). However the variant of Friedman's position which emphasises investigating the profit-related *outcomes* of philanthropy, rather than their *intentions,* would arguably justify placing his approach into the bottom-right quadrant, i.e. 'Teleological ethics', with philanthropy or gift giving to be judged in terms of outcomes rather than 'rightness'.

- *Stakeholder perspectives*: Employees, customers, suppliers etc. are seen as important, as well as shareholders. This might be more readily located on the right-hand side of Figure 6.1 with its emphasis on balancing the outcomes of corporate actions amongst the various 'interested parties' within the organisation. Of course it could be located in the top-right quadrant under 'Ethical learning and growth' should the emphasis be on individual behaviour conforming to these stakeholder principles. Here the focus would be on developing an 'atmosphere' conducive to moral behaviour at an individual level within the organisation. However, should the emphasis be on institutional behaviour being aligned with a stakeholder approach, as in the case of organisational codes of conduct, then it might more accurately be located in the bottom-right quadrant under 'teleological ethics'.

It is to these 'codes of conduct' that we now turn our attention.

Codes of conduct

As Figure 6.2 indicates, some of the pressures for organisations to exhibit ethical and socially responsible behaviour stem directly from the explicit legal environment in which the organisation operates. The only continuous and unbroken line in Figure 6.2 indicates the legally binding (mandatory) requirements as regards 'corporate' behaviour imposed on the organisation by national and supra-national (e.g. EU) governmental bodies. The broken lines represent the many ethical frameworks and codes of conduct which, while technically voluntary, provide important constraints and contexts for organisational behaviour.

Non-governmental organisations (NGOs) such as Greenpeace, Friends of the Earth, International Baby Food Action Network and other charities and pressure groups will contrast organisational performance against agreed or proposed codes of conduct and ethical frameworks. The codes of conduct the organisation itself may impose (usually these are 'top-down' initiatives!) on its own employees and operations will often be an attempt to regularise processes and steer behaviours to align the outcomes of organisational performance more closely with the external pressures and expectations from governments, NGOs and the broader society.

The 'ethics hotlines' in Figure 6.2 include mechanisms for employees to raise concerns about current behaviours and practices – giving organisations themselves early warning of possible problems as well as providing avenues for expressing concerns which might otherwise result in 'whistleblowing' to a more critical external audience.

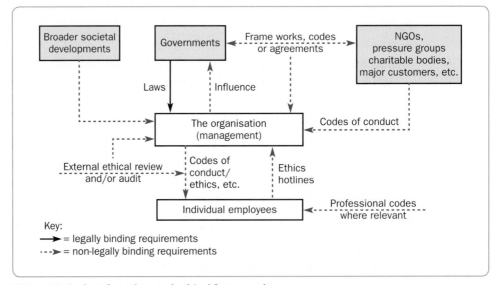

Figure 6.2 Codes of conduct and ethical frameworks

Source: *Applied Economics*, 12th ed., Financial Times Prentice Hall (Griffiths, A. and Wall, S. (eds), 2012), © Pearson Education Limited 2012.

Table 6.1 **Codes of conduct: advantages and disadvantages**

Advantages	Disadvantages
Reduces the need for governmental regulation or intervention.	Cannot enforce full implementation as voluntary codes
Limits the potential damages awarded when the organisation can be seen by the court to have an explicit policy even when not followed by individual employees	Lack rigorous mechanisms to ensure accountability
	Often written as broad philosophical statements and therefore hard to measure
Enhances trust, customer loyalty and reputation	Those adopting are often already leaders in CSR issues in those sectors
Creates benchmarks against which the organisation's practices can be compared	Often unknown to majority of employees
Creates pressure from internal and external stakeholders to follow through on commitments by formalising and publishing them	Such codes tend to be over-represented in industries and sectors with high visibility and with a focus on brand image or reputation and large environmental or social impacts (often business-to-customer products)
Creates potential for competitive advantage	
Flexible, can be uniquely adapted to that organisation	
Creates order and structure in standards and procedures acceptable to the organisation when operating globally	Often do not include complaints processes or whistleblower protections
Allows stakeholders influence in decision making	
Relatively inexpensive	

Table 6.1 provides a useful summary of some of the advantages and disadvantages of using codes of conduct.

Social contract theory

Thomas Hobbes suggested that human beings tacitly agree to laws and regulations on their behaviour so that they can live in harmony and achieve their own ends in relation to others. Donaldson and Dunfee (1999) take this argument further in their 'Integrated Social Contract Theory', by suggesting that there are basic moral minimums (or 'hypernorms') that govern all social relationships on the macro level. These are subject to debate, can be explicit or tacit, but might include:

● not causing gratuitous harm;

● honouring contracts;

● respecting human rights;

● treating people and organisations fairly.

On a micro level, however, there may be a moral 'free space' dictated by the community in question. Here communities can spell out the specific norms deemed acceptable among themselves as long as these are compatible with the hypernorms. These 'consistent norms' tend to be tacit. Figure 6.3 shows a global model of the Integrated Social Contract Theory (ISCT).

● *Hypernorms* – these moral minima include, for example, fundamental human rights or basic prescriptions common to most major religions. The values they represent are, by definition, acceptable to all cultures and organisations.

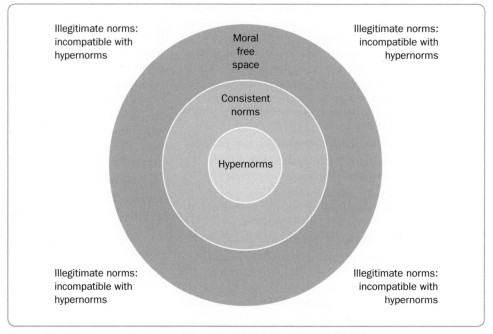

Figure 6.3 **Global norms in the Integrated Social Contract Theory (ISCT)**

- *Consistent norms* – these values are more culturally specific than those at the centre, but are consistent both with hypernorms and other legitimate norms. The ethical codes and vision value statements of companies would fall within this circle.

- *Moral-free space* – as one moves away from the centre of the circle one finds norms that are inconsistent with at least some of the other legitimate norms existing in other cultures. Such norms often reflect strongly held cultural beliefs, whether at the national, corporate or occupational level (see Chapter 5).

- *Illegitimate norms* – these are norms that are incompatible with hypernorms. When values or practices reach a point where they transgress permissible limits (as specified, say, by fundamental human rights) they fall outside the circle and into the 'incompatible' zone. Exposing workers, for instance, to unreasonable levels of carcinogens (e.g. asbestos) is an expression of a value falling outside the circle.

The ISCT model has proved helpful for evaluating ethical behaviour in organisations, especially at the international level (see p. 203).

We return to this approach in the more detailed discussion of Corporate Social Responsibility (pp. 204–208).

Ethics and profits

The conventional wisdom has long been that the more ethical the stance of a company, the lower the returns to shareholders. However, many firms are now seeing ethical and environmentally responsible behaviour as being in their own self-interest, with demand curves

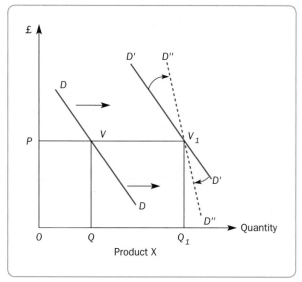

Figure 6.4 Demand increases and becomes less elastic with successful CSR campaign

Source: *Applied Economics*, 12th ed., Financial Times Prentice Hall (Griffiths, A. and Wall, S. (eds), 2012), © Pearson Education Limited 2012.

shifting to the right (increasing) the closer the alignment of products with positive social/ethical initiatives. In Figure 6.4 this is shown as a shift in the demand curve from D to D′. At any given price consumers will purchase more of the product, raising total revenue at price P in the diagram from $OPVQ$ to OPV_1Q_1. However, there is a further possible revenue-raising strategy that may now be possible! By creating a more positive ethical/environmental association with the product, CSR initiatives may also result in the demand curve pivoting from D′ to D″ in Figure 6.4. The demand curve will now be less price elastic, giving opportunities for the firm to raise price and increase revenue, since demand falls by less than in proportion to the price rise.

Firms are increasingly aware of the benefits of aligning themselves with ethical and ecological initiatives. Various 'kitemarks' exist for firms to certify that their product conforms to ethical standards in production, as for example 'Rug-Mark' for carpets and rugs, 'Forest Stewardship Council' mark (to certify wood derived from sustainable forestry extraction methods) and the 'Fairtrade' mark (guarantees a higher return to developing country producers).

Indeed, it was reported in 2014 that annual sales of Fairtrade food and drink in Britain have reached over £900 million, having grown at over 40% per year over the past decade. It has expanded from one brand of coffee ten years ago to around 1,000 foodstuffs, including chocolate, fruit, vegetables, juices, snacks, wine, tea, sugar, honey and nuts. A recent Mori poll found that two-thirds of UK consumers claim to be green or ethical and actively look to purchase products with an environmental/ethical association. At the sectoral level, many of Britain's biggest retail names have joined the Ethical Trading Initiative (ETI) which brings together companies, trade unions and non-governmental organisations in seeking to ensure that the products sold in their retail outlets have not been produced by 'sweatshop' labour working for next to nothing in hazardous conditions.

An analysis by Geoff Heal (2008) of Columbia Business School indicated that as much as $1 out of every $9 under professional investment management now involves an element of socially responsible investment (SRI), so important do firms believe the linkage to be between this type of investment and financial outcomes of that investment.

DSM and TNT, the Dutch life sciences group and postal operator respectively, have joined a growing band of companies – predominantly from the Netherlands – that link part of the bonuses senior management receive to sustainability, seen by them as an all-encompassing term that refers not only to the environment but to issues such as employee satisfaction and safety.

Pause for thought 6.2

1 Why is it suggested that the more ethically and environmentally conscious firms might actually be more profitable than those which pay little heed to the environment?
2 For what reasons might we expect UK companies to become more ethically and environmentally aware in the future?

There is an increasing awareness by companies of the importance to their stakeholders, including consumers, of an ethical stance. Case 6.2 examines efforts by Apple to develop a more ethical supply chain.

CASE 6.2 Apple in supply-chain purge at Africa mines

Apple is extending its supply chain clean-up beyond Chinese factories and into African mines, using name-and-shame tactics to cut the amount of so-called conflict minerals that end up in its iPhones and iPads. As it seeks fresh improvements to working conditions in the factories that produce its devices, the world's most valuable technology company is now combining its might in electronics component purchasing and marketing to pressure smelters to make their sourcing more ethical.

The move comes as, under Dodd–Frank rules, some US companies, including Apple, are required to provide information to the Securities and Exchange Commission about their conflict-related mineral usage before a May deadline. Jeff Williams, Apple's senior vice-president of operations, told the *Financial Times* that last month was the first time it was able to verify that none of the tantalum used in capacitors and resistors in its devices had come from mines in conflict regions. It is urging 'conflict-free' audits for gold, tin and tungsten suppliers in all areas by publishing every quarter a list of its suppliers' smelters and their compliance with ethical sourcing guidelines. 'We think it has the chance to make a difference,' Mr Williams said. 'The smelters are a choke point where all this flows through. If we can get as many smelters verified [as possible] via this pressure, then we have a real chance of influencing the nefarious activities on the ground.'

The electronics industry faces criticism from human rights organisations and impending regulations from US financial authorities over its use of conflict-related minerals mined from sites controlled by violent militias in the Democratic Republic of Congo and nearby areas.

Case 6.2 (continued)

'The fastest way for Apple to become conflict free would be to channel our demand through a couple of verified smelters,' Mr Williams said ahead of the publication of its annual Supplier Responsibility report. 'But quite honestly, if we did that, we could wave our conflict-free flag but it would do nothing to affect the workers on the ground. And so what we are focused on is getting a critical mass of suppliers verified such that we can truly influence the demand situation and change things.'

More than half of the world's tantalum flows through the electronics industry, Mr Williams said, making it easier to exert pressure to cut down the use of mines that are seen as 'unacceptable from a human rights standpoint'. For tin, tungsten and gold, Apple and other technology companies are a smaller customer, and so it is using public scrutiny to encourage change. The first publication of its quarterly report named 59 smelters that were compliant in non-conflict areas and 23 that were participating in the Conflict-Free Smelter Programme.

This scheme is run by the Electronic Industry Citizenship Coalition, an independent organisation that counts Apple, Microsoft, IBM, HP, Sony and Dell among its members. The adherence to ethical guidelines of a further 104 smelters, mainly processing gold and tin, was not known. They include smelters operated by Codelco, the world's largest copper miner, and Kazzinc, a subsidiary of Glencore Xstrata, plus Boliden of Sweden and Aurubis of Germany, Apple said.

A report by researcher HIS in 2012 found only 11.3 per cent of electronics component makers gave such data, but companies such as Samsung and LG have stepped up efforts to detail sourcing. Last month, Intel said it was making the first microprocessors with validated conflict-free gold, tin, tantalum and tungsten. After a 2012 audit found 100 instances of underage labour in 11 of its suppliers' facilities, Apple in 2013 found only 11 active cases and 12 old cases of children under 15 working in the sites. Mr Williams said that these improvements were accompanied by wider education of health and safety and working conditions among its suppliers.

 Source: Apple in supply-chain purge at Africa mines, *Financial Times*, 14/02/2014 (Bradshaw, T.), © The Financial Times Limited 2014. All Rights Reserved.

Questions

1 Why is Apple paying such attention to ethical aspects of its supply chain?

2 Why is Apple so concerned about developing a separate 'Conflict free' initiative?

International business ethics

So far we have seen that each organisation, and indeed each individual within it, has a role to play in ensuring that decisions have a conscious ethical content. However, how do people deal with one another when the ethical content varies at a cultural level? The cultural differences explored in Chapter 5 have their counterparts in ethical differences. How can managers manoeuvre through the grey areas that exist within and between organisations and cultures. Take, for example, the following illustration. As a director of a joint venture in Hungary you become aware that many of the employees are working long hours on jobs outside the company to supplement their work for the joint venture. You deem this to be not only inefficient but also possibly unethical. When you confront senior managers in the joint venture they defend their workers vigorously. They argue that the wages are not high enough to support families and that there is a tradition of 'moonlighting' which has historically been considered to be ethical. Hungarians, having suffered over 500 years of living with 'oppressors' – the Turks, the Austro-Hungarians and the Russians – typically do not confine their loyalties to any single entity. Clearly, as a director, you have been presented with what is both an efficiency and an ethical dilemma.

Similar dilemmas were highlighted by the work of Turner and Trompenaars (1993), who asked thousands of managers around the world the following question:

> While you are talking and sharing a bottle of beer with a friend who is officially on duty as a safety inspector in the company you both work for, an accident occurs, injuring a shift worker. The National Safety Commission launches an investigation and you are asked for your evidence. There are other witnesses. What right has your friend to expect you to protect him?

The choices offered were these:

1 a definite right;

2 some right;

3 no right.

Fundamental to this question is the ethical tension between a 'right' and the implicit notion of the 'duties' of friendship. The results of the survey were very revealing. To cite only a few figures, approximately 94% of US managers and 91% of Austrian managers answered 3, 'no right', whereas only 53% of French and 59% of Singaporean managers considered there to be 'no right'.

Other studies show striking differences among ethical attitudes towards everyday business problems. One study (Macdonald 1988) revealed that Hong Kong managers considered taking credit for another's work as being at the top of a list of unethical activities; in contrast to their Western counterparts, they considered this to be more unethical than bribery or the gaining of competitor information. The same study showed that 82% of Hong Kong managers thought that additional government regulation would improve ethical conduct in business, whereas only 27% of US managers believed it would.

How then do organisations deal with such ethical and cultural variations? The first step, of course, is to understand that they exist. Many multinationals fail to even acknowledge the ethical implications of cultural differences.

Approaches to ethical issues

Enderle (1995) has identified four broad types of approach which international business might take to ethical issues, each of which can be compared to a posture taken historically by nation states, as follows:

1 *Foreign country type.* This does not apply its own ethical norms to the foreign country but conforms to the local customs, taking its direction from what prevails as morality in the host country. The Swiss are often identified with this approach to business.

2 *Empire type.* This resembles the approach of Great Britain in India and elsewhere before 1947. This type of company applies domestic ethical concepts without making any serious modifications to local customs. Empire-type companies export their values in a

wholesale fashion, and often do so regardless of the consequences to the host company or its stakeholders.

3 *Interconnection type.* This regards the international sphere as differing from the domestic sphere. Companies here do not necessarily see themselves as protecting a national identity or ethical framework. The notion of national interest becomes blurred with that of the supranational (e.g. the EU).

4 *Global type.* This abstracts from all national or regional differences, viewing the domestic sphere as entirely irrelevant; citizens of all nations need to become more cosmopolitan. Only global citizenry makes sense from this perspective.

In terms of Integrated Social Contract Theory *(see p. 199)* the danger with the 'foreign country' type is that there is nothing to limit the moral-free space of the host country culture. If government corruption and environmental pollution are accepted in the host country, then the 'foreign country' type of approach to ethical issues might be regarded as colluding with this unethical framework.

The 'empire' and 'global' types fall into the opposite trap. Each acts from a fixed idea of what is right or wrong, and so will suffocate the moral-free space of the host country. The 'empire' type sees itself as the bearer of moral truth. In the same way, though perhaps more subtly, the 'global' type seeks to impose moral truth – namely that since only global citizenry makes sense, the company can be impervious to ethical differences that mark a culture's distinctiveness. The opportunity for host cultures to define their own versions of moral and economic truth is lost.

The 'interconnection' type is consistent with the ISCT approach by acknowledging both universal moral limits at the macro level (hypernorms) and also ethical consideration at the micro level. While the notion of national interest is blurred, it does manage to balance moral principles with moral-free space in a way that makes it somewhat more convincing than its three counterparts.

So what are the implications of these findings for the international manager? How can they negotiate the stormy sea of differing ethical values and behaviours? It may be instructive to attempt to use the ISCT global values (Figure 6.3) to consider the ethical problems involved with bribery or sensitive payments.

Bribery and corruption

Bribery is a major source of concern to many companies trading globally. Are such payments examples of legitimate norms or are such payments invariably a direct violation of hypernorms and other legitimate norms and hence located outside the circle and in the 'illegitimate' area? Not only does the incidence of bribery vary across nations, so too do perceptions as to its being unethical. Studies have shown Hong Kong and Greek managers to be less critical of bribery in certain scenarios than their American counterparts. An interesting question is whether bribery or 'sensitive' payments are more likely to be considered as an acceptable way of conducting international business (hence a legitimate norm) in countries where such practices are commonplace.

Donaldson and Dunfee (1999) do not think so, arguing that it is a myth to believe that bribery is accepted wherever it flourishes. In fact, there is a surprising amount of agreement to the contention that bribery is unethical. We can suggest at least three reasons for this ethical perspective on bribery using the ISCT approach.

1 Acceptance of a bribe usually violates a microsocial contract specifying the duties of the agent (the bribe recipient) to the principal (the employing body), whether the government or a private company.

2 Bribery is typically not a legitimate norm. All countries have laws against the practice. Some countries, even where the practice is flourishing, have draconian penalties. In China in 1994 the president of the Great Wall Machinery and Electronic High-Technology Industrial group, Mr Shen Haifu, was executed for bribery and embezzlement offences, despite the recorded prevalence of such practices in China. The OECD has increased its efforts to reduce bribery by launching, in March 1994, a campaign aimed at reducing the incidence of bribery in international trade transactions.

3 Bribery may violate the hypernorms of political participation and efficiency. When, in the 1970s, Japan bought planes from the American aircraft manufacturer Lockheed, Prime Minister Tanaka was subsequently found to have accepted tens of millions of dollars in bribes. The Japanese press and other sources questioned whether he was discharging his duties correctly in the context of established norms of political participation; he resigned shortly after the bribery revelation was made public. Another hypernorm, that of efficiency, may also be brought into this arena. Bribery interferes with the market mechanisms role of using 'price' alone as a signal for efficient resource allocation (see Chapter 4). Interviews with Indian CEOs have borne this out as they explicitly recognised that inefficiencies grow as decisions are made on the basis of how much money people receive under the table rather than on the basis of price and quality.

Box 6.2 looks in more detail at some of these issues involving bribery and corruption.

Paying bribes carries with it the risk of damaging the company's reputation, both within the country in which the bribes are paid and at home. There is also the risk that the corporate culture of the company itself will become more tolerant of a range of other practices at the margins of legality. There is also evidence to suggest that those host nations with a reputation for bribery and corruption damage themselves. For example, a direct link between high levels of corruption and low levels of fdi has been found, while high levels of corruption resulted in low rates of economic growth.

BOX 6.2 TI Corruption Perception Index

Transparency International (TI) is a non-governmental organisation founded in 1993 and based in Berlin. It has developed one of the more comprehensive databases on corruption, which it defines as an abuse of public office for private gain. The 'TI Corruption Perception Index' (see Table 6.2) correlates a number of surveys, polls and country studies involving the number of bribe requests which those conducting business in some 180 separate countries perceive to have been made to them. A score of 10 indicates a perception that bribe requests are never made in that country, while a score of 0 indicates a perception that bribe requests are always made. A score of 5.0 indicates a perception that there is an equal chance of a bribe being made as not being made. Of the 180 countries included in the 2012 index, 129 scored 5.0 or below; in other words, businessmen perceive that in well-over two-thirds of these 180 countries in the index it is more likely than not that a bribe request will be made in any given transaction.

Box 6.2 (*continued*)

Table 6.2 Global Corruption Perception Index 2012

Rank	The least corrupt	Score
= 1	Denmark	9.0
= 1	Finland	9.0
= 1	New Zealand	9.0
4	Sweden	8.8
5	Singapore	8.7
6	Switzerland	8.6
= 7	Australia	8.5
= 7	Norway	8.5
= 17	UK	7.4
= 17	Japan	7.4
The most corrupt		
169	Iraq	1.8
= 170	Turkmenistan	1.7
= 170	Uzbekistan	1.7
172	Burma	1.5
173	Sudan	1.3
= 174	Afghanistan	0.8
= 174	North Korea	0.8
= 174	Somalia	0.8

Source: www.transparency.org

We can see from Table 6.2 that in 2012 Denmark, Finland and New Zealand had the highest scores at 9.0, followed by Sweden, Singapore and Switzerland, with the UK joint 17th with Japan at 7.4. Afghanistan, North Korea and Somalia were jointly the most corruptly perceived countries with a score of 0.8.

While a wide range of international and national policies has been adopted in an attempt to combat bribery and corruption (see Box 6.3), a broader, more positive approach to improved business ethics and practices has involved the movement towards increasing Corporate Social Responsibility (CSR). Box 6.3 considers some recent moves to tighten legal restrictions on bribery and their impacts on international business.

BOX 6.3 Bribery and corruption

Following our earlier discussion (see pp. 205–208), it may be useful to consider in more detail some of the national/international attempts to reduce this problem. Two important international conventions and a US Act have required member countries to criminalise transnational bribery:

- *Organization of American States Inter-American Convention against Corruption (1994).*

> **Box 6.3 (*continued*)**
>
> - *OECD Convention on Combating Bribery of Foreign Public Officials (1999).* By mid-2000 some 20 countries had already adopted such laws with another 14 close to enacting them. Countries with laws that outlaw the payment of bribes to foreign officials include Austria, Belgium, Canada, Germany, Japan, Korea, the UK and the USA. In fact, the USA was the first country to pass laws to this effect.
> - *US Foreign Corrupt Practices Act 1977.* This made certain payments to foreign officials illegal even when these officials are located abroad, with penalties including prison, fines and disqualification from doing business with the US government.
>
> Although attempts to reduce corruption and bribery in these ways have been broadly welcomed, some criticisms still remain. For example, while business ventures may be prosecuted for bribing foreign officials, a wide variety of government inducements are still permissible, some of which are arguably akin to bribes. For example, governments may give substantial sums in aid on the understanding that the recipient country will grant economic and political concessions to the donor country and its companies in return.

Ecological/environmental issues

Ecological and environmental issues are of obvious concern to individuals, governments and the global community, as they are to international business. In an era of increasing governmental and popular concern with issues such as global warming and sustainability, international business must pay careful attention to the ecological and environmental perspectives with regard to all aspects of their operations.

National and global issues

The environment has become an increasingly important focus of national and international policy makers as global warming, the erosion of the ozone layer and other environmental threats are increasingly linked to worldwide growth in the emissions of harmful substances (e.g. CO_2, chlorofluorocarbons, etc.).

Role of the environment

At a more conceptual level, there is an increasing acceptance of the key role of the environment in business/economic activity in at least three respects:

- *Amenity services*: the natural environment provides consumer services to domestic households in the form of living and recreational space, natural beauty, and so on.
- *Natural resources*: the natural environment is also the source of various inputs into the production process such as mineral deposits, forests, water resources, animal populations, and so on.
- *Waste products*: both production and consumption are activities that generate waste products or residuals. For example, many productive activities generate harmful by-products, which are discharged into the atmosphere or watercourses. Similarly, sewage, litter and other waste

products result from many consumption activities. The key point here is that the natural environment is the ultimate dumping place or 'sink' for all these waste products or residuals.

Sustainable development

It is when the environment is regarded as being unable to efficiently fulfil all three functions as the economy grows over a period of time that we use the term 'unsustainable development'. In this view, the earth is a closed system in which a finite set of resources is available for current and future growth. In other words, the capacity of the economy to produce still more products is constrained or limited by the availability of natural resources. Even if resources are sufficient to permit economic growth, the extra production will simply 'draw through' more materials and energy in products, which the environment must ultimately assimilate, since matter and energy cannot be destroyed (Newton's first law of thermodynamics).

Wherever possible, materials must therefore be recycled, renewable energy sources must be used in preference to non-renewable sources and waste emissions must be limited to the extent that the earth can safely absorb these 'residuals'. This approach has led many economists to propose limiting our demand for goods and services in order to attain a level of economic growth that can be 'sustained' over future generations.

As long ago as 1987, a United Nations' report entitled *Our Common Future* provided the most widely used definition of sustainable development: 'development which meets the needs of the present without compromising the ability of future generations to meet their own needs'. Of course, there have been many different views as to how this definition should affect individual, corporate and government actions, though one theme that has been constant in most views is that of 'intergenerational equity'. This is generally understood to involve taking actions to ensure that the development process minimises any adverse impacts on future generations. *Achieving intergenerational equity* includes avoiding adverse environmental impacts such as excessive resource depletion today causing a reduction in the stock of resources available for future use, or levels of pollution emission and waste disposal today proving to be beyond the ability of the environment to absorb them, thereby imposing long-term damage on future generations.

Business issues

In this section our main concern will be with the impact of these environmental issues and concerns at the level of national and international business. In today's global economy a number of driving forces are arguably raising environmental concerns to the forefront of corporate policy debate.

Corporate responsibility

The term 'corporate responsibility' is increasingly in use, the omission of 'social' being seen by many as a recognition that the responsibilities of corporations extend over a still broader range of issues, especially those involving environmental and ethical concerns.

Environmental and ecological responsibilities

In today's global economy a number of driving forces are arguably raising environmental concerns to the forefront of *corporate* policy debate, which is the focus of this section.

- *Environmentally conscious consumers.* Consumer awareness of environmental issues is creating a market for 'green products'. Patagonia, a California-based producer of recreational clothing, has developed a loyal base of high-income customers partly because its brand identity includes a commitment to conservation. 'Every day we take steps to lighten our footprint and do less harm.' A similar successful approach has been used by Timberland ('our love for the outdoors is matched by our passion for confronting global warming') and The Body Shop. Consumers have long claimed to be more virtuous than they are. Retailers called it the '30:3 phenomenon' – 30% of purchasers told pollsters that they thought about workers' rights, animal welfare and the state of the planet when they decided what to buy, but sales figures showed that only 3% of them acted on those thoughts. Now, however, retailers are behaving as if consumers mean it. A MORI poll found that two-thirds of UK consumers claimed to be 'green' or ethical and actively look to purchase products with an environmental/ethical association. Annual sales of Fairtrade food and drink in Britain had reached over £800 million in 2013, having grown at over 40% per year over the past decade. In the UK, J. Sainsbury and Waitrose sell only bananas with the Fairtrade label, which guarantees a decent income to the grower. Marks & Spencer is stocking only Fairtrade coffee and tea and is buying a third of the world's supply of Fairtrade cotton. In the US, Dunkin' Donuts has decided to sell only Fairtrade espresso coffee in its North American and European outlets. Walmart has devoted itself to a range of 'sustainability' projects.

- *Environmentally and credit-risk-conscious producers.* International businesses are increasingly aware that failure to manage environmental risk factors effectively can lead to adverse publicity, lost revenue and profit and perhaps even more seriously a reduction in their official credit rating, making it more difficult and costly (e.g. higher interest rates) to finance future investment plans. BP has found that the Gulf of Mexico oil spill in April 2010 cost it $10 billion in clean-up operations, $1 billion in compensation to those individuals and businesses directly affected, $70 billion in market capitalisation via a 50% fall in its share price in the following six months. All this does not even include ongoing litigation for breaches in health and safety regulations prior to the explosion and oil spill, and loss of reputation and 'preferred bidder' status in many ongoing bids for new exploration in the US and elsewhere.

A 2010 Populus poll of energy consumers in the UK found that their choice of energy supplier was significantly influenced by the following factors.

- How hard the supplier is working to use resources effectively and reduce waste.
- Level of supplier investment in renewable energy.
- The extent to which the supplier is helping me to become more environmentally efficient.
- How hard the supplier is working to address climate change.
- The supplier's approach to biodiversity.

The above five factors were all in the top seven factors identified by consumers as 'important' when choosing an energy supplier, all scored over 3 on a scale from 0 (completely unimportant) to 5 (very important indeed), and all had increased their scores (by around 10%) since the previous Populus survey in 2008.

- *Environmentally conscious governments.* Businesses have a further reason for considering the environmental impacts of their activities, namely the scrutiny of host governments. Where production of a product causes environmental damage, it is likely that this will result in the imposition of taxes or regulations by government. In the EU, strict new regulations on maximum emissions of greenhouse gases by vehicles are forcing car manufacturers to change engine/chassis designs and sizes to comply with the new regulatory environment. For example, a legally binding EU regulation of a maximum emission of 130 grams of CO_2 per kilometre driven by new cars comes into force in 2015. As we note below, in 2008 the US and EU governments made it a criminal offence to import illegal timber, given environmental concerns involving deforestation.

Environmental sustainability

'Sustainable' and 'sustainability' are now key trigger words in the world of advertising for positive, emotive images associated with words such as 'green', 'wholesome', 'goodness', 'justice' and 'environment', amongst others. They are used in a sophisticated way to sell cars, nappies, holidays and even lifestyles. Sustainability sells – how has this come about and what exactly are we being encouraged to buy?

As long ago as 1987, a United Nations report entitled *Our Common Future* provided the most widely used definition of sustainable development: 'development which meets the needs of the present without compromising the ability of future generations to meet their own needs'. Of course, there have been many different views as to how this definition should affect individual, corporate and government actions, though one theme that has been constant in most views is that of 'intergenerational equity' – i.e. where the development process seeks to minimise any adverse impacts on future generations. These clearly include avoiding adverse environmental impacts such as excessive resource depletion today reducing the stock of resources available for future use, or levels of pollution emission and waste disposal today beyond the ability of the environment to absorb them, thereby imposing long-term damage on future generations.

Forests and deforestation provides a useful case, illustrating how environmental and ecological dilemmas impact on corporate interests and activities.

CASE 6.3 Forestry and corporate responsibility

The vital contribution of forests to a sustainable global environment has long been recognised, especially their ability to give out oxygen and absorb and store carbon. Of course destroying forests for wood, for increased plantation or cattle rearing works in reverse – with around half the dry weight of a tree consisting of stored carbon, much of which is released into the atmosphere when trees are burned or left to rot. In fact around half the earth's total forest area has been cleared by man-made interventions in the past 10,000 years, and today continued deforestation contributes some 15–17% of the world's annual emissions of carbon dioxide (CO_2). Of course forest clearance does still more damage than this, with the loss of plant sources of many modern medicines and animal species, as well as threatening the habitats and livelihoods of some 400 million of the world's poorest people, and resulting in increased flooding as bare hillsides fail to absorb rainfall as effectively.

The increasing emphasis of the media on such environmental issues has, of course, increased pressures on corporations and governments to advance more 'responsible' approaches to forests and their many products and uses. A UN-supported organisation, The Economics of Ecosystems and Biodiversity (TEEB), has estimated that negative externalities from forest loss and degradation cost between $2,000 billion and $4,500 billion each year!

The prominence given to the important role of forests in 'sustainability'-related concerns is providing both positive and negative incentives for corporations to adopt policies consistent with increased environmental responsibility.

> ### Case 6.3 (*continued*)
>
> - **Positive incentives:** On the positive side, governments and environmental agencies are providing incentives of various kinds to encourage a more responsible corporate attitude towards forestry. For example, agricultural companies and farmers are benefiting from incentives in the form of *Payments for Ecosystem Services* (PES) to reforest agricultural land – in China farmers in the vicinity of the Yangzi River are paid $450 a year per reforested hectare, in an attempt to lessen flooding damage. Costa Rica offers $45–$163 per reforested hectare
>
> - **Negative incentives:** On the negative side, *failure* to support sustainable forestry can result in serious damage to corporate profitability. Nestlé has been targeted by Greenpeace with negative blogs and adverts exposing links between the production of chocolate for Kit Kat bars and associated deforestation in Indonesia: around half of the forest areas cleared for crops in Indonesia are used for oil palms, mainly for chocolate production. The impact of such negative publicity was deemed so severe by Nestlé that it ceased buying palm oil from its main Indonesian supplier, Sinar Mas, and promised to remove from its supply chain any producer of palm oil linked to deforestation.
>
> #### Questions
>
> 1 Explain the reasons that environmentalists are concerned about the protection of forests.
>
> 2 What policy instruments are available to achieve this objective?

Box 6.4 reviews the case for imposing so-called 'green taxes' and regulations aimed at encouraging individuals and businesses to act in ways which are environmentally responsible.

> ## BOX 6.4 Environmental impacts, taxes and regulations
>
> If the production process results in environmental damage that the producer does not (at least initially) have to pay for, then marginal social cost (*MSC*) will be greater than marginal private cost (*MPC*). This is the case in Figure 6.6. The private cost to the firm of producing one more unit of output (*MPC*) is rising, due to extra labour, raw material or capital costs. However, the cost to society of producing that extra unit of output (*MSC*) is rising by more than the cost to the firm (*MSC > MPC*). This is because of the environmental damage (e.g. emission of CO_2) caused by producing the last unit, which is a cost to society (e.g. ill-health), even if not to the firm. The true cost to society of producing the last unit of output does include the cost to the firm (*MPC*) of using factor input (since these scarce factors are thereby denied to other firms). However, the true cost to society also includes any environmental damage caused by producing the last unit of output. We call any such damage the marginal external cost (*MEC*). We can therefore state that:
>
> Marginal Social Cost = Marginal Private Cost + Marginal External Cost
>
> $$MSC = MPC + MEC$$
>
> In Figure 6.5 a profit-maximising firm will equate *MPC* with *MR*, producing output 0Q and selling this at price 0P. However, the government may realise that from society's point of view the appropriate output is that which equates *MSC* with *MR* (here we assume *MR* to represent both marginal private benefit and marginal social benefit), producing output $0Q_s$ and selling this at price $0P_s$.

Box 6.4 (*continued*)

To achieve this 'social optimum' solution, the government may try to tax the product (e.g. by raising MPC to MSC). This would be an attempt to 'internalise the externality' by making the producer pay for any damage the producer causes. If MPC is now raised by the tax so that it is equal to MSC, then the profit-maximising firm would itself choose to produce output $0Q_S$ and sell it at price $0P_S$ (at this output and price, MPC = MSC = MR and profits are a maximum). Alternatively, the government might seek to regulate the firm by preventing it producing more than output $0Q_S$. Whatever policy instruments are chosen, business must be aware that production activities that damage the environment are likely to result in adverse impacts on themselves from host governments.

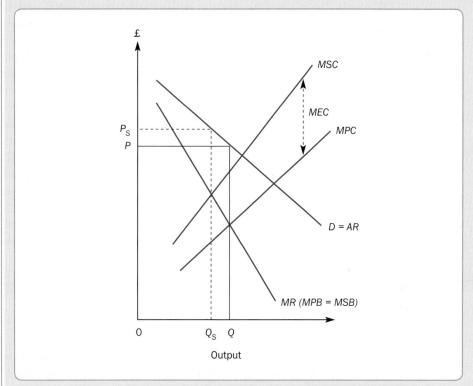

Figure 6.5 Impact of environmental damage (MSC > MPC) on price and output

Environmental codes and regulations

A number of the national/international codes and regulations involving ethical issues already considered (see pp. 198–99) have elements dealing with the environment. There are, in addition, some important environment-specific codes and regulations, which are important to international business.

- *ISO 14001*. The International Organization for Standardization has developed ISO 14001 as a means of certifying companies that adopt certain minimum standards of environmental management.

- *Regional agreements.* Bilateral investment agreements between nations (e.g. Bolivia–USA bilateral investment treaty) often contain minimum environmental standards as do broader-based 'regional' treaties such as NAFTA (North American Free Trade Agreement).
- *Multilateral agreements.* Various *protocols* have been agreed (e.g. Montreal, Kyoto) as to reductions in greenhouse gas emissions, etc. We explain the issues of global warming, sustainability and 'carbon footprints' and their impacts on international business in more detail below (pp. 216–220).

Use of private standards

This approach has been particularly successful in the US chemical industry. In 1984, toxic gas escaped from the plant of a Union Carbide subsidiary in Bhopal, India, and killed more than 2,000 people. The image of the chemical industry was damaged and it faced the threat of punitive government regulation. The industry recognised that it had to act – to forestall government regulations and improve its safety record. As a result, the leading companies in the Chemical Manufacturers Association (CMA) in the USA created an initiative called 'Responsible Care' and developed a set of private regulations that the association's members adopted in 1988.

The US companies that make up the CMA must comply with six management codes that cover such areas as pollution prevention, process safety and emergency response. If they cannot show good faith efforts to comply, their membership will be terminated. The initiative has enhanced the association's environmental reputation by producing results. Between 1988 and 1994, for example, US chemical companies reduced their environmental releases of toxic materials by almost 50%. Although other industries were also achieving significant reductions during this period, the chemical industry's reductions were steeper than the national average.

The big companies that organised 'Responsible Care' have improved their competitive positions. They spend a lower percentage of their revenues to improve their safety record than smaller competitors in the CMA; similarly, they spend a lower percentage of revenues on the monitoring, reporting and administrative costs of the regulations.

The problem with non-binding private agreements or voluntary protocols is that they depend on decisions by organisations themselves as to whether compliance is in their own self-interest.

Supporting 'environmentally friendly' activities

We have already seen in Box 6.4 how negative environmental activities can be taxed or regulated. Here we look at how positive environmental activities can be nurtured and supported. Case 6.4 looks at some of these issues in the context of organic food.

CASE 6.4 Organic farming

Recent studies show that the organic food sector has great potential for expansion. Surveys show nearly 80% of consumers, traumatised by a series of food-contamination scandals, would buy organic produce if it cost the same as conventional food. British production falls well short of meeting that demand. Britain lies in tenth place in terms of land given over to organic production, with less than 2%, compared with Liechtenstein's 17%, Austria's 8.4% and Switzerland's 7.8%.

As a result, Britain imported about 75% of the £550 million of organic food it consumed last year; much of that – humiliatingly – was root crops, cereals and dairy produce, all ideally

> ## Case 6.4 (*continued*)
>
> suited to the British climate and soil. With the annual 40% growth rate in British sales of organic foods likely to continue, and every supermarket now offering a range of products, local farmers have, belatedly, been queuing up to fill that vacuum.
>
> Nevertheless, organic farmers are worried that recent attempts by supermarkets to drastically reduce the 25% premium on prices currently charged for organic products will be passed down the line to themselves. Many believe that if the price premium over non-organic products disappears, then it will be uneconomic for the many small organic farmers to continue production. The pity is that in the long term, organic producers argue, organic farming could supply the mass market relatively cheaply. Yields will gradually increase as the size of organic farms increases, crop rotation kicks in and soil fertility rises. The gradual transformation of what is, in effect, a cottage industry into a serious commercial concern will allow economies of scale, both technical and non-technical. Steady government support, including aid that recognises the rural 'stewardship' provided by organic farmers, would narrow the cost differences with conventional farming.
>
> Only when a certain critical mass has been attained – and many organic advocates believe it must wait until 30% of British land (currently 2%) and 20% of British food is organic – can organic farm prices be expected to fall of their own accord. Until that point, their message will be: please buy organic, but be prepared to pay for it.
>
> ### Question
>
> 1 Why might the small-scale organic farmer seek to grow larger? What opportunities and threats are posed to the organic farmer by large retailers reducing the prices of organic food?

However, sometimes policies directed towards supporting an allegedly 'eco-friendly' activity may not always bring about the outcomes intended. Biofuels subsidies have been criticised for outcomes such as surging food prices and the potential destruction of natural habitats, according to the Organisation for Economic Co-operation and Development. The OECD report in 2007 argued that politicians had been rigging the market in favour of an untried technology that would have only limited impact on climate change, with biofuels cutting energy-related emissions by 3% at most. This small benefit would come at a huge cost, which would swiftly make biofuels unpopular among taxpayers.

The study estimated that the US alone spends $7 billion (£3.4 billion) a year helping make ethanol, with each tonne of CO_2 avoided costing more than $500. In the European Union, it can be almost ten times that. The study stated that biofuels could lead to some damage to the environment: 'As long as environmental values are not adequately priced in the market, there will be powerful incentives to replace natural eco-systems such as forests, wetlands and pasture with dedicated bio-energy crops.'

The report recommended governments phase out biofuel subsidies, using 'technology-neutral' carbon taxes to allow the market to find the most efficient ways of reducing greenhouse gases. The survey criticised the EU's plans to derive 10% of transport fuel from plants by 2020. It states that money saved from phasing out subsidies should fund research into so-called second-generation fuels, which are being developed to use waste products and so emit less CO_2 when they are made.

Global warming, 'carbon footprint' and tradable permits

Global warming refers to the trapping of heat between the earth's surface and gases in the atmosphere, especially carbon dioxide (CO_2). Currently some 6 billion tons of carbon dioxide are released into the atmosphere each year, largely as a result of burning fossil fuels. In fact carbon dioxide constitutes some 56% of these 'greenhouse gases', with chlorofluorocarbons (CFCs), used mainly in refrigerators, aerosols and air-conditioning systems, accounting for a further 23% of such gases, the rest being methane (14%) and nitrous oxide (7%). By trapping the sun's heat these gases are in turn raising global temperature (global warming). On present estimates, temperatures are expected to increase by a further 1°C in the next two decades, when an increase of merely half a degree in world temperature over the past century is believed to have contributed to a rise of 10 centimetres in sea levels. Higher sea levels (resulting from melting ice caps), flooding and various climatic changes causing increased desertification and drought have all been widely linked to global warming.

The importance of global warming and its association with CO_2 emission has become increasingly high profile in recent years. The increasing occurrence of extreme weather conditions across many continents, and the overwhelming collection of scientific evidence on the reality of global warming, has convinced all but a few diehard sceptics of the reality of global warming. This has led to increasing pressures on individuals and organisations to reduce their 'carbon footprint' and demonstrate a responsible attitude to the environment.

The Stern Report (Stern 2007) was regarded as a major factor in encouraging governmental policy makers to make still greater efforts to reduce CO_2 emissions. Box 6.5 outlines the main points raised in the Stern Report.

BOX 6.5 Stern Report and global warming

The Stern Report on climate change was published in late 2006, and is widely regarded as the most authoritative of its kind.
Key findings include the following.

- CO_2 in the atmosphere around 1780, i.e. just before the Industrial Revolution, has been estimated at around 280 ppm (parts per million).
- CO_2 in 2006 had risen as high as 382 ppm.
- Greenhouse gases (CO_2, methane, nitrous oxide, etc.) in 2006 were recorded at 430 ppm in CO_2 equivalents.

Do nothing scenario

This will result in the following:

- a temperature rise of 2°C by 2050;
- a temperature rise of 5°C or more by 2100;
- the damage to the global economy of such climate change is an estimated reduction in global GDP per head (i.e. consumption per head) of between 5% and 20% over the next two centuries. This occurs via rising temperatures, droughts, floods, water shortages and extreme weather events.

> **Box 6.5 (*continued*)**
>
> **Intervene scenario**
>
> - The Stern Report advocates measures to stabilise greenhouse gas emissions at 550 ppm CO_2 equivalents by 2050.
> - This requires global emissions of CO_2 to peak in the next 10–20 years, then fall at a rate of at least 1–3% per year.
> - By 2050 global emissions must be around 25% below current levels.
> - Since global GDP should be around three times as high as today in 2050, the CO_2 emissions *per unit* of global GDP must be less than one-third of today's level (and sufficiently less to give the 25% reduction on today's levels).
> - The Stern Report estimated the cost of stabilisation at 550 ppm CO_2 equivalents to be around 1% of current global GDP (i.e. around £200 billion). This expenditure will be required every year, rising to £600 billion per annum in 2050 if global GDP is three times higher.
> - Stabilisation would limit temperature rises by 2050 to 2°C, not prevent them. Otherwise temperature rises well in excess of 2°C are predicted – possibly as much as 5°C by 2100.

Tradable permits

Tradable permits are a market-based solution to the problem of pollution. With this policy option the polluter is issued with a number of permits to emit a specified amount of pollution. The total number of permits in existence places a limit on the total amount of emissions allowed. Polluters can buy and sell the permits to each other, at a price agreed between the two polluters. In other words, the permits are transferable.

The underlying principle of tradable permits is that those firms which can achieve a lower level of pollution can benefit by selling permits to those firms which at present find it either too difficult or too expensive to meet the standard set.

The market for permits can be illustrated by Figure 6.6. In order to achieve an optimum level of pollution, the agency responsible for permits may issue Qs permits. With demand for permits at D_1 the price will be set at P_1. If new polluters enter the market, the demand for permits will increase, as with D_2 in the figure. As such, the permit price will increase to P_2.

If for any reason the agency wishes to relax the standard set then more permits will be issued and the supply curve for permits will shift to the right. Alternatively, the standard could be tightened, by the agency purchasing permits on the open market from polluters, which would have the effect of shifting the supply curve to the left.

The EU Emissions Trading Scheme uses the idea of tradable permits to reduce greenhouse gas emissions, and this is outlined in Box 6.6. Many industries, sectors and nations are developing similar schemes using tradable permits.

In January 2008, the European Commission proposed a number of changes to the scheme, including centralised allocation (no more national allocation plans) by an EU authority, the auctioning of a greater share (60+%) of permits rather than allocating them freely, and inclusion of other greenhouse gases, such as nitrous oxide. These changes became effective from January 2013 onwards. The proposed caps from 2013 foresee an overall reduction of greenhouse gases in the EU of 21% in 2020 compared to 2005 emissions.

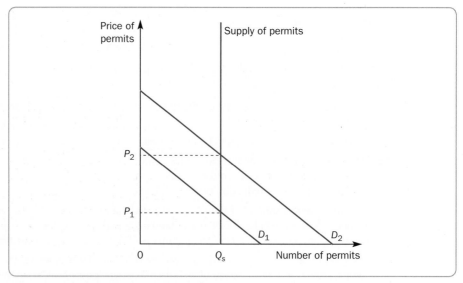

Figure 6.6 Using permits to control pollution

BOX 6.6 The EU Emissions Trading Scheme

In the EU an Emissions Trading Scheme (ETS) is being seen as a key economic instrument in a move to reduce greenhouse gas emissions. The ETS is to aid the EU in meeting its commitments as part of the Kyoto Protocol. The EU took upon itself as part of the Protocol to reduce greenhouse gas emissions by 8% (from 1990 levels) by 2008–12. The idea behind the ETS is to ensure that those companies within certain sectors responsible for greenhouse gas emissions keep within specific limits by either reducing their emissions or by buying allowances from other organisations with lower emissions. The ETS is essentially aimed at placing a cap on emissions.

Background

The emission of greenhouse gases is seen as a major cause of climate change, which has environmental and economic implications, not least in terms of floods and drought. In October 2001 the European Commission proposed that an ETS should be established in the EU in order to deal with greenhouse gas emissions. The result is that an ETS, in the first instance covering only CO_2 (carbon dioxide) emissions, commenced on 1 January 2005, and represented the world's largest market in emission allowances. In the

first phase, which ran from 2005 to 2007, the ETS covered companies of a certain size in sectors such as energy, production and processing of ferrous metals, the mineral industrial sectors and factories making cement, glass, lime, brick, ceramics, pulp and paper.

To implement the ETS an electronic registry system has been developed such that when a change in the ownership of allowances takes place there is a transfer of allowances in terms of the registry system accounts. This registry is similar to a banking clearing system that tracks accounts in terms of the ownership of money. In order to buy and sell the allowances each company involved in the scheme will require an account.

How emissions trading works?

This section details a hypothetical situation that will aid in understanding of how emissions trading will operate. In the following analysis we assume there are two companies, A and B, emitting 60 million and 45 million tonnes of CO_2 per annum respectively. Each company is illustrated in Figure 6.7. The marginal abatement cost (MAC) curves refer to the extra cost to the firm of avoiding emitting the last unit of pollution. The MAC for company A (MAC_A)

Box 6.6 (*continued*)

increases more slowly than for company B (MAC_B) indicating that the cost of abatement is more costly for company B when compared with A.

With no controls on the level of emissions then the total level of CO_2 emissions will be 210 million tonnes (120 million tonnes from company A and 90 million tonnes from company B). If we now assume that the authorities want to reduce CO_2 emissions by 50% (so that 105 million tonnes is the maximum) then this can be achieved by issuing 105 million tonnes of emission allowances. If they are issued on the basis of previous emission levels then company A would receive 60 million emission allowances (or tradable permits) and company B 45 million, based on one allowance representing the right to emit one tonne of CO_2. If this were the case then company A would have to reduce its emissions to 60

million tonnes and company B to 45 million tonnes. Based on this, company A would have a MAC of £1,200 and company B £3,000. Given this situation, company B would buy permits if it could pay less than £3,000 and company A would sell them for a price greater than £1,200. Company A would sell them since the revenue earned from the sale would be greater than the additional abatement cost incurred by reducing emissions.

There is thus a basis for trade in emission allowances and this will continue until the MAC's are identical. In Figure 6.7 this can be seen as £1,500 with 40 million tonnes of CO_2 emitted by company A and 65 million tonnes by company B, with company A selling 20 million emission allowances to company B. Overall the price of the allowances will be determined by supply and demand.

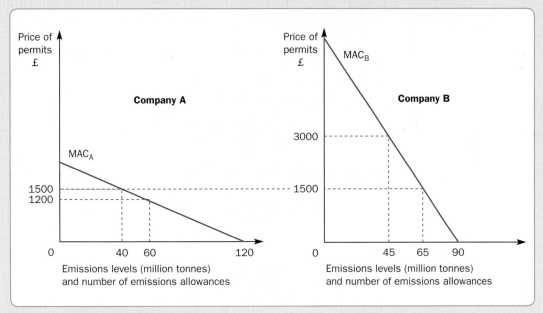

Figure 6.7 **Emissions trading schemes**

The airline industry was included in the ETS for the first time in 2012. The industry has been granted 85% of the total of emission permits allocated to the sector free in 2012, and 82% of any new permits issued between 2013 to 2020 will also be allocated free to the sector, using the 'grandfathering' principle. This has been estimated as effectively a £17 billion subsidy to the airline industry over the next decade for the 4,000 airlines operating in the 27 nations of the EU. However, the EU has estimated that the airlines will collectively have to pay around £3 billion extra to purchase such permits over the next decade, adding to the pressures on an industry already suffering from high fuel prices and weak demand.

CASE 6.5 Emissions trading: The case of cement

What is the difference between cement and clinker? To a handful of companies in the European Union's emissions trading scheme, it means millions of euros and a long-term competitive advantage. Clinker is cement's essential building block. The simple chemical reaction when limestone and clay are converted to clinker is responsible for much of cement's CO_2 emissions.

Two years ago when the European Commission launched an exercise to award carbon permits to industries based on their pollution profiles, the continent's cement industry argued that companies' allocations should be based on their clinker production. By that measure, its members would have all been treated much the same. But one company dissented. In the 1990s Switzerland's Holcim had begun pioneering ways to replace clinker with less polluting materials. These days, its cement contains roughly 10 percentage points less clinker than the European average. Holcim, which has plants across Europe, argued that the industry should be graded (given tradable permits) based not on clinker production but on cement production.

That approach would have recognised its greater efficiency in producing more cement from less clinker but would set a higher bar for the entire industry in the sense that CO_2 emissions permitted per unit of cement would now be lower. As the Swiss company pressed its case, the industry plunged into a brutal lobbying battle. At stake were the permits, each of which gives a company the right to emit a tonne of carbon dioxide and can be sold to others or banked for the future.

When the Commission published its draft proposal in October 2010, Holcim executives were heartened to see that clinker substitution had at least been recognised. But rivals including France's Lafarge and Cemex of Mexico mobilised governments that had factories and jobs at stake. Two months later, when member states amended the plan, Holcim's concession was erased. Bruno Vanderborght, environment chief at Hocim, has lamented that it was 'penalised' for making the sort of environmental investments the carbon market was supposed to reward.

 Source: Adapted from Emissions trading: cheap and dirty, *Financial Times*, 13/02/2012, p. 9 (Chaffin, J.), © The Financial Times Limited 2012. All Rights Reserved.

Questions

1 Explain how Holcim would have benefited from linking the maximum CO_2 emissions permitted per unit of cement to the best technology available (rather than to standard 'clinker' production technology).

2 Consider some of the implications of this case study for the use of emissions trading schemes.

Chapter 7

International strategic issues

By the end of this chapter you should be able to:

- examine the meaning and relevance of business strategy in today's corporate, national and international environment;
- discuss those strategic issues of particular relevance in a globalised economy;
- explain some of the techniques used by international business in developing and reviewing strategic initiatives;
- evaluate the impacts of strategic responses on the structure of the value chain, including operational, logistical and supply chain strategies;
- consider in some detail the strategic issues involved in discrete areas of international business such as mergers, acquisitions and alliances, technology and innovation.

Introduction

Many definitions have been applied to business strategy which, while differing in detail, broadly agree that it involves devising the guiding rules or principles that influence the direction and scope of the organisation's activities over the long term. Kenneth Andrews of the Harvard Business School defined corporate strategy as: 'the pattern of decisions in a company that determines and reveals its objectives, purposes or goals, produces the principal policies and plans for achieving those goals, and defines the range of business the company is to pursue'. We have already considered the contribution of the multinational enterprise (MNE) to the growth of international business activity (Chapter 1, pp. 30–36). Here we review the strategic approaches available to the MNE and the implications of those approaches for the value chain.

Before considering the evolution of business strategy within a global marketplace, it may be useful to briefly review the more conventional ideas and concepts that have dominated business strategy over the past two decades. Many of these ideas originated during the 1970s and 1980s when industrial structures were relatively stable and technical change largely incremental. After reviewing the seminal works of Michael Porter of Harvard University (1980, 1985), which helped to give a more coherent analytical structure to a broad range of managerial practices, we assess the contribution of more recent strategic approaches to international business activity.

Business strategy – ideas and concepts

Techniques such as the following have been widely applied to strategic thinking for more than three decades.

SWOT and PESTLE analysis

During the 1970s Kenneth Andrews (the academic writer) proposed a framework for strategy formulation based on the premise that the final strategy adopted by a company should achieve a 'fit' between its internal capabilities (strengths and weaknesses) and the external situation (opportunities and threats). This is commonly known as SWOT analysis (see Figure 7.1(a)) and involves undertaking (1) an analysis of the external environment within which the firm operates and (2) an objective appraisal of the organisation's current position in order to determine factors that might influence their ability to compete effectively within a particular market.

1 An *external analysis* should highlight the general environmental influences that a firm must cope with – for example, the political, economic, social, technological, legal and ecological factors (PESTLE) already considered in Chapters 4–6. This analysis of the external environment will lead to the identification of a number of *opportunities and threats*.

2 An *internal analysis* of a firm should identify those things that the organisation does particularly well (strengths) and those features that inhibit its ability to fulfil its purposes (weaknesses). The features to be assessed may include the organisation, personnel, marketing and financial features which are considered further in Chapters 8–10.

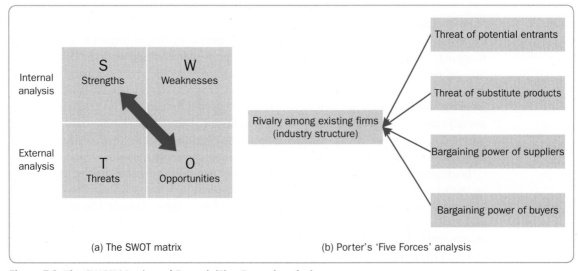

Figure 7.1 **The SWOT Matrix and Porter's 'Five Forces' analysis**

Source: Figure 7.1(b) Based on Porter, M. (1998); Griffiths, A. and Wall, S. (2011); Sloman, J. and Jones, E. (2014).

Strategic alternatives arise from matching current strengths to environmental opportunities at an acceptable level of risk. This framework was further developed during the 1980s by Michael Porter, who proposed a more analytical approach to strategy formulation.

Porter's Five Forces analysis

Porter argued that 'the essence of strategy formulation is coping with competition' and that in addition to undertaking a PEST analysis, it is also necessary to undertake a structural analysis of the industry to gauge the strengths and weaknesses of the opposition and also determine the competitive structure of a given market. The key elements in Porter's Five Forces analysis (see Figure 7.1(b)) can be identified as the threat of (1) potential entrants and (2) substitutes, as well as the power of (3) suppliers and (4) buyers, together with an exploration of (5) the degree of competitive rivalry.

(1) Threat of potential entrants

The threat of new entrants into an industry depends on the barriers that exist in the market and the expected reaction of existing competitors to the entrant. Porter identified six possible sources of barriers to entry, namely economies of scale, differentiation of the product, capital requirements of entry, cost advantages, access to distribution channels and legislative intervention.

(2) Threat of substitute products

The threat of substitute products can alter the competitive environment within which the firm operates. A new process or product may render an existing product useless. For an individual firm the main issue is the extent to which there is a danger that substitutes may encroach on its activities. The firm may be able to minimise the risks from substitutes by a policy of product differentiation or by achieving a low-cost position in the industry.

(3) Bargaining power of suppliers

Suppliers have the ability to squeeze industry profits by raising prices or reducing the quality of their products. Porter states that a supplier is powerful if few suppliers exist in a particular market, there are no substitute products available, the industry is not an important customer of the supplier, or the supplier's product is an important input to the buyer's business. Japanese firms have shown the importance of establishing a strong relationship with suppliers so that they 'become an extension of the firm itself', as in the keiretsu approach to industrial organisation (see Chapter 5).

(4) Bargaining power of buyers

In general, the greater the bargaining power of buyers, the greater is their ability to depress industry profitability. Porter identified a number of determinants of bargaining power, including: the concentration and size of buyers, the importance of purchases to the buyer in cost terms, the costs of switching between suppliers and the degree of standardisation of products. Buyers should be treated as rivals but should have a 'friendly relationship based on performance and integrity'.

(5) Rivalry among existing firms

Finally, the extent of rivalry between firms can influence the competitive environment within which the firm operates. Rivalry is influenced by the above forces but also depends on the concentration of firms in the marketplace and their relative market shares, the rate of industry growth, the degree of product differentiation and the height of exit barriers. Porter refers to the tactics used by firms to seek an advantage over their competitors as 'jockeying for position'. This usually takes the form of policies towards pricing, promotion, product innovation and service level.

The following case gives you an opportunity to review the application of Porter's five-force analysis to strategies which might be adopted by multinationals operating in emerging markets.

CASE 7.1 Strategies for MNEs in emerging markets

Only four emerging-market brands make Interbrand's list of the world's 100 most valuable: Samsung and Hyundai of South Korea, Mexico's Corona Beer and Taiwan's HTC. How can others make the leap? *The New Emerging Market Multinationals,* a book by Amitava Chattopadhyay of INSEAD and Rajeev Batra of the University of Michigan's Ross School of Business, offers some clues (Chattopadhyay *et al.* 2012).

First they must exploit their two basic advantages – economies of scale and local knowledge – to expand into new markets. Some have become so dominant in their home markets that they can hardly avoid expanding abroad. Turkey's Arcelik, for example, controls 50% of the Turkish market for domestic appliances and is now expanding rapidly in Europe. Lenovo gets 42% of its sales from China and has 40 times more stores there than Apple has worldwide. Some firms use their understanding of local markets to expand globally: India's Marico produces shampoo suited to the highly chlorinated water that flows from Middle Eastern taps. Others move swiftly to exploit opportunities: Turkey's Evyap established itself as a leading seller of cheap soaps and scents in Russia when the Soviet Union collapsed. Chattopadhyay and Batra argue that emerging market companies need to add three more ingredients to these basics.

The first ingredient is *focus*: they should define a market segment in which they have a chance of becoming world class. Natura Cosmeticos, a Brazilian cosmetics maker, zeroes in on the market for 'natural' cosmetics with ingredients extracted from the rainforest. Lenovo focused on computers for corporate clients before expanding into the consumer market. Haier, a Chinese maker of dishwashers and fridges, focuses on consumers that many of its rivals neglect, such as students.

The second ingredient is *innovation*: firms need new products and processes that generate buzz. HTC produces 15–20 new mobile phone handsets a year. Natura releases a new product every three working days. Haier keeps producing new ideas such as fridges with locks on them (to keep dormitory mates from snaffling your tofu), compact washing machines (for clothes for pampered Japanese pets) and freezers with compartments that keep ice cream soft (for impatient gluttons). Ranbaxy, an Indian drug firm, has developed controlled release systems that allow patients to take only one pill a day instead of several small doses.

The third ingredient is old-fashioned *brand building*. Emerging market bosses must grapple with many traditional branding puzzles. Should they slap the company's name on the product (as Toyota does) or another name (as Procter & Gamble does with its portfolio of brands, from Gillette razors to Pampers nappies)? How can they market themselves effectively in multiple countries without exhausting the budget? Lenovo has hired an ➡

Case 7.1 (continued)

expensive American marketing boss, but saves money by doing most of its advertising work in Bangalore.

Questions

1 Which of Porter's 'Five Forces' are suggested as helping develop innovative ideas from emerging market economy companies to become established in global markets?

2 What approaches other than 'Five Forces' are suggested for positioning these ideas?

3 Which of these approaches might be relevant for a start-up business (rather than multinational) in an emerging market economy?

Source: Based on information from *The Economist*, 4–10 August 2012, p. 58.

According to Porter, strategy formulation requires that each of the above forces be carefully analysed in order to successfully:

● *position the company* so that its capabilities provide the best defence against the competitive forces;

● *influence the balance* of the forces through strategic moves, thereby improving the company's position;

● *anticipate changes* in the factors underlying the forces and respond to them.

The following example reviews the applications of strategic thinking to the situation facing business start-up in India. It provides useful insights into approaches considered by Sachin and Binny Bansal in founding, developing and positioning their business ideas for *Flipkart,* an online book-selling company.

CASE 7.2 Flipkart formulation: strategy for an Indian start-up

Sachin and Binny Bonsal met each other during their university studies and after graduation the two friends worked together as software engineers at Amazon India. Working for Amazon they were drawn into the entrepreneurial, technology-obsessed and metric-driven culture of the firm that strives to be the world's most customer-centric company. They heard repeated stories of how Jeff Bezos, Amazon's founder, would visit the warehouses and get his hands dirty, seeking valuable insights by direct engagement with Amazon's processes and workforce. The young engineers wanted to start a business of their own and decided to try and build on their experience in Amazon. They spent a significant amount of time brainstorming ideas involving e-commerce and selling books online. They were looking for something simple, that could be operated from home and yet would be profitable from the outset. Eventually an idea came about while working on developing a comparative shopping engine, which involved them in a search for comparison-based websites. They were surprised to discover that there were no such sites involving book buying at that time in India! They soon realised they might have come across a potentially viable gap in the market. However, the discovery came with a very

➡

Case 7.2 (*continued*)

discouraging question: 'Can two guys working from home do a better job at providing a service which no other provider currently attempts to provide in the entire Indian market?'

Sachin and Binny knew very well that the general idea of selling books online was hardly new! They would have to reinvent the wheel innovatively, knowing that Amazon had itself been selling books online since 1995, alongside two other large players in the Indian market, Indiamart and Rediff Books. Sachin and Binny decided to base their business idea on 'differentiation', in the sense of offering customers something that others did not currently provide. They discovered that the free 'shipping' of books to the end-user was not the norm in India, that the information provided for consumers to pre-order books was limited, and that cash-on-delivery was unavailable for book buyers. They decided Flipkart would offer all of these things.

It took Sachin and Binny a long time to convince book distributors and vendors that they were actually serious and that the business had potential. They faced a particular challenge in dealings with third parties. They found it impossible to secure a payment gateway without having an office, phones and other infrastructure, as they were initially working from their shared room using their personal computers, so they found out about the PayPal service as a starting point. The two entrepreneurs recall the hardships of securing venture capital in order to expand their business. They initially read on most blogs that venture capital would be the best and easiest route for financing their business. They therefore embarked on various start-ups events and presentations to venture capitalists but they were constantly turned down by potential investors who did not believe they had the capabilities to scale up the business. They soon realised that as they were only two years out of university, with only a few months' work experience and no business family background, they would have to build a customer base to prove the business potential of their idea to prospective investors. They therefore decided to drop the start-up meetings and presentations with venture capitalists and to focus their energy on building their customer base.

They received their first order within ten days of launching the business website. Their first customer had ordered a book called *Leaving Microsoft to Change the World* by John Wood. It took two days to find the ordered book and they had to sell it at a loss to make up for the delay in delivery. This 'lesson' taught them to find the best couriers in India and to pay them competitive rates to avoid any service inconvenience to their customers. The two entrepreneurs did not take a salary for 18 months and had to adapt their lifestyle accordingly. They felt fortunate to have some savings, and parents who were ready and able to support them. It took the two emerging entrepreneurs six months until they could start breaking even, and soon after they began to reinvest profits into a new office space and to hire employees.

At the end of 2009, some two years after start-up, they began to be approached by very serious investors, and they received their first venture capital to the value of $1 million from the Venture Capital Fund. Sachin explains, 'From then onwards, the operation skyrocketed; we opened multiple offices, hired new engineers and boosted our catalogue.' Within a further year Flipkart was selling two books every minute and capturing a quarter of the total book market in India.

Within three years, starting with a workforce of no more than five people and mainly through word-of-mouth marketing, Flipkart was ranked in the 'Top 100' Indian sites and was credited for being India's largest online bookseller with over 10 million titles on offer. Nevertheless, Sachin and Binny knew that books alone could not give sufficient scale to the company so that diversification into other market segments was vital. Today, Flipkart not only sells books, but also mobile phones, gaming consoles, electronics, music and movies, and they have expanded further into other online market segments.

Sachin and Binny have emphasised customer excellence, with a focus on building trust, maintaining top-quality products, offering a wide range of products and practising consistent performance, as setting their company apart from rivals.

With over 1,000 employees after three years, Sachin and Binny were aware that recruiting and

Case 7.2 (continued)

retaining employees was one of their major challenges. They were well aware that India is still a cash-compensation-based economy, so it is important to find innovative ways of incentivising, attracting, retaining and training their workforce. Nevertheless, they firmly believe that being an Indian company and hiring local people has created an excitement and buzz amongst the community, which in turn creates word-of-mouth advertising for the company. They are well aware of the threat provided by the emerging trend of e-books, with Amazon's e-book sales now exceeding the sale of hardcover books, and the two partners have therefore introduced an e-book segment in their product portfolio. They are also aware that India's English-language publishing market is growing at over 10% per year, with over 50 million Indians buying English-language books in 2014.

Question

How might Porter's approach to strategy formulation (p. 223) apply to the Flipkart case?

Portfolio analysis

The Boston Consulting Group's portfolio matrix (see Figure 7.2) provides a useful framework for examining an organisation's own competitive position. The organisation's portfolio of products is subjected to a detailed analysis according to market share, growth rate and cash flow. The four alternative categories of company (or product) that emerge from the model are given the labels of 'stars', 'cash cows', 'dogs' and 'problem children' (or 'question marks').

● *Stars* have high market share, high growth, but limited cash flow due to the substantial amount of investment required to maintain growth. Successful *stars* go on to become *cash cows*.

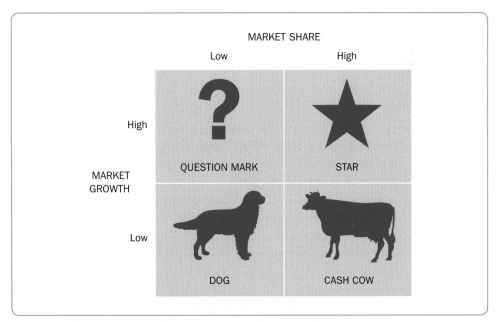

Figure 7.2 The Boston Consulting Group growth-share matrix

Source: The BCG Portfolio Matrix from the Product Portfolio Matrix, © 1970, The Boston Consulting Group

- *Cash cows* have a high market share but slow growth. They tend to generate a very positive cash flow that can be used to develop other products.

- *Dogs* have a low share of a slow-growth market. They may be profitable, but only at the expense of cash reinvestment, and thus generate little for other products.

- *Problem children* have a low share of a fast-growing market and need more cash than they can generate themselves in order to keep up with the market.

The growth-share matrix is useful in providing a visual display of the strengths of a portfolio and therefore can be helpful in guiding the strategic direction of each business. However, there have been several criticisms aimed at the Boston Portfolio, namely that it is prone to oversimplification and that it takes no account of other key variables such as differentiation and market structure.

Choice of strategy

There have been several theoretical models of strategic choice, each of which seeks to identify the main strategic options open to the business in pursuit of its objectives. The following three approaches to strategic choice are often referred to:

- *product–market strategies* – which determine where the organisation competes and the direction of growth (e.g. Ansoff);

- *competitive strategies* – which influence the action/reaction patterns an organisation will pursue for competitive advantage (e.g. Porter);

- *institutional strategies* – which involve a variety of formal and informal relationships with other firms usually directed towards the method of growth (e.g. acquisition v. organic).

Product–market strategies

Igor Ansoff (1968) presented the various strategic options in the form of a matrix (see Figure 7.3(a)).

- *Market penetration strategy* refers to gaining a larger share of the market by exploiting the firm's existing products. Unless the particular market is growing, this will involve taking business away from competitors, perhaps using one or more of the 4 Ps (see Chapter 9) in a national or international context.

- *Market development strategy* involves taking present products into new markets, and thus focusing activities on market opportunities and competitor situations.

- *Product development strategy* is where new products are introduced into existing markets, with the focus moving towards developing, launching and supporting additions to the product range.

- *Diversification strategy* involves the company branching out into both new products and new markets. This strategy can be further subdivided into horizontal, vertical, concentric and conglomerate diversification.

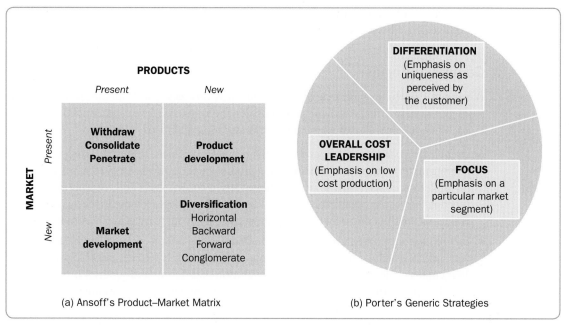

Figure 7.3 (a) Ansoff's product–market matrix; (b) Porter's generic strategies

Source: Figure 7.3(a) Reprinted by permission of Harvard Business Review. From 'Strategies of Diversification' by H.I. Ansoff, Sep/Oct 1957. Copyright 1957 by the Harvard Business School Publishing Corporation, all rights reserved.

Pause for thought 7.1

Can you define and give examples of each of these four types of diversification strategy?

Competitive strategies

Porter (1980) and later writers emphasised the contribution of strategic decisions to achieving some *competitive advantage* over the competition.

Such competitive advantages were often expressed in terms of the additional 'added value' the more successful firms in an industry were able to generate vis-à-vis the most marginal firm in that industry.

> Where no explicit comparator is stated, the relevant benchmark is the marginal firm in the industry. The weakest firm which still finds it worthwhile to serve the market provides the baseline against which the competitive advantage of all other firms can be set. (Kay 1993)

These competitive advantages could be attributed to a host of potential factors:

● *architecture* (a more effective set of contractual relationships with suppliers/customers);

● *incumbency advantages* (reputation, branding, scale economies, etc.);

● *access to strategic assets* (raw materials, wavebands, scarce labour inputs, etc.);

● *innovation* (product or process, protected by patents, licences, etc.);

● *operational efficiencies* (quality circles, just-in-time techniques, re-engineering, etc.).

Our discussion here is primarily in terms of *organisations*. Aspects of *national* competitive advantage (e.g. Porter's diamond) have already been considered in Chapter 3 (pp. 00–00).

Generic strategies

Writing in 1980 in his pioneering book, *Competitive Strategy,* Porter identifies three *generic* strategies open to firms, which may help position the firm to achieve such competitive advantages. These are overall cost leadership, differentiation and focus.

- *Overall cost leadership strategy* requires the business to achieve lower costs than other competitors in the industry while maintaining product quality. This strategy requires aggressive investment in efficient plant and machinery, tight cost controls and cost minimisation in functional areas. An organisation must understand the critical activities in the business' value chain that are the sources for cost advantage and endeavour to excel in one or more of them.

- *Differentiation strategy* is based on creating 'something unique, unmatched by its competitors' which is 'valued by its buyers beyond offering simply a lower price' (Porter 1985). This entails achieving industry-wide recognition of different and superior products compared to competitors, which might result from using superior technology or providing superior customer service.

- *Focus strategy* involves selecting 'a particular buyer group, segment of the product line, or geographic market' as the basis for competition rather than the whole industry. This strategy is 'built around serving a particular target very well' in order to achieve better results. Within the targeted segment the business may attempt to compete on a low-cost or differentiation basis.

Mintzberg (Mintzberg and Quinn 1991) examined both Ansoff's and Porter's models of strategic choice and suggested an alternative view of generic strategies. Mintzberg sees such strategies as being divided into five groupings, which can be summarised as locating, distinguishing, elaborating, extending and reconceiving the core business.

Case 7.3 reviews some current strategic thinking in the publishing market involving Amazon and the more traditional publishing companies. It also links to our discussions on price elasticity of demand (pp. 326 and 327). For example, Amazon argues that demand for an e-book is elastic, and that an e-book priced at $9.99 will sell 1.74 times as many copies as the same e-book priced at $14.99. However, this ignores the impact on hard copy books, which typically have higher prices and lower margins. The research group Forester estimates that physical book sales in the US will be $20 billion in 2014, $6 billion less than four years earlier in 2010, whereas e-book sales will be $9 billion in 2014, seven times higher than in 2010.

CASE 7.3 Publishers take on Amazon

Inefficiency is not a quality usually associated with Amazon but Jeff Bezo's company is behaving as if it is a small, disorganised bookstore that cannot quite control its stock. 'You want that book, do you? Very sorry, but we have run out. We can order you another copy but they are taking a long time to arrive at the moment. How about buying another title instead?' It is a ruse, of course. When Amazon tells its US customers that *The Silkworm,* the new novel by Robert Galbraith, a pseudonym for JK Rowling, is 'currently unavailable', it is not telling the truth. What it means is that it is not making the book available for pre-order because it is published by Hachette, from which Amazon is trying to force discounts.

This is the moment publishers have feared since they lost last year an antitrust case in the US and Europe. 'They were concerned that, should Amazon continue to dominate the sale of e-books to consumers, it would start to demand lower wholesale prices,' wrote Denise Cote, the US district judge. She ruled that the publishers had conspired with Apple to raise prices in its store. By forming a blatant cartel, the 'big six' publishers and Apple botched their effort to resist Amazon's dominance of eBooks with the Kindle. It made the strangest antitrust case of recent years – the US Government and the European Commission rushing to the aid of an emerging monopolist.

Mr Bezos once suggested that Amazon treats small publishers 'the way a cheetah would pursue a sickly gazelle', wrote Brad Stone in the *Everything Store*, his corporate biography. Hachette is one of the smaller big five – reduced from six by the Penguin–Random House merger – and is vulnerable.

I have mixed feelings about Amazon. Mr Bezos has created a remarkable company whose devotion to pleasing customers and cutting prices puts competitors to shame. It reimagined what retailing should be like, not just by putting it online, but by making it easier. He also cut through the fumblings of rivals such as Sony in creating the Kindle. It did not overtake the Sony Reader and the Nook merely because of Amazon's marketing power and manufacturing efficiency. It is a superior device and is linked to a brilliant (when Mr Bezos lets it work) online store. Despite its current tactics, Amazon has been a profitable partner to publishers – bringing innovation to a business of custom and practice. 'Amazon is the publishers' best account. It offers tremendous volume with no returns [of unsold books] and pre-ordering helps them put their books on bestseller lists on day one,' says Mike Shatzkin, consultant.

But it appears disturbingly ruthless, with a hardly disguised ambition to force other suppliers and intermediaries – including publishers and bookstores – out of business. It is a machine for squeezing margins, including its own, to near zero in order to cut prices. These margins include not only publishers' profits but royalties and advances to authors, which have been falling. 'This is a punitive, vindictive, vicious anti-culture company,' says Andrew Wylie, the authors' agent. 'If it doesn't like the way negotiations are going, it punishes the publishers and readers. I don't understand why this is not subject to legal redress.'

There lies Amazon's advantage – it need not form a cartel to squeeze its suppliers because it is already large. With a 30 per cent share of the physical book market in the US and more than 60 per cent of e-books, it clearly has market power in the antitrust sense. But there has never been a case in US competition law of a single company being declared an illegal monopsonist. 'In the US, the simple use by one company of monopsony power to extract lower prices from suppliers is not illegal. There is general intuition that buyer power means lower prices and lower prices are good,' says Jonathan Jacobson, an antitrust lawyer at Wilson, Sonsini, Goodrich & Rosati in New York.

Amazon may trigger a legal challenge over its deceptive sales practice – telling its customers that Hachette books in Germany, where it is waging a similar campaign, are 'unavailable' when they can be bought quickly from its competitors. In terms of antitrust law however, Amazon, the biggest force in books, is secure.

There is a moral for publishers: get bigger. Penguin has merged with Random House (Pearson, the owner of the *Financial Times*, holds a 47 per cent stake in Penguin Random House) and HarperCollins has just brought Harlequin, one of the biggest independents, for $415m. The remedy to market power is to bulk up.

The question is less who wins the contest between Amazon and publishers than what benefits the reader and author (I am both, having had books published by Penguin Random House), and wider society. Amazon has done some things for

Case 7.3 (*continued*)

the public good – the ability of any writer to self-publish on the Kindle platform aids freedom of expression and the spread of ideas.

It is hard, though, to see the public benefit in Amazon treating book publishers as just another bunch of suppliers, like the makers of toys or garden furniture. For now margins on e-books remain high, offsetting the squeeze on hardbacks, but Amazon's intent is clear. If it turns publishing into a lossmaking business, the profession of writing will suffer.

The irony is that publishers' efforts to set book prices themselves and treat Amazon as an agent were legal: it was the cartel that undermined them. The solution in US law is to grow into giants themselves. So much for craft industry.

Question

How might the various strategic approaches reviewed in this chapter apply to this case:

(a) as regards Amazon?

(b) as regards the more traditional publishing companies?

Institutional strategies

The focus here is on possible relationships with other firms and organisations. An initial decision for a firm seeking growth is whether to do so using its own endeavours (e.g. *organic growth*) or to short-cut the growth process by some kind of institutional tie-up with other firms. These can, of course, take many forms, including the franchise, joint venture, alliances and mergers and acquisitions considered in Chapter 2. We return to consider mergers and acquisitions in more detail later in this chapter after briefly reviewing what many believe to be the new competitive landscape of a globalised economy within which all strategic choices must now take place.

To the above we can, of course, add many other conventional techniques of business analysis such as product life cycle, strategic clock, value chain analysis, barriers to entry and contestable market theory, and so on. However, our main concern here is with international business strategies in a far less stable context than pertained in the 1970s and 1980s when many of these techniques were devised and applied.

Corporate strategy in a global economy

Prahalad (1999) has painted a vivid picture of a 'discontinuous competitive landscape', which many see as characterising much of the 1990s as well as the new millennium to the present date. Industries are no longer the stable entities they once were:

● rapid technological changes and the convergence of technologies (e.g. computer and telecommunications) are constantly redefining industrial 'boundaries' so that the 'old' industrial structures become barely recognisable;

- privatisation and deregulation have become global trends within industrial sectors (e.g. telecommunications, power, water, healthcare, financial services) and even within nations themselves (e.g. transition economies, China);

- internet-related technologies are beginning to have major impacts on business-to-business and business-to-customer relationships;

- pressure groups based around environmental and ecological sensitivities are progressively well organised and influential;

- new forms of institutional arrangements and liaisons are exerting greater influences on organisational structures than hitherto (e.g. strategic alliances, franchising).

In an increasingly less stable environment dominated by such discontinuities, there will arguably be a shift in perspective away from the previous strategic focus of Porter and his contemporaries in which companies are seen as seeking to identify and exploit competitive advantages within stable industrial structures.

Pause for thought 7.2

Think of the marginal (just surviving) firm in an industry with which you are familiar. Can you identify some of the competitive advantages of the market leader in that industry over the marginal firm?

Strategy in the new competitive environment

The more conventional strategic models focused on securing competitive advantages by better utilising one or more of the five factors mentioned above. However, the discontinuities outlined previously have changed the setting in which much of the strategic discussion must now take place. Prahalad goes on to suggest four key 'transformations' which must now be registered.

1 *Recognising changes in strategic space.* Deregulation and privatisation of previously government-controlled industries, access to new market opportunities in large developing countries (e.g. China, India, Brazil) and in the transitional economies of Central and Eastern Europe, together with the rapidly changing technological environment, are creating entirely new strategic opportunities. Take the case of the large energy utilities. They must now decide on the extent of integration (power generation, power transmission within industrial and/or consumer sectors), the geographical reach of their operations (domestic/overseas), the extent of diversification (other types of energy, non-energy fields), and so on. Powergen in the UK is a good example of a traditional utility with its historical base in electricity generation which, in a decade or so, has transformed itself into a global provider of electricity services (generation and transmission), water and other infrastructure services. Clearly the strategic 'space' available to companies is ever expanding, creating entirely new possibilities in the modern global economy.

2 *Recognising globalisation impacts.* As we discuss in more detail below, globalisation of business activity is itself opening up new strategic opportunities and threats. Arguably the distinction between local and global business will itself become increasingly irrelevant. The local businesses must devise their own strategic response to the impact of globalised players. Nirula, the Indian fast-food chain, raising standards of hygiene and restaurant ambience in response to competition from McDonald's, is one type of local response, and McDonald's providing more lamb and vegetarian produce in its Indian stores is another. Mass customisation and quick-response strategies require global businesses to be increasingly responsive to local consumers. Additionally, globalisation opens up new strategic initiatives in terms of geographical locations, modes of transnational collaboration, financial accountability and logistical provision.

3 *Recognising the importance of timely responses.* Even annual planning cycles are arguably becoming progressively obsolete as the speed of corporate response becomes a still more critical success factor, both to seize opportunities and to repel threats.

4 *Recognising the enhanced importance of innovation.* Although innovation has long been recognised as a critical success factor, its role is still further enhanced in an environment dominated by the 'discontinuities' previously mentioned. Successful companies must still innovate in terms of new products and processes but now such innovation must also be directed towards providing the company with faster and more reliable information on customers as part of mass customisation, quick response and personalised product business philosophies.

These factors are arguably changing the context for business strategy from positioning the company within a clear-cut industrial structure, to stretching and shaping that structure by its own strategic initiatives. It may no longer be sensible or efficient to devise strategic blueprints over a protracted planning timeframe and then seek to apply the blueprints mechanically given that events and circumstances are changing so rapidly. The direction of broad strategic thrust can be determined as a route map, but tactical and operational adjustments must be continually appraised and modified along the way.

Nor can the traditional strategy hierarchies continue unchallenged – i.e. top management creating strategy and middle management implementing it. Those who are closest to the product and market are becoming increasingly important as well-informed sources for identifying opportunities to exploit or threats to repel. Arguably, the roles of middle and lower management in the strategic process are being considerably enhanced by the 'discontinuities' previously observed. Top managers are finding themselves progressively removed from competitive reality in an era of discontinuous change. Their role is rather to set a broad course, to ensure that effective and responsive middle and lower management are in place to exercise delegated strategic responsibilities, and to provide an appropriate infrastructure for strategic delivery. For example, a key role of top managers in various media-related activities may be to secure access to an appropriate broadband wavelength by successfully competing in the UK or German waveband auctions. Such access is likely to be a prerequisite for competitive involvement in a whole raft of internet-related products for home and business consumption via mobile telephony.

Figure 7.4 provides a useful summary of the traditional and emerging views of international business strategy.

The emerging view of strategy contrasts dramatically with the traditional view. The difference is shown below:

Traditional view	**Emerging view**
• Strategy as *fit* with resources	• Strategy as *stretch and leverage*
• Strategy as *positioning in existing* industry space	• Strategy as *creating new industry* space
• Strategy as *top management* activity	• Strategy as *total organisational* process
• Strategy as an *analytical* exercise	• Strategy as an *analytical and organisational* exercise
• Strategy as *extrapolating* the past	• Strategy as *creating the future*

Figure 7.4 **The new view of strategy**
Source: Adapted from Prahalad (1999).

Case 7.4 on the challenges facing those operating within the 'smarter homes' market provides a useful context for reviewing some of the ideas in Figure 7.4.

CASE 7.4 Apple hopes to open door to 'smarter' homes

For more than 100 years, inventors have struggled to find ways to improve on the humble light switch. Compared with much of today's fiddly technology, it is reliable, intuitive and immediate. It never runs out of batteries, never requests a reset or never needs an operating system update. So when it comes to making home appliances 'smart' by adding mobile apps and Bluetooth or Wi-Fi connections, the bar for improvement is high and the chance of doing it without adding confusion and complexity is low.

Into this mess steps Apple, with its constant promise to bring simplicity, clarity and ease of use – even if

it is not yet clear to most people why the 'connected home' is actually useful. For many years, only the well-off could afford to install home-automation systems, which require significant structural work to houses and typically cost several thousand dollars, to control their lights, stereos or heating. Now, the ubiquity of mobile devices and falling costs of wireless chips and other electronics components has allowed companies, large and small, to experiment with cheaper alternatives.

Larger electronics groups such as Philips, with its Hue light bulbs, and Belkin, which makes a range of WeMo switches and accessories, have been selling

➡

Case 7.4 (*continued*)

products for $50 to $200 apiece that allow previously 'dumb' parts of the home to be controlled via a smart-phone. Several start-ups have also raised multimillion-dollar rounds of venture-capital funding over the past year, including Dropcam and Canary, two wireless security camera makers. At the end of last year, investment researcher CBI insights calculated that venture capital investors had put a total of $468m into smart home start-ups since 2012.

However, it is the entry of large technology companies such as Samsung, Google and Apple that hold the most promise of jump-starting the market, according to analysts. BK Yoon, co-chief executive of Samsung Electronics, in January unveiled a glimpse into the home of the future at the Consumer Electronics Show in Las Vegas, promising that customers could soon take phone calls from their fridges and make their dwellings more 'flexible and responsive'.

Google's $3.2bn acquisition in January of Nest, the smart thermostat company, was seen as an endorsement for the concept of the connected home, but the search engine company has not yet set out its broader vision for the market. Apple will beat Google to the punch next week when it reveals its own plans for the smart home, according to people familiar with the iPhone maker's preparations for its World-wide Developer Conference in San Francisco.

The smart home market 'is really a hobbyist market today', says Jan Dawson, tech analyst with Jackdaw. 'It's not mainstream at all and it's extremely fragmented. Apple could galvanise the market.' Digital music players and smart-phones existed before the iPod and iPhone, Mr Dawson notes, but Apple's entry with slickly designed products brought them mass appeal.

The connected home software platform is a departure for Apple because its system will rely on hardware made by other companies, in contrast to its typical approach of vertical integration. But it has gained valuable experience from the iPhones' App Store and more recently *CarPlay,* a system for linking iOS devices to a vehicle's dashboard. Apple will give other device makers a badge confirming their compatibility with its system, just as it has for several years to iPod and iPhone accessories such as headphones. 'The reason people want to work with Apple in the first place is it's all about quality and being

officially sanctioned,' Mr Dawson says. 'That's a very established model at Apple.'

Joi Ito, director of the *MIT Media Lab* and an investor in start-up *SmartThings,* says most companies working on smart home technology tackle just one small element rather than thinking of whole systems. SmartThings last week made its bid to solve that problem with what chief executive Alex Hankinson calls the 'fist app store for the smart home'. 'It's hard to imagine the big tech companies won't want to have a very big stake in this. But they have a huge existing business to protect, rather than nothing to lose.'

While SmartThings is growing fast, its customer base today remains relatively small, in the tens of thousands. Like other start-ups, it will be watching carefully next week to see if Apple will become a partner or a competitor. 'There are a whole bunch of technical things (Apple) could do that would improve the responsiveness and simplicity of controlling things without compromising the individual hardware companies,' says Tom Coates, co-founder of *Product Club,* a start-up targeting the 'internet of things'.

But he adds that some prospective partners may become uncomfortable if Apple tries to displace their apps with a central controller of its own. That leaves start-ups with a Catch-22 dilemma: if they do not sign up for Apple's scheme, they may miss out on the smart home's biggest sales opportunity to date, but if they do join it, Apple could 'own their customers' and relegate them to being commodity hardware manufacturers.

A similar question faced mobile operators when Apple launched the iPhone with strict conditions that diminished the network providers' role and emphasised its own. 'The big fundamental question is how much of the user interface stays with the individual manufacturers and their apps, and how much is incorporated into the Apple system,' Mr Coates says.

Question

Use Figure 7.4 to evaluate the strategic decision making in the smarter homes market.

Source: Adapted from Apple hopes to open door to smarter homes, *Financial Times*, 28/05/2014, p. 17 (Bradshaw, T.), © The Financial Times Limited 2014. All Rights Reserved.

International business and the value chain

We noted in Chapter 1 that international production is dominated by MNEs that are increasingly transnational in operation, including horizontally and vertically integrated activities more widely dispersed on a geographical basis. This brings into focus the *value chain* in Figure 7.5, which breaks down the full collection of activities that companies perform into 'primary' and 'secondary' activities.

- *Primary activities* are those required to create the product (good or service, including inbound raw materials, components and other inputs), sell the product and distribute it to the marketplace.

- *Secondary activities* include a variety of functions such as human resource management, technological development, management information systems, finance for procurement, etc. These secondary activities are required to support the primary activities.

It is useful to remember that an effective international business strategy must encompass all parts of the value chain configuration, wherever their geographical location. Later chapters of this book consider the international dimension of these various activities in their own right. Here we concentrate on international strategic approaches that might help the firm maximise the sum of these individual activities. International strategies that yield global synergies for the firm over its entire value chain are likely to be of particular interest, where synergies refer to the so-called '2 + 2 > 4 effect' whereby the whole becomes greater than the sum of the individual parts.

A number of sources can be identified as contributing to these global synergies.

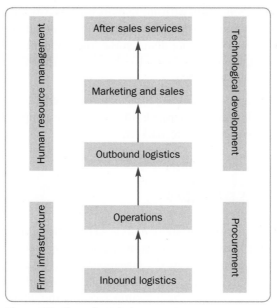

Figure 7.5 The value chain

Source: Adapted with the permission of The Free Press, a Division of Simon & Schuster, Inc. from COMPETITIVE ADVANTAGE: Creating and Sustaining Superior Performance by Michael E. Porter. Copyright © 1985, 1998 by Michael E. Porter. All rights reserved.

Sources of global synergies

Expanding internationally may allow firms to reconfigure their value chains and raise overall corporate profitability in ways that would not otherwise be available within a wholly domestic context. International businesses may be able to develop these 'global synergies' from a variety of sources.

- *Localisation on a global scale* where only the international business can disperse individual value-creating activities (both 'primary' and 'secondary') around the world to locations where they can be undertaken most efficiently (at least cost) and effectively. For example, we saw in Chapter 1 (p. 8–24) how labour costs and productivities varied markedly between different geographical locations.

- *Economies of scale* where it is only by becoming an international business that the firm can operate at such a size that all available economies of scale (technical and non-technical) are achieved for a particular activity within the value chain. This is especially important when the 'minimum efficient size' for an activity within the firm's value chain exceeds the maximum level of output achievable within the domestic economy (see Box 7.1, p. 243).

- *Economies of scope and experience* where only the international business can configure the most appropriate *mix* of activities (*economies of scope*) within the value chain consistent with efficient and effective production (see p. 245). Or where only by becoming an international business can the firm secure the *economies of experience* essential to minimising (*cumulative*) average costs.

- *Non-organic growth on an international scale* where the international business recognises that organic growth is insufficient to meet its key objectives and where some form of *institutional arrangement* with one or more overseas firm(s) is seen as the way ahead. The various institutional mechanisms available have already been touched on in Chapter 2 and are considered in more detail in the international context below. Of course these institutional linkages may themselves be a means to achieving one or more of the global synergies already identified.

- *Increase in geographical reach of core competencies* where the international business seeks to earn a still higher return from its distinctive core competencies by applying those competencies to new geographic markets.

International business strategies

The enormous variety of operations embraced by the term 'multinational' has led some writers to distinguish between four key strategies when competing in the international business environment: a global strategy, a transnational strategy, a multidomestic strategy and an international strategy. The appropriateness of the particular strategy selected will depend to a considerable extent on the pressures faced by the international business in terms of both cost and local responsiveness, as indicated in Figure 7.6. These will become clearer as we discuss the nature of these various strategies and their associated advantages and disadvantages.

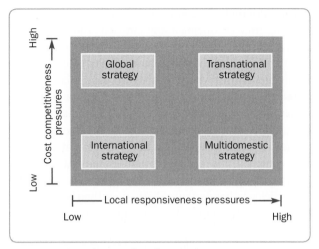

Figure 7.6 **Four international strategies**

Global strategy

This is particularly appropriate when the firm faces high pressures in terms of cost competitiveness but low pressures in terms of being responsive to local market conditions. Firms adopting a global strategy focus on being cost competitive by securing the various economies of scale and scope outlined in Box 7.1 (p. 243) and economies of experience related to *cumulative* output over many years. Production, marketing and R&D activities tend to be concentrated in a few (and in extreme cases a single) favourable geographical locations rather than being widely dispersed. The emphasis of the global firm is on a homogenous, standardised product to maximise these various technical and non-technical economies. Of course such a low-cost strategy is only possible where few pressures exist to localise either production or marketing. If localisation pressures were high, then shorter production runs of a locally differentiated product would invariably raise both technical (production) and non-technical (function/support services) costs.

The global strategy is best suited to industrial products for which there are high pressures for cost reductions but relatively low pressures for the product to be differentiated to meet local market requirements. The semiconductor industry is widely regarded as suitable for this strategy, with global standards placing a premium on firms such as Intel, Motorola and Texas Instruments producing standardised products at minimum cost. A global strategy does not suit many consumer goods markets where product differentiation is a key to local/ cultural acceptability.

Transnational strategy

This is particularly appropriate when the firm faces pressures in terms of both cost competitiveness and responsiveness to local conditions. Of course such local responsiveness may involve more than the 'local' market acceptability of a differentiated product. It might, for example, also reflect entry barriers which effectively protect the local market from the import of a standardised product, however locally acceptable to consumers.

Firms adopting the transnational strategy cannot depend on cost reductions via scale economies from producing a standardised product in a few selected geographical locations. Rather, they must seek cost reductions by exploiting *location economies* appropriate to a particular element of the value chain; for example, locating labour-intensive component production in countries where relative unit labour costs (RULCs – see p. 10) are low. Another cost reduction mechanism open to a transnational strategy might involve benefiting from *experience economies* related to cumulative production across a larger number of geographical locations. *Global learning* may be a further mechanism yielding cost reductions, as when foreign subsidiaries themselves add value to any core competencies transferred from the parent company. The foreign subsidiaries may go on to develop the expertise to become the primary centres for further, initially unforeseen, value-added activities, thereby increasing global efficiency. Foreign subsidiaries may then be able to use this 'global learning' to transfer their own (newly acquired) core competencies to other foreign subsidiaries or back to the parent company itself.

These cost reduction outcomes via a transnational strategy must, of course, remain consistent with the high pressure towards local responsiveness. For example, local responsiveness may require product differentiation and non-standardised marketing and HRM approaches appropriate to local sociocultural sensitivities.

Implementing a transnational strategy is likely to require a high degree of complex organisational co-ordination across geographically dispersed primary and secondary activities within the global value chain. There is also likely to be an element of conflict between cost reductions via the various mechanisms outlined above and cost increases resulting from an increased local responsiveness which inhibits scale economies of both a technical and non-technical nature. How then can the international business implement a transnational strategy?

There are of course many variants, but a widely used method for implementing this strategy involves the idea of 'modularity' in both design and production (see p. 267). This approach is currently being widely used in the car industry as part of a transnational strategy, whereby production activities are progressively broken down into a number of large but separate elements that can be carried out independently in different international locations, chosen according to the optimum mix of factor inputs (cost and quality) for each element. Final assembly, characterised by local responsiveness in terms of product differentiation involving design and other features, often takes place at, or near to, the intended market.

Ford is following this approach, making many different models but using the same 'platform' – the basic chassis and other standardised internal parts. Design and technological breakthroughs of this kind permit even the transnational strategy to benefit from scale economies, as in the production of the basic platform. However, Ford plans to produce ten different vehicles from this common platform, with differentiated features reflecting the need to respond to localised consumer preferences.

Multidomestic strategy

This is particularly appropriate when the firm faces low pressures in terms of cost competitiveness but high pressures in terms of local responsiveness. This strategy tends to involve establishing relatively independent subsidiaries, each providing a full range of value chain activities (primary and secondary) within each national market. The subsidiary is broadly free to customise its products, focus its marketing and select and recruit its personnel, all in keeping with the local culture and the expressed preferences of its customers in each local market.

Such a strategy is more likely to occur when economies of scale in production and marketing are low, and when there are high co-ordination costs between parent and subsidiary. A disadvantage of such local 'independence' may also be an inability to realise potential experience economies. A further disadvantage may manifest itself in the autonomous actions of subsidiaries, sometimes paying little regard to more broad-based corporate objectives. A classic example in this respect was the decision by the US subsidiary of Philips NV in the late 1970s to purchase the Matsushita VHS-format video-cassette recorders (VCRs) and put its own label on them, when the parent company was seeking to establish its own V2000 VCRs as the industry standard.

International strategy

This is particularly appropriate when the firm faces low pressures as regards both cost competitiveness and local responsiveness. The international strategy places the main focus on establishing the 'core architecture' (e.g. product development and R&D) underpinning the value chain at the home base of the MNE and seeking to translate this more or less intact to the national market overseas. Some localised production and marketing activities may be permitted, but these will be limited in scope. McDonald's, IBM, Microsoft, Wal Mart, Kelloggs and Procter & Gamble are often cited as companies pursuing an international strategy in which head office keeps a tight rein over product strategy and marketing initiatives.

Over time some additional local customisation of product and marketing has tended to accompany the international strategy, not least because of some well-publicised failures from an overly strict adherence to the 'core architecture' at head offices. For example IKEA, the Swedish furniture retailer, transferred its retailing formula developed in Sweden into other nations. While such a transfer has proved successful in the UK and elsewhere, it most certainly failed in the USA, with product ranges proving inappropriate to both the larger American physiques (e.g. beds and sofas were too small), the American preferences for larger storage spaces (drawers, bedroom chests and other containers too confined) and European-sized curtains proving incompatible with the sizes of American windows. After entering the US market in 1985, IKEA had realised by the early 1990s that it would need to customise its product range to the American market if it was going to succeed there, which it has duly done to considerable success.

Such celebrated failures, together with a growing awareness of the benefits of at least a limited amount of local responsiveness, have somewhat diluted the international strategy, though it still remains one in which a centralised core architecture persists. It is most appropriate to situations where the parent firm possesses core competencies, which are unmatched by indigenous competitors in foreign markets, and where the key characteristics of the product are broadly welcomed by consumers in those markets.

Table 7.1 reviews the advantages and disadvantages of these four international strategies.

Table 7.1 **Characteristics of four international strategies**

Strategy	Advantages	Disadvantages
Global	Standardised products become highly cost competitive Economies of scale Economies of experience Emphasise home country core competencies	Less responsive to local conditions Loss of market share if consumer behaviour becomes more responsive to localised characteristics Few opportunities for global learning
Transnational	Economies of location via a geographically dispersed value chain Economies of experience Global learning stemming from the sharing of core competencies Product differentiation, with production and marketing responsive to local conditions	Complex co-ordination to implement strategy Possible conflicts between cost competitiveness and local responsiveness
Multidomestic	Highly customised production and marketing, emphasising local responsiveness Most appropriate where the minimum efficient size (MES) is relatively low for key elements of the value chain and strong local/cultural preferences exist.	Loss of location economies (which require a geographically dispersed value chain) Loss of experience economies Little global learning where core competencies are not transferred between foreign companies Lack of corporate group cohesion
International	Core competencies transferred to foreign markets Economies of scale for centralised markets in 'core architecture' (e.g. product development, R&D)	Less responsive to local conditions Fewer location economies available, via retention of 'core architecture' Less global learning as few core competencies transferred Fewer experience economies available

Institutional strategies and international business

To a greater or lesser extent, all four strategies discussed in the previous two sections may involve the firm in devising new *institutional arrangements,* especially where 'green field' foreign direct investment (see p. 57) overseas is deemed inappropriate. Mergers and acquisitions and strategic alliances were seen, in Chapter 1, to be an increasingly prominent aspect of international business. In this section we consider these institutional arrangements within the international business environment in rather more detail.

Mergers and acquisitions (M&A)

We have already noted (see Chapter 2) how globalisation has influenced MNE perspectives of horizontal and vertical integration, with the former particularly relevant to cost-oriented MNEs and the latter to market-oriented MNEs. Laurence Capron has expressed similar views in her assertion that two types of synergy (sometimes described as the '2 + 2 > 4 effect') are typically used to justify mergers and acquisitions, namely cost- and revenue-based synergies:

● *cost-based synergies* – horizontal acquisitions have traditionally been considered an effective means of achieving economies of scale in production, in R&D and in administrative, logistical and sales functions;

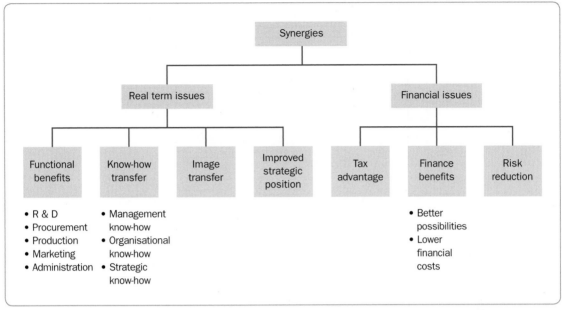

Figure 7.7 **Potential synergies from M&A**

- *revenue-based synergies* – horizontal or vertical acquisitions enable companies to develop new competencies, which may in turn enable them to command a price premium (via increased market power, higher innovation capabilities) or to increase sales volume (via increased market leverage – both geographic and product-line extension).

Figure 7.7 provides a still broader classification of the potential synergies from M&A activity, breaking them down this time into 'real term' and 'financial' issues. Box 7.1 looks in rather more detail at some of the synergies commonly ascribed to M&A.

BOX 7.1 Mergers and acquisitions incentives

Mergers and acquisitions constitute the main vehicle by which firms grow in size (accounts for around 60% of the increase in industrial concentration in the UK) and provide a more rapid alternative to organic growth via 'ploughed-back' profits. Of course, it also offers benefits in terms of cost efficiencies, risk reduction and market power.

Cost efficiencies

The suggestion here is that growth in firm size can provide economies of scale, i.e. a fall in long-run average costs (see Figure 7.8). These can be of a technical or a non-technical variety.

1 **Technical economies.** These are related to an increase in size of the plant or production unit and are most common in horizontal M&As. Reasons include:

- *specialisation of labour or capital,* which becomes more possible as output increases. Specialisation raises productivity per unit of labour/capital input, so that average variable costs fall as output increases;

- *the 'engineers rule'* whereby material costs increase as the square but volume (capacity) increases as the cube, so that material costs per unit of capacity fall as output increases;

Box 7.1 (*continued*)

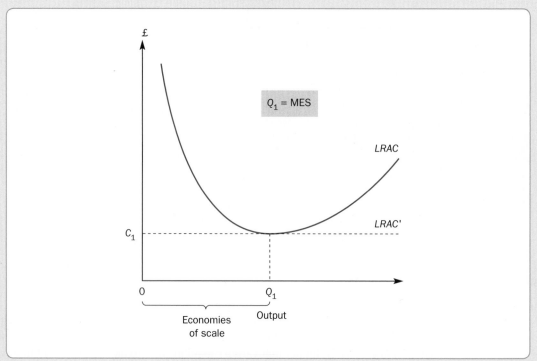

Figure 7.8 Economies of scale and minimum efficient size (MES)

- *dovetailing of processes,* which may only be feasible at high levels of output. For example, if the finished product needs processes A, B and C respectively producing 10, 20, 30 items per hour, then only at 60 units per hour can all processes 'dovetail' and avoid incurring the unnecessary cost of spare (unused) capacity.

2 **Non-technical (enterprise) economies.** These are related to an increase in size of the enterprise as a whole and are valid for both horizontal and vertical M&As. Reasons include:

- *financial economies* – larger enterprises can raise financial capital more cheaply (lower interest rates, access to share and rights issues via stock exchange listings, etc.);

- *administrative, marketing and other functional economies* – existing functional departments can often increase throughput without a pro-rata increase in their establishment;

- *distributive economies* – more efficient distributional and supply-chain operations become feasible with greater size (lorries, ships and other containers can be dispatched with loads nearer to capacity, etc.);

- *purchasing economies* – bulk buying discounts are available for larger enterprises. Also, vertical integration (e.g. backwards) means that components can be purchased at cost from the now internal supplier rather than at cost plus profit.

As can be seen from Figure 7.8, where economies of scale exist for these various reasons, the long-run average cost (*LRAC*) curve will fall as output rises over the range $0–Q_1$. The more substantial these economies of scale, the steeper the fall in the *LRAC* curve, which then means that any firm producing less output than Q_1 is at a considerable cost disadvantage vis-à-vis its competitors. This output (Q_1) at which *LRAC* is a minimum is often called the

---

Box 7.1 (*continued*)

'minimum efficient size' (MES). The larger Q_1 is relative to total industry output, the fewer efficient firms the industry can sustain. For example, if Q_1 is 50% of the usual UK output of glass, then arguably the UK can only sustain two efficient glass producers.

Some surveys suggest that if a firm attempts to produce beyond the MES (Q_1), average costs then begin to rise. These are called diseconomies of scale, and are usually attributed to managerial problems in handling output growth efficiently. However, other surveys suggest that while *LRAC* ceases to fall, there is little evidence that it actually rises for levels of output beyond Q_1 (i.e. *LRAC'* in Figure 7.8).

Other cost efficiencies can result from economies of scope via M&A Here the suggestion is that a more appropriate mix of products or activities in the company's portfolio can help reduce average costs. The joint production of two or more products by the firm or its engagement in two or more activities can bring complementarities which may yield overall cost savings (e.g. heat from energy production by the firm may be available as a by-product to support its other activities).

- *Risk reduction.* This applies particularly to conglomerate M&As, which involve diversifying the firm's existing portfolio of products or activities. Such diversification helps cushion the firm against any damaging movements which are restricted to particular product groups or particular countries.

- *Market power.* The enlarged firm can use its higher market share or capitalised value to exert greater influence on price or on competitor actions/reactions in 'game' playing situations (see p. 251). Enhanced market power can be deployed to raise corporate profit or to achieve other corporate objectives.

A *merger* takes place with the mutual agreement of the management of both companies, usually through an exchange of shares of the merging firms with shares of the new legal entity. Additional funds are not usually required for the act of merging, and the new venture often reflects the name of both the companies concerned.

An acquisition (or takeover) occurs when the management of Firm A makes a direct offer to the shareholders of Firm B and acquires a controlling interest. Usually the price offered to Firm B shareholders is substantially higher than the current share price on the stock market. In other words, a takeover involves a direct transaction between the management of the acquiring firm and the stockholders of the acquired firm. Takeovers usually require additional funds to be raised by the acquiring firm (Firm A) for the acquisition of the other firm (Firm B), and the identity of the acquired company is often subsumed within that of the purchaser.

While it has been widely accepted that successful mergers and acquisitions can create value and add growth, the outcome of such integration has often proved disappointing. Indeed, this has to some extent been anticipated by the short-run stock market return to acquiring companies, which for some time has been approximately zero. However, analysts suggest that at least three reasons underlie these disappointing outcomes: unpredictability, agency problems and managerial error.

- *Unpredictability.* The 'discontinuities' already outlined (see pp. 232–235) give ample reasons why linear predictions of the future are unlikely to be realised. Nevertheless, this may not be the whole story, with suggestions that for acquisitions where the stock market reacts negatively to the merger announcement, the subsequent break-up (divestment) of the new entity was more likely to occur. This implies that the stock market does in fact have some ability to identify those mergers and acquisitions that are more likely to fail in the future.

- *Agency problems.* Where the principal–agent problem occurs (see p. 195), there may well be a separation of interests between those of shareholders (principals) and managers (agents). It may then follow that a merger/acquisition viewed as favourable by one may actually be unfavourable to the other. In a classic study Buckingham and Atkinson (1999) noted that only 17% of mergers and acquisitions produced any value for shareholders while 53% of them actually destroyed shareholder value. However, there is ample evidence (Harris 2012) that managers' remuneration and perquisites may be more closely related to variables such as corporate turnover and growth rates than to corporate profitability. This misalignment of incentives (agency problem) may be an important factor in the continued drive towards M&A as a strategic focus.

- *Managerial errors.* Lack of knowledge, errors of judgement and managerial hubris (overconfidence) can manifest themselves in all three phases of M&A activity, i.e. the planning, implementation and operational phases. For example, in the *planning phase* imagined synergy is far more common than actual synergy, as is indicated in Case 7.5 using the Daimler-Benz and Chrysler merger. Often the actual estimates of merger benefits prove too optimistic and in reality the enhanced resource base of the company may not add value in the ways planned. In the *implementation phase* culture clashes at corporate or national levels may also occur, preventing potential synergies being realised (see Chapter 5). For example, at the corporate level, acquisitions involving a traditional bureaucratic company with an innovative entrepreneurial company will invariably bring conflicts, with the result that for some employees there will be a loss of identification with, and motivation by, the new employer. High-quality human resources are extremely mobile and key knowledge, skills, contacts and capabilities are embedded in these employees, whose loss as a result of the M&A activity will seriously diminish the prospects of the new corporate entity. Finally, in the *operational phase* the hoped for economies of scale and scope outlined in Box 7.1 may fail to materialise, for a variety of logistical reasons.

Case 7.5 on the Daimler-Benz and Chrysler merger usefully illustrates some of these aspects of a cross-border merger.

CASE 7.5 Daimler-Benz AG and Chrysler

Karl Benz constructed the first automobile in 1886, at which time Gottlieb Daimler was active in the same field of business. After years of partnership their businesses were formally integrated in 1926 as the Daimler-Benz Company. In the 1980s Daimler-Benz pursued a strategy of diversification, acquiring MTU, AEG, the aeroplane companies Dornier, MBB and Fokker, the latter completing the aviation arm of Daimler-Benz. The vision of the chairman (Mr Reuter) was to transform the firm from a car maker into an integrated technology group along the lines of General Electric or the Japanese Mitsubishi conglomerate. His vision included generating cross-border synergies between the automobile, the aeroplane and

electronics industry, exchanging skills and knowledge, and spreading the company's risks over the many businesses in its portfolio.

Daimler's first acquisition round

This round of acquisitions soon ran into trouble. The electronics industry was being pressurised by cheap components from Asia, the civil aviation industry was badly affected by the recession of the late 1980s early 1990s and the market for military aeroplanes collapsed after the end of the cold war. Further, many of the acquired businesses had needed restructuring to make them internationally cost competitive. Few of the newly acquired firms had proved to be

Case 7.5 (*continued*)

cash cows for Daimler – quite the opposite, absorbing profits as the company invested heavily in them during restructuring. In terms of Porter's 'parenting advantage' concept it would seem that Daimler provided neither benefits to its acquired businesses nor gained competitive advantages or other benefits from them. For example, Daimler proved unable to provide readily transferable skills from its core automobile business to units like AEG or Fokker. The outcome was that AEG – one of the most well-known and established German companies – was broken up, with the brand sold to Electrolux, some parts integrated into other Daimler businesses and most others closed. With Fokker (aeroplanes) the outcome was similar – Fokker was on the edge of bankruptcy after Daimler withdrew financial support in 1996. Arguably Daimler not only destroyed shareholder value, but also destroyed whole companies with its attempt to build a conglomerate based on unrealistic expectations of planned synergies.

Daimler's first round of acquisitions ended with the highest loss since its foundation (DM5.8 billion) being announced in 1995, mainly due to restructuring charges. Applying M&A success measurements it would seem that the strategy had failed. Many of the acquired firms had been sold off or closed and in terms of stock market figures the market value of Daimler had plunged during the diversification period from DM53 billion in 1986 to DM35 billion in 1995.

Daimler's merger with Chrysler

On 6 May 1998 a new chapter in Daimler's M&A history began: Daimler-Benz AG and Chrysler Corporation announced their merger and the creation of the new DaimlerChrysler AG. To understand this merger one must first consider all the environmental factors. The automobile industry is becoming increasingly mature, with only certain regions (especially Asia) offering higher than average growth opportunities. If a car maker wants to survive, it must have a global reach and be established in all markets of the triad (for example, the number of independent car producers has halved in the last 30 years). A second factor involves the time dimension. Those who wish to sustain their position must react very quickly to changing demands and must renew their product portfolio more frequently. As a result, they

are forced to share expensive fixed overheads (e.g. gain synergies in research and development) and use economies of scale and scope to keep variable costs down. Arguably only large, globalised companies can fulfil these criteria.

The Daimler–Chrysler management engaged international merger experts to assist in all the vital steps of the pre- and post-merger phases. The merger with Chrysler was undertaken with a view to capitalising on core competencies. Both companies, as car producers, sought to keep their core business in the automobile sector. Other expressed reasons involved increasing market power and sharing infrastructure, identified in Figure 7.7 as 'real term' issues. Figure 7.9 outlines some of the product range synergies stated by the participants as relevant to this particular merger.

As can be seen in Figure 7.9, except in the 'off-road' segment there were no product overlaps – rather the respective product portfolios complemented one another. This was also the case in terms of their geographical markets, with Chrysler a strong player in the NAFTA region, while Daimler-Benz was a leading company in Europe. DaimlerChrysler AG subsequently moved to acquire a third leg in the Asian market to consolidate its position in all regions of the triad.1

Further synergies were identified in fields such as procurement, common use of parts and sales. Synergies totalling DM2.5 billion were stated as having already been obtained in those fields within one year of the merger. Going forward, more synergies were targeted in sales, production, research and development and sales. For example, Chrysler brands were expected to gain entry into the European market by using the market knowledge acquired by the established Daimler sales network and some of its distribution outlets. Pilot plants in South America were already being used as test beds for combining production of Daimler and Chrysler vehicles with standardised parts to be used across the different models wherever possible. Common efforts in R& D were also undertaken in the field of future drive concepts. Further synergies of DM6.4 billion were expected by 2001. When these projected savings were compared with the estimated merger costs of DM550 million, then the advantages became obvious.

Case 7.5 (*continued*)

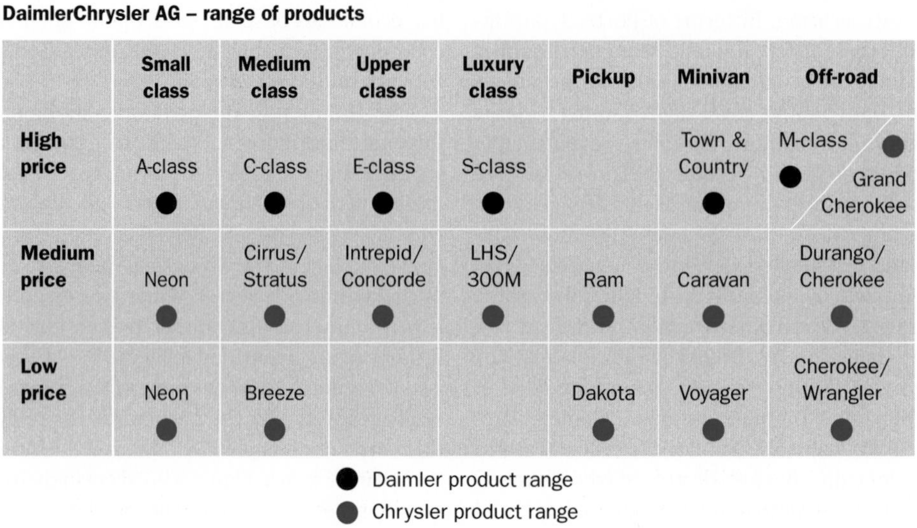

DaimlerChrysler AG – range of products

	Small class	Medium class	Upper class	Luxury class	Pickup	Minivan	Off-road
High price	A-class ●	C-class ●	E-class ●	S-class ●		Town & Country ●	M-class ● / Grand Cherokee
Medium price	Neon ●	Cirrus/ Stratus ●	Intrepid/ Concorde ●	LHS/ 300M ●	Ram ●	Caravan ●	Durango/ Cherokee ●
Low price	Neon ●	Breeze ●			Dakota ●	Voyager ●	Cherokee/ Wrangler ●

● Daimler product range
● Chrysler product range

Figure 7.9 **Product range synergies in the Daimler and Chrysler merger**

A number of critical success factors were highlighted by the chairman, Mr Barnevik.

- In the pre-merger phase
  - *Act quickly and keep it secret.* The company tried to limit the number of people involved and to act rapidly to achieve surprise and momentum. It is better to concentrate on essentials rather than be distracted by less important details.
    - *Approach M&A as a project.* The whole merger and subsequent integration should be done in the form of a series of mini-projects. Therefore, strong project managers are necessary.
    - *Negotiation team to be kept as small as possible.* This helps to keep the negotiations secret and to make decisions more quickly.

- In the post-merger phase
  - *Find key people.* They are important for accelerating projects, integrating people and cultures.
    - *Walk to talk.* Top management must engage directly with people to make sure they participate in the overall vision.

  - *Maintain centralised control.* The use of a centralised control system made information available faster and facilitated quick decisions.

The Daimler–Chrysler merger seemed to incorporate many of these factors. The merger was undertaken in a record time, with only six months elapsing between the announcement and the actual flotation of Daimler–Chrysler shares. The whole preparation took place without any leaks from the negotiation team, with the global auto industry caught unawares by the announcement of this transatlantic alliance. Key people were found and more than 90 projects for integration defined.

Daimler–Chrysler installed special post-merger integration (PMI) teams and a PMI network by which all participants had 24-hour worldwide access to an information base, obtaining details on the various integration projects. As well as the PMI teams, issue resolution teams (IRT) were installed. Their objectives included supervising and co-ordinating the PMI projects. Speed, accuracy, reliable communication, transparency and clear goals were the objectives of these developments. The achievement

Case 7.5 (continued)

of synergy potential was monitored all the time. Accordingly the PMI teams encouraged the sharing of existing resources and, if necessary, the raising of new resource allocations. Synergies to the value of more than DM2.5 billion were stated as being achieved overall in the first year of operation.

Daimler–Chrysler also introduced a new integrated controlling system (ICS) using common concepts and data to help compare the different businesses. This approach helped to eliminate contradictory rules as regards definition and to foster rationalisation and integration. A vital element for a successful cross-border integration, and arguably the most difficult, was recognised as being the creation of one common culture and corporate identity, especially where the new business involves different national as well as corporate cultures. Chrysler perceived German companies as being too comfortable, less innovative and less project-oriented than US companies. On the other hand, Daimler-Benz thought its American partner was too capitalistic and insensitive towards the German social security system.

In an attempt to combine these different cultures and mentalities, a conscious effort was made to create a culture of discussion. A senior management figure was appointed to communicate the goals company-wide, to field e-mails and to respond to the enquiries of worried employees. Interchange programmes took place to make intercultural understanding easier, involving brief information visits, shared projects, seminars or even longer stays abroad. Daimler–Chrysler sought to clarify from the outset that this was a genuine merger of 'equals'. It kept two bases: one in Auburn Hills, USA, and one in Stuttgart, Germany, and the respective CEOs, Robert Eaton and Jurgen Schrempp, led the company together. Both companies were equally represented at board level with equal rights and so avoided the victor/vanquished syndrome.

Of course, there were some negative aspects. Several high-profile former Chrysler executives left the new company. With those departures went valuable skills and personal knowledge. Nevertheless, many of the critical factors for a successful merger would seem to have been applied.

Yet many of these initial expectations for the merger ultimately proved excessively optimistic. Daimler and Chrysler de-merged in mid-2007 and, for many years prior to this, problems within the merged company had become increasingly apparent. Many of the German executives and workers resented the loss of 'Benz' in the new corporate name. Although the mantra throughout the merger process was of a 'merger of equals', most people thought this a ploy to gain acceptance of the merger by the US government and Chrysler employees, rather than reflecting reality! It was noted at the time of the de-merger in 2007 that the Daimler–Chrysler Board had changed from the equal number of 1998 to a ten-to-one ratio in favour of Daimler. Cultural differences in business practices began to emerge in many aspects of the new company, not least as regards employee reward structures. The 'Chrysler' element venture saw the need to increase employee incentives to match those in rivals GM and Ford, including a range of bonus and health care payments, estimated at as much as $2,000 per vehicle produced in the years subsequent to the merger.

Questions

1 What lessons might be learned about M&A from Daimler-Benz's first round of acquisitions?

2 What lessons might be learned about M&A from the Daimler–Chrysler merger?

As already noted, a key strategic goal used to support M&A activity is that the combined entity creates positive net value (i.e. creates potential synergies). Of course, the *realisation* of any potential synergies will crucially depend on whether the *post-integration phase* really does permit the transfer of core competencies, from acquirer to target or vice versa.

Technological change and strategic choice

Case 7.6 usefully reminds us that strategic choices are never made in a static environment but in dynamic, ever-changing environments. One of the key catalysts for such change is technology itself, which may then force a rapid re-examination of previous strategic directions.

CASE 7.6 Retail banks go Digital

When Britain's first telephone bank opened in 1989, it claimed to be from the future. In a television advert marking the launch of First Direct, a hologrammed woman was beamed from 2010, seemingly heralding a time when 24-hour call centres would replace bank branches. Twenty-five years later – and with traditional branches still very much in existence – lenders are claiming a new revolution. They say digital technology is fuelling the biggest change in consumer banking for decades.

Soon, they say, banks will be able to track customers in real time and bombard them with information and offers for shops they are walking by or transport services they are about to use. Technology will enable banks to offer loans on goods before the customer has decided to buy them; identify customers the moment they walk into a branch; and process payments without the buyer ever having to take out their wallet. 'We are in the middle of a revolution,' says Victor Matarranz, executive director at Santander UK, the British arm of the Spanish bank. 'Some people have said there have been periods like this before – like in the early 2000s with the internet coming up. But this time it is different. Technology is far more advanced than before and a whole generation is working on mobile.'

Fuelling the changes is a rapid rise in the adoption of mobile banking, enabled by the near ubiquitous status of smartphones in developed markets. A report from the BBA, a banking trade association, and EY, the consultancy, found that in the UK alone, almost £1bn of mobile and internet transactions are being processed every day. In 2014 more than 15,000 people a day have been downloading banking applications in the UK and spending on contactless cards is expected to almost double. At the same time the use of traditional branches has fallen sharply.

As banks scramble to keep pace with the likes of Google and Facebook, technology experts say it is often smaller lenders, or those that have been forced to reinvent themselves following the financial crisis, that have the edge. 'Spain is very innovative,' says Alex Bray at Misys, the financial software company. 'A lot of banks there

had near death experiences so were pushed to offer something different.' Likewise, he says, niche banks trying to differentiate themselves have to offer better services for customers.

BPH and Getin Bank, two Polish banks, have introduced high-tech cash machines that identify customers by scanning the unique vein patterns in their fingertips. This system, already established in Japan, is considered more reliable than simple fingerprint recognition. Spain's CaixaBank is advancing the 'wearable banking' trend by distributing 15,000 wristbands embedded with payment technology, enabling customers to make contactless purchases from multiple debit or credit cards without taking a wallet out. It has also created a Google Glass app that features a branch finder and currency converter. In the UK, where the top four banks control an unusually high proportion of bank accounts – at least 70 per cent – and are having to spend most of their IT budgets upgrading unreliable existing systems, experts say innovation is less advanced.

Recent changes include a service that allows customers to make instant payments by text using just the recipient's mobile phone number. Plans are also under way to allow retail and small business customers to pay in cheques by snapping them and sending them in with a smartphone rather than queuing at a branch. Meanwhile Barclays is rolling out voice biometrics to save customers time-consuming security checks. 'There has been a lot of innovation in the UK but it hasn't really taken off yet,' says Mr Bray. 'These services require a lot of investment to be broadly adopted and they haven't been promoted as hard as they could.' He says innovations such as voice biometrics and Wi-Fi in branches 'are hardly shaking the world'.

Banks in the UK and elsewhere predict dramatic changes in the coming years, however. They expect big developments in areas such as contactless payments, as wearable payment devices such as wristbands and watches are improved, and security, as banks adopt biometric identification to screen customers instantly.

Analysts say banks have a lot to gain from the switch to digital, not least cost savings from

Case 7.6 (continued)

automating services. 'The costs of complying with tougher regulation have gone up since the crisis, and the direct consequence is that the cost bases of traditional providers have to be addressed,' says Omar Ali, UK head of banking and capital markets at EY.

Also, better access to customer data means banks should be able to sell in a more efficient and effective way.

But as the banking market evolves, lenders are facing an increasing threat from rivals outside the industry, such as Google and Facebook, which have been making inroads into areas such as payments and mobile money – and peer-to-peer lenders. 'Many retail financial firms still haven't grasped the full potential of digital disruption,' says Olivia Bedak, an analyst at Forrester Research. These tech outfits could put banks' attempts to innovate in the shade. Ms Berdak says the likes of Google 'use digital technologies to deliver better or entirely new ways of meeting customer needs, often bypassing regulation and redefining a given industry in the process'.

However she – and insiders at the big banks – discount the idea of Google launching a fully-fledged bank, given the costs, regulatory requirements and its advertising revenue from financial services clients.

Perhaps a bigger challenge for banks is working out how to use data from customers without unnerving them by breaching their privacy. Lenders believe customers are generally comfortable with technology that saves them time, such as biometric identification or contactless payments, or which reduces fraud. But they fear a backlash against more intrusive actions, such as the real-time tracking of their smartphones. 'We can't just take for granted the fact that customers want to share intimate details of their lives with us,' says Simon McNamera, who is responsible for IT at RBS. Likewise, Barclays admits that it is yet to come up with an incentive that would warrant customers giving the bank live access to their whereabouts.

Steve Ellis, head of wholesale services at Wells Fargo, says lenders must seek permission from customers to use data they hold on them. 'The 'big brother' impact here can be a little scary,' he says. 'The amount of information you can get from a phone – that can definitely bother people.'

Question

Consider the changes in bank strategies that might be expected to follow from these developments in digital banking.

Techniques for strategic analysis

Again, we must be selective. We consider in detail some of the more widely used techniques for strategic analysis.

Game-based techniques

This approach has been widely used in highly concentrated industries and markets dominated by a few large firms. The idea is to estimate, for each proposed strategy the firm might adopt, the likely counter-strategies of the rival (or rivals). A variety of assumptions can be made as to how a firm views the likely counter-strategies to be adopted by the rival.

Decision rules

These assumptions are built into 'decision rules', two of which are widely adopted:

1 *maxi-min decision rule* – assumes that the rival (Firm B) reacts in the worst (for Firm A) way possible for each A strategy. Firm A then selects the best (maxi) of these worst (mini) possible outcomes.

2 *mini-max decision rule* – assumes that the rival (Firm B) reacts in the best (for Firm A) way possible for each A strategy. Firm A then selects the worst (mini) of these best (maxi) possible outcomes.

Of course, many other decision rules can be devised for such games. Box 7.2 shows an example of a market share game using the maxi-min decision rule.

BOX 7.2 Two-firm zero-sum game

We might usefully illustrate the principles involved in game theory by a simple two-firm (duopoly) game, involving market share. By its very nature, a market share game must be 'zero sum', in that any gain by one player must be offset exactly by the loss of the other(s).

Suppose Firm A is considering two possible strategies to raise its market share, either a 20% price cut or a 10% increase in advertising expenditure (note that here each strategy involves only a single-policy variable). Whatever initial strategy Firm A adopts, it anticipates that its rival, Firm B, will react by using either a price cut or extra advertising to defend its market share. Firm A now evaluates the market share that it can expect for each initial strategy and each possible counter-strategy by Firm B. The outcomes expected by A are summarised in the pay-off matrix of Table 7.2.

If A cuts price, and B responds with a price cut, A receives 60% of the market. However, if B responds with extra advertising, A receives 70% of the market. The 'worst' outcome for A (60% of the market)

will occur if B responds with a price cut. If A adopts the strategy of extra advertising, then the 'worst' outcome for A (50% of the market) will again occur if B responds with a price cut rather than extra advertising (55% of the market).

If A expects B to play the game astutely, i.e. choose the counter-strategy best for itself (worst for A), then A will choose the price-cut strategy, as this gives it 60% of the market rather than 50%. If A plays the game in this way, selecting the best of the worst possible outcomes for each initial strategy, it is said to be adopting a 'maxi-min' decision rule or approach to the game.

If B adopts the same maxi-min approach as A, and has made the same evaluation of outcomes as A, it also will adopt a price-cut strategy. For instance, if B adopts a price-cut strategy, its 'worst' outcome will occur if A responds with a price cut; B then gets 40% of the market (100% minus 60%) rather than 50% as would be the case if A responds with extra advertising. If B adopts extra

Table 7.2 **Firm A's pay-off matrix: market share game (%)**

		Firm B's strategies	
		Price cut	Extra advertising
Firm A's strategies	Price cut	60*†	70†
	Extra advertising	50*	55

*'Worst' outcome for A of each A strategy.
†'Worst' outcome for B of each B strategy.

Box 7.2 (*continued*)

advertising, its 'worst' outcome will again occur if A responds with a price cut; B then receives 30% (100% minus 70%) instead of 45% (100% minus 55%) if A responds with extra advertising. The best of the 'worst possible' outcomes for B occurs if B adopts a price cut, which gives it 40% of the market rather than 30%.

In this particular game we have a stable equilibrium (a 'Nash' equilibrium – see below), without any resort to collusion. Both firms initially cut price, then accept the respective market shares which fulfil their maxi-min targets 60% to A, 40% to B. There could then follow the price stability which has been seen to be a feature of some oligopoly situations. In some games the optimal strategy for each firm may not even have been an initial price cut, but rather non-price competition (such as advertising). Game theory can predict both price stability and extensive non-price competition.

The problem with game theory is that it can equally predict unstable solutions, with extensive price as well as non-price competition. An unstable solution might follow if each firm, faced with the pay-off matrix of Table 7.2, adopts entirely different strategies. Firm B might not use the maxi-min approach of A, but take more risk. Instead of the price cut it might adopt the 'extra advertising' strategy, hoping to induce an advertising response from firm A and gain 45% of the market, but risk getting only 30% if A responds with a price cut. Suppose this is what happens. Firm A now receives 70% of the market, but B only receives 30%, which is below its initial expectation of 45%. This may provoke B into alternative strategy formulation, setting off a further chain reaction. The game may then fail to settle down quickly, if at all, to a stable solution, i.e. one in which each firm receives a market share which meets its overall expectation. An unstable solution might also follow if each firm evaluates the pay-off matrix differently from the other. Even if they then adopt the same approach to the game, one firm at least will be 'disappointed', possibly provoking action and counteraction.

A number of other ideas are widely presented in game theory approaches.

- *Dominant strategy.* In this approach the firm seeks to do the best it can (in terms of the objectives set) irrespective of the possible actions/reactions of any rival(s).

- *Nash equilibrium.* This occurs when each firm is doing the best that it can in terms of its own objective(s), given the strategies chosen by the other firms in the market.

- *Prisoner's dilemma.* This is an outcome where the equilibrium for the game involves both firms doing worse than they would have done had they colluded, and is sometimes called a 'cartel game' because the obvious implication is that the firms would be better off by colluding.

There are different types of game to which these ideas might be applied.

One-shot game

The suggestion here is that the decision to be made by each firm is 'once for all'. We can illustrate this type of game using Table 7.3, which is a pay-off matrix that expresses the net gains for each of two firms in terms of daily profit, the first value being that for Firm A and the second value that for Firm B. The single policy variable shown here is output level, which can be set high or low, with the pay-off dependent on the rival's reaction. Clearly this is a non-zero-sum game since the total daily profit for each combination of policies varies rather than remains constant (for example, total profit is £3,000 in the bottom-right quadrant but £6,000 elsewhere).

Suppose, initially, that we treat this situation as a one-shot game.

- 'High output' would be the dominant strategy for each firm, giving both Firm A and Firm B £4,000 in daily profit should the other firm select 'low output'. However, if both firms follow this dominant strategy and select 'high output', they each receive only £1,500 daily profit.

- If each firm follows a maxi-min decision rule, then Firm A selects 'low output' as the best of the worst possible outcomes (£2,000 > £1,500), as does Firm B (£2,000 > £1,500). The combination (low output, low output) will then be a Nash equilibrium, with each firm satisfied that it is doing the best that it can in terms of its own objective, given the strategy chosen by the other firm (each actually receives £3,000).

- If each firm follows a mini-max decision rule, you should be able to show that both Firm A and Firm B will still select 'low output' as the worst of the best possible outcomes (£3,000 < £4,000 for each firm). The combination (low output/low output) remains a Nash equilibrium.

Even if one firm follows a maxi-min and the other a mini-max decision rule, the combination (low output/low output) will remain a Nash equilibrium in this particular game. We could reasonably describe this output combination (low/low) as a stable, Nash-type equilibrium.

Repeated game

However, should we view the pay-off matrix in Table 7.3 as part of a repeated game then the situation so far described might be subject to considerable change. We might expect the respective firms to alter the strategies they pursue and the game to have a different outcome.

Suppose the firms initially establish the low output/low output 'solution' to the game, whether as the result of a 'Nash equilibrium' or by some form of agreement between the firms. Unlike the one-shot game, a firm in a repeated game can modify its strategy from one period to the next, and can also respond to any changes in strategy by the other firm.

- *Cheating.* If Table 7.3 is now viewed as the pay-off matrix for a repeated game, there would seem to be a possible incentive for either firm to depart from its initial 'low output' policy in the next period. Had the initial 'low output' policy been mutually agreed by the two firms in an attempt to avoid the mutually damaging high output/high output combination had each firm followed its 'dominant strategy', we might regard such a departure as *cheating* on an agreement. By unexpectedly switching to high output, either firm could benefit by raising daily profit (from £3,000 to £4,000), though the loss of profit (from £3,000 to £2,000) by the other firm might provoke an eventual retaliation in some future time period, resulting in the mutually damaging high output/high output combination.

- *Tit-for-tat strategy.* Whether or not any 'cheating' is likely to benefit a firm will depend on a number of factors, not least the rapidity with which any rival responds to a breach of the agreement: the more rapid the response of the rival, the smaller any net benefits from cheating will be. Suppose, in our example, it takes the other firm five days to respond with higher output, then on each of these days the cheating firm gains a first-mover advantage (see also

Table 7.3 **Pay-off matrix (daily profits)**

		Firm B	
		Low output	High output
Firm A	Low output	£3,000; £3,000	£2,000; £4,000
	High output	£4,000; £2,000	£1,500; £1,500

p. 000) of an extra £1,000 in profit from breaching the agreement as compared with upholding the agreement. If the response of the rival were to be more rapid, say, in three days, then only £3,000 rather than £5,000 benefit would accrue as a first-mover advantage. Of course, once the rival has responded, both firms are damaged in Table 7.3 compared with the pre-cheating situation, losing £1,500 profit per day from the high output/high output combination. This may, of course, induce both firms to restore the initial agreement.

If it becomes known that rivals are likely to respond rapidly to any cheating on agreements (or even departures from Nash-type equilibriums) by adopting *tit-for-tat* strategies, then this may itself deter attempts by either firm to cheat. Provided that each firm believes the rival is sufficiently well informed to be aware of any change in its strategy, it will anticipate a tit-for-tat response that will ensure that any benefits from cheating are of shorter duration. When factored into the decision-making process, the anticipation of a lower profit stream may deter any attempt by either firm to cheat.

Sequential games

In the games considered so far, each firm has been able to make decisions at the same time (i.e. simultaneously). However, in a sequential game the moves and countermoves take place in a defined order: one firm makes a move and only then does the rival decide how to react to that move. Table 7.4 is a pay-off matrix showing net gains as profit per period for each of two firms. The individual pay-offs depend on the price (low or high) selected by one firm and the price response of the rival in this non-zero-sum game.

The dominant strategy for both firm A and firm B is to set a low price (£3,000 profit), but if they both follow this strategy the outcome is mutually damaging (£1,000 profit each). You should be able to see that a maxi-min decision rule followed by each firm would lead to a low price/low price outcome in which the expectations of each firm are fulfilled given that they have adopted this decision rule.

Pause for thought 7.3

What would the outcome have been had each firm adopted a mini-max decision rule?

First-mover advantages

If decisions can only be taken in sequence, an important issue is whether the firm making the first move can secure any advantage!

- *Suppose firm A is in a position to move first.* It can choose 'low price', forcing firm B to choose between 'low price' (£1,000) and 'high price' (£2,000). Firm A might now anticipate that firm B will attempt to maximise its own return given the constrained situation

Table 7.4 **Pay-off matrix (profit per period)**

		Firm B	
		Low price	High price
Firm A	Low price	£1,000; £1,000	£3,000; £2,000
	High price	£2,000; £3,000	£500; £500

(via A's first move) in which B finds itself. In this case firm B selects 'high price', and firm A receives £3,000 profit per period. The first move by A has given a net profit advantage to A of £2,000 (£3,000–£1,000) as compared to the previous low price/low price outcome.

- *Suppose firm B is in a position to move first.* It can now choose 'low price' in the expectation that firm A will respond with 'high price' (£2,000 > £1,000) as firm A now seeks to maximise its own return given the constrained situation (via B's first move) in which it finds itself. In this case, firm B receives a pay-off of £3,000 profit per period and a net profit advantage of £2,000 via the first move.

Clearly this game does contain first-mover advantages, which lie in first anticipating the likely responses of the rival and then channelling those responses in a particular direction as a result of making the first move.

Most analysts counsel against using game theory to 'solve' the game in terms of some type of equilibrium solution with a precise numerical answer, since possible solutions to the games are often extremely sensitive to the assumptions the modeller makes. These assumptions might involve:

- the timing of the moves;
- the information available to the players;
- the rationality of the decisions taken;
- the consequences of playing the game under changing 'decision rules'.

The major benefit of game theory analysis is arguably to focus attention on competitor behaviour and consequent implications for policy. For example, if British Airways understands that price warfare on Atlantic routes with Virgin is a 'prisoners' dilemma' outcome, with both parties doing worse than need be the case, then remedial action can be sought. This may involve changing the 'rules of the game' (e.g. some kind of tacit collusion) in order to remove the incentives which induced both British Airways and Virgin to engage in such price warfare. It is guidance as to an appropriate type of strategic response that is arguably more important than any hypothetical (and unrealistic) numerical solution.

Case 7.7 takes further the earlier Case 7.2 (p. 225) discussions on Flipkart and broadens the analysis to internet developments in the retail market of India. It provides a useful context for reviewing some of these game playing strategies.

CASE 7.7 E-tailers in India prepare for showdown

When two young graduates of the Indian Institute of Technology Delhi in 2007 launched *Flipkart,* an Amazon inspired online bookstore, few Indians had ever bought anything other than airline tickets over the internet. As a pioneer in the business, Flipkart had to wrestle with obstacles ranging from customers' reluctance to give credit card details online – or even a lack of credit cards at all – to suspicions that the goods would never arrive.

Flipkart might have hoped its early mover advantage would help it build an impregnable position in India's e-retail market, like China's *Alibaba,* which accounts for more than 80 per cent of e-commerce in its home market. Instead, Flipkart – with 22m registered users and selling items from apparel to electronics – is defending its turf from aggressive rivals. These include Amazon, its original role model, and local challenger *Snapdeal,* both of which are vying

Case 7.7 (*continued*)

for position in an industry that observers say is poised to boom in the coming years.

Flipkart said last month that it had raised $1bn in new equity for expansion and improvements. A day later *Amazon,* which launched in India a year ago, said it was increasing its bet on growth in the country and had found another $2bn to invest. Analysts believe it is a matter of time before Snapdeal, backed by eBay, also raises funds to remain competitive. 'Everyone is getting more aggressive in defending and growing their market share,' says Pragya Singh, a vice-president at *Technopak,* a New Delhi-based retail consultancy. 'Everybody realises the potential this market has.'

Alibaba, now preparing for an initial public offering that will value it at $100bn, is an inspiration to both Flipkart and Snapdeal. Flipkart says India too can create a $100bn ecommerce company – a role it aspires to fill – while Kunal Bahl, Snapdeal's co-founder, has described his venture as 'identical' to the Chinese group. But Indian retail analysts suggest no single company will establish such a dominant position in India e-commerce, which looks set to be a complex and bitter battleground. 'It's going to be a multiplayer tussle,' says Harminder Sahni, managing director of *Wazir Associates,* a consumer consultancy. 'India is the last big market and none of these players will give up. They are all going to want a share of this pie.'

Indian e-commerce is still in its infancy compared with China, but sales of goods over the internet – about $2.3bn annually – is projected to grow rapidly, potentially rising to as much as $32bn a year within six years, according to Technopak. India's exorbitant real estate prices give e-commerce companies a cost advantage over traditional retailers, while buying items online, and taking delivery at your doorstep is ever more appealing in India's congested urban centres. 'The cost of real estate in India is nonsensical, so e-commerce will always be able to offer better prices than brick-and-mortar,' says Raghave Gupta, a veteran retail industry consultant. 'And travel time, and

travel in general, in India is getting more and more painful.'

The proliferation of less expensive smartphones is also enabling far more Indians to go online regularly. Both Flipkart and Snapdeal say the proportion of customers accessing their sites via mobile phones has increased from less than 10 per cent last year to more than 50 per cent.

In addition to general merchandisers, India's e-commerce market has spawned niche participants in categories such as fashion, spectacles and home items. But Ms Singh says funding for start-ups has dried up during the past year, with investors focusing on larger companies.

In spite of the market promise, profitability is still on a distant horizon, with companies chasing growth, upgrading and expanding technology and logistics, and wooing new customers. 'We don't want to start thinking about profitability in the short term,' says Sachin Bansal, Flipkart's co-founder. While Snapdeal's Mr Bahl touts his company's IPO prospects within two years, Mr Bansal has ruled out Flipkart going public in the near future. 'Private investors have enough long-term appetite,' he says. 'We have not yet settled on a business model that we want to take public.'

Specialised e-commerce companies are not the only ones jostling for space in the industry. Stymied by India's ban on foreign owned hypermarkets, US giant Walmart is piloting an e-commerce platform, while Indian conglomerates involved in bricks and mortar retailing such as Reliance Industries, Kishore Biyani's *Future Group* and the *Tata Group* are also planning to go online to expand.

Manufacturers and brands are also likely to enter the electronic fray, setting up their own sales portals. Analysts say that, while consumers will surely benefit, companies face a long, hard haul. 'The jury is out on who will be the winners or the losers,' says Debashiash Mukherjee, a retail industry expert *at AT Kearney.* 'The investments and scale required to succeed are going to be quite significant. Eventually, there will only be three or four players standing.'

Question

Suggest how game theory approaches might be used by the various 'players' in developing strategies in the e-commerce retail market. You might develop your suggestion from the point of view of (a) existing e-commerce retail companies; (b) new entrants to e-commerce retail.

International operations management and logistical strategies

Both international operations management and international logistics involve the co-ordination of a set of interrelated activities directed towards the efficient production and supply of goods and services. Although there is some overlap between them, for the purposes of this chapter we deal with each approach separately.

International operations management

Operations management can be regarded as one of the key managerial roles within any organisation and is, in effect, 'the management of a system which provides goods or services to or for a customer, and involves the design, planning and control of the system'. The systems theory approach to operations management is based on the view that an organisation can be seen as a network of interconnected components, each performing a role or function. Each component within this system is influential to the extent that if one component were absent or ineffective in some way, then the behaviour of the whole system would change. These basic relationships involved in systems theory can be expressed diagrammatically in terms of inputs and outputs, as in Figure 7.10.

Although this systems approach is commonly applied to manufacturing, it can equally be used in the context of distributive activities, such as transport operations or warehousing. We first illustrate a 'traditional' approach to operations management within manufacturing, and then extend the scope of the discussion to non-manufacturing activities and consider the changing role of operations management within a globalised economy.

Operations management: a manufacturing perspective

Operations management is concerned with managing the transformation process whereby input resources are converted into outputs. Five general approaches can be used for managing the transformation process within manufacturing, namely project processes, jobbing

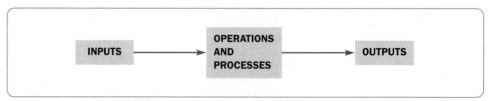

Figure 7.10 **The operations management system approach**

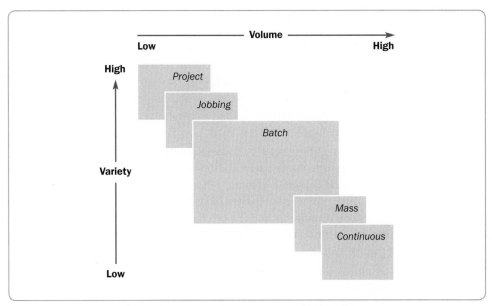

Figure 7.11 **Characteristics of some traditional methods of manufacture**

processes, batch processes, mass processes and continuous processes. Each of these methods involves utilising different approaches to organising and managing the manufacturing activities, depending on the different volume and variety of products required, as can be seen from Figure 7.11.

- *Project processes.* These are traditionally used to produce highly customised, one-off items such as the construction of a new building, the production of a cinema film or the installation of a computer system (i.e. low-volume, high-variety products). There is a sequence of operations, but this sequence can be uncertain, may require alteration during the production process itself and is not usually repeated. With this type of process, the resources necessary for transformation will usually be allocated in a manner specific to each product.

- *Jobbing processes.* These involve the manufacture of a unique item from beginning to end as a result of an individual order. Products subjected to jobbing processes are usually of a smaller stature than those subjected to project processes and may include handmade shoes, restored furniture and individualised computer systems. As with project processes, this type of process is also characterised by low volume, high variety and low repetition, but the transforming resources involved in job processes are typically shared between several products. The main features of jobbing processes are the high set-up costs, flexible multi-use equipment required, skilled and versatile labour required, high worker motivation and a high-priced product. Advantages include creating a unique product to the exact specifications of the customer, for which a premium price might be charged. Disadvantages include the limited opportunities for economies of scale.

- *Batch processes.* These involve the manufacture of a number of similar items whereby a batch of products is processed through a given stage before the entire batch is moved on to the next stage in a well-defined sequence. Examples of batch production include car components, machine tool manufacturing and the production of clothes. Batch processes are typically characterised by larger volumes but a narrower variety of products than are produced by project or jobbing processes. The larger output provides some opportunity for scale economies, resulting in lower costs per unit than jobbing processes. The main features of batch processes are less skilled labour required, use of more specialised but flexible machinery, the possibility of repeat orders, some standardisation of product and the ability to supply a larger market.

● *Mass processes.* These involve the use of a mass-production line whereby the product moves continuously from one operation to another without stopping. Mass processes typically produce goods in larger volumes but are less varied in terms of their design characteristics. Examples of mass processes include motor vehicle manufacturing, food preparation in fast-food restaurants and the production of compact discs. The operations involved in mass production processes are largely repetitive, highly predictable, very efficient but rather inflexible.

● *Continuous processes.* These can be considered as a variation of mass processes in that goods are produced in even larger volumes and are often highly standardised in their design, such as petrochemical refineries, beer, paper and electricity production. The operations involved in continuous processes are usually more automated and standardised than mass processes and are often literally produced in an endless flow. The main features of mass or continuous (flow) processes are high capital investment, a greater proportion of unskilled and semi-skilled labour; specialised plant and equipment with little flexibility; highly automated production and the huge economies of scale which are available.

Some mass production manufacturing systems have adopted the 'just-in-time' (JIT) philosophy that aims to minimise stock-holding costs by planning the arrival of raw materials and components just as they are needed. This requires a highly efficient ordering system, normally computerised, that is linked directly to the suppliers, who, in turn, must be highly reliable. Customers' orders 'pull' production and stocks through the manufacturing process, thus eliminating the need for large stock holdings and driving down the costs of production. Although this can reduce significantly the stock-holding costs, it also increases the danger of production disruption due to non-arrival of stock supplies.

Pause for thought 7.4

Why, historically, have mass and continuous processes become a predominant form of manufacture in the past few decades?

In more recent times there has been considerable focus on slimming down 'mass production' processes into more flexible or 'lean production' approaches to manufacturing (see Box 7.3).

BOX 7.3 Lean production

The Japanese have adopted a 'total approach' to removing anything that does not add value to the final product. The term lean production has been applied to this approach which aims to produce more by using less, and is to be achieved by:

● involving both management and workers in the decision-making and suggestion-making process;

● minimising the use of key resources such as materials, manpower, floor space, capacity and time;

● introducing just-in-time (JIT) materials handling in order to lower stock-holding costs and to minimise the need for buffer stocks;

● encouraging worker participation in quality circles where improvements can be suggested and discussed;

● introducing preventative maintenance;

● using multiple purpose machines for flexible production;

● employing and training multi-skilled operatives;

● encouraging teamwork.

This approach slimmed down 'mass' production into a flexible or 'lean' production system. Advantages claimed for this approach include:

● an increase in quality of product and after-sales service;

● shorter product development time;

● faster reaction to changes in consumer preferences;

● a reduction in unit costs of production without sacrificing quality;

● a better trained and more motivated workforce.

Operations management: a non-manufacturing perspective

In addition to the manufacture of goods, operations management is also concerned with the provision of services. Processes are equally relevant in both manufacturing and service delivery systems but the technologies for delivering services are clearly quite different from those used in manufacturing. As a result of this distinction, Slack *et al.* (2013) identified three process types specific to service operations: namely, professional service, service shops and mass services, ranging from low volume/high variety to high volume/low variety respectively. Some writers argue that the five general process types applied to manufacturing are also appropriate to service operations.

Case 7.8 looks at the use of operations management techniques in an essentially non-manufacturing operation. This involves the marketing of handicraft products in the context of new, global opportunities.

CASE 7.8 Operations management system: Khan Handicrafts

Some of the key operations management issues can be illustrated in the context of Khan Handicrafts, which is a medium-sized cooperative located in Dhaka, Bangladesh. Khan Handicrafts currently serves three different segments of the market, namely foreign tourists (who buy 10% of products at a premium price), local 'expatriates' (who buy 40% of products at an above average price) and middle/upper class Bangladeshis (who buy 50% of products at a lower 'local' price). The higher profit margin derived from the first two of these market segments has prompted Khan to concentrate on the tourist and expatriate markets, although this has involved increased quality control and design input. However, Khan is currently experiencing both a declining home market (reductions in aid agencies) and greater competition within that market. As a result, the organisation is reconsidering its strategic plan for the next decade. One option under active consideration involves moving into the export business.

Figure 7.12 summarises the current system in terms of systems theory. The cooperative's major systems input can be considered to be the workers within its 53 member societies. These societies are made up of poor rural men and women who utilise their woodwork, pottery, sewing, weaving and basket-work skills. Further inputs to the system include finance/capital, storage facilities, raw materials (e.g. dye, wood, clay, etc.) and the equipment necessary to produce the goods. There is also an element of design input, whereby products are produced in accordance with specific customer requirements.

Design might be subsumed within the 'information' heading, which might also include advice given by Khan to its member societies to remain solvent in terms of cash flow management.

The transformation stage of the system takes these inputs and uses them, together with the skills of the workers, to produce the desired outputs. The major output of the Khan organisation is obviously not only the goods produced but also their successful marketing. In other words, the outputs are both goods produced and a range of services which include distribution of the goods directly through Khan's own outlets and as an intermediary in using the outlets of others. In some ways the transformation process for Khan involves acting as an intermediary between producers (its member societies) and the consumers (currently foreign tourists, local expatriates and middle/upper-class Bangladeshis).

A more detailed systems diagram (Figure 7.13) can be used to express the operations of the Khan organisation incorporating the fact that its primary activity is to market the goods produced by the member societies of the cooperative. These goods are marketed either directly through one of Khan Handicraft's own marketing outlets or, more usually, through other outlets. At the central warehouse, the products are subjected to a rapid quality check, labelled with a Khan tag and securely stored until they are dispatched in batches to retail outlets. Khan also uses its extensive market knowledge to influence the design process of individual societies.

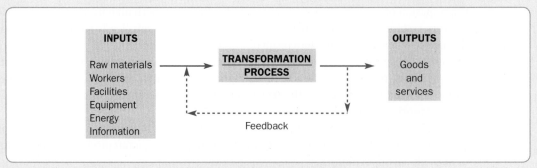

Figure 7.12 The operations management system of Khan Handicrafts

Case 7.8 (continued)

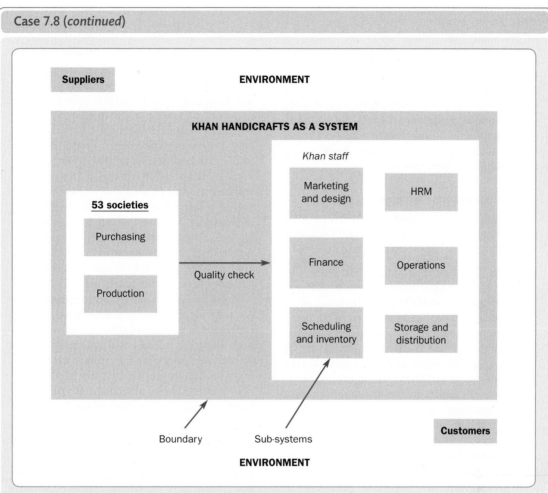

Figure 7.13 **A more detailed systems diagram of Khan Handicrafts**

The influence of the environment on the transformation process is of particular importance when using the systems theory approach to operations management. It is important to understand that the organisation is embedded in its external environment and any changes in these factors, such as political, economic, social or technological changes, may result in changes in the system or one of its components. For example, it can already be seen in the case of Khan that the restrictions on aid missions imposed by the government is affecting a key market segment, namely the demand for its products by home-based expatriates. In attempting to develop existing and new market segments (e.g. export) in response to this environmental change, Khan will

need to factor into its operations management system appropriate mechanisms for dealing with the new requirements for quality, flexibility, timeliness, capacity, etc. An important element in dealing with the environment involves the introduction of physical or organisational 'buffering' techniques wherever possible as a means of minimising the impacts of unforeseeable 'environmental' disruptions, whether on the side of supply or demand.

One of the problems of the systems approach involves precisely delineating the boundaries between the operation function and other functions involved in the production of goods and services. A broad approach is adopted for the Khan systems analysis. A further problem involves modelling the

Case 7.8 (*continued*)

hierarchy of operations appropriately, in particular the treatment given to internal customers and suppliers as compared to external customers and suppliers. Indeed, a network of micro operations, each involved in transforming inputs into outputs, are often key components of the overall macro operation. The fulfilment of customer needs will require the successful integration of all these operations.

Current operations management issues

If the organisation is to achieve its objective of moving into the export business, there are various operations management issues that must be considered.

- *Design.* The current design system utilised by Khan involves little input from its constituent societies. The Khan staff control the design activity as they feel they are more aware of the needs of customers within the market and therefore better able to design products that will satisfy those needs. As competition increases within the current market and Khan seeks to become established in the export market, the design element of the products will become increasingly important. It will be vital for Khan to identify exactly what its customers require from the product in terms of features, colour, fashion, etc. so it can meet, if not exceed, these requirements in order to gain a competitive edge. Changes to the traditional design specifications of products may require the workers to be retrained so that they have the skills to produce exactly what is required to a high standard. Khan may also need to alert workers to the fact that in export markets product design will often supersede functional aspects in terms of buyer behaviour. The company may also consider revising its current policy and encourage design input from the workers, who may be able to contribute new ideas, thereby improving the quality of products and the efficiency of the system as a whole. If Khan is to succeed in breaking into the export market, it may also consider consulting its clients to request their input in terms of design features and technical aspects of the products.
- *Manufacture.* The manufacture of the products can continue to take place locally but a stronger

emphasis must now be placed on improving the quality of the goods produced for a more discriminating export market. Obviously, if the possibility of entering the export market is to be a realistic option, Khan is going to have to seriously rethink its quality control procedures. Given the problems it currently experiences in producing goods of the standard needed by the foreign tourists segment of its market, dramatic improvements will be required. To achieve a higher quality of output, a better and more standardised quality of input (e.g. dyes) will be required. This could be done by introducing a degree of centralisation in supplying raw materials to the individual groups for the manufacturing process. There will also need to be greater quality control at various stages of manufacture, not least to control costs, e.g. if dyeing of spotted or cracked wax occurs in the batik work, this expensive process will have been wasted. It will be important for workers to inspect their own work for errors at each phase of the production process. This may involve additional training but should significantly reduce the need for quality inspections when the finished goods arrive at the central warehouse.

- *Distribution.* This will be a key component of the operations management system. Orders may be made in bulk by foreign purchasers and will often involve an element of product modification. Khan will need to ensure that these features are embodied in the design of sufficient numbers of products supplied to the central warehouse. Khan may also have to oversee the incorporation of higher quality raw materials (sometimes provided by customers themselves) into the manufacturing process, replacing previous sources of domestic supply. Flexibility will be an important element in such adjustments, as, for example, in having to meet specialised and higher quality bulk orders, compared to simply providing products, as made, in smaller batches to customers imposing less onerous time requirements.
- *Capacity.* Khan may need to expand capacity in order to cope with demand from both home and export markets, especially when the latter may involve bulk ordering. This is likely to involve

Case 7.8 (continued)

larger warehousing facilities and more careful attention to demand estimation and production possibilities in order to ensure that orders are met and capacity is not exceeded. Even though, at present, some spare capacity is available, implementation of the new strategy is likely to require the purchase or leasing of additional storage space. The location of this warehousing capacity may need to be reviewed, e.g. ease of access to ports or airports may now become an important factor. Associated with enhanced capacity may be an extra requirement for labour input, as, for example, in support of additional quality control and stock-handling activities.

- *Stock (inventory)*. Stock levels must be more carefully monitored in order to avoid 'stock-out' costs and resulting lost orders. Systems will be needed to handle the warehouse dispatch and location within the warehouse of the more differentiated products required by the export market. While sufficient stock must be held to meet urgent orders and provide adequate numbers of sample items on request, too much stock can result in excessive stock-handling costs. Improvements in inventory management will be an important component of any move into the export market.

- *Purchasing*. The current policy regarding purchasing is that the individual societies purchase their own raw materials as required. Central purchasing may be an important element in ensuring the higher quality products required by the export market. In fact bulk purchase of such inputs at discounts may also lead to the benefit of reducing the cost of purchasing for both domestic and overseas markets, thereby raising profit margins. However, the need for extra storage space already mentioned may absorb part of any additional profit. Some purchasing may now be undertaken under the direction of the clients themselves as they seek to ensure a better quality product.

- *Scheduling*. This will also be a key component of the operations management system. Any delay in receipt or dispatch of stock may endanger future orders, by adding to movement and delivery time. Efficient scheduling of inputs and outputs will also help reduce average stock levels and associated stock-holding costs.

- *Employees*. A further operations management issue that will need consideration is that of the workers and the effect any changes made to current procedures will have on them. Khan may experience resistance from the workers in trying to implement the changes necessary to successfully enter the export market. For example, the majority of rural workers are only part-time and will have difficulty displaying the flexibility required to meet delivery dates due to their other commitments. The special training required might also cause problems as it will involve trying to change ingrained concepts (as to quality and design features for example) which may take years to modify and standardise.

It is important to understand that all of these elements are interrelated; for example, the decision to enter the export market will affect the production process selected, the skills and training requirements of the labour force, the layout of facilities, the warehousing capacity required, etc. These linkages highlight the need for a feedback loop within the overall system so that the elements can be monitored, controlled and any necessary changes made. The combination and interaction of these elements clearly have important implications for the organisation's overall operations management strategy.

Question

If Khan is to broaden its market base (for example, by moving into the export market segment), what strategic issues might be involved?

Indeed, operations management approaches can be applied to a wide range of service-type activities. Case 7.9 reviews the use of an operations management approach in a hospital environment, with a view to identifying process deficiencies and then resolving them.

CASE 7.9 Surgeons adopt assembly-line ideas

The story: In recent years orthopaedic surgeons at the Franciscan Centre for Hip and Knee Surgery in Mooresville, Indiana, USA have faced increasing pressure on their income as insurance companies and the government have reduced the payments they make for such procedures. The partnership's management team recognised that although the failing joints of ageing 'baby boomers' would be a continual source of demand, something had to change if both partnership incomes and patient outcomes were to be maintained.

The challenge: Having ascertained that their own costs offered few opportunities for savings, the partnership decided that the best alternative was to increase productivity. But how could surgeons perform more operations within the working week when there are only so many hours that surgeons, like anyone, are alert enough to wield a scalpel safely and effectively?

The response: The surgeons at the Centre began to see themselves as a bottleneck on an assembly line. Instead of taking one to two hours for a typical knee or hip replacement, the surgeons worked out how they could perform operations within 45 minutes. There would be side-benefits too: for instance, infections would diminish because the wound would be open for a shorter period of time.

A new regime was introduced to make the most of the surgeons' time. Rather than doing everything in a single room, the surgeon now shuttles between two adjacent operating rooms. Each room has its own team, and each team member does the same job for every operation. The operation itself is tightly choreographed, with each team member arriving at the patient at just the right moment to advance the procedure.

The surgeon performs one step after another at a deliberately steady pace. Under the new regime, all sources of variation to the procedure are removed. The two days when operations are performed are planned meticulously. Potential problems are discussed beforehand. During the two days of surgery each week, 15 to 20 patients have replacements performed, roughly double the previous number. The surgeon spends the rest of the week visiting patients who have recently been operated on or meeting and diagnosing new patients.

Meanwhile, two new teams were set up to address pre- and post-operation issues. The pre-operative team handles just pre-operation tasks to make sure patients know what is in store during and after surgery. The job of the doctors, nurses and physical therapists is to ensure patients are in peak condition for surgery and that all necessary information is communicated to the operating team beforehand. The post-operative team monitors pain relief, recovery and the start of physical therapy.

The Centre has introduced metrics to track issues such as quality of outcomes or reduction of inefficiencies – for example, the percentage of patients discharged directly to their home, or the number of operations that did not start on time.

 Source: Treating patients faster, Financial Times, 24/07/2012 (Schmenner, R.), © Roger W. Schmenner.

Question

Identify and examine some of the 'lessons' suggested by this case as regards the use of an operations management approach.

Integration versus modularity

An important contemporary debate involving aspects of operations management is whether to remain integrated in the sense of retaining centralised control of the entire design and production processes, or whether to move in a modular direction. A 'modular product' has been defined as a complex product whose individual elements have each been designed independently and yet function together as a seamless whole. As we shall see, the role of 'enterprise resource planning' has played a part in this debate.

Enterprise resource planning (ERP)

This term refers to the wide variety of company-wide information systems that are increasingly replacing the more fragmented, stand-alone IT systems in many companies. Such ERP systems provide centralised real-time data on all elements of an organisation's operations, no matter how globalised they might be. Manufacturing strategy ceases to involve a sequence of discrete decisions which 'lock' the enterprise into a certain mode of manufacture or operation. Rather it involves the continuous application of intelligence to operational processes which at the same time may open up new product and service opportunities. The increased availability of data may permit the introduction of new and more efficient operational processes (e.g. the introduction of worldwide benchmarking standards) as well as refined and enhanced products more closely attuned to customer requirements.

Modular strategies

Globalisation has been a driving force for modular strategies, since these can help companies engage in large worldwide investments without a huge increase in fixed costs and with fewer of the problems typically associated with managing complex global operations. Modular strategies can embrace production, design and/or use (Figure 7.14).

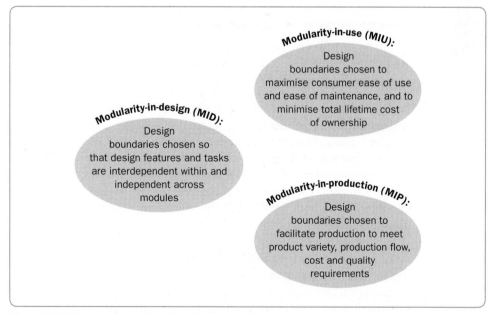

Figure 7.14 Three arenas of modularisation

- *Modularity-in-production (MIP)*. This provided the initial impetus to adopt modules in the car industry. Here production activities are broken down into a number of large but separate elements that can be carried out independently, with the finished vehicle then being assembled from these large sub-assemblies. Such modular production systems can help reduce the fixed capital overhead required for production, especially where selected modules are outsourced. Specialisation of labour and management on smaller, independent modules can also result in productivity gains and lower variable costs.

- *Modularity-in-design (MID)*. There may be more problems in establishing modularity in the design process. This will be particularly true where the finished product embodies systems as well as sub-assembly components. For example, a finished vehicle offers climate control and vehicle safety 'systems' which, to be provided effectively, require design input into a whole range of sub-assembly module operations. Modularity-in-design may therefore require that boundaries be carefully drawn so as to capture as many interdependencies as possible within the modular groupings.

- *Modularity-in-use (MIU)*. This was the main reason for the introduction of modularity in the computer industry. It became increasingly obvious that consumers required computer-related products that were both compatible and upgradeable. Much effort was therefore expended in standardising interfaces between different elements of the product architecture to give these desired user attributes. The then leader, IBM, found that the electro-mechanical system could be disaggregated without adversely affecting performance.

Of course, creating a modular product in any or all of these ways may have organisational consequences, not all of which may be foreseen. For example, a module product architecture may result in modular business organisation. This has certainly been the case in the computer industry. It can also stimulate certain types of organisational practice, such as outsourcing and shift power relationships between companies. For example, IBM's decision to outsource the development and production of its operating system to Microsoft and of its chip components to Intel was an important factor in shifting power away from the overall product architecture to these designers and producers of modular systems elements.

International logistics

Logistics is a term that has long been associated with military activities, and in particular with co-ordinating the movements of troops, armaments and other supplies to specified locations in the most efficient ways technically feasible. When first applied to business some 30 years ago the term was mainly used to refer to the total flow of finished products downstream from the plant to the customers. In more recent times it has been extended further to include the major part of the total flows of materials (finished and unfinished) and information both downstream and upstream. Activities such as transport, storage, inventory management, materials handling and order processing are commonly included within the 'logistics' heading. Indeed, over the last decade the term 'supply chain management' has sometimes been used interchangeably with 'logistics'. This still broader perspective includes the management of the entire chain from supply of raw materials through manufacture and assembly to distribution to the end consumer. As we shall see, when logistics is viewed from this broad perspective it increasingly becomes a strategic as well as an operational issue.

Logistical principles

Before turning to some specific areas of logistical concern for international business, it may be useful to review a number of logistical principles which are of general relevance.

- *Square root law.* The amount of safety stock required will decline by a fraction whose denominator is the square root of the reduction in number of stock-holding points in the logistical system. For example, a reduction from 17 separate warehouses to a single separate warehouse will lead to an approximate reduction of 25% in the safety stock required, which in turn implies an approximately pro rata reduction in stock-holding cost.

- *Logistical cost trade-offs.* It will often be the case that logistical changes will reduce certain specified costs but only at the expense of raising other costs. Such changes will only be applied where the net outcome is positive, i.e. the logistical cost trade-off is 'favourable'. For example, while the reduction in number of separate warehouses reduces stock-holding costs it may well have other impacts. On the positive side, the larger scale of warehousing operations may further reduce inventory and associated materials handling costs. On the negative side there may be additional transport costs incurred by distributions from fewer, larger warehouses to local customers. Only if the overall reduction in inventory and material handling costs more than compensates for any increases in transport-related costs will this logistical trade-off be deemed 'favourable' to the enterprise. More generally MNEs must address such logistical trade-offs whenever they consider centralising production in factories/plants to create scale economies and reduced average production costs while simultaneously incurring additional transportation costs and lengthened lead time to customers.

- *Time compression.* This refers to the various attempts to accelerate the flows of materials and information in logistical systems. It is sometimes extended to cover a variety of techniques and approaches, such as just-in-time, quick response, lead-time management, lean logistics, process mapping techniques, and so on. The idea behind many of these techniques has been to reduce the expenditure of time within various aspects of the supply chain, with particular attention paid to eliminating slack time and time used in non-value-adding activities. Even here, however, the logistical trade-offs will often apply. For example, saving time within large, highly automated and synchronised centralised warehousing systems may be at the expense of incurring more time by lengthening the geographical supply chain to the final customer.

- *Postponement principle.* The company will benefit by postponing decisions as to the precise configuration of customised product until as late a stage as possible within the supply chain. This implies that companies should hold stock in generic form for as long as possible before deciding how to extend the product range by reconfiguring that stock into the separate 'stock-keeping units' (SKUs) which correspond to customised products. The application of this 'postponement principle' reduces the volume of inventory in the global supply chain and the costs associated with under-supplying (stock-out costs) or over-supplying (stock handling costs) a particular market with a customised product. However, the logistical cost trade-off principle can be expected to apply yet again, since the reduction in overall inventory costs may be at the expense of incurring additional costs associated with extending the global supply chain (e.g. transport/distribution costs).

Box 7.4 reviews some of the key logistical principles in the particular context of inventory (stock) costs and control.

BOX 7.4 Inventory (stock) costs and control

There are three broad categories of costs involving inventories. The cost of holding stock (carrying costs), costs of obtaining stock (ordering costs) and the costs of failing to have adequate stock (stock-out costs).

Inventory costs include the following:

- *Holding or carrying costs.* These might include insurance, storage costs (staff, equipment, handling, deterioration, obsolescence, security). These might also include opportunity costs, i.e. the financial cost in terms of alternatives forgone (e.g. interest) through having capital tied up.

- *Order costs.* These occur when obtaining stock and might include the costs of clerical and administrative work in raising an order, any associated transport costs and inspection of stock on arrival, etc.

- *Stock-out costs.* These are difficult to quantify but might include the following:

Stock-out of raw materials and work-in-progress, which may result in machine and operator idle time and possibly the need for overtime payments to catch up on missed production.

Stock-out of finished goods, which may result in:

1 missed orders from occasional customers;
2 missed delivery dates resulting in a deterioration in customer/supplier relations;
3 penalty clauses incurred for late delivery.

Stock-out of tools and spares, which may result in an increase in downtime of machinery and loss of production.

Stock carrying costs can be expected to rise as the order size increases, for reasons already discussed. However, stock ordering costs can be expected to fall as the order size increases (*see* Figure 7.15).

If we ignore stock-out costs, which are notoriously difficult to quantify, then total (inventory) costs can be regarded as the sum of the carrying and ordering costs. These will be at a minimum for the following value of Q (output).

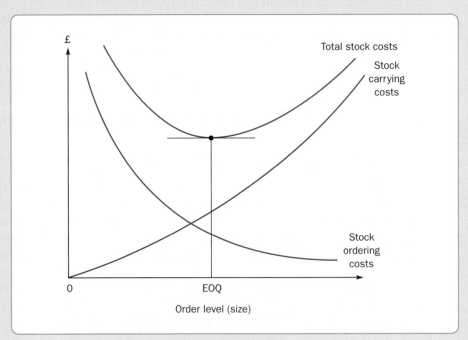

Figure 7.15 **Finding the economic order quantity (EOQ)**

BOX 7.4 (continued)

Economic order quantity

$$Q = \sqrt{\frac{2 \cdot CoD}{Cc}}$$

Where Q = economic order quantity

Co = ordering costs for one order

D = annual demand for stock

Cc = carrying cost for one item p.a.

A firm uses 100,000 components per annum in its manufacturing process, each of which cost the firm £10 to purchase from its supplier. The carrying costs of stocking these components is estimated as 15% per annum of the purchase price. The ordering costs are estimated at £10 per order. Find the economic order quantity.

Solution

$$EOQ = \sqrt{\frac{2 \cdot CoD}{Cc}}$$

Where Co = £10 per order

D = 100,000 units p.a.

Cc = £10 × 0.15 = £1.50 per item per annum.

$$EOQ = \sqrt{\frac{2 \cdot (10) \cdot (100,000)}{1.50}}$$

i.e. EOQ = 1155 units

Of course, more complex inventory control situations with variable usage rates, variable lead times and gradual (rather than instantaneous) replenishment may be encountered by firms.

International distribution systems

International business might, at one extreme, pay little heed to the logistical aspects of delivery by exporting on an ex-works basis. The responsibility in this case would be on the overseas purchaser to arrange for the collection of the goods and to bear all the insurance and freight costs. This rarely happens in practice, with the result that sellers and buyers must make an agreement as to their respective responsibilities and duties in trade, with the range of possibilities often referred to as 'incoterms'.

Incoterms

The International Chamber of Commerce has drafted standard definitions of export delivery terms to clarify these issues:

- ex works (EXW): customers collect goods from the exporters premises;
- free on board (FOB): customers only take responsibility after the goods are loaded onto the ship in the exporter's country;
- free carrier (FRC): as for FOB, but applies to any form of carrier, ship or otherwise;
- cost, insurance and freight (CIF): customers only take responsibility after the goods have reached a named foreign destination (i.e. exporter bears all transport and insurance costs to that point);
- delivered at frontier (DAF): customers only take responsibility after the goods have passed through a named frontier;
- delivered duty paid (DDP): customers only take responsibility after the goods have reached their premises. This is increasingly becoming the standard approach for export sales.

Table 7.5 **International distribution systems**

Types of system	Advantages	Disadvantages
1 Direct	No need for foreign warehouse Greater inventory centralisation/lower inventory level	Longer order lead time Less load consolidation/higher transport costs
2 Transit	Permits breaking of bulk Greater load consolidation, so lower transport costs Less packaging and administration	Extra handling costs in foreign markets
3 Classical	Permits breaking of bulk Greater load consolidation, so lower transport costs Less packaging and administration Shorter order lead times Local stock availability Lower import dues	Incurs full warehousing cost Decentralisation of inventory increases total stockholding
4 Multicountry	Higher degree of inventory centralisation and lower unit warehousing costs than 3	Longer lead times to customers Higher delivery costs Difficult to co-ordinate with nationally based sales organisation

Source: Adapted from Tayeb (2000).

Types of distribution channel

'Distribution channel' refers to the route the product takes from producer to the final consumer. Such channels must fulfil a number of functions, including the physical movement of the products, their storage prior to transit or sale, the transfer of title to the products and their presentation to the customer.

Four main types of channel are commonly identified:

1 *Direct system*: no intermediaries involved, with orders sent directly from a factory or warehouse in the home country to the overseas purchaser.

2 *Transit system*: exports sent to a transit (or 'satellite') warehouse/depot in another country. This then acts as a 'break bulk' point, with some items despatched in bulk over long distances and others in smaller units to more local destinations.

3 *Classical system*: here each foreign country has its own separate warehouse/depot. Exports are sent to these and then distributed within that national market. Such warehouses/depots both 'break bulk' and perform a stock-holding function, with nationals of that country being served by locally held inventories.

4 *Multi-country system*: as for the classical system, except that the separate warehouses/depots may serve several adjoining countries rather than one country only.

Table 7.5 summarises some of the advantages/disadvantages of each of the four types of distributional channel.

Choice of distributional channel

In practice a few key factors will determine the choice of distributional channel:

● *Foreign customer base*: the direct system is more likely to be used where a small number of large overseas purchasers are involved.

- *Export volumes*: the use of 'break-bulk' or stockholding warehouses/depots will only be economically viable when export volumes exceed certain 'threshold' levels.

- *Value density of product*: those products with a high ratio of value to weight/volume (i.e. high value density) are more suited to direct systems since they can more easily absorb the higher associated transport costs.

- *Order lead times*: where direct systems are inappropriate (e.g. low value density) yet where customers required rapid and reliable delivery, stock may have to be held locally (i.e. classical or multi-country systems).

Recent evidence suggests a rise in *direct, transit* and *multi-country systems*. The rise of e-commerce is increasing direct systems use with international and personalised delivery via parcel networks (e.g. 'just for you', J4U delivery). Transit and multi-country systems have also been increasing, with many MNEs consolidating warehousing in a few large 'pan-European' distribution centres. Sony, Rank Xerox, Philips, Kellogg's, Nike and IBM have moved in this direction and away from the classical system previously adopted. Some of these choices of distribution channels may be influenced by opportunities for 'economies of scope' (see p. 245).

Case 7.10 reviews the impact of technology in increasing the range of distributional channels available, in this case the use of 'click and collect'.

CASE 7.10 Walmart's English experiment

It is hard to imagine that the corner of a car park on the outskirts of Leeds could help determine the future of Walmart, the world's biggest retailer. But that is just what is happening at the Pudsey outpost of Asda, Walmart's UK arm. It is the first Asda supermarket to allow customers to pick up their shopping from temperature controlled lockers. After submitting their order online, shoppers collect their goods from the bright-turquoise storage units, which are unlocked when they enter their order number or scan a 'QR' code sent out after payment. Inside the lockers, their goods are divided into three zones; chilled on top, frozen on the bottom and ambient in the middle.

Walmart is watching the Pudsey 'click and collect' experiment to see whether it could be a useful innovation for its vast grocery operations in the US, which are today overwhelmingly reliant on customers driving out to stores and picking goods off the shelves themselves. 'Click and collect is an interesting idea,' says Neil Ashe, who runs Walmart's global e-commerce centre. While acknowledging that the US and UK are very different markets, he thinks it could

have an appeal for Walmart domestically as it experiments with a move into online grocery ordering. It is already trialling lockers for non-food items at several Walmart stores outside Washington DC. 'If [click and collect] turns out to be popular with customers, it could definitely make a big difference.'

Asda's importance to Walmart in this regard reflects the fact that the UK is much more advanced than the US in shifting grocery shopping on to the internet. In the UK, about 4 per cent of grocery sales are through the web, compared with less than 1 per cent in the US. Click and collect is also forecast to grow much faster than home delivery in the UK, according to strategy consultants OC&C. It predicts a 60 per cent compound annual growth rate for non-food click and collect volumes between 2012 and 2017, against 5 per cent for home delivery. 'Click and collect is every retailer's biggest growth opportunity,' says Michael Jary, a partner at OC&C.

The shift towards click and collect can be partly explained by shopper impatience. As online

➡

273

shopping has gathered pace, so customers have become more demanding. Waiting in for an order is no longer acceptable. 'One of the great myths about home delivery is that it is convenient. It is only convenient if you happen to be at home,' said Philip Clarke, former chief executive of Tesco. But there is another reason why retailers are embracing click and collect. Since the earliest days of online shopping, the last mile of fulfilling the delivery has been challenging – particularly for food.

In a traditional supermarket, the customer does much of the work – driving to the store, picking goods off shelves, then driving them home again. When an order is placed electronically, all this must be done by the supermarket. And cut-throat competition means they struggle to recoup the cost of delivery. Grocer click and collect is usually free to the customers, and the fulfilment costs (though still there) are much lower. Staff must still physically pick the products from the shelves, and put them in the car or the locker, but the last mile costs are minimised.

Asda has also been rolling out a drive-through click and collect system. In York, less than 30 miles away from Pudsey, customers drive up to a collection point and scan their QR codes. Immediately, the order flashes up on a screen inside. Already picked from the shelves, it is assembled from its ambient, frozen and chiller constituents, and an Asda employee delivers it to the car. The aim is for the whole process to take less than five minutes. Tiny sensors under the floor detect the car and start the clock ticking. 'Most customers don't get out of the car, and a colleague puts [the order] in the boot,' says Mr Ibbotson.

Asda already has 110 drive-through collection points, where customers can also pick up non-food items. This is expected to increase to half of its 600-strong estate by the end of the year, with grocer click and collect points in the remainder of its stores. Mr Ibbotson says Asda plans to have 1,000 remote click and collect locations 'where people live and work', by 2018. Drive-throughs are already being installed in petrol stations.

Lockers could go in offices, high streets, schools, universities, petrol and train stations, even airports. Asda is trialling pickups from London Underground stations, although at the moment this is served by a van outside the station. At Pudsey, the busiest time is between 2pm and 4pm, as parents pop in around the time of the school run.

Rival Tesco is also increasingly active in click and collect, creating pick-up 'pods' in car parks and drive-throughs'. One valuable benefit is that customers often buy extra items when they pick up their orders. Asda estimates that a third of the customers using its drive-through service and lockers come into the store. Another advantage is that it could help retailers reach customers where the economics of home delivery do not make sense. Drive-through grocery points began in France, where journeys can be very long and populations sparse outside urban areas. Coles, the Australian supermarket chain, has installed lockers with three temperature zones at petrol stations and supermarkets.

Theoretically, using drive-throughs or lockers could help Walmart crack grocery home-shopping in the US. It is trialling drive-throughs at 29 of its US superstores in only its second foray into online food in its home market. In the meantime, Walmart and Asda are collaborating closely. Insiders joke that Asda staff used to be constantly flying to Walmart's HQ in Bentonville, Arkansas. Now the demand is for flights to and from San Francisco, to visit Mr Ashe's global e-commerce team in Silicon Valley. But Mr Ibbotson points out that Asda also has an eye on developments outside the UK. Indeed, inspiration for the drive-throughs came from a visit to France. 'We scan the world, and Walmart operations in other countries scan our world,' he says.

The growth of click and collect is a challenge for retailers with no physical stores but some online 'pure plays' are taking steps to overcome their lack of a shop front. Amazon has lockers on both sides of the Atlantic, with approaching 300 locations in the UK.

Meanwhile, eBay recently teamed up with Argos, the British retailer. Click and collect now accounts for almost a third of Argos's sales. British consumers love click and collect.' John

Case 7.10 (*continued*)

Donahoe, eBay chief executive, said shortly after announcing the trial, whereby orders from more than 150 eBay sellers could be picked up from 150 Argos stores. Other internet-only retailers, such as Amazon and online fashion boutique Asos, use CollectPlus, which delivers to more than 5,000 local convenience stores, newsagents and petrol stations across the UK. But not all online retailers are embracing click and collect. Tim Steiner, chief executive of Ocado, the lossmaking online grocer, has been scathing about the channel. 'No Ocado customer has ever asked me if they could pick up their grocer order,' he told an industry conference last autumn.

Question

Why is Walmart paying particular attention to the 'click and collect' route to market?

Transport

Transport issues are implicit in the choice of distributional channels and in other locational decisions for the multinational organisation. In traditional heavy industries the location chosen will often depend on whether the operation is 'bulk forming' or 'bulk reducing'. Bulk-forming operations, such as in furniture manufacture, need to be close to their markets in order to cut transport costs. However, for bulk-reducing operations, such as in the steel industry, the main need is to be close to the heavy raw materials used as inputs. Modern industries increasingly use lighter raw materials so that they, together with the service industries, tend to be more 'footloose'.

For any firm, access to rail, road, sea and air links is important, both for the inward movement of inputs and the outward movement of outputs (goods and services). New electronic technologies are reducing the importance of distance in some product areas such as books, CDs and software, but in many other areas of economic activity transport costs still increase with distance.

Of course, the transport mode chosen will depend not only on cost but on the relative importance for that product or service of: speed of delivery, dependability of delivery, quality deterioration issues, transport costs, route flexibility. As shown in Table 7.6, Slack *et al.* (2013) suggest the ranking of the different modes of transport as regards these factors.

We noted in Chapter 2 that transport costs can be a factor in influencing MNE decisions as to whether to export or to produce abroad. However, transport issues can also influence other organisational and strategic decisions in international business, as indicated in Box 7.5.

Table 7.6 **The relative performance of each mode of transport**

Operation's performance objective	Mode of transport				
	Road	Rail	Air	Water	Pipeline
Delivery speed	2	3	1	5	4
Delivery dependability	2	3	4	5	1
Quality	2	3	4	5	1
Cost	3	4	5	2	1
Route flexibility	1	2	3	4	5

Source: Slack *et al.* (2013)

BOX 7.5 Economies of scope and the transport sector

Economies of scope refer to cost benefits from changing the mix of production, as, for instance, when a number of related commodities or services are produced using common processing facilities. The potential for such economies of scope can be found in the transport industry. For example, the deregulation of the aircraft industry in the USA after 1978 resulted in significant changes in the structure of carrier operations. Instead of a large number of individual routes between various cities, the carriers redesigned the route system into a hub and spoke system reminiscent of a bicycle wheel. Travel was routed from, say, a city positioned at the end of one 'spoke' through a 'hub' or central airport, then out again to another city at the end of another spoke.

For example, in Figure 7.16(a) we have five point-to-point direct links from cities A to B, C to D, E to F, G to H and I to J respectively. If these are replaced by ten services from each of the cities to a hub airport, as in Figure 7.16(b), the number of city pairs that can be served

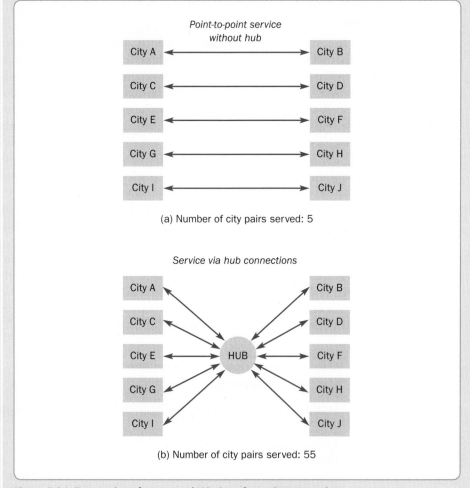

(a) Number of city pairs served: 5

(b) Number of city pairs served: 55

Figure 7.16 Economies of scope and US aircraft routing operations

---

BOX 7.5 (*continued*)

rises sharply from five to 55. The total number of city pairs that can be served is given by the formula $n(n + 1)/2$, where n is the number of spokes (cities served) emanating from the hub airport. It follows that if the number of spokes from the hub rises to 50, then the number of city pairs that can be linked rises to 1,275. This system has advantages, because all the passengers destined for a city at the end of one spoke will be collected at the hub airport from all the other cities at the end of the other spokes. This means that there will be many more passengers per flight, allowing definite economies of density: i.e. larger aircraft can be used, with associated savings in costs. On the marketing side, the hub system also facilitates more departures to a larger number of cities, making the marketing of a more integrated service network a more attractive proposition.

In this way economies of scope are realised. By serving a large number of city-pair markets through the hub, a carrier also provides many different products or combinations of products not previously available. These lead on to further economies as, for instance, airlines are now able to meet travel demands that have different characteristics from those previously met. In this case business and vacation travel can use a single network of flights instead of a variety of interconnecting networks of flights. The hub might permit still further 'common carriage' and cost reductions: for example, business-oriented routes might become still more cost-effective now that there is a greater chance (with a larger number of spokes) that vacation visitors might also wish to use these business-oriented routes.

Of course, the siting and location of depots/warehouses can provide similar benefits in terms of economies of scope.

Centralisation versus decentralisation

There has been much debate over the years of the logistical benefits and costs of centralised versus decentralised distributive systems. Certainly the predominant trend in logistics has been towards the centralisation of inventory holding in both national and international business, taking advantage of the 'square root law' previously discussed (see p. 269). We saw that moving from a decentralised system of 17 warehouses to a completely centralised system of one warehouse would cut the required amount of safety stock by one-quarter. It has generally been perceived that the resulting savings in stock-holding costs outweigh any increases in transport and related costs resulting from a geographically extended distribution system.

There has been a similar tendency towards centralisation in productive systems as MNEs operate on an increasingly global scale and seek to achieve scale economies wherever possible, even if some parts of other overall productive processes are geographically located in different international countries. This again places greater strain on the logistical system in terms of delivering rapidly and efficiently to the final consumer.

Chapter 8

International human resource management

By the end of this chapter you should be able to:

- explain why the human resource management (HRM) function is so important for managing people effectively;
- outline the key issues involved in international aspects of HRM;
- describe the methods used and the particular problems faced by MNEs in managing human resources;
- evaluate some strategic issues in international human resource management (IHRM).

Introduction

In order to create and distribute products (goods or services) every organisation needs people. Over time and in different places the ways in which people are being managed are constantly changing, though a general consensus has emerged that people are an organisation's greatest asset. This has led to an increasing interest in the way in which people are managed and how they are rewarded. After briefly reviewing the human resource management (HRM) function the emphasis shifts to defining the *international* context of that function and the problems and opportunities associated with it. Linkages are drawn with the international cultural dimensions explored in Chapter 5, wherever appropriate.

Human resource management function

Human resource management (HRM) is a concept that first emerged in the 1980s and concerns those aspects of management that deal with the human side of organisations. Armstrong (1999) defines HRM as: 'a strategic and coherent approach to the management of an organisation's most valued assets – the people working there who individually and collectively contribute to the achievement of its goals'.

A broader definition is given by Boxall and Purcell (2008: 28):

Human resource management includes the firm's work systems and its employment practices. It embraces both individual and collective aspects of people management. It is not restricted to any one style or ideology. It engages the energies of both line and specialist managers (where the latter exists) and typically entails a range of messages for a variety of workforce groups.

Managing human resources is a central function within an organisation and its effective implementation involves combining the skills and knowledge of the human resource department with the expertise of line managers in other departments. The human resource function is a wide-ranging subject that covers, among other things: management/worker communications; elements of work psychology; employee relations, training and motivation; organisation of the physical and social conditions of work; and personnel management. In contrast with 'personnel management' – which deals purely with the practical aspects of recruitment, staff appraisal, training, job evaluation, etc. – HRM has a strategic dimension and involves the total deployment of all the human resources available to the firm, including the integration of personnel and other HRM considerations into the firm's overall corporate planning and strategy formulation procedures. It is proactive, seeking to continuously discover new ways of utilising the labour force in a more productive manner, thus giving the business a competitive edge.

For the purposes of this chapter, we adopt Brewster's and Hegewisch's model of HRM (Figure 8.1) which shows that the corporate strategies, HRM strategies and HRM practices are located within both an *internal environment* (which includes organisational features such as size, structure and corporate culture) and an *external environment* (which includes national culture, power systems, legislation, education and employee representation). The model shows how the human resource strategies and practices interact with, and are part of, the broader environment in which the company operates. The model may also serve as a reminder to practitioners that their human resource strategies must reflect the organisational and national cultures in which they are operating.

Human resource management has grown in importance over the past decades largely in response to the impacts of increasing internationalisation in fragmenting product and labour markets and creating the need for ever more strategic ways of managing people competitively. In the UK, prior to the 1980s, managing the workforce was largely the responsibility of the personnel department and focused on trade unions, the collective bargaining process and the handling of grievances and disputes. As a concept, HRM has arguably been imported into Europe from the United States. Its major differences from the former personnel departments being that it is more strategic, that management speaks more directly to employees rather than through the unions, and that it is underpinned by more scientific methods of measuring people's performance. Nevertheless, although more strategic in focus, HRM issues still involve functions and aspects such as recruitment, training, pay, employee relations and workforce flexibility.

In an attempt to investigate HRM issues in a wider environmental context, including that of internationalisation, a model of human resource management was developed by Beer *et al.* (1984) at Harvard University. According to this Harvard model, HRM strategies should develop from an in-depth analysis of (i) the demands of the various stakeholders in a business (e.g. shareholders, employees, the government, etc.) and (ii) a number of situational factors (e.g. the state of the labour market, the skills and motivation of the workforce, management styles, etc.). According to the Harvard researchers, both

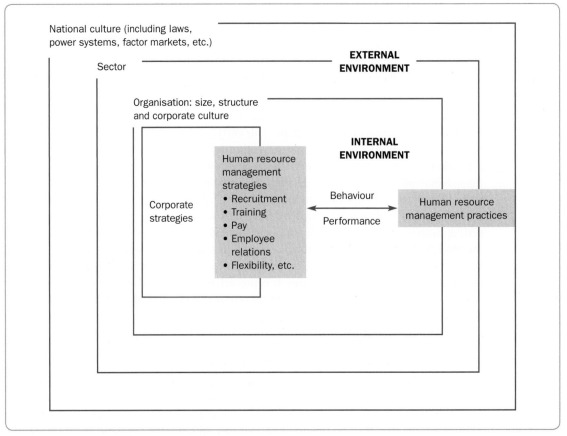

Figure 8.1 A model for investigating human resource strategies

Source: Adapted from Brewster and Hegewisch (1994).

stakeholder expectations and situational factors need to be considered when formulating human resource strategies and the effectiveness of the outcomes should be evaluated under four headings: commitment (i.e. employees' loyalty), competence (i.e. employees' skills), congruence (i.e. shared vision of workers and management) and cost efficiencies (i.e. operational efficiency). The Harvard model suggests that human resource policies should be directed towards raising attainment levels for each of these four categories; for example, competence could be increased through the provision of extra training, adjustments to recruitment policy, different incentivisation schemes, and so on.

Hendry and Pettigrew (1990) offer an adaptation of the Harvard model (Figure 8.2) that attempts to integrate HRM issues with a still broader range of external societal influences (such as socio-economic, technical, political, legal and competitive issues) which may vary considerably in different international situations. These 'outer context' issues will influence HRM strategies and practices, as will a variety of 'inner context' and business strategic issues.

The importance of these external societal influences for HRM policy formation is usefully illustrated by Case 8.1, which examines the response of McDonald's to changing demographics in Europe.

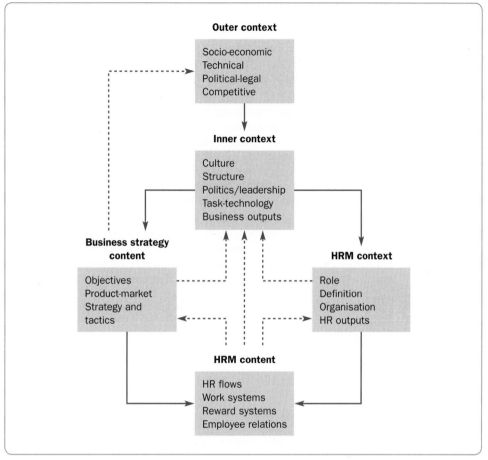

Figure 8.2 Model of strategic change and human resource management

Source: Human Resource Management: An Agenda for the 1990s, *International Journal of Human Resource Management*, vol. 1, no. 1 (Hendry, J. and Pettigrew, A. 1990), reprinted by permission of the publisher (Taylor & Francis Group, www. informaworld.com).

CASE 8.1 Hire the young and old McDonald's

McDonald's has warned that Europe faces a future of stunted growth unless employers do more to bring marginalised groups such as young people and older workers into the labour force. David Fairhust, chief people officer at McDonald's Europe, said the fast-food chain, which employs 425,000 people in 38 European markets, was already feeling the effects of what he called the 'workforce cliff'. 'The workforce is shrinking at both ends of the spectrum,' he told the *Financial Times*. 'There aren't enough young people coming into the labour markets and too many older people are leaving it.'

Mr Fairhust said the shortage of workers would soon have an impact on economic growth, despite the EU's current unemployment rate of 10.8 per cent of the workforce and a young jobless rate above 23 per cent. A report by the European Commission said the EU's average output growth of 2.25 per cent a year was made up of 1 per cent

---

Case 8.1 (*continued*)

employment growth and productivity gains a little above 1 per cent. But it said the 1 per cent employment growth could be sustained no longer than 2019. After 2021, the European workforce is set to shrink by about 6.5 per cent a year for the foreseeable future.

Mr Fairhurst said the 'workforce cliff' would arrive even earlier in some countries, such as 2015 in the Netherlands and 2016 in Germany, whereas in the UK workforce growth would not turn negative until 2023. But he added: 'If employers can enable the participation of more of the working age population, the edge of the workforce cliff can be pushed back by as much as a decade.' He said employers needed to offer more work placements, mentoring site visits and talks in schools and colleges to replace the decline of traditional entry-level jobs for young people in many industries.

Three-quarters of McDonald's staff are under 30, but it has stepped up recruitment of older workers. In the UK, nearly 60 per cent of the workforce aged 55–64 are now in employment, but across the EU it is less than half. Research for McDonald's by Lancaster University Business School found that customer satisfaction levels were on average 20 per cent higher in restaurants that employed staff aged over 60.

 Source: Hire the young and old to avoid 'workforce cliff', *Financial Times*, 31/03/2014, p. 19 (Groom, B.), © The Financial Times Limited 2014. All Rights Reserved.

Questions

1 What are the societal factors behind McDonald's changing its recruitment policy in the ways suggested?

2 What might be the advantages and disadvantages to McDonald's from such a change in recruitment practices?

Before turning to the more obviously international aspects of HRM, it will be useful to review the theoretical underpinnings as regards the motivational factors involved in managing people effectively, whatever the location. Box 8.1 provides an overview of the relevant motivational theory.

BOX 8.1 Motivation theory and HRM

The human relations approach to management relied heavily on the work of Elton Mayo, who undertook work on the link between productivity and working conditions. He found that productivity rose even when working conditions deteriorated. Mayo conducted a whole series of experiments at the Hawthorne Plant of General Electric between 1927 and 1932. His conclusions were as follows.

- *Work pacing*. The pace at which people produce is one set informally by the work group.

- *Recognition*. Acknowledgement of an employee's contribution by those in authority tends to increase output, as do other forms of social approval.

- *Social interaction*. The opportunities provided by the working situation for social interaction between fellow workers, especially if they could

Box 8.1 (*continued*)

select for interaction those with whom they were compatible, enhanced job satisfaction and sometimes influenced output.

- *The Hawthorne effect*. Regardless of what changes were made to the way the employees were treated, productivity went up as they seemed to enjoy the novelty of the situation and the extra attention – the so-called 'Hawthorne effect'.

- *Grievances*. Employees responded well to having someone to whom to let off steam by talking through problems they were having.

- *Conforming*. The pressure from workmates in the group was far more influential on behaviour than any incentive from management.

The importance of this work was to show the effect of work groups and social context on behaviour. It also helped to generate new ideas about the nature of supervision to include better communication and better management of people. It was perhaps most important in recognising the critical nature of informal processes at work as well as the rational, scientific procedures that management prescribes, the latter being the conclusions from earlier work by F.W. Taylor.

Maslow and 'hierarchy of needs'

Maslow argued that workers have a 'hierarchy of needs' (Figure 8.3). The first three needs, physiological, safety and social needs, are identified as *lower-order* needs and are satisfied from the *context* within which the job is undertaken. Self-esteem and self-actualisation are identified as *higher-order* needs and are met through the *content* of the job.

Maslow went further. He argued that at any one time one need is dominant and acts as a motivator. However, once that need is satisfied it will no longer motivate, but be replaced by the next higher-level need.

The implications of this theory for managers include their having to try to satisfy their workers'

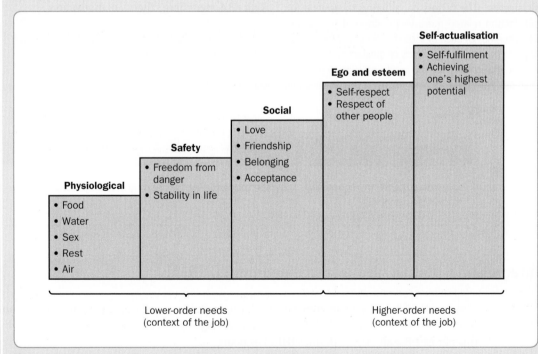

Figure 8.3 Maslow's 'hierarchy of needs'

Source: *Applied Economics*, 12th ed., Financial Times Prentice Hall (Griffiths, A. and Wall, S. (eds), 2012), © Pearson Education Limited 2012.

Box 8.1 (*continued*)

needs both in terms of the organisational context in which work takes place and what the worker is required to do. Some examples of how this might be achieved include:

- *physiological* – pay, rest periods, holidays;
- *safety* – health and safety measures, employment security, pensions;
- *social* – formal and informal groups, social events, sports clubs;
- *self-esteem* – power, titles, status symbols, promotion.

Herzberg and the 'two factor theory'

Herzberg's 'two factor theory' was based on a survey of what made managers feel good or bad about their job. He discovered that the factors which created dissatisfaction about the job related to the context within which the job was done. He termed these factors 'hygiene factors', as indicated in Figure 8.4.

However, ensuring that these factors were met while helping avoid dissatisfaction did not result in positive satisfaction. The factors contributing to positive job satisfaction related more to the content of the job. The presence of each of these factors (motivators) was capable of causing high levels of satisfaction.

The implications for the practising human resource manager were twofold. First, to ensure that the hygiene factors are met adequately to avoid dissatisfaction, but not to expect these to motivate employees. Second, to ensure that the motivators are met to create positive job satisfaction.

Hygiene factors (avoid dissatisfaction)

Company policy
Supervision
Working conditions
Salary
Relationship with peers
Personal life
Relationship with subordinates
Status
Security

Motivators (create satisfaction)

Achievement
Recognition
Work itself
Responsibility
Advancement
Growth

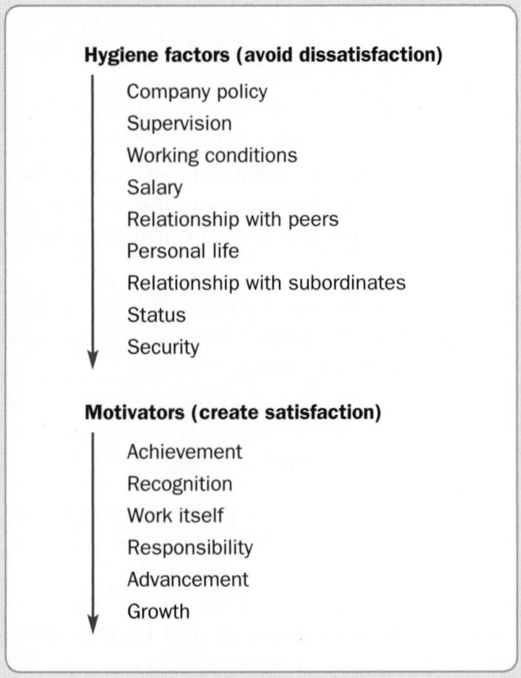

Figure 8.4 **Hertzberg's theory of motivation**

Pause for thought 8.1

Can you suggest any other ways in which motivational theory might be of practical use to the HRM specialist?

International human resource management (IHRM)

The growth of business at an international level has led to an increase in the number of publications about international human resource management. However, what do we mean by this phrase? Boxall (1992) defines IHRM as being:

> concerned with the human resource problems of multinational firms in foreign subsidiaries (such as expatriate management) or more broadly, with the unfolding HRM issues that are associated with the various stages of the internationalisation process.

Others, such as Mark Mendenhall (2000), have sought to be more specific by outlining a number of criteria relevant to a definition of IHRM.

1 IHRM is concerned with HRM issues that cross national boundaries or are conducted in locations other than the home country headquarters of the organisations within the study.

2 IHRM is concerned with the relationships between the HRM activities of organisations and the foreign environments in which the organisations operate.

3 IHRM includes comparative HRM studies; for example, how companies in Japan, Thailand, Austria and Switzerland plan for increased employee commitment, upgrading of employee skills and so on.

4 IHRM does *not* include studies that are focused on issues outside the traditional activities inherent in the HRM function. In other words, topics such as leadership style, unless specifically linked to an HRM function (e.g. developing a selection programme to measure and select global leaders) do not qualify to be in the domain of IHRM. Such studies would arguably lie within the domain of *organisational behaviour.*

5 IHRM does *not* include studies of HRM activities in single countries. A study of personnel selection practices in Saudi Arabia, whether undertaken by an English, German or Canadian researcher, is still a study about domestic HRM in Saudi Arabia. Though such studies may have interest for those who work in international HRM issues, they are essentially examples of domestic HRM research.

A recurrent theme throughout this chapter will be the importance of MNEs operating outside their home base to adapt their IHRM policies to the national cultural settings in which their subsidiaries are operating. This brings directly into focus the earlier national cultural analyses of Hofstede, Trompenaar and others in Chapter 5. The following case usefully indicates these cultural linkages with IHRM policies, by emphasising differences in 'uncertainty avoidance' among employees of an Indian-based clinical research company with major subsidiaries in Germany and the US.

CASE 8.2 Uncertainty avoidance and IHRM policies

High levels of uncertainty avoidance are expressed and reinforced by beliefs and practices that increase predictability of outcomes and therefore provide a sense of safety. These may include tightly articulated agendas, processes and procedures, strict and detailed rules and laws controlled by recognised authorities and unambiguous belief in the absolute truth-value of existing knowledge at the philosophical, scientific or religious level. They will also strive towards the 'correct' answer, solution or decision.

In more explicitly IHRM contexts, the level of uncertainty avoidance has equally important ramifications.

High UA organisations (e.g. German subsidiaries), are more likely to focus on operational excellence and incremental process improvement leading to reliable, consistent and replicable results. Employees will value stable employment and low job mobility. Roles and responsibilities will be clearly and unambiguously defined. Fear of failure, avoidance and mitigating of perceived risks, and conforming to relatively narrow cultural norms are pervasive motivators of behaviour and highly valued attributes. Loyalty, seniority and 'fitting in' will be the main criteria for promotion. Surprises will be avoided or kept to a minimum through the practice of informal

Case 8.2 (continued)

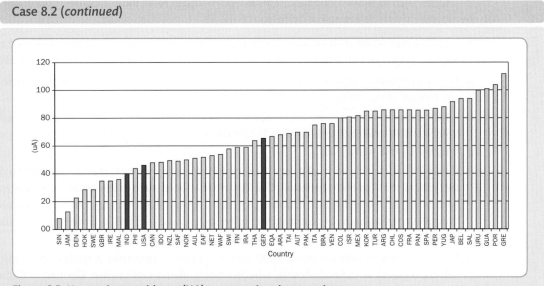

Figure 8.5 Uncertainty avoidance (UA): cross-national comparisons

Source: http://globallearningpractices.wikispaces.com/Hofstede%27s+Index+Comparisons

meetings before the formal meetings. Precise guidelines and instructions will be expected, as much as detailed plans and agendas.

Low UA organisations (e.g. Indian or US subsidiaries) are more likely to lead through innovation or embrace transformational change in response to changing conditions. They are more tolerant of novel situations and open to a diversity of people, thoughts and ideas. Deviations from established procedure tend not just to be tolerated, but are even encouraged and valued. Conflict and calculated risk taking are considered desirable. Such organisations will be comfortable learning from mistakes and tolerant of conflict and dissent. Improvisation and a broad and adaptable outlining of goals, roles and responsibilities will be the norm.

Questions

1 Can you suggest some specific HRM policies *more likely* to be acceptable in the German organisation than in the Indian or US organisations?

2 Can you suggest some specific HRM policies *less likely* to be acceptable in the German organisation than in the Indian or US organisations?

Source: Sastry (2014).

IHRM and organisational structure

The type of international organisational structure adopted by the MNE will provide the context for many of the IHRM issues faced by the company. There are at least five widely recognised types of international organisational structures available to MNEs. There is no 'standard model' in this respect. A multinational enterprise may change from one type to another at different stages of the internationalisation process or as senior management perceives that emerging corporate needs are better served by one particular type.

The five readily identified 'types' of organisational structure include:

1 international division structure;
2 international geographic/regional structure;
3 international product structure;
4 international functional structure;
5 matrix or mixed structure.

Figure 8.6 outlines the first four of these types.

1 *The international division structure* is often used in the early stage of internationalisation with an 'international division' merely added to the existing divisional structures. As the activity within the international division grows (e.g. sales volume/value, number of overseas markets, etc.) then this division may itself need to be reorganised according to function, product or geographic area.

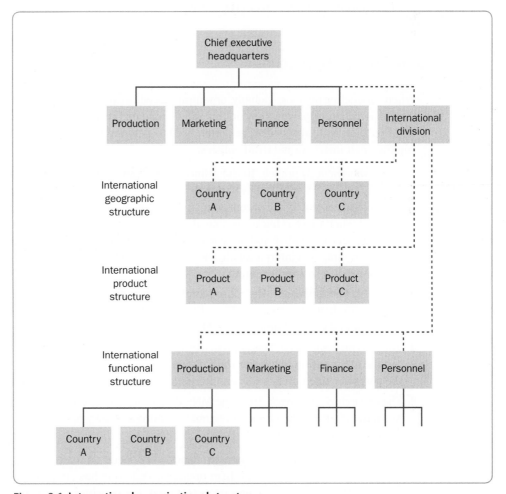

Figure 8.6 **International organisational structures**

2 *The international geographic/regional structure* involves separating out the different geographic/regional areas in which the MNE operates. Each geographic area may be given its own division with its own functional departments; MNEs with a wide variety of products in their portfolio sold across many geographic areas often adopt this organisational structure.

3 *The international product structure* is where an MNE's divisions are established on the basis of related product lines rather than geographic area. Each product division is responsible for all functions relating to those items in that particular product portfolio – e.g. production, marking, finance and personnel relating to chocolate products for an MNE with confectionery interests. This structure is often adopted by MNEs with a variety of unrelated product lines (e.g. conglomerate MNEs).

4 *The international functional structure* gives each functional department of the MNE (production, marketing, finance, etc.) responsibility for the international operations of that function.

Matrix (or mixed) structures bring together the functional, geographic and product structures and combine them in an attempt to meet the needs of a *specific activity or project*. Once that activity or project is completed, the 'team' is often disbanded and return to their original position within the divisional or other structures of the MNE.

International HRM approaches

When conducting business globally, organisations will also need to integrate HRM into their international strategy. How they do this will depend on the approach they adopt as regards HRM policies. Four approaches are often used to describe the ways in which MNEs might conduct their international HRM policies.

1 *The ethnocentric approach.* In the ethnocentric approach, all key positions in the host country subsidiary are filled by nationals of the parent company. This approach offers the most direct control by the parent company over the host country subsidiary, and is often adopted when there is felt to be a need to maintain good communications between the headquarters of the MNE and the subsidiary. This ethnocentric approach is often followed in the early stages of internationalisation when the MNE is seeking to establish a new business or product in another country.

2 *The polycentric approach.* Here, host country nationals are recruited to manage the subsidiaries in their own country. This allows the MNE to take a lower profile in sensitive economic and political situations and helps to avoid intercultural management problems.

3 *The geocentric approach.* This approach utilises the best people for all the key jobs throughout the organisation, whatever their nationality or whatever the geographic location of the post to be filled. In this way an international executive team can be developed.

4 *The regiocentric approach.* Here the MNE divides its operations into geographic regions and moves staff within particular regions, e.g. Europe, America, Asia, rather than between regions.

Choices between these different approaches will depend on the culture, philosophy and the local conditions in which the firm operates. Vodafone has adopted the ethnocentric approach with its UK HR team and processes used as a benchmark in its ethnocentric and global model for people management. The model will see the firm's local HR teams across 25 countries adopting a standardised structure with four key areas: HR services, including administrative and process support; business partnering; centres of expertise; and 'other functions', such as health and safety. Adidas, however, uses a mainly regiocentric approach, with HRM staff familiar with the cultural context of the region of operation responsible for leading the HRM functions of the subsidiaries located within the international region and country in question. Some international companies may adopt an ethnocentric approach in some countries and a polycentric approach in others. However, a key element in this choice will involve the question as to how an international firm can manage a dispersed and diverse workforce responsively and effectively, retaining a measure of overall cohesion while being sensitive to local conditions.

Some firms have sought to resolve this dilemma by maintaining an international group of HRM managers with an ethnocentric orientation at the centre, who can be moved in and out of the worldwide operations, yet at the same time devolving HRM responsibility down the line so that the firm can remain responsive to local developments. This approach is followed by BMW, as indicated in its 2007 annual report:

> [BMW] guidelines are defined and steered centrally and lived and implemented by the human resources departments and executives across the globe . . . once a management board is set up in a foreign subsidiary, the local HRM takes responsibility for management of middle management and operative levels. This includes aspects such as recruitment, training and employee relations. The key is that the [central] IHR management provides guidance and supervises the application of BMW's HR policies. Cultural issues and differences may be a challenge, and IHRM should provide means to analyse these and adjust the local HR approach accordingly.

Finding the right balance between integration and decentralisation for IHRM is complex, and the mix will depend on the following factors.

- *Degree and type of internationalisation.* We have seen (Chapter 2) that there is a range of options for international firms as to how they may expand, from exporting through to using wholly owned subsidiaries. In general an integrated and more ethnocentric approach to HRM is often adopted for the wholly owned subsidiary, with the MNE retaining centralised control over the way in which its employees are managed.

- *Type of industry and markets served.* Porter (1986) distinguishes the multi-domestic industry, in which competition within each country is largely internal (retailing, distribution and insurance), from the global industry in which competition is worldwide (electronic equipment, branded food, defence products). Porter suggests that strategies for the global industry are more likely to involve the firm in integrating its activities worldwide, especially where strong brand images are involved. For the global industry, therefore, IHRM is more likely to be ethnocentric while for the multi-domestic industry IHRM is more likely to be polycentric and to resemble that typically used in the particular country in which the subsidiary operates.

- *Characteristics of staff.* The types of employees may well influence the degree to which the IHRM function is decentralised. For example, if the employees of a subsidiary consist of highly skilled, experienced and fully committed staff, the IHRM function may be decentralised. However, where the employees mainly consist of unskilled and temporary staff (perhaps where the MNE has bought into a cheap labour market) then headquarters will usually wish to exercise a greater degree of control over the corporate foreign subsidiary.

● *Cultural preferences*. The degree of integration or decentralisation will also depend on the cultural preferences towards either of these approaches to management in both the organisation and in the country in which the subsidiary operates. The latter reflects Hofstede's idea of national 'cultural distance' (see Chapter 5), and is considered further in the context of Greece in Box 8.2.

BOX 8.2 Greek national culture and decentralisation of the IHRM function

While the global nature of multinational activity may call for increased consistency, the variety of cultural environments in which the MNE operates may call for differentiation. Workplace values and behaviours are widely regarded as being influenced by national as well as corporate cultural characteristics. As Laurent (1986) claims, 'if we accept the view that human resource management (HRM) approaches are cultural artefacts reflecting the basic assumptions and values of the national culture in which organisations are embedded, international HRM becomes one of the most challenging corporate tasks in multinational organisations.'

Greece is clustered in the 'Mediterranean culture' sector of managerial models; native managers are assumed to be less individualistic and more comfortable with highly bureaucratic organisational structures in order to achieve their objectives. In Hofstede's terms, Greece is characterised by large power distance and strong uncertainty avoidance (see Figure 5.1, p. 162). Since the early 1960s, Greece has been the host country for many foreign firms, initially in manufacturing and more recently in services.

It is broadly accepted that management practices which reinforce national cultural values are more likely to yield better outcomes in terms of performance, with a mismatch between work unit management practices and national culture likely to reduce performance. The suggestion here is that multinationals which have established their affiliates in Greece will be more efficient if their management practices are better adapted to the national culture of Greece. Theory suggests that this adaptation will be better achieved where the national culture of the home country of the MNE is close to that of Greece. In other words, MNEs from collectivist, large power distance and strong uncertainty avoidance countries will be at a small cultural distance from Greece and will better integrate into the organisational culture of the Greek affiliate. The following hypothesis is therefore suggested by Kessapidou and Varsakelis (2000).

Hypothesis: MNEs from home countries at a large cultural distance from Greece will prefer to employ local managers and permit more decentralised IHRM practices.

This hypothesis would then predict that MNEs from home countries with national cultural characteristics of the individualist, small power distance and weak uncertainty avoidance variety (i.e. the opposites to Greece) will prefer to employ local managers and permit more decentralised IHRM practices.

In their analysis of the operations of 485 foreign affiliates in Greece over the years 1994–96, Kessapidou and Varsakelis found considerable evidence to support this hypothesis. MNEs from home countries at a large cultural distance from Greece (e.g. UK, the Netherlands and USA, with cultural distance factors of 4.27, 4.03 and 3.47 respectively) were much more likely to employ local managers and adopt a decentralised approach to IHRM than countries at a small cultural distance from Greece (e.g. Italy, France and Spain, with cultural distance factors of 1.46, 0.99 and 0.58 respectively).

Source: Adapted from Kessapidou and Varsakelis (2000).

> **Pause for thought 8.2**
>
> Look back to Table 5.3 in Chapter 5. Which of these four approaches to IHRM might you expect an MNE which has Great Britain as its headquarters to adopt as regards an overseas affiliate in (a) Japan, (b) Canada?

Case 8.3 indicates why a decentralised approach to IHRM may be appropriate for achieving employee-related outcomes in different countries. The requirement for retaining employee loyalty and increasing employee productivity in China may require a country-sensitive approach to IHRM.

CASE 8.3 China factory chiefs struggle to maintain worker loyalty

As China prepared to usher in the Year of the Horse, *Crystal Group*, a garment manufacturer that produces clothes for retailers such as Abercrombie & Fitch and Mothercare, added a new task to its holiday 'to do' list. Dennis Wong, executive director at Crystal, says it bought 9,000 return train tickets for migrant workers to Dongguan who wanted to return home for the lunar New Year – the biggest holiday in the Chinese calendar – and also helped them buy snacks for the often long trip from Guangdong province to their towns and villages. While workers receive a free trip, more importantly they no longer have to queue – or go online as is increasingly common – to buy tickets. Crystal also gains as workers are less likely to leave Guangdong earlier to secure a train or bus seat for the biggest annual migration on earth. 'This whole programme is to attract them to stay as long as they can,' says Mr Wong, explaining that the company also boosts the amount it pays in efficiency bonuses by up to 8 per cent from November until the New Year period.

Many factories across the Pearl River Delta, the manufacturing workshop of the world in Guangdong, are trying to find ways to keep workers. This has become more important as demographic changes – particularly the one-child policy and a government push to create jobs inland – have made staffing harder. Melissa Taul at *Eagle*, an electronics manufacturer in Dongguan, says workers get a bonus of Rmb 100–Rmb 1,000 for returning on time after New Year. She says this has helped keep retention rates high – about 80 to 90 per cent – in contrast to some factories that can lose more than 30 per cent of their workforce over the holiday.

In another part of Dongguan, *TAL*, an apparel company that supplies Brooks Brothers and other retailers, tried to retain staff with a lucky draw. Any worker who stayed between November 15 and January 24 was eligible to win one of eight prizes of Rmb 8,888 ($1,500), an auspicious number in Chinese as it suggests financial success.

Crystal will also hold a draw for Rmb 9,999, another lucky number that signals longevity, in February to entice more workers to return. Mr Wong says that over the past five years, 98 per cent of workers have returned on the first day after the holiday. But he stresses that such measures are part of a year-along push. 'It is really like a "package". More important is how you treat the workers during the year and not just Chinese new year,' says Mr Wong, adding that the company has introduced initiatives to 'make them feel like it [Dongguan] is their second home', including organising parties and day trips. That echoes with Alan Cuddihy, Head of Sustainability at *PCH*, the supply chain company in Shenzhen that works with clients such as Apple, which has built a library with free Wi-Fi, organises outings such as beach barbecues and issued discount cards at local businesses. It has also set up a worker hotline. Mr Cuddihy says efforts have helped cut average monthly turnover from 31 per cent in 2012 to

Case 8.3 (continued)

less than 10 per cent. 'Workers from different cities around China inevitably feel homesick, lonely and often change jobs when you don't get to know anyone in the immediate area,' says Mr Cuddihy. 'They are looking for more social work environments and communities . . . this is one of the main reasons for frequent job changes.'

But the world's factories cannot simply rely on outings, returning bonuses and lucky draws. What workers want is better pay and benefits, says Geoff Crothall of *China Labour Bulletin*.

While wages in Guangdong have posted double-digit rises in recent years, the minimum monthly wage in Shenzhen, the highest in China, is still only $300. Gerhard Flatz, general manager at KTC, which makes skiwear in Guangdong, adds that measures such as returning bonuses are not sustainable solutions for retention issues. 'These kinds of tools are very similar to painkillers,' says Mr Flatz. 'In the short term, they may help to repress the urgent symptoms to a certain degree, but alone are likely to fail in solving or even addressing the actual root problem.'

 Source: China factory chiefs struggle to maintain worker loyalty, *Financial Times*, 04/02/2014 (Sevastopulo, D.), © The Financial Times Limited 2014. All Rights Reserved.

Questions

1 Discuss the reasons behind the innovative HRM policies outlined.

2 What are the advantages and disadvantages of these policies?

3 Can you identify any linkages with the Chinese cultural characteristics reviewed in Chapter 5?

Table 8.1 outlines some advantages and disadvantages of a decentralised approach to IHRM.

Figure 8.7 outlines a number of internal organisational influences which will influence the extent of integration or decentralisation of the IHRM function by MNEs.

Box 8.1 above looked in more detail at the suggestion that national cultural attributes may also play a key role in an MNE's choice of a centralised or decentralised approach to IHRM.

Of course, corporate culture and national culture can exert separate, and sometimes opposing, influences. Morosini *et al.* (1998) suggest that specific absorptive mechanisms (such as job rotation, incentives, internal reporting systems and global co-ordination functions) involving people from different national backgrounds sharing a strong corporate culture can help to facilitate the cross-border transfer of routines and repertoires. Nevertheless, when national cultural characteristics are particularly strong and diverse these may dominate these internal absorptive mechanisms which seek to reinforce aspects of corporate culture irrespective of national identity. This would certainly seem to be indicated by Case 8.4, which considers the impacts on IHRM of theocratic (religious-based) cultures within Islamic countries.

Table 8.1 Advantages and disadvantages of a 'decentralised' approach to IHRM

Advantages	Disadvantages
Groups within the subsidiary can gain in status	Tendency to become 'exclusive'
Groups within the subsidiary become more cohesive, fostering group identity	Loss of central control, higher administrative costs as HRM function is sent 'down the line'
IHRM takes place within a culture appropriate to the local workforce and customers	Loss of organisational control and organisational identity

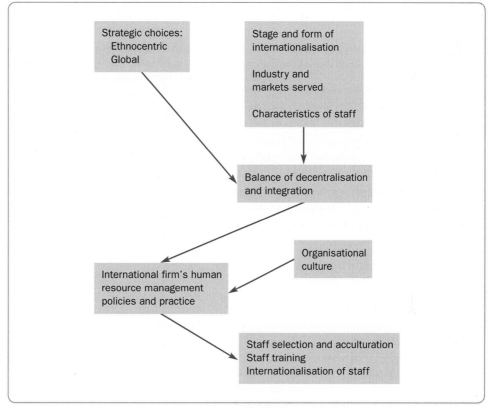

Figure 8.7 Impacts of internal organisational considerations on human resource management

CASE 8.4 Islamic culture and IHRM

Islam has grown enormously over the past three decades. In the countries where it is prevalent, from West Africa to the Lebanon, Malaysia to Indonesia, Muslims are returning to Islamic traditions as a way of rediscovering their identity and as an alternative to the materialism and tensions of the twentieth century.

Islam is an all-encompassing creed, governing every aspect of public and private life. The Koran is regarded as containing the revealed words of God which can act as a guide and a direction. Nevertheless, humans are able to choose and intervene in their own destiny, and must be held responsible for the consequences of their deeds. The economic ideas of the Koran are quite close to those of the West, with the Koran advocating a system based on individual enterprise and reward. As for the Muslim individual,

he or she should be guided by his/her conscience to treat employees and others responsibly. Individuals should pay a reasonable wage, charge a fair price and be restrained in the way in which they use any profits. They also have a responsibility for protecting the environment.

However, the way in which Islam is manifest is very different across nations. At the extreme end, the Taliban regime in Afghanistan does not allow women to work outside their homes, and girls do not attend schools or colleges. In Iran, however, while women have to follow a strict dress code at work and there is a policy of segregation on public occasions such as prayers, Iranian women are doing relatively well in public life. Women can go into most jobs and professions, and, unlike their peers in Saudi, they can drive cars and vote.

Case 8.4 (continued)

The following work-related values of Islamic culture in Iran have been identified by Latifi (1997):

- equality before God;
- individual responsibility within a framework of cooperation with others;
- a view that people in positions of power should treat subordinates kindly, as if their subordinates are brothers or sisters;
- fatalism, but also a recognition of personal choice;
- encouragement of consultation at all levels of decision making, from family to the wider community.

Latifi closely observed a sample of Iranian managers and found traces of Islamic values in the HRM style. Iranian employees thought of their managers as sympathetic brothers and sisters or compassionate fathers and mothers. The family-like relationship seemed to have been extended to include social and teacher roles for the managers, and they were frequently involved in their subordinates' private lives and family matters. A high proportion of managers were willing to make their time and organisations available for high-school and university students who might wish to conduct a research project or acquire work experience as part of their courses. They viewed this as part of their responsibility to society and to the next generation of managers.

In Malaysia, Endot (1995) also found that Islam had filtered down to the HRM practices. One of the companies offers its employees interest-free loans for vehicle or house purchase, or for preparation for a wedding ceremony. Another organises Islamic study circles for managers. These are segregated, but help create cohesiveness of relationships among the members. Another company sends its employees on short courses in Islamic teachings, in order that the employees understand Islam and its values. Yet another organisation recruits individuals who have graduated in Islamic studies, only later exposing them to techniques of modern management.

In a study carried out in the Arab Middle East, decision making and management–employee relationships were found to be characterised by a process of consultation, rooted in Islamic traditions. For example, the Koran asserts that those who conduct their affairs by consultation will receive favour. However, this does not take the form of the Western model of consultative decision making. Rather, consultation is used to avoid potential conflicts between executives and their subordinates: to please, placate or win over people who may be potential obstacles. It is also an information-gathering mechanism. So while consultation may occur, it usually involves only a few selected people and is not part of a hierarchical decision-making structure.

Questions

1 What type of approach to IHRM would you expect to be adopted if a Western MNE acquires an Iranian-based company which has been operating successfully for some time?

2 What results might you expect if the MNE were to use the Harvard model to evaluate the outcomes of the current HRM function within the Iranian firm? (Use commitment, competence, congruence and cost efficiencies.)

IHRM policies and practices

At this point it may be useful to consider in rather more detail some of the key elements within an IHRM programme.

Training and development in an international context

Obviously, training and development increases in complexity as MNEs move abroad. The type of training that takes place would usually depend on a number of factors:

- the degree to which management is centralised;
- the types of workers employed in subsidiaries or joint ventures;

- the importance of branding, and the extent to which employees are expected to reflect the brand;

- the cultural expectations of training.

In a global company, the training may well be centralised so that suppliers, employees and distributors are aware of the brand image that needs to be communicated. In Ford, for example, training programmes are set up centrally, and then translated and delivered to all main suppliers, subsidiaries and distributors. If, however, a more polycentric approach is taken, then the training may well be far more local, and more in line with the local culture.

Again the training needs of the MNE may need to be fine-tuned to the national setting in which the MNE is operating. Case 8.5 provides a useful context for skills training policies which may be appropriate for MNEs operating in the UK.

CASE 8.5 Skills training urged for low paid

Britain's chronic productivity problem will not be solved unless action is taken to help the low paid improve their skills so that they can progress to higher-paid jobs, according to research published today. Almost 3m workers have been stuck in low-paid jobs for more than a year and many for more than a decade, with serious consequences for household incomes, taxpayers and the economy, the Social Market Foundation think-tank found. It said being in work did not offer a route out of poverty and that low pay necessitated 'colossal' state spending of £21bn a year on tax credits for those in employment. The problem is also a factor in the UK's poor productivity record. Output per hour worked is 26 per cent behind the US and 24 per cent behind Germany and France.

The findings echo the concerns of employers, who say 656,000 workers in the three bottom-level occupations lack sufficient skills to do their job, according to a survey by the UK Commission for Employment and Skills. 'We do need to deal with the large number of people in the UK economy who have low-level skills or no qualifications,' said Nigel Keohane, co-author of the report. The SMF found that investing at least £2,000 per person by paying employers to train low-paid employees over the age of 24 for vocational qualifications would be cost-neutral for the government. Those who took part would earn more by moving up the occupational scale, which would increase tax and national insurance revenue and cut tax credit and housing benefit payments, the think-tank said.

As a way of dealing with low pay, the idea may appeal more to businesses than above-inflation rises in the minimum wage, and has the added benefit of raising productivity. Labour proposes tax breaks for employers that pay the higher 'living wage'.

But Mr Keohane said: 'Instead of regulating wages, we were more interested in thinking about how to improve the skills of those workers so that they were worth a higher wage to the economy, and businesses are ready to pay more. The SMF said one in five British workers, or nearly 5m, were low paid, defined as earning less than two-thirds of the median hourly wage – a higher proportion than in any developed country except the US. The highest percentage of those with low pay are in retail and hospitality.

Case 8.5 (*continued*)

One in eight, or 2.9m workers, remain in low pay for at least a year. More than a quarter of the low paid stay there for a decade or more. Studies show the low paid are far more likely than others to progress up the occupation bands if they receive training but are also the least likely to be offered it by their employer or to take it up when offered, for reasons including cost and time constraints. Under the SMF plan, the government would fund at least £15,000 of workplace training per employer and £400–£500 payments to workers as an incentive to take it up.

Employers would provide training for a nationally recognised qualification and would be expected then to move the employees into more highly paid jobs. If their earnings had not increased within two years, the employer would have to repay a portion of the funds to the government. Employers would be able to form partnerships to engage in the scheme, while local enterprise partnerships in England would commission training on behalf of small businesses. According to research by the business department, achieving a basic 'level one' qualification adds, on average, about 10 per cent to a worker's earnings.

Questions

1 How might the UK government policies outlined above be relevant to overseas MNEs operating in the UK?

2 Review some of the advantages and disadvantages to various stakeholders of these proposed policies.

Other problems may arise with team-working. There has been a great deal of work done over the past three decades on how to train teams, and how to ensure that there is synergy in teamwork. Business psychologists such as Belbin, for example, have drawn up the types of characters that would make an ideal team, and have devised methods for testing the personalities of the team members in order that teams could be composed of a balance of types. In a cross-cultural context, it is not only the personality types that have to be taken into account, but also the very real cultural differences and approaches between team members. Attempts at cross-cultural team training are becoming increasingly prominent in MNEs.

A further problem for MNEs is how to ensure that employees sent abroad (expatriates) are fully immersed in the foreign culture. Many MNEs run extensive training programmes for employees going overseas, designed to provide individuals with information and experience related to local customs, cultures and work habits so that they can interact and work more effectively with local colleagues. Indeed, such programmes may also be run for spouses and children.

Research shows that the following are the most popular:

● environmental briefings used to provide information about such things as geography, climate, housing and schools;

● cultural orientation designed to familiarise the individual with cultural institutions and value systems of the host country;

- cultural assimilations to provide participants with intercultural encounters;
- language training;
- sensitivity training designed to help develop attitudinal flexibility;
- field experience which sends the participant to the country of assignment to get them used to the emotional stress of living and working with people of a different culture.

The following case looks at the implications for IHRM within Toyota subsidiaries operating outside Japan.

CASE 8.6 Mindset of a Toyota manager

In 1983 John Shook became the first westerner to work at Toyota's headquarters in Japan. His job was to help the Japanese carmaker transfer production to the US, which involved interpreting and explaining Toyota's legendary 'lean' manufacturing to people who had never heard of it. While even Toyota cannot escape the effects of the current recession – Fitch, the ratings agency, has just lowered its credit rating – it remains the case that since the mid-1980s, Toyota has overtaken Ford to become the US's second biggest carmaker. Every gain in its market share has come at the expense of the big three – Ford, GM and Chrysler – and it is a real possibility that they will not survive this recession in their current form.

Toyota's rise generated a flood of books, starting with *The Machine That Changed the World*, about its many tools, techniques and practices, broadening recently to a growing interest in its approach to management. Somehow, however, its 'secret' of success has remained elusive. In *Managing to Learn*, Shook, now director of the Japan technology programme at the University of Michigan, distils lessons from decades of experience of Toyota, which he tries to present in a way westerners can not only understand but also apply for themselves. Although written mainly for lean 'converts' and published by a lean specialist, this may be the first book that actually helps outsiders connect the dots and get a glimpse into how Toyota ticks. It does so using an extended invented story about how a young middle manager and his boss set about tackling a problem with the translation of technical documents from Japanese to English.

Ostensibly, it is all about their application of a single Toyota management tool – 'A3 decision making' – which forces managers to put on a single piece of paper everything anyone needs to know about a problem: why it matters, what is causing it, what we want to achieve, how to achieve it and how we will know we have been successful. The book charts the young manager's journey. He starts out jumping to a conclusion and investing his ego in promoting and defending it, only to discover he is wrong. Thanks to his boss's coaching, he realises that his real contribution lies in researching the facts and letting them speak for themselves. He must leave ego behind to become a detective who gets to the root of the problem. Then he must learn another lesson: how to build consensus around the answer and promote it entrepreneurially to the rest of the organisation.

As the story unfolds, Shook peels away Toyota's thinking and management philosophy layer by layer. Western managers think their job is to get results. Toyota thinks a manager's job is to design and sustain processes that generate these results as a matter of course. Western managers think they employ workers to do a job. Toyota employs workers to learn how to do the job better – to keep improving that process,

> **Case 8.6 (*continued*)**
>
> and therefore the results. Western managers think management is about knowing the answers and telling other people what to do. Toyota disagrees again: if managers tell staff what to do they take responsibility away.
>
> The manager's job is to help staff learn problem-solving skills and work out what they need to do for themselves. Real organisational leadership is about doing both – improving operations and developing people – at the same time in such a way that they are mutually supporting. As Shook shows, Toyota embeds the philosophy in day-to-day decision making and management tools such as the A3 so that staff have no choice but to learn it in a way they never forget.
>
>   *Source*: Mindset of a Toyota manager revealed, *Financial Times*, 27/11/2008 (Mitchell A.), © The Financial Times Limited 2008. All Rights Reserved

> **Questions**
>
> 1 Identify some of the differences between Japanese and Western approaches to the HRM function.
>
> 2 Examine the IHRM strategies that might help to embed the Toyota management philosophy within a Western organisation.

Pay, reward mechanisms and international employee relations

The way in which an organisation seeks to reward its employees may be critical to its success. As Hegewisch (1991: 28) points out:

> the pay package is one of the most obvious and visible expressions of the employment relationship; it is the main issue in the exchange between employer and employee, expressing the connection between the labour market, the individual's work and the performance of the employing organisation itself.

As a result of competitive pressures, organisations are constantly looking to increase the 'added value' of their employees by encouraging them to increase their efforts beyond any minimal standard and, indeed, to remain loyal to the company so that it can avoid the disruptions that result from a rapid turnover of employees. The theoretical understanding of pay and other reward structures stems from theories of motivation.

To design an appropriate reward strategy for employees taking up an international position may require a number of factors to be considered. These include a knowledge of the laws, customs, environment and employment practices of the foreign countries; familiarity with currency relationships and the effect of inflation on compensation; an understanding of the allowances appropriate to particular countries, and so on.

Awareness of employment-related legislation in the country of operation is vital to an appropriate international reward structure. India has as many as 45 labour laws at national level and close to four times that at the level of state governments (Kaushik 2006). Table 8.2 outlines some of these most important laws a human resource department in India needs to consider as regards a proposed reward structure.

The main method of drawing up a compensation package is known as the 'balance sheet' approach. This approach is, according to Reynolds (1986): 'a system designed to equalise

Table 8.2 Indian employment legislation and reward mechanisms

Labour law	Content
Minimum Wages Act 1948	Prescribes minimum wages for all employees in all establishments or working at home in certain employment specified in the schedule of the Act
Payment of Wages Act 1936	Regulates issues relating to time limits within which wages shall be distributed to employees and that no deductions other than those authorised by the law are made by the employers
Child Labour (Prohibition & Regulation) Act 1986	Prohibits the engagement of children in certain employments and regulates the conditions of work of children in certain other employments
Apprentices Act 1961	Provides regulation and control of training of apprentices
Payment of Bonus Act 1965	Provides for the payment of bonuses to persons employed in certain establishments on the basis of profits or on the basis of production or productivity. The Act is applicable to establishments employing 20 or more people
Payment of Gratuity Act 1972	Provides for a scheme for the payment of gratuity to all employees in all establishments employing ten or more employees
Maternity Benefit Act 1961	Regulates the employment of women in certain establishments for a prescribed period before and after childbirth and provides certain other benefits
Workmen's Compensation Act 1923	Compensation shall be provided to a workman for any injury suffered during the course of his employment or to his dependants in the case of his death

Source: Various including **www.citehr.com/80534-labour-laws-india.html**

the purchasing power of employees at comparable position levels living overseas and in the home country, and to provide incentives to offset qualitative differences between assignment locations'.

In order to achieve such 'balance', the organisation must take into account a number of factors when sending employees to a different country:

● income taxes incurred in both home and host country;

● housing allowances (which might range from financial assistance to employees to providing company housing);

● cost-of-living allowances (to make up any differences in prices between home and foreign country);

● contributions to savings, pension schemes, etc. while abroad;

● relocation allowances (including the moving, shipping and storage of personal and household items and temporary living expenses);

● education allowances for expatriate's children (e.g. language tuition and enrolment fees in the host country or boarding school fees in the home country);

● medical, emergency and security cover.

However, there is arguably much more to identifying appropriate international pay and remuneration packages than merely being aware of legal pay-related requirements and equalising global purchasing power at similar positions in the organisations, as Case 8.7 indicates.

CASE 8.7 Reward mechanisms in cross-cultural contexts

Both India and the UK have minimum wages, but they differ a great deal from one another. The UK minimum wage per hour is £6.31 in 2014 for those aged 21 and over, whereas the Indian minimum wage per day varies between states and occupation, but averages around one third of that at around £2.11. A multinational operating in India must consider those laws, but also take care that its wages are competitive in the market. If it fails to do so, the skilled people will work for other companies.

Another aspect needing thought is the payment of bonuses. The UK is a short-term-oriented country, whereas India is much more long-term-oriented (see Chapter 5, p. 165). As bonuses are mostly performance-related and paid when achieving a set goal for the year, they are arguably more suitable for employees based in short-term-oriented countries, such as the UK, but might offend or not be appreciated by Indian employees.

China has different priorities compared to Western societies and current motivation methods/rewards such as flexible hours, health services and pension funds need to be reconsidered. In the context of BMW, using the Trompenaars model (see Chapter 5, p. 179–180), Germany has an achieving culture whereas China has an ascribing one, meaning its focus is on collectivism and moral responsibilities. Using Hofstede's model (Chapter 5, p. 165–170) China is a long-term-oriented country compared to Germany and so dedication is valued and delayed gratification is acceptable. For instance, pay, although significant, is less appreciated in comparison to other rewards: 'pay is less important than the range of benefits (housing, food, childcare, etc.) typically provided for employees' (Harris *et al.* 2003: 96). Although Western countries are likely to be motivated by economic gains, in China this is not enough to ensure commitment. Pay should be fair but offering incentives with a higher value attached are recommended, such as contributory housing payments or childcare facilities which would help maintain BMW's reputation for having the industry's largest female workforce. China is a collectivist society where 'group interests prevail over individual interests and the individual derives his/her social identity from the groups of which he/she is a member – including family, school class, work unit' (Mead 2005: 44). Therefore group rewards, such as the corporate profit-sharing scheme currently run by BMW, are suitable as everyone is equally rewarded and such group rewards could be more appropriate compared to an individual focus on reward structures.

Jackson (2002) concurs with this approach, suggesting that as China is a particularistic-ascribing country, reward and promotion should be based on group performance or seniority criteria, rather than individual achievement. Further, not only financial rewards, such as pay and bonuses, should be integrated into the reward package, but also social benefits, such as 'lifetime' employment, housing allowances and insurance. Even though there are some discrepancies, awareness is needed of the new labour law and the rising bargaining power of trade unions.

New labour laws may also influence the reward mechanisms proposed, as for example the 2008 change in labour laws in China. A new labour contract law came into effect on 1 January 2008 requiring that every employee in China must be employed based on a written contract. Oral contracts are not permitted, and the contract must include the contents of work, labour protection and working conditions, labour remuneration and conditions for the termination of a labour contract.

Article 36 limits the working time per week to 44 hours on average. This restricts work to not more than eight hours per day on five days per week plus Saturday as a half work day of four hours. Working hours may be extended due to requirements but this should not

> ## Case 8.7 (*continued*)
>
> exceed one hour per day. If the extension is due to special reasons, overtime should not exceed three hours per day. It is illegal to work more than nine hours overtime per week or more than 36 hours overtime per month. Thus, the longest legal working week is set at 49 hours. Overtime is to be paid at least 150% of the normal wages. Employers are required to guarantee that staff have one day off in a week. The minimum age for employment is 16, and probationary periods may be agreed upon in the contract, yet they shall not exceed six months. Article 7 states that workers have the right to participate and organise trade unions.
>
> ### Questions
>
> 1 Using the content in this case and in Table 5.3 (p. 165) and Figure 5.2 (p. 167) consider how the cultural factors might influence an organisation's rewards policies.
>
> 2 How might the 2008 labour laws in China influence reward-related policies?

Appraisal

A formalised and systematic appraisal scheme will enable a regular assessment of an individual's performance, highlight potential, and identify training and development needs. A comprehensive appraisal system can provide the basis for key managerial decisions, such as those relating to the allocation of duties and responsibilities, pay, levels of supervision or delegation, promotion, training and development, and so on.

The benefits of a comprehensive appraisal system include the following:

- it can identify an individual's strengths and weaknesses, and show how these can be overcome;
- it can reveal organisational obstacles blocking progress;
- it can provide useful feedback to help improve human resource planning;
- it can improve communications by giving staff a chance to talk about expectations.

According to James (1988), performance appraisal has its roots in three key principles. People learn/work/achieve more when they are given:

1 adequate feedback as to how they are performing;
2 clear and attainable goals;
3 involvement in the setting of tasks and goals.

Again, there are cultural factors which need to be taken into account when drawing up appraisal schemes for workers in foreign countries.

Performance appraisal is, for example, less emphasised in India where there is relatively low coverage of employees under formal performance appraisal. India is very seniority based, so that the older a person, the more respectful and rewarding the work is expected to become, arguably restricting the perceived relevance of performance appraisal to career progression (Chatterjee 2007). The 'reservation system', which seeks to allocate employment opportunities to specific social groups (e.g. 15% of jobs must go to scheduled castes) may be another factor restricting career planning within Indian organisations.

Table 8.3 highlights the cultural influences on appraisal systems with a key aspect being whether the country is regarded as 'low context' or 'high context' (see Chapter 5, Table 5.1).

Table 8.3 Cultural variations: performance appraisals

Dimension General	USA Low context	Saudi Arabia High context	Japan High context
Objective of performance appraisal	Fairness, employee development	Placement	Direction of company/ employee development
Who does appraisal?	Supervisor	Manager several levels up Appraiser has to know employee well	Mentor and supervisor Appraiser has to know employee well
Authority of appraiser	Presumed in supervisory role or position Supervisor takes slight lead	Reputation important (prestige is determined by nationality, sex, family, tribe, title, education) Authority of appraiser important	Respect accorded by employee to supervisor or appraiser Done co-equally
How often?	Once a year	Once a year	Developmental or periodically once a month Evaluation appraisal after first 12 years
Assumptions	Objective appraiser is fair	Subjective appraiser more important than objective Connections are more important	Objective and subjective Japanese can be trained in anything
Manner of communication and feedback	Criticism direct Criticism may be in writing Objective, authentic	Criticism subtle Older more likely to be direct Criticism not given	Criticism subtle Criticism given verbally Observe formalities in writing
Rebuttals	American will rebut appraisal	Saudi Arabian will rebut appraisal	Japanese would rarely rebut appraisal
Praise	Given individually	Given individually	Given to entire group
Motivators	Money and position Career development	Loyalty to supervisor	Internal excellence

Source: Adapted from Harris and Moran (1991).

Chapter 9

International marketing

By the end of this chapter you should be able to:

- outline the principal activities of marketing;
- differentiate between international marketing and domestic marketing;
- conduct some basic international market research;
- outline the key stages in international marketing;
- specify the key elements in the international marketing mix and discuss how to balance them.

Introduction

Many people see marketing in terms of the advertising that accompanies products – such as that seen on advertising hoardings scattered throughout the world, or encountered on television, radio and the internet. In fact, marketing is a far more sophisticated and complex activity and for many organisations can mean the difference between success and failure.

The Chartered Institute of Marketing (CIM) defines marketing as 'the management process responsible for identifying and satisfying customer needs profitably'. The American Marketing Association's definition is: 'The process of planning and executing the conception, pricing, promotion and distribution of ideas, goods and services to create exchanges that satisfy individual and organisational goals.'

Arguably at least three major elements are involved in the marketing role.

1 *Customer orientation*. This sounds obvious, but in practice many organisations can become so preoccupied with manufacturing processes or technology that they lose sight of what the customer wants, leaving themselves vulnerable to the activities of competitors who have a keener eye for customer needs.

2 *Integrated effort*. A key role of marketers is to build bridges between the requirements of the customer and the capabilities of the organisation. For example, senior managers may not have a marketing orientation; they might focus on keeping costs down, as the route to success, when what is actually required might be more investment in research and design, or more stock on the shelves. 'Integrated effort' means a focus on marketing throughout the organisation.

3 *Goal focus*. Many business activities can be focused on achieving short-term profit, rather than looking to the longer-term strategic aims of the organisation. Marketers may play a part in keeping these longer-term strategic aims in focus.

The principal activities of marketing

We have seen that marketing is an integrated activity that takes place throughout the organisation and seeks to align customer needs with the capabilities and goals of the organisation. We can therefore break marketing down into the following activities.

Analysis

Market analysis can itself be broken down into at least three elements.

1 *Environmental analysis*. This may involve scanning the environment for risks and opportunities, and seeking to identify factors outside the firm's control (see also Chapters 4–6).

2 *Buyer behaviour*. Firms need to have a profile of their existing and potential customer base, and to know how and why their customers purchase. Marketing seeks to identify the buyers, their potential motivation for purchase, their educational levels, income, class, age and many other factors which might influence the decision to purchase.

3 *Market research*. This is the process by which much of the information about the firm's customers and its environment is collected. Without such market research, organisations would have to make guesses about their customers. Such research may involve using data which already exist (secondary data) or using surveys and other methods to collect entirely new data (primary data). Box 9.1 gives a useful insight into the importance of such market research.

BOX 9.1 Baseball thrives on desk research

If you ever thought business decision making had little to do with detailed data analysis, then you haven't seen the film *Moneyball* released in late 2011. It tells the true story of how using published secondary data on baseball performance helped a previously little known team, Oakland A, to compete effectively and win against all the richer and better established US baseball teams. Billy Beane, the general manager of Oaklands A, adopted the language and practices of Wall Street and the use of computer simulations using spreadsheets to transform the fortunes of the team. Beane's idea was to use extensive published data on the performance of baseball players and then input this into spreadsheets for analysis. The results of using the spreadsheets helped him to find 'undervalued assets in an inefficient market', i.e. players for which the actual data demonstrated that they were far better in terms of their actual achievement in key aspects of baseball than other key people in baseball seemed to appreciate! As a result their cost (transfer price) on the market was much lower than the actual data on their performance merited, and Oakland A could then 'buy' these players at a bargain price.

Strategy

Once the environment has been scanned, then the organisation must develop a marketing strategy to give a sense of direction for marketing activity. The concepts of market segmentation and marketing mix invariably appear in such strategies.

Market segmentation

Major decisions need to be taken as to which *market segments* to target. A market segment is a group of potential customers who have certain characteristics in common, for example being within a certain age range, income range or occupational profile (see Box 9.2). Some of these market segments may be identified as more likely to purchase that product than others. When these segments have been identified, the organisation needs to decide whether one segment or a number of segments are to be targeted. Once that strategic decision is made, then the product can be positioned to meet the particular needs or wants which characterise that segment. The task here is to ensure that the product has a particular set of characteristics which make it competitive with other products in the market.

BOX 9.2 Market segmentation

Producers tend to define markets broadly, but within these markets are groups of people who have more specific requirements. Market segmentation is the process by which a total market is broken down into separate groups of customers having identifiably different product needs, using characteristics such as income, age, sex, and ethnicity and so on.

Occupational profile

There are many different methods of segmenting a market. One widely used technique is to classify people according to the occupation of the head of the household as shown in Table 9.1, since market research suggests that consumer buying behaviour changes as individuals move from one such group or 'class' to another.

Table 9.1 **Occupation of head of household**

Group	Description	% of population
A	Higher managerial and professional	3
B	Middle management	11
C1	Supervisory and clerical	22
C2	Skilled manual	32
D	Semi-skilled and manual workers	23
E	Pensioners, unemployed	9

VALS framework

Originally developed by Arnold Mitchell in the US in the 1960s, this framework has been much refined and is increasingly used by national and international marketers. It focuses on psychological, demographic and lifestyle factors to segment consumer groups.

The latest version of VALS segments the English-speaking population aged 18 or older into eight consumer groups.

> **Box 9.2 (*continued*)**
>
> - *Innovators* – High self-esteem, take charge, sophisticated, curious. Purchases reflect cultivated tastes for up-market, niche products and services.
> - *Thinkers* – Motivated by ideals, mature, well-educated and reflective. Purchases favour durability, functionality and value.
> - *Believers* – Strongly traditional and respect authority. Choose familiar products and established brands.
> - *Achievers* – Goal-oriented lifestyles centred on family and career. Purchase premium products that demonstrate success to their peers.
> - *Strivers* – Trendy and fun-loving. Purchase stylish products that emulate the purchasers of higher income groups.
> - *Experiencers* – Unconventional, active and impulsive. Purchase fashionable products and those related to socialising and entertainment.
> - *Makers* – Practical, responsible and self-sufficient. Purchase basic products, reflecting value rather than luxury.
> - *Survivors* – Lead narrowly focused lives with few resources, seek safety and security. Purchase low-cost, well-known brands (i.e. exhibit brand loyalty) and seek out available discounted products.

The use of 'softer skills' in marketing, reflecting the VALS-type approach, is usefully illustrated by the approach of Lego in Case 9.1.

CASE 9.1 How Lego and others turned to anthropology

A decade ago, Lego's plastic brick empire was starting to crumble. Half a century after patenting its click-fit system, the Danish toy company reported heavy losses and gave a sign of the depth of its troubles: the grandson of the founder relinquished his place as chief executive to a McKinsey consultant. In setting out to turn round the business, the new boss inevitably turned to outside advice. Unusually, though, he embedded anthropologist researchers into families in US and German cities for months, taking photos, compiling diaries, talking to parents and spending time shopping and playing with children.

The result was to help reverse Lego's decline by ceasing its diversification away from its classic nerdy brick building: a trend driven by the erroneous assumption that its customers no longer had time to play, and that the advent of electronic 'plus and play' games meant they wanted instant gratification. To the contrary, the researchers – known as 'anthros' by the company – discovered that many children still had plenty of free time, that they enjoyed difficult problems and that they often behaved differently when unsupervised.

The approach, according to Christian Madsbjerg and Mikkel Rasmussen, founding partners of ReD associates, a consultancy that applies the human sciences in business, demonstrated the value of what they call 'sensemaking'. In their book *The*

Case 9.1 (*continued*)

Moment of Clarity, they argue that companies need to pull back from the narrowly focused and generalised approach of questionnaires and spreadsheets, and apply softer skills to understand customers. 'The hard sciences involving mathematics and universal laws tell us the way things are,' they write. 'This tendency is so common, we often disregard, . . . the way things are experienced in culture.'

In other words, conventional market research to identify perceptions and desires does not always equate to what people ultimately buy and why. For example, a man may focus on the technical performance of a new music system but ultimately purchase a different one because of the 'wife acceptance' factor at home.

The authors describe the experiences of one of their own consultants who finally gained insights into a Chinese man's perceptions of modernisation only on a fourth visit, once the two of them had built up confidence and travelled together from his own old family apartment to the different environment of a new flat he had bought for his son. This tactic is no great revelation to a journalist, though no doubt insufficiently applied in business.

 Source: How Lego and others turned to anthropology, *Financial Times*, 26/02/2014, p. 14 (Jack, A.), © The Financial Times Limited 2014. All Rights Reserved.

Question

What national and international marketing approaches are suggested by this case?

Segmentation has allowed the growth of small specialist or 'niche' markets. As people have become more affluent, they have been prepared to pay the higher price for a product that meets their precise requirements. The growth of niche markets has also been important in supporting the existence of small firms. In many cases the large firm has found many of these segments to be too small to service profitably.

Pause for thought 9.1

Explain what is meant by the following terms: benefit segmentation; behaviour segmentation; geodemographic segmentation; lifestyle segmentation.

Marketing mix

Strategy will also involve selecting a suitable *marketing mix*, which will take into account the following factors:

● the product itself (what particular defining characteristics should the product have?);
● price (what pricing strategies might be pursued?);
● promotional activity (how do we make consumers aware of this product?);
● place (is it available to key customers?).

Table 9.2 **Marketing responses to the product life cycle**

	Introduction	Growth	Maturity	Decline
Marketing emphasis	Create product awareness Encourage product trial	Establish high market share	Fight off competition; generate profits	Minimise marketing expenditure
Product strategy	Introduce basic products	Improve features of basic products	Design product versions for different segments	Rationalise the product range
Pricing	Price skimming or price penetration	Reduce prices enough to expand the market and establish market share	Match or beat the competition	Reduce prices further
Promotional strategy	Advertising and sales promotion to end-users and dealers	Mass media advertising to establish brand image	Emphasise brand strengths to different segments	Minimal level to retain loyal customers
Distribution strategy (Place)	Build selective distribution outlets	Increase the number of outlets	Maintain intensive distribution	Rationalise outlets to minimise distribution costs

These four elements are often referred to as the '4 Ps' and are considered in more detail in the context of international marketing strategies (see below). However, they can also play a part in the shorter-term action/reaction patterns ('tactics') of firms in the context of marketing responses to the product life cycle (Table 9.2).

Tactics

The tactics to be used are a shorter-term and more detailed extension of the marketing strategy. Many of these 'tactics' can involve individual elements of the '4 Ps'.

- *Product tactics* may involve attempts to utilise or modify the various stages (introduction, growth, maturity, decline) of the 'product life cycle'. For example, attempts may be made to extend the 'maturity stage' by finding new markets for existing products, new uses for the products and/or modifying the product.

- *Price tactics* may involve selecting particular pricing approaches for the product. For instance, 'price skimming' may be adopted whereby the price is initially set at a high level to 'skim' as much revenue and profit out of the product as possible. Alternatively, 'price penetration' may be used whereby a low price is set in order to reach as large a market as possible in a short period of time. 'Discriminatory pricing' may also be considered where the same product is priced lower in some markets than in others (e.g. lower price in those market segments with a higher price elasticity of demand – see Box 9.5, pp. 326–327).

- *Promotion tactics* may involve the degree of emphasis given to personal selling, advertising, public relations, sales promotion, etc. 'Push' tactics might focus on the producer offering incentives to key players in each distributional 'channel' to promote their products (e.g. the firm may offer incentives to wholesalers so that they 'push' the firm's products to retailers, etc.). 'Pull' tactics focus on the final consumer, the idea being to stimulate consumer demands which will then stimulate ('pull') retailers/wholesalers into stocking the firm's products.

● *Place tactics* might involve placing a particular emphasis on one or more *distributional channels* for the products in question. For example, pre-eminence in distributional policy might be given to distributional channels such as direct selling, producer to retailer, producer to wholesaler or franchising.

Planning and management

These various marketing activities need to be integrated throughout the organisation, and this can only be done through careful planning and managing of the whole process.

Planning is the process of assessing market opportunities and matching them with the resources and capabilities of the organisation in order to achieve its objectives. However, planning is not just a one-off exercise. It needs to be integrated into the ever-shifting environment of the firm so that new issues are constantly addressed and met. Forecasts made at this stage will have a major effect on production, financial decisions, research and development and human resource planning.

Managing the process can involve many aspects. For example, in order for the planning to be ongoing, the whole process needs to be monitored to ensure that customer needs are being met effectively. This may involve measuring the outcomes of marketing strategies against objectives that may have been set at the strategic stage, such as checking whether specific targets have been met for individual products. Customer surveys may also be used to audit the quality of the services delivered. Whatever the method, it is important that monitoring is built into the plan, so that major or minor adjustments can be made. Managing may also involve *organising* the marketing function, for example allocating different tasks to different individuals or different departments.

Clearly any rapid changes in market characteristics will mean that both those market planning and market managing activities must be kept under constant review, as Case 9.2 on the use of smart devices would certainly suggest.

CASE 9.2 Britons use smart devices for longer than they sleep

British people spend more time glued to screens than they do sleeping, according to the annual report on the nation's communications habits by the industry watchdog. Ofcom paints a picture of a country obsessed with consuming media in all formats but in particular on digital devices such as smartphones and tablets. The regulator found that television viewing has dropped below four hours a day for the first time since 2009.

Instead, led by the 'millennium generation' that rarely uses a phone to make calls, but to update a social media status and check for instant messages, the average adult spends more time using media or communications – at 8 hours 41 minutes – than they do sleeping.

Ofcom found people using several devices at the same time – for example, making calls while surfing the internet on a tablet – meant that total use of media and communications has averaged more than 11 hours a day so far in 2014. This was an increase of more than two hours since Ofcom conducted equivalent research in 2010,

Case 9.2 (*continued*)

and reflects the sharp increase in internet use on the move as mobile data networks have improved. 'Our research shows that a "millennium generation" is shaping communications habits,' said Ed Richards, Ofcom chief executive. 'The convenience and simplicity of smartphones and tablets are helping us cram more activities into our lives.'

The 16–24 age group is the largest user of media and communications, Ofcom found, making time for more than 14 hours of activity by using different devices simultaneously each day. The digital divide between age groups is becoming more pronounced – almost 90% of 16–24s own a smartphone, compared with only 14% of those aged over 65.

Young adults are glued to their smartphones for 3 hours 36 minutes a day, nearly three times the one hour 22 minutes average for all adults. Younger generations also use their phones in different ways: children aged 12–15 spend just 3% of their time on voice calls, turning almost entirely to instant messaging and social networking instead.

Ofcom found digital literacy fell sharply after a certain age. In a study of nearly 3,000 adults and children, Ofcom found six year olds have the same knowledge of technology as 45 year olds. Peak understanding of digital communications is reached at 14–15, it said, with few born at the turn of the millennium remembering life without access to fast mobile data networks.

 Source: Britons use smart devices for longer than they sleep, *Financial Times*, 07/08/2014, p. 3 (Thomas, D.), © The Financial Times Limited 2014. All Rights Reserved.

Question

Consider some of the marketing implications of these changes in market characteristics/consumer behaviour.

International marketing

We have outlined the general activities of the marketing process, but how do these apply to international markets? While the basic activities remain the same, the picture is far more complex. International marketing can simply be defined as involving marketing activities that cross national borders. However, such marketing activities can take place at different levels.

- Firms exporting to international markets but which have the majority of their sales in the domestic market. Here the international market is considered secondary to the domestic market.

- Multinational enterprises which have operations and sales worldwide and which regard the home or host country as but one of many equally important market environments.

- Firms (usually MNEs) which seek to adopt global marketing strategies. The basis of global marketing is to identify products or services for which similarities across several markets enable a single, global, marketing strategy to be pursued. Examples today might include

Coca-Cola, Heinz, Kellogg's, McDonald's, Marlboro, etc. All the examples given are of consumer products but the potential for globalisation in industrial markets is also great, in particular where there is little or no need to adapt a product to local needs. Thus, a global market exists in areas such as telecommunications, computers, pharmaceuticals, construction machinery, bio-engineering, etc.

Pause for thought 9.2

Can you list some of the differences between domestic marketing and international marketing?

We return to issues of brand value later in the chapter (p. 323).

Reasons for international marketing

Obviously international marketing activities at all these levels involve additional risks and uncertainties as compared to selling in a domestic market only. It may be worth briefly reviewing the reasons why firms commonly seek to extend the geographical scale of their marketing activities.

- *Increasing the size of the market.* Developing new markets abroad may permit the firm to fully exploit scale economies (see Chapter 7), which is particularly important when these are substantial for that product. In some cases the minimum efficient size for a firm's production may be greater than the total sales potential of the domestic market. In this case the firm's average costs can only be reduced to their lowest level by finding extra sales in overseas markets.

- *Extending the product life cycle.* Finding new markets abroad may help extend the maturity stage of the product life cycle. This can be particularly important when domestic markets have reached 'saturation point' for a product.

- *Supporting international specialisation.* In an attempt to reduce overall production costs, separate elements of an overall product may be produced in large scale in different geographical locations worldwide. For example, labour-intensive components will often be produced in low-cost labour locations, whereas capital-intensive components are more likely to be produced in high-technology locations. The final product, once assembled, must by definition be marketed internationally to achieve the huge sales volumes which are a pre-requisite for international specialisation.

- *Establishing first-mover advantages.* From a less cost and more market-oriented perspective, being the first entrant within an overseas market may be an advantage. By becoming a 'first mover' a firm may make it difficult for new entrants to compete. For example, advantages include established customer loyalty, greater choice in terms of suppliers and the experience that comes with being the first entrant. The UK cider producer HP Bulmer became a first mover when it decided to produce cider in Qufu, China. The company established a joint venture with the Chinese firm San Kong Brewery in the knowledge that it would be the first foreign company to produce cider in China.

- *Helping reduce investment pay-back periods*. Finding overseas markets helps achieve high-volume sales early in the product life cycle, thereby reducing the pay-back period needed to return the initial capital outlay and making many investment projects more attractive. This may help to compensate for modern trends towards shorter product life cycles which are tending to inhibit investment expenditure.

- *Reducing stock-holding costs*. Overseas markets may provide new sales outlets for surplus stocks (inventories), thereby reducing warehousing and other stock-holding costs.

Decision making and international marketing

It is often said that at least five decisions must potentially be made by those involved in the international marketing process (see Figure 9.1), namely:

1 whether to internationalise;

2 which foreign market(s) to enter;

3 how to enter these foreign markets (market-entry strategies);

4 what international marketing mix to adopt (the 4 Ps);

5 how to implement, co-ordinate and control the international marketing programme.

International marketing research can be regarded as a support activity, providing evidence and analysis of patterns and trends to support these five key decisions. We might usefully review each of these decisions and support mechanisms, some of which are considered in rather more detail elsewhere in this text.

International marketing research

This function supports all five 'phases' outlined in Figure 9.1, providing vital information and analysis to underpin the decisions associated with each phase. A key aim of market research is to reduce the risk involved in taking effective decisions in these five phases. This is particularly important where the environment in which the firm is operating is unfamiliar. Market research can be divided into two types: desk research, which means using information which has already been gathered for another purpose (secondary data), and field research, which involves obtaining information specifically directed towards a particular marketing issue and which is usually original (primary data).

From Figure 9.1 we can see from the 'Information needed' column that data will be required on both a macro level (e.g. GNP, demographic changes, inflation, exchange rates, etc.) and a micro level (e.g. firm sizes, productivities, cost structures, competitor reactions, consumer buying patterns, distribution channels available, etc.).

Desk research

There are numerous sources of secondary information available to the international marketer.

- *International organisations*. The OECD, UN, EU, IMF and World Bank all collect large volumes of mainly macro data on an annual basis for both developed and developing countries. For example, the EU, apart from its many statistical publications, has established over 300 'European Documentation Centres' around the UK (and similar centres in other

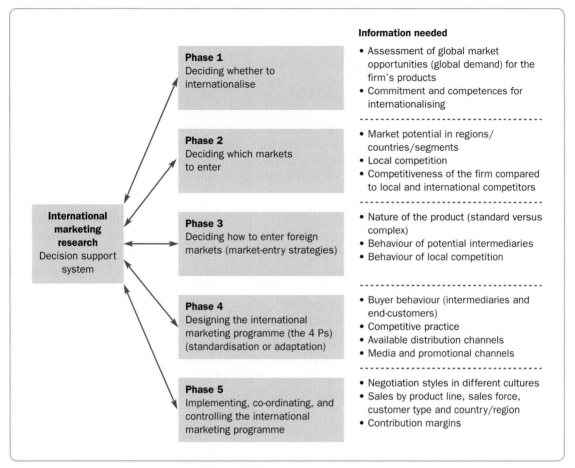

Figure 9.1 Major international marketing decisions

Source: International Business: Theories, Policies and Practices, Financial Times Prentice Hall (Tayeb, M. 2000), © Pearson Education Limited 2000.

member countries). These centres are regularly updated with documents (often originating from the European Commission and Parliament) which impact on the single market.

- *National publications*. In the UK National Statistics (formerly the Office for National Statistics (ONS)) publishes detailed annual (sometimes monthly or quarterly) data on most types of economic and socio-economic indicator. Similar information is available in most advanced industrialised economies.

- *National Trade Associations and Chambers of Commerce (or equivalents)*. These business agencies in the various countries can be invaluable in providing up-to-date market information.

- *Trade journals*. These often provide up-to-the-minute profiles of various aspects of industries, countries or specific market sectors.

- *Financial press*. The various FT indices and ratios (and their equivalents elsewhere) provide an invaluable source of up-to-date information on firms and industrial sectors.

- *Internet*. Finally, of course, there is the internet, though information found here is only as good as the researcher who is using it. Remember that many of the Web pages are commercially based, and companies will not reveal any secrets that they feel might be useful to their competitors.

Field research

Primary data may be obtained from a variety of sources. The main advantage of field research is that it is customised to the firm and is unavailable to competitors. However, it is expensive and time-consuming and may present particular problems, such as collecting data in some national cultures which has little experience of using scientifically based research methods. Survey methods that assume a high level of literacy, certain education levels, access to telephones, or a willingness to respond by those surveyed, may need to be reassessed in some international situations.

- *Research agencies.* In most countries there are many enterprises that are specialists in research. Companies can specify the type of data they are interested in and the agency will carry out the research on their behalf.

- *Company networks/personnel.* Original data may be obtained from company networks (e.g. suppliers who also work for rival firms). Sometimes members of a company are sent to investigate the nature of specified markets through 'shopping trips' which, while not rigorously scientific, can help the organisation 'get a feel' for the types of markets they may enter.

Of course market entry and market research are not only the preserve of MNSs! Case 9.3 provides background on the market-related issues involved for a start-up business seeking to enter the South African market for mobile media.

CASE 9.3 Moving ADS

Moving ADS began when the three individuals, who were initially strangers, met and became friends through a social setting, namely a church. Fanana, Richard and Tinashe found that although they had different backgrounds, they shared a common experience of being university drop-outs! Many youths in Africa still face the problem of being forced to follow a particular field of study, often predetermined by their parents as the best career choice on the basis of both financial rewards and in maintaining a certain family status within the society, resulting in many students eventually changing their studies or dropping out of university.

As foreigners living and working in Johannesburg, South Africa, the three friends always dreamt of developing their own business. They had regular discussions to assess their individual areas of expertise which they might combine to establish their own company. Before establishing Moving ADS, Fanana had worked in a creative advertising firm for six years, while his partners Tinashe and Richard had worked in banking and call centre industries respectively.

The young entrepreneurs sought to find a suitable business idea while still working in their respective industries. Fanana elaborates: 'It was then that one of the partners, who came originally from Zimbabwe, suddenly mentioned that his father owned an advertising business that had originated in Europe, and which might be worth trying.' While the severe economic challenges and conditions in Zimbabwe had resulted in the business ceasing to be active, the trucks they would need were sitting in Zimbabwe and not being utilised. Fanana convinced his partners that they could revitalise the business concept and adapt it to the South African market.

Case 9.3 (*continued*)

Fanana recalls: 'Knowing the viability of advertising and media, I immediately realised the potential to enter the market with a novel tool that wasn't available in South Africa.'

Fortunately their early market research had shown that their basic business idea was already being successfully applied in other parts of the world including France, Canada, Spain and the United States. The partners were therefore convinced that the business idea was feasible, and that they could still keep their daily jobs. The partners decided to bring the trucks into South Africa one by one, starting with a single truck and a driver to test the waters in the South African media and advertising market. Like many entrepreneurial ventures, Fanana and his partners started their business in one of their apartments. They chose the most central and upmarket apartment in order to attract clients and save costs, channelling the funds saved into business cards and refurbishing their trucks.

Moving ADS provides an advertising service that specialises in outdoor promotional and marketing solutions. Simply put by the co-founders: 'Our flagship brand is a novel piece of mobile media that's designed for marketing, advertising and promotional purposes.' The Moving ADS trucks are polished multi-utility vehicles that can be deployed for various promotional activities. They offer:

- three-sided poster display unit;
- three-sided mobile billboard;
- transit media;
- events, field and promotional marketing opportunities;
- branded mobile showroom: experiential marketing;
- distribution centre.

Fanana explains: 'I can simply sum up our service as "Outdoor Media Portal". However, the trucks can also be transformed into showrooms and events vehicles. They offer ample storage space and a window showroom effect through the transparent display screens.'

One of the main challenges the three partners faced was in penetrating a highly competitive and closed market in South Africa. Fanana says, perhaps rather surprisingly, that it was probably wise that they did not undertake extensive research because this may well have scared them from taking the plunge. He explains: 'The market was not too open to business newcomers. We were young, black and unknown in an industry that's very white and ruthless. But I knew there was a huge potential for our business model because there was a clear demand.' Similar to many other entrepreneurs, venture capital was their next greatest challenge. Fanana elaborates: 'Venture capital in South Africa is very elusive. Banks don't fund start-ups with no collateral. As the business grew and whenever we needed money, we had to source venture capital at very high interest rates.' Without any external funding, the three partners reinvested all of their savings back into the business and decided to live a frugal lifestyle and to work full time in their respective jobs to help finance the business.

In little more than a year, however, the three partners found that their attention to detail and to customised service has led to a solid customer base. Fanana states: 'With service excellence focused on our individual customers, we managed to build a loyal customer base and as a result we now enjoy repeat business. We always strive to satisfy our clients because satisfaction means our clients will keep coming back.'

To move the company onwards and upwards, the three partners are exploring many different avenues and they would like to see Moving ADS progress into different sectors. They have recently developed an alternative media platform of branded car washes. Moreover, the three partners are planning to increase their fleet by acquiring more trucks and expanding the car wash business. As Fanana says, 'We currently have 20 car wash structures and we want to double their growth by the end of the year. We have also identified other business opportunities that aren't media related which we plan to explore to increase our income and grow our business.'

The three partners perceive the unpredictable South African and global economy and technological change as amongst their greatest challenges. Fanana clarifies: 'These challenging financial times are resulting in many of our clients cutting their marketing and media spend. Hence the importance

Case 9.3 (continued)

of venturing into other unrelated fields that may complement our business.' The partners also predict that new technology may threaten their business. They foresee advertising becoming increasingly digital, requiring an increasingly innovative response if they are to offer services equivalent to the new digitalised media trends within their industry. Fanana is also concerned about legal developments. 'Legislation might hinder our progress as by-laws are getting more and more rigid. We are an outdoor transit company and we are obliged to abide by such laws.'

Questions

1 Can you identify and assess some of the methods used to research and develop these initial business ideas?

2 Can you see any linkages between the positioning approaches of the three entrepreneurs and Porter's five forces?

3 Are there any other positioning strategies you might recommend to the entrepreneurs?

Market selection

The first two of the five phases for the international marketer in Figure 9.1 involve the decision on whether or not to internationalise and the decision on which markets to enter. The first of these decisions has already been considered in some detail in Chapter 2 of this text. Here we focus on the market selection decision (Phase 2 in Figure 9.1).

Segmentation and targeting

As in domestic marketing, once the larger market has been identified, the potential market has to be segmented as the firm's products are unlikely to appeal to the entire market. Segmentation, as we have seen, is the grouping together of customers with similar needs and characteristics. In international marketing, this means grouping countries with similar wants together or looking for similarities between specific groups of customers in different countries.

Shampoo provides a useful example of market segmentation. Shampoo was once considered one market, but new product development, branding and packaging have segmented this market in many ways. Shampoo products can be segmented into medicated hair products (Head & Shoulders), two-in-one (Wash & Go), children's shampoos (L'Oréal Kids), 'balanced' shampoos (Organics, Fructis) and environmentally sensitive shampoos (The Body Shop range). Such strategies permit manufacturers such as Unilever and Procter & Gamble to place a premium price on many of their shampoo products. These forms of lifestyle segmentation are now used by many firms in preference to the social class distinctions of the previous four decades.

Accessibility/actionability

The viability of a particular market segment is determined to a large extent by issues of 'accessibility' and 'actionability' which arguably are even more important in the international context.

- *Accessibility*. This refers to the ability of the firm to reach the potential foreign customers with promotional and distributional techniques and channels. Market segmentation involves identifying groups of customers with common characteristics, but even where such groups exist they may be particularly difficult to access when they cross national borders. For example, finding a media source to host a promotional campaign that is equally effective in reaching high-income female professionals in London, Frankfurt and Milan may prove difficult, as indeed it may in finding a distribution channel to actually supply product to this market segment. It may be that adjustments will have to be made (e.g. narrowing down the intended market segment) because of such accessibility problems for the international marketer.

- *Actionability.* This refers to the ability of the firm to increase its scale of operations to match (with no diminution in efficiency) the now enlarged total market. All too often firms encounter logistical problems in raising capacity which, in effect, prevent the firm from realising the benefits of these new market opportunities. For example, various diseconomies of scale (see Chapters 2 and 7) may raise average costs or adversely affect product quality. One of the methods firms often use in seeking to overcome this problem of 'actionability' is to seek out alliances and collaborative agreements with existing players in overseas markets (see Chapters 2 and 7).

PEST analysis

The whole external environment is particularly important when selecting viable overseas markets. Firms often resort to PEST analysis to broadly evaluate the potential of markets for entry. Of course, these various political, economic, sociocultural and technological (and some would add ecological/environmental and legal) factors may be still more uncertain in an international context. Chapters 4–6 have already looked at these factors in some detail.

Targeting strategies

Having selected some potentially attractive international market segments, the firm will often adopt one of three possible targeting strategies: concentration, undifferentiated (or mass) marketing, differentiated marketing.

- *Concentration.* This refers to targeting a single market segment and developing an appropriate marketing mix for it. In international terms, this means concentrating marketing efforts on one or a small number of market segments to maximise the use of resources. For example, Rolls-Royce has targeted the luxury segment of the car market. Brand value may be crucial to successfully using concentration targeting strategies.

- *Mass (global) marketing.* This is where a single marketing mix is used worldwide. Very few companies attempt this because enormous resources are required to exploit world markets. It also assumes that markets are relatively homogeneous and that customers will respond to promotions in uniform ways.

- *Differentiated marketing.* This involves developing a different marketing mix for each of the market segments identified. Here, there is an assumption that the market is heterogeneous, with consumers likely to respond in different ways and to different types of products.

Segmentation and targeting take place within a dynamic, ever-changing world business environment. No longer can organisations assume that things will stay the same for any significant period. Segmentation decisions often seek to identify sectors with high and growing levels of demand, but they must also focus on the trading environment that prevails. Any attempts at overt or covert protectionism by individual countries or regional trading blocs can have major impacts on market selection decisions. Indeed, the growth of regional trading blocs has led to 'insiderisation' with companies seeking a presence within a protected market through joint ventures with domestic firms or through founding a subsidiary company providing jobs and tax revenues within the host country. The strength of the competition also needs to be taken into account when deciding which markets to target. Organisations do not want to be crowded out by existing competitors who already have entrenched positions in terms of price, quality or consumer allegiance.

Market-entry strategies

The third decision phase in Figure 9.1 involves deciding how to enter the foreign market. Figure 9.2 outlines a number of possible methods which might be chosen.

These methods are by no means mutually exclusive: firms may be using one or more of these methods for market entry. Figure 9.2 suggests a broad spectrum ranging from minimum risk/minimum reward methods (e.g. indirect exporting) to maximum risk/maximum reward methods (e.g. foreign direct investment). These have already been discussed in some detail in Chapter 2.

However, Figure 9.3 shows how Starbucks has tended to use a variety of joint ventures and licensing arrangements with local partners to move into new overseas markets as well as increasing its penetration within these markets. Its 'capital-light' market entry strategy is clearly towards the minimum risk/minimum reward end of the spectrum of Figure 9.2.

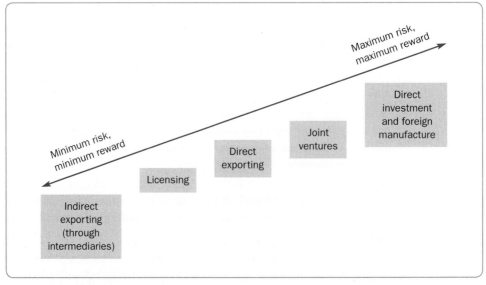

Figure 9.2 **Market entry methods**

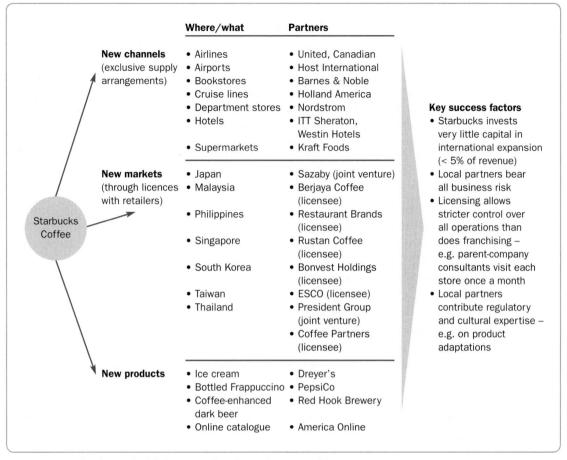

Figure 9.3 Starbucks: capital-light expansion through partnerships

International marketing mix

The fourth decision phase in Figure 9.1 involves the international marketing mix. The marketing mix of the 4 Ps can take on additional characteristics when viewed from an international perspective.

Box 9.3 shows how the importance of the various elements in the international marketing mix can vary between countries and regions.

BOX 9.3 Variations in the international marketing mix

International businesses are increasingly aware of consumer differences between countries and regions, even when these consumers otherwise have similar profiles (e.g. in terms of age, income, occupation). As a result, businesses which aspire to a global marketplace are

319

Box 9.3 (*continued*)

devoting more resources to identifying these differences before selecting the appropriate international marketing mix for that country or region.

Research led by Dawn Lacobucci of Northwestern University's Kellogg Graduate School of Management tries to get behind the cultural differences that might skew consumer responses to identical surveys in different countries. In other words, the research seeks to identify differences in consumer behaviour that are 'real' rather than 'apparent' as between nations and regions. In a recent test of their model, the researchers found important differences between consumers in four major geographical market segments (namely Asia, Latin America, northern Europe and southern Europe) in rating the products and services of a given company:

- price was seen as a key indicator of quality in Asia, northern Europe and southern Europe, but not in Latin America;
- product quality was seen as driving a company's repeat purchases in Asia, northern Europe and Latin America, but not in southern Europe;
- product after-sales service was seen as influencing repeat purchases in Asia, Latin America and southern Europe, but not in northern Europe;
- product 'value for money' was only seen as driving repeat purchases in Latin America;
- promotion was seen to have most impact on repeat purchases in Latin America and Asia, and least impact in northern Europe and southern Europe. (Here the number of sales representatives was used as a proxy variable for promotion in the sales of a given product in the different areas.)

Lacobucci concluded that 'companies that probe deeper to figure out what their global customers are thinking and feeling stand to create smarter branding strategies'.

Pause for thought 9.3

1. If you were devising a marketing mix for selling the company's products used in the survey in northern Europe, where might you place the emphasis?
2. What other factors might play a part in adjusting the marketing mix between different nations and regions?

Product

This is the fundamental component of the marketing mix, since price, promotion and place are usually related in various ways to the characteristics which the product itself offers consumers. A key issue in international marketing is the extent to which a standard or differentiated product should be provided.

Standardised or differentiated?

There are good business reasons for trying to make a standard product acceptable to as many customers as possible – for example, it can help reduce average costs in design, production, promotion and distribution. Theodore Levitt of the Harvard Business School contends that tastes and preferences in many cultures are becoming more homogeneous due to the increased frequency of world travel and improved worldwide telecommunications. He claims that when marketers appreciate the fact that consumers share basic interests they can market the same product worldwide and achieve economies of scale. A global marketing strategy is one that maintains a single marketing plan across all countries and yields global name recognition. Coca-Cola and McDonald's are examples of companies that use a global approach to market their products in different countries. Even when arguments for standardisation are strong, those who follow this path may still make subtle variations – for example, McDonald's uses chilli sauce in Mexico instead of ketchup, while in India it serves the 'Maharaja Mac' which features two mutton patties. The motto 'Think global, and act local' symbolises a patterned standardisation strategy which involves developing global product-related marketing strategies while allowing for a degree of adaptation to local market conditions. Some product types would appear more suitable for standardisation than others. Office and industrial equipment, toys, computer games, sporting goods, soft drinks are usually standardised across national borders.

On the other hand, arguments can also be advanced in favour of *product differentiation*. Where international market segments differ from one another, even when some group characteristics are held in common, then a more differentiated product strategy may be advisable. For example, if high-income households in Spain display different wants and needs from high-income households in Germany, products may have to be adapted in an attempt to sell to both groups of consumers simultaneously. Where products are highly culturally conditioned (as with many types of food, some types of drink, clothing, etc.), differentiated products and marketing strategies are commonplace.

Table 9.3 outlines some of the factors supporting internationally standardised products and some of the factors supporting differentiated products.

Ariel washing powder has used nine different formulae throughout Europe, reflecting country-to-country differences in a wide range of factors, such as in water softness, types of washing machine, consumer preferences and legal restrictions on ingredients.

Differentiation can also include the product portfolio offered by the business, as is illustrated in Case 9.4 on Flipkart (see earlier Cases 7.2, p. 225, and 7.7, p. 256).

Table 9.3 **Factors supporting product standardisation or product differentiation**

Factors supporting standardisation	Factors supporting product differentiation
Rapid technological change, reducing product life cycles (places a premium on rapid global penetration)	Slow technological change, lengthening product life cycles
Substantial scale economies	Few scale economies
International product standards	Local product standards
Short cultural distance to overseas market	Large cultural distance to overseas market
Strong and favourable brand image	Weak and/or unfavourable brand image
Homogeneous consumer preferences (within a given group characteristic, e.g. high income)	Heterogeneous consumer preferences (within a given group characteristic, e.g. high income)
Global competition	Local competition
Centralised management of MNE operations	Decentralised management of MNE operations

CASE 9.4 Flipkart aims to make shoe fit

Of all the items being sold over the internet, apparel and shoes would seem to be one of the trickiest categories, given customers' usual desire to try on items to determine whether the look and fit is really right. But as it faces growing competition 'Flipkart', the online e-commerce book and etext retailer (see Case 7.7, p. 256) is focusing heavily on expanding into fashion, which it believes has tremendous potential in a vast country where major brands have struggled to expand beyond the largest cities. In May 2014, the company acquired Myntra, one of a number of niche Indian e-commerce companies dedicated to fashion and apparel.

Part of the challenge is that Flipkart has a guaranteed returns policy, which means customers who buy fashion items can return them free of cost if they decide they are not quite right. Though that would seem to set the company up for high costs in handling returns, Sachin Bansal, Flipkart's chief executive, says margins in apparel are significantly higher than margins in other categories, which counters the attendant risk of a higher return rate, which for the company as a whole is in the low single-digits.

Binny Bansal, Flipkart's co-founder and chief operating officer, says the company sees great promise in the retailing of apparel and accessories. 'We are bullish about fashion – we think it's going to be the biggest category,' he says. 'In China, a huge chunk of the business is fashion. Although it is more difficult than electronics, if you have the right solution for it, we believe it can really take off.'

 Source: E-tailers in India prepare for showdown, *Financial Times*, 12/08/2014, p. 15 (Kazmin, A.), © The Financial Times Limited 2014. All Rights Reserved.

Question

Why is Flipkart extending into a more differentiated product portfolio, beyond books only?

McDonald's has moved further along the product differentiation path in recent years in its various international operations, for a number of reasons.

- *Reason*: Meeting different consumer tastes. *Examples*: US portion sizes larger; French menu includes traditional snacks such as Croque Monsieur, French pastries, stronger coffee; Chinese New Year menu includes authentic cultural dishes and packages; 'McCafe's' used in mature markets such as Australia, the US and the UK, with lattes, cappuccinos and other speciality drinks.

- *Reason*: Religion. *Examples*: lamb-based 'Maharajah Mac' to meet Hindu aversion to beef and Muslim aversion to pork.

- *Reason*: Local commitment. *Examples*: emphasis on British beef in the UK and on local rice in China.

- *Reason*: Demographics. *Examples*: 20% of all sales are to children so 'Happy Meal', food with toys themed with popular films, etc. for children up to nine years; 'Mighty Kids meal', for children over nine years who have grown out of the ('fun food with a toy') Happy Meal; 'Giant burger' (40% bigger) to appeal to young men in the 15–32 year age group, identified as important but with poor market penetration by McDonald's.

As most companies are looking for some standardisation, they will often use a *modular product* design that allows the company to adapt to local needs while still achieving economies of scale. Car makers are beginning to adopt this form of production, with a basic body shape forming the shell around which different features are built (e.g. windscreen designs, sun roofs – see Chapter 7, p. 267).

Branding

Establishing product characteristics which are different from those of the firm's main competitors may be important in helping the firm establish a brand image. Of course, brand image may depend not so much on *actual* product differences but on consumer *perceptions* of product differences, created and reinforced by extensive advertising.

Certainly the potential benefits of brand image may influence the product characteristics sought at the introduction stage of the product life cycle or the modifications considered during the growth or maturity stages of that life cycle. For example, a product may be modified in order to reposition it and/or extend the reach of the brand at the maturity stage of the product life cycle. Such 'brand extension strategies' often appeal to larger companies that are well aware of the value to sales and profits resulting from past investment in brands.

A brand is an element or group of elements that help distinguish the product of a particular supplier or the image of the supplier itself. When attempting to set up brands, organisations need to consider whether the brand should be local (developed for a specific market), regional or global. Branding can sometimes extend into a communication that is separate from the product itself. Kotler and Armstrong (2010) make a distinction between the *utterable brand* (a name like Persil or Guinness) and the *unutterable brand* (a symbol, logo, colour scheme, or even typeface in which the name of the brand appears – such as Coca-Cola). Because of the difficulties of translation into words, the unutterable brand often works best at international level.

When brands are developed successfully, they may allow higher prices to be charged, over and above those charged for non-branded, generic products. These higher prices help create what is often called 'brand value'.

Calculations of brand value involve comparing the prices of similar generic (own-brand) products with the higher price of the branded product. Data from *Interbrand* in 2013 ranked the top five global brands and their associated brand values as follows:

Apple	$98.3bn
Google	$93.3bn
Coca Cola	$79.2bn
IBM	$78.8bn
Microsoft	$59.5bn

The annualised growth in brand value over the previous 12 months is an astonishing 28% for Apple and 34% for Google, with more modest annual growth of 2% (Coca Cola), 4% (IBM) and 3% (Microsoft) for the other three brands.

Many brand names do not travel well. There are many examples of companies that have adopted a standardised approach to their branding, but have not researched the implications of translation when launching a brand into another country. For example, when it first launched in China Coca-Cola realised the name translated as 'bite the wax tadpole'. Fortunately, Estée Lauder was quick to notice the proposed export of Country Mist make-up to Germany could experience problems. This is because 'mist' in Germany is slang for 'manure'. Subsequently the product became Country Moist in Germany.

Very often brand names are changed in order to follow a standardisation strategy. For example, in the UK the following products have changed names to fall in line with the same product in other countries. Starburst was formerly Opal Fruits, Cif formerly Jif, and Snickers formerly Marathon. Mars (the manufacturers of Snickers and Starburst) decided the sweets should be called the same name in the UK as they are in the rest of the world. Reasons for having one universal brand name can be attributed to cost savings by producing a single global advertising and marketing campaign for all countries. Also, with increased travel, consumers are able to recognise a brand abroad. Usually companies adopt expensive advertising campaigns advising of the name change. This needs to be done in a positive way to ensure the brand image maintains its current position in the mind of the consumer.

Corporate branding

Traditionally new drugs in the pharmaceutical sector are given new names to indicate a departure from previous alternatives available. The downside of this strategy is that large corporate investment in branding previous drug products is disassociated from the new products and may be regarded as largely wasted. It has been suggested that pharmaceutical companies might be well advised to consider *corporate branding* as a replacement for individual drug branding, so that company loyalty embedded in consumer allegiance to earlier products can then be transferred to successor products. A customer looking for a treatment for allergies, for example, would not look for Claritin but for the latest Shering-Plough medicine.

Positive marketing may even help turn disadvantages of individual drugs into brand benefits. For example, it was noted that Zyrtec, an antihistamine drug developed by Pfizer, induced rather more sleepiness in users than alternative therapies. Rather than allow rivals to use this as a negative, Pfizer sought to stress the positive benefits of drowsiness in increasing the likelihood of a good night's sleep and in reducing the itchiness which often accompanies the use of such drugs.

Successful branding can help to bind consumers to particular products for reasons other than price. This will cause the demand curve to pivot, becoming less steep (i.e. less price elastic – see p. 334). This in turn gives greater opportunities for considering a price-raising policy, since fewer consumers will be lost when there is a conviction that the branded product is of a higher quality than the now lower-priced rivals. The linkage between price elasticity of demand and revenue is explored below in Box 9.4.

Price

Price in any marketing context is governed by competition, production costs and company objectives. Case 9.5 suggests that the pricing strategy of Tesco (and other supermarkets) is certainly influenced by the behaviour of competitors.

CASE 9.5 Tesco steps up battle against pound shops

Tesco has stepped up its offensive against the hard discounters and pound stores, dedicating aisles in its stores to cut-price products. Britain's biggest retailer, which is striving to turn round its UK business, plans to transform aisles into zones selling products priced at a pound or below. It already has the feature in 60 stores and could extend it. The items could be smaller packs of products sold elsewhere.

The move comes as the German discounters – Aldi and Lidl – gain traction with consumers. They have been boosted by the squeezed middle classes flocking to their stores as they have moved into upmarket areas and improved the quality of their products to compete with the mainstream supermarkets. Britain's big four grocers – Tesco, Asda, J. Sainsbury and Wm Morrison – are also battling a growing number of pound shops. These include Poundland and B&M, some of which have opened outlets near the big four.

In a sign of this shift in power, Poundland is chaired by former Tesco finance director Andrew Higginson, while B&M is chaired by Sir Terry Leahy, who was chief executive of Tesco, transforming it from a struggling domestic grocer to an international brand. The discount retailers have been particularly effective during events, such as Halloween, when parents can stock up on cheap novelty goods.

Underlining the growth of the discount and pound shop sectors, Poundland said its sales rose 13.3 per cent in the year to March 30, 2014, compared with the previous year.

Question

Explain the reasoning behind Tesco's decision to engage in a significant price-cutting initiative.

Source: Morrison's discounts all pain and no gain, *Financial Times*, 09/05/2014, p. 21 (Felsted, A.), © The Financial Times Limited 2014. All Rights Reserved.

Box 9.4 reviews some commonly used strategic pricing initiatives.

BOX 9.4 Strategic pricing initiatives

- **Penetration pricing** Here price for a new product may even be set below average cost in order to capture market share. The expectation is that prices can be raised and profit margins restored later on in the growth/maturity stages, helped by the fact that average costs may themselves be falling in those stages via the various economies of scale.

- **'Price-skimming'** Here a high price is set for a new product in the introduction/early growth stages which 'skims off' a small but lucrative part of the market. Producers of fashion products, which have a short life and high innovative value as long as only a few people own them, often adopt a skimming strategy. Companies such as IBM, Polaroid and Bosch have operated such price-skimming systems over time. Bosch used a successful skimming policy, supported by patents, in its launch of fuel injection and antilock braking systems.

Box 9.4 (*continued*)

- **Loss leader (bait) pricing** Where a limited number of products are priced at or below cost to entice customers who may then pay full price on other purchases (e.g. for selected products in supermarkets).
- **Clearance pricing** Where rock-bottom prices are charged to clear stock and make resources available for alternative uses.
- **Transfer pricing** (see below, p. 331) Here the price (at least notionally) of a product or part of a product is set with regard to the tax regimes which exist in different countries.
- **Parallel pricing** Where several firms change prices in the same direction and by broadly the same amount.
- **Product line pricing** Where the pricing of one item is related to that of complementary items, with a view to maximising the return on the whole product line. For example, the price of a 'core' product might be set at a low level to encourage sales and then the 'accessories' priced at high levels.
- **Prestige pricing** Where higher prices are associated with higher quality ('Veblen effect').
- **Competitor pricing** As, for example, where the firm follows the prices set by the market leader or engages in price warfare under oligopoly market structures (see Chapter 7).
- **Price discrimination** (see below, p. 329) If demand for a given product can be broken down into market segments, some being more price sensitive than others, then revenue and profits can be increased by charging a different price in each market segment.

International pricing decisions will reflect these aspects and will also need to take into account market differences between countries, exchange rates, difficulties of invoicing and collecting payment across borders, the effects of tariffs and purchase taxes on competitiveness, governmental regulations of the host country and the long-term strategic plan of the company in the different markets in which it operates.

We now review some of the major issues faced by those setting prices in different countries.

Price elasticity of demand (PED) (Box 4.3, p. 149) has already been identified as a key element in the pricing decision, with the decision on whether to raise or lower price crucially dependent on how 'sensitive' consumers are expected to be in responding to that price change. Box 9.5 considers the *revenue* linkage with PED in rather more detail.

BOX 9.5 Price elasticity of demand (PED) and revenue

We have already considered aspects of PED in Box 4.3 (p. 149). For a business to make sensible decisions as to the price it should charge, it will help to be aware of the linkage between PED and total revenue (turnover), where:

$$PED = \frac{\%\ \text{change in quantity demanded of}\ X}{\%\ \text{change in price of}\ X}$$

Box 9.5 (*continued*)

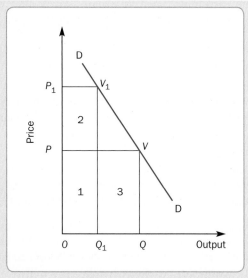

Figure 9.4 Box diagram to show how revenue varies with price and output

The 'box' diagram shown in Figure 9.4 helps explain this linkage using a straight line (linear) demand curve (DD).

We can see that with the initial price at OP, total revenue (price × quantity) is shown by area $OPVQ$. A rise in price to OP_1 will lead to a contraction of demand to OQ_1 and a new total revenue indicated by area $OP_1V_1Q_1$. Clearly Area 1 is common to both total revenue situations, but here Area 3 is lost and Area 2 gained. The loss of Area 3 is due to consumers no longer buying the $Q_1 - Q$ units because of the higher price; the gain of Area 2 is due to the higher price being paid by the Q_1 consumers who still buy the product.

The relationships listed in Table 9.4 below will hold true for the box diagram.

Table 9.4 PED and revenue

Numerical value of PED	Relationship between Area 2 and Area 3
1	Area 3 = Area 2
>1	Area 3 > Area 2
<1	Area 3 < Area 2

We can now use these relationships to make a number of predictions involving price rises and total revenue.

Price changes and total revenue

- For price rises along a unit elastic demand curve (PED = 1) or segment of a demand curve, there will be no change in total revenue (Area 2 = Area 3).

- For price rises along a relatively elastic demand curve (PED > 1) or segment of a demand curve, total revenue will decrease as there is a more than proportionate response of lost consumers to the now higher price (Area 2 < Area 3).

- For price rises along a relatively inelastic demand curve (PED < 1) or segment of a demand curve, total revenue will increase as there is a less than proportionate response of lost consumers to the now higher price (Area 2 > Area 3).

Pause for thought 9.4

Now rework these predictions for a price decrease in each of the three situations.

Case 9.6 uses the significant increases in the price of letters by the Royal Mail to further reflect on the linkages between price elasticity of demand and revenue.

CASE 9.6 Royal Mail, pricing and letters

The Royal Mail used its monopoly power to sharply increase the price of both first and second class letters in April 2012. The revenue and volume results over the following six-month period to end September 2012 are shown below and compared to the previous six-month period (October 2011 to March 2012).

The 9% fall in total letter volume following these price increases was around 4% more than the projected fall of 5% expected over this period from the already well-established trend of a loss of letter post volume to internet-driven substitutes for letters (e-mail, texts, etc.). However, while the higher prices led to a loss of volume this was more than compensated in revenue terms, with total letter revenue actually rising by 2% over these successive six-month periods.

The Royal Mail also increased the price of its parcel deliveries in April 2012 by an average of 16% across the various parcel sizes. However, the volume of its parcel deliveries actually increased by 5.6% over the following six months, with revenues from parcel deliveries rising by as much as 13%. The rapid growth of parcel deliveries is seen as linked to rapid growth in B2C (business-to-customer) business for Royal Mail, fuelled by the success of Amazon and other e-commerce firms using Royal Mail parcel deliveries.

Questions

1 What barriers to entry apply to the business activities of the Royal Mail?

2 Can you use the earlier ideas of price elasticity of demand to explain the results in Table 9.5?

3 What limitations are there to the monopoly power of the Royal Mail in terms of price setting?

Table 9.5 Royal Mail letters outcomes over two six-month period 2011–12

Price 1st class stamp 2011 46p
Price 1st class stamp 2012 60p
Price 2nd class stamp 2011 36p
Price 2nd class stamp 2012 50p
Total letter volume −9% over the two periods
Total letter revenue +2% over the two periods

Market differences

Clearly some overseas markets are more attractive for a particular product than others in terms of population size, standard of living (e.g. real GNP per head), age profile, purchasing patterns, etc. Of particular interest in terms of international price setting is the possibility and profitability of setting different prices in different geographical markets. When the same product is priced higher in one (international) market than another, this is termed price discrimination.

For this to be possible, there must be barriers preventing purchase in one country at the lower price and resale in another country at the higher price (transport costs, tariff barriers, etc.). For this to be profitable, there must be different 'price elasticities of demand' in the different geographical markets. Where consumers in one country are more responsive to changes in price (i.e. have a higher price elasticity of demand), it can be shown that a firm can earn higher profits by charging a lower price in that country (see Box 9.6).

BOX 9.6 Price discrimination

This involves charging different prices for an identical product.

In Figure 9.5 the firm faces two international markets: Market A with a relatively inelastic demand and Market B with a relatively elastic demand. To maximise profit the marginal cost of total firm output to both markets (MC_{A+B}) must equal aggregate marginal revenue from both markets (MR_{A+B}). This occurs at output Q_I, giving overall marginal cost of C. Now the conditions for maximum total profit is that the marginal cost of total firm output (C) must equal marginal revenue in each separate market.

$$\text{i.e. } MC_{A+B} = MR_A = MR_B \quad \text{i.e. } Q_A \text{ and } Q_B \text{ respectively}$$

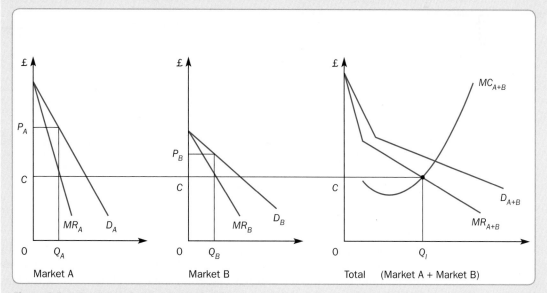

Figure 9.5 **International price discrimination**

That price discrimination occurs in practice is well illustrated by Table 9.6, which shows considerable differences in the US dollar price of the 'Big Mac' burger across a range of countries using current exchange rates.

Table 9.6 Variations in the US$ price of 'Big Macs'

Country	Price	Country	Price
India	$1.54	Canada	$5.01
China	$2.74	Turkey	$3.76
Indonesia	$2.30	UK	$4.63
South Africa	$2.16	Brazil	$5.25
Egypt	$2.43	Euro-zone area	$4.96
Russia	$2.62	Switzerland	$7.14
Japan	$2.97	Norway	$7.80
US	$4.62		

Source: Adapted from *The Economist*, 25 January 2014, p. 67 © The Economist Newspaper Limited, London 2014.

Pause for thought 9.5

Can you suggest reasons for the price differences observed in Table 9.6?

Variations in real national income per head (living standards) are another market difference which may result in price variations for a given product across different countries. Figure 9.6 usefully illustrates this relationship. Since only some 6% of the cost of a 'Big Mac' can be attributed to the cost of the ingredients, the clearly positive relationship between the dollar price of a 'Big Mac' and real national income per head (capital) has little to do with different cost factors in the various locations.

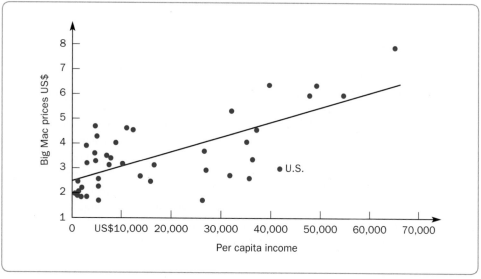

Figure 9.6 Big Mac prices and per capita income
Source: Landry (2004).

Transfer pricing

We have already noted in Chapter 4 that multinational enterprises are well placed to take advantage of any differences in national tax and subsidy regimes. One particularly important aspect which might influence pricing policy involves attempts to reduce the corporate tax burden by 'transfer pricing' – that is, by adjusting the pricing of internal transactions between international subsidiaries of the multinational enterprise.

Multinationals are widely accused by governments of arranging intra-company transactions in order to minimise their tax liabilities, effectively forcing countries to compete to provide the lowest-tax regime. Here we consider a simplified example in which a multinational's production is vertically integrated, with operations in two countries. Basic manufacture takes place in country A and final assembly and sale in country B (see Table 9.7). In country A, the corporate tax rate is 25%, while in country B it is 50%. Suppose the company's costs (inputs, labour, etc.) in country A are $40 million and it produces intermediate products with a market value of $50 million; if it were to sell these intermediate products on the open market, it would declare a profit of $10 million in country A, incurring a tax liability of $2.5 million in that country.

Table 9.7 Multinational tax avoidances

$m	Scenario 1		Scenario 2	
	Country A	Country B	Country A	Country B
Costs	40	90	40	100
Sales	50	100	60	100
Profit	10	10	20	0
Tax liability	2.5	5	5	0
Total tax	7.5		5	

However, suppose the products are actually intended for the parent company's subsidiary in country B. In Scenario 1, the 'transfer price' (i.e. the internal price used by the company to calculate profits in different countries) is set at the market price of $50 million in country A for the intermediate products which are now to be 'shipped' to country B for $100 million, thus the subsidiary will declare a profit of $10 million and incur a tax liability of $5 million. The company as a whole will face a total tax liability of $7.5 million in countries A and B taken together.

Consider an alternative scenario (Scenario 2), in which the company sets a transfer price above the market price for the intermediate products manufactured in the low-tax country, A. With a transfer price of $60 million rather than $50 million and the same costs of $40 million the subsidiary in country A incurs a higher tax liability (25% of $20 million), but this is more than offset by the lower (in fact, zero) tax liability incurred by the subsidiary in country B. Because the latter is now recording its total costs (including the cost of the intermediate products 'bought' from the subsidiary in country A) as being $100 million rather than $90 million, its profits and tax liability fall to zero. As a result, the total tax liability faced by the company on its international operations is only $5 million, rather than $7.5 million.

The basic issue is that the multinational has earned a total profit of $20 million on its vertically integrated operation, i.e. $100 million actual sales revenue in B minus $80 million costs in A + B. However, by setting transfer prices on intra-company sales and purchases of intermediate products appropriately, the company can 'move' this profit to the lowest-tax country, thereby denying the higher-tax country (in this case, country B) the tax revenue to which it is entitled. Such transfer pricing can, of course, only succeed when there is no active market for the intermediate products being traded. If the tax authorities in country B can refer to an open market price for the intermediate product, the inflated transfer price being paid can be identified. However, to the extent that many multinationals internalise cross-border operations because they have ownership-specific advantages (e.g. control of a specific raw material or technology), it may be that comparable intermediate products are not available on the open market. For this reason, high-tax countries may find they lose tax revenues to lower-tax centres as business becomes increasingly globalised. This creates, in turn, an incentive for countries to 'compete' for multinational tax revenues by offering low tax rates; the result of such competition is a transfer of income from national governments to the shareholders of multinational companies.

Exchange rates

When exchange rates fluctuate this can change the potential profitability of international contracts. For example, marketers must be alert as to any potential movements in the exchange rate between the date of quotation/invoicing and the date of payment so that the profit margin is not eroded. Price may have to be adjusted to cover adverse exchange rate movements. To reduce the impact of such problems currencies may be purchased on futures markets (see p. 351), or products may be priced in 'harder', more stable currencies. Of course, when both parties have a single currency, such as the euro, these problems will be avoided.

Cross-border payments

In contracts for internationally traded products it is important to specify exactly what a price covers. For example, does it cover cost, insurance and freight?

Tariffs and other taxes

Increases in tariffs (purchase taxes) or raw materials used in production or on overseas sales can force a firm to raise the quoted price of its exports in order to retain its profit margin. In 2008 L'Oréal was faced with a rise in costs of its raw materials when the EU imposed a 7.8% duty on a chemical (dihydromurcenol) imported from India and used in several of its cosmetics lines. Whether the firm will be able to pass these taxes on to the consumer as a higher price will, of course, depend on the price elasticity of demand for the product. The less price elastic the demand, the more of any tax increase can be passed on to the overseas consumer. Tariffs and taxes can have other impacts on trade issues. In an attempt to avoid such tariffs (and sometimes to overcome currency problems) there has been a growth in countertrade, namely the barter of goods and services between countries. Some 5% of all international trade has been estimated as being of this type. Further, any increases (or differences between countries) in *profit-related taxes* (e.g. corporation tax) can result in MNEs adopting a policy of 'transfer pricing'. Here firms sell products on to subsidiaries within another country at prices which bear little relation to the true costs incurred at that stage of the overall production process (see p. 331).

Government regulations

As well as taxes, overseas governments may influence the firm's price-setting policies by regulations, perhaps setting maximum or minimum prices of products or minimum quality standards for particular products. Regulations may also inhibit other promotional techniques; for example, L'Oréal could not use the successful UK free samples promotion of mascara in Norway or Germany, where such free offers are prohibited.

Strategic objectives

Overseas price setting may, of course, be influenced by the strategic objectives of the firm. For example, where market share or revenue maximisation are primary objectives, then prices will tend to be lower (e.g. penetration pricing) than they might be under, say, a profit-maximising objective.

Promotion

The objective of promotional campaigns is often expressed as being both to increase the commitment of existing consumers to the product and to capture new consumers. Box 9.7 looks at these objectives in more detail.

BOX 9.7 Promotion/advertising and demand

The intention of a promotional strategy which emphasises the superior quality or characteristics of your product is often twofold.

- First, to shift the demand curve to the right, so that more of product X is purchased at any given price. This is shown as an increase in demand from DD to D'D' in Figure 9.7, with Q_1 now demanded at price OP. The promotional campaign seeks to change the

Box 9.7 (*continued*)

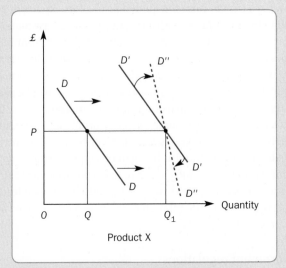

Figure 9.7 Demand increases and becomes less elastic with successful promotion/advertising campaign

tastes/preferences of consumers in favour of your product X, either by capturing new consumers for that product or attracting existing consumers away from a competitor product.

● Second, to cause the demand curve to pivot and become steeper (D″D″ in Figure 9.7), i.e. become less price elastic (see p. 149). A successful promotion will bind consumers to your product for reasons other than price, convincing them that your product really does have an extra 'edge' on rival products in the marketplace. The benefit of this is that a less price elastic demand curve will allow you to raise the price of your product X above OP without losing as many customers as previously, thereby increasing revenue from the product (see Box 9.5).

Pause for thought 9.6

What would be the result of a promotional campaign which succeeded in alerting unaware consumers that the existing price of your product was below that of your rivals?

This is one of the most challenging areas of international marketing, since it is particularly affected by technological, sociocultural and regulatory factors. Promotion may involve press and media campaigns, direct mail, exhibitions or direct selling. When planning international campaigns, companies will need to ask the following questions:

● *What is the technological infrastructure of the country?* This will influence the prospects for reaching the final consumer. For example, in most industrialised countries over 90% of households own a TV, but this is often only a minority in the developing countries. If using direct selling by telesales, what proportion of the target market in that country possesses a telephone? If planning a poster campaign, what are the panel sizes available in different countries? Panel sizes are different, for example, in France and the UK, which can be important given the high costs of preparing and printing panels of varying sizes.

- *What appeals culturally in the advertisement?* English advertisements quite frequently use humour; French ones use erotic imagery, while in Germany the advertisements tend to be very factual. Great attention therefore needs to be paid to style and content in terms of the cultural impact of the campaign. If using direct selling, what type of sales force will be acceptable? For example, should we use local salespeople, an expatriate sales force or nationals from third countries?

- *What are the regulations on advertising in this particular country?* The UK, Belgium, the Netherlands and Denmark ban TV commercials for tobacco products but allow press adverts. In the UK any advertisement for tobacco products must carry a health warning. Are there any legal restrictions on the use of direct marketing (such as the use of information stored on computer databases)? Are there any legal restrictions on sales promotions? (Some countries do not allow certain types of free offers to be made; for example, money-off coupons are not allowed in Norway.)

- *What are the different media habits of the country?* For example, the current circulation figures per 1,000 of population of women's weekly magazines is around 29 in Germany, compared to 15 for the UK and five for Spain. Similar figures for TV guides are 37 for Germany, ten for the UK and seven for Spain.

- *What type of packaging do we use to retain the brand image yet meet country requirements* (e.g. ecological requirements demanded in Germany)? Do we need special types of labels? How much information needs to be presented about the content of the product?

We can see from these questions that international marketing is not an easy proposition. It requires an intimate knowledge of the market in each country. As market segmentation analysis becomes ever more sophisticated, this too can impact on promotion/advertising strategies.

Psychographic factors and promotion

Attempts are being made to segment markets in terms of psychographic factors, i.e. in attitudinal and behavioural characteristics resulting from cultural differences. For example, Roper Starch Worldwide (a leading market research company) claimed to identify four distinct shopping styles worldwide after surveying around 38,000 consumers in 40 countries, namely 'deal makers', 'price seekers', 'brand loyalists' and 'luxury innovators'. To the extent that such psychographic segmentation is shown to be reliable, companies can only adopt global promotion/advertising campaigns to clearly defined groupings across various countries. Cultural differences will prevent a more comprehensive advertising approach.

The FCB (Foote, Cone and Belding) two-by-two grid can be used to categorise a product in terms of its consumer orientation, using two key dimensions (see Figure 9.8):

1 an 'involvement' spectrum, with the *higher involvement* products reflecting those which are generally believed by consumers to further their personal objectives or have important personal consequences, as opposed to the *lower involvement* products;

2 a 'think–feel' spectrum, where *think products* possess characteristics which are primarily associated with functional outcomes and *feel products* with emotional outcomes.

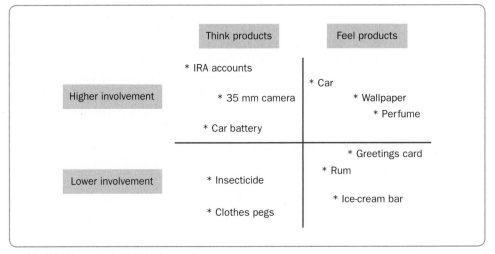

Figure 9.8 **Consumer–product relationships**

Only where a product falls in a clearly defined quadrant in all its international markets can a global promotion campaign be applied with any confidence.

Ethnographic factors and promotion

Companies are increasingly sending their market researchers to live in consumers' homes to understand better their consumption patterns and perceptions of products. This practice, known as *ethnography,* is based on the study of anthropology and the idea that you get more detailed and accurate information by immersing yourself with the subject (here the consumer). It is an attempt to overcome the known distortions that regularly occur when consumers fill in diaries or questionnaires, where subconsciously respondents often write what they think the researchers want to read. Brewers, for example, have found that men typically overstate how much they actually drank whereas women understate the true quantities. More accurate figures arguably require researchers to live alongside the consumer and record what, and how often, they actually do drink.

'Buzz' marketing and promotion

In some ways this is an attempt to promote with minimal expenditure on conventional promotional media. 'Buzz' marketing involves getting the trendsetters in any community themselves to convey the key message of the brand, creating interest in the product with little overt promotion or advertising. The message may be conveyed physically (the avant-garde seen with the product), verbally (spoken about in conversation) or virtually (via the internet). Ford used this approach to promote its new Focus. Having identified 120 people in six core markets as trendsetters (e.g. local DJs), each was given a Focus to drive for six months and promotional materials to distribute to interested acquaintances. Red Bull has also used this approach. For example, in its eight US sales areas, representatives identify the bars and clubs visited by trendsetters and offer the owners branded refrigerators and other free goods along with their first order.

Place (distribution)

This is one of the major challenges for the international marketer, and mastery of this aspect can give the firm an edge over its competitors. A common problem in international marketing is for the firm to concentrate too much on the channels closest to the producer rather than channels closest to the customer. Some of these logistical issues involving type of channel selected are considered in more detail in Chapter 7.

The following aspects will influence the type of channel selected:

● the value and type of product;
● the cost and speed of alternative types of transport;
● the ease with which a channel can be managed;
● what the competitors are doing.

It is more difficult to control these channels from outside the overseas country itself. The type of distribution channel selected will also depend on the type of market entry a company has pursued. If it is operating from subsidiaries in that country (internalisation) then the subsidiary itself will often handle the distribution. If, however, products are simply being imported, then a third party such as a local agent may be employed to ensure that the quickest, cheapest and safest method is used. The company must adapt itself to local conditions, using strategies such as employing local distributors or buying such distributors and using them as part of the firm's internal operations, as appropriate to each circumstance.

Case Study 9.7 emphasises the importance of a distribution approach and infrastructure which must be compatible with the cultural behaviour of consumers in the host country.

CASE 9.7 Indian stores in search of drama

When Kishore Biyani tried a 'clean Italian look' of glass and minimalist lines in one of his Big Bazaar stores, he was surprised by the effect on his customers – it drove them away. The sleek section of the store remained empty while the rest of the store bustled. Mr Biyani, head of the Future Group, India's largest retailer, realised the decor was intimidating and alienating the middle-class Indian consumers who were more used to crowded bazaars and shops. 'You need hustle and bustle,' says Mr Biyani. 'The Indian model of shopping is theatrical – there is buzz and haggling. If you have wide aisles you have a problem.'

Mr Biyani's Big Bazaar 'hypermarket' stores, which are India's closest equivalent to Wal-Mart, are clean, air-conditioned and well lit. But they have deliberately narrow aisles and overflowing display bins that simulate the feel of open-air markets common in India. Drama and theatre are important elements in Mr Biyani's stores, which also include the Pantaloons and Food Bazaar chains. At one store in a Mumbai shopping mall, dance music popular in Indian nightclubs blasts from loudspeakers while customers jostle to reach the best goods.

Modern retail stores are relatively new to India, so Mr Biyani and other retailers are having to adapt to the evolving shopping habits of Indians. The biggest mistake that retailers make is thinking that 'just because you have set something up people will come', says Anirudha Mukhedkar, chief executive of Restore Solutions, a retail consultancy in Bangalore. Shopping in so-called organised stores accounts for only 4% of India's $322 billion (£218 billion) retail industry but this share is expected to grow to 22% or $427 billion by 2010, according to the Federation of Indian Chambers of Commerce and Industry.

Case 9.7 (*continued*)

Unlike their struggling counterparts in the West, India's retailers are looking at an attractive growth market. But getting it right will be tricky, given the country's diverse population and distinct regional cultures. Understanding India's wide diversity – socio-economic, religious, regional and linguistic – is key to that strategy. 'When you say Indian consumers, there are at least ten Indias,' says Mr Mukhedkar. Cultural preferences vary widely between regions. For example, types of rice and how people buy it differs in the north and south, says Harminder Sahni, managing director of Technopak, a retail consultancy based in Delhi. In the north, rice might be sold in open sacks so consumers can inspect the goods. But in some parts of the south, rice is a common staple sold in sealed packets. Store lay-outs will also vary according to region. In big grocery stores in Kolkata, eastern India and other coastal cities, fish is a staple sold in the vegetable section, whereas it is categorised with meat in inland areas.

Because of these distinct regional tastes, retailers 'don't look at India as India', says Mr Sahni. 'They pick a region or market or city . . . The first two years might be in one city.' He says that most do not have ambitions to open pan-Indian stores: 'Many start in one part of India and just stick to that.'

The Future Group has found another way of capitalising on regional variations: it has 72 annual promotions linked to local festivals. The company says the Big Bazaar store in Bhubaneswar, capital of the backwater eastern state of Orissa, took the group record for a single day's turnover after promoting a sale linked to a festival.

William Bissell, managing director of Fabindia, a chain of upscale boutiques that sells clothing and housewares, says 'Every store has to offer a different mix. That's why retailing in India is so complicated.' Mr Bissell notes that Fabindia, founded in 1960, has an inventory of 200,000 items to cater to consumer tastes that vary dramatically across regions. 'Any retailer will say that is crazy,' says Mr Bissell. To manage its enormous inventory, Fabindia has installed an IT system to track the flow of goods at nearly 100 stores in India. Capacious Western-style malls are also cropping up,

especially for luxury goods. But when catering to the mass consumer, 'it makes sense to have smaller stores with more workers', says Mr Mukhedkar of Restore Solutions. He points out that India's cities command some of the highest real estate prices in the world but labour costs are among the lowest. Packed shelves are also preferable to give the consumer a sense of abundance and choice. 'If a shelf can take 50 things, try to fit in 75,' Mr Mukhedkar advises. 'Density per square foot has to be as high as possible.'

For practical reasons, Mr Bissell favours smaller stores. He dismisses the notion of a 100,000 sq ft Ikea-style store in India, except where 'enormous' volumes might justify high maintenance costs. 'At 40 to 44 degrees in the summer I'm going to have to air-condition the whole thing. That would be an environmental disaster.' And it would be too expensive, he adds, in a country where electricity rates are high, and power cuts force many businesses to buy costly diesel-run generators.

The biggest misunderstanding about retail in India, says Mr Bissell, is that Indians consume as copiously as Westerners. Instead, Indians are more selective, value-conscious and price-sensitive. Mr Sahni of Technopak agrees. In a grocery store, an Indian consumer will not fill up a trolley as is common practice in the West. 'Indians will shop with a basket. Below a certain income level, people won't want to spend so much with each transaction.' Smaller refrigerators and limited storage space at home are also factors. 'People will buy more frequently and in smaller packets,' says Mr Sahni.

But some aspects of retail in India are more abstract. To stay attuned to India's pulse, Mr Biyani has a special unit devoted to tracking the country's social trends to incubate ideas for new store brands and strategies.

The 'Future Ideas' group includes sociologists, interior designers, graphic designers and other cultural experts. One of their biggest tasks is analysing the changing tastes of Indian youth. With more than half of India's population under the age of 25, understanding their consuming habits and aspirations is a priority for the Future Group. 'India is still family-centred, and young people influence purchases,' says Mr Biyani. But by far his biggest

Case 9.7 (*continued*)

challenge as a retailer is managing the speed of change in India. 'How do you make an organisation that is not permanent in thought, structure or design?' asks Mr Biyani. 'Retail in the next five years will be different. Nothing is permanent.'

Source: Indian stores in search of drama, *Financial Times*, 30/12/2008 (Yee, A.), © The Financial Times Limited 2008. All Rights Reserved.

Questions

1 What lessons does this case suggest for multinational retailers seeking to increase their sales in the Indian marketplace?

2 What more general lessons can be learned from this case by international marketers?

International marketing planning

The fifth and final phase of the international marketing approach, outlined in Figure 9.1, involves implementation, co-ordination and control.

Implementation does, of course, presume that there is an international marketing plan to implement! The nature of that plan will depend on some of the issues already discussed – for example, whether the product is standardised or differentiated, the stage of the product life cycle reached in different countries, the national regulatory environment, whether prices are to be uniform internationally or whether price discrimination is to be pursued, the nature of the distributional channels selected, and so on. Of course, such an international marketing plan must be consistent with the key corporate objectives.

Implementation of the international marketing plan, whatever its characteristics, will depend in part on the corporate structure of the firms in question. For example, when a firm grows from exports into international alliances such as those involving joint ventures, licensing or the establishment of subsidiaries it will often create an international division. This can be organised by geographical area or by product and can even take the form of an independent subsidiary. Such divisions usually specialise in international areas of marketing, manufacturing, finance, personnel and research, with responsibilities for the overall planning and control of these international activities. The degree of centralisation of the marketing function will usually depend on the strength of the particular brand. Strong brands need centralised marketing to preserve the integrity of the brand, but for weaker brands there will usually be a great deal of local adaptation so that marketing decisions will also tend to be localised.

International market planning, co-ordination and control face a number of particular problems:

● despite technological advances, the market intelligence available for many international operations may be of poor quality and incomplete, especially in the developing/transitional economies;

● few tried and tested models of international marketing exist and those that do are often based on North American constructs which may have little relevance to many international markets.

Chapter 10

International finance: theory and practice

By the end of this chapter you should be able to:

- outline the differences of accounting treatment followed by various countries and assess the need for international harmonisation of accounting practices;

- discuss the background to accounting and financial information available to organisations and identify the main users of such information, including the credit rating agencies;

- examine the functions of the main international financial markets (including the foreign exchange market) and analyse the impacts of these international financial markets on international business;

- identify and evaluate some of the financial instruments used in the finance of foreign trade;

- examine some of the key issues facing the firm in the management of international finance and when operating under different financial and fiscal regimes.

Introduction

The first part of this chapter looks at the role and nature of international accounting – its main divisions, key financial statements and the regulatory frameworks which govern it. It also contrasts the differing accounting principles used within certain groups of countries, which might produce misleading results if used for comparative purposes. There is a growing trend towards international harmonisation and in particular more use of International Accounting Standards (IASs). Over time it is expected that 'national' accounting regulations will be of less importance than agreed worldwide frameworks, and there is continuing pressure from international stock markets and organisations such as the European Union for the introduction of more unified and cohesive financial reporting standards.

The second part of this chapter looks at some of the key issues in international financial management and some of the instruments used in the finance of foreign trade. The operation of the international currency and money markets are reviewed. Particular attention is given to a key 'price', namely the *exchange rate,* which is determined on the foreign exchange market. The broader international institutional environment, such as the role of the International Monetary Fund, World Bank and other international financial institutions has already been considered in Chapter 3. Here we emphasise the interconnectedness of global financial markets, the emergence of new methods and financial instruments within financial intermediation, and the contribution of these to current international liquidity problems. We also review some possible strategic international financial responses available to global business organisations and national governments.

Accounting, financial information and decision making

Accounting has been defined as: the process of identifying, measuring and communicating economic information about an organisation or other entity, in order to permit informed judgements by users of the information. It can be divided into two types: financial accounting and management accounting.

- **Financial accounting.** This is concerned with the production of the principal accounting statements that provide stakeholders in the business (management, employees, shareholders, creditors, consumers and government) with an accurate view of the firm's financial position. It uses historic data and is predominantly *backward looking* in that it summarises what has happened in the previous accounting period. The principal output would include profit and loss accounts, balance sheets and cash flow statements.

- **Management accounting.** This generates information for internal use to aid the analysis, planning and control of the firm's activities. Management accountants are principally *forward looking,* acting as 'information providers' to senior management. This information might be in the form of financial forecasts, budgets, contribution statements and break-even charts.

Together the two types of accounting provide insights for stakeholders into the success or failure of *past* decisions and operations and help management be better aware of the *future* opportunities and difficulties likely to be encountered.

Accounting concepts and conventions

Concepts

There are four fundamental concepts that underlie the production of a set of accounts.

- *Going concern* – assumes the business will continue to trade 'for the foreseeable future'.
- *Accruals or matching principle* – relates revenues and costs to the period in which they occur.
- *Prudence or conservatism* – avoids an over-optimistic view of the performance of the business; the accountant recognises revenue only when it is realised in an acceptable form but provides for all expenses and losses as soon as they are known.
- *Consistency* – maintains the same approach to asset valuation and the allocation of costs so that comparisons can be made over time.

Conventions

Many accounting conventions have been adopted over time as tried and tested general rules. Here are five key accounting conventions.

- *Objectivity* – accounts are based on measurable facts that can be verified.
- *Separate entity* – the company is recognised as a legal person in its own right, entirely separate from its managers and owners.
- *Money measurement* – all assets and liabilities are expressed in money terms.
- *Historic cost* – all valuations are based on the original cost rather than current worth. Where items fall in value through use, they are depreciated or written down in value. This gives the company an objective valuation of its assets.
- *Double entry* – all transactions involve two sides: giving and receiving. This is acknowledged in the double-entry system of bookkeeping where the source of funds is balanced by the use made of them.

The concepts, conventions and legal requirements which shape the presentation of the accounts have become a matter of intense debate following recent corporate 'scandals'. The attempts to harmonise accounting standards between countries has also become a key issue for businesses.

Accounting standards

The International Accounting Standards Board (IASB) was formed in 2000 with the aim of developing accounting standards that 'require high quality, transparent and comparable information in financial statements and other financial reporting to help participants in the world's capital markets and other users make economic decisions'. In 2001 the IASB adopted a *Framework for the Preparation and Presentation of Financial Statements* which set out certain concepts that underlie the preparation and presentation of financial statements. The Framework identified the following seven groups of users (see Table 10.1) together with the information which they need from the financial statements.

The International Accounting Standards Board (IASB) is seeking a global convergence on accounting standards. More than 110 countries, including most of Europe and Asia, use the International Financial Reporting Standards drawn up by the IASB. US companies continue to report under Generally Accepted Accounting Principles (GAAP) while its regulators consider whether to endorse IFRS. Case 10.1 suggests that it really does matter as to which converged accounting standards are to be used.

Again, the outcome of any such convergence will be important for international business. For example, the proposed converged standard for accounting for pensions is modelled on rules introduced in the UK by Sir David Tweedie, the then IASB chairman who wrote FRS 17, as the UK rule is known. Some companies in the UK have blamed it for forcing the closure of their relatively generous defined benefit pension schemes. The FRS 17 rule on pensions puts a heavy emphasis on 'fair value' accounting, with the measurement of the assets in a defined benefit pension scheme now having to reflect their fair or market value. FRS 17 also tells accountants how to arrive at the present value for future liabilities; it adds them up and discounts back at an interest rate equal to that on AA-rated corporate bonds. Credit ratings agencies are responding to FRS 17 by downgrading the debt of companies such as BAE Systems, the defence group, where they have concerns about pension deficits. Many UK employers,

Table 10.1 **User groups and information needs**

User group	Information needs
Investors	Investors need to assess the financial performance of the organisation they have invested in to consider the risk inherent in, and return provided by, their investments
Lenders	Lenders need to be aware of the ability of the organisation to repay loans and interest. Potential lenders need to decide whether to lend, and on what terms
Suppliers and other trade creditors	Suppliers need to take commercial decisions as to whether or not they should sell to the organisation, and if they do, whether they will be paid
Employees	People will be interested in their employer's stability and profitability, in particular that part of the organisation (such as a branch) in which they work. They will also be interested in the ability of their employer to pay their wages and pensions
Customers	Customers who are dependent on a particular supplier or are considering placing a long-term contract will need to know if the organisation will continue to exist
Governments and their agencies	Reliable financial data helps governments to assemble national economic statistics which are used for a variety of purposes in controlling the economy. Specific financial information from an organisation also enables tax to be assessed
The public	Financial statements often include information relevant to local communities and pressure groups such as attitudes to environmental matters, plans to expand or shut down factories, policies on employment of disabled persons, etc.

Source: International Accounting Standards Board (IASB) (2001) *Framework for the Preparation and Presentation of Financial Statements,* IASB.

CASE 10.1 Accounts shake-up

Britain's economy is going to change abruptly and profoundly in four months' time – at least on paper. For the first time in 15 years, the Office for National Statistics (ONS) will, in September 2014, tear up the way it measures the economy to take account of new international standards and to make the UK as comparable as possible with other countries. If the ONS's preview yesterday was anything to go by, the results will be dramatic. Most eye-catching was the decision to include prostitution and illegal drugs in the national accounts for the first time. Britain is not an outlier in this: all EU countries will be making adjustments for illegal activity in an attempt to make it easier to compare their economies. In the UK, the ONS thinks this will add £10bn to the level of gross domestic product in 2009. Altogether, the changes for September 2014 will add between 4 and 5 per cent to the level of gross domestic product going back to 2009 – the most recent year for which the ONS has calculated the figures so far. The path of real

GDP growth is also likely to change, although statisticians have not calculated that as yet.

Prostitutes and drugs dealers are not the only ones who are set to play a bigger role in the economy. They will be joined by people who build their own houses: the ONS has found a new data source on the value of that activity which it thinks will add £4bn to the economy. Bankers will chip in too: the ONS will change the way it measures 'FISIM' – the gap between interest paid to and received from banks – which will add another £5bn to GDP. On the other side of the ledger, some adjustments to the measurement for investment and stock building will reduce the level of GDP by about £10bn.

But yesterday's announcements are only the beginning. New global accounting standards will also be applied to the national accounts in September 2014. Under these rules, research and development spending will count towards GDP, rather than being seen as a cost of production,

Case 10.1 (*continued*)

and building aircraft carriers and other weapons will also add to the economy's size. One of the biggest changes will be in how savings are measured. The official figures will start to count future pension rights as if they were present income. With Britain one of the few countries to have a large, funded defined benefit pension system, this will significantly raise measured household incomes, thereby increasing the savings ratio. Officials said last month the savings ratio would rise 'by around 5 percentage points', practically doubling the current 5.1 per

cent and putting it at about 10 per cent, far closer to other European countries. That would mean Britons could cast off their reputation as a nation of profligate borrowers and spenders. Instead they would look like a nation of savers.

The full implications of the planned changes are not yet clear. But they come at a sensitive time for the Bank of England. As the central bank weighs how soon to raise interest rates from their record lows, it will be acutely aware that the economy might look entirely different on the morning of September 30 2014 than it does today.

 Source: Accounts shake-up promises boost for growth, *Financial Times*, 30/05/2014, p. 3 (O'Connor, S.), © The Financial Times Limited 2014. All Rights Reserved.

Questions

1 What does this case suggest about the importance of accounting standards and conventions?

2 What are the likely impacts of the changes identified and how might they affect international business activity?

however, argue that FRS 17 is misleading: although a pension shortfall is presented as a liability, it is not one about to come due in full any time soon.

Nevertheless, there is considerable support for a common set of rules by which international investors, whether organisations or individuals, will be better able to compare and contrast the revenue and cost outcomes of international businesses. Case 10.2 reports on a new converged standard for international revenue reporting.

CASE 10.2 New accounting rule a boost for investors

Investors will find it easier to compare this performance of companies around the world following the culmination of a 12 year project to bring together US and international revenue reporting. Accounting regulators in the US and Europe in May 2014 published a joint standard on how companies report revenue from contracts with customers. Eliminating the differences in reporting makes it easier for investors to compare companies in different countries and also remove the risk that some companies may be exploiting the varied rules to flatter their bottom lines. Christophe Hutten, chief accounting officer at German computer software company SAP, called this initiative a 'crown jewel of the effort of global standards'.

A company's revenue, known as its top line, is the amount of money that it receives during a specific period. Costs are taken off the revenue figure to determine a company's net income. Companies in the telecoms, construction, real estate and software industries are likely to be the most affected by the new standard. Many sell packages of goods or services, such as a car dealer selling a vehicle with extended

Case 10.2 (continued)

warranties and insurance, or a telecoms company selling a mobile phone package on a fixed-period contract. Peter Elwin, head of accounting research at JPMorgan, said: 'The joint standard should give more consistency within sectors and provide greater comparability of revenue components in sectors such as telecoms.'

Since the process of converging US and European accounting standards began a decade ago, revenue recognition has been seen as a priority. Regulators have become increasingly vigilant over the ways that companies book sales in the wake of the financial crisis. They are concerned that companies may be tempted to be optimistic and report sales earlier than they should. Under the current approach to revenue recognition, US companies are overseen by the Generally Accepted Accounting Principles and face a more prescriptive regime with specific guidance for different sectors. In Europe, accounts are supervised by the International Financial Reporting Standards, which revolves around principles rather than rules.

Dr Nigel Sleight-Johnson, head of the financial reporting faculty at ICAEW, the UK accountancy body, said implementing the new standard could be a challenge. 'This will involve assessing the impact of the standard on all the company's revenue streams and determining what customers pay for each element of goods and services sold as packages. This can be a complicated task. It may also raise questions about executive pay, which some companies link to revenue. The global standard will take effect in 2017 and is subject to endorsement by individual jurisdictions.

FT *Source*: Adapted from New accounting rule a boost for investors, *Financial Times*, 28/05/2014 (Agnew, H. and Burgess, K.), © The Financial Times Limited 2014. All Rights Reserved.

Questions

1 Identify the main impacts from this new revenue-related accounting rule.

2 How might this change affect international business activity?

Impacts of different accounting standards

The practical implications of countries adopting differing accounting procedures can be seen in the two extracts below which appeared on the same day in an accounting magazine. While somewhat historical, the extracts usefully indicate the reason behind strong support for common international standards in accounting practice.

Extract 1: 'Rover trouble was avoidable'

'Sacked BMW chairman Bernd Pischetsrieder might have retained his job if he had persuaded colleagues not to impose harsh German accounting policies on Rover when the company bought the British car maker in 1994, analysis by *Accountancy Age* has shown. Though the British company is now widely blamed as jeopardising BMW's future as an independent business, Rover's results compiled under British accounting standards, quietly filed at Companies House, paint a picture quite different from the enduring story of huge losses that ultimately led to Pischetsrieder's downfall.

As shown in the table below, figures reveal that Rover made a profit of £147m between 1994 and 1997. Headline figures from consolidated accounts published by BMW, which took the company over in March 1994, however, show Rover making a loss of £363m in the same period. It is these figures that the press, analysts and indeed BMW's board have pounced on as proof of the British car maker's inefficiency.

(Losses in brackets)	Rover net profit using British accounting rules £m	Rover net profit using German accounting rules £m	Difference £m
1994	279	Unpublished	–
1995	(51)	(163)	2112
1996	(100)	(109)	29
1997	19	(91)	272
Total	**147**	**(363)**	**2216**

Source: Accountancy Age, 18 February 1999.

German accounting policies are notoriously harsh. Investments are depreciated faster; there are more possibilities for making provisions and different rules for valuing stocks. All these have the effect of depressing profits.'

Extract 2: 'UK standards add £200m to British Airways results'

'Differing international accounting systems are affecting airlines' reported profit levels by hundreds of millions of pounds each year, according to an aviation industry expert. Using an analysis of the results of British Airways, Richard Shaylor, a financial analysis lecturer with Signal Training, says the differences are confusing investors. The airline publishes its results according to UK standards and has no plans to move to an international standard. But, because it has shares listed on both the London and New York Stock Exchanges, it also includes a revised profit and loss account constructed according to US generally accepted accounting practice in its annual report. As the table below shows, one of the larger distortions arises from BA's 1996 figures. Under UK rules, it made a profit of £473m, whereas using US rules the figure was £267m.'

	BA net profit using British accounting rules (£m)	BA net profit using US accounting rules (£m)	Difference (£m)
1994	274	145	−129
1995	250	297	147
1996	473	267	−206
1997	553	548	−5
1998	460	654	1194
Totals	**2,010**	**1,911**	**−99**

Source: Accountancy Age, 18 February 1999.

Pause for thought 10.1

Comment briefly on how the issues raised in these two extracts have implications for international business.

Table 10.2 **Reasons for different accounting standards**

The legal system	Some countries (e.g. France and Germany) have all-embracing sets of rules and regulations which apply to businesses, whereas countries such as the UK and the USA have more general statute laws backed up by case law, allowing more flexibility for individual companies. For example, in the USA, individual companies decide the rates at which assets depreciate, but in Germany the government decides what is appropriate.
Types of ownership patterns	Countries with wide share ownership (e.g. UK, USA) have developed strong independent professional accountancy associations to provide reliable financial data to shareholders. Those countries with predominantly small, family-run businesses (e.g. France) or with banks owning most shares of large companies (e.g. Germany) have had less need for providers of independent financial information.
The accounting profession	Strong independent professional associations of accountants developed in those countries (e.g. UK, USA) with the most liberal company laws and widest share ownership. Countries with restricted patterns of business ownership and rigid company statutes (e.g. France, Germany) had weak groupings of accountants, and sometimes the governments themselves controlled the profession.
Conservatism	Financial statements produced by independent accountants should ideally show a 'true and fair view'. This is open to many interpretations, not least being the problem of asset valuation. Should assets be valued at original cost, what they might be sold at today, what it would cost to replace them or a depreciated value based on usage, wear and tear, etc.? US practice is conservative – don't revalue, but depreciate on a reasonable basis over the asset's lifetime. German practice is also conservative – don't revalue, but depreciate on a basis decreed by the government. UK practice is liberal – allowing companies either to revalue at intervals or show assets at cost, and depreciate on a reasonable basis.

As seen in the extracts above, major industrialised nations have developed their own specific accounting regulations. This rarely has a major impact when applied to domestic companies within those countries, but as we have seen can have dramatic implications when international investment decisions have to be made.

Some of the reasons why countries have previously adopted different accounting standards are briefly reviewed in Table 10.2.

Risk assessment and the credit rating agencies

The standards used in reporting revenues, costs and profits in the various published accounts are of obvious interest to the credit rating agencies. The well-known companies, Moody's Investors Service and Standard & Poor's, both based in New York, dominate the ratings industry, with the creditworthiness of countries or organisations having major impacts on the availability and cost of raising finance. Two smaller firms, Fitch IBCA and Duff & Phelps Credit Rating Co., also issue ratings internationally. The firms' ratings are not always in agreement, as each uses a different methodology. Table 10.3 interprets the default ratings of the four major international firms.

A downgrading of the credit ratings of either a private company or a government can have serious implications for the borrowers. Lenders will insist on higher interest rates on any future loans to that company or government in order to cover the increased risks of

Table 10.3 **Credit risk assessments**

	Moody's	Standard & Poor's	Fitch IBCA	Duff & Phelps
Highest credit quality; issuer has strong ability to meet obligations	Aaa	AAA	AAA	AAA
Very high credit quality; low risk of default	Aa1 Aa2 Aa3	AA+ AA AA−	AA	AA+ AA AA−
High credit quality, but more vulnerable to changes in economy or business	A1 A2 A3	AA+ AA AA−	AA	AA+ AA AA−
Adequate credit quality for now, but more likely to be impaired if conditions worsen	Baa1 Baa2 Baa3	BBB+ BBB BBB−	BBB	BBB+ BBB BBB−
Below investment grade, but good chance that issuer can meet commitments	Ba1 Ba2 Ba3	BB+ BB BB−	BB	BB+ BB BB−
Significant credit risk, but issuer is presently able to meet obligations	B1 B2 B3	B+ B B−	B	B+ B B−
High default risk	Caa1 Caa2 Caa3	CCC+ CCC CCC−	CCC	CCC+ CCC CCC−
Issuer failed to meet scheduled interest or principal payments	C	D	DDD DD D	DD

making such loans. This can be important for both individual businesses and for the macro-environment in which they operate since higher interest rates are likely to depress aggregate demand (both consumption and investment) in the country and increase the prospects of economic recession.

What is clear is that when a country or business is downgraded by one or more credit rating agencies, the impacts can be substantial. Case 10.3 reviews one such ratings downgrade for Puerto Rico in 2014.

CASE 10.3 Moody's cuts Puerto Rico deeper into junk

Puerto Rico securities are widely held among pension and mutual funds, which have benefited from the bonds' exemption from municipal, state and federal taxes. A move by Puerto Rico in 2014 to allow some public companies to restructure their debts has rattled the $4,000bn US municipal debt market, sparking a credit downgrade by Moody's, a leading rating agency. Alejandro Garcia Padilla, the island's governor, signed a bill at the weekend that allows some of Puerto Rico's largest utilities, such as the Puerto Rico Power Authority, to negotiate with bondholders to reduce their mounting debt loads. The bill was seen as a departure from the Caribbean island's commitment to bondholders.

Moody's on Tuesday cut its credit rating on the US territory to B2 from Ba2, deeper into 'junk' territory, after warning that the new legislation provided 'a clear path to default' for public companies. Standard & Poor's also signalled it may cut

Case 10.3 (*continued*)

Puerto Rico's credit rating within 60 to 90 days. Unlike some US municipalities, the constitution of Puerto Rico, a US territory, prevents the government and public companies from seeking protection from creditors in bankruptcy courts. While some public companies could default under the new law, officials were adamant it did not apply to bonds issued and backed directly by the commonwealth, which make up the bulk of the island's $7.3bn debt. 'We will continue to honour our obligations to Puerto Rico's creditors. We are focused on assuring that Puerto Rico regains its economic growth, and we will stand by this promise, the governor said in a statement.

The public bodies have combined debt of almost $20bn and, under the law, they would be able to negotiate repayment to bondholders for a period of several months. Any restructuring would require approval of 75 per cent of bondholders. Governor Padila defended the bill, saying it allowed public companies to address their financial difficulties without compromising any essential services.

Funds managed by Franklin Funds and Oppenheimer, which hold Puerto Rico Power Authority bonds, have challenged the new law, saying it is unconstitutional and only the US Congress is allowed to change bankruptcy rulings. In the past month following the ratings downgrade, yields on Puerto Rico's general obligation bonds have risen 21 basis points, to 7.96 per cent on Monday, according to Thomson Reuter's data.

 Source: Adapted from Moody's cuts Puerto Rico deeper into junk, *Financial Times*, 01/07/2014 (Rodrigues, V.). © The Financial Times Limited 2014. All Rights Reserved.

Questions

1 Why has Puerto Rico debt been downgraded by the credit rating agencies?

2 What impacts might this have for Puerto Rico itself and for international business activity in Puerto Rico.

Case 10.4 is a useful reminder of why organisations and governments often challenge the ratings given by a particular agency.

CASE 10.4 Moody's faced new conflict of interest claim

Moody's appears to show favouritism towards its top shareholders – including Warren Buffett's Berkshire Hathaway – when rating the bonds of companies, a new academic study has found. The study's conclusion – which Moody's disputes – could revive concerns over potential conflicts of interest at credit rating agencies, which are paid to evaluate the riskiness of billions of dollars' worth of bonds.

These concerns zoomed into focus in the years following the financial crisis, with rule makers working to decrease the link between credit ratings and financial regulation and even pressing for limits on Moody's ability to rate Berkshire-related products. The study, due to be presented at the American Accounting Association's annual meeting in August 2014, looks at ratings made by Moody's between 2001 and 2010 and

Case 10.4 (*continued*)

compares them with ratings issued by Standard & Poor's, the larger competitor. It finds that Moody's had a 'tangible bias' in favouring companies in which Berkshire or Davis Selected Advisors – the two biggest shareholders of Moody's – owned at least a 0.25 per cent stake. On average Moody's ratings of these bonds are almost half a notch higher than ratings on the same bonds given by S&P. That would equate to interest savings of roughly half a million dollars for the issuing firms per year, according to the authors of the paper. 'All we can show is some kind of statistically circumstantial evidence,' says Shivaram Rajgopol, a professor at Emory University and one of the study's authors.

Moody's said: 'Moody's ratings are based on a thorough, independent analysis of credit quality by our ratings committees, conducted according to publicly available methodologies. Any coincidental ownership of Moody's Corporation shares has absolutely no bearing on our ratings actions, and we have long had measures in place to maintain a strong separation between the analytical and commercial aspects of our business.'

The rating agency became a publicly traded company in 2000 with Berkshire Hathaway and Davis – (the New York-based asset manager) – taking large stakes in the company. The initial public offering has previously been highlighted as a turning point in Moody's more than century-long history. In testimony made to the US Congress in late 2008, Jerome Fons, a former Moody's director, said: 'management's focus increasingly turned "to maximising revenues" in the post-IPO period'. The new study – by Simi Kedia, Shivaram Rajgopal and Zing Zhou – builds on their previous work analysing credit rating agencies and finds that Moody's was slower than S&P by an average 71 days to downgrade bonds related to its long-term large shareholders. It also identifies a similar pattern in the ratings awarded to commercial mortgage-backed securities, which bundle together loans secured by shopping malls, office buildings and the like.

Questions

1 What is the basis for criticising Moody's approaches to credit rating?

2 Does it matter that the various credit rating agencies adopt different approaches?

The credit ratings agencies have been strongly criticised, especially during the recent 'austerity years', for regularly downgrading the credit ratings of economies such as Greece, Spain, Portugal and Ireland. Indeed, even the US lost its AAA rating in 2009.

International financial markets

The international financial markets are usually regarded as those involved in trading foreign exchange and various types of paper assets such as equities (shares), government debt (bills, bonds, etc.) and financial derivatives (options, etc.). They are important to firms, individuals and governments in raising finance to support international production, trade and investment, in reducing risks and in providing a potentially income-generating repository for any surplus funds they might hold. Of course, in recent times any such 'certainties' as to the role of these international financial markets and their various financial instruments have been shaken by a global liquidity crisis. We return to this issue, its underlying causes, its impact on international business and proposed remedies at various points in the chapter.

The foreign exchange market

The foreign exchange market is the market on which international currencies are traded. It has no physical existence: it consists of traders, such as the dealing rooms of major banks, who are in continual communication with one another on a worldwide basis. Currencies are bought and sold on behalf of clients, which may be companies, private individuals or banks themselves. A distinction is made between the 'spot' rate for a currency and the forward rate. The *spot rate* is the domestic currency price of a unit of foreign exchange when the transaction is to be completed within three days. The *forward rate* is the price of that unit when delivery is to take place at some future date – usually 30, 60 or 90 days hence. Both spot and forward rates are determined in today's market; the relationship between today's spot and today's forward rate will be determined largely by how the market *expects* the spot rate to move in the near future. The more efficient the market is at anticipating future spot rates, the closer will today's forward rate be to the future spot rate.

The spot market is used by those who wish to acquire foreign exchange immediately. Forward markets are used by three groups of people:

1 *hedgers* who wish to cover themselves (*hedge*) against the risk of exchange variation. For instance, suppose an importer orders goods to be paid for in three months' time in dollars. All his calculations will be upset if the price of dollars rises between now and payment date. He can cover himself by buying dollars today for delivery in three months' time; he thus locks himself into a rate which reduces the risk element in his transaction;

2 *arbitrageurs* who attempt to make a profit on the difference between interest rates in one country and another, and who buy or sell currency forward to ensure that the profit which they hope to make by moving their capital is not negated by adverse exchange rate movements;

3 *speculators* who use the forward markets to buy or sell in anticipation of exchange rate changes. For instance, if I think that today's forward rates do not adequately reflect the probability of the dollar increasing in value I will buy dollars forward, hoping to sell them at a profit when they are delivered to me at some future date.

London is the world's largest centre for foreign exchange trading, with an average daily turnover in 2014 of over US$5,300 billion. The market is growing all the time; indeed, the average daily turnover in 2014 was more than eight times the value recorded in 1992. Some 39% of transactions are 'spot' on any one day, some 12% are forward, and the remaining 49% involve foreign currency futures, options and swaps of one kind or another, especially swaps. The following have been the fastest growing currency transactions:

- *foreign currency futures,* which are standardised contracts to buy or sell on agreed terms on specific future dates (see pp. 362–363);
- *foreign currency options,* which give the right (but do not impose an obligation) to buy or sell currencies at some future date and price (see pp. 362–363);

- *foreign currency swaps* – rather than purchase the foreign currency, countries and firms swap agreed values of one currency for another, to be returned at a specified future date (see p. 000).

Foreign exchange market business in London is done in an increasingly wide variety of currencies with the £/$ business now accounting for only 11% of activity.

Supply and demand for a currency

Prices of currencies are determined, as on any other market, by demand for and supply of the various currencies. Tourists coming to the UK will sell their own currency in order to buy (demand) sterling. Businessmen wishing to import goods will often sell (supply) sterling in order to buy currency with which to pay the supplier in another country. Other types of transactions, too, will have exchange rate repercussions. For instance, if an American company wishes to buy an office or a factory in the UK, it will need to convert dollars into sterling. A similar demand for sterling will result from foreign banks wishing to make sterling deposits in London, or residents abroad who wish to buy UK government bonds.

Another way of presenting this is to say that in any given period of time the factors that determine the demand for and supply of foreign exchange are those which are represented in the balance of payments account. For example, demand for sterling results from the export of UK goods and services and inflows of foreign capital into the UK (short and long term), which are all plus signs in the balance of payments accounts. Similarly, a supply of sterling results from imports of goods and services into the UK and outflows of capital from the UK (short and long term), which are all minus signs in the balance of payments accounts.

Of course companies and individuals are not the only clients of foreign exchange market dealers. In the case of the UK the Bank of England buys and sells foreign currency, using the official reserves in the Exchange Equalisation Account. In order to reflect on why this might be the case, we have to remember that governments have an interest in the level of the exchange rate (see Chapter 4) and that they may on occasion wish to intervene in the workings of the foreign exchange market to affect the value of their currency. Indeed, it was estimated that on the day sterling was forced to withdraw from the Exchange Rate Mechanism (ERM) (16 September 1992), the Bank of England spent an estimated £7 billion, roughly a third of its foreign exchange reserves, in buying sterling. In particular, it bought sterling with deutschmarks in an unsuccessful attempt to preserve the sterling exchange rate within its permitted ERM band. A current criticism by the US administration is that the Chinese authorities are continually intervening in the foreign exchange market to keep the exchange rate between the yuan and the dollar artificially low.

The worldwide demand for and supply of a currency will determine its price (the exchange rate) on the foreign exchange market.

The exchange rate

The exchange rate is the price of one currency in terms of another. The exchange rate for sterling is conventionally defined as the number of units of another currency, such as the dollar, that it takes to purchase one pound sterling on the foreign exchange market. In the market,

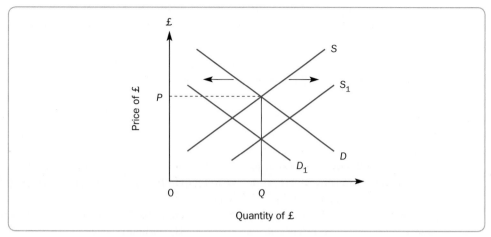

Figure 10.1 **The foreign exchange market**

however, it is usually quoted as the number of units of the domestic currency that it takes to purchase one unit of the foreign currency. In general terms the sterling exchange rate is perhaps the most important 'price' in the UK economic system. It affects the standard of living, because it determines how many goods we can get for what we sell abroad. It influences the price of UK exports and hence their sales, thereby determining output and jobs in the export industries. It structures the extent to which imports can compete with home-produced goods, and thereby affects the viability of UK companies. Because the price of imports enters into the retail price index (RPI), any variation in the exchange rate will also have an effect on the rate of inflation.

Figure 10.1 presents a stylised picture of how the sterling exchange rate is determined on the foreign exchange market. Suppose we start with the supply of sterling S and the demand for sterling D, giving an initial equilibrium exchange rate 0P with 0Q pounds sterling bought and sold on the foreign exchange market. Anything which shifts one or other of the curves will change the equilibrium price (exchange rate) on the foreign exchange market. Supply and demand curves for sterling can shift for a number of reasons:

- A shift (increase) in supply from S to S_1 might be due to a change in the tastes of UK residents in favour of foreign products. More expenditure by UK residents on imports will mean more sterling being supplied in order to buy the foreign currencies to pay for those imports (more investment overseas by UK residents will have the same effect). The same increase in supply from S to S1 could be the result of a rise in *capital outflows* from sterling deposits to overseas currency deposits in different currencies.

- A shift (decrease) in demand from D to D_1 might be due to a change in the tastes of overseas residents away from UK products. Less expenditure by overseas residents on UK exports will mean less sterling being demanded in order to pay for those exports (less investment in the UK by overseas residents – firms and individuals – will have the same effect). The same decrease in demand from D to D_1 could be the result of a fall in *capital inflows* into sterling deposits from overseas currency deposits in different countries.

Each of these changes (increase in supply or decrease in demand) will result in the pound falling in value (depreciating). We have already noted how a fall in the exchange rate makes exports cheaper abroad and imports dearer at home (see Chapter 3, p. 104).

Pause for thought 10.2

In recent times the pound has been rising in value (appreciating against both the euro and the US dollar). Can you use Figure 10.1 to explain the factors that might cause the pound to rise above OP?

In actual fact there are different types of exchange rate, as is noted in Box 10.1.

BOX 10.1 Types of exchange rate

In a foreign exchange market where exchange rates are allowed to 'float', every currency has a price against every other currency. In order to allow for measurability three different types of exchange rate may be used.

1 **The nominal rate of exchange.** This is the rate of exchange for any one currency as quoted against any other currency. The nominal exchange rate is therefore a bilateral (two country) exchange rate.

2 **The effective exchange rate (EER).** This is a measure that takes into account the fact that each currency (e.g. sterling) varies in different ways against each of the other currencies, some of which are more important than others in the UK's trading relationships. It is calculated as a trade-weighted average of the individual or bilateral rates, and is expressed as an index number relative to the base

year. The EER is therefore a multilateral (many country) trade-weighted exchange rate.

3 **The real exchange rate (RER).** This concept is designed to measure the rate at which home goods exchange for goods from other countries, rather than the rate at which the currencies themselves are traded. It is thus essentially a measure of competitiveness. When we consider multilateral UK trade, it is defined as:

$$RER = EER \times \frac{P(UK)}{P(F)}$$

In other words, the real exchange rate is equal to the effective exchange rate multiplied by the price ratio of home, P(UK), to foreign, P(F), goods. If UK prices rise, the real exchange rate will rise unless the effective exchange rate falls.

Case 10.5 reviews the current suggestion that these various exchange rates for sterling have become overvalued in recent times, with various adverse effects.

CASE 10.5 IMF says 'overvalued' pound preventing rebalancing

The international Monetary Fund warned in July 2014 that the pound was 'overvalued' and preventing the rebalancing of the UK economy away from a reliance on spending and imports. In its annual assessment of the UK economy, the IMF said sterling was between 5 and 10 per cent overvalued because of a 'lack of competitiveness and limited export diversification.' Although sterling's rise will be a boon to UK tourists abroad, the IMF called for Britain to be less reliant on public and private

spending if it was to rectify its unsustainable external position.

The IMF focus on sterling came after the pound has strengthened about 10 per cent over the past year against the dollar and the IMF's assessment of current real effective exchange rates – taking into account the UK's trading patterns and inflation – is 6 per cent stronger than the 2013 average. Sterling's strength was impeding the efforts to close Britain's trade deficit and leaving

Case 10.5 (*continued*)

too high a current account deficit, a measure that also includes investment income on foreign-owned assets. 'The IMF estimates that the current account balance is 2.6 per cent weaker than its equilibrium level and that the real exchange rate is overvalued by about 5–10 per cent, the IMF said. It recommended continued cuts in public spending and efforts to boost productivity to make the UK more competitive.

The IMF criticised the UK government for blocking skilled immigration as a route to higher productivity. 'Relaxing immigration requirements in areas with labour shortage, such as manufacturing, could provide a boost to productivity and facilitate the rebalancing of the UK economy,' it said. The IMF also favoured 'loosening' the visa regime for foreign students 'to improve skills and facilitate educational exports'. Without a rise in productivity, the IMF warned that the Bank of England would have to raise interest rates sooner rather than later because the economy would run out of slack for rapid non-inflationary growth. Should productivity fail to pick up, the MPC which sets interest rates in the UK would eventually have to tighten monetary conditions to dampen inflationary pressures, in keeping with its mandate, the IMF staff concluded.

 Source: Adapted from IMF says 'overvalued' pound preventing rebalancing, *Financial Times*, 28/07/2014 (Giles, C.), © The Financial Times Limited 2014. All Rights Reserved.

Questions

1 What are the reasons for the IMF believing that the pound is overvalued?

2 What policies might help remove this overvaluation of the pound? Explain your reasoning.

3 What are the likely impacts of an overvalued pound?

International debt financing

Firms can raise short- and long-term loans on international as well as domestic financial markets. The term 'money markets' is usually applied to the buying and selling of short-term (less than one year to maturity) debt instruments, whereas the term 'bond markets' refers to trading longer-term (more than one year to maturity) debt instruments.

Here we select a number of important international financial markets by way of illustration. In doing so we examine the sources and impacts of the so-called 'credit crunch' and the associated financial derivatives and instruments which have been widely traded across the world, and which underpin many of the contemporary issues that have arisen within global finance and trade. It may be helpful to begin with the market in a wide range of structured investment vehicles (SIVs) and the origins of that market.

Structured investment vehicles (SIVs) market

These are the financial instruments that have emerged in recent years and which consist of not one but a variety of securities, some of which involve mortgage debt (see Figure 10.2). Before reviewing the contribution of SIVs to current international financial developments, it will help to consider the so-called *subprime* market, and the impact this has had on the value of SIVs, many of which involve a mortgage-backed 'slice' of their overall portfolio.

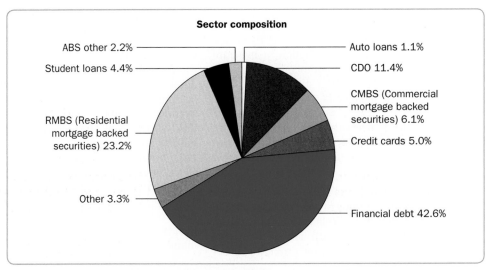

Figure 10.2 The Structured Investment Vehicle (SIV)

Source: SIV manager dig out their manuals, *Financial Times*, 30/08/2007 (Davies, P.), © The Financial Times Limited 2007. All Rights Reserved.

Subprime market

The term 'subprime' was widely used to refer to excessive lending for mortgage purposes in the US to low-income borrowers at high risk. When economic slowdown occurred in the US in 2006/07, many of these high-risk borrowers lost their jobs and/or found themselves unable to pay the higher monthly repayments as US interest rates rose substantially in 2006/07 (by around 4% in little over one year). Nor did these low-income/high-risk borrowers have assets to help cushion falls in their current income. As a result many defaulted on their loans and the bad debt provision of the lenders soared, putting huge pressure on themselves and on other financial firms worldwide which had invested in the mortgage-related securities.

House prices fell by over 30% in the US in the following three years to 2010, and a simulation by economists at the UBS bank had suggested that a 10% drop in US house and share prices would reduce US economic growth by as much as 2.6 percentage points. The negative impacts on US and, via contagion, world economic growth did indeed materialise, with standards of living in the global economy of 2014 barely higher than that in 2006/07 before the 'austerity years'.

Box 10.2 takes a closer look at what exactly constitutes a SIV.

Problems in this market for SIVs and associated financial instruments such as collateralised debt obligations (CDOs) have played a key role in the events unfolding globally over recent years.

'Contagion' is a word much feared by analysts of the subprime market. Many innovative financial instruments which were developed and used ('securitisation') to stimulate extra lending and borrowing are now viewed with much greater suspicion by the financial markets. Lending between financial intermediaries themselves has also diminished, as they have become more unsure of the true creditworthiness of the borrowers, given that there is now serious concern over the value of many of these new financial instruments in their portfolios. This reluctance of financial intermediaries to lend to each other was a key factor in the problems experienced in 2007/08 by Northern Rock in the UK, whose business model depended

> ### BOX 10.2 The Structured Investment Vehicle (SIV)
>
> 1 A structured investment vehicle (SIV) exists to help those acquiring it make a profit from the difference between the low cost of short-term debt funding and the higher returns, or yields, of longer-term debt investments.
>
> 2 A SIV consists of a pool of debts of financial companies, such as banks and insurers, including asset-backed securities, or bonds, backed by mortgages, loans or other debt (see Figure 10.2).
>
> 3 The SIV funds these more profitable longer-term investments by issuing debt itself. A small portion of this debt (between 5% and 12%) is longer term and carries the first risk of losses if assets in the pool of investments start to go bad. This debt is also the last to be repaid, but it shares some of the profits made by the vehicle. This is the *junior debt,* otherwise known as the capital notes.
>
> 4 The lion's share of debt issued by the SIV is very low-cost short-term commercial paper, which has a life span of days or weeks, and medium-term notes, which have a life span of three to six months. This is the *senior debt.*

on regular inter-bank loans which were no longer forthcoming. The share price of Northern Rock collapsed in late 2007, forcing the Bank of England to step in as 'lender of last resort' and to avoid a systemic banking failure in the UK.

Collateralised debt obligations (CDOs) are themselves bundles of other securities and have been traded on international financial markets singly, or as part of broader SIVs. The linkage of slices of these securities to the falling value of mortgages and to other assets of diminishing value has been a major element in the declining portfolio and capital values of many international organisations.

Case Study 10.6 suggests that the international financial markets are still making use of such financial instruments.

CASE 10.6 Sliced and diced debt deals

In early June 2009, the world's securitisation bankers congregated at a London hotel on Edgware Road, not far from the prison cells at Paddington Green police station. It was a location symbolic of the state of the securitisation industry in the aftermath of the financial crisis, when the bankers who had sliced and diced loans into bonds were in the collective doghouse. 'Regroup and rebuild' was the humble slogan for that year's Global ABS or asset-backed securities conference.

Five years later in 2014 and bankers are now heading to the summer climes of Barcelona for the annual ABS gathering. The location is, once again, suggestive of the wider state of securitisation markets – one that features a much brighter outlook. Certain securitisation deals have roared back in the US. The European market could soon come back to life after a prolonged hibernation.

➡

Case 10.6 (*continued*)

The Bank of England and the European Central Bank are now arguing that restarting parts of the securitisation market could help funnel credit to the wider economy and help transfer risk away from still struggling banks. The ECB is also said to be considering purchasing ABS as part of an effort to jump start Eurozone growth: it is a far cry from the days when the products were branded by regulators as 'toxic sludge'. The ECB potentially buying ABS is an important symbolic indication that the policy paradigm has shifted,' says Mark Hale, chief investment officer at Prytania Investment Advisors, a London-based structured finance specialist.

In the US, the resurgence has been swift. While this kind of subprime mortgage-backed securities that played a prominent role in the build-up to the financial crisis remain dormant, other securitisation deals have rebounded thanks to investors' hunger for yield and low corporate default rates. US sales of collateralised loan obligations, or packages of loans made to low-rated companies, are on course to hit a record high this year. Issuance of commercial mortgage-backed securities totalled $102bn in 2013, according to Dealogic data, the highest since the $231bn sold just before the crisis.

In Europe, by contrast, sales of securitised bonds have been anaemic. Given a choice, local banks have opted to tap central bank facilities for their funding instead of creating securitisation to sell to an investor base still wary of the products. 'Investor-placed European ABS issuance had been around €60bn to €70bn a year since 2010 and has not really been increasing,' says Christian Aufsatz, European ABS strategist at Barclays. He estimates that sales of securitisation to investors between 2004 and 2006 ranged from €250bn to €400bn a year.

The BoE and ECB are aiming to revive the simplest of ABS structures. They now argue that securitisation 'can contribute to enhancing the issuer's risk management culture' rather than jeopardise it. Nevertheless, there are critics who warn that the industry has yet to learn the lessons of the crisis.

Questions

1 Why is there a renewed interest in CDOs and other types of asset-backed securities?

2 What are the potential benefits and costs to international business activity of this renewed interest?

Box 10.3 identifies some of the other, more conventional instruments used in the finance of international trade.

The relevance of the availability, as well as cost, of international debt financing to global trade has had major impacts on supply chain strategies and their financing by dependent organisations. There has been a distinct lack of trust between financial intermediaries themselves, given that no party knew the extent to which the other had CDOs or other mortgag-backed securities in their portfolios or SIVs. As a result there has been a reluctance to lend even to other financial institutions, given the uncertainty arising from this information asymmetry. Such liquidity shortages have also had significant impacts on the global supply chain.

Companies' supply chains have become far more global in the past decade, with the consequence that stress from the financial crisis has spread quickly to suppliers large and small,

BOX 10.3 Financial instruments and international trade

The following is a brief review of some of the more traditional financial instruments associated with the finance of international trade.

- *Bills of exchange.* An exporter may send this to an importer ordering the importer to pay a certain sum of money to the exporter on receipt of the bill or at a specified date in the future (often three months). The exporter (seller) is the *'drawer'* of the bill and the importer (buyer) is the *'drawee'*; the exporter's bank is the *'remitting bank'* and the importer's bank the *'collecting bank'*. The bill of exchange must be *'accepted'* (endorsed) by the foreign importer (*drawee*) before it becomes a 'negotiable instrument' – that is, once accepted the bill can be sold to a third party for less than the face value (i.e. discounted) if the exporter needs immediate cash or held for the full three months, etc.

- An *'avalised bill of exchange'* carries a guarantee from the importer's bank that the bill will definitely be honoured. If the bill is not avalised, then the exporter's bank will expect the exporting company to repay the loan itself should the importer default. *'With recourse financing'* is a term used whenever a bank can demand compensation from an exporter should the importer default.

- *Forfaiting.* For large-scale (and often long-term) finance a company may issue a bundle of bills of exchange, each one maturing on a different date (e.g. six months, 12 months, 18 months, 24 months, etc.) up to the completion of the project. Once 'accepted', these bills can be sold in their entirety to the company's own banker should immediate cash be required.

- *Letters of credit.* These may be required by exporters who wish to have proof that they will be paid before they send their products abroad. Such letters are an order from one bank to a bank abroad authorising payment to a person named in the letter of a particular sum of money or up to a limit of a certain sum. Letters of credit are not negotiable but can be cashed at the specified bank. A 'confirmed' letter of credit is one which has been guaranteed by a bank in the exporter's own country; the confirming bank has no claim on the exporter should there be any default. Normally the exporter is paid by the confirming bank which then collects the money from the foreign bank issuing the credit. Almost all letters of credit are 'irrevocable', i.e. they cannot be cancelled at any time by the customer (importer).

- *Factoring.* Here the debt is sold on to another company for a price (usually well below the face value of the debt), with the new company now responsible for collecting the original debt.

- *Invoice discounting.* Similar to factoring, except that the exporter retains responsibility for debt collection and for an agreed proportion of bad debts. However, the exporter does receive a cash payment (loan) from the invoice discounter issued to customers.

- *Securitisation.* The process of converting any existing (non-tradable) loan into a security which is tradable. The seller of the asset (security) guarantees payment of interest in the new bundled security, which now becomes more liquid than the assets it replaces.

- *Options, futures* and *swaps* (pp. 362–363).

encouraging companies in industries from aerospace to retailing to take extraordinary measures. VT Group, a leading British defence group, summoned its leading 100 suppliers – which accounted for about 70% of its £500 million annual supply budget – to a meeting in which it offered to help solve cash flow problems in its supply chain, paying suppliers in cash earlier, giving them longer orders or even lending them workers.

Counterparty risk refers to the chance one side of an agreement will default, and it has become a key concept as producers more closely check their exposure to risk in the supply chain. 'Is your overseas supplier financially sound? Are they capable of maintaining your supply?' is an increasingly familiar question for supply chain analysts.

Many organisations now seek double or triple sourcing with suppliers for the same part or component spread across the world. But doubts remain. One is over how quickly a supplier can respond to take over the capacity if one of its rivals collapses. Another is the fact that some components are so complex they are manufactured only by one supplier. Additionally, companies such as car makers often use one supplier for each model or project, meaning changing component makers could take months.

Just-in-time delivery – long the mantra of many manufacturers worldwide – is also turning into a possible weakness in the supply chain. A problem with just one supplier can throw the entire system into chaos, as can shipping difficulties. Manufacturing experts say that for these and other reasons they are starting to see Western companies bring back operations or suppliers from far-off countries in Asia to closer to home: Eastern Europe or Mexico.

Other international financial markets

We now review some of the other important international financial markets.

Eurocurrency market

Eurocurrency is currency held on deposit with a bank outside the country from which that currency originates. For example, loans made in dollars by banks in the UK are known as Eurodollar loans. The Eurocurrency market is a wholesale market and has its origins in the growing holdings of US dollars outside the USA in the 1960s. Since that time, Eurocurrency markets have grown rapidly to include dealing in all the major currencies, and have become particularly important when oil price rises have created huge world surpluses and deficits, resulting in large shifts in demand for and supply of the major world currencies.

The major participants are banks, who use the Euromarkets for a variety of reasons: for short-term inter-bank lending and borrowing, to match the currency composition of assets and liabilities, and for global liquidity transformation between branches. However, the market is also extensively used by companies and by governmental and international organisations. Lending which is longer term is usually done on a variable-rate basis, where the interest is calculated periodically in line with changing market rates.

There are two important factors which make Eurocurrency business attractive. The first is that the market is unregulated, so that banks which are subject to reserve requirements or interest rate restrictions in the home country, for instance, can do business more freely abroad. The other factor is that the margin between the lending and borrowing rates is narrower on this market than on the home market, primarily because banks can operate at lower cost when all business is wholesale and when they are not subject to reserve requirements.

Euro-paper and Euro-note markets

The Eurocurrency markets have led to the issue of various types of *Euro-paper* and *Euro-note* debt instruments.

- *Euro-commercial papers* (ECPs) are short-term debt instruments usually denominated in dollars. They can be issued by multinational companies with excellent credit ratings, and holders obtain a return by purchasing them at a discount (i.e. paying less than face value at issue and receiving face value on maturity).

- *Euro notes* are short- to medium-term debt instruments (up to five years to maturity) which again can be issued by multinational companies, but with an interest return (rather than discount) to those holding them to maturity. Euro medium-term notes (Euro MTNs) have been growing rapidly in recent years, often being seen as much more flexible than more conventional debt instruments (e.g. more choice in terms of value, maturity date, currency, fixed/variable interest, etc.).

Eurobond markets

Longer-term bonds typically have maturity dates ranging up to 30 years. A *Eurobond* is underwritten by an investment bank and can be sold only outside the country from which the bond originates. Eurobonds are usually issued by large multinational firms (of high credit standing), governments and international institutions. The interest paid may be fixed or variable; in the latter case a linkage is made with other interest rates (e.g. the London Interbank Offer Rate, or LIBOR – notorious in recent years for alleged rate fixing). Some Eurobonds are 'convertible' in the sense that holders can convert the bond at a set price ('warrant' price) prior to the maturity date. The Eurobond market has grown substantially, partly because there is less regulation and fewer disclosure requirements than in other bond markets and various tax advantages (e.g. interest on Eurobonds has been exempt from the EU income-withholding tax).

Sharia bond markets

The issue of bonds which comply with Islamic law is a growth area for international finance, as indicated in Case 10.7.

CASE 10.7 Tunisia and Pakistan join rush for Sharia Bonds

Countries including Pakistan, Tunisia and South Africa are drawing up plans to issue government bonds that comply with Islamic law as they seek to capitalise on strong investor demand for sovereign debt from emerging markets. Pakistan, which racked up orders worth $7bn for a $2bn sale of government debt earlier this year, says it plans to issue the bonds, known as sukuk, before the end of 2014. Officials in Islamabad say they hope to announce which banks have been hired for the sale within the next few weeks.

In Kenya, where investors placed orders of $8bn for the country's first international sale of debt in June, the central bank has told local banks that new regulations will enable the sale of bonds that adhere to Sharia, or Islamic law. Tunisia is working with the Islamic Development Bank to issue a 1bn dinar ($700m) sukuk this year, while Jordan has instructed a committee to look into the possibility of issuing sukuk next year. South Africa and the Philippines also say they are considering raising money by selling Islamic debt.

Global sukuk issuance reached $66bn in the first half of 2014, an increase of 8 per cent on the same period last year, according to the Malaysia International Islamic Finance Centre, which says it expects new sovereign issues to drive growth throughout the rest of the year. Entrants to the market this year include Senegal, which launched sub-Saharan African's biggest sukuk this summer. Analysts say that Africa, home to about a quarter of the world's Muslims, could be a fertile source of future growth for Islamic finance, though some question whether all countries will go through with a sale. 'There has been a lot of

Case 10.7 (continued)

rumours about potential sovereign sukuk issuance this year,' said Souhail Mahjour, emerging markets debt specialist at HSBC. 'Not all are likely to come to the market. Those that already issue regularly and want to diversify, and countries with a large Muslim population or a strong link to Islamic countries, are most likely.'

Islamic bonds are structured to adhere to Muslim prohibition on interest payments. The market remains small compared with that for conventional sovereign debt and is dominated by Malaysia. However, strong investor appetite for government bonds issued by other emerging market countries has encouraged more governments to consider raising money through Islamic bonds. 'Countries with Islamic populations are natural borrowers through sukuk, but we have increasingly seen other countries consider this market as well,' said Stefan Weiler, a debt banker at JPMorgan.

The UK hopes to become a global hub of Islamic finance. Its £200m sale of Islamic debt in June 2014, which attracted orders 10 times higher than the amount sold, has been hailed as the start of a movement to broaden the market in Islamic bonds.

Bankers and others working closely with countries that issue Islamic debt say that demand has been equally strong from Islamic and non-Islamic investors.

FT *Source*: Moore, E., 'Tunisia and Pakistan join rush for sharia bonds', *Financial Times*, 11 August 2014.

Questions

1 Why is there a growing demand for Sharia bonds as a source of international finance?

2 How might this affect international business activity?

Futures and options markets

Exchange rates became highly volatile in the early 1970s as countries moved away from the system of pegging their exchange rates to the dollar. Futures and options markets have therefore developed as a means of reducing the risks of companies requiring foreign currencies for international transactions. Both of these instruments are referred to as 'financial derivatives'. Attempts to avoid future risks of this kind are sometimes referred to as 'hedging'.

Futures markets

A foreign currency futures contract is an agreement to deliver or receive a fixed amount of foreign currency at a future specified time and price. The 'margin requirement' refers to the price the purchaser of the future foreign currency must pay for others taking the risk of exchange rate volatility. Typically such margin requirements are 5% or less. The International Monetary Market (IMM) on the Chicago Mercantile Exchange is the main US market for foreign currency futures. Eurex is the German equivalent and LIFFE (London International Finance and Futures Exchange) is the UK equivalent.

- *Holder* is the purchaser of the option.
- *Writer (or grantee)* is the seller of the option.
- *European options* are those which can only be exercised on the specified expiration date.

- *American options* are those which can be exercised at any time before the expiration date.
- *Premium* is the initially agreed difference between the selling and buying price of the currencies (i.e. the cost of the option to the purchaser).

Clearly those involved in buying and selling options must negotiate the premium. However, the other avenue for gain/loss is the difference between the exercise (strike) price agreed at the outset and the spot (current) price at the time at which the option is exercised.

Such options can be traded on formal exchanges or on less formal, over-the-counter (OTC) markets. Important formal exchanges include LIFFE in the UK, Chicago Mercantile Exchange and Philadelphia Stock Exchange in the USA, the European Options Exchange in Amsterdam and the Montreal Stock Exchange.

Options markets

There are obvious similarities between the futures and options markets. The main difference, however, is that the forward and future contracts markets involve a legal obligation to buy or sell a fixed amount of foreign currency at a specified point in time (expiration date), whereas the options markets only involve a right to such a transaction.

- A *call option* purchaser has the right to buy foreign currency (sell domestic currency).
- A *put option* purchaser has the right to sell foreign currency (buy domestic currency).

Currency and interest rate swaps

The IMF introduced (in 1961) the idea of 'currency swaps' by which a country in need of specific foreign exchange could avoid the obvious disadvantage of having to purchase it with its own currency by simply agreeing to 'swap' a certain amount through the Bank for International Settlements. The swap contract would state a rate of exchange which would also apply to the 'repayment' at the end of the contract.

Multinational firms as well as governments are now making use of swap facilities, with the swaps arranged by dealers located in various international financial centres. These can involve both currency swaps and interest rate swaps. For example, one multinational may borrow funds in its own financial market in which it has low-interest access to funds and swap these loans with those similarly obtained by another multinational located overseas. As well as removing the exchange risk on low-cost borrowings, such swap transactions have the further advantages of not appearing on the firm's balance sheet! Interest rate swaps can also involve changing the maturity structure of the debt. Here one party to the swap typically exchanges a floating-rate obligation for a fixed-rate obligation.

International equity markets

As well as raising international finance by trading in various types of debt instruments, business can raise funds by issuing share capital (equity) in financial centres throughout the world. Equities (or shares) are non-redeemable assets issued by companies, and investors are actually buying part-ownership (a share) of a company. Investors in ordinary shares receive dividends if companies are able to pay them, but their major advantage as an asset lies in the possibility of capital appreciation if strong profit growth is anticipated. In the case of *preference shares* the company pays a fixed annual sum to the shareholder, and there is also the possibility of capital appreciation when the share is sold. *Ordinary shareholders* bear the largest risks since if the company goes out of business, the 'preferred' shareholders are entitled to a share of the money raised by selling assets first (although only after the Revenue and Customs and secured bank borrowers are paid). However, in good times, the ordinary shareholder will earn the greatest returns as dividend payments may be much greater than the fixed return received by preference shareholders. As always in the financial markets, those who bear most risk have highest potential for returns.

A high proportion of equities are traded on the stock exchanges throughout the world. Strictly speaking, 'stock' refers to the issued capital of a company other than that in the form of shares (equities). In more recent times the term 'stock' has become synonymous with the issue of securities of any type (bonds, shares, etc.). The stock exchanges we consider below are markets for all these securities, though our main concern here is with equities.

London Stock Exchange (LSE)

The London Stock Exchange (LSE) is the second largest market for equities in the world. The largest is in the hands of Euronext, the company that controls the Paris exchange. In recent times the securities markets in Germany, France and Italy have all become 'integrated', i.e. with cash and derivatives trading, settlement and clearing all done under one roof. In contrast the UK securities market on the London Stock Exchange remains fragmented, with different institutions responsible for settlement, clearing and trading.

Individual share prices may move for a whole host of reasons: stockbrokers' reports; bid rumours; executive departures; adverse press reports; results which beat, or fall short of, market expectations. This last factor is one of the most important. Outsiders are often puzzled when a company which reports a 30% rise in profits sees its shares fall.

Markets indulge in what one might call the 'White Queen syndrome', after the character in *Through the Looking Glass*. The White Queen screamed before she pricked her finger and when the injury actually occurred, made only a small sigh, as she had got all her screaming over with in advance. Similarly, stock markets are forever looking to the future and anticipating what will happen. Expectations are built into the market; thus, if a company is expected to increase profits by 40% and only reports a rise of 30%, its shares will fall.

International financial risk management

A number of issues involving international financial management have already been discussed. These are:

- *sources of international finance,* including the use of various international money, bond and equity markets as sources of funds and the various financial instruments associated with these markets;

- *the management of foreign exchange risk,* including the use of options, swaps and futures markets to 'hedge' against unpredictable changes in exchange rates.

We now look in rather more detail at some further aspects of international financial management, with our main concern being to review strategic issues in risk management, and especially the new possibilities of 'integrated' or 'enterprise' risk management. The suggestion here is that, via the identification and assessment of all the collective risks, the company can then implement a company-wide strategy to manage them. As we shall see, the early discussion on new financial instruments and associated derivatives markets will be relevant here.

Methods of integration

Lisa Meulbroek (2000) suggests that there are three ways of implementing integrated risk management objectives: modifying the company's operations, adjusting its capital structure and employing targeted financial instruments. Managers assess the advantages and disadvantages of each method before identifying the most appropriate mix for their particular enterprise.

1 *Modifying the company's operations.* The strategy adopted here will depend on the nature of the company's operations. Microsoft has chosen to use a higher ratio of temporary to permanent staff than is typical for activity within its sector. By reducing the fixed overhead of a more permanent workforce, it seeks to reduce the risks to its permanent workforce of unexpected and adverse shifts in demand, technology or regulation in an intrinsically volatile industry.

2 *Adjusting the company's capital structure.* Managers cannot always predict the magnitude of a particular operational risk or indeed any specific risk. However, they can adjust the company's capital structure to give a general reduction in risk exposure, as for example by reducing the debt-to-equity ratio. Such low levels of leverage policies have been practised by Microsoft, which helped it to avoid having outstanding debt over the past decade, thereby using equity as a risk cushion.

3 *Employing targeted financial instruments.* Here companies seek to focus on a specific risk and to hedge against it at the lowest feasible cost. This method is, of course, only feasible where financial instruments exist for the specific risk the company seeks to target. The development of liquid markets for a broad set of financial instruments has greatly helped this method in recent years. Although its figures are now in doubt, Enron, the Houston-based power and industrial group, bought and sold options and forwards (see p. 362) in the electricity and gas markets to reduce its risk exposure. In contrast, Microsoft will, arguably, find that few of its major risks are correlated with existing financial instruments and must depend on the other two methods of risk management control.

Finding the appropriate mix

The essence of an integrated approach is to combine elements of these three methods to minimise the aggregate net exposure to risk from all sources. By aggregating risk, some individual risks within the company will partially or completely offset each other. Thus, by concentrating on covering the (lower) aggregate net risk instead of each risk separately, an integrated approach to risk management can add value to the company by reducing costs. The technology products group Honeywell purchased an insurance contract in 1997 that for the first time covered a company's aggregate losses. By aggregating individual risks and then insuring the total net risk, Honeywell was able to make a 15% saving on its previous contract. Since such an integrated approach to risk management clearly requires a thorough understanding of the company's operations and financial policies, it must be implemented by senior management only. It cannot be delegated to managers of functional areas.

Alternative risk transfer (ART)

Traditionally companies have used the capital and money markets to raise much of their finance and the *insurance markets* to cover many of the individual risks to which they are exposed, with the two market types being quite distinct. However, a vast array of new financial products are now available from both market types which, together with the impact of the internet, is causing considerable convergence between these previously separate markets. This broad trend is often referred to as 'alternative risk transfer' (ART) and is reflected in Figure 10.3.

One driving force behind ART has involved the provision of financial instruments which can now be broken down into their smallest constituents, giving opportunities to price different bundles of risks in entirely new ways. The ability to identify and strip out individual risks and devise specific financial instruments to cover even the most complex bundle of such risks is arguably a revolutionary development. So much so that the term *'nuclear financial economics'* has been applied to this process of stripping down any complex situation into its constituent 'risk particles' which can then be priced. Many insurance companies are now able to diversify into providing financial instruments to cover foreign exchange and other contracts that were previously only available from the more traditional capital and money markets.

As can be seen from Figure 10.3, just as some insurance companies are developing financial instruments, which were once the preserve of the capital markets, the capital markets are themselves developing a variety of risk-related financial instruments, involving options, futures markets and swaps. The net result is a vast array of traditional and non-traditional instruments from all market sources able to meet the particular circumstances ('finite risk contract') of almost any corporate client. For example, since September 1999 the Chicago Mercantile Exchange has traded weather-linked securities (derivatives) whose value varies with the temperature, measured by an index of warmth in four large cities in the USA.

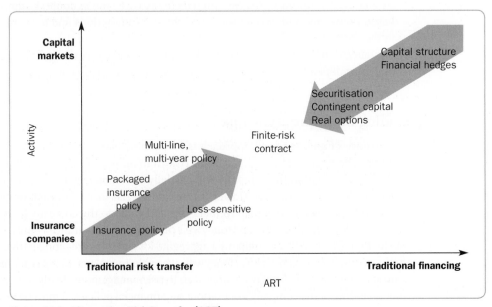

Figure 10.3 **Alternative Risk Transfer (ART)**

Such financial instruments can be the basis of 'contracts' to cover situations which previously would be regarded as entirely unpredictable and beyond mankind's control. Of course, the fears of such haphazard future contingencies often deterred firms from entering into a project, especially so the more risk-averse the firm's senior management. Now firms can take such risks explicitly into account and insure against them. For example, British Aerospace paid some $70 million in 1999 for an insurance policy that helped take £3 billion of aircraft-leasing risks off its balance sheet. Within six weeks of taking out the policy British Aerospace shares had outperformed the market by some 15%, the argument being that its future profitability now depended on its skill in operating its core business of building aircraft rather than on haphazard events (involving leasing issues) outside its direct control.

A second driver behind ART has been the rapid development in telecommunication and computer-related technologies. Clearly the internet has reduced search costs and times close to zero as regards finding the lowest price for various products. Intelligent automated asset managers are progressively able to seek out the financial instruments that best fit an investor's particular risk-profile. The availability of these technologies is clearly aiding the unbundling process, enabling providers to parcel risks into different classes of security on which prices can be readily quoted.

Case Study 10.8 looks at the impact of these automated risk valuation models in rather more detail.

CASE 10.8 Risk needs a human touch

In extraordinary and treacherous conditions, aircraft passengers would almost certainly prefer a human pilot to be at the controls than the autopilot – and for good reasons. No matter how powerful and sophisticated our computers are, there are always subtleties and nuances of experience that we cannot yet program them to judge. A computer would never have pulled off that emergency landing on New York's Hudson river in January 2009.

Investigators into the global financial crash landing are already producing remedies even as the disaster continues. A major realisation has been that banks and their supervisors trusted too much in the risk management autopilot. Lord Turner, chairman of the US's Financial Services Authority, has highlighted attempts by the Basel Committee to overhaul the use of 'value at risk' (VaR) models, which predict how much a bank can lose on a given day. These models have allowed the systematic underestimation of risk, which in turn has meant that only very small capital cushions were required in banks' trading operations. VaR models used unduly short historical data sets

to predict future developments and discounted the worth of incorporating rare, but extremely painful outcomes. VaR, he said, 'fails to allow for the fact that historically low volatility may actually be an indication of irrationally low risk-aversion and therefore increased systemic risk.' Lord Turner gave an example of a bank whose trading assets made up 57% of its total book, but which set its market risk capital requirement at just 0.1% of trading assets. This is extreme, but others in the sample chose 0.4% and 1.1% – better, but hardly a paradigm of prudence.

The Basel Committee, unsurprisingly, wants to raise these capital charges as swiftly and comprehensively as possible. The key driver for its action is the mind-boggling losses suffered in 2008 in the trading books of banks such as UBS, Merrill Lynch and Citigroup. Institutions exploited the low capital demands of VaR models to keep very large and long-term complex structured bond positions in a book really meant only for temporary asset positions.

The Basel Committee is cracking down hard on this area and their changes look likely to

Case 10.8 (*continued*)

handicap seriously the potential for any recovery in securitisation. It will prohibit banks from recognising any capital benefits from securitisations, even as hedging tools. This is because the Committee believes that 'the state of risk modelling in this area is not sufficiently reliable as to warrant recognising hedging or diversification benefits attributable to securitisation positions'.

For the most part, banks seem only too willing to accept these changes. Many bankers with global responsibility for credit trading are seeking different kinds of risk managers in their businesses. The new risk manager's human judgement would be the final arbiter rather than the strict letter of the VaR law, which could only act as a guide.

Most important would be 'intent'. People in risk management should not be allowed to work for themselves, embattled and concerned mainly with their own job security. 'They need to be close to the action, but not so close that they lose their perspective. In volatile, liquidity-strained times, traders need to be given more freedom around risk limits, but everyone needs to have a rounded view, across asset classes, markets and the full trading room.' What is needed, it is suggested, is a greater spirit of collectivism – an attitude of solving for the greater good.

Fine words, but markets are social phenomena riddled with dysfunction. They pursue bad leads and develop sustained distortions. As the lending drought shows, there are conflicts between what is rational for the individual and what is rational for the whole. And as investors have felt repeatedly in this crisis, markets can stay insane longer than they can stay solvent.

But the biggest difficulty and the reason VaR dominates is the business case. It is very difficult to turn human, qualitative judgement into numbers in the boardroom. Banks more than most demand quantitative assessment and as long as bonuses need to be calculated, this will not change.

 Source: Insight: Risk needs a human touch but models hold the whip hand, *Financial Times*, 23/01/2009 (Davies, P.), © The Financial Times Limited 2009. All Rights Reserved.

Question

Consider the advantages and disadvantages of the use of automated risk management models.

Centralised versus decentralised financial decisions

The financial decisions taken by MNEs reflect a variety of influences, such as choosing the types and sources of financing, the need for foreign exchange management, the short- versus long-term goal orientation of the company, the financial reporting requirements of different nations, tax, interest rate, inflationary and other financial considerations, and so on. Nevertheless, an important issue is whether the MNE seeks to take such decisions centrally or to direct many of these decisions to the management of affiliates in host countries. The facts would suggest a tendency towards centralisation: for example, around 57% of fundraising by MNE affiliates took place in host country financial markets in 1989, but this figure had fallen to below 45% by the late 1990s.

We might usefully review some of the arguments for and against such centralisation.

Centralised financial management

A number of arguments support this approach.

1 *Minimising cost/maximising return.* The rapid growth in type and source of financial instrument already considered suggests a global rather than local approach to financing.

Specialist financial managers with a global perspective can help the MNE borrow funds wherever in the world they are cheapest and invest them wherever the expected returns are highest.

2 *Flexibility.* Only centralised control can permit a rapid corporate response to changed conditions. For example, moving cash away from nations with high projected rates of inflation/currency depreciation and towards nations with high projected rates of economic growth/currency appreciation, etc.

3 *Scale economies.* Large-scale centralised borrowings can secure lower interest rates from lenders and reduce transaction costs per pound/dollar borrowed. Similarly, large-scale centralised deposits of cash surpluses can secure higher interest rates from borrowers.

4 *Professional expertise.* Higher-paid and more expert financial managers can be expected to better appraise the vast array of financial alternatives open to the MNE. Specialisation in such operations can be expected to further develop these skills.

5 *Synchronisation.* Centralised control permits a more uniform approach across all affiliates with regard to financial matters, one more likely to be consistent with stated corporate objectives.

Decentralised financial management

A number of counterarguments can be used to support a more decentralised approach.

1 *Generality.* The financing requirement of particular foreign affiliates may be overlooked by managers at headquarters who focus on more global needs. Pump-priming and other longer-term objectives of foreign affiliates may be sacrificed if funds are unavailable for new developments. Headquarter financial management may be unaware of the particular circumstance of local financial markets, so that low-cost sources of funds are overlooked.

2 *Motivation and morale.* These may be diminished among employees within the foreign affiliate as they perceive a lack of control over their own financial destiny.

3 *Conflicts.* Headquarter policy may conflict with policy deemed appropriate by host countries to firms operating there – for example, rationalisation of production involving unemployment in foreign affiliates where host governments are seeking to expand output and employment. Similarly, only affiliate financial managers may be able to appraise which financial reporting, control and cash management systems are appropriate to accurately reflect their local operations.

4 *Inflexibility.* Local financial managers may experience delays in receiving the go-ahead for new initiatives from an overburdened and bureaucratised headquarters.

In practice most MNEs centralise some of the financial management decisions and decentralise others, the extent of such decentralisation sometimes depending on the host country in which the affiliate operates.

References

Alexander, M. and Korine, H. (2008) 'Why you shouldn't go global', *Harvard Business Review,* December.

Andrews, K. (1980) *The Concept of Corporate Strategy* (2nd edn), Dow-Jones Irwin.

Ansoff, H.I. (1968) *Corporate Strategy,* Penguin.

Armstrong, M. (1999) *A Handbook of Human Resource Management* (7th edn), Kogan Page.

Barro, R. (1991) 'Economic growth in a cross-section of countries', *Quarterly Journal of Economics,* vol. 106, no. 20, pp. 407–43.

Beer, M., Spector, B., Lawrence, P.R., Quinn Mills, D. and Walton, R.E. (1984) *Managing Human Assets,* Free Press.

Bentham, J. (1823) reprinted in Burns, H. (ed.) (1970) *The Collected Works of Jeremy Bentham,* The Athlone Press.

Beyer, J. and Nino, D. (1999) 'Ethics and cultures in international business', *Journal of Management Inquiry,* vol. 8, no. 3.

Black, J. (2002) *A Dictionary of Economics,* Oxford Business Dictionary, Oxford University Press.

Boxall, P. (1992) 'Strategic HRM: beginnings of a new theoretical sophistication', *Human Resource Management Journal,* vol. 2, no. 3, pp. 60–79.

Boxall, P. and Purcell, J. (2008) *Strategy and Human Resource Management,* Palgrave Macmillan.

Brett, J., Behfar, K. and Kern, C. (2006) 'Managing cultural teams', *Harvard Business Review,* November.

Brewster, C. and Hegewisch, A. (1994) *Policy and Practice in European Human Resource Management,* Routledge/Thomson Learning.

Brewster, C., Sparrow, P. and Vernon, G. (2007) *International Human Resource Management* (2nd edn), Chartered Institute of Personnel and Development.

Buckingham, L. and Atkinson, D. (1999) 'Whisper it. . . takeovers don't pay', *Guardian,* 30 November.

Chatterjee, P. (2007) **www.inter-asia.net/conferences/2007-inter-asia-cultural-studies-society-shanghai-conference/speakers/**

Chattopadhyay. A., *et al.* (2012) *The New Emerging Market Multinationals,* McGraw Hill.

Chu, G.C. and Ju, Y. (1993) *The Grand Wall in Ruins,* State University of New York Press.

Claugue, C., Keefer, P., Knack, S. and Olson, M. (1999) 'Contract – intensive money: contract enforcement, property rights and economic performances', *Journal of Economic Growth,* vol. 4, pp. 185–211.

Collins, J.C. and Porras, J.L. (1994) *Built to Last,* Harper Business.

Croucher, S. (2003) *Globalization and Belonging: The Politics of Identity in a Changing World,* Rowman & Littlefield Publishers.

Czinkota, M. and Ronkainen, I. (1999) *International Marketing* (5th edn), South Western.

D'Iribane, I., cited in Hofstede, G. (1996) 'Problems remain but theories will change: the universal and the specific in 21st century global management', *Organizational Dynamics,* vol. 1, pp. 34–43.

Dichtl, E. and Koeglmayr, H.G. (1986) 'Country risk ratings', *Management International Review,* vol. 26, no. 4.

Donaldson, T. and Dunfee, T.W. (1999) 'When ethics travel: the promise and peril of global business ethics', *California Management Review,* vol. 41, no. 4.

Dunning, J.H. (1993) *Multinational Enterprises and the Global Economy,* Addison-Wesley.

Elashmawi, F. (1998) 'Overcoming multicultural clashes in global joint ventures', *European Business Review,* vol. 98, no. 4, pp. 211–16.

Elias, N. (1994) *The Civilizing Process,* Blackwell.

Encyclopedia Britannica (2014), Encyclopedia Britannica (UK) Ltd, online London.

Enderle, G. (1995) 'What is international? A topology of international spheres and its relevance for business ethics', Paper presented at the Annual Meeting of the International Association of Business and Society, Vienna, Austria.

Endot, S. (1995) 'The Islamisation process in Malaysia', PhD thesis, University of Bradford.

Fedor, K.J. and Werther, W.B. Jr (1996) 'The fourth dimension: creating culturally responsive international alliances', *Organizational Dynamics,* vol. 1.

Fisher, C. and Lovell, A. (2009) *Business Ethics and Values,* FT Prentice Hall.

Frankel, J. (1997) *Regional Trading Blocs in the World Economic System,* Institute for International Economics.

Friedman, M. (1970) 'The social responsibility of business', *New York Times Magazine,* 13 September.

Fuller, E. (2012) 'Mergers and acquisitions in the growth of the firm', in *Applied Economics* (12th edn), Griffiths, A. and Wall, S. (eds), Financial Times Prentice Hall.

Giddens, A. (1990) *The Consequences of Modernity,* Polity Press.

Griffin, R.W. and Pustay, M.W. (1996) *International Business: A Managerial Perspective,* Addison-Wesley.

Griffiths, A. (2000) 'Cultural determinants of competitiveness: the Japanese experience', in *Dimensions of International Competitiveness: Issues and Policies,* Lloyd-Reason, L. and Wall, S. (eds), Edward Elgar.

Griffiths, A. and Wall, S. (2011) *Economics for Business and Management* (3rd edn), Pearson.

Griffiths, A. and Wall, S. (eds) (2012) *Applied Economics* (12 edn), Financial Times Prentice Hall.

Hampden-Turner, C. and Trompenaars, F. (1994) *The Seven Cultures of Capitalism,* Piatkus.

Harris, N. (2012) *Service Operations Management,* Cassell.

Harris, P.R. and Moran, R.T. (1991) *Managing Cultural Differences,* Gulf Publishing.

Harris, H., Brewster, C. and Sparrow, P. (2003) *International Human Resource Management,* CIPD.

Heal, G. (2008) *When Principles Pay: Corporate Social Responsibility and the Bottom Line,* Columbia Business School Publishing.

Hegewisch, A. (1991) 'The decentralisation of pay bargaining: European comparisons', *Personnel Review,* vol. 20, no. 6.

Held, D., McGrew, A., Goldblatt, D. and Perraton, J. (1999) *Global Transformations: Politics, Economics and Culture,* Polity Press.

Hendry, J. and Pettigrew, A. (1990) 'Human resource management: an agenda for the 1990s', *International Journal of Human Resource Management,* vol. 1, no. 1.

Hill, C. (2005) *International Business: Competing in the Global Marketplace* (5th edn), McGrawHill/Irwin.

Hill, C. (2013) *International Business: Competing in the Global Marketplace* (9th edn), McGrawHill.

Hofstede, G. (1980) *Culture's Consequences,* Sage.

Hofstede, G. (1991) *Cultures and Organizations: Software of the Mind,* McGraw-Hill.

Hofstede, G. and Hofstede, G.J. (2005) *Cultures and Organisations: Software of the Mind,* McGraw Hill.

International Herald Tribune (2007) 'Japan merger culture: an investors' guide', 4 May (**http://iht.com/articles/2007/05/04yourmoney/mjapan.php**).

Jackson, J. (2002) 'Reticence in second language case discussions: anxiety and aspirations', *System,* vol. 30, 65–84.

James, G. (1988) *Performance Appraisal,* Occasional Paper 40, ACAS Work Research Unit.

Johanson, J. and Wiedersheim-Paul, F. (1975) 'The Internationalisation of the Firm – Four Swedish Cases', *Journal of Management Studies,* 19, 3.

Kaushik, B. (2006) 'Teacher truancy in India: the role of cultural norms and economic incentives', Working Paper, Centre for Analytic Economics, Cornell University.

Kay, J. (1993) 'Economics in business', *Economics and Business Education,* vol. 1, part 1, no. 2.

Kessapidou, S. and Varsakelis, N. (2000) 'National culture, choice of management and business performance: the case of foreign firms in Greece', in *Dimensions of International Competitiveness: Issues and Policies,* Lloyd-Reason, L. and Wall, S. (eds), Edward Elgar.

Kidd, J. and Xue, Li (2000) 'The modelling of issues and perspectives in MNEs', in *Dimensions of International Competitiveness,* Lloyd-Reason, L. and Wall, S. (eds), Edward Elgar.

Kotler, P. and Armstrong, G. (2010) *Principles of Marketing,* Prentice-Hall.

Landry, A. (2004) 'The Big Mac: a global-to-local look at pricing', *Federal Reserve Bank of Dallas, Economic Letter,* vol. 3, no. 9.

Latifi, F. (1997) 'Management learning in natural context', PhD thesis, Henley Management College, cited in Tayeb, M. (2000).

Laurent, A. (1986) 'The cross-cultural puzzle of international human resource management', *Human Resource Management,* 25.

Lei, D., Slocum, J.W. and Pitts, R.A. (1997) 'Building competitive advantage: managing strategic alliances to promote organizational learning', *Journal of World Business,* vol. 32, no. 3.

Lipsey, R.E. (1999) 'The location and characteristics of US affiliates in Asia', *National Bureau of Economic Research* (NBER) Working Paper, Cambridge, Mass.

Macdonald, G.M. (1988) 'Ethical perceptions of Hong Kong Chinese business managers', *Journal of Business Ethics,* vol. 7.

McGrew, A. (1992) 'A global society', in *Modernity and its Futures,* Hall, S., Held, D. and McGrew, A. (eds), Open University Press.

Mead, W.R. (2005) **www.articles.latimes.com/writers/walter-russell-mead**

Mendenhall, M. (2000) 'Mapping the terrain of IHRM: a call for ongoing dialogue', Paper presented at 15th Workshop on Strategic HRM, Fontainebleau, France, 30 March–1 April.

Meulbroek, L. (2000) 'Total strategies for risk control', *Financial Times,* 9 May.

Mintzberg, H. and Quinn, J.B. (1991) *Strategy Process: Concepts, Contexts, Cases,* Prentice Hall.

Morosini, P., Scott, S. and Harbir, S. (1998) 'National cultural distance and cross-border acquisition performance', *Journal of International Business,* vol. 29, no. 1.

OECD (2008) *Removing Barriers to SME Access to International Markets,* OECD.

Peters, T. and Waterman, R.H. (1982) *In Search of Excellence,* Harper & Row.

Porter, M.E. (1980) *Competitive Strategy,* Free Press, Collier Macmillan.

Porter, M.E. (1985) *Competitive Advantage,* Free Press.

Porter, M.E. (1986) *Competition in Global Industries,* Harvard Business School Press.

Porter, M.E. (1990) *The Competitive Advantage of Nations,* Macmillan.

Prahalad, C.K. (1999) 'Changes in the competitive battlefield', *Financial Times,* 4 October.

Reuer, J. (1999) 'The logic of alliances', *Financial Times,* 4 October.

Reuer, J. and Koza, M. (2000) 'Asymmetric information and joint venture performance: theory and evidence for domestic and international joint ventures', *Strategic Management Journal,* vol. 1.

Reynolds, C. (1986) 'Compensation of overseas personnel', in *Handbooks of Human Resource Administration* (2nd edn), Farnularo, J. (ed.), McGraw-Hill.

Roberts, M. and Deichmann, U. (2008) 'Regional spillover estimation', Background paper for the *World Development Report,* 2009.

Sastry, S. (2014) 'Optimising intercultural synergies in post-merger integration contexts: an alternative framework for organisational leadership', PhD thesis, Anglia Ruskin University, Cambridge.

Schwab, K. (ed.) (2014) *The Global Competitiveness Report 2013–2014,* World Economic Forum.

Slack, N., Chambers, S., Harland, C., Harrison, A. and Johnson, R. (2013) *Operations Management* (7th edn), FT Prentice Hall.

Sloman, J. and Jones, E. (2014) *Essential Economics for Business* (4th edn), Pearson.

Snow, C.C., Davison, S.C., Snell, S.A. and Hambrik, D.C. (1996) 'Use of transnational teams to globalize your company', *Organizational Dynamics,* vol. 24, no. 4, pp. 90–107.

Stern, N. (2007) *Stern Review on the Economics of Climate Change,* Office of Climate Change.

Tayeb, M. (1994) 'Japanese managers and British culture: a comparative case study', *International Journal of Human Resource Management,* vol. 5.

Tayeb, M. (2000) *International Business: Theories, Policies and Practices,* Financial Times Prentice Hall, especially Chapters 4, 13 and 19.

Tiplady, R. (2003) *One World or Many? The Impact of Globalisation on Mission,* Authentic.

Trompenaars, H. (1993) *Riding the Waves of Culture: Understanding Cultural Diversity in Business,* The Economist Books.

Turner, C.H. and Trompenaars, A. (1993) *The Seven Cultures of Capitalism,* Doubleday.

UNESCO (2002) *Universal Declaration on Cultural Diversity* (Adopted by the 31st Session of the General Conference of UNESCO), Paris, 2 November 2001, p. 11.

United Nations Conference on Trade and Development (UNCTAD) *World Investment Report* (annual publication).

Wallsten, S. (2001) 'Ringing in the 20th century', *World Bank Research Working Paper,* World Bank.

Weber, M. (1930) *The Protestant Ethic and the Spirit of Capitalism,* Allen & Unwin.

World Bank, *World Development Report* (annual publication).

Yeung, I.Y.M. and Tung, K.L. (1996) 'Achieving business success in Confucian societies: the importance of Guanxi (connections)', *Organizational Dynamics,* vol. 1.

Zak, P. (2001) 'Institutions, property rights and growth', *The Gruter Institute Working Papers,* vol. 2, no. 1: Article 2.

Zonis, M. and Wilkin, S. (2000) 'Driving defensively through a minefield of political risk', *Financial Times,* 30 May.

Index

Page references to Figures or Tables will be in *italics*